Andrew J. Indovina,
Pierre Boutquin,
David Jung

SAMS
Teach Yourself
Visual Basic® 6
Online
in Web Time

SAMS

*201 West 103rd Street,
Indianapolis, Indiana 46290*

Sams Teach Yourself Visual Basic® 6 Online in Web Time

Trademarks

All terms mentioned in this book that are known to be trademarks or service marks have been appropriately capitalized. Sams Publishing cannot attest to the accuracy of this information. Use of a term in this book should not be regarded as affecting the validity of any trademark or service mark.

Visual Basic is a registered trademark of Microsoft Corporation.

Warning and Disclaimer

Every effort has been made to make this book as complete and as accurate as possible, but no warranty or fitness is implied. The information provided is on an "as is" basis. The authors and the publisher shall have neither liability nor responsibility to any person or entity with respect to any loss or damages arising from the information contained in this book or from the use of the CD-ROM or programs accompanying it.

EXECUTIVE EDITOR
Robert Linsky

ACQUISITIONS EDITOR
Charles Drucker

TECHNICAL EDITOR
Alfonso Hermida

MANAGING EDITOR
Jodi Jensen

PROJECT EDITOR
Heather Talbot

PROOFREADER
Megan Wade

MEDIA DEVELOPER
Craig Atkins

INTERIOR DESIGN
Gary Adair

COVER DESIGN
Alan Clements

COPY WRITER
Eric Borgert

LAYOUT TECHNICIANS
Susan Geiselman
Mark Walchle

Sams Teach Yourself Online in Web Time Guided Tour

The best-selling computer tutorial series just got even better.

The *Sams Teach Yourself* series now has its own Web site. When you buy a book in the *Sams Teach Yourself Online in Web Time* series, you open the door to a new world of online learning. These books give you a full year of access to http://www.samsteachyourself.com, a virtual classroom and online educational community that offers in-depth, online courses to help you master the book's material more thoroughly and more rapidly.

When you take a *Sams Teach Yourself Online in Web Time* course, you can do the following:

- Assess your progress with interactive tests.
- Improve your skills and understanding with online exercises.
- Discuss technology topics online with other students and subject matter experts.
- Expand your knowledge with a complete searchable reference work.

Because these courses are offered in Web Time, you can take them at any hour of the day or night—at your convenience and at your own pace. And when you enroll in a *Web Time* course, you're not alone; you join an online community of students and computer professionals who can help you work through the more difficult material.

What's on the Web Site

Sams Teach Yourself Online in Web Time courses follow the chapter-and-lesson organization of the *Sams Teach Yourself Online in Web Time* books, with an online section for each chapter. Online quizzes for every lesson help you gauge your progress. The quizzes are scored automatically, and your grades are stored in a database, so you can always review your work.

Each chapter in the Web course also contains a set of online exercises. Specially designed to enhance your understanding of the accompanying chapter in your *Sams Teach Yourself* book, these exercises give you hands-on practice with real-life problems. Sample solutions for the exercises are also provided online, along with hints on alternative solutions and tips on where to go for more information.

There's also a threaded discussion list overseen by a technical expert in the field, so if one of the exercises has you stumped or if an online solution doesn't appear to be the only way to work the problem, just post a message. One of the other students is likely to have passed this way before.

What You'll Need

The *Sams Teach Yourself Online in Web Time* course site is easy to access and use. First, though, you need to purchase one of the *Sams Teach Yourself Online in Web Time* books. The CD-ROM envelope in the back of this book contains a card with an authorization number that you'll need to register for your online course, so be sure that the seal on the envelope is intact.

After you've purchased a book, all you need is Internet access and browser software. The online course system works with most browsers that support frames, but is best viewed with recent versions of Netscape Navigator (4 or higher) or Microsoft Internet Explorer 5. You'll also need to configure your browser to accept JavaScript and cookies because the online course engine requires both of these features.

Finding the *Sams Teach Yourself Online* Site

To access the *Sams Teach Yourself Online* site, launch your browser and go to http://www.samsteachyourself.com. This is the gateway for all *Sams Teach Yourself Online* courses. When you're at the site, you'll find instructions on how to register as a student and how to access the *Sams Teach Yourself Visual Basic 6 Online in Web Time* course. There's also a Guest area where you can sample the courses that accompany the other *Sams Teach Yourself Online in Web Time* titles.

Logging In

After you've registered and chosen your username and password, you'll be able to log in to the *Sams Teach Yourself Visual Basic 6 Online* class (see Figure 1).

FIGURE 1

The Login page.

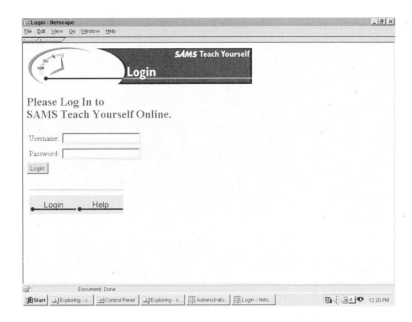

Be sure to set your browser to accept cookies because this is how the system keeps track of you as a student.

The Student Home Page

After you've registered and logged in to the *Sams Teach Yourself Visual Basic 6 Online* course, you'll be taken to the Student Home page (see Figure 2). From this point, you can view course materials, review your work on earlier chapters, check class announcements, go to the course discussion area, or search through the online reference materials for this course.

FIGURE 2

The Student Home page.

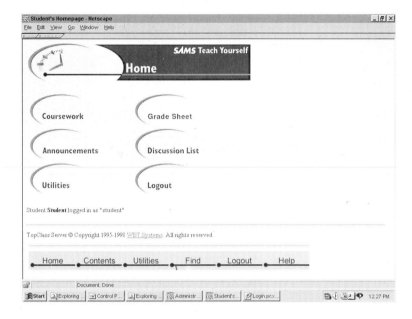

When you reach the Home page, you might see New tags on the class Announcements or Discussion List banners. It's always a good idea to check the Announcements folder first for messages about your course or the *Sams Teach Yourself Online* site.

Click the class Announcements banner to open the Announcements folder. Then click the highlighted Announcements link to view the folder's messages.

Wherever you are in the *Sams Teach Yourself Visual Basic 6 Online in Web Time* course, you can always return to the Home page by clicking the Home button at the bottom of the page.

The Student Home page also gives you access to a threaded discussion list. Only students who have registered for the *Sams Teach Yourself Visual Basic 6 Online* course can read and post messages. The discussion is overseen by a professional subject matter expert to steer the discussion threads, provide guidance, and come up with answers to the more difficult questions that are posed. Click the Discussion List banner to use this online community feature.

Online Course Materials

Click the Coursework banner on the Home page to access your course materials (see Figure 3).

FIGURE 3

The Coursework page.

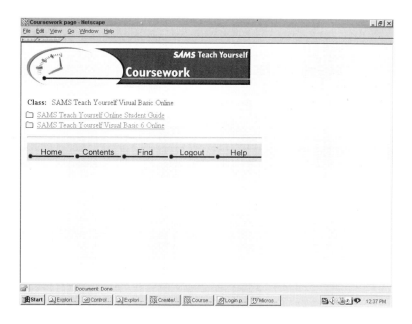

One of the courses, in the folder Sams Teach Yourself Online Student Guide, is designed to teach you how to use this system. It also contains a complete reference section that provides full details on the system's features and how to use them. Even if you've taken online classes before, it's a good idea to step through the Sams Teach Yourself Online Student Guide course to familiarize yourself with the messaging system and the navigation tools.

Click the Sams Teach Yourself Visual Basic 6 Online folder to see the main coursework for your class. Each chapter in the textbook has a corresponding folder of online material (see Figure 4). (The blue *U* means that a folder contains unread material; a red *N* means that a folder contains new material.) You'll also see a midterm and final exam, as well as a complete, searchable reference work.

If you open one of the chapter folders, you'll see that it contains a number of self-scoring quizzes—one for each lesson in the chapter—as well as a set of programming exercises (see Figure 5). Sample solutions for these exercises are also available online. Check the discussion board for any threads relating to exercises you're working on—or start a thread of your own, if there is something you want to talk about or don't fully understand.

FIGURE 4

The chapter folders.

FIGURE 5

Each chapter folder contains quizzes and exercises, as well as sample solutions for the exercises.

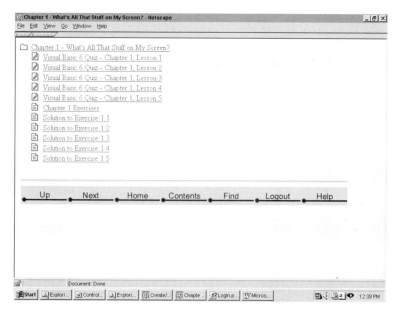

Searchable Reference Material

As a further benefit for *Sams Teach Yourself Online in Web Time* students, the full text of *Visual Basic 6 Unleashed* has been made part of your course materials. This 980-page book, by Visual Basic expert Rob Thayer, is one of the most extensive reference works available on the subject. *Visual Basic 6 Unleashed* provides the reader with a comprehensive reference to virtually all the topics that are used in today's leading-edge Visual Basic applications. It's a $39.99 value, and it's available free to registered students in the *Sams Teach Yourself Visual Basic 6 Online in Web Time* course.

You can use this reference work in two different ways. First, you can open the course folder containing the text and browse the material by chapter and section. Or you can use the simple but powerful text search engine that's part of the *Sams Teach Yourself Online* system. Just click the Find button at the bottom of any page and enter the words or phrases that interest you into the text box (see Figure 6). You can do a quick search by titles or a more complete search by titles and text.

FIGURE 6

An example of a search.

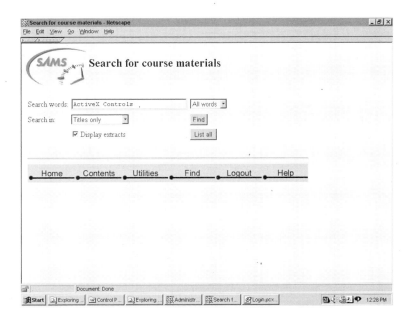

The search engine will supply you with links to the pages where the text was found. When you jump to those pages, you might want to use your browser's Find function to locate the specific line containing the text you searched for (press Ctrl+F or open the Edit menu and click Find).

Be Our Guest

The best way to find out more about *Sams Teach Yourself Online* courses is to go to the Guest area of the site, which you'll find at `http://www.samsteachyourself.com`. There you'll find the course material for the first chapter of each of the *Sams Teach Yourself Online in Web Time* books, as well as a portion of the reference material.

Overview

Contents

About the Authors

MARK SPENIK is the manager of emerging technologies at Keiter Stephens Computer Services, Inc., located in Richmond, Virginia. Mark, a graduate of George Mason University in Fairfax, Virginia, entered the computer industry in 1985. He has designed and coded large-scale applications and has consulted with numerous firms in application development, implementation, and migration. He has a broad programming background including assembly language, C, C++, HTML, Active Server Pages, and Visual Basic.

Mark is a Microsoft Certified Solution Developer and charter member and is frequently invited to speak at various development conferences and seminars. He is one of the co-authors of *Visual Basic 5 Interactive Course* by Waite Group Press. Mark is also a co-author of the *Microsoft SQL Server 7.0 DBA Survival Guide* by Sams Publishing and has contributed to various other books on Visual Basic and SQL Server development. Mark can be reached via the Internet at mspenik@kscsinc.com.

ANDREW J. INDOVINA is currently a freelance programming consultant, working in both Visual Basic and C during the past five years. He lives with his wife in Rochester, New York. You can reach him at aindovin@eznet.net.

PIERRE BOUTQUIN is a senior analyst in the corporate treasury of a major Canadian bank, where he develops leading-edge market risk management software. He has more than 10 years of experience implementing PC-based computer systems with in-depth knowledge of object-oriented analysis and design, C++, Visual Basic, and SQL. He co-authored *Visual Basic 5 SuperBible*, published by Waite Group Press.

When not held captive by Sasha and Koshka, the two Burmese cats owning him, or reading (or writing) computer books, Pierre likes to research finance, play chess, and keep up with news from Belgium, his native country. You may reach him at boutquin@istar.ca.

DAVID JUNG has been developing programs in BASIC ever since he discovered personal computers back in the early 1980s. A graduate of California State Poly-technic University, Pomona, David has a Bachelor of Science degree in business administration emphasizing computer information systems. His development expertise is in designing and constructing cross-platform client/server and distributed database solutions using Visual Basic, Java, Access, SQL Server, Oracle, DB2, and Internet technology.

David is a member of the Pasadena IBM Users Group's technical staff and leads its Visual Basic Special Interest Group. He is a frequent speaker at seminars and user groups, showing how Visual Basic, Java, and the Internet can be integrated into business solutions. David has co-authored several Waite Group Press books, including *Visual Basic 5 & 6 Client/Server How-To* and the *Visual Basic 4 & 5 SuperBible*.

When David isn't programming, writing, and presenting, he can be found on the bike trails in Southern California, the golf course, and with his wife, Joanne, and two dogs (that he pretends he likes!). He can be reached at `davidj@vb2java.com` (`http://www.vb2java.com`).

Dedication

To Lisa and Hope for showing me true love and happiness.

—Mark Spenik

This book is dedicated to my wife, Denise, who gives me incredible love and support in everything I choose to do. I also dedicate this book to my parents, for without them, none of this would have been possible. And this book is also dedicated to the memory of Michael R. Eisenman, the best friend a person could ever have.

—Andrew J. Indovina

To my wife Sandra—thanks for letting Koshka and Sasha into our home.

—Pierre Boutquin

To the memory of our fellow author, John Harrington, whom we lost before this project began.

—David Jung

Acknowledgments

We want to acknowledge and thank the authors who wrote *Visual Basic 5 Interactive Course*, which this book is based on: John Harrington, Mark Spenik, Heidi Brumbaugh, and Cliff Diamond. Thanks also to the editorial and production staffs of that edition, especially Lisa Goldstein, John Crudo, Joanne Miller, and Cecile Kaufman, for paving the way for this book.

Sams Teach Yourself Visual Basic 6 Online in Web Time is largely drawn from *Visual Basic 6 Interactive Course*. Many people at Waite Group Press were involved in acquiring and developing *Visual Basic 6 Interactive Course*, including Charles Drucker, Susan Walton, Stephanie Wall, Laura Brown, Carmela Carvajal, Andrea Rosenberg, Dan Scherf, and Kurt Stephan. Thank you to the members of the advisory board who contributed to the development of this book's table of contents: Steve Smith, Dr. Robert Detjen, C.C. Hommer, and Chang-Shyh Peng. Much credit for refinement of the manuscript goes to content editor Russ Jacobs and technical reviewer Don Sticksel; their in-depth evaluations were essential to this project. Thank you also to the editorial and production staff at Macmillan Computer Publishing, including Caroline Roop, Sherri Fugit, and many more, for putting the final product together.

Finally, thank you to Mitchell Waite for his vision and inspiration, and for making it all possible in the first place.

—Waite Group Press

I want to thank my wife and best friend Lisa for her patience and support while enduring the rigors of my writing a book. To my family Bonnie, John, Denise, David, Kim, Adam, Chris, Gary, Debbie, Lisa, David, and all my nieces and nephews (whose numbers are steadily increasing), thanks for the support! Thanks also to the Meyer (Sam, Marge and Jonathan) and the Rimes (Denise and Pat) families for all their encouragement. Thank you to my father John and my late mother Anna Jane for being such remarkable role models. A belated thanks to John McVicker and Danny Mcie for giving me the opportunity as well as teaching me Visual Basic so many years ago.

—Mark Spenik

I want to thank my wife, Denise, for her enduring love and support. She tolerated our sacrifice of free time and more while this book was being written. I would also like to thank Susan Walton, who got me started in the whole book writing thing in the first place. Thank you to John Harrington for answering all the questions a beginning writer asks. Thanks to Andrea Rosenberg and Kurt Stephan for their support and assistance in getting the book written. Finally, I would like to give thanks to Michael Platania for introducing me to Visual Basic, encouraging my interest in the language, and for being a great mentor; to Nick Gray for his computer expertise in every area; and to all my friends at Manning & Napier Advisors, Inc.

—Andrew J. Indovina

I would like to thank Andrea Rosenberg, Kurt Stephan, Susan Walton, and all the other Waite Group editors for the opportunity to co-author another book. Russ Jacobs and Don Sticksel are both appreciated for their help in making me look like an accomplished writer. Most importantly, I must acknowledge the enthusiastic encouragement provided to me by my wife Sandra. Without her, I surely would have faltered in this effort. Finally, I must thank Jennifer and "Tindy & Doel" for the occasional free helpings of fast food.

—Pierre Boutquin

I want to thank my wife, Joanne, for her enduring love and support. As crazy as things might have become, she was always there with positive encouragement and support (and understood when I couldn't take the dogs for their walk). Thanks to the rest of my family and friends who understood that I "couldn't come out and play." A special thanks to everyone at Waite Group Press for their support, especially to our editor, Kurt Stephan. Without his encouragement, understanding, and organization, this project wouldn't have been put together as efficiently as it was (especially when I needed "just one more day"). I would also like to acknowledge John Harrington and his family. His spirit is definitely within the contents of this book. My thoughts and prayers are with his family.

—David Jung

Tell Us What You Think!

As the reader of this book, *you* are our most important critic and commentator. We value your opinion and want to know what we're doing right, what we could do better, what areas you'd like to see us publish in, and any other words of wisdom you're willing to pass our way.

As a Publisher for Sams Publishing, I welcome your comments. You can fax, email, or write me directly to let me know what you did or didn't like about this book—as well as what we can do to make our books stronger.

Please note that I cannot help you with technical problems related to the topic of this book, and that due to the high volume of mail I receive, I might not be able to reply to every message.

When you write, please be sure to include this book's title and authors as well as your name and phone or fax number. I will carefully review your comments and share them with the authors and editors who worked on the book.

Fax: 317-581-4770

Email: blee@mcp.com

Mail: Benjamin Lee, Ph.D.
          Executive Editor
          Sams Publishing
          201 West 103rd Street
          Indianapolis, IN 46290 USA

Introduction

Sams Teach Yourself Visual Basic 6 Online in Web Time is a hands-on course in Visual Basic 6, the Microsoft programming language that makes developing for Windows as visual as Windows itself. This book is designed to be used by a beginning programmer: It assumes no previous programming knowledge. However, if you already program in another language, you will find this book an easy and enjoyable way to get up to speed on Visual Basic.

About Visual Basic 6

Sams Teach Yourself Visual Basic 6 Online in Web Time not only guides you through the powerful and rich language of Visual Basic that programmers have appreciated for years, but also shows you how to take advantage of the exciting new features and enhancements in the most recent release: Visual Basic 6.

So how does Visual Basic 6 differ from earlier versions of this popular programming language? The biggest and most obvious difference is in data access, where the long-time data access object model, Microsoft DAO (Data Access Objects)—which shipped with Visual Basic 3, 4, and 5—has been replaced with Microsoft ADO (Advanced Data Objects). Data access has been further enhanced with new data-aware controls, such as data grid and data list box. Also, the report writer used in Visual Basic 3, 4, and 5, Crystal Reports, has been replaced with Microsoft's Data Report. Data Environment has been added to provide visual programming and drag-and-drop features to ADO's objects.

Of course, Microsoft did not stop with the database enhancements. Visual Basic 6 includes many new Internet and intranet features, including the capability to create DHTML (Dynamic HTML) applications with Visual Basic. To make your life much easier and more productive, this latest version of Visual Basic includes many new and enhanced wizards. Of course, Visual Basic 6 includes many new ActiveX controls, such as `CoolBar` and `DateTimePicker`. And last but not least, several new language features have been added, such as the File System objects and several new string functions (`Split`, `StrReverse`, `Join`, and more).

What's in the Book?

Sams Teach Yourself Visual Basic 6 Online in Web Time progresses logically through introductory material and beginning concepts all the way to advanced and complex professional programming techniques.

Chapter 1, "What's All That Stuff on My Screen?" starts by guiding you through the Visual Basic 6 workspace, and familiarizes you with the windows and dialog boxes of the development environment. Once you're comfortable with the look and feel of the Visual Basic interface, you'll be ready to learn about the concepts of object-oriented programming (OOP). Chapter 2, "Object-Oriented Programming," fearlessly demystifies OOP, which is at the heart of Windows programming.

After these basic concepts are covered, the book takes you step by step through program creation. By writing dozens of sample programs, you'll understand how each line of code works, and better yet, why it is important.

Chapter 3, "Variables, Constants, and Associated Functions," defines variables and constants, and shows you how to use and declare them. It also expands your programming horizons by explaining numeric variables, strings, and date variables. Chapter 4, "Subroutines, Functions, and the Visual Basic 6 Language," builds on this knowledge and introduces the concept of program flow using subroutines and functions—the building blocks of modular programming.

Chapter 5, "Controls," defines and shows the variety of controls and forms you can use to make your Visual Basic projects really take shape. Chapter 6, "Building the GUI with Forms, Menus, and MDI Forms," takes what you've learned in Chapter 5 even further by introducing and explaining the design aspects you need to consider when creating the graphical user interface for your application.

In Chapter 7, "Building Classes: The Foundation of Visual Basic OOP," you'll learn how to use classes, as well as discover the relationship between a class and an object—knowledge that will allow you to make the most of Visual Basic 6's object-oriented features. You will then be introduced to a collection of Microsoft controls that enable you to add a professional look and feel to your applications in Chapter 8, "Using ActiveX Controls." Because applications you develop will almost always require some type of printed output, Chapter 9, "Printing," teaches you the ins and outs of Visual Basic's Printer class and object, the Printers collection, and the printer itself.

Chapter 10, "Problem Solving: Handling Errors and Debugging Your Program," dives into error handling and the noble art of debugging. You will learn how to troubleshoot your programs and prevent bugs instead of having to fix them.

Once your programs have a professional interface and are bug-free, you'll want to jazz up their appearance. Chapter 11, "Adding Pizazz with Graphics," shows you how to do just that by introducing you to graphics programming. You'll learn to use graphics controls and methods, and do simple animations.

When it's time for your applications to go public, it's essential that you understand the Windows file system and the different types of file input and output access methods. Chapter 12, "Reading and Writing Disk Files," teaches you all that and more. You'll learn about file system controls and how to handle sequential access, random access, and binary access file types.

Much of business programming involves databases. In Chapter 13, "Database Programming," you'll learn simple techniques for creating and managing database files. The chapter provides an introduction to databases, database design, and the new ADO (Active Data Objects), and shows you how to create stylish custom reports from database files.

Chapter 14, "Advanced Features," proves that you haven't yet learned all there is to know about Visual Basic. This chapter teaches you how to use the Timer control to perform background processing, introduces DDE implementation, shows you how to create setup programs to distribute your applications using the Setup Wizard, and much more.

Chapter 15, "Doing the Impossible (and More) with the Windows API," will teach you how to tap into the powerful Windows Application Programming Interface (API). You'll learn to use its hundreds of functions and procedures to perform tasks that normally cannot be done in Visual Basic or that offer improved processing speed over standard VB programming methods.

You'll learn how to use object linking and embedding (OLE) in Chapter 16, "Interfacing with Excel and Other Programs." This chapter explains how to create applications that use the Visual Basic OLE container control to link and embed documents from Microsoft Word and Microsoft Excel, describes OLE automation, shows how to create ActiveX client and server applications, and much more.

Chapter 17, "Advanced ActiveX and Registry API Techniques," builds on lessons taught in Chapters 8 and 15. First, it introduces you to the ActiveX Interface Wizard and gives you valuable advice on compiling and distributing your controls. In the second half of the chapter, you'll learn how to save data to, and retrieve data from, the system registry, review the Registry API, and perform subkey operations.

Chapter 18, "Using Visual Basic for Communications," shows how to apply your Visual Basic programming knowledge to the Internet. You'll learn how to communicate through modems with the MSComm control, connect to the Internet, build your own Web browser, use the Winsock control, and more.

Sams Teach Yourself Visual Basic 6 Online in Web Time concludes with Chapter 19, "Using Visual Basic for Internet/Intranet Applications." You'll take the knowledge you gained in Chapter 18 and add to it with some advanced techniques: creating an ActiveX Document application, using Message Application Program Interface (MAPI) controls to create your own email program, and incorporating Dynamic HTML (DHTML) to create powerful Internet applications.

How This Book Is Different

Every chapter of *Sams Teach Yourself Visual Basic 6 Online in Web Time* is divided into a number of short, easily digestible lessons, and each is followed by a convenient summary that recaps the key points. Each lesson is devoted to a specific topic and requires approximately an hour to read and understand. This makes it easy to complete lessons every time you sit down with the book, even if your time is limited.

Each lesson is followed by four quiz questions to test your understanding of the material, and most lessons include exercises that suggest ways to expand and enhance your knowledge. Quiz answers for all lessons are included in the appendix, so you can check your results as you progress.

About the CD

The CD that accompanies *Sams Teach Yourself Visual Basic 6 Online in Web Time* includes all the source code developed in the book, and adds several useful utilities and controls. The source code is organized by chapter. Please see the "Installing the CD-ROM" page at the back of the book for more details.

CHAPTER 1

What's All That Stuff on My Screen?

Even if you've been programming for a while, your first look at Visual Basic 6 (VB 6) is likely to startle you. There sure is a lot of stuff there, and a lot of it is new to Visual Basic 6. In this chapter, you learn to maneuver around the Visual Basic 6 integrated development environment and to set it up for convenient programming. You won't be writing any programs, but learning these techniques can be a big timesaver for you. Even if you are upgrading from a previous version of VB, you will find something new here. In particular, you'll learn about:

- The different windows in the development environment
- Tailoring the development environment to your preferences
- The Application Wizard
- Visual Basic add-ins
- Using the Help system

LESSON 1

Getting Started

If you haven't done so already, double-click the VB 6 icon, and let's take a ride. (If you haven't yet installed Visual Basic, consult the Visual Basic documentation for instructions.)

The Opening Screen

After the splash screen, the first thing you get when you double-click the VB 6 icon is an opening dialog box that offers a confusing array of choices. The dialog box is shown in Figure 1.1.

FIGURE **1.1**

The opening dialog box of Visual Basic 6.

Your Mileage May Vary

There are three different versions of Visual Basic 6. Some of the features available in the Professional and Enterprise Editions are not available in the Learning Edition. The screens shown throughout this book are from the Enterprise Edition. They might vary in some detail from the screens you see.

Let's take a look at what all those icons mean. The various choices exist because Visual Basic 6 can compile your programs into several different types of files:

- Standard .EXE files, which are normal programs.

- ActiveX .EXE files, which are programs that allow other programs to access their data. These are known as *out of process servers,* because they operate in their own process space: memory that Windows sets aside for programs to use.

- ActiveX .DLL files (dynamic link libraries), which are collections of functions and procedures that can be accessed by other programs. DLL files are known as *in-process servers*; they operate in the same memory space as the program that uses them.

- ActiveX controls, which are components that you add to your program. You will learn about controls in Chapter 5, "Controls."

- ActiveX Document .DLL and .EXE files, which are programs that have been modified to work within Web browser programs, such as Internet Explorer. They are suitable for distribution and viewing over the Internet.

- Add-in files, which can be *added in* to the Visual Basic programming environment. They are used to automate tasks that you do over and over again.

- The VB Application Wizard, which builds a part of your program for you. Obviously, it doesn't know what you want the program to do, but it can create a large part of the program's user interface.

- An Internet Information Server (IIS) application, which is executed on a Web server. It uses Visual Basic to process browser requests and respond to events in the browser and uses HTML to present its user interface.

- A DHTML (Dynamic HTML) application, which uses Visual Basic on the client to process events in HTML pages.

Most of the applications in this book use the standard EXE option.

There are three tabs on this opening screen. To open a project file from the disk, select the Existing tab. A dialog box such as the one shown in Figure 1.2 opens.

As you can see, this is a lot like the standard Windows 98 Explorer window, and you navigate it in the same way. Later in the book, you will learn to include windows such as this in your own programs.

Figure 1.2

The Existing tab.

The third tab is the Recent tab. As you might expect, it contains a list of the most recent projects you have been using. Figure 1.3 shows the Recent tab. You will find this tab handy as you work through the lessons in this book.

Figure 1.3

The Recent tab.

The Development Environment

Go back to the New tab and select Standard EXE. Click Open to begin a new project. Let's take a look at where you will work. The default development environment is shown in Figure 1.4.

FIGURE 1.4

The default development environment.

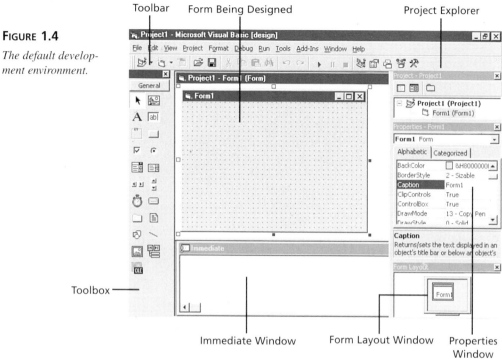

There's a lot there! Let's take a closer look at the default items on the screen:

- Visual Basic 6 creates Windows programs. The user interface for Windows programs is a window. Each window your program uses is created on a form in the development environment. Think of a form as a blank window on which you will draw the part of the program that the user sees.

- When you are writing the program that makes a form work (called the code), you use the Code window.

- The items on a form are called controls. All the controls that you can use in your project are in the toolbox. Microsoft supplies several controls that are not automatically included in the toolbox. You can also purchase or download other controls, called third-party controls. These extra controls add functionality to your VB programs. Later in this book, you will see how to add more controls to the toolbox.

- The toolbar provides quick access to things that are found in the menus. There are several specialized toolbars, too. The standard toolbar is the one you will use the most.

- The Project Explorer window enables you to access the different parts of your project. You might have several forms and any number of classes and program modules in a single project. (Don't worry if some of this is mysterious right now. It won't be that way for long!) The Project Explorer gives you instant access to any part of the project at any time.

- Properties are attributes of your form or an object on your form. You have properties, too. You have a height property, a weight property, and a hair color property. You can set the properties of the form or a control on the form in the Properties window.

- The Form Layout window lets you set the position your form will take when your program begins to run. It is a visual way to set two of the form's properties, Top and Left.

- The Immediate window is a kind of scratch pad. You can try out some of your program's instructions there. When you are troubleshooting a program, this becomes a Debug window where you can change the values that your program is manipulating.

Dockable?

All the windows except the Form window have a property of their own: They are dockable. A *dockable* window is one that attaches itself to the nearest edge of the screen or to the nearest other dockable window. When you move a dockable window, it "snaps" to the location. A docked window is dominant. If you drag the toolbox to the top of the screen, for example, it docks there and all the other windows change size to accommodate it.

Windows that have their Dockable property enabled also have another property. They are always on top. If they are open, they are visible and not hidden behind another window.

You can view the Dockable property by right-clicking your mouse inside the window. If the word Dockable is checked, it is a dockable window. You can, of course, change that property. If a window is not docked, it is a *floating* window.

Whether you choose to have a window docked or not is a matter of personal preference.

Lesson Summary

In this lesson, you have started exploring the Visual Basic development environment. We will continue this exploration in the next lesson.

Quiz 1

1. The New tab offers several choices for creating a new project. If you just want an ordinary program, you should select:

   a. Standard EXE

   b. ActiveX EXE

   c. ActiveX DLL

   d. ActiveX Control

2. If you want to open an old project that is stored on your disk, select the:

   a. Recent tab

   b. Existing tab

   c. Application Wizard

   d. Project Retrieval Wizard

3. The _____ window helps you access the different parts of a project.

   a. Properties

   b. Immediate

   c. Project Explorer

   d. Toolbox

4. Set the attributes of your form in the _____ window.

   a. Properties

   b. Immediate

   c. Project Explorer

   d. Toolbox

LESSON 2

Customizing the Development Environment

All these wonderful windows are handy, but you don't really need all of them all of the time, and the screen is awfully cluttered. If you increase the size of your form, for example, the dockable windows on either side of the form will hide part of it, and you will have to use the scroll bars to view different parts. Worse yet, you will have problems visualizing the overall appearance of the form. It makes sense, then, to close at least some of the windows and undock others.

Start by clicking the Maximize button of the form. Find Window State in the Properties window. Set Window State to Maximized by clicking the Window State label, clicking the drop-down arrow that appears, and selecting Maximized from the drop-down list. Note that a portion of the Form window is clipped and that scroll bars let you view the hidden parts. You might find it more convenient to see more of the form and to close most of the other windows.

The Project Explorer

The Project Explorer is an essential window. As your project grows, you will need it to get from one part of the project to another. But while you are designing the user interface (the form), the Project Explorer is in the way. Click the Close button in the upper-right corner of the Project Explorer to close this window. You can get it back when you need it by selecting Project Explorer under the View menu, by pressing Ctrl+R, or by selecting the Project Explorer icon on the toolbar. Close this window now.

The Form Layout Window

You use the Form Layout window only once for each form in the project—and some-times not at all. The form in the current project opens maximized: It takes up the entire screen. There is no need to position it. Also, you often position your program's forms in the program code. As a rule, use the window when you first add a form to your project and then close it. You can reopen it from the View menu or select its icon on the toolbar, but there is no keyboard shortcut. Close it now.

The Immediate Window

You won't need the Immediate window very often. When you do, it is accessible from the View menu or by pressing Ctrl+G. Close it now.

The Properties Window

You need the Properties window to set the properties of the form and all of the controls you place on the form. If you also want to view parts of your form that the Properties window normally covers, you can drag it to another part of the screen. If you close the Properties window, you can reopen it from the View menu by pressing F4 or by selecting it on the toolbar. You can also drag it into another part of the screen. Leaving it floating is often more convenient than docking it.

The Toolbox

While you are designing the user interface of a form, the form's layout, you need the toolbox available. After you have placed all of your controls, however, you might want to close it to give yourself a better view of the form for setting properties and positioning the controls more precisely. You can reopen the toolbox from the View menu by pressing Ctrl+X or by selecting it on the toolbar. Leaving the toolbox floating is often more convenient than docking it.

On the Toolbar

Thought we weren't going to tell you? Figure 1.5 shows the right end of the standard toolbar, where you can find the icons for these necessary windows. There is no reason to worry about closing one of these windows because they are all so easy to recover.

FIGURE 1.5

Part of the standard toolbar.

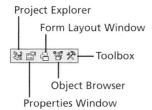

Project Explorer
Form Layout Window
—— Toolbox
Object Browser
Properties Window

A More Convenient Work Space?

Figure 1.6 shows a work space that we find convenient for form layout. The toolbox is showing, but it is floating instead of docked. It is easy to drag around the screen to get it out of the way. All the other windows are closed, but they are only a mouse click away. Your own preferences dictate the most convenient work space for you.

This arrangement provides good access to the form, most of which can be accessed without using the scroll bars. It is a great aid for form design.

Note

Don't forget that all these windows are sizable, too.

Customizing Your Toolbars

There are several options that are not on the standard toolbar that you might like to have available with the click of your mouse. For example, the Immediate window is not part of the default toolbar settings, but you may want to add it. As you gain more experience in programming, you will probably find other features that you use frequently that are not on any of the available toolbars.

FIGURE 1.6

A more convenient
work space.

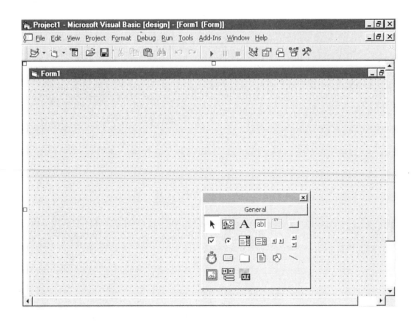

Fortunately, it is easy to customize a toolbar. Let's add a few items to the standard toolbar so that you can see how it is done.

1. Right-click the standard toolbar and select Customize from the pop-up menu that
   appears. The Customize window opens, as shown in Figure 1.7.

FIGURE 1.7

The Customize
window.

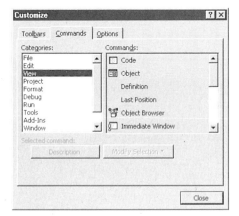

2. Select the Commands tab.
3. Click View in the Commands list box

4. Grab the icon for the Immediate window and drag it to the standard toolbar, as shown in Figure 1.8. Drop it just to the right of the Toolbox icon. This is called *drag and drop.*

FIGURE 1.8

Dropping the Immediate window icon on the toolbar.

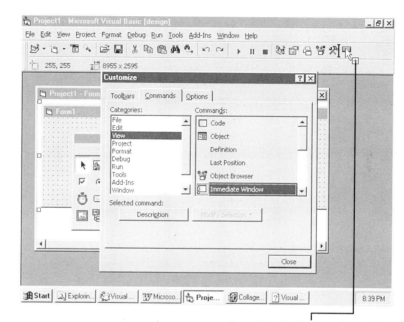

Dropping the icon on the toolbar

5. Repeat with the View Object and View Code icons. They will come in handy later.

Setting the Dockable Property

You can set the Dockable property of all the windows in a single step. Click the Tools menu and select Options. When the dialog box appears, select the Docking tab. Figure 1.9 shows the Docking tab. The check boxes indicate which windows are dockable and which are not. As an experiment, click the check box for the Properties window and then click OK. When you have returned to the development environment, open the Properties window by clicking its icon.

You may find this version of the Properties window more convenient to use. Note, however, what happens when you click the form. The Properties window disappears! It is no longer always on top. When it does not have the focus, it falls behind the window that does have the focus.

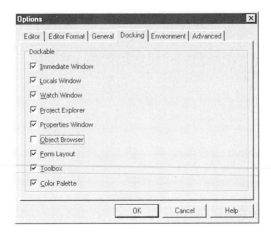

FIGURE **1.9**

The VB 6 Docking tab.

It is all a matter of taste; set your development environment up the way you like it. You can always change it.

While you are in the Options window, make one more change. Select the Environment tab and click the check box next to Prompt To Save Changes, then click OK. When you run a Visual Basic program, VB 6 asks whether you want to save any changes you have made. In most cases, the correct answer is Yes.

Lesson Summary

In this lesson, you have learned how to customize the Visual Basic development environment so that the screen is not too cluttered. In the next lesson, you will use a wizard to generate a Visual Basic program.

Quiz 2

1. What windows could you close while you are laying out a form?

    a. Properties, Toolbox

    b. Toolbox, Project Explorer

    c. Project Explorer

    d. Properties, Project Explorer

2. You can open the Properties window by pressing what?

    a. Ctrl+R

    b. F4

    c. Ctrl+G

    d. Ctrl+X

3. You can set the runtime position of a form by using the _____ window.

    a. Immediate

    b. Customize

    c. Options

    d. Form Layout

4. You can select which windows are dockable using the _____ window.

    a. Immediate

    b. Customize

    c. Options

    d. Form Layout

LESSON 3

The Application Wizard

Microsoft has added wizards to almost every software it produces, and Visual Basic 6 is no exception. In this lesson, you will use the Application Wizard to see how VB 6 creates a ready-to-modify application framework that can make your programming efforts look professional with a minimum amount of work. This book is dedicated to teaching you how to write and understand the code, so we will not use the wizards a lot. After you have mastered the art of programming, you might find some of them very helpful.

Running the Application Wizard

Select New Project under the File menu. (The keyboard shortcut is Ctrl+N if you prefer keys.) When the opening dialog box appears, select the VB Application Wizard. The Application Wizard—Introduction screen appears, as shown in Figure 1.10. As you are about to see, before the wizard creates your application, you will be presented with many choices. You can save these choices in a profile and select it as a shortcut the next time you want to make the same choices in the Application Wizard. Because you have not yet saved any choices in a profile, just click Next.

FIGURE **1.10**

*The Application
Wizard—Introduction
screen.*

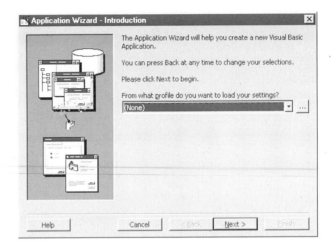

Note

If the Application Wizard is not available in the startup dialog box, click
Cancel. Then check whether the Application is available under the Add-Ins
menu. If it is not available, you can load the Application by selecting the
Add-In Manager under the Add-Ins menu. Find the Application Wizard entry
in the list, click it, and select Loan on Startup in the Load Behavior options.
After you click OK, you will find the Application Wizard listed under the
Add-Ins menu.

This brings up the Application Wizard—Interface Type screen, as shown in Figure 1.11,
which offers three types of user interfaces. It's too early to get really fancy, so select
Single Document Interface. Enter GeeWhiz (all one word) in the project name text box
and click Next.

Note

A Single Document Interface (or SDI) assumes that only one document will
be open at all times. Notepad is an example of a SDI application. We will
talk about the other interface types later in the book.

The next screen you see is the Application Wizard—Menus screen, as shown in Figure
1.12. Most Single Document Interface programs will have four standard menus—File,

Edit, View, and Help. The wizard gives you complete control over the menus and sub-menus included in your program. Let's get rid of a few submenus we do not need. Click the File menus to display its submenus in the right list box. Disable the Sen&d submenu and the separator above it. Click the View menu and disable the Web Browser submenu. The wizard adds all four menus with the selected submenus to your program. Click Next to move on.

FIGURE 1.11

The Application Wizard—Interface Type screen.

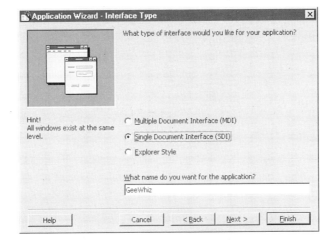

FIGURE 1.12

The Application Wizard—Menus screen.

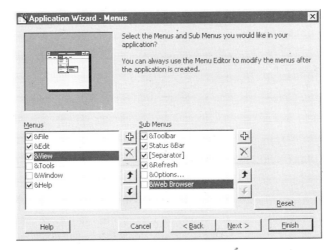

The next screen is the Application Wizard—Customize Toolbar screen, as shown in Figure 1.13. You can now customize the icons show in the toolbar. For now, we will settle for the default icons, so just click Next to move on.

FIGURE 1.13

The Application Wizard—Customize Toolbars screen.

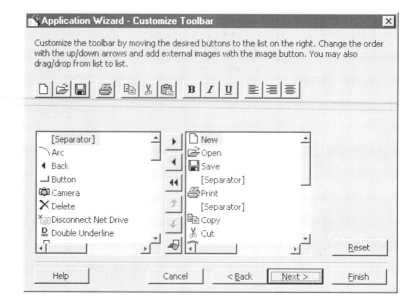

The next screen is the Application Wizard—Resources screen. Building resource files is an advanced topic that we will not cover in this book. Note that the No option is already selected. Just click Next to keep moving.

You see the Application Wizard—Internet Connectivity screen. Yep, it can be that easy! Well, almost that easy. As nice as it would be to add an Internet browser to your new application, it is far too early. Chapter 18, "Using Visual Basic for Communications," shows you how to build a Web browser. Be sure that No is selected and click Next.

This brings you to the Application Wizard—Standard Forms screen, as shown in Figure 1.14. Now you have some choices to make.

You can design forms that you will use again and again and save them in a standard forms template collection. Actually, Microsoft has provided you with a set of standard form templates in the TEMPLATE\FORMS subdirectory for Visual Basic 6, but you can add as many more as you want. Click the Form Templates button to get an idea of the choices. They don't all show up because most of your selections are made using the check boxes. Close the Form Templates dialog box. Now let's make our choices.

FIGURE 1.14

*The Application
Wizard—Standard
Forms screen.*

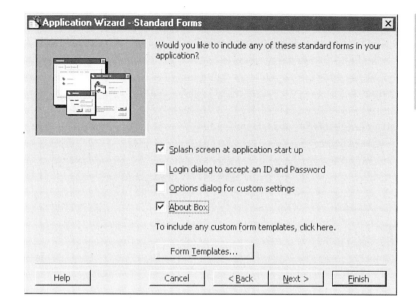

Splash Screen

A splash screen is a screen that comes up immediately and gives the user something to look at while the real working screens are being loaded. You see them all the time; Visual Basic 6 starts out with a splash screen, as do most other large programs. Splash screens give the illusion that your program loads more quickly than it actually does.

Based on the questions that appear in the Visual Basic Internet newsgroups, splash screens are not easy to do. Not any more! VB 6 can create one for you. All you have to do is modify it a little to make it uniquely your own. Click the Splash Screen check box to select it.

Note

You can get a lot of help and a lot of ideas from the Usenet newsgroups. As of this writing, four are devoted to Visual Basic. They are as follows:

```
comp.lang.basic.visual.3rdparty
comp.lang.basic.visual.announce
comp.lang.basic.visual.database
comp.lang.basic.visual.misc
```

There are also special newsgroups available at Microsoft's Visual Basic Web site, http://www.microsoft.com/vbasic. And if you enjoy the World Wide Web, a recent search found more than 83,000 documents about Visual Basic.

Login Dialog Box

Some programs need security, which requires a login screen where the user must enter a name and a password before entry to the program is granted. VB 6 can build the login screen for you, but you are not ready to use it yet, so skip this choice.

Options Dialog Box for Custom Settings

The best programs let you customize the way they look and, to some degree, the way they work. You have already customized Visual Basic 6, so you have a pretty good idea what that is all about. Customizing settings is pretty sophisticated for a first effort, so skip this choice.

About Box

If you pull down the Help menu in any good Windows program, you see an option called About. The program's makers use the About box to display copyright notices and version information. Really sophisticated programs include a choice here to enable the user to get system information.

VB 6 can build the About box for you. Some modification is required to personalize it, but the hard part is done. Put a check mark next to About Box; then click Next.

The next screen is the Application Wizard—Data Access Forms screen. You aren't writing a database application yet, so just remember that this option is available and click Next.

The Finished! Screen

The next and final screen you see is the Application Wizard—Finished! screen. There's no end to the wonders of this program! By clicking View Report, you can even receive a set of instructions about what you can do next! You can read the instructions on this screen and choose to close the screen or save the instructions to a text file and then close the screen.

For now, just ignore this option and click Finish. Your hard drive whirs and whizzes for a while, your screen flashes and flickers and gives you tantalizing views of sophisticated-looking forms, and finally you are rewarded with the screen shown in Figure 1.15.

If your Project Explorer is not open, open it now.

FIGURE 1.15

Your application has been created.

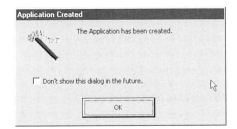

The Wizard-Created Program

According to the Project Explorer, you have three forms and a module in your program. This might not make a lot of sense to you right now, but you will get it. For now, you just want to see what VB 6 has wrought. Press F5 to run the program.

Pretty neat! And you have yet to write a single line of code! There you are with a nifty (so we exaggerate a bit!) splash screen; when the main form comes up, just look at everything there—four menus, a toolbar, and a status bar at the bottom of the screen.

Check out the menus. Under the File menu, select Open. You get a standard Windows file selection screen. Go ahead and select a file, perhaps a text file or a bitmap. It seems to load, but nothing happens. Try Print under the File menu. Aha! Now you begin to see what your job is.

Try a few of the icons on the toolbar. Except for File Open, none of them have any working code. Let your mouse pointer rest on one of the icons for a moment. You'll see a ToolTip—another new toy from Visual Basic 6.

Now let's look at some real sophistication. Select About under the Help menu. The About box has a place to put a picture—your logo, perhaps? There is space for the version number and a description of the application, or maybe a plug for your company. There is an ominous space labeled Warning..., which is where you will put your copyright notice.

And there is a System Info button. Go ahead: Click it! (If you are scared, take a look at Figure 1.16.)

FIGURE 1.16

Everything you always wanted to know about your system—and then some.

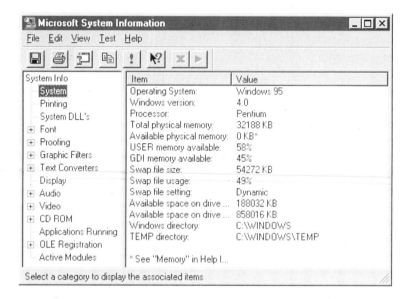

The System Info window is a standard Microsoft component that can be accessed from Visual Basic 6. Not too long ago, people spent a couple hundred dollars for programs that could tell them some of what this utility provides in your About box!

What's Missing?

You can see that the wizard did a lot of useful work for you, but a lot of work remains to be done. Except for a few standard functions, you must write the code to make all of the menu items work. And the main form is blank except for the menus and the toolbar. That's a good thing. After all, if Visual Basic could write the whole program, there wouldn't be a need for programmers!

The purpose of this book is for you to learn how to fill in the blanks, the remainder of the program, as well as how to create programs that differ from the standard patterns that the wizard will develop. To adapt the output of the wizards to your own tasks, you must understand the details of the programming language. Read on!

Lesson Summary

In this lesson, you used the Visual Basic Application Wizard to generate a skeletal SDI application. The generated program had a very complete user interface but very limited functionality. In the next lesson, you will learn about other utilities and wizards included with Visual Basic.

Quiz 3

1. What type of program interface will the Application Wizard create?

    a. Multiple Document Interface

    b. Single Document Interface

    c. Explorer Style Interface

    d. All of the above

2. Several standard menus are available in the wizard. The ones found in most programs are

    a. File, Edit, Window

    b. File, Edit, Help

    c. View, Edit, About

    d. File, Edit, Insert

3. Application wizard choices that you use over and over again can be saved as:

    a. Profiles

    b. Templates

    c. Patterns

    d. Formats

4. The _____ is used while the application loads.

    a. Login screen

    b. Splash Screen

    c. Options dialog box

    d. About box

LESSON 4

Add-Ins

Visual Basic 6 comes with several add-ins. Add-ins are extensions of the Visual Basic development environment: utilities and wizards that simplify some of the more common tasks. If you have the Professional or Enterprise Edition of Visual Basic 6, you can even create your own add-ins.

Adding Add-Ins

Add add-ins? Well, the default setup for VB 6 includes only one of the add-ins as a standard, the Visual Data Manager. You might find other add-ins that have not yet been added to the add-in menu lurking around in the `Samples` directory.

Select the Add-Ins menu. The default Add-Ins menu is shown in Figure 1.17.

FIGURE 1.17

The Add-Ins menu.

There are only two items in the Add-Ins menu at the moment: the Visual Data Manager and the Add-In Manager. Select the Add-In Manager. Your screen looks something like that in Figure 1.18.

FIGURE 1.18

The Add-In Manager screen.

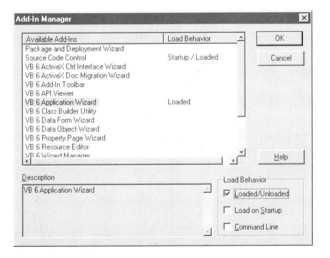

> **Note**   Some of the add-ins might not show up on your system. Different versions of Visual Basic support different features. As of this writing, full information on which features will be included with which version is not available.

Let's take a quick look at the add-ins shown in Figure 1.18.

Visual Data Manager

The Visual Data Manager lets you create databases without having to go to the expense of purchasing Microsoft Access. You will learn to work with databases in Chapter 13, "Database Programming."

API Viewer

Windows programs are built around a standard set of features known as the application program interface, or API. All programs call on the API for most of their functions. But some of the API functions are not accessed directly from Visual Basic. You can still use them, as you will see in Chapter 14, "Advanced Features," and again in Chapter 17, "Advanced ActiveX and Registry API Techniques."

Using the API is not difficult, but the API is picky. Everything must be just so, and much of what you have to add to your programs is quite detailed. The API viewer enables you to cut and paste the required declarations. It helps you avoid errors and is a great time saver.

The Microsoft Data Tools

The Data Tools add-in helps you build data-aware Internet applications. It requires Internet Explorer and Microsoft's SQL Server software. Its use goes beyond the scope of a beginning programmer's book.

SQL Debugger

SQL stands for Structured Query Language. You will learn some SQL in Chapter 13 but the SQL Debugger add-in is meant to be used with Microsoft's SQL Server software. Its use goes beyond the scope of a beginning programmer's book.

The VB ActiveX Control Interface Wizard

Visual Basic 6 lets you build your own ActiveX controls, which you will do in Chapter 8, "Using ActiveX Controls." The ActiveX Control Interface Wizard helps you create the public interface for a Visual Basic-generated ActiveX control after you have created your user interface. The public interface includes properties, methods, and events. (Yes, you will understand all this terminology—and soon, too!)

The VB ActiveX Document Migration Wizard

The programs you create with Visual Basic 6 can become ActiveX documents. That means that they can be viewed and operated with browsers such as the Internet Explorer and can be made available on the Internet or in company-wide intranets. The Document Migration Wizard does most of the work for you. You will migrate an application in Chapter 18.

What is ActiveX, anyhow? ActiveX is a programming standard that integrates software components in a networked environment. ActiveX controls can be integrated into Web pages. They can also be integrated into any application that supports ActiveX controls, including Microsoft Internet Explorer, Microsoft Office 97, Visual Basic, and Netscape Navigator via plug-ins.

Note

> Other companies are also building ActiveX capabilities into their products, enabling developers (that's you!) to include new controls in their applications.

The VB Add-In Toolbar

The VB Add-In toolbar lets you use all your selected add-ins with a single mouse click instead of having to use the Add-In menu.

The VB Application Wizard

We covered the Application Wizard in Lesson 3. Should you feel you need a refresher, do not hesitate to go back to this lesson.

The VB Class Builder Utility

Classes are the blueprints for object-oriented programming, and object-oriented programming is the foundation of all modern programming languages, including Visual Basic 6; you will be exposed to the concepts of object-oriented programming throughout this book. Although you don't need it, the Class Builder utility helps you build and organize your classes.

The VB Data Form Wizard

Database programming involves a lot of attention to detail. Databases can store tremendous amounts of data arranged in a bewildering array of tables and fields. The Data Form Wizard creates forms (screens) that display your data. Like all the other wizards, the Data Form Wizard leaves some of the finer details to you, but it can be a big time saver.

The VB Property Page Wizard

As you work with some of the controls in Visual Basic, you will discover that they have property pages, which are tabbed pages that help you customize the way a control looks and behaves. When you create your own ActiveX controls, the Property Page Wizard helps you add this sophisticated feature to your own controls.

The Wizard Manager

Just in case there aren't enough wizards to satisfy your taste, the Wizard Manager helps you build your own wizards. If you find yourself building the same kind of application time after time, or adding the same functionality to all your applications, you can build a wizard that automates the process for you.

Lesson Summary

Add-ins, builders, wizards! Visual Basic 6 makes every effort to provide you with the tools that simplify and speed the process of creating your own applications. If you already program in a previous version of Visual Basic or in another language, you will be amazed to discover how quickly Visual Basic 6 can do things that you used to spend hours doing. If you are a new programmer, you will be able to turn out professional-looking (and professional-acting) applications even while you learn Visual Basic.

Quiz 4

1. An add-in is
   a. A program that has been modified to work within Web browser programs
   b. An extension of the Visual Basic development
   c. A collection of functions and procedures that can be accessed by other programs
   d. A component that you add to your program

2. The _____ add-in is an advanced tool used with Microsoft SQL Server.
   a. SQL Debugger
   b. Property Page Wizard
   c. Data Form Designer
   d. ActiveX Document Migration Wizard

3. You can create your own ActiveX controls for Visual Basic with the help of:
   a. The ActiveX Control Interface Wizard
   b. The Visual Data Manager
   c. The ActiveX Document Migration Wizard
   d. The Wizard Manager

4. You can build your own wizards with:

    a. The ActiveX Control Interface Wizard

    b. The Visual Data Manager

    c. The ActiveX Document Migration Wizard

    d. The Wizard Manager

LESSON 5

Help!

This might be the single most important lesson in the entire book. There is no way that any book can hope to cover all the features of Visual Basic 6 or all the possibilities you may uncover for using them. Finding and solving new problems is one of the joys of programming.

Visual Basic 6 comes with a large collection of Help files. Knowing how to find what you need by using the Help files is one of your most valuable skills.

Using Help

If you have been using Windows for any length of time, you already know how to use Help. You might be surprised to know how many Visual Basic users ask questions that are answered in the Help files! Open the Help menu; a menu something like the one shown in Figure 1.19 appears.

FIGURE 1.19

The Visual Basic 6 Help menu.

Hmmm. There's more here than the usual Help and About listings. Let's take a look at them.

Microsoft Visual Basic Help Topics

This is where you will spend most of your time in Help. You will spend some time visiting this section later in this lesson.

Search Reference Index

As of this writing, this choice takes you to exactly the same place as Help Topics.

Search Master Index

Included on the Visual Basic 6 CD is a version of Microsoft's Books Online database. The Master Index referred to here is the index of the VB Books Online file.

Obtaining Technical Support

Microsoft offers technical support in several different venues. The information in this menu provides the latest information on how to get official Microsoft technical support.

Microsoft on the Web

This menu option provides the URL for Microsoft's Web pages. It also includes the Internet address of the Microsoft FTP sites for Visual Basic. If you have Internet access, the WWW pages are the best way to keep up with changes, problem solutions, and ideas.

About Microsoft Visual Basic

This option displays the standard About box, including, of course, that System Info button you found in GeeWhiz.

A Closer Look

Let's take a closer look at the Microsoft Visual Basic Help Topics selection. Click that now. A menu such as the one shown in Figure 1.20 appears.

FIGURE 1.20

Visual Basic Help topics.

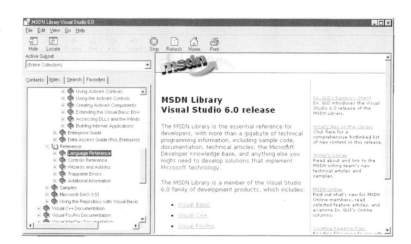

Familiar enough, of course—Microsoft did not suddenly reinvent the Help system just for Visual Basic. What it has done is used the Help system to its fullest potential. Double-click Objects, then the C: book, and finally the CheckBox control icon. A screen like that shown in Figure 1.21 appears.

FIGURE 1.21

Help on the CheckBox *control.*

You selected the check box because you are already familiar with it, although this gives you a lot more detail than you had before, when you just clicked it. Don't pay a lot of attention to what it says about the CheckBox control for now; you will work with that in Chapter 2, "Object-Oriented Programming." Notice, instead, the choices offered at the top of the screen. As we discuss each one, click it to see what it offers.

See Also

The See Also choice points you to other Help topics that have some bearing on the CheckBox control. Because some Help topics cover items that are closely related to other Help topics, you will find this invaluable in tracking down all the references you need to get a task done.

Example

If you are looking up a command or a function, the Help system will often give you an example of how to use it. You can even cut and paste the example into your own programs! There are no examples for most of the controls, and Example is grayed out in that case.

Properties

Properties are attributes or characteristics, such as color and size. If you click the Properties choice, you see a list of the control's properties, as shown in Figure 1.22.

FIGURE 1.22

The properties of a check box.

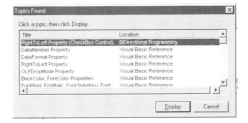

Again, don't pay a lot of attention yet. What you need is to learn how to find things in the Help files. You will have plenty of time to dig out more details later.

Methods

Methods are things you can do to a control. You can, for example, move it or give it focus (make it the active control). Methods are often thought of as verbs (subroutines and functions in programming lingo), such as MoveThis or DoThat. Try clicking the Methods choice to get an idea. The CheckBox has only a few methods. Other controls have many more.

Events

Events are procedures that are triggered when things happen to a control. For example, you can click a check box. When you do, the Click event is fired and the control can respond to what you have done. Once again, there are only a few events for a CheckBox control, whereas other controls have dozens.

Specifics

When a topic requires a lot of detail, the Specifics choice is enabled. Because a check box is a pretty simple control, Specifics is grayed out.

Summary

The Summary choice is not shown for a check box. It is displayed for topics such as the Database Object, where the topic you are viewing is a small part of a collection of related controls.

The Control Buttons

There are also three control buttons at the top of the screen. Let's take a look.

Help Topics

The Help Topics button takes you back to the Table of Contents screen.

Back

Windows Help keeps a history of the choices you have made during a Help session. If you have selected a series of Help topics, the Back button lets you move backward through the list of topics you have viewed. This is often handier than trying to find the topic again.

Options

The Options button offers several more choices. You can

- *Annotate the topic:* Write notes on the topic that you can then view the next time you bring the topic up. The same choice lets you read notes you have written.
- *Copy the topic to the clipboard:* After the topic is copied, you can paste it into any Windows document.
- *Print the topic:* Use this sparingly unless you have reams of paper and are an excellent organizer.
- *Change the font size:* The three choices are small, normal, and large, which is helpful on those late nights after a 16-hour stint at the keyboard.
- *Keep Help on top, or not, depending on your taste*: It is always on top by default.
- *Use System Colors for Windows Help:* If you have a favorite color scheme, you can have Help use the same colors.

But Wait! There's More!

The main Help screen has three tabs, and you have looked at only one of them. The others can sometimes be your biggest help.

The Index Tab

The Help files have an index, which can usually help you find what you are looking for faster than the Table of Contents. Switch to the Index tab now and type check into the text box at the top. You see something like Figure 1.23.

It turns out that there is more to this topic than you originally saw! Not really—but the index seems to be a quicker way to find things.

The Find or Search Tab

The Find or Search tab is even more flexible. The first time you select Find, the computer wants to do a conversion of the word list. Tell it OK, then go get some coffee and a couple of donuts—it can take a while. Even after the Find or Search database has been created, the Find or Search tab takes a few seconds the first time you click it so that it can load the word list. It is more than worth the wait.

FIGURE **1.23**

Index finding check.

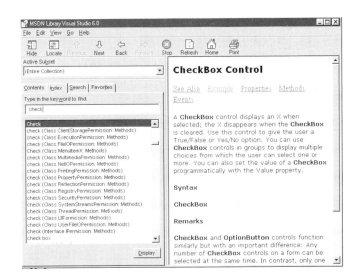

Click Find or Search now and type check in the text box at the top of the Find or Search tab's dialog box. The Find or Send tab looks something like that in Figure 1.24.

FIGURE **1.24**

Find finding check.

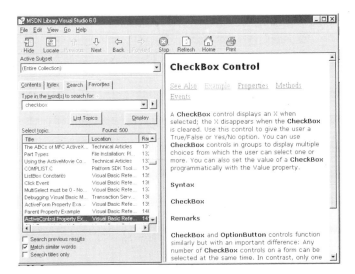

Now there is a collection of information! You can even tailor the search if you are looking for something in a specific area. You can change the time when the search begins and how much of what you type in is a required part of the search key, all of which is handled by the Options button.

By default, the Find or Search tab begins searching when there is a pause in your typing; it searches for all references that begin with the characters you typed, and it searches through the entire collection of VB 6 Help files.

Lesson Summary

Practice using the Visual Basic Help files. Practically everything you need to know is included in there somewhere, and it is available whenever you need it. You might have to dig for your information, but if you persist, you can find it.

This lesson has concentrated on the Visual Basic 6 Help files. The Contents tab offers well-organized, single-topic selections; the Index tab widens the scope of your search; and the Find tab gives you the broadest search capabilities. You will find that all these tabs are handy, but chances are, you will find yourself using one more than the other two combined. Which one that is will be a matter of personal taste.

Quiz 5

1. The VB 6 Help system provides information about the _____ for controls.

    a. Properties, methods, and events

    b. Color, position, and size

    c. Syntax

    d. None of the above

2. The Search Master Index is the _____.

    a. Complete list of all events, methods, and properties

    b. Index of VB Books Online

    c. Complete list of all Controls

    d. Index of all Visual Basic Help files

3. The _____ button lets you visit topics related to the one you're currently viewing.

    a. Contents

    b. See Also

c. Help

d. Back

4. The _____ button lets you change the font size or add annotations to the Help files.

a. Index

b. Options

c. Find

d. Contents

Chapter Summary

In this chapter, we explored the Visual Basic development environment. Along the way, we customized it so that we could be more productive. Then, we used Visual Basic Application Wizard to create a skeletal SDI application with all graphical elements in place, but with limited functionality. We looked at the other add-ins available in Visual Basic 6. Finally, we took a close look at the VB 6 Help system.

In Chapter 2, we discuss the method used to write Visual Basic programs.

CHAPTER 2

Object-Oriented Programming

Effective Visual Basic 6 programming is based on the concept of objects. An *object* is a distinct unit in a program that has certain characteristics and can perform certain actions. In object-oriented programming, you approach a programming problem by asking the following questions:

- How can I break down this task into objects?
- What will each object look like?
- How will it behave?
- How do the objects interact?

The advantage of object-oriented programming, or OOP, is that well designed objects are reusable in other applications. The most visible example of this technique is Microsoft Windows itself. The elements you commonly use to interact with your computer—windows, buttons, menus, and so on—are all objects. As a Visual Basic programmer, you add these types of objects to your programs.

You control their characteristics—such as whether or not a window is sizable—and what happens when your program's user interacts with them; for example, by clicking a button. However, many of the tasks that are common to all objects of the same type are handled automatically by Windows.

LESSON 1

Objects

The word object has a particular meaning in software development terminology. An object also means different things to different people. We are going to concentrate on the definition of objects and OOP from the perspective of Visual Basic 6.

The Evolution of Object-Oriented Programming

In the past, programmers were taught to take complex problems and break them down into smaller, less complex ones. This process, termed *decomposition*, might be familiar to you as the traditional top-down approach to software design. Decomposition continues until you are left with a finite set of procedures—small units of code—that fully define the solution to the problem.

The problem with *procedural design* is that the resulting software is inherently inflexible. Small changes to one localized section of the design can affect code in a large number of source files. Even well-structured software designed by highly experienced analysts is affected in this way. Eventually, the software becomes difficult, or even impossible, to maintain and debug. When it reaches this stage, the only option is to start all over again.

When the computer software industry was in its infancy, the idea that software had to be ultimately disposable was largely accepted. As software became more complex and, therefore, more expensive, the fact that the software itself needed to be more durable and accepting of change became clear. It also became clear that the design techniques themselves were flawed.

To understand more about software design, software designers and methodologists turned to other industries to see if anything could be learned from their design and construction techniques. The construction industry itself is a good example. After all, it would be ridiculous if you had to dismantle your house every time you wanted to redecorate. Yet this was what had been happening to software for many years.

Eventually, it was recognized that although computing was a new industry, it didn't necessarily require new design strategies. Like a construction project, a software project could be seen as a system that programmers would build up from lots of small, self-contained objects.

Objects surround us. This is obvious. We intuitively know what a real-world object is because we can use our senses to determine that it exists. Some examples of real-world objects are trees, cars, people, computers, desks, and chairs. Let's have a look at the characteristics that all objects have in common:

- Each individual object is a self-contained unit. The existence of one particular object is not dependent on the existence of another.

- Although individual objects are unique, each object can be identified as belonging to a particular classification through its properties.

- Objects can respond to certain predefined external stimuli only.

- Objects can interact with each other and with the outside world in a predefined and limited manner.

- Although each object behaves in a different way, many of the things objects know how to do can be given the same name. For example, for humans to walk, we have to coordinate moving two legs. For dogs to walk, they have to coordinate four legs. Both can walk, but neither is concerned at a strategic level with the actual processes involved.

- Some methodologists have strict criteria for naming a programming language *object-oriented* and a set of broader criteria for naming it *object-based*. By these standards, Visual Basic 6 is object-based. For simplicity's sake, we are ignoring this theoretical distinction in this text.

And So What?

How does this understanding of objects relate to computer software?

Imagine that a sports equipment manufacturer has hired you as an information technology consultant. The company has decided to launch a new range of soccer balls for both the professional and the home markets. To achieve its goal, the company has to transform a basic design concept into a fully operational manufacturing process.

To begin with, the company only has a vague idea about the final products and their performance specifications. For example, it knows that the top-of-the-line professional ball will have to be made of a number of black and white hexagonal and square pieces of leather, stitched together to form a sphere. It knows that the ball will contain an inner tube that will have to be inflated to a certain air pressure, with the air inlet protected by a valve to prevent the air from escaping.

Compare this with the bottom-of-the-line ball for the home market. This will be made of two molded hemispherical pieces of plastic, which will then be bonded together. Unlike the professional ball, this version will be inflated during the manufacturing process and, instead of a valve, a solid piece of plastic will be molded into the air inlet hole to prevent the air from escaping.

The company needs to determine the type and grade of materials that will be used in the construction of the various versions of the ball. Criteria such as durability, bounce, and burst pressure will all affect the choice of materials and the manufacturing processes eventually chosen. Factors such as the grade of leather and thread used, as well as the stitching technique itself, will affect the durability of the professional ball. Similarly, the type of plastic and the plastic welding technique used to bond the two halves of the domestic ball together must produce a strong enough bond to meet the specification for that product.

Traditionally, the company has relied on prototyping to determine that both the materials and manufacturing processes will meet the required standards. However, prototyping is expensive and time-consuming, so instead, the company has come to you to write a computer system to model the performance of balls made from different materials and manufacturing processes.

Thinking in Objects

Object-oriented programming requires you to think first of the things you are trying to model in your software. (In *procedural-oriented* design, by contrast, you would first think about how those things work.) This does not imply that analyzing how things work is unimportant, but it is not of central importance and does not influence the higher-level design.

The first problem most software analysts have is working out what an object is in their particular project. They often have difficulty identifying where the boundaries between objects lie. Some objects have boundaries that are fairly intuitive. For example, it is easy to tell that, in your prototyping system, you need to think of a ball as an object, because it directly relates to something that exists in the real world. Although the objects in each particular project vary each time, there is a broad rule that you can apply. Try to think of every thing in object-oriented terms. In other words, assume that everything you can represent by a noun in the system that you are trying to model is an object. Examples in this project would include a ball, an inner tube, and an air inlet.

Object-oriented analysis is all about understanding the properties and behavioral characteristics of the objects in your project. Once you have identified what the objects are, you need to consider the following:

- An object's properties, which help identify it as being an object of a particular type
- The common external events to which objects of a particular type need to respond
- The common capabilities that objects of a particular type need to exhibit to make them useful

Objects Have Properties

To classify objects as belonging to a particular type, you need to identify the properties that distinguish them from other types of objects.

In the prototyping example, the professional ball might have the following properties:

- *The length of one side of one hexagonal shape:* Because the number and arrangement of hexagonal and square shapes is fixed, you only need to vary the size of each component piece to produce a ball of a different size. It is possible to write an algorithm to calculate the entire surface of the ball from this one measurement. (An *algorithm* is a way of going about solving a problem. In our example, it will be the formula used to calculate the surface of the ball.)

- *Internal and external air pressure expressed in pounds per square inch:* You would need this property to model how well the ball might bounce.

- *Strength of outer skin expressed on a percentage scale:* You would need this property to assess the durability of different grades of leather over time.

Obviously, a real prototyping system would need to implement more properties than these for an accurate representation of a soccer ball. This list does, however, convey the kinds of properties that objects have.

Objects Have Events

To exist in an environment, objects must be able to react with that environment and with other objects that share that environment. For example, in the prototyping system, consider how you might model how well a soccer ball bounces. Provided you have an algorithm for modeling how a ball moves when it comes into contact with some external surface, you simply have to recognize that, to make the ball bounce, it has to be able to respond to the event of hitting the other surface. Let's call this event Touch. Therefore, every time a ball comes into contact with another surface, a Touch event occurs, and your simulation of the ball reacts to the event.

Similarly, each time the ball moves to a different position, it will be necessary to redraw the ball on the screen. So the list of events that the ball would have to respond to would have to include a ReDraw event.

Objects Have Methods

Objects also have to perform functions of their own. It isn't usually enough that the object exists. After all, the whole point of creating an object is that the object does something useful. These additional functions are known as *methods* in OOP terms.

In the prototyping example, one of the methods that the soccer balls would have to implement would be the functionality that draws the ball on the screen. Earlier, we talked about the example of humans and canines, who both know how to walk. The processes are different, but the verb is the same. Similarly, you'll be able to draw a ball in your project simply by using the verb *draw* because each ball will contain the source code it needs to be able to draw itself on the screen.

It is legitimate to connect an object's methods to the events that it responds to so that the object can perform useful tasks in response to external events. Given the example of a ball object responding to a ReDraw event, the ball could simply call its Draw method every time it receives a ReDraw event to update the screen.

Objects Are Instances of Classes

Until now, we have talked about different classifications or types of objects. You have also seen how an object can be defined by its properties, events, and methods. Object-oriented terms use the word *class* to refer to the properties, events, and methods that uniquely define a type of object.

Note   When we refer to a class, we are not referring to a tangible object, either in the real world or in the context of the computer program. Rather, a class is the information that we need to create an object of that class.

Each object in a program is said to be an instance of its class. The form and controls you use to build a program are actually instances of their respective classes.

You should now be able to see another benefit of object-oriented design. Each object is a separate unit, consisting of the code and the data, which together refer to that particular instance of the class. In the prototyping example, it would therefore be a simple matter to model more than one ball on the screen at the same time. You could simply create a new instance of one particular class of ball. To model two or more professional balls at the same time, you could just create the number of professional ball objects that you require. It would also be a simple matter to create instances of different types of balls and model them all on the screen at the same time.

Some objects naturally fit into a schema in which multiple instances of the objects might exist. The soccer ball is a good example. Others do not, however. For instance, take the screen around which the soccer balls are bouncing. Remember that everything in your object-oriented world should be considered an object. Accordingly, the environment in which your soccer ball objects bounce around must be an object itself. It would not make sense, however, to have more than one screen object.

Objects Have Life Cycles

Now that you have seen that objects are instances of their classes, you may recognize that objects have life cycles. That is to say that in order to be used, they have to be created. At some point, when they are not needed any more, they can be destroyed. You should also note that, before an object is created, it doesn't exist and therefore it doesn't take up any of the computer's resources (memory). Similarly, when an object is destroyed, the memory that was being used by that object is freed and is then available for reuse.

Note

> If you have trouble identifying the classes used in an application or their interaction, it may be helpful to use a design technique known as *use cases*. In a use case, you describe what the application does from a user's perspective in user terms. Each user interaction is simplified to a basic level and described in a use case. When designing an ATM application, you would identify several dozens of use cases, such as User Logs on to ATM (first attempt, password correct). A first attempt with an incorrect password would be another use case, and so on. After having described a fairly substantial portion of the application in this way, you can look for classes (nouns) and methods (verbs).

Lesson Summary

In this lesson, you have been introduced to the terms used when talking about object-oriented programming. You should now understand what is meant by the terms object, instance, class, property, event, and method. In next lesson, we will start putting these concepts to work.

Quiz 1

1. A property is best defined as

    a. Something that an object has

    b. Something that an object knows how to do

    c. The size of something, such as the side of a soccer ball

    d. A characteristic of an object

2. A method is best defined as

   a. A function that calls an object

   b. A function that an object knows how to do

   c. Walking

   d. A type of event

3. Which of the following is not an object that might appear in a printing application?

   a. A printer driver

   b. A file

   c. A font

   d. The number of pages to print

4. After defining the characteristics of a class, how do you add an object of that class to your program?

   a. Generate an instance of that class.

   b. Generate a method of that class.

   c. Add a Name property to refer to it.

   d. You don't have to do anything further; defining the class automatically creates the object.

Exercise 1

Complexity: Moderate

1. What properties, methods and events do you think a bank account as used in ATM software might have?

Complexity: Advanced

2. What classes do you think would be used to design ATM software?

LESSON 2

Forms: Your First Program

Sure, you've heard how easy it is to program in Visual Basic. Let's find out how easy it really is!

Off and Running

Double-click the Visual Basic 6 program icon and select Standard Exe. From the Run menu, select Start. The program that's running represents Visual Basic's default project: a single blank window called Form1. Even though you haven't done anything, this window, shown in Figure 2.1, behaves as you would expect it to. You can move it around, minimize or maximize it, or resize it. This is because Windows already knows how this object is supposed to behave.

FIGURE 2.1

This really is a program.

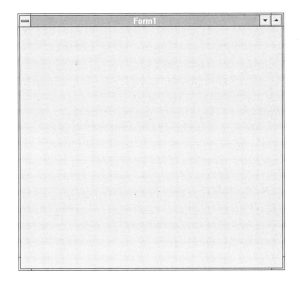

Now close the program by clicking the window's Close box and selecting the Close menu option. (The Close box and its menu are shown in Figure 2.2.) You return to the Visual Basic design screen.

FIGURE 2.2

Click the Close option to quit.

In Visual Basic, this window object is called a *form*. The form contains most of the other objects that make up your program. In Figure 2.2, the form is a generic sizable window.

Note

> A form can be large, such as a program's main screen, or small, such as a dialog box. A form can even be hidden from view, performing tasks in the background. You specify all the characteristics of the forms in your program. When your program is running, Microsoft Windows handles much of the form's behavior automatically.

Looking Pretty

A program can have one or many forms. The form that comes up when the user first runs your program is called the *startup form*. By default, this is called Form1. Let's change this name to something more descriptive.

The description of the form that appears on the title bar is called a *caption*. A caption is one of the many characteristics or properties that an object can have.

You can change most properties at design time, which is when you are laying out your application and writing code. You can also change most properties at runtime as well, which is when your program is running.

Note

> The Visual Basic title bar indicates whether you are currently in design or runtime mode.

Notice the Properties window, shown in Figure 2.3. The property names are in the left column; the corresponding values are in the right. The long list of properties for Form1 gives you an idea of the power Visual Basic provides over your form design. Luckily for you, the default settings describe a fairly typical window and are fine for now. Click the Caption property and type in File Picker. Note that VB copies the caption to the title bar as you type it.

Visual Basic's visual editing system lets you "draw" your program to your specifications. What you see on the screen is pretty much what you'll get when the program runs. Test this by resizing the form and running the program again to see your changes reflected.

Stay in Control

Tired of looking at an empty window? Let's add some objects to the form.

Visual Basic has several types of objects. Forms are one type. Controls are another. A Visual Basic control is the most common component of VB programs. Typical controls are small, with a specific function, such as a Command button or check box. Other controls offer more elaborate functionality, such as the Data control and MCI (multimedia) control.

FIGURE 2.3

The Properties window.

Under the View menu, click Toolbox. This brings up the selection window for the Visual Basic 6 controls, as shown in Figure 2.4. Note that the ToolTips feature is implemented; when you hold the mouse cursor over an icon for a few seconds, you can see the name of the control that icon represents.

FIGURE 2.4

The toolbox enables you to add controls to your project.

Click the Command button icon indicated in the figure. The CommandButton control puts a standard gray Windows button on the screen. When the program is running, the user can click the button to issue a command.

Now draw the button onto the form by holding down the mouse button and drawing a rectangle. When you let go of the mouse, the button appears in the size and location you specified. Notice how you can pick up the button with the mouse and move it around, or resize it as you would a window.

Let's change the text that the user sees on the Command button. Like a form, a Command button uses the `Caption` property to specify a label. Click the Command button once to select it. Note the properties available to this control.

Note

> The Properties window lists the properties for the currently selected form or control. The name of this control is noted on the title bar of the Properties window. It's a good idea to get in the habit of checking to make sure the correct object is specified. Otherwise, you may change a property value for the wrong control; if the change is minor, it might take some time before you catch the mistake. To change the active object in the Properties window, select a new property from the drop-down list box right beneath the title bar.

Select the `Caption` property for the Command button and enter `Done`. The change is reflected immediately.

Run the program again by clicking Run under the Start menu. You can click this button to your heart's content and it automatically receives the focus and "presses" in and out. What's that, you say? But it doesn't do anything? Microsoft Windows can handle common tasks, but unfortunately it can't read our minds. If you want that button to do something, you have to tell it what to do! Quit the program by clicking the Close box and then selecting Close.

Lesson Summary

In this lesson, you have created your first Visual Basic program. This program did not require any code, but you were able to move the window around, minimize or maximize it and resize it. You also added a command button to the window, thereby getting a taste of visual programming. In the next lesson, you will add code to make the button functional.

Quiz 2

1. Although there are many advantages to OOP, the main advantage is
   a. You get to feel you're on the leading edge of software design.
   b. It's easier to learn.
   c. Breaking a task down into objects is less work than breaking it down into functions.
   d. Well-designed objects can be reused in different applications.

2. A Visual Basic form is most like
   a. A window
   b. A list of items you can select from
   c. A file selector
   d. A button

3. The `Caption` property
   a. Lets the user type in a new value for the title bar
   b. Is a value you set at runtime or design time to label an object for the user
   c. Requires complicated programming to define
   d. Is always Command1

4. Which of the following tasks is likely not handled automatically by Microsoft Windows?
   a. Displaying a window on screen
   b. Minimizing or maximizing a window
   c. Performing a specific task, such as adding a list of numbers, in response to the user's request
   d. Making a button looked pressed when the user clicks it

LESSON 3

Getting Things Done

Objects have things, they do things, and they can respond to things. In Visual Basic lingo, the characteristics that describe an object are known as its properties. An action that an object performs is called a *method*. Finally, an object responds to system events. In this lesson, we'll talk about events.

The Main Event

An event is something that happens in the environment. This can be triggered by a user (clicking a control), by another program (messages), or by something such as a timer going off.

In Lesson 2, you saw the Properties window, which shows all the properties associated with each control. Now let's take a look at the events associated with each control. While still in design mode, double-click the button labeled Done. You'll see the Code window shown in Figure 2.5. The list box to the left contains all the objects in the current project that have events associated with them. A list box is a standard Windows interface element that gives the user a list of items and lets the user select one of them.

FIGURE 2.5

The Code window.

By Any Other Name

Notice that the name of the current object is Command1, not Done. That's because the Caption property value—the label the user sees—is completely separate from the name that you use to identify the object within the program. Internally, the property that identifies a control is the Name property. The Name property is a unique name that lets you refer to the object's other property values, the events associated with the object, and the methods the object can perform. You've already seen this property used in the Properties window. Visual Basic assigns all objects a default name (Form1, Command1) when you create them. Later, you'll change these names to make them more descriptive.

Take another look at Figure 2.5. The list box to the right contains all the events that can be triggered for the current object. The Code window comes up with a default event for the current object. In this case it's the Click event, which is what you want. The Click event is fired when the user clicks the form or control.

Events are processed in subroutines or procedures: logical groupings of code. This subroutine is bracketed by the keywords `Private Sub` and `End Sub`. The name of this routine is `Command1_Click()`. Whatever source code you place inside this routine executes whenever the associated event is fired.

> **Note**
>
> Event routine names are always in the form:
>
> ```
> ControlName_Event([parameters])
> ```
>
> (Don't worry about parameters for now.)

Know the Code

It's time to start adding source code.

Visual Basic 6 has a rich and powerful language in which you'll write the procedural aspects of your projects. Visual Basic has a nice feature called *automatic syntax checking*. When you press Enter after typing in a line of code, Visual Basic alerts you if there's an error in that line.

> **Note**
>
> A *programming language* is a command set that lets you instruct the computer to perform certain tasks. Types of commands typically include assignments, system commands, conditional instructions, and looping instructions. Additionally, you can call subroutines and functions to perform complex tasks and build subroutines and functions of your own. Because Visual Basic 6 is an object-oriented language, many (if not most) of the routines you'll be working with will have to do with defining the behavior of the objects that make up your program.

Make sure the cursor is between the `Private Sub` and `End Sub` lines and enter the following line of code:

```
Unload Me
```

The `Unload Me` statement removes the active window, thus ending the program and returning control to the operating system or shell (if the program is compiled) or the Visual Basic development environment (if not). `Me` refers to the form (we will explain this in greater detail in Chapter 4, "Variables, Constants, and Associated Functions") that will be unloaded. The screen should now look like that shown in Figure 2.6. Go ahead and run the program; clicking the Done button now ends the program.

FIGURE 2.6

Real source code in place.

> **Note**
>
> In some programming languages, instructions are case sensitive. That is, something called student is different from something called STUDENT. Other languages are not case-sensitive; you could use the two expressions interchangeably. Visual Basic handles case in a slightly different way.

Instructions are not case sensitive; you can type unload me, Unload Me, or UNLOAD ME and it all means the same thing. *However, Visual Basic has a preferred case usage for keywords*, and it automatically converts whatever you type to that usage. Thus, if you type in

```
unload me
```

as soon as you press Enter, Visual Basic changes the command to

```
Unload Me
```

VB 6 similarly changes form1 to Form1, label1 to Label1, and so on.

Furthermore, VB forces all your variable names to have the same case usage everywhere they appear. Thus, if you declare a variable to be named NumStudents, and enter a line such as

```
numstudents=5
```

when you press Enter, VB will change it to

```
NumStudents=5
```

Moving Right Along

By now you should be getting a feel for the Visual Basic development process, sketched out in broad strokes in Figure 2.7. Visual editing lets you draw the interface for the program. Then you add the code, the functionality, to your program. Finally, you test your work.

FIGURE 2.7

The VB 6 development process.

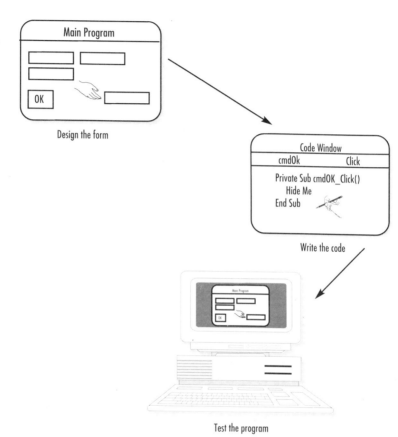

Design the form

Write the code

Test the program

In practice, this process is cyclical; once you've tested a component, you move on to add the next piece. This illustration also omits the design and architecture phase, which takes place before you even load up Visual Basic.

Visual Basic's File Controls

Let's add some more controls to the form to make this program more functional. Drag three new controls onto the form: a FileListBox control, a DirListBox control, and a DriveListBox control. The icons for these controls are indicated in Figure 2.8. These three controls pack a lot of functionality. In fact, you'll notice that as soon as you put them on the form, they fill in with information about the current directory and drive, even though you're still in design mode.

FIGURE 2.8

The file selection controls.

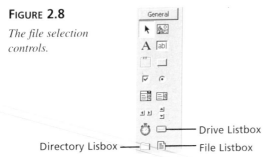

Directory Lisbox ——— □ ▤ ——— File Listbox

——— Drive Listbox

The `FileListBox` control is a list box that Visual Basic automatically fills with the contents of the current directory. The `FileName` property of the control contains the currently selected filename.

The `DirListBox` control is a list box that Visual Basic automatically fills with the current directory's subdirectories. The `Path` property of the control contains the currently selected directory name. This selection defaults to the current directory.

The `DriveListBox` control is a list box that Visual Basic automatically fills with the drives currently available on the system. The `Drive` property of the control contains the currently selected drive name. This selection defaults to the current drive.

Sizing Things Up

The standard Windows file selector is adequate, but we always find we have to spend a lot of time on the scroll bars. Let's make the `FileListBox` and `DirListBox` controls nice and long. To resize a control, click it to select it, then grab (hold down the left mouse button) the lower-right sizing square to the new position. Run the program again; the screen should look roughly like that shown in Figure 2.9.

Looking good! Notice that even though the file selection controls and the `CommandButton` control have vastly different functionality, from your perspective they work more or less the same. You drop them where you want them and let them do their thing. If you play with this program a little, you'll notice it doesn't really work; selecting a new drive or directory has no effect. Here, again, is where Windows leaves off and we pick up. You'll add this functionality via code in Lesson 4.

FIGURE 2.9

Program with file selection controls.

Lesson Summary

In this lesson, you made the Done command button functional with a single line of code. You also set the stage for the next lesson by adding a DriveListBox, a DirListBox, and a FileListBox to the form. Next, you will add the code needed to make these controls functional.

Quiz 3

1. In Visual Basic terms, an event is

   a. Something the user does, such as clicking something or moving a form

   b. Something that Windows does, such as setting off a timer or letting you know when something's changed

   c. Something another program does, such as sending a message to your program

   d. Any of the above

2. The Code window

   a. Is where you enter code for your program

   b. Can be accessed only at runtime

   c. Is where you output debugging statements

   d. Is accessible only via a secret decoder ring

3. The property used internally to identify an object is

   a. The `Caption` property

   b. The `Name` property

   c. The `Variable` property

   d. The `Label` property

4. When the user clicks an object

   a. The mouse cursor changes to a button.

   b. You need to detect which object was selected by analyzing the x,y coordinates of the mouse.

   c. Windows figures out what you probably want that object to do and does it.

   d. A `click` event is generated for that object.

LESSON 4

The File Picker Gets Better

So far, you've built a little program that looks like it should do something but actually doesn't. Let's go back into the file picker and add some functionality. Recall that the program is made up of the components shown in Table 2.1.

TABLE 2.1   The File Picker Objects

Object	Property	Value
Form	Name	Form1
	Caption	File Picker
CommandButton	Name	Command1
	Caption	Done
FileListBox	Name	File1
DirListBox	Name	Dir1
DriveListBox	Name	Drive1

The `File` Control's Properties

The file selection controls all have built-in functionality. To access this functionality, you'll have to get to know the properties of the controls that relate to this functionality. These properties are summarized in Table 2.2.

TABLE 2.2 Important File Selection Properties

Property	Applies to	Description
Drive	DriveListBox	Sets or returns the currently selected drive. Not available at design time.
Path	DirListBox, FileListBox	For the DirListBox, sets or returns the currently selected path. For the FileListBox, sets or returns the path containing the currently displayed list of files. Not available at design time.
FileName	FileListBox	Sets or returns the name of the currently selected file. Not available at design time.

Because these are all runtime properties, you won't see them in the Properties window. You'll need to access them directly in code.

> **Note**
>
> To access the value of an object's property, create an identifier consisting of the object's name, a period, and the property name. For example:
>
> ```
> Form1.Caption = "The Amazing File Picker"
> File1.Path  = Dir1.Path
> ```

Zeroing In on the Task

Figure 2.10 illustrates how the controls need to interrelate. When the user selects a new drive, the directory list box is updated. When the user selects a new directory, the file list box is updated. To implement this behavior, rely on the Change event, which occurs whenever the contents of the control change. Another feature you're going to add to your program is to change the current drive and directory whenever one of these changes occurs. This way, the user will always go back to the last directory chosen.

Let's enter some code. Double-click the drive list box to bring up the code window. You should already be in the Change event. Enter the code shown in Listing 2.1. You don't need to retype the first and last lines; they are included in the listing, so you can be sure where the code is supposed to go.

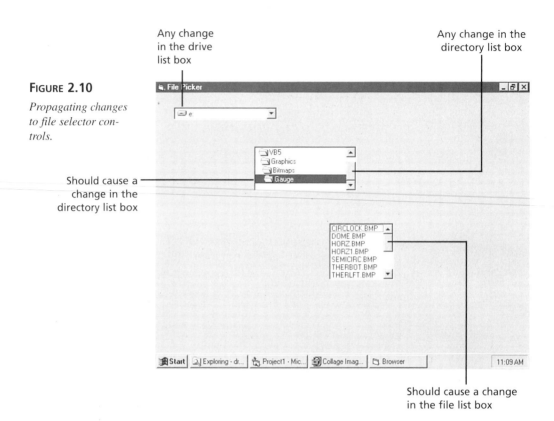

FIGURE 2.10

Propagating changes to file selector controls.

Any change in the drive list box

Any change in the directory list box

Should cause a change in the directory list box

Should cause a change in the file list box

LISTING 2.1 A Change to the Drive List Box Propagates a Change to the Directory Box

```
Private Sub Drive1_Change()
    Dir1.Path = Drive1.Drive
    ChDrive Drive1.Drive
End Sub
```

We'll discuss the first statement below. The ChDrive statement changes the current drive. The current drive and directory are the first places programs (or file selectors) look for files.

Now let's add corresponding code in the directory list box Change event. From the Object: drop-down list on the top-left of the Code window, select Dir1. This puts you in the Change routine. Now enter the code in Listing 2.2.

LISTING 2.2 A Change to the Directory List Box Propagates a Change to the File Box

```
Private Sub Dir1_Change()
      File1.Path = Dir1.Path
      ChDir Dir1.Path
End Sub
```

The ChDir statement changes the current directory.

All set, no kidding! Run the program again. Double-click a drive to select it, and see the changes in the other controls.

Assignments

Let's take a closer look at what you did. (If you're not new to programming, you can skip ahead to the quiz.) The statement

```
Dir1.Path = Drive1.Drive
```

makes an assignment. In computer programming, an assignment means you take a value and copy it somewhere else. In this case, you assign the value in the Drive1 control's Drive property to the Dir1 control's Path property.

The = Operator and Expressions

The equal sign has two functions in Visual Basic: It works as an assignment operator, and it works as a comparison operator. (We'll cover comparison operations in Chapter 3, "Variables, Constants, and Associated Functions.") When you invoke the equal sign as an assignment operator, it evaluates the expression on the right side of the equation and then puts the result into the contents of the left side of the equation. An expression can be the following:

- A constant, such as File Picker
- The result of an operation, such as 4+5
- The return value of a function, such as Sqr
- The contents of a variable (or property), such as NumStudents or Form1.Caption
- Any combination of the above

An expression yields a numeric or string result.

Assignments to and from property values are simple to carry out and are immensely powerful. It's as if you can reach in with your virtual fingers and tweak, twist, and fine-tune the object instances you've created, molding them in your hands to the perfect form to carry out the function you want.

Lesson Summary

In this lesson, we made our file picker functional by adding code to propagate changes to the file selector controls. In doing so, we also discussed the use of the = operator in Visual basic. In next lesson, you will take a close look at the Visual Basic development environment.

Quiz 4

1. The property you'd use for accessing the path currently being pointed to by the `DirListBox` is

    a. `ChDir`

    b. `DirListPath`

    c. `Path`

    d. `Drive`

2. The `FileName` property

    a. Is common to the `DirListBox`, `FileListBox`, and `DriveListBox` controls

    b. Is set automatically by Visual Basic to the current project name

    c. Needs to be typed in by the user

    d. Returns the name of the currently selected file in the File List box

3. Which of the following does not identify an object's property?

    a. `Form1.Caption`

    b. `Dir1.Path`

    c. `frmMain_Click`

    d. `cmdOk.Caption`

4. The Change event

    a. Is fired whenever the contents of the control are changed

    b. Is of no use whatever

    c. Happens only when another program sends you a message

    d. Was inspired by a David Bowie song

Exercise 4

Complexity: Moderate

Run four or five of the Windows programs on your desktop, such as the calculator, the notepad, your word processor, or spreadsheet. Note which elements all the programs have in common. Think about these elements as objects. How might you use similar types of objects in your own programs?

LESSON 5

The Development Environment

Visual Basic programs are called *projects*, which are made up of various components. So far, you've seen a project with a single form and the source code associated with that form. In fact, a project can contain many forms and code modules, which perform functions in the background, as well as class modules, which are new to VB 6. Although we expect the components of our project to come together flawlessly and become something greater than the sum of its parts, keeping track of all the pieces can be troublesome.

Visual Basic 6 doesn't require a project's files to be in a separate directory. However, it's a good practice to create a new directory for each project. This prevents confusion and possibly overwriting other projects. Switch over to the File Manager or Windows Explorer to create a new directory (folder in Windows 98) called FILEPICK.

So far, you've been taking the Visual Basic development environment for granted. Let's take a closer look at Visual Basic's main screen and the tools it makes available to you. If you've had any experience with Microsoft Windows, many of the elements shown in Figure 2.11 might already be familiar to you.

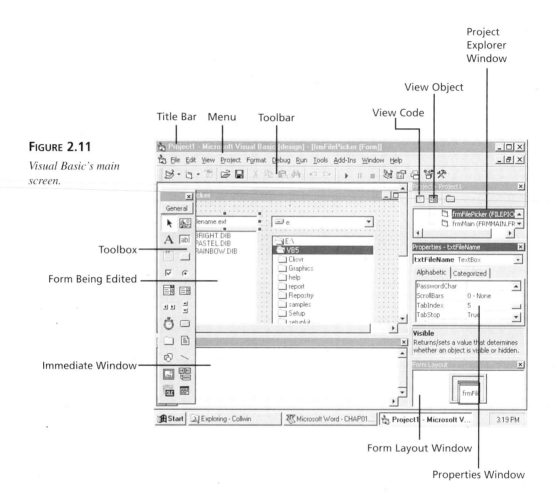

FIGURE 2.11

Visual Basic's main screen.

Project Explorer Window

View Object

View Code

Title Bar   Menu   Toolbar

Toolbox

Form Being Edited

Immediate Window

Form Layout Window

Properties Window

The Menu Bar

Visual Basic's menu bar is pretty typical. Click the File menu (shown in Figure 2.12). Notice that there are different options for files and projects. Each module of a project is saved in a separate file; the project file pulls all the information together. Click Save Project As. Because you haven't saved the form to a file yet, VB asks if you want to do this. Click Yes, and then switch to the FILEPICK directory and enter FILEPICK.FRM and press Enter. Next it's time to save the project; enter FILEPICK.VBP.

FIGURE 2.12

The File menu reflects the fact that projects are made up of one or more files.

```
File  Edit  View  Project  Format  Debug  Run
   New Project                    Ctrl+N
   Open Project...                Ctrl+O

   Add Project...
   Remove Project

   Save Project
   Save Project As...

   Save FILEPICK.FRM              Ctrl+S
   Save FILEPICK.FRM As...

   Print...                       Ctrl+P
   Print Setup...

   Make FILEPICK.exe...
   Make Project Group...

   1 ...\...\CHAP01\FILEPICK\FILEPICK.VBP
   2 FilePicker.vbp

   Exit                           Alt+Q
```

> **Note**   Visual Basic 6, Visual Basic 5, and 4 projects have the extension .VBP; previous versions of Visual Basic used the extension .MAK. Visual Basic converts older projects into the latest format when you load them with VB 6.

So far, the only other menus you've used are View and Run. As with most larger software products, Visual Basic 6 has a range of options that won't be important to you until later. We'll be talking about more advanced options as the book unfolds.

Click Code under the View menu. You'll see the Code window you've previously brought up by double-clicking an object. There is actually one other way to get to this screen.

The Project Window

If the Project window is not showing, click Project Explorer under the View menu. This brings up the Project window. Right now this isn't a very useful feature, because you have only one file in your project. Let's add another file to make things more interesting.

Click Add Form under the Project menu. A blank form labeled Form2 comes up. Now look at the Project Explorer window (shown in Figure 2.13). You can select between the elements that compose a project (that is, forms and modules) and choose to view either the code or the form by clicking on the View Code or View Object icons, respectively.

FIGURE 2.13

*The Project window
helps you manage the
elements of your
project.*

View Object

View Code

Notice that as you add to the project, you'll realize that the default names Visual Basic
assigns aren't very helpful. Let's make the project a little more understandable.

The Properties Window, Part 2

Make sure Form2 is selected in the Project window. Then bring up the Properties window, either by selecting it and pressing the right mouse button or by clicking Properties
under the View window.

> **Note**   You can also bring up the Properties window for the current form by
> pressing F4.

Let's change the caption of the new form. Click the `Caption` property, then enter
`Browser`. At this point, you should also give your forms better names. Click the `Name`
property and enter *frmMain*. To change the name of the other form, you first need to
select that form. You can do this either by clicking it or by selecting its name from the
Project window and then clicking View Object. Next, go back to the Properties window
(which should now say Properties—Form1 on the title bar) and click the `Name` property.
Enter *frmFilePicker* as the new name.

You'll be using `frmFilePicker` as a dialog box, which you'll use in `frmMain` in response
to certain user actions.

The Menu Editor

Let's advance the professional look of the program by adding a menu to the main screen.
Select the `frmMain` form by clicking it (or using the Project Explorer window). Click
Menu Editor under the Tools menu to bring up the dialog box shown in Figure 2.14. The
first two fields are the familiar Caption and Name. Menus and menu items look and act
like the other objects you've seen. As with the Command button you entered earlier, the
Caption is the label, and the Name refers to the object internally. When you're ready to
add code, the `Click` event will let you know when the user selected the item.

FIGURE 2.14

The Menu Editor.

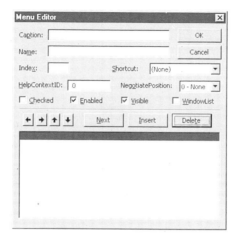

Enter File in the caption field, a standard first menu. Press Tab to advance to the next field and type mnuFile as the name. Although this dialog box has other options, this is all the information you need to enter for now.

Note

The Visual Basic 6 development environment has extensive context-sensitive help. You can press F1 to bring up a description of any dialog box.

Click the Next button. This adds another item to the menu. Type Open for the caption and mnuFileOpen for the name. The horizontal arrow icons to the left of the Next button set the level of the menu item. Click the right arrow button now to make Open subordinate to the File menu.

Press Enter to start a new entry. (This is the same as clicking Next.) Let's add a separator bar. In the Caption field, enter a single hyphen. The hyphen has a special meaning to the menu editor. It tells the editor to create a separator bar, such as the one between Open Project and Save File in the Visual Basic File menu.

Even though you won't be assigning code for this entry, each menu item needs a name. Call this item mnuSeparator. Finally, create a menu item with the caption Exit and name it mnuFileExit. Your screen should look like that shown in Figure 2.15.

Exit the Menu Editor by clicking OK. Look at the menu as it appears on the design-time form. Note that the separator bar automatically extends across the menu box. Click a menu item to bring up the Code window for that item's Click event. You'll be filling in the code in Lesson 6.

FIGURE 2.15

Creating a file menu.

Each Form in Its Place

Let's run the program now. Rather than selecting Start from the Run menu, you can use the VCR-style controls on the toolbar, as shown in Figure 2.16. Other toolbar buttons you might find useful are the ones to switch to the menu editor, Properties window, and Project window. Remember, you can find out what a button does by holding the mouse over it for a few seconds and reading the drop-down ToolTip.

FIGURE 2.16

The Visual Basic 6 toolbar.

Currently, only the Start button is enabled. Click it now to run the program. This also enables the Break and End buttons, but that's not what you want! When the program runs, the file picker comes up, not the main menu screen. Once again, Visual Basic fails miserably at reading your mind. Exit the program, this time by pressing the toolbar End button to exit.

What's happening is that the first form in a project is assumed to be the startup form—the one first displayed. To change which form is the startup form, click Properties under the Project menu. The Properties dialog box has five sets of options: settings for General, Make, Compile, Component, and Debugging. Select a set of options by clicking the tab label. For now, click the General tab to bring up the screen shown in Figure 2.17. This dialog box is mostly used for setting options relating to projects that will be used as OLE

Automation Servers. (This topic is covered in Chapter 14, "Advanced Features.") The Startup Object drop-down list is the one you want. As you saw when you ran the program, this is currently set to frmFilePicker. Change this now to frmMain.

FIGURE 2.17

The Project Properties dialog box.

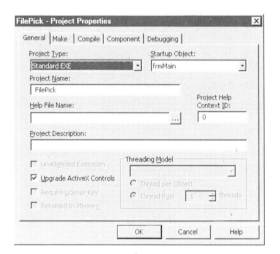

Note that there is a third item on the list: Sub Main. Occasionally, you may not want a form to gain control when your project starts. If this is the case, you can pass control to a special subroutine called Main. The Main subroutine must appear in a code module somewhere in your project, and there can be only one Main subroutine per project. You can use this feature to produce hidden Windows programs that do not have a visible interface but that perhaps add functionality to a client application via OLE automation.

At this point, you don't need to worry about the other options on this screen. The Project Name setting, for example, is confusingly not where you need to name your project. This is for OLE automation naming purposes. You already saved the name of the project file when you saved the project to disk.

Click OK to close the dialog box. Now, when you run the program, the main screen comes up first. Because you still haven't added any functionality, exit the program by pressing the End button on the VCR-style controls on the toolbar. For now, disregard the middle Break button in Figure 2.16; you'll use that when you learn about debugging in Chapter 10, "Problem Solving and Handling Errors and Debugging Your Program."

Lesson Summary

In this lesson, you were introduced to the Visual Basic development environment: its menu bar, the project window, the properties window and the menu editor. In the next lesson, you will take a closer look at forms.

Quiz 5

1. A Visual Basic project
    a. Can be made up of multiple forms and modules
    b. Refers to the source code that tells the computer what to do
    c. Must start with the first (default) form
    d. Can have a maximum of eight class modules

2. The Visual Basic Project window
    a. Is where you enter code for your projects
    b. Isn't very helpful, because you have to use the default names of Form1 and Form2
    c. Lets you switch between your forms in design mode
    d. Lets you switch between your forms in runtime mode

3. The menu editor
    a. Is a Visual Basic menu
    b. Lets you name your menu items, but then you use a resource editor to draw them on the screen
    c. Is where you enter code to respond to menu selections
    d. Is where you define the menu characteristics, information VB uses to draw and maintain your window

4. To bring up Visual Basic's context-sensitive help
    a. Press F1
    b. Press F2
    c. Press F3
    d. Press CTRL+H

Exercise 5

Complexity: Moderate

Start a new project and add the following menus to it:

File	Edit
New	Undo
Save	Cut
Save As	Copy
Close	Paste
Exit	

Give the menu items names that tell you something about the functionality so that you will remember them.

LESSON 6

Looking Closely at Forms

When you run the File Browser program, the main window comes up on the screen. So far, you've pretty much taken this for granted, but that's what's happening only from a user's perspective. What's happening from your (more sophisticated, of course) programming perspective?

The Mother Load

Running a program causes the startup form to load. Windows generates an instance of the window and sets up all the internal housekeeping it needs to keep track of it. Put another way, running a program generates a Load event for the startup form. In addition to letting Windows perform its necessary functions, Visual Basic also executes any code the programmer has placed in the form's Load event.

The Load Event

The Load event occurs when a form loads. A form loads

- When the application runs, if the form is a startup form
- Via code by calling the Load statement for a form
- When any reference is made to an unloaded form's properties or controls

Let's add some source code to the main form's Load event and watch this happen. Double-click frmMain, or select frmMain from the Project window and click View Code. Notice that the Load event is the default event for this object. Enter the following code:

```
Private Sub Form_Load()
    MsgBox "Hello world"
End Sub
```

The MsgBox function displays a box on the screen with a message to the user. Chapter 4, "Subroutines, Functions, and the Visual Basic 6 Language," covers this function in detail.

Run the program, and you'll see the message box shown in Figure 2.18.

FIGURE 2.18

Inside the Load *routine.*

A Method to the Madness

Now let's invoke a Load event from inside the program. The type of command you're going to use to do this is called a method. A *method* is a command that is applied to an object.

Note

A method is invoked with the following syntax:

```
[objectname.]methodname [parameters]
```

The following is an example:

```
picButterfly.Move 100,100,200,200
```

The details of this syntax, of course, depend on the particular method you're invoking.

In the discussion of classes, we said you could think about humans and canines as being examples of classes. In that analogy, a task, such as walking, is a method: It is a function the members of both types of objects can carry out. Thus, if you have an instance of a human named Julia and an instance of a canine named Fido, you could invoke their respective walk methods by saying

```
Julia.Walk
Fido.Walk
```

These commands would actually call different routines, because walking is a different procedure, depending on whether you have two legs or four. However, once the classes and the methods for those classes are defined, you can access the methods without any further consideration as to how the task is accomplished. You tell the object, in effect, to just go do it.

Visual Basic objects such as forms and controls have a wide range of built-in methods, as you might imagine. Visible objects contain methods to move, drag, and refresh the display of themselves. Objects to hold and manipulate data, such as list boxes, contain methods to manipulate the data they contain. Specialized controls often have methods that contain powerful functionality; the Database object contains a method to execute an SQL query on any ODBC database, for example.

Calling All Forms

Let's invoke a fairly straightforward method, the Show method. Its syntax is

```
[form.]Show [style]
```

Show displays a form and gives that form the focus. A form or a control with the focus is the object that will receive input.

Remember from the event description of Load that a Load event is invoked automatically whenever you reference a form or a form's controls or properties. Therefore, just by calling the Show method, you automatically load the form if it isn't loaded already.

Remove the MsgBox function from the Form_Load routine. While in design mode, click Open under the frmMain File menu. This brings you to the Code window. Enter the code in Listing 2.3.

LISTING 2.3   Displaying the File Picker Form

```
Private Sub mnuFileOpen_Click()
     frmFilePicker.Show
End Sub
```

While you're at it, let's implement the Exit option. In the Code window's Object dropdown list box, select mnuFileExit and enter the code in Listing 2.4.

LISTING 2.4   Code to End the Program

```
Private Sub mnuFileExit_Click()
     Unload Me
End Sub
```

Run the program once again. This time when you click Open, the file picker comes up.

Note

> In Windows, you can tell which window has the focus, because its title bar is highlighted. In a dialog box, you can tell which control has the focus because its caption is surrounded by a dotted rectangle.

The program is starting to behave, at least a little bit. But again things aren't quite right.

Going in Style

Switch over to your program's main window by clicking it. Now switch back to the file picker dialog box. Any problem? OK, that was a trick question. You shouldn't be able to switch back and forth—at least, not from the standpoint of typical Windows interface design.

Exit the program by clicking the Exit option, which now works. Under the Visual Basic 6 File menu, click Save Project As. When the file selector comes up, without clicking Save or Cancel, try to get back to Visual Basic's main screen. Clicking an area outside the dialog box causes VB to beep in protest. This is because the Save Project As dialog box is modal; nothing else can happen in the program until the dialog box closes. Click Cancel now and look at the VB environment from this new perspective.

Note that while you're in design mode, you can freely move between the forms in your project. Additionally, you can move between the Project Explorer window, the Properties window, and so on without restriction. These windows are said to be *modeless style*.

Note

> Modal Versus Modeless: Although the difference between these types of forms is simple enough to grasp (either you temporarily give up control of the program flow or you don't), sometimes it's hard to remember which style is which. Here's an easy way to remember the difference between the terms: A modal dialog box takes over *all* of the running program.

You don't want the user to do anything else after selecting Open until he picks a filename. This is because, eventually, the line after the Show command will go off and open the file. The program won't behave predictably if the user can do something else in between.

Change the frmFilePicker dialog box to a modal style by modifying the Show method in the mnuFileOpen_Click subroutine. The value for the style parameter can be modal or modeless. Modeless style is the default. Bring up the mnuFileOpen_Click routine in the Code window and change the command as shown in Listing 2.5.

Note

> Use Visual Basic Constants: Instead of forcing you to remember the meaning of numeric parameter, Visual Basic gives you the option to use predefined constants. For example, you can use vbModal and vbModeless as parameters for the Show method. The use of these constants is strongly recommended because the code is much clearer without any speed penalty.

LISTING 2.5   Showing the Form in Modal Style

```
Private Sub mnuFileOpen_Click()
     frmFilePicker.Show vbModal
End Sub
```

Now when you run the program and click Open, you can't go back to the main form. To exit, click the Done button.

Lesson Summary

In this lesson, you have learned how forms get created and destroyed and what event corresponds to these actions. In the next lesson, we continue to improve the File Picker program we started in the first lesson of this chapter.

Quiz 6

1. Which event is generated when Windows creates an instance of a window?

    a. Show

    b. Load

    c. UnHide

    d. No event is generated; Windows handles everything.

2. In the example of a human and a dog both walking, what point is being made about class methods?

    a. Walking is always the same function, no matter how many legs you have.

    b. Julia.Walk and Fido.Walk both call the same routine, because the name is the same.

    c. Even though Julia and Fido use different functions to walk, you can invoke the method without particular concern as to how the task is accomplished.

    d. The best approach to programming is to break down a task such as walking into small, manageable subtasks, such as extending a leg.

3. In the File menu's Open Click event, you didn't need to load the file picker form explicitly because

    a. It was implicitly loaded when it was referenced by the Show method.

    b. All forms are loaded when the program runs.

    c. It was the startup form.

    d. The code is wrong; you were supposed to load it explicitly.

4. A modal window

    a. Is the same as a form

    b. Is any window that operates in some kind of mode

    c. Lets you switch freely between windows

    d. Takes over ALL of the application

Lesson 7

The File Picker: Better Still

Thus far, you've been throwing controls around without really thinking much about what you wanted to do with them. Let's formalize what we want this application to do!

It Slices, It Dices!

Let's make the program a browser so the user can pick a file from the file picker and view the file's contents on the main screen. Because you don't know anything about file operations yet, you'll view only files that Visual Basic can handle for you. It turns out the PictureBox control has a built-in method to load pictures, so let's make the program a picture browser for now.

When the user runs the program, the form is blank. When he clicks Open, the file picker comes up. You want the file picker to act a little more like a standard file selector, so make a few changes to it. For example, you want functional OK and Cancel buttons instead of the Done button you have now, and you need a place to put the filename. You also want to limit the file list to picture files, because that's all you know how to view. Finally, if the user clicks OK, you need a place to view the picture.

Everything Is OK

Select the File Picker form. Click the Done button once to select it. Now go to the Properties window. Click Caption and type OK, then click Name and type cmdOk. Now go to the toolbox and select another Command button, draw it on the form, and change the Caption property to Cancel and the Name property to cmdCancel.

Note

From here onward, we'll use tables to show you concisely which controls to create and what the property values should be. Only the properties you need to change will be listed, for example:

Control	Property	Value
CommandButton	Caption	OK
	Name	cmdOk

Now add a text box to the form. Figure 2.19 shows the icon for the TextBox control. The TextBox is a remarkably powerful control that displays—or lets the user enter—alphanumeric characters. We'll explore the text box in more detail in Chapter 5, "Controls," when we use it as the centerpiece of a notepad application.

FIGURE 2.19

The TextBox *control.*

Text Box on Toolbar

Text Box on Form

Edit the text box's properties, as shown in Table 2.3. Size and arrange the controls so that the design is pleasing and the layout seems accessible. The finished form looks something like that shown in Figure 2.20.

Table 2.3   Property Values for the File Picker TextBox Control

Control	Property	Value
txtFileName		
	Text	filename.ext

Getting It Working

Because you'll view only picture files, let's limit the file list box to list only those files. This makes it easier for the user to find the picture files and prevents the user from selecting a file you can't display. Fortunately, the `FileListBox` control has a built-in property to limit which files are displayed: the `Pattern` property.

FIGURE 2.20

*The smoothed-over
File picker.*

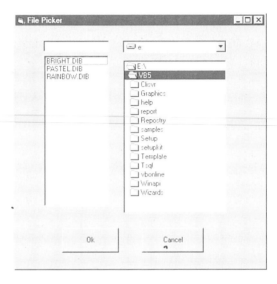

The `Pattern` Property

The `Pattern` property limits the files displayed in the list box. The value of the property follows the standard Windows/MS-DOS convention of using wildcards to mean *any* value. An asterisk matches any number of characters, for example, `*.*` or `*.EXE`. A question mark matches any single character, for example, `CHAP??.*` matches CHAP01.DOC and CHAP24.DOC but not CHAPTERS.TXT.

The default value of the `Pattern` property is `*.*` (all files). You can specify more than one pattern by separating the values by semicolons, for example, `*.EXE;*.BAT`.

To limit the file list box to all the image types the picture box knows how to read, enter the following for the pattern value:

`*.bmp;*.wmf;*.emf;*.rle;*.ico;*.dib;*.cur;*.jpg;*.gif`

Because you won't change this value at runtime, this is all you need to do with this property.

The `Text` Property

You saw in Lesson 4 how to propagate changes across the drive, directory, and file controls. Let's see how to get the selection from the file list box into the text box. You'll use two properties: FileName and Text. The Text property sets or returns the text in the editable area of the control.

Double-click the FileListBox control to bring up the Code window. Again, the default event for this control is what you want, the Click event. Enter the following code:

```
Private Sub File1_Click()
    txtFileName.Text = File1.FileName
End Sub
```

That should handle the user's selections. There's one other detail to handle, however. Back when you defined the text box, you initialized the Text field to filename.ext. This made it so it was easy to see what the runtime result would look like when you positioned the controls on the form. You could clear this value in the Properties window, but it's just as easy to do it at runtime in code. This approach enables you to retain the design-time self documentation.

Double-click the File Picker form to get to the Load event and enter the following code:

```
Private Sub Form_Load()
    txtFileName.Text = ""
End Sub
```

The two quotation marks in a row set the value to nothing.

Note

A *string* is a type of value that can contain any combination of alphanumeric characters. The contents of the text box's Text field is a string, as is the Caption property and a few other properties you've seen. We'll be covering strings extensively in Chapter 3, "Variables, Constants, and Associated Functions." For now, the important thing to keep in mind is that when you set these values in code, you must enclose the string in quotation marks. Two quotation marks in a row are called an *empty string* and clear the property's value.

Now you know where the value you want will be. How do you get at it?

The Hide Method

After selecting a filename, the user clicks OK or Cancel to dismiss the dialog box. At that point, you need to shut down the File Picker form so that program control goes back to the main form. The command to do that is the Hide method. The syntax is

```
[object.]Hide
```

This method hides a form from view but doesn't unload it from memory. It hides the form that has the focus if object is omitted.

Bring up the `cmdOk_Click` event procedure and enter the following code into it.

```
Private Sub cmdOk_Click()
      Hide
End Sub
```

Because this form was shown in the modal style, everything else in the program essentially came to a halt. Hiding the form returns you to where you were before file picker was displayed—in other words, right after the `Show` command in the `mnuFileOpen_Click` event. Let's go back to the main form and see what you need to do to display a picture.

A Thousand Words

The `PictureBox` control displays a graphic .GIF image file, .JPG image file, bitmap (.BMP) file, icon (.ICO) file, Windows metafile (.WMF), run-length encoded (.RLE) file, or Windows enhanced metafile (.EMF). Select a picture box from the toolbox (shown in Figure 2.21) and place it on the main form. Because you don't know how big the picture is going to be, don't worry about how big to draw the box.

FIGURE **2.21**

The PictureBox icon.

The `AutoSize` Property

In the Properties window for this control, select the `AutoSize` property, which is currently set to `False`. The `AutoSize` property determines whether or not a control is automatically resized to fit the image it contains.

Notice that when you select this property, a drop-down arrow appears to the right of `False`. Click the arrow and select `True` to change the value.

 Note Whenever a property has a limited set of values it can contain, you can select from those values at design time, using a drop-down list in the Properties window.

The `Picture` Property

The `Picture` property determines the graphic to be displayed in the control. At design time, you set the `Picture` property in the Properties window. Click the `Picture` property and notice that an ellipsis icon appears to the right of the property name. This means you need to use a dialog box to fill in the value of the property. Click the ellipsis now. A file selector box comes up. This is where you load the image at design time. Click Cancel for now; you want to start with a blank picture.

To set the value of the `Picture` property at runtime, you need to learn one more command, the last new language element of the chapter: the `LoadPicture` function.

The `LoadPicture` Function

The `LoadPicture` function loads an image from a file into an object. The syntax is

```
LoadPicture([filename])
```

For example,

```
Picture1.Picture = LoadPicture("happy.bmp")
```

Remote Control

Now the question is simply, "How do we get the filename from the file picker?" From inside the file picker, the filename value is

```
txtFileName.Text
```

It turns out that accessing a control from outside the form is a simple matter of putting the form name, separated by a period, in front of the control.

Note

To access controls outside the current form, use the following syntax:

```
formname.controlname.propertyname
```

The following are examples:

```
Form1.CommandButton1.Caption
frmMain.mnuOption.Checked
```

Go back to the `mnuFileOpen_Click` routine and add the highlighted line after the existing code, as shown in Listing 2.6.

LISTING 2.6   Loading the Picture

```
Sub Open_Click
    frmFilePicker.Show 1
    Picture1.Picture = LoadPicture(frmFilePicker.txtFileName.Text)
End sub
```

Run the program and try it out. Click Open, select a file, and click OK. Majestic! Load another file. Live it up! However, if you experiment with all the buttons, you'll soon see you have a slight problem: The Cancel button doesn't work yet. (Sigh.) A programmer's work is never done. Exit the program, and go into the frmFilePicker Code window. Select the cmdCancel Click event. There are (you'll see later) a few fancy techniques you can use for forms to communicate with each other about what the user did. However, in this case, you're kind of going to cheat.

It turns out that assigning a blank string to the LoadPicture function clears the contents of the picture box. This effect will be fine if the user presses Cancel. All you need to do, then, is clear the contents of the text box and hide the form as you did when the user pressed OK. This code is shown in Listing 2.7.

LISTING 2.7   The Cancel Button

```
Private Sub cmdCancel_Click()
    txtFileName.Text = ""
    Hide
End Sub
```

Save your work now. Run the File Picker and watch everything working the way you coded it.

Lesson Summary

The file picker might not have the broadest functionality, but it's not bad for your first project. You know only a handful of controls and language statements, yet you have all the tools to build something that performs a useful function in the real world. In Lesson 8, we'll review what you've learned, and apply it to another project.

Quiz 7

1. The TextBox control

    a. Is a modal dialog box to request input from the user

    b. Has a Caption property so you can use it as a label

    c. Is read-only at runtime

    d. Is a control you add to a form to let the user type in alphanumeric characters

2. Which of the following is not an example of a valid `Pattern` property?

    a. *.*

    b. INV*.DOC

    c. FIG??.BMP

    d. D:\MYDIR

3. A null string is

    a. Two quotation marks in a row ("") designating an empty string

    b. The same as the space bar

    c. 0

    d. Illegal in many string operations

4. To assign a value to the `Picture` property of a picture box

    a. Assign the filename, as in Picture1.Picture = "SMILEY.BMP"

    b. Set the `AutoSize` property to `True`

    c. Use the `Show` method on the `Picture` control

    d. Call the `LoadPicture` function, as in `Picture1.Picture` = `LoadPicture` ("SMILEY.BMP")

Exercise 7

Complexity: Moderate

Modify the file picker so that the user can enter a pattern in the text field and then press a Change Pattern button to adjust the contents of the list box.

LESSON 8

It's a Wrap

Visual Basic 6 and Windows handle so many details for you, you can focus on the fun part of programming: Designing and building a project that performs exactly how you tell it to. You still have a lot to learn about programming—variables, program flow and structure, object design, logic, and debugging—but as we move from this introduction through the book to more advanced topics, you'll see that a large part of learning Visual Basic 6 will be absorbing more of the same type of things you learned here.

You'll need to learn the rest of the common controls, more property values, events, and methods. If you already understand the concepts in this chapter, the work ahead won't be particularly difficult: We'll combine the same types of tools in different ways. If you feel some of the concepts are still a little fuzzy, that's OK too. As you do more of this type of work, these concepts will come into clearer and clearer focus.

Summary

Let's take a look at the VB language elements you've learned thus far and review vocabulary. Tables 2.4, 2.5, 2.6, 2.7, and 2.8 summarize the language elements covered in this chapter.

TABLE 2.4 Objects

Object	Description
CommandButton	A control that draws a button on the screen for the user to click.
DirListBox	A list box the user can select from that is automatically filled with the directories in the current drive.
DriveListBox	A list box the user can select from that is automatically filled with the drives available to the system.
FileListBox	A list box the user can select from that is automatically filled with the files in the current directory.
Form	The main window that contains the other objects in your program.
Menu	A control that puts up a menu on the screen from which the user can make selections.
PictureBox	Displays a graphic bitmap, icon, or metafile.
TextBox	Displays or lets the user enter text.

TABLE 2.5 Properties

Property	Description
AutoSize	Determines whether or not a control is automatically resized to fit the image it contains
Caption	Provides a label to describe the form or control to the user
Drive	Sets or returns the currently selected drive on the DriveListBox
FileName	Sets or returns the filename of the currently selected file in the FileListBox
Name	A descriptor that identifies the object internally

Property	Description
Path	Sets or returns the currently selected path for the DirListBox; for the FileListBox, sets or returns the path containing the currently displayed list of files
Pattern	Limits the files displayed in the FileListBox
Picture	Determines the graphic to be displayed in the control
Text	Sets or returns the text in the editable area of the control

TABLE 2.6 Events

Event	Description
Change	Occurs when the contents of the control change
Click	Occurs when the user clicks an object
Load	Occurs when a form is loaded

TABLE 2.7 Statements and Functions

Statements and Functions	Description
ChDir	Changes the current directory on the system
ChDrive	Changes the current drive on the system
LoadPicture()	Loads an image from a file into an object
MsgBox()	Puts up a message on the screen
Unload Me	Unloads the form in which this code appears

TABLE 2.8 Methods

Method	Description
Show	Displays a form and gives that form the focus
Hide	Hides a form from view but doesn't unload it from memory

Table 2.9 lists the terms related to OOP you've seen in this chapter.

TABLE 2.9   OOP Terms

Terms	Definition
Class	The properties, events, and methods that uniquely define a type of object.
Decomposition	The traditional, top-down approach to software design in which you break down complex problems into smaller, less complex ones.
Event	Something that happens in the environment.
Instance	An object in a program is an instance of its class.
Method	A function that an object knows how to do.
Object	A distinct unit in a program that has certain characteristics and can do certain things.
Object-oriented programming	An approach to programming in which you first break a programming task into theobjects that make it up.
Programming language	A command set that lets you instruct the computer to perform . certain tasks
Property	A characteristic of an object.
Subroutines/ procedures	Logical groupings of code.

Lesson Summary

Use this lesson and the following quiz to help you ensure that you understand all terms introduced in this chapter. Do not hesitate to go back over sections that are not crystal clear. Without the fundamentals of this chapter, you will struggle with many of the concepts introduced later.

Quiz 8

1. Which property was common to all the controls you learned about in this chapter?

    a. Caption

    b. Name

    c. Pattern

    d. Text

2. Which of the following commands unloads a form from the screen?

    a. End

    b. Hide

    c. Change

    d. ChDir

3. Which is the best definition of a programming language?

    a. An approach in which you first break down a task into smaller tasks to perform

    b. A tool that lets you draw forms and controls on the screen

    c. A command set that lets you instruct the computer to perform certain tasks

    d. An object

4. In which of the following tasks do you already possess all the tools to perform in Visual Basic?

    a. Track the mouse's movements to draw on the screen

    b. Create a new program that displays a different picture at regular intervals

    c. Modify the file picker to read text files as well as pictures

    d. Modify the browser to clear the text box field before the file picker comes up

Chapter Summary

In this chapter, you learned all the building blocks of object-oriented programming in Visual Basic. You incrementally built a program with real-world functionality to illustrate the objects, properties, events, statements and functions, and methods discussed.

In Chapter 3, "Variables, Constants, and Associated Functions," we introduce variables and the functions associated with them.

CHAPTER 3

Variables, Constants, and Associated Functions

In Chapter 2, "Object-Oriented Programming," you learned about many of the fundamentals of the Visual Basic 6 (VB 6) development environment and the components of a VB 6 program. This chapter concentrates on the different types of variables and constants. You learn how to declare them and use them. This chapter also covers many support functions provided by Visual Basic that perform specific actions on different variable types. Additionally, you'll explore the VB environment a little more and start to learn about program flow.

LESSON 1

Variables: Getting Started

Variables are containers that store data in our programs. A variable is like a placeholder for a value. In programming, variable names are usually descriptive of the contents they hold. For example, a program to analyze student test scores might contain variables called NumberOfStudents, TotalScores, and AverageScore.

Variables come in different types, which we will discuss in lesson 3. Until then, we will use the Integer type. Integers are whole numbers, for example, –4, –3, –2, –1, 0, 1, 2, 3, and 4, and, in Visual Basic 6, have a range of –32,768 to 32,767.

To learn how to use variables, you'll create a new project called CD Maker. This program analyzes data about a list of songs and computes whether the songs will fit on an audio CD.

CD Maker

Create a new directory called CDMAKER. Create a new project by clicking New Project under the File menu. Select the program's main form (all right, the only form) by clicking it; then bring up the Properties window, and set the property values shown in Table 3.1.

TABLE 3.1   The Property Values of the CD Maker's Main Form

Object	Property	Value
Form	Name	frmCDMaker
	Caption	CD Maker

Visual Basic 6 comes with an icon library from which you can import images to spice up your programs. Let's add a CD image to the program. Select the PictureBox control from the toolbox and draw it in the upper-left region of the form. Don't worry about the size. Set the property values described in Table 3.2. Note that the path to your Visual Basic Graphics directory may be different.

TABLE 3.2   The Picturebox Property Values

Object	Property	Value
PictureBox	AutoSize	True
	Picture	\Program Files\Microsoft VisualStudio\Common\Graphics\ Icons\Computer\CDROM01.ICO

Note   If a property value has a limited set of values to choose from—such as the AutoSize property, which can be either True or False—you can quickly switch between them in the Properties window by double-clicking the property name or the property value.

The Label Control

Next we'll add another common control to your repertoire: the Label control.

The Label control lets you display textual information to your user via the Label's Caption property. The Label control is typically used for display purposes only, not for input. You can set the label's caption at design or runtime.

Draw a label next to the CD icon. Again, you don't need to worry about the size because the Label control also has an AutoSize property. Assign the property values shown in Table 3.3.

TABLE 3.3   The Label Control Property Values

Object	Property	Value
Label	AutoSize	True
	Caption	This program figures out how many songs will fit on a CD.
	Font	Arial, bold, 10 points

The Font Property

Notice that we used a new property, the Font property. In design mode, setting this property is easy. Click Font in the Properties window and then click the ellipsis points button that appears to bring up the Font selection dialog box shown in Figure 3.1. Setting the property in code is a little more complicated. We'll get to that in Chapter 9, "Printing."

FIGURE 3.1

The font dialog box enables you to set font characteristics easily at design time.

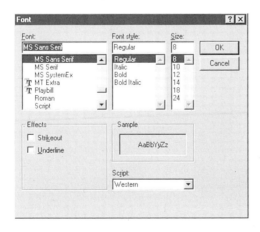

Add one more label and also an Exit Command button to the form, as described in Table 3.4.

TABLE 3.4   More Property Values for CD Maker

Object	Property	Value
Label	Name	lblTimeAvailable
	AutoSize	True
	Caption	There are x minutes available.
CommandButton	Name	cmdExit
	Caption	Exit

The screen should look like that shown in Figure 3.2.

FIGURE 3.2

The CD Maker thus far.

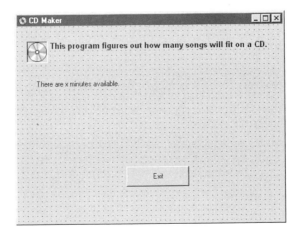

Declaring Variables

Let's add some source code to the program. First we'll program the Exit button. Enter the code in Listing 3.1 in the cmdExit button's Click event routine. This should be familiar to you by now.

LISTING 3.1   The Exit Routine

```
Private Sub cmdExit_Click()
    Unload Me
End Sub
```

Now you need to declare the variables you'll use. Declaring a variable tells Visual Basic about that variable: what its name is and what type of value it contains. Visual Basic uses different declaration statements to cope with different situations. The most commonly used declaration statement is the `Dim` statement. The `Dim` statement has the following syntax:

```
Dim varname [([subscripts])] As [New] type [, varname ...]
```

for example,

```
Dim MyVar As Integer
```

Variable declarations for a form are handled outside the event routines. In the Code window, click the drop-down list next to Object:. Select the very first item, General. This will take you to the Proc: item (Declarations), which is what you want. Enter the following declaration:

```
Dim iTotalCDTime As Integer
```

This tells VB, in effect, that you're going to be using a variable in this program called `iTotalCDTime` that will contain integer values.

Initializing Variables and the & Operator

Now let's use this variable to store some data. Go to the `Form_Load` routine and add the code in Listing 3.2.

LISTING 3.2 Initializing Values

```
Private Sub Form_Load()

' Initialize
iTotalCDTime = 60
lblTimeAvailable.Caption = "There are " & iTotalCDTime & _
                           " minutes available."
End Sub
```

The & operator lets you build string expressions by combining integer and string expressions.

Before we move on, notice there's a new element to this code. The line

```
' Initialize
```

is a comment, a notation that explains what the code is doing but isn't itself source code to be executed. You can precede comments with either an apostrophe or the keyword Rem (short for Remark). Commenting source code is part of good programming. Even if you use meaningful variable names, it's sometimes hard, when you go back later, to remember what each section of code does. It is even harder to read someone else's code that hasn't been well commented.

In this case, we're initializing variables—that is, setting them to an initial value. The startup form's Form_Load event is typically a good place to initialize values, because it's the first code that gets executed when the program runs.

Run the program, and you'll see that the variable was correctly assigned and used in the expression, as shown in Figure 3.3. Exit the program.

Figure 3.3

The first variable.

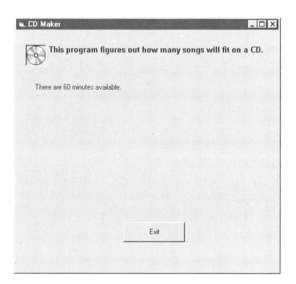

Manipulating Variables

Assigning values to variables is pretty straightforward. This is, of course, the same operation you performed in Chapter 2, "Object-Oriented Programming" with property values. Let's add a few more variables to the program and see how to manipulate them.

Add the controls shown in Table 3.5 to the form. The form should now look like that in Figure 3.4.

FIGURE 3.4

CD Maker expands.

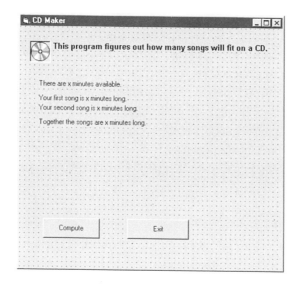

TABLE 3.5   More and More Property Values for CD Maker

Object	Property	Value
Label	Name	lblLengthSong1
	AutoSize	True
	Caption	Your first song is x minutes long.
Label	Name	lblLengthSong2
	AutoSize	True
	Caption	Your second song is x minutes long.
Label	Name	lblTotalLength
	AutoSize	True
	Caption	Together the songs are x minutes long.
CommandButton	Name	cmdCompute
	Caption	Compute

Add the code shown in Listing 3.3 to the (General) Declarations section. Changes are in bold.

LISTING 3.3 Variables to Hold Song Lengths

```
Dim iTotalCDTime As Integer
Dim iSong1Length As Integer
Dim iSong2Length As Integer
Dim iTotalLength As Integer
```

Add the code in Listing 3.4 to the Form_Load routine.

LISTING 3.4 Giving the User More Information

```
Private Sub Form_Load()

' Initialize
iTotalCDTime = 60
iSong1Length = 3
iSong2Length = 5

' Update Captions
lblTimeAvailable.Caption = "There are " & iTotalCDTime & " minutes available."
lblLengthSong1.Caption = "Your first song is " & iSong1Length & " minutes long."
lblLengthSong2.Caption = "Your second song is " & iSong2Length & " minutes
long."

End Sub
```

Finally, add the code in Listing 3.5 to the cmdCompute button's Click event routine.

LISTING 3.5 Adding the Lengths

```
Private Sub cmdCompute_Click()
iTotalLength = iSong1Length + iSong2Length
lblTotalLength.Caption = "Together the songs are " & iTotalLength & _
                               " minutes long."
End Sub
```

Arithmetic Operators

The arithmetic operators built into the Visual Basic language are summarized in Table 3.6.

TABLE 3.6   Arithmetic Operators

Operator	Name	Example	Description
^	Exponentiation	x^y	Raises x to the power of y
-	Negation	-y	Negates y
*	Multiplication	x*y	Multiplies x and y
/	Division	x/y	Divides x by y and returns a floating point result
\	Integer division	x\y	Divides x by y and returns an integer result
Mod	Modulo	x Mod y	Divides x by y and returns the remainder
+	Addition	x + y	Adds x and y
-	Subtraction	x - y	Subtracts y from x

Precedence

In programming terms, precedence refers to the order in which arithmetic operations are carried out. For example, the expression 4+5*2 evaluates to 14, because the multiplication operator has a higher precedence than does the addition operator. Table 3.6 lists the arithmetic operators in order of precedence, with exponentiation being the highest. (Multiplication and division actually have the same precedence, as do addition and subtraction.)

You can override operator precedence by enclosing expressions in parentheses. Operations inside parentheses are always evaluated first (although, if there are multiple operators inside the parentheses, normal rules of precedence apply). Thus the equation (4+5)*2 evaluates to 18, because the addition is performed first.

In Lesson 2 you'll expand the program further, using more arithmetic operators and learning some new language features.

Lesson Summary

You have studied variables and the operations you can perform on them. In the next lesson, you will explore the Visual Basic environment and be introduced to your first math function.

Quiz 1

1. A variable is

   a. A kind of property

   b. A container to store data

   c. Any arithmetic operation

   d. A number

2. Which of the following controls is typically not used for input?

   a. `Label`

   b. `TextBox`

   c. `CommandButton`

   d. `DriveListBox`

3. When you click a property name in the Properties window and an ellipsis points button appears next to the property value, it means that

   a. You must enter a string value.

   b. The property is read-only at design time.

   c. You can click the button to bring up a dialog box from which you can select the value.

   d. You can't set the value in code.

4. Which of the following lines declares an integer value to store a high score?

   a. `Dim iHighScore as Integer`

   b. `Declare iHighScore as Integer`

   c. `Initialize iHighScore as Integer`

   d. `Dim iHighScore as Integer = 0`

Exercise 1

Complexity: Moderate

1. Write a program that displays two numbers and their sum.

Complexity: Advanced

2. Expand the program above to include all arithmetic operations covered in this chapter.

LESSON 2

The Code Window Explored

In this lesson, you'll expand your program to include some further math operations and use the first math function. You'll also explore the Visual Basic environment some more, especially the Code window.

Still More Labels

Add two more labels to the CD Maker screen, as described in Table 3.7.

TABLE 3.7 Two More CD Maker Labels

Object	Property	Value
Label	Name	lblAverage
	AutoSize	True
	Caption	The average song length is x.
Label	Name	lblRoom
	AutoSize	True
	Caption	You have room for x more songs.
Label	Name	lblResult
	AutoSize	True
	Caption	Your songs will/will not fit.

Because lblRoom, lblAverage, and lblResult don't really apply until after the user has clicked the Compute button, let's hide these values until then.

The Visible Property

The Visible property specifies whether or not the user sees the object. Set the Visible property to False for lblRoom, lblAverage, and lblResult.

Note

You can set property values for more than one control at once. Click the controls to select while holding down the Ctrl key. Notice that the Properties window now contains the properties common to all the selected controls. Set the values you want. Remember you can toggle a value by double-clicking it.

Computer Computes

Now let's program some more computations. Go into the Code window and select the (General) Declarations section. You'll need a few more variables. Enter the declarations shown in Listing 3.6.

LISTING 3.6 Variables to Hold Computation Results

```
Dim iTotalCDTime As Integer
Dim iSong1Length As Integer
Dim iSong2Length As Integer
Dim iTotalLength As Integer
Dim iAverageLength As Integer
Dim iRoomLeft As Integer
```

You'll add some source code to the cmdCompute_Click event routine, but first let's learn a little more about the Code window and its features.

Splitting the Screen

In a case like this, it would be helpful to see both the Declarations section and the routine where you're going to use those variables. That way you can make sure you're using the same variable name as the one you declared. Fortunately, there's a way to see two routines at once in the Code window.

To split the screen, move the mouse to the space directly above the vertical scroll bar, as shown in Figure 3.5, until the mouse cursor turns into two vertical arrows separated by a bar. (This icon is also used in Word for Windows and other programs with split-screen functionality.) Now hold down the mouse button, and you'll see a line appear across the width of the window. Move that line, holding down the mouse button, to about halfway down the screen. When you release the mouse button, you'll see the window is separated into two panes, which can be scrolled independently of one another.

Now select cmdCompute under the Object: list box of the Code window. The Click event routine displays in whichever window currently contains the cursor, as shown in Figure 3.6.

Enter the computations in Listing 3.7 in the cmdCompute_Click event routine.

LISTING 3.7 Computing Average Length and Room Left

```
Private Sub cmdCompute_Click()
' Compute the songs'total length
iTotalLength = iSong1Length + iSong2Length
lblTotalLength.Caption = "Together the songs are " & iTotalLength & _
```

```
                                    " minutes long."

    ' Find the average length
    iAverageLength = iTotalLength / 2
    lblAverage.Caption = "The average song length is " & _
                                iAverageLength & "."

    ' See how much room is left over.
    ' Use parentheses to force precedence.
    iRoomLeft = (iTotalCDTime - iTotalLength) / iAverageLength
    lblRoom.Caption = "You have room for " & iRoomLeft & " more songs."

    End Sub
```

FIGURE 3.5

Click the area above the scrollbar to split the screen.

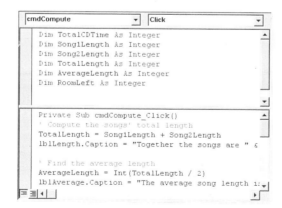

FIGURE 3.6

The split screen.

The `Int` Function

Both `AverageLength` and `RoomLeft` are integer values, so if the division results in a fractional value, it will automatically be converted to an integer. If you attempt to put a real number (numbers with fractional parts are called real numbers) into an integer variable, VB automatically truncates it into an integer. You can make this more explicit by using the `Int` function, which removes the fractional portion of a value.

Functions are routines that return a value. Visual Basic has numerous built-in functions of different types. You can also create your own functions. Functions often take arguments, values that you pass to the function. Argument is another word for parameter, which was mentioned in Chapter 2. For example, the `Int` function takes as an argument the value to convert to an integer. The syntax of the `Int` function is therefore

```
Int(expr)
```

Because functions return a value, they can be used in expressions, just as you've been using variables, property values, and numbers. Some valid uses of this function might be

```
Answer = Int(Question)
LblAnswer.Caption = "The answer is " & Int(3.4) & "."
Result = msgbox ("The integer value is " & int(OtherValue) & ".")
```

Similarly, you can include an entire expression as an argument to a function, as in

```
Answer = Int(Question/3)
```

Modify the lines shown in bold in the compute routine shown in Listing 3.8.

LISTING 3.8   Forcing Integer Values

```
Private Sub cmdCompute_Click()
' Compute the songs'total length
iTotalLength = iSong1Length + iSong2Length
lblTotalLength.Caption = "Together the songs are " & iTotalLength & _
                                    " minutes long."

' Find the average length
iAverageLength = Int(iTotalLength / 2)
lblAverage.Caption = "The average song length is " & _
                              iAverageLength & "."

' See how much room is left over.
iRoomLeft = Int((iTotalCDTime - iTotalLength) / iAverageLength)
```

```
lblRoom.Caption = "You have room for " & iRoomLeft & " more songs."

End Sub
```

The True and False Keywords

Next you need to display the labels. In the Properties window, you changed the Visible property from True to False. It turns out that True and False are keywords in Visual Basic. That means they have predefined values and you can use them naturally in an expression. Add the final bits of code to your routine, as shown in Listing 3.9.

LISTING 3.9 Making the Controls Visible

```
Private Sub cmdCompute_Click()
' Compute the songs'total length
iTotalLength = iSong1Length + iSong2Length
lblTotalLength.Caption = "Together the songs are " & iTotalLength & _
                              " minutes long."

' Find the average length
iAverageLength = Int(iTotalLength / 2)
lblAverage.Caption = "The average song length is " & _
                          iAverageLength & "."

' See how much room is left over.
iRoomLeft = Int((iTotalCDTime - iTotalLength) / iAverageLength)
lblRoom.Caption = "You have room for " & iRoomLeft & " more songs."

' Make the labels visible
lblTotalLength.Visible = True
lblAverage.Visible = True
lblRoom.Visible = True

End Sub
```

Notice the color scheme VB uses as you type in code. Comments are green, keywords are blue, and the rest of the code is black.

Tip

Your color scheme may be different. You can select the colors that you want to use. Open the Tools menu and select Options. The color scheme is set on the Editor Format tab.

Run the program and click the Compute button. The result should look like Figure 3.7.

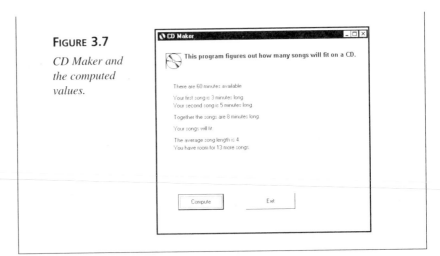

FIGURE 3.7

CD Maker and the computed values.

Context-Sensitive Help in the Code Window

Before we move on, go back to the design-mode Code window. Visual Basic 6 implements extensive context-sensitive help as you're programming. In the `cmdCompute_Click` event routine, move the cursor so that it's on the property name `Caption`. Press F1. If the help system finds more than one instance of the word, you'll see the dialog box shown in Figure 3.8. At this point you'll generally pick VB (or VBA for Visual Basic for Applications). Click Help to continue to the help system.

FIGURE 3.8

Sometimes you need to specify which Help screen is applicable.

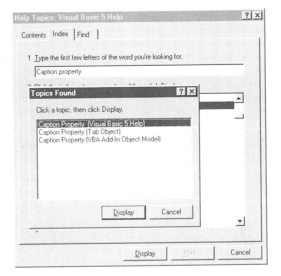

Next go back to the Code window (either by exiting Help or by pressing Alt+Tab to switch between Windows applications). Put the cursor on the word Int and press F1. You'll see the Int, Fix Functions help screen. Click See Also and then select Math Functions. You'll see the hypertext list shown in Figure 3.9. It's never too soon to get in the habit of using VB 6's online help engine as a primary reference. It's faster to look up keywords in here than it is to look them up in the manual, and it's easier to move around in Help. Putting the cursor on a keyword and pressing F1 is particularly helpful when you know the command you want but don't remember the exact syntax or order of arguments.

FIGURE 3.9

The math functions.

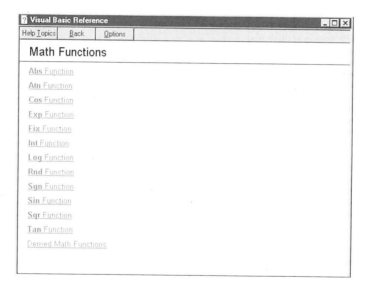

Note

Another convenient feature of VB 6 is the Auto Quick Info feature, which displays the correct syntax for a keyword as you type it. If Auto Quick Info is not turned on, open the Tools menu and select options. Auto Quick Info is on the Editor tab. You can also access Quick Info by placing your mouse pointer on a keyword and pressing Ctrl+I.

Math Functions

Let's take a closer look at the list of math functions shown in Figure 3.9. Some of these functions—particularly the trigonometric functions Sin(), Cos(), and so on—are self-explanatory. Others, such as the Rnd() function, require more explanation and will be covered in detail later. Table 3.8 summarizes the math functions. Don't worry about memorizing all the functions at once. This is just to give you an idea of what's available.

TABLE 3.8 The Visual Basic 6 Math Functions

Function	Example	Description	Note
Abs	Abs(x)	Returns the absolute value of x.	
Atn	Atn(x)	Returns the arctangent of x.	Returns an angle in radians.
Cos	Cos(x)	Returns the cosine of x.	x expresses an angle in radians.
Exp	Exp(x)	Returns e (the base of natural logarithms) raised to the power of x.	
Fix	Fix(x)	Returns the integer portion of x.	See the online help screen for the difference between Int and Fix.
Int	Int(x)	Returns the integer portion of x.	See the online help screen for the difference between Int and Fix.
Log	Log(x)	Returns the natural logarithm of x.	
Rnd	Rnd	Returns a random number less than 1 but greater than or equal to 0.	
Sgn	Sgn(x)	Returns: 1 if x is greater than 0; 0 if x equals 0; −1 if x is less than 0.	
Sin	Sin(x)	Returns the sine of x.	x expresses an angle in radians.
Sqr	Sqr(x)	Returns the square root of x.	
Tan	Tan(x)	Returns the tangent of x.	x expresses an angle in radians.

Function	Example	Description	Note
Derived Math Functions		See the online help system for formulas to derive functions that aren't predefined, such as cotangent.	

Lesson Summary

In this lesson, you have become more familiar with the Visual Basic development environment. The Help system, in particular, will come in very handy from time to time to refresh your memory. You were also introduced to the Visual Basic math functions. In next lesson, we discuss the variable types and program flow.

Quiz 2

1. Which of the following statements shows a label that was previously invisible to the user?

   a. `lblTotalSongs.Visible = True`

   b. `Show lblTotalSongs`

   c. `Show lblTotalSongs.Visible`

   d. `lblTotalSongs.Show = True`

2. Which of the following statements puts an integer value in `Result`?

   a. `Result = TotalLength\2`

   b. `Result = Int(TotalLength/2)`

   c. `Dim Result As Integer Result = TotalLength/2`

   d. All of the above

3. In order to make an assignment to `True` or `False` valid, you first need to

   a. Declare `True` and `False` as Booleans.

   b. Do nothing; they are predefined keywords.

   c. Assign `-1` to `True` and `0` to `False`.

   d. Assign `1` to `True` and `0` to `False`.

4. Most VB math functions are pretty self-explanatory. The Cos function, for example

    a. Returns the sine of an angle

    b. Returns the cosine of an angle

    c. Returns the cosine of an exponent

    d. Converts the angle to degrees

Exercise 2

Complexity: Moderate

1. Add text boxes to the CD maker program to enable the user to specify the length of each of the two songs and the length of the CD. For now, assume that all input is valid.

Complexity: Advanced

2. Write a program that enables you to enter two integers in a text box and displays the sum of these numbers in a label. For simplicity's sake, you may assume that only integers will be entered in the text boxes.

LESSON 3

If and More Variable Types

In this lesson you'll learn some new variable types. But first, we'll start with a discussion of program flow. So far, all the source code you've written has been linear within the routine it's contained in. That is, first one statement is executed, then the next, and so on until the end of the routine. Although this is fine for very short tasks, soon you'll need to know program flow statements to make your programs do what you want. Most program flow statements fall into one of the following categories:

- Conditional, or decision statements, in which code is executed based on whether or not a condition is met

- Looping statements, in which code is executed repeatedly either a certain number of times or until a condition is met

- Branching statements, in which program execution switches to a different part of the program, usually based on some condition

This lesson deals with a very common decision statement, the If statement.

The `If` Statement (Introduction)

It's time to make a decision.

The `If...Then...Else` statement lets you say, in effect, "If this is true, then do this; otherwise, do that." This statement can be used in two different ways:

- As a single-line statement
- As a multiple-line statement

The syntax for the single-line `If` statement is

```
If expression Then statement [Else statement]
```

The multiline `If` statement syntax is

```
If expression Then
    [statement]
[Else]
    [statement]
End If
```

The statements following the `If` statement are executed if the expression evaluates to `True`. Conversely, the `Else` block of statements is executed if the expression evaluates to `False`. The expression used in `If...Then` is a Boolean expression. Boolean expressions have two possible values: `True` or `False`. Numerically, `False` is equal to `0`, and `True` is equal to a value of `-1`.

Note
> The use of the `Else` block in both versions of the `If` statement is optional.

Here is an example of the single-line syntax (note the line continuation):

```
If lblScore.Visible = True Then lblScore.Caption = Score _
                            Else Score = 0
```

The multiline structure of this statement is preferred, as it is generally much easier to read:

```
If lblScore.Visible = True Then
    lblScore.Caption = Score
Else
    Score = 0
End If
```

Comparison Operators

Note that, in the above example, the equal sign is being used both as an assignment statement (`Score = 0`) and as a comparison operator (`lblScore.Visible = True`). A comparison operator compares two values and returns the result of the comparison (either True or False). Table 3.9 lists the arithmetic comparison operators in Visual Basic, in order of precedence.

TABLE 3.9   Comparison Operators

Operator	Name
=	Equality
<>	Inequality
<	Less than
>	Greater than
<=	Less than or equal to
>=	Greater than or equal to

CD Maker Gets Smarter

Let's use these new language elements to give CD Maker a little logic. On the main form, add the label described in Table 3.10.

TABLE 3.10   Yet Another CD Maker Label

Object	Property	Value
Label	Name	lblResult
	AutoSize	True
	Caption	Your songs will/will not fit.
	Visible	False

Go to the cmdCompute click event and modify the code, as shown in Listing 3.10.

LISTING 3.10   Implementing a Conditional Statement

```
Private Sub cmdCompute_Click()
' Compute the songs'total length
iTotalLength = iSong1Length + iSong2Length
lblTotalLength.Caption = "Together the songs are " & iTotalLength & _
                                " minutes long."

' Find the average length
iAverageLength = Int(iTotalLength / 2)
lblAverage.Caption = "The average song length is " & _
```

```
                            iAverageLength & "."
' Can they fit on the CD?
If iTotalLength <= iTotalCDTime Then
   lblResult.Caption = "Your songs will fit."

   ' See how much room is left over.
   iRoomLeft = Int((iTotalCDTime - iTotalLength) / iAverageLength)
   lblRoom.Caption = "You have room for " & iRoomLeft _
                                   & " more songs."
   lblRoom.Visible = True
Else
   lblResult.Caption = "Your songs will not fit."
   lblRoom.Visible = False
End If

' Make the labels visible
lblResult.Visible = True
lblTotalLength.Visible = True
lblAverage.Visible = True

End Sub
```

The conditional statement in this code segment reads as follows:

```
If the total length is less than or equal
to the total time on the CD, then...
```

Notice that the lblRoom property assignments are now inside the conditional statement block, because if there isn't enough room on the CD for the two songs, there won't be room for any more. Run the program again and click the Compute button. You'll see the screen shown in Figure 3.10. Try changing the values of iSong1Length and iSong2Length to 45 and 20 and running the program again.

That about does it for the CD Maker. Go ahead and save the form as CDMAKER.FRM and the project as CDMAKER.VBP inside the CDMAKER directory. After a few digressions, we'll start a new sample project.

Constants

So far, we have considered only variables in the programs. Visual Basic enables you to declare constants as well. Constants are rather like variables, except that their value never changes. Consider the following example:

```
If Action = 3 Then
    ' execute code for action number 3
End If
```

FIGURE 3.10

The CD Maker knows
what will fit.

The problem with the above example is that action number 3 isn't very meaningful. It would be much better if we could write the code as:

```
If Action = CANCELORDER Then
    ' execute code to cancel the order
End If
```

In this example, CANCELORDER is a constant that we have predefined to take the number 3. Constants are declared anywhere in your project, but you will most likely declare your constants in the General Declarations sections of your modules. Constants are declared using the Const keyword, which has the following syntax:

```
[Public ¦ Private] Const constname [As type] = expression
```

For example:

```
Const CANCELORDER As Integer = 3
```

The keywords Public and Private refer to scope, which we'll talk about in Chapter 4, "Subroutines, Functions, and the Visual Basic 6 Language."

Variable Types

So far, the variables you've declared have all been integers (although we talked in Chapter 2, "Object-Oriented Programming," about string values for some properties). VB 6 has a range of additional types as well. Table 3.11 lists all of VB's built-in types.

TABLE 3.11 The VB 6 Variable Types

Type	Range	Note
Byte	0 to 255	Occupies only 1 byte of memory.
Boolean	True or False	This is actually stored internally as an integer.
Integer	−32,768 to 32,767	Each integer occupies 2 bytes of memory.
Long	−2,147,483,648 to 2,147,483,647	Longs hold integers, but use 4 bytes of memory.
Single	See below.	Single-precision floating-point variable; occupies 4 bytes of memory.
Double	See below.	Double-precision floating-point variable; occupies 8 bytes of memory.
Currency	−922,337,203, 685,477.5808 to922,337,203 685,477.5807	Occupies 8 bytes of memory.
Dec	+/−79,228,162, 514,264,337,593, 543, 950,335 as a whole number; +/−7.92281625142 643375935439503 35 with decimal places	Occupies 12 bytes of memory.
String		Strings hold alphanumeric values and are discussed in Lessons 4 and 5.
Date		The Date data type holds dates and times and is discussed in Lessons 6 and 7.
Variant		Variant is a generic data type and is covered in Lesson 8.
Object		Object is advanced data type, covered in Chapter 14, "Advanced Features."

Byte

A byte is the smallest numeric data type. It can hold unsigned numbers (positive only) between 0 and 255. Bytes are quite useful when you want to conserve memory space and you know that the numbers you need to process will never be greater than 255. Consider the example in Listing 3.11, which assumes that the form has the Command buttons `cmdApples`, `cmdBananas`, `cmdOranges`, and `cmdGroceryOrder`.

LISTING 3.11   Replacing Numbers with Meaningful Constants to Help Readability

```
Const APPLES As Byte = 1
Const BANANAS As Byte = 2
Const ORANGES As Byte = 3
Dim Fruit As Byte

Private Sub cmdApples_Click()
Fruit = APPLES
End Sub

Private Sub cmdBananas_Click()
Fruit = BANANAS
End Sub

Private Sub cmdOranges_Click()
Fruit = ORANGES
End Sub

Private Sub cmdGroceryOrder_Click()
If Fruit = ORANGES Then
    MsgBox "Sorry, oranges are out of season."
End If
End Sub
```

By replacing the numeric values with symbolic constants, you made the code easier to read. Because you know you'll have less than 255 kinds of fruit, you're conserving memory as well by using the Byte data type.

Boolean

Boolean types are special in that they can be set to only one of two values: `True` or `False`. Internally, the Boolean type is actually an Integer data type. The value `True` is represented by the value `-1` and `False` is represented by `0`. When you print the value of a `Boolean` variable, Visual Basic converts these internal representation to the string `"True"` or `"False"`.

Booleans are generally used in two ways:

- To hold the result of an expression evaluation
- As flags to indicate whether or not a particular condition has been satisfied

Booleans to Hold the Result of an Expression Evaluation

To use a Boolean to hold the result of an expression, simply assign the expression to the Boolean as in Listing 3.12.

LISTING 3.12 Code Fragment to Assign a Value to a Boolean

```
Dim bHigher As Boolean
Dim iNum1 As Integer, iNum2 As Integer

' Perform assignments or get data here.

bHigher = iNum1 > iNum2
If bHigher Then
   ' Do whatever
EndIf
```

You might want to do this if you'll be using the result of the expression in more than one place or if the value of Num1 or Num2 might change, but you still want to remember the results of the original comparison.

Booleans to Keep Track of Whether a Condition Has Been Satisfied

Start a new Visual Basic project with the Command buttons listed in Table 3.12. It doesn't matter where on the form you put the buttons.

TABLE 3.12 Controls for the Boolean Flag Example

Control	Property	Value
CommandButton	Caption	Click once, at least!
	Name	cmdClick
CommandButton	Caption	Exit
	Name	cmdExit

This program uses a Boolean flag, Clicked, to keep track of whether the user has clicked the first button. You'll use the value in the Exit routine to prevent the user from quitting before clicking. The code to do this is shown in Listing 3.13.

LISTING 3.13 Boolean Flag Example

```
Dim bClicked As Boolean

Private Sub cmdClick_Click()
```

continues

LISTING 3.13 continued

```
' Set flag to True
bClicked = True
End Sub

Private Sub cmdExit_Click()
If Not bClicked Then
    MsgBox "Sorry, you have to click at least once!"
Else
    MsgBox "Good! You clicked!"
    Unload Me
End If
End Sub

Private Sub Form_Load()
' Initialize flag to False
bClicked = False
End Sub
```

Integer

You have already seen integers in action in the CD Maker program. Integers are whole numbers in the range of –32768 to 32767. Each integer occupies two bytes of memory.

Long

Longs are another type of integer, except they occupy four bytes of memory rather than two. Correspondingly, they can hold much larger numbers.

A long can hold numbers in the range of –2,147,483,648 to 2,147,483,647.

Single

Single-precision floating-point variables occupy 4 bytes of memory. Singles and doubles are used for storing numbers that have a decimal point. You should be aware, however, that the accuracy of the representation of floating-point numbers is as dependent on how many digits there are before the decimal point as on how many there are after.

For example:

```
Dim fMySingle As Single
fMySingle = 123456.123456
lblOutput.Caption = fMySingle
```

The original value assigned to MySingle doesn't survive the assignment. This is because, although single-precision floating-point variables can store very large or very small numbers, by using their exponent component, they can hold only a small number of actual numbers (seven at the most).

The full ranges of valid numbers for singles are

- $-3.402823E38$ to $-1.401298E{-}45$ for negative numbers
- $1.401298E{-}45$ to $3.402823E38$ for positive numbers
- 0

The numbers above are expressed in scientific notation. Scientific notation is a system used to express very large and very small numbers using the powers of ten. Briefly, 1E3 evaluates to 1000 and 1E–3 evaluates to 0.001. The number following the E tells you how far to move the decimal point and the sign of the number tells you which way to move it.

Double

Double-precision floating-point variables use 8 bytes of memory for each variable and, accordingly, can store a greater range and precision of numbers. The full range of valid numbers for doubles is

- $-1.79769313486232E308$ to $-4.94065645841247E{-}324$ for negative numbers
- $-4.94065645841247E{-}324$ to $1.79769313486232E308$ for positive numbers
- 0

Be careful when using single- and double-precision floating-point variables in the same program unless it doesn't matter if you lose some decimal places during your calculations. For example, if you need to do monetary calculations, use the Currency data type rather than Single or Double.

Currency

The Currency data type is provided for the express purpose of holding money values. It can hold amounts in the range –922,337,203,685,477.5808 to 922,337,203,685,477.5807.

Currency data types can hold numbers down to four decimal places, because some currencies around the world need such accuracy.

Currency variables use 8 bytes of memory space.

Decimal

If you are calculating really big numbers, like this month's electric bill, you can use the new Decimal data type. This little gem uses 12 bytes of memory and holds numbers in the range (hold on to your hat!) +/–79,228,162,514,264,337,593,543,950,335 for zero-scaled numbers, that is, numbers with no decimal places. If you need decimal places, you can have up to 28 of them, and the range becomes +/–7.9228162514264337593543950335. The smallest possible non-zero number is 0.0000000000000000000000000001.

As of this writing, you can't declare a Decimal data type, but you can create one from a variant. To see how to do this, open a new form and put a text box on it. Enter the following code in the form's Load event:

```
Private Sub Form_Load()

Dim cMyCurr As Currency, vMyDec As Variant
cMyCurr = CCur(234.456784)    ' cMyCurr is a Currency.

' Convert result to a DecimalvMyDec = CDec(cMyCurr * 8.2 * 0.000000000000001)
Text1.Text = vMyDec

End Sub
```

Now run the program by pressing F5.

Note the use of the variant data type in the code. A variant is a catch-all data type that can be used to hold any kind of data. Most programmers avoid them when possible because they use more memory than the other data types, but sometimes, as in this code, they are required.

Lesson Summary

In this lesson, you learned how to use the if statement to code decisions. The numeric data types were discussed at length and you were briefly introduced to the non-numeric data types, that will be covered in detail later on. In the next lesson, we start the discussion of non-numeric data types with strings.

Quiz 3

1. If is an example of
   a. A looping statement
   b. A branching statement
   c. A conditional statement
   d. A function

2. What is the difference between

    ```
    If...Then...Else...
    ```

    and

    ```
    If...Then
    ...
    Else
    ...
    End If
    ```

    a. The first usage can execute only one statement per condition.

    b. The first usage cannot really implement an `Else` clause.

    c. They are functionally equivalent, but the second usage is easier to read.

    d. Both a and b are true.

3. In which of the following statements is = being used as a comparison operator?

    a. `HighScore = 50`

    b. `HighScore = lblScore.Caption`

    c. `lblScore.Caption = HighScore`

    d. `If HighScore = 50 Then ...`

4. How would you declare a constant to hold a value representing a grocery item?

    a. `Dim Const FRESHDILL As Integer = 23`

    b. `Dim FRESHDILL = 23`

    c. `Const FRESHDILL As Integer = 23`

    d. `Dim FRESHDILL As Integer FRESHDILL = 23`

Exercise 3

Complexity: Moderate

1. Write a program that enables you to enter two numbers in a text box and displays the result of the division of the first number by the second one in a label. Make sure you catch attempts to divide by zero. For simplicity's sake, you may assume that only numbers will be entered in the text boxes.

Complexity: Advanced

2. Add text boxes to the CD maker program to enable the user to specify the length of each of the two songs and the length of the CD. Check whether the input is valid before the calculations.

LESSON 4

Introduction to Strings

Strings are variables and constants that hold alphanumeric values. These are values that you want to display but will not usually use for mathematical calculations. You've already been using strings since Lesson 2 in Chapter 2, "Object-Oriented Programming." In Visual Basic, a sequence of alphanumeric characters treated as a single value is considered a string. The `Caption` property, `Text` property, `FileName` property, and so on all contain string values. Literal strings are assigned by enclosing the value in quotation marks, as you've already seen. For example:

```
lblMessage.Caption = "Sorry, oranges are out of season."
```

Working with a string's contents is more complicated than working with numbers because the characters that make up the string give you not just one value, but have a separate value for each character in the string. Fortunately, VB has a wealth of string manipulation functions. How you use them depends on how closely you need to analyze a string's contents. Before we proceed, let's take a look at a new, fast way to look at the value of a variable.

The Immediate Window

The Immediate window is a window to which you can output information that you might need for purposes of program development and debugging. You might use the Immediate window to quickly check a variable's value or to evaluate an expression without interrupting the flow of your program.

The Immediate window is actually Visual Basic's built-in `Debug` object. The `Debug` object is an example of a class that has only one instance. The `Debug` object is automatically created by Visual Basic for you, so there is no need for you to provide any additional programming support to create it. The `Debug` object provides you with a single method: the `Print` method.

The `Print` Method

The `Print` method outputs a value. What `Print` does depends on the object being acted on. To try out the Immediate window, start a new project, double-click the form to bring up the Code window, and enter the code in Listing 3.14 in the `Form_Load` event.

LISTING 3.14   Testing the Immediate Window

```
Private Sub Form_Load()
    Dim FullName As String
    FullName = "c:\vb\vb.exe"
    Debug.Print FullName
End Sub
```

Run your program. The Immediate window may be hidden behind the main form. To bring it to view, click Immediate Window under the View menu. You'll see your output, as shown in Figure 3.11.

FIGURE 3.11

The Immediate window.

You can leave the Debug statements in your program when you compile it, because they are ignored by the compiler. We will often use the Immediate window in this way to help demonstrate the values that variables take in our examples.

Note

> In the future, when we use short code snippets with Debug.Print as examples, we won't specify the Form_Load event every time. This will be assumed, because that's the natural place to put code you want to run immediately. You may want to resize or move the main form and the Immediate window in design mode so that the Immediate window is visible when the program runs.

To learn to use strings, you will create a new project called Address Book. This program accepts data entry and separates it into the appropriate strings for address book entries. (The program will not save your entries. Chapter 12, "Reading and Writing Disk Files," and Chapter 13, "Database Programming," deal with techniques for saving data like this to disk for later use.)

Address Book

Create a new directory called ADDRESS BOOK. Create a new project by clicking New Project under the File menu. Select the program's main form and press F4 to bring up the Property window. Set the form's property values, as shown in Table 3.13.

TABLE 3.13 The Address Book Form Property Values

Object	Property	Value
Form	Name	frmAddressBook
	Caption	Address Book

The Icon Property

You will add an icon to this project to change its look. When you compile a project that has one or more icons set, the first icon the compiler finds will become the icon for the project's EXE file. Click the Icon property of the form; then click the ellipsis points that appear in the right edge of the property list. A File Open list box will appear. The collection of icons is in the GRAPHICS\ICONS directory. Select the WRITING directory; then select NOTE14.ICO.

Note | If you select an icon or a bitmap picture that you later decide to delete, you cannot remove it by selecting None again—VB will not offer you that choice. You can remove it by highlighting the word Icon or Bitmap (by dragging the mouse pointer across the selection in the Properties window) and pressing Del.

Add three labels, a text box, and a Command button to frmAddressBook. Assign the property values shown in Table 3.14.

TABLE 3.14 New Properties for the Address Book Project

Object	Property	Value
Label	Name	lblInstructions
	Caption	Enter Last Name, First Name
	AutoSize	True
TextBox	Name	txtName
	Text	txtName
Label	Name	lblFirstName
	AutoSize	False
	Caption	leave field blank

Object	Property	Value
Label	Name	lblLastName
	AutoSize	False
	Caption	leave field blank
CommandButton	Name	cmdSave
	Caption	&Save

For lblFirstName and lblLastName, select the BackColor property and change the color to white (&H00FFFFFF&).

Arrange the controls on the form, as shown in Figure 3.12. The two white blocks in the center are lblFirstName on the left and lblLastName on the right. Note that txtName, lblFirstname, and cmdSave are aligned on the left.

FIGURE 3.12

The Address Book project.

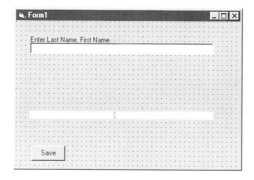

Note

You can align controls easily in VB 6. Select all the controls you want to align by holding down Shift as you click each control. Now select Align from the Format menu. You will get a cornucopia of alignment and sizing options. Try it!

Before we add code to this project, let's look at some basic facts about strings.

Strings

Strings hold character data. Visual Basic 6 can store strings up to 2 billion characters in length! There are two types of strings:

- Variable-length
- Fixed-length

Variable-Length Strings

Variable-length strings are declared simply by using the `String` type name when you declare the variable. For instance:

```
Dim MyVarString As String
```

Variable-length strings have an overhead of 10 bytes per string. They occupy 10 additional bytes over and above the length of the string itself.

Fixed-Length Strings

Fixed-length strings are declared by specifying the length of the string in the declaration of the string variable. For instance:

```
Dim MyFixedString As String * 30
```

declares a 30-character string. It will always be 30 characters, even if you assign less data to it. For example:

```
MyFixedString = "ABCDE"
```

automatically right-pads the string with 25 spaces.

String Functions

Sometimes you don't care what's in a string. A string is just a thing that you pass from one part of your program to another without regard for its contents. Other times, however, you need to know what's inside. You might need to verify its contents, modify it in some way, or extract a specific piece of information from it. There are enough core string functions that two lessons are required in order to cover them all. The string functions you'll learn in this lesson are summarized in Table 3.15.

TABLE 3.15   The First Batch of String Functions

Function	Example	Description
Len	Len(String)	Returns the integer length of String
InStr	InStr([StartPosition,] String, SubString [, Compare])	Searches String for occurrences of SubString
Left	Left(String,Length)	Returns the leftmost Length characters of String
Right	Right(String, Length)	Returns the rightmost Length characters of String
Mid	Mid(String, Start, Length)	Returns Length characters from String, starting at position Start

Many of these functions are helpful in parsing, extracting smaller pieces from the string. Throughout this session, you'll explore the task of breaking a string into components and checking the values of specific parts of a string.

Code for Address Book

Now let's add the code for the Address Book project. Because you will be doing the same thing to several different strings before you are done, add some functions to the project.

All the work to begin with will be done in the cmdSave_Click event. Enter the code in Listing 3.15, or copy it from the CD that comes with this book.

LISTING 3.15   The cmdSave_Click Event

```
Private Sub cmdSave_Click()

' message for sMsgbox
Dim sSMsg As String
' The name, separated into first and last names
Dim sFirstName As String, sLastName As String
' where is the comma in the name
Dim iCommaPosition As Integer
' The length of the name as entered
Dim iLength As Integer
' Where the space is
Dim iSpacePosition As Integer
' The city, state and ZIP code
Dim sCity As String, sState As String, sZip As String

' First make sure the name was entered
If Len(txtName.Text) = 0 Then
    ' Create the warning message
    sMsg = "No Name Entered"
    ' make it visible
    MsgBox sMsg
    ' set focus back to txtName
    txtName.SetFocus
    Exit Sub
End If
' now check for the comma
If InStr(txtName.Text, ",") = 0 Then
    ' Create the warning message
    sMsg = "Must have a comma between" & vbCrLf
    sMsg = sMsg & "Last Name and First Name"
    ' make it visible
    MsgBox sMsg
    ' set focus back to txtName
```

continues

3

LISTING 3.15   continued

```
        txtName.SetFocus
        Exit Sub
End If
' if we got here the name was probably entered correctly
' get the length
iLength = Len(txtName)
' find the comma
iCommaPosition = InStr(txtName.Text, ",")
' Pull the First name from the textbox
' The -1 is so we don't get the comma, too
sLastName = Left(txtName, iCommaPosition - 1)
' Pull the last name from the textbox
' Start by testing for a space after the comma
If Mid(txtName, iCommaPosition + 1, 1) = " " Then
        iCommaPosition = iCommaPosition + 1
         'move the start position one place to the right
End If
sFirstName = Right(txtName.Text, iLength - iCommaPosition)
' display the separated names
lblFirstName.Caption = sFirstName
lblLastName.Caption = sLastName

End Sub
```

A Look at the Code

Let's take a look at the code to see what is happening.

```
' message for sMsgbox
Dim sSMsg As String
' The name, separated into first and last names
Dim sFirstName As String, sLastName As String
' where is the comma in the name
Dim iCommaPosition As Integer
' The length of the name as entered
Dim iNameLength As Integer
```

This section of code declares the variables you will be using in the Click event. It is using a naming convention that helps you remember what kind of variable you are using. For example, the s in sMsg reminds you that it is a string variable and the i in iNameLength reminds you that it is an integer variable. Naming conventions like this can help avoid mistakes, especially on large projects.

Because computer users are human, input errors are quite possible. The code in cmdSave_Click begins with a couple of tests to be sure the data was input in the correct format. (Sorry, we can't do anything about spelling!)

```
If Len(txtName.Text) = 0 Then
    ' Create the warning message
```

```
        sMsg = "No Name Entered"
        ' make it visible
        MsgBox sMsg
        ' set focus back to txtName
        txtName.SetFocus
          'the entry is incorrect, do not process it
        Exit Sub
End If
```

The first routine checks to make sure that something was actually entered in txtName. It uses the len() function to verify that something is in the box.

The Len Function

The Len function counts the characters in a string and returns the length as an integer. The syntax is

```
Length = Len(String)
```

Knowing how long a string is can help you in cases for which you need to verify that the string will fit in a certain field. You also might use this function when you need to perform some operation for every character in the string, when you need to compare the relative sizes of two strings, or in other situations.

In this case, if Len returns a 0, it tells you there are no characters in the string. If that is the case, the program uses a built-in Visual Basic function, the Message Box, to let the user know that there is no text in the text box. The code lines

```
sMsg = "No Name Entered"
MsgBox sMsg
```

build a message to be displayed and then display the message in a modal form. A modal form is one that must be closed before the program can continue. Much more can be done with the MsgBox object, but we will stick to this simple method for now.

When the user clicks OK in the message box, the line

```
txtName.SetFocus
```

sets the focus back to the text box so a name can be entered.

Remember that spaces are characters, too, and will be counted.

Back to the Code

The next block of code makes sure that the user has followed instructions by separating the last name and first name with a comma.

```
If InStr(txtName.Text, ",")= 0 Then
    ' Create the warning message
```

```
        sMsg = "Must have a comma between" & vbCrLf
        sMsg = sMsg & "Last Name and First Name"
        ' make it visible
        MsgBox sMsg
        ' set focus back to txtName
        txtName.SetFocus
         'the entry is incorrect, do not process it
        Exit Sub
End If
```

This code uses the InStr function to be sure that a comma has been entered. If there is no comma, a MsgBox informs the user and focus is returned to the text box. Note that when the message is built, this time we use string concatenation. Concatenation is a 75-cent word for *pasting together*. The first line,

```
sMsg = "Must have a comma between" & vbCRLF
```

ends with & vbCRLF. The & tells VB to add two strings together. The vbCRLF is a built-in Visual Basic constant that represents a carriage return and a linefeed. The next line,

```
sMsg = sMsg & "Last Name and First Name"
```

adds another string to the first. Because of the vbCRLF at the end of the first line, the message will be shown on two lines in the MsgBox.

The InStr Function

The Instr function returns the first position of a string inside another string. If the substring (the string you're looking for) isn't found, InStr returns a 0. The syntax of InStr is

```
InStr([StartPosition,] String, SubString [, Compare])
```

The components of the InStr syntax are as follows:

- StartPosition is a numeric expression that sets the start position for the search of SubString in String. (The first character is position 1.) If StartPosition is omitted, InStr begins searching at the first position.
- String is the string being searched.
- SubString is the string you are looking for in String.
- Compare determines how to go about the comparison of the two strings. If you omit Compare or specify a value of 0, InStr performs a straight comparison, which is usually the type you want to use. If you are working mostly with text and want to use a Compare that is not case sensitive, specify 1 for the Compare parameter.

Here's a simple example of `InStr`:

```
Debug.Print InStr("Hello in there","in")
```

This line displays 7. On the other hand,

```
Debug.Print InStr(8,"Hello in there","in")
```

returns a value of `0` because the substring `"in"` doesn't appear at or after the eighth character.

`InStr` is helpful simply to see whether a string is in a substring, as in this example to validate input.

```
If  InStr(txtName.Text,",") = 0 Then
    lblMessage.Caption = "Please separate names with a comma."
Else
    ' (Go off and process the data.)
End If
```

However, `InStr` really shows its power when you need it to track the position of characters. We'll be looking at this use more below, in conjunction with the other string functions.

The Rest of the Code

Both of the tests will detect a problem with the data entered (or not entered) in `txtName`. You don't want to process that bad data, so both tests have the line

```
Exit Sub
```

just before the `End If`. `Exit Sub`, of course, exits from the sub `cmdSave_Click` without executing any more of the commands.

The next block of code assumes correct entry of the data; the name has been entered last name first, with a comma separating the last name from the first name. Data processing applications should really be written so that the two names are entered separately, but this program uses the next block of code to do the separation.

```
' get the length
nLength = Len(txtName)
```

gets the length of the string.

```
iCommaPosition = InStr(txtName.Text, ",")
' Pull the Last name from the textbox
' The -1 is so we don't get the comma, too
sLastName = Left(txtName, iCommaPosition - 1)
```

uses the left function to extract the left end of the string in `txtName` into its own variable, `sLastName`. We will look at the `Left`, `Right`, and `Mid` functions after these blocks of code.

```
' Pull the First name from the textbox
' Start by testing for a space after the comma
If Mid(txtName, iCommaPosition + 1,1) = " " Then
    iCommaPosition = iCommaPosition + 1
End If
```

You don't want a space as the first character of the first name, so check to see if the user entered one by using the `Mid` function. If you find one (you should) then increment `iCommaPosition` by 1.

```
sFirstName = Right(txtName.Text, iLength - iCommaPosition)
```

Next, use the `Right` function to extract the first name from `txtName`. Then, using techniques you already know, display the separated names in their own labels.

```
' display the separated names
lblFirstName.Caption = sFirstName
lblLastName.Caption = sLastName
End Sub
```

The Left Function

The `Left` function returns characters from the left-hand side of `String`. For example, the `Left` function has the following syntax:

```
Left(String, Length)
```

The components of the `Left` function syntax are as follows:

- String is the string from which you are returning characters.
- Length is the number of characters to return. If Length = 0, then a zero-length string is returned. If Length is greater than the length of the string, then the entire string is returned. You can try out the sample code by placing it in Form_Load and viewing the results in the Immediate window.

```
Dim sAlphabet As String, sEasyPart As String
sAlphabet = "ABCDEFGHIJKLMNOPQRSTUVWXYZ"
sEasyPart = Left(Alphabet,3)
Debug.Print "It's easy as " & sEasyPart
```

This creates and prints out a new string consisting of `Alphabet`'s first three characters, `ABC`. Here's another example.

```
Dim sFullPathName As String, sDrive As String
sFullPathName = "C:\Program Files\Microsoft Visual Studio\VB6\VB6.exe"
sDrive = Left(sFullPathName,1)
Debug.Print "Searching drive " & sDrive & "..."
```

The Right Function

The Right function returns characters from the right-hand side of the string. It has the following syntax:

```
Right(String, Length)
```

The components of the Right function syntax are as follows:

- String is the string from which you are returning characters.
- Length is the number of characters to return. If Length = 0, then a zero-length string is returned. If Length is greater than the length of the string, then the entire string is returned.

The Mid Function

The Mid function returns characters from any part of a string.

The Mid function has the following syntax:

```
Mid(String, Start [,Length])
```

The components of the Mid function syntax are as follows:

- String is the string from which you are returning characters.
- Start is the character position in string at which the part to be taken begins. If Start is greater than the number of characters in the string, Mid returns a zero-length string.
- Length is the number of characters to return. If this is omitted or if there are fewer than Length characters in the text (including the character at the start), all characters from the start position to the end of the string are returned.

For example,

```
Dim sMyString As String, sNewString As String
sMyString = "ABCDEFGHIJKLMNOPQRSTUVWXYZ"
sNewString = Mid(sMyString, 11, 10)
Debug.Print sNewString
```

outputs

```
KLMNOPQRST
```

Note that the third parameter refers to the length of string that you want to return, not the end character in the original string. If Length is omitted, all characters from Start to the end of the string are returned.

Running the Code

Now run the code for Address Book.

- Start by clicking the Save button without putting any text in the text box. Note the appearance of the message box.

- Enter a name in the text box, but omit the required comma. Note what happens when you click the Save button; the two-line message adds a touch of professionalism to the box.

- Add the comma between the first and last names in the text box. Again note what happens when you click the Save button: The first and last names now appear in their specified display labels.

- Save the project. You will be working with it more in Lesson 5.

Lesson Summary

In this lesson, we started our discussion of the String data type. You learned how to look into a string using the Len and InStr functions and how to chop up a String using the Left, Right and Mid functions. In the next lesson, we conclude our discussion of strings.

Quiz 4

1. The statement

   ```
   Debug.Print "The answer is 10."
   ```

   a. Outputs a single string to the Immediate window

   b. Won't do anything until you create an instance of the Debug object

   c. Will have to be removed manually before you can ship the compiled version of your product

   d. Won't work, because the argument is a string literal

2. String functions such as Mid, InStr, and Len are useful

   a. When you need to perform close analysis of a string's contents

   b. When you are passing a string as a single value from one part of your program to another

    c. When you need to assign a string variable to an object property

    d. All of the above

3. The statement

```
Debug.Print InStr(4, "c:\windows\system.ini","\")
```

prints out

    a. 3

    b. 4

    c. 11

    d. 10

4. The statement

```
Dim sMyString As String
sMyString = "ABC;123;QRS"
Debug.Print Mid(sMyString,InStr(sMyString,";"),3)
```

outputs

    a. 123

    b. QRS

    c. ;12

    d. Nothing; the line has a syntax error

Exercise 4

Complexity: Moderate

1. Write a program that accepts a person's name in a text box. Assume the last name is entered first and that a comma separates it from the first name, for example, "Gates, Bill." Add an exit button to the form that says bye using the first name from the text box when pressed; for example, "Bye, Bill!"

Complexity: Advanced

2. Write a program to print out the drive or device name of a file, given the full path name. Assume the device name is preceded by a colon and may be more than one character long. Let the user know if there isn't a device name present.

LESSON 5

String Manipulation

This session covers such string-handling techniques as converting a string to upper- or lowercase and trimming the excess spaces from a string. These functions are summarized in Table 3.16. After that, we'll round out our string machinations with sections on string concatenation and string comparison.

TABLE 3.16   The Second Batch of String Functions

Function	Example	Description
UCase	UCase(String)	Converts string to all uppercase
LCase	LCase(String)	Converts a string to all lowercase
LTrim	LTrim(String)	Strips leading spaces from a string
RTrim	RTrim(String)	Strips trailing spaces from a string
Trim	Trim(String)	Strips leading and trailing spaces from a string
Asc	Asc(StringChar)	Returns the numeric equivalent of a character
Chr	Chr(Number)	Returns the character corresponding to a code value
Space	Space(Number)	Returns a string consisting of a number of spaces
String	String(Number, Character)	Returns a string consisting of a single character repeated a number of times
LSet	LSet String1 = String2	Left-justifies one string within another
RSet	RSet String1 = String2	Right-justifies one string within another
StrComp	StrComp(string1, string2 [,compare])	Returns a value indicating the result of a string comparison

Improving Address Book

Open the Address Book project and add two new text boxes and six new labels to the form.

Note

Look ahead at Figure 3.13. You will see that the new text boxes are exactly the same size as the original text boxes. You can make copies of VB controls just the same way you make copies of text in a word processor. Click `txtName` and press Ctrl+C to copy the control to the clipboard. Then press Ctrl+V to paste it on the form. VB will ask you if you are making a control array. Answer No, and it will insert a copy of the control in the upper-left corner of the form.

FIGURE 3.13

The improved Address Book form.

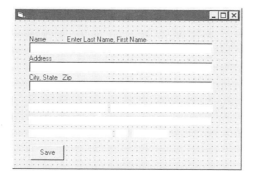

Note

While the control is selected, you can move it by holding down Ctrl and using the arrow keys to move the control or by dragging it with the mouse. If you need to resize a control, select it and use Shift and the arrow keys to adjust the size, or use the mouse to resize the control.

Set the properties of the new controls according to Table 3.17.

TABLE 3.17 Properties for the New Controls

Object	Property	Value
TextBox	Name	txtAddress
TextBox	Name	txtCityStateZip
Label	Name	lbl1
	AutoSize	True
	Caption	Name

continues

TABLE 3.17   continued

Object	Property	Value
Label	Name	lbl2
	AutoSize	True
	Caption	Address
Label	Name	lbl3
	AutoSize	True
	Caption	City, State Zip
Label	Name	lblAddress
	Caption	lblAddress
	BackColor	&H00FFFFFF&
Label	Name	lblCity
	Caption	lblCity
	BackColor	&H00FFFFFF&
Label	Name	lblState
	Caption	lblState
	BackColor	&H00FFFFFF&
Label	Name	lblZip
	Caption	lblZip
BackColor	&H00FFFFFF&	

Use Figure 3.13 as a guide to placing the new control objects.

Changing the Tab Order

Move from control to control in a running VB program by pressing the Tab key. The order, or sequence of the controls as you tab through a form is initially set to be the same as the order in which you created the controls. On this form, with all its new controls, the tab order is no longer correct. If you enter data in txtName and press Tab, you may want to go to txtAddress, but you will go to cmdSave.

The following steps make it easy to change the tab order:

1. Select the control you want to be last in the tab order and change its Tab Index property to 0.

2. Select the next to last control and change its Tab Index property to 0.

3. Continue to work your way backward through the controls, setting each control's Tab Index property to 0.

As you change each control's Tab Index property to 0, all the controls below it are automatically changed to the next higher index. The effect ripples through all the previously set controls and your tab indexes are automatically reset to the order you wanted.

Enabling Enter

You want to make some improvements to what you already have before you add code for the new controls. For example, some people find it more natural to finish entering data into a text box by pressing the Enter key rather than by pressing Tab, which is the standard way to move from field to field. You could do that by placing the following code in the KeyPress event of every text box:

```
If KeyAscii = 13 then
    KeyAscii = 0
    SendKeys "{Tab}"
End If
```

That wouldn't be too hard now—you have only three text boxes. But some programs have a lot more text boxes. Instead, you can use a formwide technique:

- Set the KeyPreview property of frmAddressBook to True.
- Put the code shown above in the Form_KeyPress event.

It is standard Windows practice to use Enter to operate a default key, usually either OK or Close. This alternative use of Enter is included because some clients just don't want to be "standard."

KeyAscii

The KeyPress event occurs (surprise!) every time a key is pressed in a control. KeyAscii is the ASCII value of the key that was pressed. ASCII stands for American Standard Code for Information Interchange and represents the binary number for the letters, numbers, and control characters you can generate from the keyboard. Each character has its own code number. For example, the ASCII code for the letter A is 65 and the ASCII code for the letter a is 97. There is a table of ASCII values under Character Set in online help.

ASCII 13 is the value of the carriage return, or Enter. By default, if you press Enter in a text box, the computer will beep. But if you detect the 13 and change it to a 0, the beep will disappear.

SendKeys

The SendKeys event sends one or more keystrokes to the active window as if typed at the keyboard.

The syntax for SendKeys is

```
SendKeys string[, wait]
```

The components of the SendKeys syntax are as follows:

- String is the keystroke or keystrokes you want to send.
- Wait is a Boolean value specifying the wait mode. If it is False (default), control is returned to the procedure immediately after the keys are sent. If it is True, keystrokes must be processed before control is returned to the procedure. If Wait is missing, it is False by default.

The only way out of the text box without using the mouse is the Tab key, so you will fool the computer by sending Tab out of the KeyPress event using the SendKeys statement. The string "{Tab}" represents Tab for SendKeys. The listing of special keystrokes is in online help.

More Improvements to Address Book

Users might enter their data in all uppercase or all lowercase letters, whereas we want to store (later) and display them in more normal fashion, with only the first letter capitalized. Find

```
sLastName = Left(txtName, iCommaPosition - 1)
```

in the code and add the following lines after it:

```
' convert to all lower case
sLastName = LCase(sLastName)
' Change first letter to upper case
Mid(sLastName, 1, 1) = UCase(Mid(sLastName, 1, 1))
```

Then find

```
sFirstName = Right(txtName.Text, nLength - iCommaPosition)
```

in the code and place the following lines after it:

```
' convert to all lower case
sFirstName = LCase(sFirstName)
' Change first letter to upper case
Mid(sFirstName, 1, 1) = UCase(Mid(sFirstName, 1, 1))
```

These few lines of code use two new VB functions and a new VB statement.

The LCase Function

The LCase function returns a string with all letters converted to lowercase.

The syntax for LCase is

```
LCase(string)
```

The string argument is any valid string expression. If string contains Null, Null is returned.

The UCase Function

The UCase function returns a string with all letters converted to uppercase.

The syntax for UCase is

```
UCase(string)
```

The string argument is any valid string expression. If string contains Null, Null is returned.

For UCase and LCase, only the alphabetic characters are acted on; these functions will not affect numbers or punctuation or other printable symbols.

The Mid Statement

The Mid statement replaces a specified number of characters in a string variable with characters from another string. At first glance, it looks exactly like the Mid function, which returns the value of a specified part of a string, but its behavior is completely different.

The syntax for the Mid statement is

```
Mid(stringvar, start[, length]) = string
```

The components of the Mid statement syntax are as follows:

- stringvar is the name of the string variable to modify.
- start is the character position in stringvar where the replacement of text begins.
- length is the number of characters to replace. If this is omitted, all of string is used.
- string is the string expression that replaces part of stringvar.

In this code, the strings that are extracted from txtName.Text are first converted into lowercase letters; then the Mid statement is used to replace the first character of each string with an uppercase letter.

The New Code for Address Book

Now you are ready to add the code for handling the two new text boxes on frmAddressBook. You will add some declarations at the beginning of the cmdSave_Click event, immediately following the last Dim statement:

```
Dim sCity As String, sState As String, sZip As String
Dim iSpacePosition As Integer
```

The following code will be placed at the end of the cmdSave_Click event. Between the last line,

```
lblLastName.Caption = sLastName
```

and

```
End Sub
```

insert the code shown in Listing 3.16.

LISTING 3.16   The New Code for Address Book

```
' new code for Lesson 5
'    Copy Address
'    First check for length, if there is nothing here
'    skip these steps
If Len(txtAddress) = 0 Then Exit Sub
lblAddress.Caption = txtAddress.Text
'    Separate city, State and Zip
'    First check for length, if there is nothing here
'    skip these steps
If Len(txtCityStateZip) = 0 Then Exit Sub
' Check for comma between city and state
iCommaPosition = InStr(txtCityStateZip, ",")
If iCommaPosition = 0 Then
    ' Create the warning message
    sMsg = "Must have a comma between" & vbCrLf
    sMsg = sMsg & "City and State"
    ' make it visible
    MsgBox sMsg
    ' set focus back to txtName
    txtCityStateZip.SetFocus
    Exit Sub
End If
' Get length
nLength = Len(txtCityStateZip)
' Extract City
'again -1 to skip the comma
sCity = Trim(Left(txtCityStateZip, iCommaPosition - 1))
' Make only first character upper case
```

```
sCity = LCase(sCity)
Mid(sCity, 1, 1) = Chr(Asc(Mid(sCity, 1, 1)) - 32)
' Check for a space after the comma
If Mid(txtCityStateZip, iCommaPosition + 1, 1) = " " Then
    iCommaPosition = iCommaPosition + 1
End If
' Find the space after the state
iSpacePosition = InStr(iCommaPosition + 1, txtCityStateZip, Chr(32))
' Extract State
If iSpacePosition > iCommaPosition Then
sState = Trim(Mid(txtCityStateZip, iCommaPosition, iSpacePosition _
                            - iCommaPosition))
End If
' Make only first character upper case
sState = LCase(sState)
If Len(sState) <> 0 Then _
    Mid(sState, 1, 1) = Chr(Asc(Mid(sState, 1, 1)) - 32)
' Extract Zip
If nLength > iSpacePosition + 1 Then
    sZip = Trim(Right(txtCityStateZip, nLength - iSpacePosition + 1))
End If
' display the results
lblCity = sCity
lblState = sState
lblZip = sZip
```

What's New in Address Book?

Much of what you added to Address Book in this session is only more of the same stuff you've seen before. There are a couple of new functions, though.

The Trim Functions

The Trim functions return a copy of a string without leading spaces (LTrim), trailing spaces (RTrim), or both leading and trailing spaces (Trim).

The syntax of the Trim functions is

```
LTrim(string)
RTrim(string)
Trim(string)
```

The string argument is any valid string expression. If string contains Null, Null is returned. In this program, you used Trim to remove all leading and training spaces. In some cases, you may want to remove spaces from only one end. Then you would use either LTrim or RTrim.

The Asc Function

The Asc function returns the character code corresponding to the first letter in a string.

The syntax of the Asc function is

```
Asc(string)
```

The string argument is any valid string expression. If the string contains no characters, a runtime error occurs.

The Chr Function

The Chr function returns the character associated with the specified character code.

The syntax of the Chr function is

```
Chr(charcode)
```

The charcode argument is a number that identifies a character. The numbers are the ASCII character set, which includes numbers from 0 to 255. You should remember that ASCII codes above 127 represent what is called the Extended ASCII character set. These codes are valid only in IBM-type computers.

Explanation of the New Code

Some of the things you did in the new code are different ways of doing things you did in earlier code. The line

```
If Len(sState) <> 0 Then _
    Mid(sState, 1, 1) = Chr(Asc(Mid(sState, 1, 1)) - 32)
```

is really a difficult way of converting the first character to uppercase.

```
Asc(Mid(sState, 1, 1))
```

returns the ASCII code for the first character in the string. In the ASCII character set, the numbers for lowercase letters are higher than the numbers for the uppercase letters by exactly 32. So subtracting 32 from a lowercase letter converts it to an uppercase letter. The Chr function then converts the number back to a letter so you can put it back into the string. (Yes, this is the hard way, but now you know about the Asc and Chr functions and something about the ASCII character set.)

Running the New Code

Now run the code for Address Book. Enter names, cities, and states in all uppercase or all lowercase or mixed-case letters. Leave txtCityStateZip empty to see what happens.

Enter text in `txtCityStateZip` without the comma to see what happens. Try leaving out the space between `AnyCity,State`.

More String Functions

You have learned a lot about string manipulation in the last two lessons, but there are still a number of string functions that we have not covered! We will provide examples of them, displaying their results in the Immediate window.

The `Space` Function

The `Space` function returns a string consisting of the specified number of spaces.

The syntax of the `Space` function is

```
Space(number)
```

The `number` argument is the number of spaces you want in the string.

Use the `Space` function to fill a fixed-length string with spaces. Strange as it may seem, when you create a fixed-length string, it is still an empty string. The following code demonstrates that fact by using `InStr` to look for the first space before and after you use the `Space` function.

```
Dim sString As String * 20
Debug.Print Len(sString),
Debug.Print InStr(sString, " ")
sString = Space(10)
Debug.Print Len(sString),
Debug.Print InStr(sString, " ")
```

The string length is always 20 characters, but until you run `sString = Space(10)`, all the characters are composed of the empty string.

The empty string is represented by `""` (quotation marks with nothing between them). The empty string is a handy way of clearing text boxes and string variables. The code `sFirstName = ""` would fill `sFirstName` with the empty string. In other words, you would clear any other string from the variable. You also use the empty string to see if code has assigned a value to a string:

```
If sFirstName = "" Then debug.print "sFirstName is Empty"
```

The `String` Function

The `String` function returns a repeating character string of the length specified.

The syntax of the `String` function is

```
String(number, character)
```

The components of the String function syntax are as follows:

- *number* is the length of the returned string. If number contains Null, Null is returned.
- *character* is the character code specifying the character or string expression whose first character is used to build the return string. If character contains Null, Null is returned.

If you specify a number for a character greater than 255, String converts the number to a valid character code using the formula character Mod 256.

This code demonstrates the effect of String:

```
Dim sString As String * 20
sString = String(20, 169)
Debug.Print sString
```

If you have changed the default font for your form, the results will vary, but you will get 20 of them, whatever they are.

The LSet Statement

The LSet statement left-aligns a string within a string variable.

The syntax is

```
LSet stringvar = string
```

The components of the LSet syntax are as follows:

- stringvar is the name of the string variable.
- string is the string expression to be left-aligned within stringvar.

The LSet statement replaces any leftover characters in stringvar with spaces.

If string is longer than stringvar, LSet places only the leftmost characters, up to the length of the stringvar, in stringvar. Try the following code:

```
Dim sString As String * 20
sString = String(20, 169)
Debug.Print sString
LSet sString = "Hello"
Debug.Print sString
```

The RSet Statement

The RSet statement right aligns a string within a string variable.

The syntax is

```
RSet stringvar = string
```

The components of the RSet syntax are as follows:

- stringvar is the name of the string variable.
- string is the string expression to be left-aligned within stringvar.

Leftover characters in stringvar are replaced with spaces, back to its beginning.

Try the following code:

```
Dim sString As String * 20
sString = String(20, 169)
Debug.Print sString & " Dolly"
RSet sString = "Hello"
Debug.Print sString & " Dolly"
```

LSet, RSet, and String are especially useful when you are working with data files stored on disk, where the different fields are of a specific length.

String Comparison

Now that you know how to manipulate strings, you need to know how to tell if two strings are equal. Not only that, you need to be able to test for equality in two different ways: case sensitive and not case sensitive. In case-sensitive comparisons, capital letters have a different *value* than lowercase letters. Remember that the ASCII value of a lowercase letter is greater than the capital letter by 32; Asc("A") = 65 and ASC("a") = 97. In case-sensitive comparisons, "A" < "a", and comparisons that are not case sensitive, "A" = "a". If you are doing a case-sensitive comparison, "A" = "a" returns False.

The StrComp Function

The StrComp function returns a value indicating the result of a string comparison.

The syntax is

```
StrComp(string1, string2[, compare])
```

The components of the StrComp function syntax are as follows:

- string1 is any valid string expression.
- string2 is any valid string expression.
- compare specifies the type of string comparison.

The compare argument can be omitted, in which case Visual Basic does a case-sensitive comparison. This is the same result you would get if you specified 0. Specify 1 to perform a textual comparison, which is not case sensitive, as shown in Table 3.18.

TABLE 3.18 The Return Values for StrComp

Return Value	Comparison
-1	string1 < string2
0	string1 = string2
1	string1 > string2
Null	string1 or string2 is Null

The following code snippet demonstrates the different possibilities for the StrComp function:

```
Dim sString1 As String, sString2 As String
sString1 = "Abcdefgh"
sString2 = "AbcdefgH"
Debug.Print "Result    Comparison"
Debug.Print StrComp(sString1, sString2, 0); "      s1>s2,Compare = 0"
Debug.Print StrComp(sString2, sString1, 0); "      s2<s1,Compare = 0"
Debug.Print StrComp(sString1, sString1, 0); "      s1=s1,Compare = 0"
Debug.Print StrComp(sString1, sString2, 1); "      s1>s2,Compare = 1"
Debug.Print StrComp(sString2, sString1, 1); "      s2<s1,Compare = 1"
Debug.Print StrComp(sString1, sString1, 1); "      s1=s1,Compare = 1"
```

In this code, sString2 is less than sString1 by virtue of the uppercase H in the string. The two strings evaluate as equal when the control parameter = 1, but the comparison is case-sensitive when the control parameter = 0.

Lesson Summary

In this lesson, you learned how to use more string manipulation functions, giving you a powerful tool set to deal with strings. In the next two lessons, you will learn all about times and dates.

Quiz 5

1. The Mid statement is used for

   a. Testing for the presence of one string within another

   b. Changing one or more characters within a string

    c. Counting the number of characters in a string

    d. Testing a string for a null string

2. The `Chr` function returns

    a. The characters in a string, sorted into ascending order

    b. The number of characters in a string

    c. The ASCII value of a character

    d. The character represented by an ASCII value

3. `StrComp ("One", "one", 0)` returns

    a. `1`

    b. `-1`

    c. `0`

    d. Nothing; there is a syntax error in the statement

4. What function would you use to remove all spaces from both ends of a string?

    a. `LSet`

    b. `LTrim`

    c. `RTrim`

    d. `Trim`

Exercise 5

Complexity: Moderate

1. Write a program that enables you to enter two numbers in a text box and displays the result of the division of the first number by the second one in a label. Make sure you catch attempts to divide by zero and non numeric characters entered in the text box.

Complexity: Advanced

2. Write a program that takes a number less than 1 million as input in a text box and puts the words that describe this number in a label.

LESSON 6

Times and Dates

Visual Basic has a powerful Date data type and some useful functions to go with it. Both this lesson and Lesson 7 discuss this data type, which you will find extremely useful in your programs.

First, the Basics

The Date data type is capable of storing dates and times in the range January 1, 100, to December 31, 9999, inclusive. Each date that you declare occupies 8 bytes of memory.

The Date data type is actually stored internally as a double-precision floating-point number. The integer portion (the whole part) to the left of the decimal point is used to represent the date. The decimal portion (to the right of the decimal point) is used to represent the time. Times can be stored to single-second accuracy in the range 00:00:00 (midnight) to 23:59:59.

The Timesheet Program

To show you how the time and date functions work, we'll create a new sample program. Create a new directory called TIMESHET. Click New Project under the File menu. Add the objects and property values described in Table 3.19 to the form.

TABLE 3.19   Objects and Properties for the Timesheet Program

Object	Property	Value
Form	Name	frmTimeSheet
	Caption	Timesheet
Label	Caption	Date:
	AutoSize	True
Label	Caption	Time In:
	AutoSize	True
Label	Caption	Time Out:
	AutoSize	True
Label	Caption	Total
	AutoSize	True

Object	Property	Value
Label	Name	lblTotal
	Caption	x hours and x minutes
	AutoSize	True
	Visible	False
TextBox	Name	txtDate
	Text	[blank]
TextBox	Name	txtTimeIn
	Text	[blank]
TextBox	Name	txtTimeOut
	Text	[blank]
CommandButton	Name	cmdCompute
	Caption	Compute
CommandButton	Name	cmdExit
	Caption	Exit
CommandButton	Name	cmdNowIn
	Caption	Now
CommandButton	Name	cmdNowOut
	Caption	Now

Lay out the controls so the form looks like that in Figure 3.14. Program the Exit button, as shown in Listing 3.17, to make it a little easier to run and test the program.

LISTING 3.17 The Exit Button

```
Private Sub cmdExit_Click()
    Unload Me
End Sub
```

Representing Dates and Times as Literals

You often need to represent dates and times as literal values in your programs. Visual Basic allows tremendous flexibility over how you do this. All the following are valid date formats and result in the same date (February 1, 1998) being placed in the `MyDate` variable.

```
Dim dtMyDate As Date

dtMyDate = "2/1/98"
dtMyDate = "2/1/1998"
dtMyDate = "2 1 98"
dtMyDate = "2 1 1998"
dtMyDate = "1 Feb 98"
dtMyDate = "Feb 1 1998"
dtMyDate = "February 1 1998"
dtMyDate = "1 February 1998"
dtMyDate = "1998 Feb 1"
dtMyDate = "1998 2 1"
dtMyDate = "98 1 Feb"
```

FIGURE 3.14

Layout for the Timesheet program.

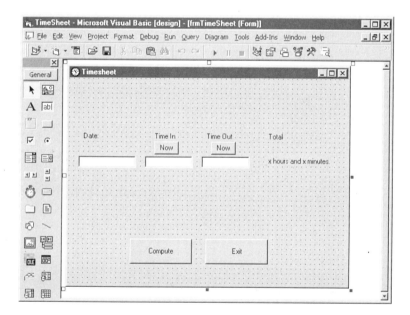

Visual Basic is even sensitive to the locale settings in the control panel. For example, if you set the country setting to the United Kingdom and rerun the above example, the first four dates are interpreted as the 2nd of January, rather than the 1st of February. If you are writing programs for international use, you need to take care that your program can adapt to such occurrences.

Visual Basic's date handling goes a little way toward solving this problem. Consider the following date literal:

```
15/1/98
```

Depending on which country you are in, this date could be interpreted as either a valid date (January 15, 1998) or an invalid date. However, if you try this with the country setting set to the United States, an error does not occur. Visual Basic recognizes that even though this date has not been entered in the correct format for the current locale, it would be a valid date if the month and day were swapped.

Date Literals

The above examples assign string values to dates. This works fine and, indeed, you would need to work with string values if you were assigning the date from a value entered by the user as a string. However, what's happening internally is that Visual Basic needs to create a temporary string variable before making the assignment. In the above examples, it would be more efficient to tell the VB compiler to treat the date literal as a Date type from the outset. You do this by surrounding the date with # (the pound sign) rather than with quotation marks.

```
dtMyDate = #1 Feb 1998#
```

Enter this line of code, and you can see Visual Basic converting the type up front. VB changes the representation of the date literal as soon as you type it into the Code window. It appears as

```
dtMyDate = #2/1/98#
```

Note that the displayed representation of the date when used with literals in your program remains fixed. It does not vary with the locale setting.

Date Functions

Visual Basic provides a wealth of date functions that can be used to manipulate dates. The first set of date functions we'll look at is summarized in Table 3.20. You'll learn about the remaining date functions in Lesson 7.

TABLE 3.20 VB 6 Time and Date Functions

Syntax	Type of Language Element	Description
Now	Function	Returns the current date and time from your computer's built-in clock
Date	Function/ Statement	Reads or sets the date from your computer's clock
Time	Function/ Statement	Reads or sets the time from your computer's clock
IsDate(strexp)	Function	Returns a Boolean indicating whether or not the string is a valid date
DateValue(date)	Function	Optional, Returns a Date data type from a string representation of a date
TimeValue(time)	Function	Optional, returns a Date data type from a string representation of a time
Day(date)	Function	Returns an integer representing the day portion of the date parameter
Month(date)	Function	Returns an integer representing the month portion of the date parameter
Year(date)	Function	Returns an integer representing the year portion of the date parameter
Hour(time)	Function	Returns an integer representing the hour portion of the time
Minute(time)	Function	Returns an integer representing the minute portion of the time
Second(time)	Function	Returns an integer representing the second portion of the time

The Now Function and Statement

The Now function returns the current date and time from your computer's built-in clock in a single Date variable.

For example:

```
Dim dtToday As Date
dtToday = Now
Form1.Caption = "Running: " & dtToday
```

The Date Function and Statement

The Date function/statement reads or sets the date portion of the current system date. You can change the date on your system's clock simply by assigning Date a new value. Let's use this value in the Timesheet program to set the default date in the text box. In the Form_Load routine, enter the code in Listing 3.18.

LISTING 3.18   Assigning the Current Date to the Text Box

```
Private Sub Form_Load()
    txtDate.Text = Date
End Sub
```

The Time Function and Statement

Visual Basic provides you with a built-in Time variable that you can use to read or set the time from your computer's clock. Let's add functionality to the two Now buttons so the user doesn't have to type in the current time. Add the code in Listing 3.19.

LISTING 3.19   Giving the User Access to the System Clock

```
Private Sub cmdNowIn_Click()
    txtTimeIn.Text = Time
End Sub

Private Sub cmdNowOut_Click()
    txtTimeOut.Text = Time
End Sub
```

The IsDate Function

The IsDate function returns a Boolean value to indicate whether the string passed contains a valid date. Let's enable the user to edit the date field directly, but verify that he or she entered a valid date. To do this, you need to know about a new event, the LostFocus event.

The GotFocus and LostFocus Events

Recall that the object with the focus is the object that is currently receiving input. An event is fired both when the object gets the focus (GotFocus) and when it loses the focus (LostFocus). The LostFocus event of a text box is a good place to verify input, because it gives the user a chance to enter (and, if necessary, edit) the value. Add the code in Listing 3.20 to the Timesheet program.

LISTING 3.20   Validating the Date the User Entered

```
Private Sub txtDate_LostFocus()
If Not IsDate(txtDate) Then
    txtDate = "<Invalid date>"
End If
End Sub
```

The Not Operator

Notice that we slipped in a new operator, Not. As you'd expect, this operator negates the current expression. Using it in context has the benefit of being very easy to read. We'll talk more about Not and other logic operators in Chapter 4, "Subroutines, Functions, and the Visual Basic 6 Language."

The DateValue Function

The DateValue function returns a Date data type from a string representation of a date that is passed to it.

For example:

```
Dim dtMyDate As Date
Dim sMyString As String
sMyString = "1 May 1998"
dtMyDate = DateValue(sMyString)
```

You may have noticed that the DateValue function is optional. As you saw in the section Representing Dates and Times as Literals, you could have written the above code as simply:

```
Dim dtMyDate As Date
Dim sMyString As String
sMyString = "1 May 1998"
dtMyDate = sMyString
```

In this case, Visual Basic converts the string data type to a Date data type implicitly. Although this works, performing the operation explicitly is more pedantic and possibly more reliable. We will look at other types of conversion in Lesson 8 and you will see that Visual Basic does quite a lot of data type conversion behind the scenes.

The TimeValue Function

Similarly to the DateValue function, TimeValue takes a string representation of the time and converts it to a Date data type. For example:

```
Dim dtMyDate As Date
Dim sMyString As String
```

```
sMyString = "15:30:00"
dtMyDate = TimeValue(sMyString)
```

You can also use implicit conversions rather than calling `TimeValue`. However, in the interest of clarity, let's use `TimeValue` to get at the times in your program. Add the code in Listing 3.21 to the `cmdCompute` click event.

LISTING 3.21   Computing the Time Difference

```
Private Sub cmdCompute_Click()
Dim dtTimediff As Date
Dim dtTimeIn As Date, dtTimeOut As Date
dtTimeIn = TimeValue(txtTimeIn)
dtTimeOut = TimeValue(txtTimeOut)
dtTimediff = dtTimeOut - dtTimeIn

' Output the results
lblTotal.Caption = dtTimediff
lblTotal.Visible = True

End Sub
```

Run the program and try it out. See what happens if you enter an invalid date in the Date box. (Because you didn't check the time formats, trying to compute using bad values will cause the program to crash.) Play with the Now buttons. Notice that you can use either a 12- or a 24-hour clock. If you use a 12-hour clock, you'll need to specify PM values, as shown in Figure 3.15. Although the program correctly computes the time difference, it displays the value in a time format, which is not what you want. You need to learn a few more functions before adding the last bit of code.

FIGURE 3.15

Entering values in the Timesheet program.

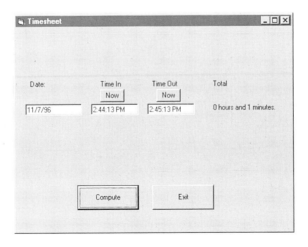

Day, Month, and Year Functions

The Day, Month, and Year functions are used to extract integer representations of the day, month, and year, respectively, from a Date data type.

Try the example in Listing 3.22.

LISTING 3.22   Displaying the Date in the Form Caption

```
Private Sub Form_Load()
Dim dtMyDate As Date
Dim iMyDay As Integer, iMyMonth As Integer, iMyYear As Integer
dtMyDate = Now
iMyDay = Day(dtMyDate)
iMyMonth = Month(dtMyDate)
iMyYear = Year(dtMyDate)
frmTimeSheet.Caption = "Today: " & iMyMonth & "/" & iMyDay & "/" & iMyYear
End Sub
```

Obviously, the actual values printed depend on the current setting of your computer's clock; however, using these three functions, you can extract integers that you can then use for date calculation or for some other purpose, such as storing information in a database.

Hour, Minute, and Second Functions

Visual Basic provides functions for displaying the components of the time as well. Add the final code to the cmdCompute routine, as shown in Listing 3.23.

LISTING 3.23   Outputting the Difference in a More Readable Format

```
Private Sub cmdCompute_Click()
Dim dtTimeDiff As Date
Dim iHoursDiff As Integer, iMinutesDiff As Integer
Dim dtTimeIn As Date, dtTimeOut As Date
dtTimeIn = TimeValue(txtTimeIn)
dtTimeOut = TimeValue(txtTimeOut)
dtTimeDiff = dtTimeOut - dtTimeIn
iHoursDiff = Hour(dtTimeDiff)
iMinutesDiff = Minute(dtTimeDiff)

lblTotal = iHoursDiff & " hours and " & iMinutesDiff & "
➥ minutes."_lblTotal.Visible = True
End Sub
```

Save the Timesheet program as TIMESHET.FRM/TIMESHET.VPB. You've been dated!

Lesson Summary

As you saw in this lesson, Visual Basic gives you access to every component of the Date data type. We'll cover the remaining date functions in Lesson 7.

Quiz 6

1. The most explicit way to represent a date literal in code is

   a. `"2/1/98"`

   b. `"Feb 1 1998"`

   c. `#2/1/98#`

   d. It depends on the date settings of the Control Panel.

2. The difference between `Date` (used as a function) and `Now` is that

   a. `Now` returns the date and time; `Date` returns just the date.

   b. `Now` returns the time; `Date` returns the date.

   c. `Date` returns the date and time; `Now` returns just the date.

   d. Nothing. The functions are equivalent.

3. Because a user may type many characters or make corrections in a text box, a good time to get input from the text box is in the _____ event.

   a. `GotFocus`

   b. `LostFocus`

   c. `Change`

   d. `Click`

4. Which of the following statements assigns a time to the `Date` variable declared

   `Dim dtMyTime As Date`

   a. `dtMyTime = Time`

   b. `dtMyTime = "03:45 PM"`

   c. `dtMyTime = TimeValue("03:45 PM")`

   d. All of the above

Exercise 6

Complexity: Moderate

1. Write a program that asks for your birth date. Add a compute button that displays how many years, months and days you have lived.

Complexity: Advanced

2. Write a program that asks for your birth date. Add a compute button that displays how many years, months and days until the next birthday.

LESSON 7

Other Date and Time Support Functions

Some other useful functions relate to dates and times. Let's complete our look at the Date data type by considering these functions, summarized in Table 3.21.

TABLE 3.21 Remaining Date/Time Functions

Type of Language Syntax	Element	Description
DateSerial	Function	Returns a Date data type from a year, month, and day
TimeSerial	Function	Returns a time from the hours, minutes, and seconds
Weekday	Function	Returns the day of the week
Timer	Function	Returns the number of seconds past midnight

The `DateSerial` Function

The `DateSerial` function returns a Date data type from the individual `year`, `month`, and `day` parameters that you pass to it. The syntax is

```
DateVar = DateSerial(Year, Month, Day)
```

For example:

```
Dim dtMyDate As Date
dtMyDate = DateSerial(1998, 5, 1)
Debug.Print dtMyDate
```

This code prints out

```
5/1/98
```

You can also use `DateSerial` to do some date calculations. Let's say you want to work out what the date will be in 50 days from May 1, 1998. Using the following:

```
dtMyDate = DateSerial(1998, 5, 1 + 50)
```

Visual Basic correctly determines that the new date is June 20, 1998.

The `DateSerial` function isn't doing anything particularly clever when you phrase this parameter as 1 + 50. Visual Basic does the calculation 1 + 50 first, and then passes the number 51 to the function. The `DateSerial` function is capable of taking the date that you've asked for (May 51, 1998, effectively) and turning that into a correct date representation. It's quite a useful feature.

The `TimeSerial` Function

The `TimeSerial` function returns a time from individual hours, minutes, and seconds. The syntax is

```
TimeVar = TimeSerial(Hour, Minute, Second)
```

For example:

```
Dim dtMyDate As Date
dtMyDate = TimeSerial(13, 0, 5)
Debug.Print dtMyDate
```

This example returns a time of 1:00:05 PM.

You can also use `TimeSerial` to perform some math operations on times. For example:

```
Dim dtMyDate As Date
dtMyDate = TimeSerial(13, 0, 75)
Debug.Print dtMyDate
```

returns a time of 1:01:15 PM.

Consider the following example:

```
Dim dtMyDate As Date
dtMyDate = TimeSerial(23, 59, 75)
Debug.Print dtMyDate
```

This outputs

```
12/31/1899 12:00:15 AM
```

Why did this happen? Remember that Date data types are no more than double-precision floating-point numbers internally. You simply overflowed the decimal portion of the `Date` variable and accidentally placed an integer value in the floating-point number.

Let's prove this by rerunning that example; however, instead of directly printing the value of the date in the Immediate window, first assign it to a standard Double data type and then print that. The new example is shown in Listing 3.24.

LISTING 3.24   Viewing a Date as a Double

```
Dim dtMyDate As Date
Dim dMyDouble As Double
dtMyDate = TimeSerial(23, 59, 75)
dMyDouble = dtMyDate
Debug.Print dMyDouble
```

You see that the value printed is `1.00017361111111`. It just so happens that the date represented by the integer number 1 is December 31, 1899.

Try rerunning some of the above examples, but this time assign the `Date` values to `Doubles` and print them out. This will give you a good understanding of how dates are represented internally in `Date` variables.

Weekday Function

In Lesson 6, you saw functions to return the month, year, and day of a date. Occasionally, however, you need to determine what the day of the week is. Luckily, VB 6 has a built-in function to give you this information: the `Weekday` function. The syntax is

```
DayVar = Weekday(date [, firstdayofweek])
```

`Weekday` returns an integer value representing the day of the week. For example:

```
Debug.Print Weekday(Now)
```

displays a number from 1 to 7, representing Sunday through Saturday. The number corresponds to whatever day today is.

Visual Basic 6 provides built-in constants for the values 1 to 7 to use in your programs so that you don't have to refer to a particular day as just a number. The constants are as summarized in Table 3.22.

TABLE 3.22   The Visual Basic Weekday Constants

Constant	Value
vbSunday	1
vbMonday	2
vbTuesday	3
vbWednesday	4
vbThursday	5
vbFriday	6
vbSaturday	7

This, of course, assumes that you expect the week to begin on Sunday. You might want the week in your program to start on a different day, say, Monday. You can tell the Weekday function that it should return 1 for Monday by adding one parameter to the function: the day of the week constant that you want to be the first day of the week. Therefore:

```
Debug.Print Weekday(Now, vbMonday)
```

will return 1 if today is a Monday and 7 if today is a Sunday.

The Timer Function

The Timer function is useful for implementing simple timed operations. It returns a value representing the number of seconds that have elapsed since midnight. Because there are 86,400 seconds in a day (24 hours * 60 minutes * 60 seconds) and an integer cannot hold values greater than 32,767, Timer cannot return an integer. Let's see what type of variable it returns:

```
Dim vMyVar As Variant
vMyVar = Timer
Debug.Print TypeName(vMyVar)
```

You might be surprised to find that Timer returns a single-precision variable. This is because of the way the timer is implemented inside Visual Basic. Again, the reason is largely historical, but Timer is capable of timing to subsecond intervals. However, the subsecond values are not really accurate because they are not tied to any hardware time base.

To see how you might use Timer in a typical timed operation, let's implement a loop that executes repeatedly until a predetermined number of seconds (10 in this case) has passed:

```
Dim fEndTime As Single
fEndTime = Timer + 10
Do While Timer < fEndTime
    ' these statements will be executed repeatedly until
    ' the value returned by Timer is greater than or equal to fEndTime
Loop
```

Although you will see how to use loops in detail in Chapter 4, "Subroutines, Functions, and the Visual Basic 6 Language," it should be clear how Timer might be used to implement a simple timer.

Date and Time Calculation Functions

You saw earlier how DateSerial and TimeSerial could be used to perform date calculations. Visual Basic 6 also provides some specific functions to do this job more explicitly. These functions are

- DateAdd
- DateDiff
- DatePart

The DateAdd Function

The DateAdd function has the following syntax:

```
DateAdd(Interval, Number, Date)
```

The first parameter, Interval, is a string that represents the type of interval that is being added to or subtracted from the date in the third parameter. The Interval string must be one of the values summarized in Table 3.23.

TABLE 3.23   Values for the DateAdd Interval Parameter

Interval	Description
yyyy	Year
q	Quarter
m	Month
y	Day of year
d	Day
w	Weekday
ww	Week
h	Hour
m	Minute
s	Second

The second parameter, Number, is a Long integer that represents the number of units of type Interval to add to the date in the third parameter. If Number is negative, the function subtracts the number of intervals, rather than adding. The DateAdd function, despite its name, can therefore be used for both adding to and subtracting from dates.

The third parameter, Date, must be a date variable that contains a valid date. The function acts on the date contained in the variable and returns the resulting date.

Let's see `DateAdd` in action. The example in Listing 3.25 returns the date one week from October 1, 1998.

LISTING 3.25   The `DateAdd` Function

```
Dim dtDateVar As Date
Dim dtNextWeek As Date
dtDateVar = #10/1/98#
dtNextWeek = DateAdd("ww", 1, dtDateVar)
Debug.Print dtDateVar
Debug.Print dtNextWeek
```

This code outputs

```
10/1/98
10/8/98
```

The `DateAdd` function always tries to return a valid date. For example, try the following code:

```
Dim dtMyDate As Date, dtNextMonthEnd As Date
dtMyDate = #31 Jan 2000#
dtNextMonthEnd = DateAdd("m", 1, dtMyDate)
Debug.Print dtNextMonthEnd
```

The `DateAdd` function hasn't just added one month to the date and produced an invalid date of February 31, 2000. Instead, it has done exactly what you asked of it, and found the last day of the next month (February 29, 2000). Try the example again, but this time use a start date of February 29, 2000.

```
Dim dtMyDate As Date, dtNextMonthEnd As Date
dtMyDate = #29 Feb 2000#
dtNextMonthEnd = DateAdd("m", 1, dtMyDate)
Debug.Print dtNextMonthEnd
```

This time, because March 29, 2000, is a valid date, that is the date returned.

The `DateDiff` Function

The `DateDiff` function returns the difference between two dates in the interval that you select.

The full syntax for `DateDiff` is

```
DateDiff(Interval, Date1, Date2[, FirstDayOfWeek[, FirstWeekOfYear]])
```

The `Interval` parameter is a string that denotes the interval in which the difference should be expressed. The same settings are used as those listed in Table 3.23 for `DateAdd`.

Date1 and Date2 are the two dates to be used. Date1 is subtracted from Date2, and the result is returned in the unit specified in Interval.

For example:

```
Debug.Print DateDiff("m", #2/29/96#, #3/29/96#)
```

returns 1 (one month).

For that matter, so does

```
Debug.Print DateDiff("m", #2/29/96#, #3/31/96#)
```

However, the following example returns two months:

```
Debug.Print DateDiff("m", #2/29/96#, #4/1/96#)
```

This is because, although two months have not elapsed, the difference in the two dates spans two calendar months. You have to be careful when using DateDiff that you ask for the answer you expect.

The DateDiff function has two optional parameters: FirstDayOfWeek and FirstWeekOfYear. Most of the time, you can probably ignore these, because they customize how the function works. The FirstDayOfWeek parameter is the same parameter as you saw in the Weekday function. It uses the day constants (vbSunday to vbSaturday) to specify which day should be treated as the first day of the week.

The FirstWeekOfYear parameter works slightly differently. It controls calculations for which the function has to calculate the first week of the year.

This parameter takes the constants summarized in Table 3.24.

TABLE 3.24   Constants for DateDiff's FirstWeekOfYear Parameter

Constant	Meaning
vbFirstJan1	Week in which January 1 appears
vbFirstFourDays	First week in January with at least four days
vbFirstFullWeek	First full week in January

The DatePart Function

The DatePart function uses the same interval string settings to return the part of the date specified.

Its full syntax is

```
DatePart(Interval, Date [, FirstDayOfWeek [,FirstWeekOfYear]])
```

In its simple form, DatePart returns the same information as the Day, Month, Year, Hour, Minute, Second, and Weekday functions.

For example:

```
Debug.Print DatePart("m", Now)   ' these two statements
Debug.Print Month(Now)           ' are equivalent
```

However, DatePart can also be used with the FirstDayOfWeek and FirstWeekOfYear parameters to customize your view of when the week and the year begin.

Lesson Summary

In this lesson, you learned more date and time support functions, completing your knowledge of the Date data type started in previous lesson. In the final lesson of this chapter, we conclude our coverage of variables with a discussion about variable declaration and variable types.

Quiz 7

1. What date does the following line print out?

   ```
   Debug.Print DateSerial(1985,3,32)
   ```

   a. 3/32/85

   b. 3/31/85

   c. 4/1/85

   d. None. VB prints an error message.

2. Assuming April 1, 1985, is a Monday, what will the following line print out?

   ```
   Debug.Print Weekday("April 1 85",3)
   ```

   a. 7

   b. 3

   c. 5

   d. 6

3. What sort of data type does the Timer function return?

   a. Long

   b. Integer

   c. Single

   d. Date

4. What does the following statement print out?

```
Debug.Print DateAdd("m",1,#8/31/90#)
```

   a. 9/31/90

   b. 9/30/90

   c. 9/28/90

   d. 10/1/90

Exercise 7

Complexity: Moderate

1. Write a program that asks for your birth date. Add a compute button that displays on what weekday you were born and the weekday of the next birthday.

Complexity: Advanced

2. Write a program that can be used as an on-screen clock.

LESSON 8

Variables Concluded

By now, you should have a good idea of what variables are and how to use them. We'll conclude this chapter by talking in a little more detail about variable declaration and variable types.

Variable Declaration

Variables can be declared in two different ways: explicitly (via the Dim statement) or implicitly.

Explicit Declaration

To use explicit declaration, you simply declare the variable using one of Visual Basic's declaration statements. This is what you've been doing all along in this chapter with the Dim statement. Typical declarations are

```
Dim iTestScore As Integer
Dim sFullFileName As String
```

Visual Basic's declaration statements are not executed in the same way as other language statements. Instead, they are really instructions to Visual Basic 6's compiler to create the variable when the program is compiled rather than when it is run.

> **Note**
>
> There is one caveat when regarding the <u>As</u> keyword. Although you can declare more than one variable on a line, As refers only to the variable immediately preceding it. For example,
>
> ```
> Dim Var1, Var2 As Integer
> ```
>
> looks as though it declares two integer variables. However, because Var1 has no corresponding As statement, it's actually declared as a variant.

Let's take a look at how variables are treated by VB before you assign a value to them. Add the following code after the declarations above:

```
Debug.Print TestScore
TestScore = 5
Debug.Print TestScore
```

Now run the project by pressing F5. Visual Basic outputs

```
0
5
```

Before you actually assign anything to MyVar, it has the value 0. Visual Basic automatically initializes all variables when they are declared. All numeric variables are therefore initialized to 0. This can be quite useful: You do not need to assign 0 expressly to a variable, as you do with some other languages.

You can force the use of explicit declarations by adding Option Explicit as the first line in the Declarations section of your code. That requires that you explicitly declare every variable before you use it in your programs, which helps you detect mistyped variable names in your code. Visual Basic will add Option Explicit to your code automatically if you select Options under the Tools menu and place a check beside Require Variable Declaration on the Editor tab. Option Explicit is discussed in more detail later in this chapter.

Implicit Declaration

Let's repeat the above test. This time, though, let's use implicit declaration. Remove the Dim statements from the Form_Load subroutine and run the project again.

You don't actually need to remove these statements. Instead, you can just comment out both lines.

```
'Dim TestScore As Integer
'Dim FullFileName As String
Debug.Print TestScore
TestScore = 5
Debug.Print TestScore
```

When Visual Basic encounters the assignment statement, it declares the variable and performs the assignment. This is implicit declaration and works only because the Option Explicit statement is not present in the module. When you run the example above, only 5 is printed out.

Consider the following example using implicit declaration:

```
MyVar = 5
MyVar = 5.1
```

The above code would cause a runtime error if you had explicitly declared MyVar to be an integer. What type of variable is Visual Basic declaring?

Visual Basic is actually declaring MyVar to be a variant type variable. A variant is a special data type that is capable of becoming any of the other built-in types. This is why MyVar can be an integer one moment and something else the next.

Let's prove that this is happening by using the TypeName function.

The TypeName Function

The TypeName function returns a string containing the name of the type of the variable passed to it.

For example, enter the code in Listing 3.26.

LISTING 3.26   The TypeName Function

```
Debug.Print TypeName(MyVar)
MyVar = 5
Debug.Print TypeName(MyVar)
MyVar = 5.1
Debug.Print TypeName(MyVar)
MyVar = "Five point 1"
Debug.Print TypeName(MyVar)
```

This program fragment outputs

```
Empty
Integer
Double
String
```

When the first statement is executed, `MyVar` hasn't been declared yet, so Visual Basic implicitly declares it as a variant. However, because you haven't assigned any data to it, the variant is uninitialized and has the type name of `Empty`.

The second time you call `TypeName`, you have already assigned an integer number to `MyVar`. When that assignment took place, Visual Basic changed the variant from the uninitialized type `Empty` to an `Integer`.

The third time, `MyVar` has changed to a `Double`; the fourth time, it has become a `String`.

At first sight, implicit declaration appears to have some distinct advantages over explicit declaration. However, there are some distinct disadvantages to using implicit declaration, as follows:

1. Variants occupy more memory than most other variable types. If you rely on implicit declaration, your programs consume more memory than they would using explicit declaration.

2. Implicit declaration is a little too forgiving of typing errors. If you incorrectly entered `MyVar` as `MuVar`, for example, Visual Basic would simply declare another variable. In a real program, the error might be difficult to find.

3. Because variants can change type, there is a small overhead in their use. Each time some data is assigned to them, Visual Basic has to determine whether or not the type needs to change. This happens very quickly, of course, but if you use variants in long loops, for example, the code will take slightly longer to execute than if you used specific data types and explicit declaration.

Good programming practice dictates, and we firmly recommend, that you use explicit declaration in your programs. You can use variants in your programs on those rare occasions when they are necessary, as long as you explicitly declare the variables as such.

```
Dim MyVar As Variant
```

Option Explicit

The `Option Explicit` statement is placed in the General Declarations section of a module. It tells Visual Basic that all variable declarations in that module must by explicit declaration only. In other words, you must declare every variable you use. In Chapter 9, "Printing," you will learn that this helps avoid a common programming error. The Environment Options dialog box controls whether Visual Basic automatically puts this statement in the General Declarations sections of your modules. Display the Environment Options dialog box now by opening the Tools menu and selecting the Options menu option from the Tools menu. The Editor tab, as shown in Figure 3.16, is displayed automatically because it is the first tab in the dialog box.

FIGURE 3.16

The Environment Options dialog box.

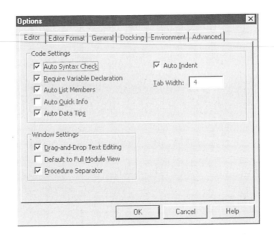

The setting you want is a check box labeled Require Variable Declaration. If it is not already set, click it now. If the check box is off, any modules that you add to your project will not have the `Option Explicit` statement added to them automatically. This does not mean that you cannot add `Option Explicit` to a module manually; it is just that Visual Basic will not do it for you. If the `Option Explicit` statement is present, Visual Basic insists that you explicitly declare your variables and generates an error at compile time if you try to use a variable without declaring it first. Note that checking this option will not add `Option Explicit` to modules that already exist in your projects; it will only cause it to be added to future modules that you create.

Variants

You have already seen variants in action. Variants are capable of becoming any of the other built-in data types. However there is a small overhead in their use because Visual Basic has to do some behind-the-scenes work to determine whether or not it needs to change the data type represented by the variant.

Sixteen bytes of memory are used when variants are combined with numeric data. If you use variants to hold string data, each variant has an overhead of 22 bytes of memory on top of the space required to store the string.

Variants can, in addition to storing the built-in data types, take three further values:

- `Empty`
- `Null`
- `Error`

Empty

You have already seen that uninitialized variants are declared as `Empty`.

Null

`Null` is different from `Empty` and the two should not be confused with each other. `Null` is an explicit value that you can assign to variants only. It indicates that you intend the variant to contain no data. If you use variants in your programs, you will find it useful to be able to distinguish between variants that contain no data because they have not been initialized yet (`Empty`) and variants that intentionally contain no data (`Null`).

To set a variant to `Null`, just assign `Null` to the variant:

```
MyVariant = Null
```

Error

Variants can also hold special error values when used in conjunction with functions. We will look at this aspect of variant behavior later when we consider functions and error handling (see Chapter 10, "Problem Solving: Handling Errors and Debugging Your Program").

Variable Assignment

In the examples in this chapter, we have assigned values to variables by using the assignment operator =. This is actually a shorthand way of assigning data to variables. There is a special keyword that you can use, called `Let`.

Let

The `Let` keyword assigns a value to a variable.

```
[Let] Var = Expression
```

The use of the Let statement is entirely optional and largely ignored by programmers. Its inclusion in the language is historical, because the earliest BASIC languages required its use.

Type Declaration Characters

Visual Basic offers a shorthand way of forcing a number to be a particular data type. Consider the following:

```
Dim MyInteger As Integer
Dim MyDouble As Double
MyInteger = 5
MyDouble = 5
```

You saw earlier when you took a quick look at variants that Visual Basic treats whole numbers within the range of an integer as integers. Therefore, the first assignment statement is self-explanatory. You are simply assigning an integer number to an integer variable.

The second assignment, however, requires a little more work on the part of Visual Basic. In the second case, 5 still starts out life as an integer. However, Visual Basic does a little bit of conversion work behind the scenes to turn the integer 5 into a double-precision floating-point variable.

To prevent Visual Basic from doing this work at runtime, you can use type declaration characters with both numbers and variables to force Visual Basic to treat them as specific data types. For example, we could have written

```
MyInteger = 5%
MyDouble = 5#
```

The % symbol is the type declaration character for an integer and # is the character for a double-precision floating-point number.

You can also use type declaration characters when you declare your variables. For example:

```
Dim MyInteger%
```

```
Dim MyDouble#
```

The use of the type declaration character obviates the need for the As keyword part of the declaration.

The full range of type declaration characters is summarized in Table 3.25.

TABLE 3.25 Type Declaration Characters

Data Type	Character	Data Type	Character
Byte	None	Date	None
Boolean	None	Currency	@
Integer	%	String	$
Long	&	Object	None
Single	!	Variant	None
Double	#		

Most of the time, you do not need to use type declaration characters, although you may prefer to if you feel it makes your choice of type declaration more obvious.

One occasion when it makes sense to use type declaration characters is when you use implicit declaration. For example, if you implicitly declare the following:

MyVar1 = 5

MyVar2% = 5

this code declares MyVar1 as a variant and MyVar2 as an integer.

Just My Type

Before wrapping up this chapter, let's take a look at a few functions that help you work across string and numeric types. These functions are particularly helpful because many of your input mechanisms (text boxes) and output mechanisms (captions) assume a string variable, but your program data may be numeric.

The `Val` Function

The `Val` function takes a string that contains the string representation of a number and converts it into a true numeric data type.

The `Val` function has the following syntax:

```
Val(String)
```

Because `Val` is designed to cope with any numeric type, it always returns a double-precision floating-point number. For example:

```
Dim sMyString As String
sMyString = "123"
Debug.Print TypeName(Val(sMyString))
```

outputs

```
Double
```

If you change the code to sMyString = "Fred", Val(sMyString) returns 0.

The Str Function

The Str function is the opposite of the Val function. It takes a numeric value and converts it to a string. The Str function has the following syntax:

```
Str(Number)
```

Listing 3.27 is an example.

LISTING 3.27   The Str Function on a Positive Value

```
Dim sMyString As String
Dim iMyInteger As Integer
iMyInteger = 123
sMyString = Str(iMyInteger)
Debug.Print sMyString
```

Note that sMyString is set to a string that has a leading space. This is because Str works according to some very basic formatting rules that state that if the number being converted is negative, then the string representation of that number will begin with a minus sign, as in Listing 3.28.

LISTING 3.28   The Str Function on a Negative Value

```
Dim sMyString As String
Dim iMyInteger As Integer
iMyInteger = -123
sMyString = Str(iMyInteger)
Debug.Print sMyString
```

When that number is positive, Str places a space at the beginning of the string so that both negative and positive numbers line up if displayed. Again, this behavior has more historical than practical significance nowadays. This behavior was required by versions of the BASIC language before we had graphical user interfaces. Today, if we want our numbers to line up when displayed (or printed), we have access to other functions and techniques that give us more control over how numbers display than is possible with the simple Str function.

One of those techniques is the use of the Format function, which we discuss in more detail in Chapter 8, "Using ActiveX Controls."

Lesson Summary

In the final lesson of this chapter, we concluded our discussion of variables with coverage of variable declaration, type declaration characters and Variants. You also learned how to convert between strings and numbers, using Val and Str.

Quiz 8

1. To declare a variable implicitly

    a. Use the Dim statement.

    b. Use the variable in a statement.

    c. Declare the variable a variant.

    d. Set the Option Explicit field of the Environment dialog box.

2. To find out a variable's type, call the _____ function.

    a. Type

    b. TypeName

    c. TypeAs

    d. MyType

3. Which of the following is never a valid type for a variant?

    a. Empty

    b. String

    c. Null

    d. All are correct

4. Why might an implicitly declared variable have a type declaration character, as in:

    Alphabet$ = "ABCDEFGHIJKLMNOPQRSTUVWXYZ"

    a. No reason.

    b. It forces the variable to be a string, avoiding the overhead of a variant.

    c. To prevent confusion with another variable of the same name.

    d. Variants can't take alphabetic characters as values.

3

Exercise 8

Complexity: Moderate

1. Add a column to the Timesheet program that displays (from the date) the day of the week corresponding to an entry.

Advanced

2. Add an output label to the Timesheet program, called lblCumulative, that updates a cumulative time variable every time the user presses Compute, so that the user can use the program to add up more than one time period. Add a text box where the user enters an hourly rate, and compute from that the total paycheck due for the cumulative time. (Hint: Use the Currency data type as appropriate.)

Chapter Summary

In this chapter, you expanded your programming horizon by learning about numeric variables, strings, and date variables. For each variable type, you studied several support functions allowing for easy manipulation of variable of that type.

In Chapter 4, "Subroutines, Functions, and the Visual Basic 6 Language," you will learn the control flow statements available in Visual Basic. These language elements will enable you to create "intelligent programs"—programs that act differently depending on circumstances. You will also learn how to use the building blocks of modular programming: subroutines and functions. With these, you will be able to reduce the complexity of writing programming by breaking the task into smaller, more manageable modules.

CHAPTER 4

Subroutines, Functions, and the Visual Basic 6 Language

This chapter builds on what you've already learned about variables and their related functions to complete the tutorial of the VB 6 programming language. Specifically, this chapter covers in detail:

- `For...Next` and other loop statements
- Decision statements
- Subroutine and function syntax
- Procedure and variable scope
- Arrays

You've already seen many of the main elements of a VB 6 program. You know how to add controls to a form; how to customize the look of your program by setting object properties at design or runtime; and how to attach source code to events, such as quitting the program when the user presses a button.

Additionally, you've learned the rudiments of computer programming. You can assign values to variables, call functions to manipulate your data, make decisions based on what your variables contain, and output results to the user.

Of course, there's still a lot to learn. But much of the work ahead of you has to do with expanding your familiarity with these basic building blocks and, with practice, gaining confidence in creatively combining these processes. We hope that as you proceed through the exercises in this book, you take time to experiment and to test your own theories about what's happening by modifying the code to see the new result or by outputting variable values to the Debug window. You won't hurt anything by experimenting. But, as always with computers, you may want to save your work first!

LESSON 1

A Project Skeleton

In this chapter, you'll learn about program flow. We'll try out new language elements by progressively expanding a new project: the Number Adder. Create a new directory called ADDER.

The World's Most Annoying Adding Machine

Build the "skeleton" of the project first, just as you've done in previous chapters. Fill in the source code as you go along. Start a new project with the objects and properties summarized in Table 4.1. Lay out the controls as shown in Figure 4.1.

FIGURE 4.1

The Number Adder (initial design).

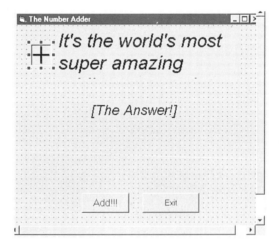

TABLE 4.1 Initial Objects and Properties for the Number Adder

Object	Property	Value
Form	Name	frmAdder
	Caption	The Number Adder
Picture	Picture	c:\Program Files\Microsoft Visual Studio\Common\Graphics\Icons\Misc\ misc18.ico
	AutoSize	True
Label	Caption	It's the world's most super_amazing adding program!
	Font	Name: Monotype Corsiva (or other script font)
		Size: 24
Label	Name	lblOutput
	AutoSize	True
	Caption	[The Answer!]
	Font	Name: Monotype Corsiva (or other script font)
		Size: 18
CommandButton	Name	cmdAdd
	Caption	Add!!!
	Font	Name: MS Sans Serif
		Size: 12
CommandButton	Name	cmdExit
	Caption	Exit
	Font	Name: MS Sans Serif
		Size: 12

4

Add source code to quit the program, as shown in Listing 4.1.

LISTING 4.1 The Familiar Exit Routine

```
Private Sub cmdExit_Click()
    Unload Me
End Sub
```

You have now implemented the program skeleton, all the visual elements with only the Exit button being functional. Next, you will be adding the guts to the program.

Overblown Fanfare: The First OLE Object

The theme of this project is "much ado about nothing." This program takes way too much pride in accomplishing a simple task. We'll convey the program's personality by adding a sound effect that plays when the program adds a number. Because playing a sound effect is a task the Sound Recorder that comes with Microsoft Windows already knows how to do, you'll add the sound as an OLE object. This will be easy.

Click the OLE container control icon indicated in Figure 4.2.

FIGURE 4.2

The OLE container control icon.

Draw the control anywhere on the form. When you let go of the mouse cursor, the Insert Object dialog box shown in Figure 4.3 comes up. Click Create From File, and then enter (or select via the Browse button) the filename c:\windows\tada.wav. Click OK.

FIGURE 4.3

The Insert Object dialog box.

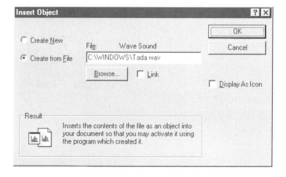

The sound object is represented by a microphone, as shown in Figure 4.4. OLE container control objects have a special popup menu that can access them. To bring up this window, click the right mouse button on the microphone icon. If you have a sound card, you can click Play now to hear the sound.

In Chapter 14, "Advanced Features," you'll learn amazing things about OLE automation and programmable objects. For now, however, all you need to know is that objects have methods (that shouldn't surprise you!), just as the controls you've been using all along have methods. Although the methods available depend, of course, on the object and its features, many objects have a default method. You can access this method using the DoVerb method:

```
objectname.DoVerb
```

(This is actually just a small part of what DoVerb can do; you'll learn more about it in Chapter 14, "Advanced Features.") Give your OLE object a meaningful name— oleTada—and go into the cmdAdd_Click routine. Enter the code to add numbers, as shown in Listing 4.2.

FIGURE 4.4

The microphone icon represents the sound.

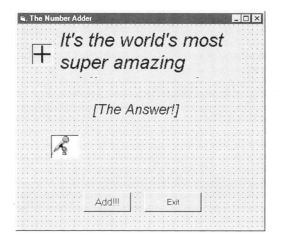

LISTING 4.2   Ta Da!

```
Private Sub cmdAdd_Click()
Dim Sum As Integer
'  If there is no sound card, skip to following line
On Error Resume Next
Sum = 2 + 2

lblOutput.Caption = Sum & " !!!"
oleTada.DoVerb

End Sub
```

The line On Error Resume Next is a simple error handler to take care of those of us who do not have sound cards in our computers. You will learn about error handlers in Chapter 9, "Printing."

Note	OLE controls don't just have methods. They have methods, properties and events, just like the built-in Visual Basic controls you have studied in the previous chapters.

Because you probably don't want the microphone icon on your program's main screen, you can either set the OLE container control's Visible property to False, or just move it out of sight by enlarging the frmAdder window. Drag the icon off out of the way, and then put the form back to its previous size.

Go ahead and save the form as ADDER.FRM and the project as ADDER.VBP. Run the program and see what you have implemented: a very basic adding machine, complete with sound.

Lesson Summary

With just a few lines of Visual Basic code, you have created a skeletal project that adds two numbers and makes a sound as it displays the total. This project will provide a good place to experiment with the language flow commands coming up in this chapter.

Quiz 1

1. Adding an OLE object that has a narrow function, such as a sound effect, to a program is
    a. Not going to be covered until Chapter 14
    b. Incredibly difficult
    c. Incredibly, impossibly difficult, something you shouldn't even aspire to
    d. Actually not all that hard

2. Which of the following are valid techniques for watching what's happening in a program?
    a. Printing out variables with Debug.Print
    b. Showing values or state information with MsgBox
    c. Changing things around a little and watching what happens
    d. All of the above

3. Which statement best describes computer programming?

    a. Analyzing data (from user input or other sources), manipulating the data, making decisions based on the data's contents or from a program's state, and continuing this process until a desired result is achieved

    b. Using the Debug.Print statement for output

    c. Assigning values to variables

    d. Evaluating True/False expressions

4. The OLE object method DoVerb

    a. Requires a verb name as a parameter

    b. By itself, executes a default action for an object

    c. By itself, always opens the object for user editing

    d. Is restricted to use by Microsoft-anointed gurus

Exercise 1

Complexity: Moderate

1. Create a program with three buttons: Make Changes, Save and Exit. Make sure one cannot exit the program without saving after Making Changes.

Complexity: Advanced

2. Add a New button to the previous program. Make sure one cannot start a new file without saving after Making Changes. Allow it to exit after a new file is started as long as no changes were made.

LESSON 2

For Loops

Visual Basic 6 provides a number of different types of loops that you can use to implement repetitive operations. We will start our look at loops by considering the most commonly used loop: the For...Next loop.

For...Next

The For...Next loop executes a series of statements a specific number of times. The basic syntax is

```
For countervariable = start To end
      ' Do something
Next countervariable
```

Here's how it works.

When VB executes the For line, the variable countervariable takes on the value of start. Thus, if the line is

```
For I = 1 to 10
```

then I starts life holding the value 1.

After the first line is executed, all the commands up until the Next statement are executed. The code inside the For...Next loop can be any combination of regular Basic commands.

When VB gets to the line Next countervariable, it increments countervariable by 1. In the example above, I would now have a value of 2.

Then VB loops—goes back to the For... line. This time I is compared to the end value, 10. If I is less than or equal to 10, the statements through Next are executed again. Otherwise, program execution resumes at the line following the Next statement.

Let's watch a simple loop in action. In the Form_Load event of the Adder program, enter the following code:

```
Dim I As Integer
For I = 1 to 10
      Debug.Print "Hi, I =  & I
Next I
Debug.Print "Out of loop, I = " & I
```

Run the program to see the word Hi and the value of I printed 10 times. When the value of I reaches 11, program flow will exit from the loop, just as you might expect. Then the program will tell you the value that I has reached when it exits from the loop.

The Counter variable, in this case I, is a variable like any other variable. You can use it in an expression, print it out—even change its value (not a good idea). Printing out the value of the loop counter is also a frequent debugging tool. It lets you see exactly what your loop is up to.

Now remove this code from the program.

Adding Up

Let's do something useful—well, marginally useful. Replace the cmdAdd_Click routine contents with the code in Listing 4.3. This adds the numbers 1 through 10.

LISTING 4.3   Adding the Numbers 1 Through 10

```
Private Sub cmdAdd_Click()
' Declare variables
Dim I, Sum As Integer

' Add the numbers from 1 to 10.
For I = 1 To 10
    Sum = Sum + I
Next I

Sub Output(Result As Variant)

' Output the results with fanfare
' if there is no sound card, skip to next line
On Error Resume Next
lblOutput.Caption = Result & " !!!"
oleTada.DoVerb

End Sub
```

Let's look at the For...Next loop a little more closely. Its full syntax is

```
For countervariable = start To end [ Step step ]
    [ statements ]
    [ Exit For ]
    [ statements ]
Next [ counter ]
```

The counter must be a numeric variable—any numeric variable type will do. Generally, you use an integer for the counter, but this is by no means a requirement of the statement.

The start and end values are numeric expressions that evaluate to numbers of the type that can be stored in the Counter variable. By numeric expression, we mean any valid Visual Basic statement that returns a number.

Consider the example in Listing 4.4.

LISTING 4.4   Using Variable Loop Parameters

```
Dim StartVar As Integer
Dim EndVar As Integer
Dim Counter As Integer
StartVar = 1
EndVar = 1000
For Counter = StartVar To EndVar
    ' your statements
Next Counter
```

In this example, the start and end values have been replaced by variables. Using variables makes the code more flexible than entering the numbers directly (referred to as "hard-coding" numbers). Now, if you wanted to use StartVar and EndVar somewhere else, you could be sure the values were the same. If you need to change the values, you need to do so only once.

Numeric expressions also can be the result of functions that return numeric values. Listing 4.5 is an example of using a function's return value in a For expression.

LISTING 4.5   Using a Function's Return Value in a Loop Parameter

```
Dim MyString As String
Dim Counter As Integer
MyString = "Visual Basic 6"
For Counter = 1 To Len(MyString)
    ' your statements
Next Counter
```

The Step Keyword

In its simplest form, the For...Next loop increments the Counter variable by 1 each time it goes through the loop. You can change the increment amount by using the Step keyword.

For example:

```
Dim QuarterMonth As Integer
For QuarterMonth = 1 To 12 Step 3
    ' your statements
Next QuarterMonth
```

In this example, the loop will execute four times, with the Counter variable QuarterMonth taking the values 1, 4, 7, and 10, respectively, on each pass through the loop. On the fifth pass through the loop, QuarterMonth will take the value 13, which is greater than the end expression 12. Accordingly, on the fifth pass through the loop, the loop will terminate.

You can also use the `Step` keyword to reverse order through the loop. For _example:

```
Dim I As Integer
For I = 10 To 1 Step -1
    Debug.Print I
Next I
```

prints out

```
10
 9
 8
 7
 6
 5
 4
 3
 2
 1
```

What do you think will happen if you leave out the `Step -1` part of the statement in the previous example? Try it. Your code should appear as follows:

```
Dim I As Integer
For I = 10 To 1
    Debug.Print I
Next I
```

The loop terminates without executing the `Debug.Print` statement. This occurs because the `Step` value is ommited; therefore, VB defaults to `Step = 1` and since the start value (`10`) for `I` is already greater than the end value (`1`), the loop exits immediately.

Remember that the `Step` amount does not have to be a whole integer; it just has to be an expression that evaluates to the same type of variable as `Counter`, `Start`, and `End`.

The `Exit For` Command

There are occasions where you need to break out of a `For...Next` loop. Consider the example in Listing 4.6.

LISTING 4.6 The `Exit For` Command

```
Dim FileName As String
Dim Counter As Integer
FileName = "VB.EXE"
For Counter = 1 To Len(FileName)
```

continues

LISTING 4.6   continued

```
        ' Search for period
        If Mid(FileName, Counter, 1) = "." Then
            Exit For
        End If
    Next Counter
    Debug.Print Counter
```

In this example, you are searching a filename for a period. Once you find the period, you use the Exit For statement to terminate forcibly the For loop. The Debug.Print statement shows that Counter is set to 3 after the end of the loop—the position of the character . in the string FileName.

Nested Loops

You can put a For...Next loop inside of another For...Next loop. Consider the example in Listing 4.7.

LISTING 4.7   Nested For...Next Loops

```
Dim Counter1 As Integer
Dim Counter2 As Integer
For Counter1 = 1 To 10
    For Counter2 = 1 To 10
        ' your statements
    Next Counter2
Next Counter1
```

This example demonstrates nested For...Next statements. The statements inside the inner loop will execute 10 * 10 times.

It turns out that VB doesn't require you to use variables after the Next statement. The following code is functionally the same:

```
For Counter1 = 1 To 10
    For Counter2 = 1 To 10
        ' your statements
    Next
Next
```

Visual Basic treats each Next statement as the end of the last specified For loop. Therefore, the first Next statement terminates the Counter2 loop, and the last Next statement terminates the Counter1 loop. However, it is good practice to specify the Counter variable in the Next statement, because it makes your code more readable. You will find it much easier to keep track of nested loops when the variable names are put in the Next statement.

When you use nested `For...Next` statements, you can terminate all your loops with one `Next` statement by specifying each `Counter` variable in the `Next` statement, separated by commas. You must specify the `Counter` variables with the one specified in the innermost `For` statement first. For example:

```
For Counter1 = 1 To 10
    For Counter2 = 1 To 10
        ' your statements
Next Counter2, Counter1
```

Onward

Save the Adder program for now. You'll continue building that project a little later in the chapter. If you want to do some experimentation of your own, you can either start a new project now to use for entering short examples in the `Form_Load` routine or enter the code examples directly in Adder's `Form_Load` event and simply delete them when you've seen how they work.

Lesson Summary

You have just learned how to use `For...Next` loops to execute the same bit of code repeatedly. Next, we'll examine VB 6's other looping constructs.

Quiz 2

1. Which of the following code fragments will output the following line:

   ```
   10  10.1  10.2  10.3  10.4  10.5
   ```

   a.
   ```
   Dim I As Integer
   For I = 10 to 10.5
       Debug.Print I;
   Next I
   ```

   b.
   ```
   Dim I As Double
   For I = 10 To 10.5
       Debug.Print I;
   Next I
   ```

   c.
   ```
   Dim I As Double
   For I = 10 to 10.5 Step .1
       Debug.Print I;
   Next I
   ```

   d.
   ```
   Dim I as Double
   For I = 10.1 To 10.5 Step .1
       Debug.Print I;
   Next I
   ```

2. Which of the following code segments outputs the number 5?

    a.
```
Dim I As Integer
For I = 5 To 1
Next I
Debug.Print I
```

    b.
```
Dim I As Integer
For I = 1 To 4
Next I
Debug.Print I
```

    c.
```
Dim I As Integer
For I = 1 To 10
    If I = 5 Then Exit For
Next I
Debug.Print I
```

    d. All of the above

3. Which of the following types is not a valid loop counter?

    a. `Variant`

    b. `String`

    c. `Integer`

    d. `Double`

4. Which of the following is an invalid statement?

    a. `For I = 1 To EndVar`

    b. `For Counter = 0 To Len(SomeString)`

    c. `For J = StartVar To StartVar + 10 Step Increment`

    d. `For 2 = StartVar To EndVar Step 2`

Exercise 2

Complexity: Moderate

1. Write a program that verifies the formula for the sum of the first 15 numbers: Sum of first N numbers = N * (N – 1) / 2.

Complexity: Advanced

2. Modify the previous program to accept any number between 1 and 20.

LESSON 3

Other Loops

Although For...Next loops are useful when you know in advance how many times you want to execute the loop, there are occasions when you do not have this information in advance. Visual Basic provides other types of loops that you can use in these circumstances:

- Do loop
- While...Wend loop

The Do Loop

Visual Basic provides a very flexible general-purpose loop known as a Do loop. It has the following syntax:

```
Do [{ While | Until } expression ]
    [ statements ]
    [ Exit Do ]
Loop
```

or

```
Do
    [ statements ]
    [ Exit Do ]
Loop [{ While | Until } expression ]
```

This type of loop is very flexible because the expression that controls whether the loop continues or terminates can be phrased in two different ways using the keywords While or Until. Furthermore, the expression can be placed at either the beginning or the end of the loop.

You can even leave out the expression. See what happens when you enter the following code in the Form_Load event:

```
Do
    Debug.Print "Hi!"
Loop
```

Run the program and behold: Computers really are stupid enough to do exactly what you tell them. This is an example of an *infinite*, or *endless*, loop. Because nothing inside the program will get it to stop, you need to cause a break from the interpreter. To do this, hold down the Ctrl key and press the Break key on your keyboard. You can now end the program by clicking the square, VCR-style stop button on the toolbar or by selecting End from the Run menu.

Let's move on to a less reckless example.

Do While

Using the While keyword and an expression tells VB to execute the loop while the expression is True. Let's program the adding program's poor relation. Replace the infinite loop tester code with the following:

```
Sum = 0
Do While Sum < 100
        Sum = Sum + 1
Loop
Debug.Print Sum
```

When this loop is finished, it prints out 100. This routine can add, but only up to 100. Each time through, the loop evaluates Sum < 100. When the expression is no longer True, that is, when Sum is equal to (or greater than) 100, program execution continues with the line after the Loop statement.

Do Until

The While loop executes until a condition is False; the Until keyword instructs the loop to execute until a condition is True. Replace the tester code with the example in Listing 4.8.

LISTING 4.8   The Do Until Loop

```
FileName = "vb.exe"
Pos = 0
Char = ""
Do Until Char = "."
    Pos = Pos + 1
    Char = Mid(FileName, Pos, 1)
Loop
Debug.Print Char & " found at position " & Pos
```

This program assigns each character in the filename in turn to Char. The loop terminates when Char is a period. This code outputs

```
. found at position 3
```

What happens if the exit condition is met even before the loop is executed? Try the example in Listing 4.9.

LISTING 4.9   Checking the Do Until Exit Condition

```
I = 10
Do Until I >= 10
    Debug.Print "In the loop."
    Debug.Print "Incrementing I..."
    I = I + 1
Loop
Debug.Print "Out of loop; I is " & I
```

Guess what the output will be before trying it out. Here's what happens:

```
Out of loop; I is 10
```

With both Do While and Do Until, the loop isn't necessarily executed at once. The program always evaluates the exit condition before entering the loop.

Loop While

To make sure that the loop executes at least once, place the exit condition at the Loop statement, rather than at the Do statement, as in Listing 4.10.

LISTING 4.10   Loop While

```
I = 10
Do
    Debug.Print "In the loop."
    Debug.Print "Incrementing I..."
    I = I + 1
Loop While I < 10
Debug.Print "Out of loop; I is " & I
```

This version outputs

```
In the loop.
Incrementing I...
Out of loop; I is 11
```

Note

When checking a variable for an exit condition, you might not get the result you anticipate if you just check for equality or inequality. It is safest to use comparison operators such as less than, greater than, less than or equal to, and greater than or equal to. In the previous example, if the exit condition had been

```
Loop While I <> 10
```

> the program would have gone into an infinite loop, because I is increment-
> ed past its initial value of 10 before the value is checked.

Loop Until

You can similarly put the Until condition at the end of a loop. In the previous example, where you were searching a string for a character, you knew you wanted to go through the loop at least once. By putting the Until statement at the end, you don't need to worry about the initial value of Char. Listing 4.11 demonstrates this principle.

LISTING 4.11   Loop Until

```
FileName = "vb.exe"
Pos = 0
Do
    Pos = Pos + 1
    Char = Mid(FileName, Pos, 1)
Loop Until Char = "."
Debug.Print Char & " found at position " & Pos
```

The variations of the Do...Loop statement are summarized in Table 4.2.

TABLE 4.2   The Do...Loop Statement

Loop	Description
Do While condition Loop	Enters loop if condition is True.
Do Until condition Loop	Enters loop if condition is False.
Do Loop While condition	Always executes loop once. Loops if condition is True.
Do Loop Until condition	Always executes loop once. Loops if condition is False.

The While...Wend Loop

Visual Basic 6 also provides another general-purpose loop statement called the While ...Wend loop. (The Wend keyword is short for *while end*.) The While...Wend loop is equivalent to the Do While loop and is really provided only for compatibility with soft-ware written for earlier versions of Visual Basic that may not have the Do Loop state-ment. Because the Do loop is more expressive, we recommend that you use Do While rather than While...Wend.

The `While...Wend` loop has the following syntax:

```
While [ expression ]
    [ statements ]
Wend
```

Boolean Expression Evaluation

Both the `While` and `Until` loops work by evaluating Boolean expressions, just as you did in Chapter 3, "Variables, Constants, and Associated Functions," when you learned the `If` statement. Now it's time to talk a little more about what's really going on behind the scenes.

You have seen how `Do` and `While` loops use Boolean expressions to decide whether to continue or terminate the loop. For example:

```
Dim I As Integer
Do Until I = 3
    I = I + 1
Loop
```

The previous loop executes three times. Why? Each time the Boolean expression in the `Do Until` statement is evaluated, Visual Basic actually determines whether the Boolean expression is `True` or `False`. Each time the loop goes around, Visual Basic asks the question, "Is I equal to 3?"

The first time around the loop, `I` is equal to `0` because it has not yet been initialized to anything. Therefore the Boolean expression `I = 3` evaluates to `False`. Just before we go around the loop for the second time, the Boolean expression `I = 3` is evaluated again. This time, `I` equals `1`, so the Boolean expression evaluates to `False` again. This continues until after we have been around the loop three times. Just before we go around for a fourth time, the Boolean expression is evaluated again. This time `I` does equal `3`, so the Boolean expression evaluates to `True`, and this loop terminates.

You can see how expressions evaluate by looking at the result directly. To do this, we'll begin using the Debug window in a new way.

Break Mode

So far, you've dealt with Visual Basic in only two modes: runtime and design time. There is actually a third mode, called *break mode,* or sometimes *immediate mode.* During this time, the program is still running, but it's temporarily stopped. You can examine or change variable values at this point or access a range of debugging features we'll talk about more in Chapter 9, "Printing." For now, what interests us is that break mode provides full access to the Debug window.

Run whatever program is currently up. Click Debug window under the View menu. Try to type something in the Debug window. Because the program is running, you can use Debug only for output, from inside your code.

There are several ways to enter break mode. The one we'll use here is to click the Break button on the toolbar, shown in Figure 4.5. Click the Break button now.

FIGURE 4.5

The Break button.

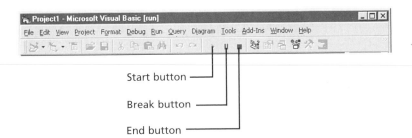

Start button ——
Break button ——
End button ——

The Visual Basic title bar notes the change in the mode. Both the Play and Stop buttons on the toolbar are active, except now the Forward button actually means *continue*. Put the cursor in the Debug window and notice that you can now type. In fact, in immediate mode, you can use this window to type in a VB 6 command and it executes immediately. Try typing

```
Print 2+3
```

You don't need to specify `Debug.Print`, because the method acts on the active object by default.

Note

A question mark is shorthand notation for the `Print` method. Thus

```
Print FullName
```

and

```
? FullName
```

both do the same thing.

In immediate mode, you can access the current program variables. Try typing

```
FullName = "c:\winword\winword.exe"
Print FullName
```

You can even exit the program by typing `End`, as shown in Figure 4.6.

FIGURE 4.6

You can execute basic commands in immediate mode.

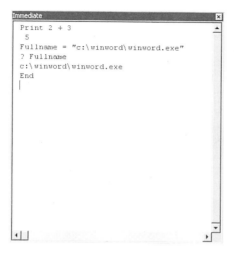

```
Immediate                                    ×
Print 2 + 3
  5
Fullname = "c:\winword\winword.exe"
? Fullname
c:\winword\winword.exe
End
```

Immediate Boolean Expression Evaluation

While in break mode, try executing the following statement in the Debug window:

```
Print 0 = 3
```

VB prints the word False in the Debug window, because 0 is definitely not equal to 3. Now try

```
Print 3 = 3
```

Yes, as expected, VB prints the word True.

Realizing that Boolean expressions evaluate to a simple True or False value is important, because Boolean expressions are used frequently in Visual Basic. Sometimes they can become very complex indeed. Part of a programmer's skill in debugging software is the ability to determine what the result of a Boolean expression should be.

Now consider the following example:

```
Dim I As Integer
I = 5
Do While I
   I = I - 1
         Debug.Print I
Loop
```

In this example, the Boolean expression being evaluated is actually a straightforward integer variable. How does Visual Basic evaluate such Boolean expressions? It turns out that Visual Basic treats any nonzero value as True and any value of 0 as False. Therefore, this program prints out

```
4
3
2
1
0
```

Combining Boolean Expressions: Logical Operators

You can combine Boolean expressions using Visual Basic's logical operators, such as And, Or, and Not. (You already saw this in Chapter 3, "Variables, Constants, and Associated Functions," when you used Not to evaluate an If expression.) For an example, see the code in Listing 4.12.

LISTING 4.12   Combining Boolean Expressions

```
FileName = "vb.exe"
Pos = 0
Char = ""
Do
    Pos = Pos + 1
    Char = Mid(FileName, Pos, 1)
Loop Until Char = "." Or Pos > Len(FileName)
If Char = "." Then
    Debug.Print Char & " found at position " & Pos
Else
    Debug.Print "Couldn't find period."
End If
```

The program now exits the loop either when the period is found, or when Pos is greater than the length of the string. This neatly handles the case of a FileName value without a period.

The logical operators are summarized in Table 4.3. Tables 4.4, 4.5, 4.6, 4.7, 4.8, and 4.9 show the results of the operators' behavior.

TABLE 4.3   The Logical Operators

Operator	Syntax	Behavior
And	Expr1 And Expr2	Returns True if (and only if) both expressions are True.
Eqv	Expr1 Eqv Expr2	Equivalence: Returns True if both expressions are the same.

Operator	Syntax	Behavior
Imp	Expr1 Imp Expr2	Implication: Returns True unless Expr1 is True and Expr2 is False.
Not	Not Expr	Returns True if Expr is False and False if Expr is True.
Or	Expr1 Or Expr2	Returns True if Expr1 or Expr2 (or both) are True.
Xor	Expr1 Xor Expr2	Exclusive or: Returns True if either (but not both) of the expressions are True.

TABLE 4.4   The And Operator

Expr1	Operator	Expr2	Result
True	And	True	True
True	And	False	False
False	And	True	False
False	And	False	False

TABLE 4.5   The Equ (Equivalence) Operator

Expr1	Operator	Expr2	Result
True	Eqv	True	True
True	Eqv	False	False
False	Eqv	True	False
False	Eqv	False	True

TABLE 4.6   The Imp (Implication) Operator

Expr1	Operator	Expr2	Result
True	Imp	True	True
True	Imp	False	False
False	Imp	True	True
False	Imp	False	True

TABLE 4.7   The Not Operator

Operator	Expr2	Result
Not	True	False
Not	False	True

TABLE 4.8   The Or Operator

Expr1	Operator	Expr2	Result
True	Or	True	True
True	Or	False	True
False	Or	True	True
False	Or	False	False

TABLE 4.9   The Xor (Exclusive Or) Operator

Expr1	Operator	Expr2	Result
True	Xor	True	False
True	Xor	False	True
False	Xor	True	True
False	Xor	False	False

Bitwise Operations

You can also apply these operators to numeric values. In that case, the operators perform a bitwise operation on the numbers. That means each bit in a binary (base 2) representation of the number is evaluated. Bitwise operations are sometimes used in advanced programming techniques, particularly graphics techniques. Let's look at the example of 6 And 4.

In a bitwise And operation, the result is 1 if and only if both bits in the same position are 1.

The binary representation of 6 is 110; the binary representation of 4 is 100. Line these numbers up to see that 110 And 100 evaluate to 100; 1 And 1 evaluate to 1; 1 And 0 evaluate to 0; and 0 And 0 evaluate to 0. The result, converted back to decimal, is 4. You can test this out in the Debug window with

```
Print 4 And 6
```

If you want to experiment with bitwise operations, a quick way to convert numbers to and from binary is to use the Windows calculator in scientific view.

Lesson Summary

You have now studied all Visual Basic constructs you can use to execute repeatedly a piece of code: the For...Next loop in previous lesson, and the Do While, Do Until and While...Wend loop in this lesson. You also learned how to combine Boolean expressions using the Visual Basic logical operators And, Or, and Not. Next, we'll take an in-depth look at the If statement.

Quiz 3

1. What is the output of the following program segment?

```
I = 25
Do While I < 30
    I = I + 1
Loop
Debug.Print I
```

   a. 25

   b. 30

   c. 29

   d. 31

2. Assume I and Pos are implicitly declared variants. Which code segment outputs
   `Position found at 6.`

   a. ```
For I = 1 To Len("Split¦Me")
            Pos = Mid("Split¦Me", I, 1)
    Next I
    Debug.Print "Position found at " & Pos
```

   b. ```
Do
            I = I + 1
            Pos = Mid("Split¦Me", I, 1)
    Loop Until I >= Len("Split¦Me")
    Debug.Print "Position found at " & Pos
```

   c. ```
Do While I <= Len("Split¦Me")
    If Mid("Split¦Me", I, 1) = "¦" Then
            Pos = I
        End If
    Loop
    Debug.Print "Position found at " & Pos
```
```

```
        d. Do While I <= Len("Split¦Me")
                    I = I + 1
                    If Mid("Split¦Me", I, 1) = "¦" Then
                            Pos = I
                    End If
           Loop
           Debug.Print "Position found at " & Pos
```

3. What is the output of this code?

```
Debug.Print (5 ^ 2) + 12 = 37
```

    a. `True`

    b. `False`

    c. `37`

    d. `0`

4. Which loop is not executed at least once? Assume `I` is initialized to `10`.

```
        a. For I = 1 To 10
                Debug.Print "Loopy"
           Next I
```

```
        b. Do
                Debug.Print "Loopy"
                I = I + 1
           Loop Until I = 10
```

```
        c. Do Until I = 10
                Debug.Print "Loopy"
                I = I + 1
           Loop
```

```
        d. Do While I = 10
                Debug.Print "Loopy"
                I = I + 1
           Loop
```

Exercise 3

Complexity: Moderate

1. Write a program that displays the filename extension found in "c:\Program Files\Microsoft Visual Studio\Common\Graphics\Icons\Misc\misc18.ico."

Complexity: Advanced

2. Modify the previous program to display also the filename, and change the path being parsed to "c:\Program Files\Microsoft Visual Studio\Common\Graphics\Icons.01\Misc\misc18.ico."

LESSON 4

Decision Statements

In Chapter 3, "Variables, Constants, and Associated Functions," you used the If statement to make a decision. In this lesson, we'll look at the If statement in more detail. We'll also look at the VB application language's other decision statement: Select Case.

If...Then...Else

As you saw in Chapter 3, "Variables, Constants, and Associated Functions," the two forms of the If statement are

```
If expression Then statement [Else statement]
```

and

```
If expression Then
    [statement]
[ElseIf]
    [statement]
[Else]
    [statement]
End If
```

The statements following the If statement are executed if the Boolean expression evaluates to True. Conversely, the Else block of statements is executed if the expression evaluates to False.

The Statement Separator

You can execute multiple statements in a single-line If statement by separating the individual statements with statement separators as follows:

```
' "Move" the traffic light pictures.
Car = (Car.Visible = True)
If Car Then Green.Visible = True: Car.Visible = False: _
                         Message.Caption = "Go!"
```

In fact, you can use the statement separator on any VB line:

```
Dim Counter As Integer : Counter = 0
```

performs the same task as

```
Dim Counter As Integer
Counter = 0
```

However, most programmers prefer only a single statement per line. This makes the code easier to read, analyze, and debug. If you use longer (more meaningful) variable names, placing more than one command on a line could make the code extend past the visible part of the window. In fact, you may want to break your statements into more than one line. To do this, place a space and the underscore character before the carriage return.

The following If statement could be all on one line without the _ character, but it is easier to read this way.

```
If InStr(filename, ".") = 0 And _
   InStr(filename, "\") = 0 And _
   InStr(filename, ":") = 0 Then
        MsgBox "Nothing to parse!"
End If
```

The Picture Pusher

For this section, you will create a new test project named PUSH. This project will display a different picture each time you click the arrow picture, showing the changing colors of a traffic light.

Create a directory for the project. Add the objects and properties summarized in Table 4.10. Arrange the controls as shown in Figure 4.7.

FIGURE 4.7

The Picture Pusher project at design time.

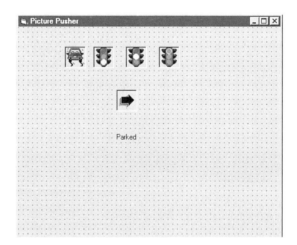

TABLE 4.10   The Picture Pusher Project

Object	Property	Value	
Picture	Name	Car	
	AutoSize	True	
	Picture	Picture	c:\Program Files\Microsoft Visual Studio\Common\Graphics\Icons\Traffic\trffc16.ico
Picture	Name	Green	
	AutoSize	True	
	Picture	Picture	c:\Program Files\Microsoft Visual Studio\Common\Graphics\Icons\Traffic\trffc10A.ico
Picture	Name	Yellow	
	AutoSize	True	
	Picture	Picture	c:\Program Files\Microsoft Visual Studio\Common\Graphics\Icons\Traffic\trffc10B.ico
Picture	Name	Red	
	AutoSize	True	
	Picture	Picture	c:\Program Files\Microsoft Visual Studio\Common\Graphics\Icons\Traffic\trffc10C.ico
Picture	Name	Right	
	AutoSize	True	
	Picture	Picture	c:\Program Files\Microsoft Visual Studio\Common\Graphics\Icons\Arrows\arw04rt.ico
Label	Name	Output	
	AutoSize	True	
	Picture	Picture	c:\Program Files\Microsoft Visual Studio\Common\Graphics\Icons\Arrows\arw04rt.ico
Label	Name	Output	
	AutoSize	True	
	Caption	Parked	

4

Else and ElseIf

Let's generate some code that performs multiple actions based on a variety of circumstances. If the car is present, turn on the green light. If the green light is on, turn on the yellow light. If the yellow light is on, turn on the red light. If the red light is on, show the car. Add the code in Listing 4.13 to the right arrow button Click routine.

LISTING 4.13   Moving the Pictures

```
Private Sub Right_Click()
' "Move" the traffic light pictures.
    If Car.Visible Then
        Green.Visible = True
        Car.Visible = False
        Message.Caption = "Go!"
    Else
        If Green.Visible = True Then
            Yellow.Visible = True
            Green.Visible = False
            Message.Caption = "Slow!"
        Else
            If Yellow.Visible = True Then
                Red.Visible = True
                Yellow.Visible = False
                Message.Caption = "Stop!"
            Else
                ' Red must be visible
                Car.Visible = True
                Red.Visible = False
                Message.Caption = "Parked"
            End If
        End If
    End If
End Sub
```

Making sure the opening/closing blocks line up helps readability, but this code is still hard to read. You can improve it by using the ElseIf statement. Add the improved code in Listing 4.14 to the right arrow picture's Click event.

LISTING 4.14   More Readable Routine with ElseIf

```
Private Sub Right_Click()
' "Move" the traffic light pictures.
    If Car.Visible Then
        Green.Visible = True
        Car.Visible = False
        Message.Caption = "Go!"
    ElseIf Green.Visible = True Then
```

```
            yellow.Visible = True
            Green.Visible = False
            Message.Caption = "Slow!"
        ElseIf yellow.Visible = True Then
            red.Visible = True
            yellow.Visible = False
            Message.Caption = "Stop!"
        Else
            ' Red must be visible
            Car.Visible = True
            red.Visible = False
            Message.Caption = "Parked"
        End If
End Sub
```

This method is somewhat easier to read and is equivalent to the nested If statements used before. The If statement now requires only one End If. Go ahead, save the project, then run it and see it work as expected.

Select Case

The Select Case statement differs from the If (and nested If) statement by providing a structured way to execute alternative blocks of code depending on the value of a numeric expression, rather than on a True/False evaluation of the expression. The syntax of Select Case is as follows:

```
Select Case expression
    Case expression
        [statements]
    [Case Else]
        [statements]
End Select
```

Chapter 3, "Variables, Constants, and Associated Functions," showed the listing for a sample Grocery program. This program used a set of constants and the Byte variable Fruit, as shown in Listing 4.15. If you created this program, load it now; otherwise, load it from the book's CD.

LISTING 4.15   Constants for the Grocery Program

```
Const APPLES As Byte = 1
Const BANANAS As Byte = 2
Const ORANGES As Byte = 3
Dim Fruit As Byte
```

Replace the Grocery button code with the code in Listing 4.16.

LISTING 4.16   Expanded Grocery Program

```
Private Sub cmdGroceryOrder_Click()
Select Case Fruit
    Case APPLES
        lblMessage.Caption = "An apple a day..."
    Case BANANAS
        lblMessage.Caption = "Monkeyin' around!"
    Case ORANGES
        lblMessage.Caption = "Sorry, oranges are out of season."
    Case Else
        lblMessage.Caption = "Please click a fruit button."
End If
End Sub
```

The Select Case statement selectively executes a piece of code depending on the value of Fruit. So, in the previous code, if Fruit has the value APPLES, then An apple a day[el] is displayed; if Fruit is equal to BANANA, then Monkeyin' around! is displayed; if Fruit is equal to ORANGES, then Sorry, oranges are out of season. is displayed. The Case Else is a catchall for all values that were not explicitly mentioned.

Select Case Ranges and Types

The Select Case statement can be used with all variable types. An example is shown in Listing 4.17.

LISTING 4.17   Select Case with Strings

```
Dim I As String
I = "A String"
Select Case I
    Case "A"
        'This block will not be executed
    Case "B"
        'This block will not be executed
    Case "A String"
        'This block will be executed
    Case Else
        'This block will not be executed
End Select
```

Note   You cannot use the Like comparison operator in a Case statement.

You can also specify ranges in the `Case` expressions. Listing 4.18 is an example.

LISTING 4.18   Case Ranges

```
Dim I As Integer
'set I to something
Select Case I
    Case 1 To 5
        'all values of I in the range 1 through 5
    Case Else
        'all other values of I
End Select
```

If you want to execute the same block of code for different values of the test expression, you can do so by specifying the different case expressions in one `Case` statement, separated by commas, as shown in Listing 4.19.

LISTING 4.19   Evaluating More Than One Condition

```
Select Case I
    Case 1,5,9
        'this block of statements will be executed
        'when I is equal to 1 or 5 or 9
    Case 10 To 15
        'this block of statements will be executed
        'when I is equal to any number in the range 10 through 15
    Case Else
        'this block of statements will be executed
        'when I is equal to any value other than 1 or 5 or 9 or 10 to 15
End Select
```

You can nest `Select` statements, but you must ensure that each `Select` has a corresponding `End Select`. Listing 4.20 is an example.

LISTING 4.20   Nested Select Case Statements

```
Select Case I
    Case 1 To 3
        Select Case I
            Case 1
                'This block of statements will be executed
                'when I equals 1
```

continues

LISTING 4.20   continued

```
            Case 2
                'This block of statements will be executed
                'when I equals 2
            Case 3
                'This block of statements will be executed
                'when I equals 3
        End Select
    Case Else
End Select
```

The Is Keyword

You can also use the >, <, >=, and <= operators to set up ranges in a Case statement. If you do so, you must use the Is keyword to refer to the Select Case value.

```
Select Case I
    Case Is > 15
        'This block of statements will be executed
        'when I is greater than 15
    Case Is < 10
        'This block of statements will be executed
        'when I is less than 10
End Select
```

In all the previous examples, if the value being tested does not fall within the range of one of the Case statements, program flow falls through the Select statement without executing any code, unless a Case Else statement is present.

To combine more than one range of values in a single Case statement, you can use the logical operators And and Or. Note that the example in Listing 4.21 uses Is for the first reference to the Select Case variable, but not for references after And or Or.

LISTING 4.21   Combining Ranges

```
Select Case NumVar
    Case Is > 15 Or NumVar <= 10
        'This block of statements will be executed
        'if NumVar is greater than 15 or less than or equal to 10.
    Case Is >= 11 And NumVar <= 13
        ' executes when NumVar is 11, 12, or 13
    Case Else
        'This block of statements will be executed
        'for any other value of NumVar
End Select
```

The Select Case statement is remarkably flexible. Any time your If...Then... Else constructions start to get unwieldy, analyze whether you could be using a Select Case statement instead.

Now that you've got more programming skills under your belt, let's move on to subroutines and functions.

Lesson Summary

You have studied the Select Case statement, often a good way to organize If...Then... Else unwieldy constructions.

Now that you've got more programming skills under your belt, let's move on to subroutines and functions.

Quiz 4

1. Recall that a semicolon after a Print statement prevents the output from advancing to the next line. Using a comma enters tabs, so you can space your output by columns. With that in mind, which segment prints the following:

```
stopped          True           True
```

   a. Go = True
```
If Go Then Stopped = True: Go = False: Msg = "stopped"
Debug.Print Msg, Stopped, Go
```

   b. Go = True
```
If Go Then
    Stopped = True
    Go = False
    Msg = "stopped"
End If
Debug.Print Msg, Stopped, Go
```

   c. Go = True
```
If Not Go Then
        Stopped = False
        Go = False
        Msg = "Not going"
End If
Debug.Print Msg, Stopped, Go
```

   d. Go = True
```
If Not Go Then
        Stopped = False
```

```
                Go = True
                Msg = "Not going"
        Else
                Stopped = True
                Msg = "stopped"
        End If
        Debug.Print Msg, Stopped, Go
```

2. Which symbol lets you put more than one statement on a line? Which symbol (respectively) lets you extend a statement across more than one line?

   a. _ and :

   b. : and _

   c. : and '

   d. ' and :

3. In the following program, which condition needs to be True for Umbrella to evaluate to True?

```
If Cold Then
    Wear = "Coat"
    If Rainy Then
        Umbrella = True
    Else
        Umbrella = False
    End If
ElseIf Sunny Then
        Wear = "T-Shirt"
        Umbrella = False
ElseIf Patchy Then
        Wear = "Sweater"
        Umbrella = False
Else
        Wear = "Unknown"
End If
```

   a. Rainy

   b. Cold and Patchy

   c. Cold and Rainy

   d. Cold

4. In the following program, what does the numerical value of Sky have to be for the output to be, Let's go to the beach!?

```
Const CLOUDY = 1
Const OVERCAST = 2
Const FOGGY = 3
Const RAINY = 4
Const CLEAR = 5
Const BEAUTIFUL = 6

' (Sky is assigned in here.)

Select Case Sky
    Case CLOUDY Or OVERCAST
        Debug.Print "Brrrrr."
    Case FOGGY
        Debug.Print "Drive carefully."
    Case RAINY
        Debug.Print "Please run umbrella program."
    Case CLEAR, BEAUTIFUL
        Debug.Print "Let's go to the beach!"
    Case Else
        Debug.Print "Unknown forecast."
End Select
```

   a. Less than 6

   b. Greater than or equal to 6

   c. 1, 2, or 4

   d. 5 or 6

Exercise 4

Complexity: Moderate

1. Modify the grocery program to keep track of all the fruits being selected, not just the last one being clicked.

Complexity: Advanced

2. Modify the Picture Pusher program so that all 4 pictures are always displayed and change the Message label to the name of the picture, but only if the pictures are clicked in the right order (from left to right).

LESSON 5

Subroutines and Functions: An Introduction

You shouldn't need much of an introduction to subroutines and functions: You've already used them! Look at the following examples of routines from previous lessons. A *routine* is a generic term that refers to either a subroutine or a function.

```
Private Sub mnuFileExit_Click()
    Unload Me
End Sub

Private Sub Form_Load()
    txtFileName.Text = ""
End Sub

AverageLength = Int(TotalLength / 2)
Length = Len(String)
EasyPart = Left(Alphabet,3)
```

In the first two examples, the event routines are actually subroutines you're defining.

Note

> When you define a subroutine or function, you are specifying the name of the subroutine or function, the parameters it takes (if any), and the code that executes when the routine is called.

The last three examples all call a routine (actually, in these cases, a function).

Note

> When you call a subroutine or function, you tell Visual Basic to execute the code associated with that routine. When you call a subroutine or function, you specify the arguments you want to pass to the routine; that is, the value or values you want the routine to work on.

In this lesson, you'll learn how to define and call your own subroutines and functions.

A Dip in a Sub

The basic syntax for defining a subroutine is

```
Sub name [( argumentlist)]
    [ statements ]
    [ Exit Sub ]
    [ statements ]
End Sub
```

Lesson 6 will expand on this syntax, but this is all you need to know to define a subroutine. Similarly, here is the basic syntax to define a function:

```
Function name [( argumentlist)] [As type]
    [ statements ]
    [ name = expression ]
    [ Exit Function ]
    [ statements ]
    [ name = expression ]
End Function
```

Note

The only difference between a subroutine and a function is that a function returns a value. This distinction becomes clear when you use a subroutine, that is aSubRoutine aParameter or a function, aVariable = aFunction(aParameter).

Programmers use subroutines and functions to break code into smaller tasks. This makes code easier to read and debug. Also, routines can be called from different sections of the program, reducing duplication and making the program easier to maintain.

Load the Adder program from Lessons 1 and 2. Let's separate some of the code into a subroutine. We'll devote the cmdAdd_Click routine to actual addition and create a new subroutine to output the sum.

To begin a new subroutine, simply place the cursor at the beginning of a line either just before another Sub statement or just after an End Sub statement and enter

```
Sub Output(Result As Variant)
```

Visual Basic automatically creates the new routine in the General section of the form and makes this the prominent routine in the Code window. Note that the closing line

```
End Sub
```

is also added automatically. The Output routine takes one parameter, Result, which is the number to output. Fill in the subroutine as shown in Listing 4.22.

LISTING 4.22 The Output Subroutine

```
Sub Output(Result As Variant)

' Output the results with fanfare
' if there is no sound card, skip to next line
On Error Resume Next
lblOutput.Caption = Result & " !!!"
oleTada.DoVerb

End Sub
```

Your screen should look like that in Figure 4.8.

FIGURE 4.8

The Output *subroutine in the Code window.*

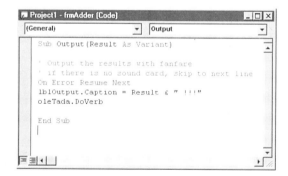

Now, if you decide to reformat the output in any way, the changes you make get compartmentalized in the Output routine. The rest of the code doesn't need to know about the details. If you expand the program and include routines to, say, perform subtractions (sacrilege!), you can call this routine to output a different value.

Next, you need to remove the output code from the cmdAdd_Click routine and call this subroutine instead. Here is the syntax to call a subroutine:

```
[Call] subname [argumentlist]
```

The Call keyword is optional. If you use the Call keyword, the argument list must be included in parentheses, as in

```
Call Output(Sum)
```

If you don't include the Call keyword, you must not use parentheses, as in

```
Output Sum
```

Modify the Add button routine as shown in Listing 4.23.

LISTING 4.23   Calling the Output Routine

```
Private Sub cmdAdd_Click()
' Declare variables
Dim I, Sum As Integer
' Add the numbers from 1 to 10.
For I = 1 To 10
    Sum = Sum + I
Next I

Output Sum

End Sub
```

One thing to notice is that cmdAdd_Click calls the routine with the argument name Sum, whereas the function definition is Output(Result). The reason this works is that Result takes on any value that is passed to the function; the variable names are completely separate. We could just as easily have said

```
Output ANumber
Output 35
Output Len(SomeString)
```

Note

> Why use Call? Because the Call statement is optional, you might wonder why you should bother to use it. The fact is, there is no good reason. Some programming languages require Call, and programmers who were trained in those languages tend to use Call from force of habit.

An Added Routine

Functions, as we said above, differ from subroutines in that they return a value. One way to describe functions is to think about a black box that processes input, as shown in

Figure 4.9. The code calling the function doesn't need to know how the function calculates the result; it just takes the output it needs and goes on its merry way.

FIGURE **4.9**

The black box.

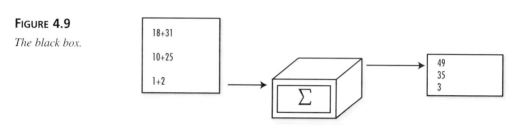

Let's write a short function for the adding program: a function to add two numbers. Visual Basic already knows how to add two numbers, but our silly program thinks addition is important enough to merit its own function. Add the Sum routine shown in Listing 4.24. As before, you just need to type the first line of the function anywhere in the Code window, and VB creates the function definition block.

LISTING 4.24   The Sum function

```
Function Sum(Num1 As Variant, Num2 As Variant) As Variant
    Sum = Num1 + Num2
End Function
```

Listing 4.24 sets the function's return value by assigning the value to the name of the function. The function definition includes a type identifier at the end. You're using variants here, because you don't know what kinds of numbers you'll add. Because variants are the default data type, you don't actually need the As Variant statement, but including it makes it clear that you explicitly decided to use variants.

You call a function anytime you use that function's return value in an expression:

```
Answer = Sum(1,2)
Output Sum(Start, End)
lblOutput.Caption = "2 + 2 make " & Sum(2,2)
```

are all valid ways of calling the function. You can also call a function without using the return value, as in

```
MsgBox "Hello!"
```

In this case, MsgBox would have returned the button the user clicked, but because you're using the default message box, which contains only one button, disregard the return value.

Note that user-defined functions look exactly like VB's functions when you call them:

```
Answer = Sum(x,y)
Answer = Sin(x)
```

Function Type Casting

Functions don't have to return numbers; they can return any data type. Let's create a function that returns a Boolean, expressing whether or not the user has already clicked the Add button. Enter the function definition in Listing 4.25.

LISTING 4.25   The AlreadyAdded Function

```
Function AlreadyAdded() As Boolean
    'See if output label has changed.
    If lblOutput.Caption = "[The Answer!]" Then
        AlreadyAdded = False
    Else
        AlreadyAdded = True
    End If
End Function
```

Now integrate these functions into the main cmdAdd_Click routine, as shown in Listing 4.26.

LISTING 4.26   Calling Our Routines

```
Private Sub cmdAdd_Click()
' Declare variables
Dim I, Number As Integer
' Add the numbers from 1 to 10.

' Don't bother to do anything if answer is already displayed.
If Not AlreadyAdded Then
    For I = 1 To 10
        Number = Sum(Number, I)
    Next I

    Output Number
End If

End Sub
```

Because the Number Adder is so short, you didn't really gain much by separating things out as procedures. The program still works much the same as before. (But it won't

"Ta da" more than once per run now.) But then, you already knew these routines were for demonstration purposes. By keeping them simple, it makes it easy to see the basic syntax and usage.

Next, we'll talk about procedures in more detail and variable scope in particular.

Lesson Summary

You have just been introduced to subroutines and functions, enabling you to break your programs into smaller tasks. Next, we look at subroutines and functions in more detail.

Quiz 5

1. An argument to a procedure is

    a. A value that is passed when the procedure is called.

    b. Available only to functions.

    c. It is necessarily numeric.

    d. Passed with a variable that has the same name in the called procedure as the calling procedure.

2. The difference between a function and a subroutine is

    a. There is no difference.

    b. Only a function can have arguments.

    c. A function can return a value.

    d. You always call a function with the `Call` statement.

3. A function definition that doesn't include a type definition character

    a. Generates a syntax error

    b. Generates a runtime error

    c. Defaults to a variant type, just like variables without type declaration

    d. Must return a number

4. In the Adder program examples, which would be a valid way to call the `Sum` function?

    a. `Call Sum(2,2)`

    b. `Answer = Sum(2,2)`

    c. Sum 2,2

    d. All of the above

Exercise 5

Complexity: Moderate

1. Write a function that takes a string and modifies the case of every letter (uppercase becomes lowercase, and lowercase becomes uppercase).

Complexity: Advanced

2. Write a function that uses a loop to convert the characters in a string to asterisks. Return the result. Spaces don't get converted. If the function reaches a || character, it should chop off the || and everything past that point. Thus,

```
hello there
```

becomes

```
***** *****
```

and

```
hello out¦ there
```

becomes

```
***** ***
```

Include code to test the function with several strings, and print the result.

LESSON 6

Subroutines and Functions: The Sequel

The Visual Basic programming environment is modular, in some cases to a fault. Take the Code window, for example. Load the Adder program and, in design mode, double-click the Add button. The Code window that comes up compartmentalizes the cmdAdd routine, as shown in Figure 4.10, to the point where you might think the routine was alone in the universe. This layout is useful when you are focusing on a specific event or function, but there are times when you want to get the big picture.

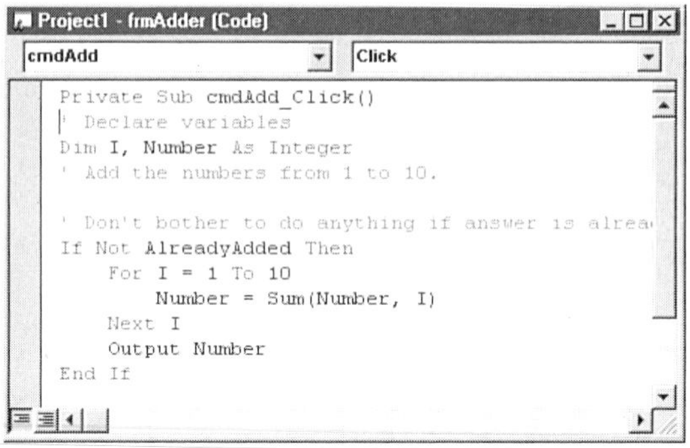

FIGURE **4.10**

The Code window showing a single routine.

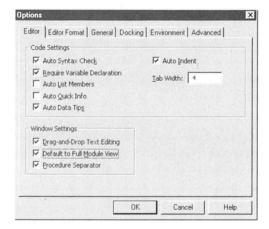

Under the Tools menu, click the Options item. The Options dialog box looks like Figure 4.11. Select the Editor tab, and then click to turn on the check box labeled Default to Full Module View. If the Procedure Separator box is not checked, click that, too. Click OK and go back to the Code window.

FIGURE **4.11**

Set full module view in the Options dialog box.

The code for the form module is really just a collection of subroutines, as shown in Figure 4.12. But then, you were probably starting to suspect that.

The Big Picture

So, the code for the form module is really just a collection of subroutines. What does that mean to us? To explore this question, let's work through another example.

This will be a multiple-form project called Sender. Each form will have a text box and a button. All the forms will be accessible at all times. The Main form's button will exit the program. The buttons on the other forms will send the contents of that form's text box to the Main form's text box. The user can change the contents of a text box and then send the results to the Main form's text box. Granted, this isn't a very useful program, but it will provide a chance to practice communication between forms.

FIGURE 4.12

The Code window in full module view.

```
cmdAdd                              ▼   Click                              ▼

   Function AlreadyAdded() As Boolean
        'See if output label has changed.
        If lblOutput.Caption = "[The Answer!]" Then
            AlreadyAdded = False
        Else
            AlreadyAdded = True
        End If
   End Function

   Sub Output(Result As Variant)

   ' Output the results with fanfare
   ' if there is no sound card, skip to next line
   On Error Resume Next
   lblOutput.Caption = Result & " !!!"
   oleTada.DoVerb

   End Sub
```

Create a directory called SENDER for the project files. Click New Project under the VB 6 File menu. Make the window rather small and put it near the center of the screen. Add the objects and properties described in Table 4.11 to the form. The result will look something like Figure 4.13.

FIGURE 4.13

Sender's Main form (design mode).

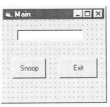

TABLE 4.11   Objects and Properties for the Main Form

Object	Property	Value
Form	Name	frmMain
	Caption	Main
TextBox	Name	txtBox
	Text	
CommandButton	Name	cmdExit
	Caption	Exit

Now add another form to the project by clicking Add Form under the Project menu. This form looks very similar to the Main form. It is about the same size and has the same controls. The objects' names and captions are slightly different, however, as seen in Table 4.12.

TABLE 4.12   Objects and Properties for the Sender Forms

Object	Property	Value
Form	Name	frmSender1
	Caption	Sender
TextBox	Name	txtBox
	Text	
CommandButton	Name	cmdSend
	Caption	Send

Next, create two more forms that are exactly the same, except the form names are frmSender2 and frmSender3. It doesn't matter that the control names are the same in different forms, because you can use the form names to identify them.

Note   To copy one or more controls, click each of the controls while holding down Shift. The selected controls will turn light gray. Select Copy from the Edit menu, select a new form by clicking it, and then select Paste from the Edit menu.

Select Form Layout window under the View menu. Drag it from its corner of the screen and resize it so you can get a good idea of how the forms will appear at runtime. Arrange the forms as shown in Figure 4.14.

Code It

This program won't require much code. In the Code window for the Main form, enter the code in Listing 4.27. The Exit button is self-explanatory. The code in the Load routine shows the other three forms, so that all four forms are available at runtime.

Note   As shown in the Exit button code, you need to unload all loaded forms for a program to stop executing.

FIGURE **4.14**

The sender forms.

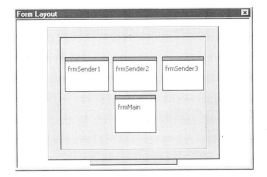

You want the user to be able to switch freely between all the forms, so call the Show method in the default *modeless* state.

LISTING 4.27   The Main Form Routines

```
Private Sub cmdExit_Click()
    Unload frmSender3
    Unload frmSender2
    Unload frmSender1
    Unload Me
End Sub

Private Sub Form_Load()
    frmSender1.Show
    frmSender2.Show
    frmSender3.Show
End Sub
```

Now double-click one of the Send buttons. You want to put the contents of the text box into the main text box, so let's use the technique of specifying the text box that is outside the current form with the destination form name followed by a period. Add the code in Listing 4.28 to the Click event routine.

LISTING 4.28   Sending Text Across Forms

```
Private Sub cmdSend_Click()
    frmMain.txtBox.Text = txtBox.Text
End Sub
```

Copy this command into the cmdSend_Click routines in the other two Sender forms as well. To copy a single line of text, move the mouse to the left of the line until the cursor turns into a right-pointing arrow, and then click once to select the line. Click Copy under the Edit menu to copy it and Paste to paste it to the destination.

Run the program. Type into any of the text boxes, and then click the Send buttons to see how it works. The runtime program is shown in Figure 4.15.

FIGURE 4.15

Sending, sending.

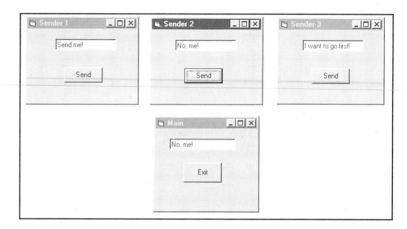

Now let's keep track of when messages are sent. In the Sender 1 form, double-click the Send button. Add the first attempt at keeping track of message sending by entering the code shown in Listing 4.29. (Additions are in boldface.)

LISTING 4.29   Sender 1 Form's First Attempt at Keeping a Log

```
Private Sub cmdSend_Click()
    Dim MailTime As Date
    Dim MessageSent As Boolean
    frmMain.txtBox.Text = txtBox.Text
    MailTime = Time
    MessageSent = True
End Sub
```

Now add a new button to that form, as described in Table 4.13.

TABLE 4.13   The View Mail Log Button

Object	Property	Value
CommandButton	Name	cmdViewMailLog
	Caption	View Mail Log

The design-time form should look like that in Figure 4.16. Add the code shown in Listing 4.30.

FIGURE 4.16

Sender 1's new button.

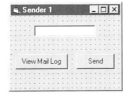

LISTING 4.30   Sender 1 Form Trying to Read the Log

```
Private Sub cmdViewMailLog_Click()
If MessageSent Then
    MsgBox "Message sent at " & MailTime & ", boss."
Else
    MsgBox "Message hasn't been sent!"
End If

End Sub
```

Run the program, enter a message in the Sender 1 text box and send it to the Main form, and then click the View Mail Log button. You get the message shown in Figure 4.17. What happened?

FIGURE 4.17

Message not sent: You didn't think it would be that easy, did you?

Scoping Out Scope

All variables, procedures, and objects have what is called *scope.* Scope defines the visibility of the item to other parts of the program.

All variables declared with the Dim statement have private scope within the routine in which they are declared. This means they are available only to that procedure. This is true for variables whether they have been explicitly or implicitly declared. Keep in mind that because variables are private, you can have variables with the same name in different procedures that won't influence each other whatsoever. Save the Sender program, start a new project, and enter the program in Listing 4.31.

LISTING 4.31   Private Variables Are Separate, Even if They Have the Same Name

```
Option Explicit
Sub Proc1()
    Dim Message As String
    Message = "Hello from Proc1"
    Debug.Print Message
End Sub

Private Sub Form_Load()
    Dim Message As String
    Message = "Hello from Form_Load"
    Debug.Print Message
    Call Proc1
    Debug.Print Message
End Sub
```

This program outputs

```
Hello from Form_Load
Hello from Proc1
Hello from Form_Load
```

Even though `Proc1` assigns a value to its `Message` variable, the separate `Message` variable in `Form_Load` isn't affected.

In the Sender example, the `cmdViewMailLog_Click()` couldn't "see" the variables that had been defined in `cmdAdd_Click`. When VB came to the line

```
If MessageSent Then
```

it implicitly declared `MessageSent`, and then evaluated its contents to `False`. (If your program has an `Option Explicit` statement in the Sender General Declarations section, you won't even get this far. Try it!)

Module Scope

What happens if you declare a variable in the General Declarations section of a module? Well, it too has private scope, but within the module as a whole. Type in Listing 4.32 to see an example.

LISTING 4.32   Module Scope

```
Option Explicit
Dim Message As String
Sub Proc1()
    Debug.Print Message
End Sub
```

```
Private Sub Form_Load()
    Message = "Hello from Form_Load"
    Debug.Print Message
    Call Proc1
    Debug.Print Message
End Sub
```

This version prints out

```
Hello from Form_Load
Hello from Form_Load
Hello from Form_Load
```

Okay, so what happens if you declare a variable in the General Declarations section of a module that has the same name as a variable in one or more procedures? For example, look at Listing 4.33.

LISTING 4.33   Competing Variables?

```
Option Explicit
Dim Message As String
Sub Proc1()
    Dim Message As String
    Message = "Hello from Proc1"
    Debug.Print Message
End Sub

Private Sub Form_Load()
    Dim Message As String
    Message = "Hello from Form_Load"
    Debug.Print Message
    Call Proc1
    Debug.Print Message
End Sub
```

This listing outputs

```
Hello from Form_Load
Hello from Proc1
Hello from Form_Load
```

This is the same output as Listing 4.31. When the program runs, the Message string in the General Declarations section is immediately created and has module scope. Any subroutine or function in the form can see and use it. But in Form_Load, you declare another Message. Any reference to Message in Form_Load automatically refers to the variable declared in that subroutine.

Note that although the Message in the Form_Load subroutine takes precedence, both Message variables are still in scope. Visual Basic 6 enables you to identify the module-level Message within Form_Load by placing the name of the module (Form1), followed by a dot, before its name. For example,

```
Debug.Print Form1.Message
```

Now reload the Sender program. Move the Dim statements from the cmdAdd routine to the General Declarations section of Sender. Listing 4.34 shows the new code. Now these variables have module scope, so the program works as advertised.

LISTING 4.34   Sender 1 with Module Scope Variables

```
Dim MailTime As Date
Dim MessageSent As Boolean
Private Sub cmdSend_Click()
    frmMain.txtBox.Text = txtBox.Text
    MailTime = Time
    MessageSent = True
End Sub
```

The World at Large

Let's try to poke around in Sender 1's private stuff. Add a Command button form named cmdSnoop and labeled Snoop in the frmMain. Add the line in Listing 4.35 to the Click event routine.

LISTING 4.35   The Snoop Button

```
Private Sub cmdSnoop_Click()
If frmSender1.MessageSent Then
    MsgBox "Sender 1 sent a message at " & frmSender1.MailTime
End If
End Sub
```

Run this program. When you try to snoop, you get a message that says Method or data member not found. Read along to discover why you get this message.

Private and Public Declarations

So far, we've used only the Dim statement to declare variables. Normally, you don't need to specify whether a variable is declared as public or private, because most of the time you want your variables to have private scope. Furthermore, variables declared within a subroutine or function are automatically private and cannot be declared public.

Visual Basic has two additional declaration statements that affect the scope of variables declared in the General Declarations section of a module, however. These are `Public` and `Private`.

Both `Public` and `Private` statements have the same syntax as the `Dim` statement. In fact, the `Private` statement is equivalent to the `Dim` statement. You might use it instead to underline the fact that you intend a particular variable to have private scope in the General Declarations section of a module.

In the Sender program, change the declarations in Sender 1 from

```
Dim MailTime As Date
Dim MessageSent As Boolean
```

to

```
Public MailTime As Date
Public MessageSent As Boolean
```

Run the program, send a message, and then try the Snoop button again. You're a regular private eye!

Procedure Scope

It's now time to consider subroutines and functions in more detail. Let's start by looking at the full syntax for subroutines and functions.

Subroutines have the following syntax:

```
[Private ¦ Public] [Static] Sub name [( argumentlist)]
    [ statements ]
    [ Exit Sub ]
    [ statements ]
End Sub
```

Whereas the syntax for functions is

```
[Private ¦ Public] [Static] Function name [( argumentlist)] [As type]
    [ statements ]
    [ name = expression ]
    [ Exit Function ]
    [ statements ]
    [ name = expression ]
End Function
```

Private Versus Public

The `Private` or `Public` keyword determines the scope of the subroutine or function. If you omit this part of the declaration, the subroutine or function will be public by default.

Public subroutines and functions can be called from any module in your project, whereas private ones can be called only from within the module in which they are declared.

Standard Modules

So far, all the source code you've entered has been in form modules. There are two other types of modules in Visual Basic 6: class modules (which we'll discuss in Chapter 6, "Building the GUI with Forms, Menus, and MDI Forms") and standard modules. (In previous versions of Visual Basic, these were called code modules.) Standard modules contain only declarations and source code. Standard modules are a good place to put routines that may be common to several other forms or modules in a project.

Let's add a standard module to Sender. Under the Project menu, click Add Module. VB opens up a Code window for the module. Notice that there is only one item under the Object drop-down menu in the Code window: General. Add the routine in Listing 4.36. Next, bring up the Properties window for the module by pressing F4. There is only one property to change: the Name property. Change it now to Code.

LISTING 4.36   A Public Sub in a Standard Module

```
Public Sub Notify()
    MsgBox "Message has been sent to main form."
End Sub
```

Now you can call the routine from any of the other modules with the command

```
Code.Notify
```

To finish up, add this line to the Send button routines. For example, the Send button routine for the Sender 2 form looks like Listing 4.37.

LISTING 4.37   Calling a Standard Module Routine

```
Private Sub cmdSend_Click()
    frmMain.txtBox.Text = txtBox.Text
    Code.Notify
End Sub
```

Now when you save the project, VB prompts you to save the standard module, which uses the extension .BAS. Save it as CODE.BAS. As you build up module libraries of useful routines, you can add them to future programs simply by selecting the Add File option of the File menu.

Note You can call public routines from outside a module without specifying the module name. For example, you could say `Notify` instead of `Code.Notify`. If you have a routine of the same name in the calling module, however, remember that Visual Basic always looks inside the current module first when trying to resolve references. This applies to subroutines, functions, variables, and constants. Visual Basic will not complain that there is a naming conflict because, as far as it is concerned, there isn't. It simply will look no further in trying to resolve a reference once it has been found.

Persistence of Variables

The life of a variable is called its *persistence*. Normally, unless you expressly state otherwise, a variable has *automatic persistence*. This means that the variable is automatically created when the procedure in which it exists is called.

To demonstrate this, consider Listing 4.38.

LISTING 4.38 Automatic Persistence

```
Private Sub Form_Load()
    AddSub
    AddSub
End Sub

Private Sub AddSub()
Dim Sum As Integer
    Sum = Sum + 1
    Debug.Print Sum
End Sub
```

The example outputs

```
1
1
```

In this example, when `AddSub` is called for the first time, `Sum` is declared with automatic persistence. This means that when `AddSub` ends, `Sum` is destroyed. (Do not confuse scope and persistence. They are two separate effects.)

You can alter the way you declare a variable if you want it to have static persistence. Instead of using the `Dim` statement to declare it, use the `Static` statement. The `Static` statement has the same syntax as `Dim`, except that the variables declared with it survive between calls to the procedures in which they are contained. Change the AddSub routine in the above example, as shown in Listing 4.39.

LISTING 4.39   Static Persistence

```
Private Sub AddSub()
Static Sum As Integer
    Sum = Sum + 1
    Debug.Print Sum
End Sub
```

The Sum statement now keeps its value between calls, so the program now outputs

```
1
2
```

Compare the persistence of a variable declared in a subroutine or function with one declared in the General Declarations section of a module. Remember that variables declared in the General Declarations section are no different from variables declared anywhere else, except that they have module scope. The persistence of such variables doesn't change. They are created when the module is created, and they are destroyed when the module is destroyed.

The Static Keyword

You saw how the Static keyword controls the persistence of variables within the subroutine or function. The Static keyword in a subroutine or function declaration controls how all the variables in that procedure are declared. If you declare a procedure with the Static keyword, any variables declared within the body of the procedure will be static by default. You cannot override the persistence of variables in a procedure that has been declared Static.

Listing 4.40 shows the AddSub routine from the previous example rewritten to apply static variable persistence to all variables in the routine.

LISTING 4.40   Static in Subroutine Definition

```
Private Static Sub AddSub()
    Dim Sum As Integer
    Sum = Sum + 1
    Debug.Print Sum
End Sub
```

Lesson Summary

You have learned two key concepts in programming: scope and persistence. Scope is the visibility of a variable, persistence is the lifetime of a variable. Make sure you thoroughly understand the concepts of this lesson, before going on to the next, which deals with arguments.

Quiz 6

1. What does the following code print out?

```
Const Dingo = "Dingo"
Const Salamander = "Salamander"
Private Sub Form_Load()
    Const MuskRat = "Loaded_MuskRat"
    Const Salamander = "Loaded_Salamander"
    Debug.Print Salamander, Dingo, MuskRat
End Sub
```

   a. Loaded_Salamander   Dingo   Loaded_MuskRat

   b. Salamander   Dingo   Loaded_MuskRat

   c. Salamander   Dingo   MuskRat

   d. Loaded_Salamander   Loaded_Dingo   Loaded_Muskrat

2. What does the following program print out?

```
Private Sub Form_Load()
    Dim Platypus, Dingo
    Dim Jack
    Platypus = "Platypus"
    Dingo = "Dingo"
    Jack = Hopping(Dingo)
    Debug.Print Jack, Platypus, Dingo
End Sub

Function Hopping(Animal)
    Platypus = "Jump, jump, platypus!"
    Hopping = "Hopping " & Animal
    If Animal = "Dingo" Then Dingo = "Hopping Dingo"
End Function
```

   a. Hopping Dingo   Platypus   Dingo

   b. Hopping Dingo   Jump, jump, platypus!   Dingo

   c. Hopping Dingo   Jump, jump, platypus!   Hopping Dingo

   d. Hopping Dingo   Platypus   Hopping Dingo

4

3. If a form named `frmDataSource` wants to make a variable called `InterestingStuff` available to a form named `frmWantsStuff`, which of the following declarations would produce this result?

   a. ```
Private Sub Form_Load()
      Dim InterestingStuff
   End Sub
```

   b. ```
Private Sub Form_Load()
      Public InterestingStuff
   End Sub
```

   c. ```
Dim InterestingStuff
   Private Sub Form_Load()
   End Sub
```

   d. ```
Public InterestingStuff
   Private Sub Form_Load()
   End Sub
```

4. If `frmWantsStuff` wants to display this value, which statement would it use?

   a. `MsgBox InterestingStuff`

   b. `MsgBox Public.InterestingStuff`

   c. `MsgBox frmDataSource.InterestingStuff`

   d. `MsgBox frmWantsStuff.InterestingStuff`

Exercise 6

Complexity: Moderate

1. Write a program that verifies the formula for the sum of the first N numbers: Sum of first N numbers = N * (N – 1) / 2. Use two functions to compute the result.

Complexity: Advanced

2. Add an optional parameter to the previous functions to print the intermediate results to the immediate window.

LESSON 7

Argument Lists

Both functions and subroutines can take arguments, values that they need to manipulate. The argument list has its own syntax that requires separate consideration.

The syntax for each argument in an argument list is

```
[Optional][ByVal ¦ ByRef][ParamArray] varname As VarType [, ...]
```

Passing Multiple Arguments

You can declare as many parameters as you want in the argument list of a subroutine or function, provided you separate each parameter with a comma. The basic syntax is to specify a name for the variable and the type of variable.

For example:

```
Private Sub PrintNumbers(Var1 As Integer, Var2 As Integer)
Debug.Print Var1
Debug.Print Var2
End Sub
```

You then call PrintNumbers from Form_Load, specifying the arguments after the subroutine name as follows:

```
Private Sub Form_Load()
PrintNumbers 1, 2
End Sub
```

Execute the above example, and the values 1 and 2 are successfully passed to Var1 and Var2.

Var1 and Var2 require no further declaration syntax. It is enough to declare them in the parameter list of the subroutine or function. Don't forget that when you pass arguments to functions, or to subroutines with the Call statement, you must enclose the arguments within parentheses.

4

ByVal and ByRef

When you pass parameters to a subroutine or function, you can do so in two ways: either by value (ByVal) or by reference (ByRef). Let's look at the distinction between the two methods.

ByVal means that the value of the variable used in the parameter list of the call will be passed to the called procedure. The contents of the variable in the calling routine will be unchanged by anything you do to the destination variable in the called procedure. This is demonstrated by the example in Listing 4.41.

LISTING 4.41   Passing Parameters by Value

```
Private Sub Form_Load()
    Dim ANumber As Integer
    ANumber = 1
    Inc ANumber
    Debug.Print "Value after function is: " & ANumber
End Sub

Private Sub Inc(ByVal IncSubsNumber As Integer)
    Debug.Print "Inc was passed: " & IncSubsNumber
    IncSubsNumber = IncSubsNumber + 1
    Debug.Print "New value is: " & IncSubsNumber
End Sub
```

This program outputs

```
Inc was passed: 1
New value is: 2
Value after function is: 1
```

ANumber in Form_Load is unaffected by the addition in Inc. This is because only the value of ANumber has been passed to IncSubsNumber. IncSubsNumber is a completely separate variable.

Now try this example again, but change ByVal in Inc to ByRef as follows:

```
Private Sub Inc(ByRef IncSubsNumber As Integer)
```

This time the output is

```
Inc was passed: 1
New value is: 2
Value after function is: 2
```

A reference to ANumber is passed to IncSubsNumber, not the value. Therefore, as far as the computer is concerned, both ANumber and IncSubsNumber are referencing the same integer in memory.

You can remove the keyword ByRef and the routine will still increment ANumber. This is because unless you specify otherwise, all variables are passed by reference.

Optional Arguments

There are times when it is inappropriate to pass all the variables in a parameter list to a subroutine or function. This is typically the case when parameters later in the list are dependent on specific values of variables earlier in the list. To declare a parameter as optional, include the Optional keyword in the parameter declaration.

For example, in the subroutine in Listing 4.42, Var1Length applies only if Var1 is a string.

LISTING 4.42   Optional Arguments

```
Private Sub MySub (Var1 As Variant, Optional Var1Length As Variant)
If TypeName(Var1) = "String" Then
    Debug.Print Var1Length
Else
    Debug.Print "Not a string"
End If
End Sub
```

4

There are some restrictions in the use of optional parameters. For example, when you declare a parameter as optional, all subsequent parameters in the list must also be optional.

Named Arguments

Normally, when you pass parameters to subroutines and functions, you do so in the order specified in the parameter list of the called procedure. You do not have to do this, however, because Visual Basic enables you to name which parameter applies to which variable. For example, the following subroutine requires three parameters:

```
Private Sub MySub (IntVar As Integer, StringVar As String, _
                             NumVar As Double)
Debug.Print IntVar
Debug.Print StringVar
Debug.Print NumVar
End Sub
```

You could call this subroutine in the following way:

```
Private Sub Form_Load()
MySub 5, "Hi", 3.14
End Sub
```

Alternatively, you can name the parameters in the call and vary the order in which the parameters appear when you make the call:

```
Private Sub Form_Load()
MySub NumVar := 3.14, IntVar := 5, StringVar := "Hi"
End Sub
```

The := syntax ensures that the correct parameter is referenced by the compiler. Most of VB 6's built-in procedures support named parameters. To find out the parameter names, look up the online help topic entry.

Type Declaration Characters

In Chapter 3, "Variables, Constants, and Associated Functions," you saw type declaration characters used in variable declaration. However, you can also use them when declaring functions and subroutines. For instance, the following two functions are equivalent:

```
Public Function MoneyFunction (Var1 As Integer, Var2 As String) _
                                          As Currency

End Function

Public Function MoneyFunction@(Var1%, Var2$)
End Function
```

Note how the second declaration of MyFunction doesn't require the As Currency syntax at the end of the declaration. It is simply enough to append the type declaration character @ to the function name to indicate that it returns a currency data type.

You're almost finished with your tour of the Visual Basic 6 applications language. There's one last topic to master before you graduate, however: arrays.

 Note

As a rule, avoid the use of type declaration characters. (There are places where they are necessary, as you will see in Chapter 12, "Reading and Writing Disk Files.") It is far easier to declare variable types explicitly and to name your variables with a naming convention that tells you what type they are than to try to remember whether to use # or % with a variable name.

Lesson Summary

You should now master passing arguments to functions and subroutines. You have also learned the important distinction between passing by value and by reference. In the last lesson of this chapter, you learn about arrays.

Quiz 7

1. Which subroutine cannot change the value of the argument passed to it?

   a. `Sub Changes(ByRef var)`

   b. `Sub Changes(ByVal var)`

   c. `Sub Changes(var)`

   d. `Sub Changes(Optional var)`

2. What is the output of the following program?

```
Dim A
Public C
Private Sub Form_Load()
   Dim B
   A = 1
   For C = 1 To 3
    B = PartyTime
   Next C
   Debug.Print A, B, C, D
End Sub

Function PartyTime
   Static A
   A = A + 1
   PartyTime = D
  D = D + 2
End Function
```

   a. 2, 1, 4

   b. 4, 3, 4

   c. 4, 3, 3

   d. 1, 1, 4

4

3. Which of the following is the only valid function call for:

```
Sub SendMe(AString$, ANumber%, ADate@, Optional MaybeMe)
```

   a. `Call SendMe(Him$, It%, ThisString$)`

   b. `SendMe Her$,ADate := LastDay@, It%`

   c. `SendMe ADate:=LastDay@, AString:=It%, ANumber:=Num%`

   d. `SendMe Its$, Num%, MaybeMe:=Her$, ADate:=LastDay@`

4. What is the output of the following program?

```
Private Sub Form_Load()
    Var1 = 0
    Process Var1
    Debug.Print Var1
End Sub

Sub Process(ByVal Var)
    Var = Var + 10
    Wring Var
End Sub

Sub Wring(ByVal Var1)
    Var1 = Var1 * Var1
    ShakeOut Var1
End Sub

Sub ShakeOut(Var1)
    Var1 = Var1 + 159
End Sub
```

   a. 10

   b. 100

   c. 259

   d. 0

Exercise 7

Complexity: Moderate

1. Write a program that verifies the formula for the sum of the first N numbers: Sum of first N numbers = N * (N – 1) / 2. Use a function and subroutine to compute the result.

Complexity: Advanced

2. Write a program that counts the words in a sentence. Use a function to find where the next word starts.

LESSON 8

Arrays

An *array* is essentially a grouping of identical variable types, arranged together in one or more dimensions. One way to think about an array is as a list of related values. You can look at any one element in the list by accessing its index, its position in the list. This is best explained by looking at a working example. Let's assume you need to store a set of four currency variables, representing the sales figures for four departments of a company for one month of the year. To do this, you could simply declare four separate variables, as follows:

```
Dim SalesDept1Jan As Currency, SalesDept2Jan As Currency
Dim SalesDept3Jan As Currency, SalesDept4Jan As Currency
```

Although this would work, it is not the most efficient way of programming a solution to this particular problem. For instance, if you wanted to add all the figures together, you would have to do so explicitly, as follows:

```
TotalSalesAllDeptsJan = SalesDept1Jan + SalesDept2Jan + SalesDept3Jan _
                                      + SalesDept4Jan
```

If the number of departments were much larger, say 100, it would be impractical to refer to each variable individually in any calculation. There is also the inherent inflexibility of such a solution. If the number of departments were to change, it would be a lot of work to make the corresponding changes to your program.

The `Dim` Statement Revisited

Declaring an array in your program is called *dimensioning* an array, and was, once upon a time, the exclusive use of the `Dim` statement. Arrays cannot be implicitly declared. Recall that the `Dim` statement syntax is

```
Dim varname [([subscripts])] As [New] type [, varname ...]
```

In the basic array declaration, the subscript's parameter is the array's upper bound. In the previous example, you could achieve the same functionality using an array of four elements, where each element represents one department, as follows:

```
Dim SalesJan(4) As Currency
```

This declaration creates the currency variables with the same variable name. Each variable in the array can be accessed by specifying its index, in parentheses, after the name of the array. Start a new project and enter Listing 4.43 to see how this works.

LISTING 4.43   Array

```
Private Sub Form_Load()
Dim SalesJan(4) As Currency
Dim TotalSales As Currency
Dim Counter As Integer

SalesJan(1) = 150000
SalesJan(2) = 220000
SalesJan(3) = 125000
SalesJan(4) = 183000

For Counter = 1 To 4
    TotalSales = TotalSales + SalesJan(Counter)
Next Counter
Debug.Print TotalSales
Stop
End Sub
```

Run the program. The output is

```
678000
```

Index Numbering

When you declared the array, you specified the upper bound of the highest-numbered element in parentheses. The first (base) element in the array, however, has an index of 0. This is because index numbering in Visual Basic begins at 0, unless you specify otherwise. Listing 4.43 has a Stop statement, so when you run the program you go into break mode. Go to the Debug window and type

```
Print SalesJan(0)
```

This statement outputs

```
0
```

because you haven't assigned a value to element 0, ignoring the fact that arrays start at 0.

Changing the Base Index

You can change the index number that represents the first element in the array in two ways:

- Using the Option Base statement
- Within the Dim statement itself

Option Base

The `Option Base` statement sets the number of the first element in an array (the base element) to either 0 or 1. If you do not include an `Option Base` statement in your program, the default option base is 0, as you have already seen.

You must place the `Option Base` statement in the General Declarations section of a module. It cannot appear inside a subroutine or function. When it appears in a module, it affects all the arrays in that module.

`Dim` Statement

You can specify the base index at the time you declare your array by using the `To` keyword in the declaration of the array subscript as follows:

```
Dim SalesJan(1 To 4) As Currency
```

This way, you can use index ranges that apply to the particular situation you are coding for. Note that when you use this method, you can use any numbers you choose as lower and upper boundaries.

```
Dim HighArray(100 To 200) As Integer
Dim LowArray(-200 To -100) As Integer
```

 Note

> If you try to access an array element outside the lower or upper bound, you get the `Subscript out of Range` runtime error.

Multiple Dimensions

All arrays must have some dimension. The simplest array, the type you have seen, has one dimension. More complex arrays may have two, three, or more. For example, let's expand the array by keeping track of the whole year's sales at each of the four departments:

```
Option Base 1
Dim Sales(12, 4) As Currency
```

Here, the first dimension in the array represents the month of the year, and the second dimension represents the department. For example, `Sales(1,1)` refers to the January figures in the first department. So, to display the sales figures for December for the third department, you would write

```
Debug.Print Sales(12, 3)
```

To access each element in the array, you would write a nested loop, such as:

```
Dim Month As Integer, Dept As Integer
For Month = 1 To 12
    For Dept = 1 To 4
        ' Do something with Sales(Month, Dept)
    Next Dept
Next Month
```

Dynamic Array Sizing

Some of the time, you will find that you know the number of elements that you will need for an array when you write your program. For instance, an array such as ours has 12 elements in the first dimension, corresponding to the 12 months of the year. Because this figure is static, you can safely hardcode the number of elements in the first dimension.

However, you can also allow for situations in which the number of elements is not fixed. In these situations, use the Dim statement in conjunction with the ReDim statement. When you declare your array using Dim, leave the number of elements and dimensions blank, so that your array declaration is as follows:

```
Dim Sales() As Currency
```

You have told Visual Basic that Sales is to be an array, but you do not yet know the array's dimensions. Before you can use the array, you have to provide this information using the ReDim statement. For example:

```
ReDim Sales(12, 4)
```

These two statements are equivalent to the single Dim statement used earlier, except that the ReDim statement can be called as many times as you want and the array bounds can be passed as variables. (Array boundaries declared with Dim must be numbers or constants.)

You could therefore write

```
Dim Sales() As Currency
Dim Months As Integer, Depts As Integer
Months = 12
Depts = 4
ReDim Sales(Months, Depts)
```

When you use dynamic array sizing, you must use one of the two standard base index numbering schemes (0 or 1). You cannot use the To keyword in the Dim statement to declare your own base index.

Each time you ReDim the array, the contents of the array are destroyed. In fact, the array is completely destroyed, and the memory it was using is released. Then a new array is created according to the new specification.

There are times when you want to retain the contents of the array and just change the size of one of its dimensions. Visual Basic enables you to do this using the Preserve keyword in the ReDim statement. This is particularly useful when you want to "grow" an array at runtime.

For example, assume you want to read some information from a file, but you do not know how many items of information are in the file. You could read through the file once, counting how many items there are, and then use a single ReDim statement to allocate an array large enough. However, what if the information were coming from a communications line? In that situation, you wouldn't have the opportunity of preparsing the data to determine the number of items. The solution is to use the Preserve keyword in conjunction with ReDim, as shown in Listing 4.44.

LISTING 4.44   The Preserve Keyword

```
Dim MyArray() As String
Dim NumElements As Integer
Dim MoreData As Boolean

'Read data from communications line
' and set MoreData to True if data was read
Do While MoreData
    NumElements = NumElements + 1
    ReDim Preserve MyArray(NumElements)
    'code to assign data to MyArray
    'Read data from communications line
    'and set MoreData to True if data was read
Loop
```

For Each...Next Loop

The For Each...Next loop is a special type of loop designed to be used with arrays and collections. We will consider collections in Chapter 6, "Building the GUI with Forms, Menus, and MDI Forms," when we look at classes and objects. The For Each...Next loop has the following syntax:

```
For Each element In array
    [statements]
    [Exit For]
```

```
    [statements]
Next [element]
```

The `For Each...Next` loop works by cycling through each element in an array without you having to specify the element's index. Each time through the loop, the variable element is assigned the contents of the next item in the array. To continue the previous example, which involved growing an array using `ReDim Preserve`, you could then use a `For Each...Next` loop to print out each element of the array as follows:

```
Dim Element As Variant
For Each Element In MyArray
   Debug.Print Element
Next Element
```

The loop starts at the first element in the array (`MyArray`) and loops for each element in that array. Notice that the `Element` variable has to be `Variant`, no matter what type of array `MyArray` is.

The Erase Statement

The way the `Erase` statement works depends on the type of array you are using it with. If you use it with a statically sized array, it sets each element in the array to its pre-initialized value. For example:

```
Dim StringArray(10) As String
Dim IntArray(10) As Integer
Erase StringArray    'Each element set to ""
Erase IntArray       'Each element set to 0
```

If you use it with an array of variants, each variant is set to `Empty`. However, if you use it with a dynamically sized array, the memory used by the array is freed:

```
Dim MyArray() As Currency
ReDim MyArray(6,7,8)
Erase MyArray    'memory used by MyArray is freed,
                           'as if the ReDim statement had not been executed
```

You can specify more than one array to erase by separating the names of the arrays with commas. For example:

```
Dim MyStringArray(10) As String
Dim MyCurrencyArray(10) As Currency
Dim MyIntegerArray(10) As Integer
Erase MyStringArray, MyCurrencyArray, MyIntegerArray
```

LBound and UBound

These two functions return the lower and upper bound indexes in the array. For example:

```
Dim MyArray(10) As String
Debug.Print LBound(MyArray)
Debug.Print UBound(MyArray)
```

If an array has more than one dimension, you can specify the dimension as an optional second parameter to these functions:

```
Dim MyArray(10, 11, 6 To 12)
Debug.Print LBound(MyArray, 3)
```

This code prints 6—the lower bound index of the third dimension.

ParamArray

In Lesson 7, you learned about passing arguments to procedures. There is one additional keyword you can use in procedure declarations: ParamArray. The ParamArray keyword enables you to pass an arbitrary number of different types of arguments in an argument list.

To use a ParamArray, just specify the last parameter in a parameter list as a ParamArray Variant array, as shown in Listing 4.45.

LISTING 4.45   The ParamArray Keyword

```
Private Sub Form_Load()
Dim A As Integer, B As String
Dim C As Single, D As Currency, E As Double
A = 5
B = "Some Text"
C = 3.14
D = 100.45
E = 1 / 5.6
MySub 1, 2, A, B, C, D, E
End Sub

Private Sub MySub(Num1%, Num2%, ParamArray Param3() As Variant)
Dim Var As Variant
Debug.Print "Lower bound: " & LBound(Param3)
Debug.Print "Upper bound: " & UBound(Param3)
For Each Var In Param3
    Debug.Print Var
Next Var
End Sub
```

This code outputs

```
Lower bound: 0
Upper bound: 4
 5
Some Text
 3.14
 100.45
 0.178571428571429
```

Wow! You know a lot. In Chapter 5, "Controls," you'll start to have some real fun using these wonderful commands to explore the VB controls in more detail.

Lesson Summary

In the final lesson of this chapter, you have learned about arrays, lists of related values. Jokingly, it is often said that arrays are most important because there is not a single programmer alive that has not asked his/her manager for "arrays."

Quiz 8

1. An array is

   a. Kind of like a list

   b. A grouping of identical variable types

   c. A way of thinking about (and treating) similar variables together

   d. All of the above

2. How many elements are in the following array?

   ```
   Option Base 0
   Dim Sales(4) As Currency
   ```

   a. 4

   b. 5

   c. 0

   d. Impossible to tell without more information

3. What is the output of the following program?

   ```
   Option Base 1
   Private Sub Form_Load()
       Dim UnderWater(-10 To 10)
       Dim Normal(10)
       Dim AbNormal(0 To 10)
       Debug.Print LBound(UnderWater), LBound(Normal), LBound(AbNormal)
   End Sub
   ```

    a. 0, 1, 0

    b. 10, 0, 0

    c. -10, 1, 0

    d. -10, 0, 1

4. What is the total number of elements in the following array?

```
Option Base 1
Dim TwoLevel(2,3) As Integer
```

    a. 2

    b. 3

    c. 5

    d. 6

Exercise 8

Complexity: Moderate

1. Write a program that uses an array to compute a requested amount of Fibonacci numbers. The first two Fibonacci numbers are 0 and 1, the next ones are the sum of the two preceding numbers. Thus, the first 8 numbers are 0, 1, 1, 2, 3, 5, 8, 13.

Complexity: Advanced

2. Rewrite the Sum routine for the Adder program so that it takes an arbitrary number of arguments, adds them all, and returns the result. Include code to test the program with several sets of input and output the results.

Chapter Summary

In this chapter, we discussed the control flow statements. These language elements enable you to create *intelligent programs*—programs that act differently depending on circumstances. You also learned how to use the building blocks of modular programming: subroutines and functions. With these, you are able to reduce the complexity of writing programming by breaking the task into smaller, more manageable modules.

In Chapter 5, "Controls," we revisit the command button and the label, and introduce a few new ones. Armed with these, you will be able to create more elaborate programs.

CHAPTER 5

Controls

Learning to program in Visual Basic isn't just about learning the language. As you've already seen, Visual Basic comes complete with a wide variety of controls that you can use in your programs. Because these controls offer so much built-in functionality, learning to use the controls adeptly is half the game.

In this chapter, we'll look in more detail at the controls you've already used, and we'll introduce many of VB's other controls. To demonstrate the controls, we'll build a data entry application. This will help you understand not only *how* to use the individual controls but *when* to use them.

The controls you'll explore in this chapter are

- TextBox
- Label
- CommandButton
- CheckBox
- OptionButton
- Frame
- ListBox
- ComboBox

Additionally, we'll talk about tab order, accelerator keys, how to use the values in one control to affect the behavior of other controls, and some other useful properties. Finally, we'll cover the advanced topic of control arrays.

LESSON 1

The TextBox Control

Different controls perform different roles in your programs. As you've seen, however, they all conform to the same fundamental programming interface. When you've learned how to use one control, you should find it quite straightforward to apply what you've learned to a different one.

Let's begin our look at controls with the TextBox control. As you saw in Chapter 1, "What's All That Stuff on My Screen?" TextBox is a control that enables the user to type in text from the keyboard and store it in your program. Some people call it an edit control because it enables you to edit text.

The Data Entry Program

Here's the scenario: You've been given the task of writing a data entry program as part of a suite of programs that store and retrieve information about the members of a video library and the videotapes they have borrowed. You need to design a data entry form that can be used for a number of different purposes:

- To allow registration of a new member
- To allow an existing member's personal details to be retrieved
- To register when a member withdraws or returns a tape

Start a new project and place a text box on the default form. (Peek ahead at Figure 5.2 to get an idea about placement.)

TextBox Properties

Select the text box and press F4 to bring up the Properties window. Let's take a closer look at how property values work.

Select the Appearance property and click to view its possible values. Notice that the actual text is 0 - Flat and 1 - 3D, as opposed to simply Flat and 3D (see Figure 5.1). Remember that properties are simply variables that exist inside the control. Therefore, each property must be a specific type of variable.

It turns out that the Appearance property is an integer. The list box that lets you set the value of the Appearance property provides you with a textual description of the two possible values. When you change the property from 3D to Flat, you are actually changing it from 1 to 0. It is often important to know what type of variable a particular property is, particularly if you want to read or set the property value in your program code. For example, to change the TextBox style to Flat, you would code

```
Text1.Appearance = 0
```

When you change the appearance from 3D to Flat, the text box is immediately redrawn, but without the 3D appearance it had earlier. (Change it back to 3D now because you want to keep the 3D appearance throughout this data entry program.)

FIGURE 5.1

Changing the Appearance *property from 3D to flat.*

> **Note**
>
> An easy way to find out what a particular property does and what the values mean is to select the property using the mouse and then press the F1 key. Visual Basic displays a Help window telling you how to use that property.

Now change the name of this text box to txtMemID. The three-letter prefixes we've been using, txt, lbl, and cmd, are conventions that many programmers use to help identify their controls by their type. We'll introduce other prefixes for the other standard controls as we go along, although there's nothing to stop you from choosing your own conventions.

The Text Property

You've already used the Text property for input in other example programs. The Text property is a string that contains the text that the user has typed in.

The default value of the Text property is Text1. If you don't delete this text from the Text property prior to running your program, the text box will display Text1 when the program runs. There will probably be times when you want to use this feature of pre-loading the Text property with some text to serve as a default value. However, you don't want to do this now, so remove the text before you continue.

Now add three more text boxes to Form1. The text boxes you've added to the form so far are summarized in Table 5.1.

TABLE 5.1 The TextBox Controls

Object	Property	Value
TextBox	Name	txtMemID
	Text	None
TextBox	Name	txtFirstName
	Text	None
TextBox	Name	txtSurname
	Text	None
TextBox	Name	txtAddress
	Text	None

Try to position the controls so that they appear in roughly the same positions as those shown in Figure 5.2.

FIGURE 5.2

View of Form1 *after name and address text boxes have been added.*

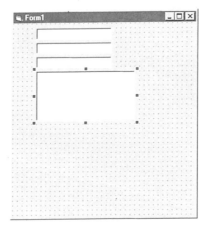

The `MultiLine` Property

The difference between the address text box and the other text boxes is that you want the address text box to store more than one line of text. If you run the program as it stands and attempt to enter an address into `txtAddress`, you'll find that making the address text box large enough isn't sufficient to make it accept multiple lines of text.

To add functionality, you need to change the `MultiLine` property of the text box `txtAddress` to `True`. Rerun the program and enter an address (street, city, state, and Zip code). You'll find that you can now enter more than one line of text by pressing Enter at the end of a line.

Note

> By setting the text box's `MultiLine` property to `True`, you will need to be concerned with line Feeds and carriage returns in your text. This can be an issue if you're storing this information in a database.

The `ScrollBars` Property

The only remaining problem with the address text box is that you cannot enter an address that is wider than the actual width of the text box. The text box automatically wraps the text for you, rather like a word processor. It would be better if the text box displayed a scrollbar to enable the user to scroll the contents of the text box. The `ScrollBars` property enables you to switch on this functionality.

This property can be set to `None`, `Horizontal`, `Vertical`, or `Both`. If you like, experiment with the different settings to see how they affect the text box's behavior. When you're done, set the value to `3` - `Both`.

Now that you've added all the text boxes that you need, let's look at how you can interact with them in your program.

The `KeyPress` Event

Let's say that to adhere to the product specification, the text box containing the member ID should automatically capitalize all the text typed into it. Double-click the `TextBox` control to bring up the Code window. This puts you in the `Change` event, the default event for the text box. This particular event is one that is called after the text in a text box has changed. You need to convert each character typed into uppercase before the character has been added, so you want the `KeyPress` event.

Select the Code window's `Proc ComboBox` to create an event subroutine for the `KeyPress` event. Visual Basic adds the full declaration for the subroutine for you. This is nice, especially for routines such as this one with parameters.

Add the code in Listing 5.1 to the `KeyPress` subroutine.

LISTING 5.1   Converting the Key Pressed to Uppercase

```
Private Sub txtMemID_KeyPress(KeyAscii As Integer)
    KeyAscii = Asc(UCase(Chr(KeyAscii)))
End Sub
```

The `KeyAscii` parameter is an integer that represents the character that's been pressed. When the user presses a key on the keyboard, Visual Basic converts that key to a number in the ASCII character set. For example, the lowercase letter *a* is converted by Visual Basic to the ASCII number 97.

You passed the number to the `Chr` function, which, as you saw in Chapter 2, "Object-Oriented Programming," converts ASCII numbers to strings. You then take the character that's been returned to you by the `Chr` function and passed that to the `UCase` function, which converts lowercase characters to uppercase characters.

Finally, you converted the result back to an ASCII value with the `Asc` function. Note that in cases like this, when you use *nested* function calls, the innermost expression, in this case, `Chr(KeyAscii)`, is always evaluated first. Note also that because the `KeyAscii` parameter is passed by reference, changing its value in the function changes the character the user sees on the screen.

Run your program now and see the effect this one line of code has had on your text box.

 Note

> If you don't want the text box to accept the key that the user has entered, you can "throw it away" by setting the value of `KeyAscii` to 0.

Validating User Input

Many data entry programs need to perform some sort of validation on the text that has been entered into a text box. Typically, you want this validation to take place after the user has completed the entry in the text box.

You'll use the LostFocus event here, as you did to validate the date the user entered in the Timesheet program in Chapter 3, "Variables, Constants, and Associated Functions." You'll also learn a new method—SetFocus—that you'll use to force the user to stay in the text box until he or she enters valid data.

The SetFocus Event

Let's add some new functionality to txtMemID. You want to make sure that only alphabetical (A to Z) or numeric characters (0 to 9) have been entered. If the user enters invalid characters, the SetFocus method forces the cursor to move back onto the text box so the user can correct the input. Recall that the syntax for calling an object's method is

```
ControlName.MethodName
```

Use the Code window to add the declaration for the LostFocus event subroutine for the txtMemID control, and then add the code in Listing 5.2 to the subroutine.

LISTING 5.2   Validating User Input

```
Private Sub txtMemID_LostFocus()
    Dim I As Integer
    Dim sCharacter As String

    For I = 1 To Len(txtMemID.Text)
        sCharacter = Mid(txtMemID.Text, I, 1)
        If (sCharacter < "A" Or sCharacter > "Z") And _
           (sCharacter < "0" Or sCharacter > "9") Then
            Beep
            txtMemID.SetFocus
            Exit For
        End If
    Next I
End Sub
```

The If statement in the listing is saying that an invalid character has been entered if the character is outside the range A to Z and the range 0 to 9. The check relies on the ordering of characters in the ASCII character set. The character A has the lowest ASCII value of the uppercase characters, and the character Z has the highest. Similarly, the digit 0 has the lowest value in the character range 0 to 9.

When you've detected that there's a character outside either of these ranges in the Text property of the control, beep the speaker once and return the focus to the text box. Now run your program, and type the following into the membership number text box:

ABCD****1234

5

You can type the four asterisks, but when you try to move the focus to one of the other text boxes, you will find that you are unable to do so.

The program is a little user unfriendly now, though. The user can type in that text box all day long and never figure out why he or she can't seem to leave it. You need a touch more code. Change the original code in the LostFocus event by adding the new code, shown in bold print in Listing 5.3.

LISTING 5.3   Changes to the LostFocus Procedure

```
Private Sub txtMemID_LostFocus()
    Dim I As Integer
    Dim sCharacter As String
    For I = 1 To Len(txtMemID.Text)
        sCharacter = Mid(txtMemID.Text, I, 1)
        If (sCharacter < "A" Or sCharacter > "Z") And _
           (sCharacter < "0" Or sCharacter > "9") Then
                MsgBox "Enter only letters and numbers, please", 48, "Note:"
            txtMemID.SetFocus
            Exit For
        End If
    Next I
End Sub
```

Notice that the beep has been removed; your user does not want everybody in the office to know he or she has made a mistake. Now a message box tells the user how to fix the problem. When the user clicks OK, he or she will be back in txtMemID, ready to fix the problem.

Lesson Summary

This lesson focused on the usage of the TextBox control. It is the most common type of control and is used to accept one or more lines of input. The next lesson will look at the MsgBox function more closely.

Quiz 1

1. If you don't change the default value of the Text property for a text box, what displays in it when the program runs?

    a. Nothing

    b. No answer; you must set this value

    c. The caption

    d. The same default value that VB gives the Name property, such as Text1

2. How do you set up a text box to allow more than one line of input?

    a. Instruct the user to press Enter or Shift+Enter at the end of a line

    b. Set the MultiLine property to True

    c. Set the ScrollBars property to 1-Horizontal

    d. Set the ScrollBars property to 2-Vertical or 3-Both

3. What are the type and contents of the variable passed to the KeyPress event routine?

    a. String; the key pressed

    b. String; the text entered so far

    c. Integer; 1 for A, 2 for B, and so on

    d. Integer; the ASCII value of the key pressed

4. Validate input in the KeyPress routine if it's important to

    a. Catch the input before it appears onscreen

    b. Validate an entire string of input

    c. Validate input after the control loses focus

    d. Use SetFocus to force the user to stay on the control

Exercise 1

Complexity: Easy

1. Create a simple login screen with a text box for a User ID and a Password. Program the password text box to allow only numeric characters.

Complexity: Easy

2. Create a form with the following text boxes:

    A text box that allows multiple lines for the shipping address.

    A text box named Country that can accept up to 30 characters and has a default value of USA.

LESSON 2

Labels and the `MsgBox` Function

You've already used `Label` controls both for captions and for message output. In this lesson, you'll learn more about how to use these ubiquitous objects. Additionally, we'll take a closer look at one of Visual Basic's more versatile functions, `MsgBox`.

`Label` Controls

You should try to make your forms as intuitive as possible to use. Where you position your labels will have an important effect on the overall form design. Typically, labels are to the left of the controls they describe. Also, if your form's width space is limited, it is typical to place the label above the control it is supposed to describe.

Add the four labels described in Table 5.2 to the form. Table 5.2 also includes a command button; add this now so you have a place to output results.

TABLE 5.2   The Video Membership Labels

Object	Property	Value
Label	Caption	Membership Number
Label	Caption	First Name
Label	Caption	Surname
Label	Caption	Address
CommandButton	Caption	Ok
	Name	cmdOk

 Note   It is a good programming practice to change your label's Name property using the naming convention of lbl. For example, Label1 could be named something like lblMbrNbr. This naming convention is known as Hungarian notation.

The `Alignment` Property

The `Label` control has an `Alignment` property. You can use this to left-, right-, or center-align the label's caption on the form. Try right-aligning the labels. It's more pleasant to look at a form that has right-aligned labels because the gap between the end of the caption and the beginning of the text box to which the caption relates is kept to a minimum. Try to make your form appear as it is shown in Figure 5.3.

FIGURE 5.3

Form1 *with right-aligned labels.*

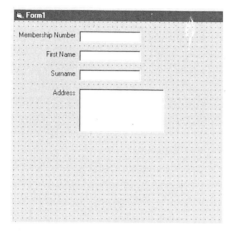

Tab Order and the `TabIndex` Property

When your program is running, you can move from control to control on the form by pressing Tab or Shift+Tab. Each time you press Tab, the cursor jumps to a different control. In fact, the cursor is following a set order when it jumps from one control to another. This order is called the tab order, and it is controlled by the value of the `TabIndex` property. Any control that is capable of receiving the focus has a `TabIndex` property.

Accelerator Keys

When forms have many controls on them, it can be helpful to your program's users to give them shortcuts for moving about a form. Many people still prefer to use the keyboard. This is where accelerator keys come in. Your users' hand doesn't have to leave the keyboard to use to mouse to move to different text boxes.

Visual Basic's development environment uses accelerator keys all the time. Take a look at any of the dialog boxes, for example the Options dialog box in the Tools menu. You'll see that each label has a caption in which an underline appears below one of the letters. That letter is the accelerator key for that control in that dialog box.

Accelerators work by letting the user press a combination of Alt and the character under which the underline appears. In the Environment Options dialog box, therefore, you can press Alt+A to set or clear the Align Controls to Grid check box.

You can provide the same functionality in your own programs by adding an accelerator to an object's caption or, if the object doesn't have a caption, to the caption of the label preceding the object.

To add an accelerator key to a caption, simply place an ampersand just before the letter in the caption that you want to be the accelerator. Label1's caption should therefore read &Membership Number, Label2's &First Name, Label3's &Surname, and Label4's &Address.

Note

> If you want to use an & character (an ampersand) in a label without its being interpreted as an accelerator, there are two techniques you can use. One is to use two ampersands in a row. The Label control will interpret an && sequence as a single ampersand character.
>
> Another way to achieve the same effect is to set the Label control's UseMnemonic property to False. This has the effect of turning off the interpretation of & characters as accelerators.

After you add the ampersand character to a caption, you'll see the caption has an underline underneath the accelerator character (see Figure 5.4).

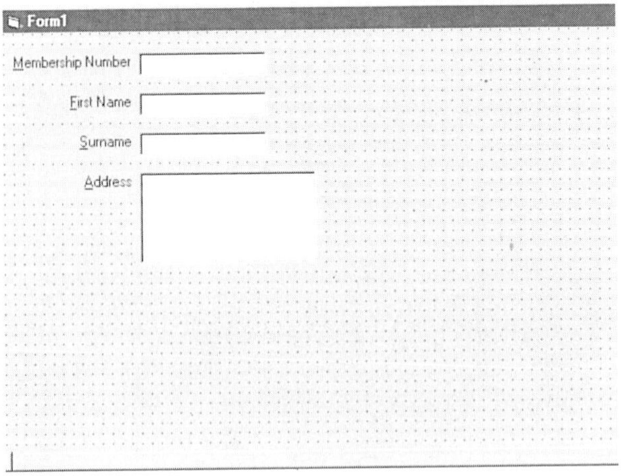

FIGURE 5.4

Form1 *after accelerators have been added.*

You should try to place the ampersand in front of unique letters. If you place the ampersand in front of the same letter in different labels and your user uses the accelerator key, the cursor's focus will go to the first available control. For example, you place the ampersand in front of the letter *L* within two different labels. When your user presses

Alt+L, the cursor's focus may go the first control or the second control. It depends where the cursor's focus is when the user presses the accelerator key combination.

If you run the program now, your accelerators may not work as expected. Go back to design mode and take a look at the TabIndex values for your labels and text boxes. If you've added the controls to the form in the order that we've prescribed, you'll find that they are set as in Table 5.3.

TABLE 5.3 Default TabIndex Values

Control	TabIndex *Value*
txtMemID	0
txtFirstname	1
txtSurname	2
txtAddress	3
Label1	4
Label2	5
Label3	6
Label4	7
cmdOk	8

Visual Basic sets the TabIndex value to the next available number when you add controls to a form. In addition to controlling the order in which the focus jumps from one control to another, the TabIndex value is important because it also controls how the accelerators on a Label control work. The focus will jump to the next control in the tab order when you press the accelerator key for a particular label because the label itself is unable to receive the focus. It is therefore important that you set the TabIndex values for all your controls in a logical order; otherwise, the accelerators on your labels will not work as expected.

Set the TabIndex values for the nine controls as in Table 5.4.

TABLE 5.4 TabIndex Values for Accelerator Keys

Control	TabIndex *Value*
Label1	0
txtMemID	1
Label2	2

continues

5

TABLE 5.4   continued

Control	TabIndex *Value*
txtFirstname	3
Label3	4
txtSurname	5
Label4	6
txtAddress	7
cmdOk	8

Sometimes you may have a control that you do not want to receive focus in the tab order. The TabStop property provides the answer. Set TabStop to False and the control will no longer be part of the tab sequence.

> **Note**
>
> Make sure you start changing the TabIndex values of the control that you want to take the lowest value. Change Label1 first. If you don't do this and try to change the values in a random order, you might not get the results you want. When you change the TabIndex value, Visual Basic will renumber the other controls.

The MsgBox Function

Now that the Video Store program has enough of an interface to begin testing it, it's time to program a routine to do something with the input. You'll use the MsgBox function inside cmdOk's click routine to display the data the user enters.

You've used the MsgBox statement a few times already to output brief messages with a single OK button to the user. This usage, such as

```
MsgBox "Hello out there!"
```

is simple and will serve you well for as long as you program in Visual Basic. However, this example barely scratches the surface of MsgBox. Its complete syntax is

```
MsgBox(prompt[, buttons][, title][, helpfile, context])
```

> **Note**
>
> There are two different types of MsgBox procedures. The most common one, which you have already used, is known as the MsgBox statement. The other method, which you will use later, is the MsgBox function.

> The MsgBox statement only displays a dialog box with a message, an OK button, an optional icon, and title. The MsgBox function returns the value of the button your user presses, described later in this lesson.

As you've seen, the prompt parameter gives the message (or prompt) to show to the user. If you need to build a long output string, as you'll do in a little while, you may want to put this value in a variable.

We'll talk about the buttons parameter later. The title parameter is simply the text that appears across the title bar of the message box. This defaults to your application's name. The helpfile and context arguments implement context-sensitive help for the message box. See the VB Online help for more details about how to use the helpfile and context arguments in your program, as well as creating help files for your applications.

The MsgBox function can have one, two, or three buttons. The function returns the value of which button your user pressed. Before we talk about these values, however, we need to take a quick detour and talk about VB 6's predefined constants.

Predefined Constants

Recall that a constant is a way of representing a number symbolically. In the grocery program example in Chapter 3, "Variable, Constants, and Associated Functions," for example, you assigned numbers to constant fruit names. You could therefore refer to an apple as APPLE, rather than having to remember that an apple is number 1. Using constants in code prevents bugs because you are less likely to assign incorrect values. Also, constants make the code easier to write and read.

Visual Basic has a number of predefined constants you can use with its functions, properties, and commands. These constants all have the prefix vb. Like constants you define in your own programs, predefined constants make code more readable. Constants also save you from having to remember (or spend time looking up) values for parameters. Using predefined constants, you can show a form as modal, for example, with the statement

```
Form2.Show vbModal
```

rather than

```
Form2.Show 1
```

Note   To browse through VB's predefined constants, search the help system for *Visual Basic constants*, or just *constants*.

MsgBox **Constants**

The `buttons` parameter of `MsgBox` can take the values summarized in Table 5.5. You can combine values by adding them. For example, if you want to have a message box displaying the Abort, Retry, and Ignore buttons and have the Ignore button the default, your `buttons` parameter would be

```
vbAbortRetryIgnore & vbDefaultButton3
```

TABLE 5.5   Constants for the `MsgBox` `buttons` Parameter

Constant	Description
vbOKOnly	OK button only (default).
vbOKCancel	OK and Cancel buttons.
vbAbortRetryIgnore	Abort, Retry, and Ignore buttons.
vbYesNoCancel	Yes, No, and Cancel buttons.
vbYesNo	Yes and No buttons.
vbRetryCancel	Retry and Cancel buttons.
vbCritical	Critical message.
vbQuestion	Warning query.
vbExclamation	Warning message.
vbInformation	Information message.
vbDefaultButton1	First button is default (default).
vbDefaultButton2	Second button is default.
vbDefaultButton3	Third button is default.
vbApplicationModal	Application modal message box (default).
vbSystemModal	System modal message box.

Visual Basic also has `MsgBox` constants you can use to analyze the value the function returns. They are summarized in Table 5.6.

TABLE 5.6 Constants for the `MsgBox` Return Value

Constant	Button User Clicked
vbOK	OK
vbCancel	Cancel
vbAbort	Abort
vbRetry	Retry
vbIgnore	Ignore
vbYes	Yes
vbNo	No

Finally, you can use the `Chr` constants defined in Table 5.7 to format your output. In fact, you can use these constants in other strings as well, for example, any time you need to extend output across multiple lines.

TABLE 5.7 Nonprinting Character Constants

Constant	Description	Chr Equivalent
vbCrLf	Carriage return/linefeed	Chr(13)+Chr(10)
vbCr	Carriage return	Chr(13)
vbLf	Linefeed	Chr(10)
vbTab	Tab	Chr$

Next are a few example calls to `MsgBox` and the resulting message boxes.

```
Answer = MsgBox("Do you want to continue?", _
        vbYesNo + vbQuestion, "Continue")
```

This produces the message box in Figure 5.5.

FIGURE 5.5

`MsgBox` *with* `vbYesNo` + `vbQuestion`.

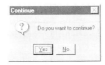

```
Continue = MsgBox("Error:" & vbTab & "File not found.", _
    vbAbortRetryIgnore + vbCritical)
```

This produces the message box in Figure 5.6.

FIGURE 5.6

MsgBox *with*
VbAbortRetryIgnore +
vbCritical.

```
If MsgBox("Do you want to perform another search?", _
        vbYesNo + vbDefaultButton2, "Search") = vbYes Then
    ' Perform Search
End If
```

This produces the message box in Figure 5.7.

FIGURE 5.7

MsgBox *with* vbYesNo +
vbDefaultButton2.

Add the source code for the OK button, as shown in Listing 5.4.

LISTING 5.4   The OK Button

```
Private Sub cmdOK_Click()
    ' Ouput name and address
    Dim sMsg As String
    Dim nAnswer As Integer

    sMsg = txtMemID.Text & vbCr
    sMsg = sMsg & txtFirstname.Text & " " & txtSurname.Text & vbCr
    sMsg = sMsg & txtAddress.Text & vbCr

    sMsg = sMsg & vbCr & "Are these values correct?"

    ' Check info
    nAnswer = MsgBox(Msg, vbYesNo, "Video Store")
    If nAnswer = vbYes Then
        ' Do something; possibly store data to file
        ' and clear values for next entry
        ' For now, just quit.
        End
    End If
    ' (If user clicked no, we'll just return to form
    ' where they can make corrections.)

End Sub
```

The program's output is shown in Figure 5.8.

FIGURE 5.8

Output from MsgBox.

Note	During software development, it's often helpful to give controls values that you use only for testing purposes. For example, after you're done testing the member ID validation routine, you could preset text box values to a membership number and your name and address. That way you don't have to retype them every time you run the program. It's a simple enough matter to clear the values before distributing the application when everything's working.

Lesson Summary

Aside from the text box control, the Label control is the next most commonly used control because all other controls need to be described and you will want to use the accelerator key to allow your users quicker navigation on your form.

Remember that the msgbox is both a statement and a function. Whether you use it as a statement or function, the amount of arguments is the same. The way it is used makes the difference. As a statement, you call the msgbox statement like any other procedure, by using the following:

```
msgbox "Message to user", buttontype, "Messagebox Caption"
```

When calling the msgbox as a function, you use it like any other function where a value is supposed to be returned after some user intervention.

This lesson worked with the usage of buttons. Although you already know how to use buttons, the next lesson talks about these important controls in more detail. You'll learn, for example, how to make the Video Store OK button look and act like a standard OK button.

Quiz 2

1. The tab order is best defined as

   a. A constant you define to insert a tab indent in a string

   b. The order in which controls are accessed when the user presses Tab

    c. An index

    d. The order of the command buttons only

2. Which of the following caption definitions will result in a label that reads exactly
   `Reilly & Sons`

    a. `Reilly & Sons`

    b. `Reilly "&" Sons`

    c. `Reilly && Sons`

    d. `Reilly _& Sons`

3. Which of the following message boxes cannot be generated by the `MsgBox` function?

    a. The message "Are you sure you want to continue?" with the buttons Yes, No,
   and Cancel

    b. The message "Continue?" with the buttons Ok and Cancel and a big question
   mark icon

    c. The message "I'm going to continue." with the button OK and a big excla-
   mation point

    d. The message "Do you want to continue?" with the buttons Continue and
   Stop

4. To advance to the next line within a `MsgBox` prompt string

    a. Insert a carriage return character (`vbCr`)

    b. Insert a tab character (`vbTab`)

    c. Press Enter in the Code window

    d. Press Enter and an underscore in the Code window

Exercise 2

Complexity: Easy

1. Add the appropriate labels with accelerator keys to both forms created in Exercise
   1. Correct the `TabIndex` order so that the accelerator keys work properly.

Complexity: Easy

2. Write a routine that will display a message box saying "The System shut down 5
   minutes ago" when the focus is changed from the login `TextBox` to the Password
   `TextBox`. The message box should only have the OK button, and the title should
   say "Login."

LESSON 3

Command Buttons and Check Boxes

Look around at the appliances in your home. There are buttons everywhere: push buttons, light switches, round buttons, square buttons, buttons that stay in when you push them, and buttons that don't. Even the keys on a computer keyboard are buttons.

Buttons are an important part of the design of your program's user interface, just like they are an important part of the panel of a stereo.

Visual Basic provides you with three standard button controls for you to use in your forms:

- CommandButton
- CheckBox
- OptionButton

This lesson discusses the Command button in more detail than you've seen before, and introduces the CheckBox. Lesson 4 covers the option button.

Command Button

You've already seen how easy it is to program a command button and how it acts from the user's point of view. Let's take a look at some of its other properties and events.

On dialog boxes, users are used to seeing two buttons on this type of form: the OK button to tell the program to accept information and the Cancel button to tell the program to ignore what the user has entered. You already have an OK button, so add the Cancel button shown in Table 5.8.

TABLE 5.8 The Cancel Button

Object	Property	Value
CommandButton	Name	cmdCancel
	Caption	Cancel

There's a bit more to these controls than just setting the captions, however.

The Default Property

You gave accelerators to the text boxes, and you could do that for the command button as well by including an ampersand in the caption name. However, your user will probably expect your OK button to follow convention and respond to Enter. To do this, Visual Basic provides the Default property. The Default property is a Boolean value that, when set to True, sets that particular command button to be the default one for the form.

The default command button is the one that is pressed when a user presses Enter on the keyboard, even if the focus is set to a different control. Only one command button on a form can have the Default property set to True.

Set the Default property of the cmdOK button to True. When you do this, you will find that the OK button is redrawn slightly differently: It now has a thicker border (see Figure 5.9).

FIGURE 5.9

The default command button has a slightly thicker border.

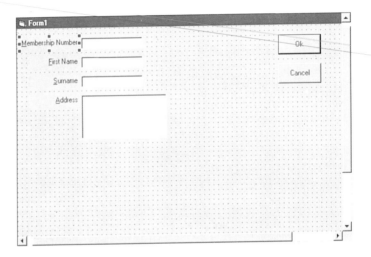

Note

When a command button has focus, the Default value on a command button no longer applies. In the previous example, if the Cancel button had focus and you pressed the Enter key, the Cancel button's event would trigger, not the Default button's.

You might have noticed a small inconsistency here regarding the effect that a default button has on a multiline text box. Earlier, you set the MultiLine property of the txtAddress text box to True so that the user could use Enter to end each line. Now, however, you're using Enter for the default button. You'll find that now, if you press Enter while the focus is set to the txtAddress text box, the OK button is pressed.

You now have to press Shift+Enter to terminate each line.

In fact, it's good practice to instruct users of your software to get into the habit of pressing Shift+Enter on a MultiLine text box. This is because the text box will always accept Shift+Enter as the line break regardless of whether or not the form also has a default command button.

The Cancel Button

There is also a convention for the Cancel button's accelerator: Esc (the Escape key). To support this, the command button also has a Cancel property, which you can set to True. Do this now for your Cancel button so that it will respond correctly to Esc. Like the Default property, only one button on the form can have the Cancel property set to True at any one time.

Add the code shown in Listing 5.5 to end the program in the Cancel routine.

LISTING 5.5   The Cancel Event Routine

```
Private Sub cmdCancel_Click()
    End
End Sub
```

Run the program. Notice that Enter presses the OK button regardless of which control in the form has the focus. Esc now ends the program.

Next you'll learn how to use a different type of button: the check box.

The CheckBox Control

Although it looks quite different from the command button, the check box is really just another type of button. It is typically used where you want to provide your users with a way to indicate a Boolean choice: something that may be either True or False.

Let's add a check box to the form in the example to indicate whether or not the member has provided proof of identity. Of course, the video club requires a member to provide proof of identity before he or she can rent films. This shouldn't prevent a member's details from being entered into the system, however. Market research shows that 25 percent of all video club members decide to join on impulse and don't have the required proof of ID with them. We have to allow someone to join the club now, but show an ID later.

Add a CheckBox control to the form. Figure 5.10 shows you what the check box looks like on the toolbox. Set the property values as shown in Table 5.9.

5

FIGURE 5.10

The CheckBox *control.*

TABLE 5.9   The Check Box Property Values

Property	Value
Name	chkID
Caption	Proof of &ID

Note that this time you're using an accelerator character directly in the caption of the button. The form should appear as in Figure 5.11.

FIGURE 5.11

Form1 *with check box added.*

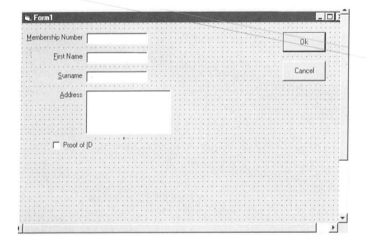

The check box's caption displays next to the check box. It's a bit like having a built-in Label control.

The Check Box Alignment Property

You can vary which side of the caption the check box appears on by changing the value of its Alignment property. Change it now so that it appears to the right of the caption by setting its Alignment property to 1 - Right Justify. Adjust the size of the check box so that it appears as in Figure 5.12.

The check box will now work automatically when you run the project. Let's see it in action. Run the project now and experiment with the check box at runtime. You'll find that there are several ways you can set and clear the checkmark in the check box. You can click the check box itself, click its caption, pressing its accelerator key (Alt+I), or by pressing the spacebar when the check box has the focus. Like the command button, the check box will generate a Click event when it is clicked.

FIGURE 5.12

View of Form1 *with right-aligned check box.*

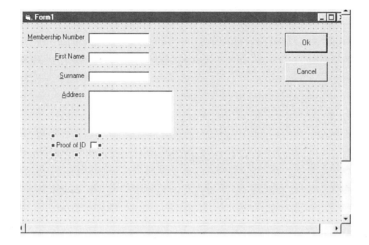

The Value Property

The Value property reflects the current state of a button. For example, when the command button is in its normal, unpressed state, its Value property is set to False. However, when you click it, its Value property changes to True. Because a value of True means the button is pressed, you could use this value in code to invoke a command button's Click routine programmatically.

Although you normally don't need to worry about the Value property for command buttons, this property is important for the check box. The Value property sets or returns the current state of the check box. You can set this value at design time if you want the control's default state to be checked. To check the box in code, you would write

```
chkID.Value = True
```

and to turn it off, you would write

```
chkID.Value = False
```

Note The Value property for the command button is not available at design time. You can only check the value of the property when the program is executed.

5

Add the highlighted code in Listing 5.6 to the cmdOK button's Click event subroutine to print the current Value setting for the check box when the OK button is pressed.

LISTING 5.6   Evaluating the Check Box Value

```
Private Sub cmdOK_Click()
    ' Ouput name and address
    Dim sMsg As String
    Dim nAnswer As Integer

    sMsg = txtMemID.Text & vbCr
    sMsg = sMsg & txtFirstname.Text & " " & txtSurname.Text & vbCr
    sMsg = sMsg & txtAddress.Text & vbCr

    If chkID.Value Then
        sMsg = sMsg & "Member has shown ID." & vbCr
    Else
        sMsg = sMsg & "Note: Member has not yet shown ID." & vbCr
    End If

    sMsg = sMsg & vbCr & "Are these values correct?"

    ' Check info
    nAnswer = MsgBox(sMsg, vbYesNo, "Video Store")
    If nAnswer = vbYes Then
        ' Do something; possibly store data to file
        ' and clear values for next entry
    End If
    ' (If user clicked no, we'll just return to form
    ' where they can make corrections.)

End Sub
```

The Enabled Property

Let's add another button to the form. This will be where you'll add the functionality to rent a videotape. However, don't give the user access to the videotape until the Proof of ID button is checked. To disable controls and make them appear gray, set the Enabled property. Add the button with the properties described in Table 5.10.

TABLE 5.10   Properties for the Rent Button

Object	Property	Value
CommandButton	Name	cmdRent
	Caption	Rent a &Tape
	Enabled	False

When the program runs, the Rent button is disabled, as shown in Figure 5.13. Note that you also can't access the button via the accelerator key while the Enabled property is False.

FIGURE 5.13

The button's initial state is disabled.

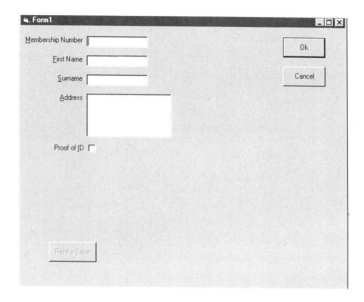

To enable the button at the appropriate time, enter the source code for the chkID_Click routine shown in Listing 5.7.

LISTING 5.7   Enabling a Button If a Value Is Checked

```
Private Sub chkID_Click()
    If chkID.Value Then
        cmdRent.Enabled = True
    Else
        cmdRent.Enabled = False
    End If
End Sub
```

Alternately, you can shorten this code by replacing the entire If...End If block with the statement

```
cmdRent.Enabled = chkID.Value
```

Note how easy it is to express relationships between the values of the controls on a form. Of course, if this were a complete application, you'd probably need more validation. For

5

example, you might want to make sure the name, address, and membership number were completed before enabling the Rent button. But the procedure to do this would be essentially the same as in Listing 5.7.

Lesson Summary

Applications use command buttons to enable the user to tell the application when to do something, such as OK to accept the current input or Cancel to ignore the current input. The Default property of a command button enables a user to press the Enter key in lieu pressing the button itself. Just remember that a different command button has focus, the Enter key will activate the button that has focus.

Check boxes enable you to help limit a user's selection to discrete values. A key thing to remember is that an option you display next to a CheckBox control does not have to be the data that gets transmitted when that option is selected. The data is transmitted as check or unchecked. The next lesson will cover another data selection method similar to the check box, the option button and how to scope them properly within a form.

Quiz 3

1. To make a button the default button for a form,
   a. Set the Ok property to True
   b. Set the Default property to True
   c. Program an accelerator using &+Enter
   d. Enter a caption of Ok; Visual Basic is smart enough to know what you mean

2. To advance to a new line of a multiline text box on a form that has a default OK button,
   a. Press Enter (VB temporarily disables the default button functionality)
   b. Press Shift+Enter
   c. Press the down-arrow key
   d. Use the horizontal scrollbar

3. Setting the Value property of a command button to True
   a. Has no effect
   b. Makes the button look pressed
   c. Calls the Click event routine for that button
   d. Does nothing; the command button doesn't have a Value property!

4. For which situation is a CheckBox control not a good choice?

    a. When there is a button to turn on or off other options on a form

    b. When there is a button the user can press to indicate whether or not a condition is true

    c. When there is a box to display whether a condition is true and that the user can't click

    d. When there is a box on a form for the user to answer a yes/no question

Exercise 3

Complexity: Easy

1. On the OK and Cancel buttons to both the login form and the Shipping form, set the properties such that the Enter key activates the OK button and the Esc key actives the Cancel button.

Complexity: Easy

2. On the shipping information form, add the following question:

```
What are your main areas of interest?
Hiking
Rafting
Mountain Biking
Scuba
None
```

5

LESSON 4

Option Buttons and Frames

In this lesson, we're going to look at two new controls. One of these, the option button, is a button similar to the Command button. The other, the frame, is the first control you've met that is not really used on its own. Intrigued? Read on.

The OptionButton Control

Option buttons are sometimes called *radio* buttons. The idea is that only one button can be pressed at one time, just like the preset buttons on a radio. Option buttons, therefore, work in groups, which is the one fundamental difference between them and the other types of buttons.

Figure 5.14 shows how the option button appears on the toolbox.

FIGURE 5.14

Adding an option button to the form.

Option buttons are useful when you have a small number of options of which only one can apply at a time. Let's add some option buttons to Form1 to show the member's marital status. Add option buttons to Form1 now with the property settings described in Table 5.11. Lay out the controls as shown on Figure 5.15. To make the label's accelerator work correctly, be sure to add the Label control first.

FIGURE 5.15

View of Form1 *after option buttons have been added.*

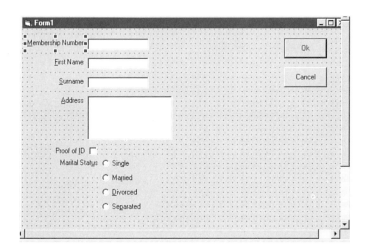

TABLE 5.11   The Marital Status Option Buttons

Object	Name	Caption
Label	lblMaritalStatus	Marital Stat&us
OptionButton	optSingle	Sin&gle
OptionButton	optMarried	Ma&rried
OptionButton	optDivorced	&Divorced
OptionButton	optSeparated	Se&parated

Option buttons respond to the same stimuli as the CommandButton and CheckBox controls. They also generate a Click event and have a Value property. The difference is that only one at a time in a group can have its Value property set to True. By contrast, any number in a group of check boxes may have a value of True at any one time.

Add the highlighted code in Listing 5.8 to the OK button routine. Select Case is a natural way to access the Option button values. Run your program now and see how the option buttons operate at runtime.

LISTING 5.8   Using Select Case to Access the Option Button Values

```
Private Sub cmdOK_Click()
    ' Ouput name and address
    Dim sMsg As String
    Dim nAnswer As Integer

    sMsg = txtMemID.Text & vbCr
    sMsg = sMsg & txtFirstname.Text & " " & txtSurname.Text & vbCr
    sMsg = sMsg & txtAddress.Text & vbCr

    sMsg = sMsg & "Marital Status:" & vbCr
    ' Output marital status.
    Select Case True
        Case optSingle.Value
            sMsg = sMsg & vbTab & "Single" & vbCr
        Case optMarried.Value
            sMsg = sMsg & vbTab & "Married" & vbCr
        Case optDivorced.Value
            sMsg = sMsg & vbTab & "Divorced" & vbCr
        Case optSeparated.Value
            sMsg = sMsg & vbTab & "Separated" & vbCr
        Case Else
            sMsg = sMsg & vbTab & "Unknown" & vbCr
    End Select

    sMsg = sMsg & vbCr & "Are these values correct?"

    ' Check info
    nAnswer = MsgBox(sMsg, vbYesNo, "Video Store")
    If nAnswer = vbYes Then
        ' Do something; possibly store data to file
        ' and clear values for next entry
    End If
    ' (If user clicked no, we'll just return to form
    ' where they can make corrections.)

End Sub
```

5

The Frame Control

The Frame control (shown in Figure 5.16) is different from the other controls that you have seen because it doesn't really do anything by itself. Instead, you use it to group other controls, both visually and functionally. A Frame control works by letting you add other controls on top of it.

FIGURE 5.16

Adding a frame to the form.

Add a Frame control to your form.

The Frame control is a rectangle with a caption along the top. As you size the control, the size and shape of the frame change. Figure 5.17 shows you how the frame appears when you first add it to the form.

FIGURE 5.17

Form1 *with* Frame *control added.*

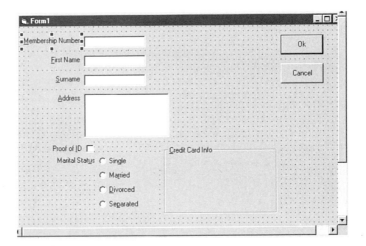

The frame has a Caption property just like a label does. Like the Label control, the Frame control can have an accelerator in its caption that, when keyed at runtime, will set the focus to the control with the next TabIndex value. Set the Frame control's Caption property as shown in Table 5.12.

TABLE 5.12   The Frame Control Caption

Object	Property	Value
Frame	Caption	&Credit Card
	Name	fraCreditCard

You're going to use the Frame control to store some further details about each member. This time you're going to record the type and number of the credit card the member has selected to use in case he or she fails to pay for a rental or overdue tape. The video rental store accepts Visa, MasterCard, and its own store card.

Add controls to a frame simply by drawing them on top of the frame. You can tell an object belongs with a frame because if you drag the frame around the control, all its objects move with it. Also, you can move controls around on a frame, but you cannot move them outside the frame.

Note   If a control is already on a form, you can't simply drag it onto a frame to make the object belong to the frame. Here is a way to move it onto a frame: Select the control by clicking it. Cut it out by clicking Cut under the Edit menu. Now select the frame you want to own the control. When the frame is selected, click Paste under the Edit menu.

Add three additional OptionButton controls to the frame, one for each type of card. This raises another important issue. You already have a set of OptionButton controls on the main part of the form. If you add more option buttons to the form, how can you tell Visual Basic to treat the two groups separately? As well as acting as a visual frame to group controls, the Frame control groups OptionButton controls functionally.

Add the controls shown in Table 5.13 to the frame.

TABLE 5.13   The Credit Card Option Buttons

Object	Property	Value
OptionButton	Name	optVisa
	Caption	&Visa
OptionButton	Name	optMastercard
	Caption	&Mastercard

continues

5

TABLE 5.13 continued

Object	Property	Value
OptionButton	Name	optStore
	Caption	&Store card
Label	Caption	&Number:
	Autosize	True
TextBox	txtCardNum	
	Text	<none>

You'll also need to add an additional TextBox control to store the credit card number. Call it txtCardNum. Your form should now look like that shown in Figure 5.18.

FIGURE 5.18

View of Form1 *after controls have been added to the frame.*

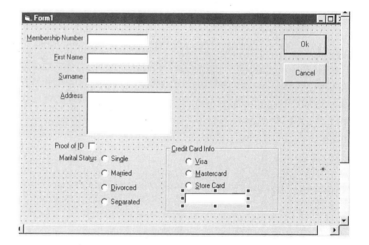

Now check the TabIndex values of your controls. If necessary, modify them so that they appear in the same order as listed in Table 5.14.

TABLE 5.14 The Form's Tab Order

Control	TabIndex	Control	TabIndex
Label1	0	optSingle	10
txtMemID	1	optMarried	11
Label2	2	optDivorced	12
txtFirstname	3	optSeparated	13
Label3	4	fraCreditCard	14

Control	TabIndex	Control	TabIndex
txtSurname	5	optVisa	15
Label4	6	optMastercard	16
txtAddress	7	optStore	17
chkID	8	txtCardNum	18
lblMaritalStatus	9	cmdRent	19

Note

If more than one control on a form has the same accelerator, pressing the accelerator once advances you to the first control in the tab order that has that accelerator, pressing it again advances you to the next control with that key, and so on.

Now add the highlighted lines in Listing 5.9 to the OK button's Click event subroutine. This code accesses the Credit Card option buttons. You should note that even though these new controls are contained within the Frame control, there is no special syntax to use to access them. You can treat controls positioned within a frame for programming purposes as if they were placed directly on the form.

LISTING 5.9 Accessing the Credit Card Info

```
Private Sub cmdOK_Click()
    ' Ouput name and address
    Dim sMsg As String
    Dim nAnswer As Integer

    sMsg = txtMemID.Text & vbCr
    sMsg = sMsg & txtFirstname.Text & " " & txtSurname.Text & vbCr
    sMsg = sMsg & txtAddress.Text & vbCr

    sMsg = sMsg & "Marital Status:" & vbCr
    ' Output marital status.
    Select Case True
        Case optSingle.Value
            sMsg = sMsg & vbTab & "Single" & vbCr
        Case optMarried.Value
            sMsg = sMsg & vbTab & "Married" & vbCr
        Case optDivorced.Value
            sMsg = sMsg & vbTab & "Divorced" & vbCr
        Case optSeparated.Value
            sMsg = sMsg & vbTab & "Separated" & vbCr
```

5

continues

LISTING 5.9 continued

```
        Case Else
            sMsg = sMsg & vbTab & "Unknown" & vbCr
    End Select

    sMsg = sMsg & "Credit Card:" & vbCr
    Select Case True
        Case optVisa.Value
            sMsg = sMsg & vbTab & "Visa" & vbCr
        Case optMastercard.Value
            sMsg = sMsg & vbTab & "Master Card" & vbCr
        Case optStore.Value
            sMsg = sMsg & vbTab & "Store Card" & vbCr
        Case Else
            sMsg = sMsg & vbTab & "None" & vbCr
    End Select

    sMsg = sMsg & vbTab & txtCardNum.Text & vbCr
    sMsg = sMsg & vbCr & "Are these values correct?"

    ' Check info
    nAnswer = MsgBox(sMsg, vbYesNo, "Video Store")
    If nAnswer = vbYes Then
        ' Do something; possibly store data to file
        ' and clear values for next entry
    End If
    ' (If user clicked no, we'll just return to form
    ' where they can make corrections.)

End Sub
```

You are now ready to run the project. Note how the option buttons work and how they are evaluated when you click Ok.

Lesson Summary

Option buttons are also referred to as *radio* button because of they work like buttons on a radio. On a radio, when you press one button, like the preset station button, another button becomes disabled. The Frame control enables you to logically group your option buttons and other controls. By keeping option buttons grouped within a Frame control, you can keep their values exclusive from one another.

In the next lesson, you will learn another method of method of controlling your user's selection items through the use of the list box control.

Quiz 4

1. The option button differs from the command button and check box in that

   a. It has a `Value` property that tells whether the button option is on or off

   b. It doesn't have a `Click` event

   c. You can't use an accelerator to access it

   d. Only one option in a group may be selected at any time

2. If you have three option buttons in a group—`optRockyRoad`, `optMintChocolate`, and `optFudgeSwirl`—and Rocky Road is selected, what's the easiest way to turn off `optRockyRoad` and turn on `optFudgeSwirl` in code?

   a. `optFudgeSwirl.Value = True`

   b. `optRockyRoad.Value = False : optFudgeSwirl.Value = True`

   c. `optRockyRoad.Value = False`

   d. `optFudgeSwirl.Pressed = True`

3. An accelerator key implemented on a frame's caption

   a. Sets the focus to the `Frame` control when pressed

   b. Sets the focus to the first editable control inside the frame when pressed

   c. Sets the focus to the next editable control in the tab order when pressed

   d. Isn't implemented because it wouldn't make sense to put the focus on a frame

4. To distinguish two or more sets of option buttons on a form functionally

   a. Put at least one other control between the tab orders of the sets of buttons

   b. Put one or both of the groups on its own frame

   c. Give options in the same group the same prefix name

   d. Give options in the same group the same accelerator name

5

Exercise 4

Complexity: Easy

1. Add a frame with a caption of Address Location. Within the frame, add two option buttons:

   ```
   Home
   Business
   ```

Complexity: Moderate

   2. On the same shipping form, add a series of option buttons for the following payment methods:

```
COD
MasterCard
Visa
American Express
Discover
```

Add a text box near the list of payment methods and set the property to `Disabled`. It should be labeled Credit Card Nbr. If any of the payment methods are selected other than COD, enable the text box.

LESSON 5

The `ListBox` Control

The data entry program is beginning to take shape, but it's not yet complete. What you need is a way to display a list of any video titles that a member has borrowed. Because the number of titles that a member could borrow at any one time can vary, you need a flexible way to display as many titles as needed. The control that will let you do this is the list box.

Figure 5.19 shows you how the list box appears on the toolbox. You add it to the form in the same way you added the previous controls. A list box lets your user select an item from a list of choices. In the Windows file selector, for example, you use list boxes to select the filename and directory. A `ListBox` control is a little more complicated than the other controls you've seen because you need to manage the items it contains, but its usage is nonetheless not very difficult.

FIGURE 5.19

Selecting the `ListBox` *control from the tool-box.*

Add a label and a list box to the form, as described in Table 5.15. Remember to add the label first so the accelerator key works correctly.

TABLE 5.15   Adding a List Box and Label to the Form

Object	Property	Value
Label	Caption	Tit&les Rented
	Name	lblTitlesRented
ListBox	Name	lstTitlesOut

Make the list box roughly the same size and position as that shown in Figure 5.20.

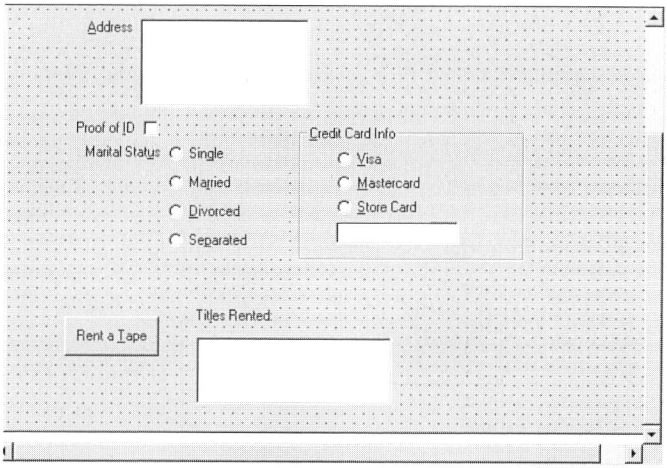

FIGURE 5.20

View of Form1 *after the list box has been added.*

Adding Items to the List

Now you'll program the Rent a Tape button to let the user type in a videotape name and add the name to the list. Visual Basic has a nice built-in function to accept text from the user. Of course, if this were a complete program, you'd probably get a list of all the videos in the store from a database and let the user select from that instead of having to type in the title.

The InputBox Function

The InputBox function accepts one or more lines of text from the user. It has its limitations, though. It isn't nearly as versatile as the text box; however, there may be times when you need an input box's ease of use. The syntax for this function is

```
InputBox(prompt[, title][, default][, xpos][, ypos][, helpfile, context])
```

For this example (and probably for most cases), you need only the prompt argument. The input box is a dialog box that displays the prompt, a text box for data entry, and an OK and Cancel button. The `title` parameter is the text displayed in the title bar (if this is omitted, Visual Basic uses the application name). You can set the upper-left x and y positions the input box with the `xpos` and `ypos` arguments; if these parameters are omitted, the box is centered on screen. (See the online help page of this function for more details.)

The `AddItem` Method

Add the video title to the list box using the `AddItem` method, which appends the string to the list. The `AddItem` method has the following syntax:

```
object.AddItem item [, index]
```

Enter the `cmdRent` function in Listing 5.10. This is the most basic way to use the `AddItem` method, where you simply specify the string expression (a variable will do) to add to the list box. In this case, the string is always added to the end of the list box. If you were adding text to the list box from a real database, you would probably want to place the call to the list box's `AddItem` method in a loop, calling it once for each line of data extracted from the database.

LISTING 5.10   Adding a Video Title to the List Box

```
Private Sub cmdRent_Click()
    Dim sTapeName As String

    sTapeName = InputBox("What tape would you like to rent?")
    If sTapeName <> "" Then
        lstTitlesOut.AddItem sTapeName
    End If
End Sub
```

Run the program and see how the Proof of ID check box enables the Rent button, and how that button in turn lets you add titles to the list, as shown in Figure 5.21. The ease with which Visual Basic controls interrelate makes building this type of functionality a snap.

FIGURE 5.21

The input box in action.

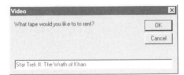

One thing to note about the InputBox function is that it returns a zero-length string if the user cancels, regardless of the text box's contents. Because the cmdRent_Click routine checks for this, if the user cancels (or doesn't enter a string) then nothing happens.

Add two or three video titles using the Rent a Tape button. When there are some items to choose from, notice how you can use the mouse to select items or use arrows to scroll down the list when the list box has the focus. Notice also that when there are more items than will fit on the box, VB 6 automatically adds scrollbars, as shown in Figure 5.22. Next we'll look at how to read user input from the list box.

FIGURE 5.22

VB 6 adds scrollbars automatically when the list gets long in the Titles Rented list box.

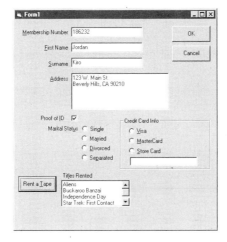

Selecting List Box Items

When you select an item in a list box, the list box generates a Click event that you can trap using the list box's Click event subroutine. Similarly, when the user double-clicks an item in a list box, VB generates a DblClick event. Often, nothing happens right away when the user clicks an item, but if he or she then clicks OK (or some other button), the choice is read and processed. As a shortcut, the user can often simply double-click an item to select it and perform the default processing.

Text, List, ListIndex, and ListCount Properties

There are two ways you can find out which item was selected. If you need the full text of the item, simply read the list box's Text property, which returns the text of the currently selected item. For example,

```
UserChoice$ = lstSomeListOfStuff.Text
```

The other way to access the selected item is to treat the contents of a list box as an array—which, it turns out, is what it really is. The array is accessed via the List property; the ListCount property contains the number of elements in the list. Because List is a zero-based array, a loop to print out the contents of a list box would look like this:

```
For Index = 0 to lstSomeListOfStuff.ListCount - 1
   Debug.Print lstSomeListOfStuff.List(Index)
Next Index
```

You may need to know the index number of the line the user selected. You can do this by referring to the list box's ListIndex property. This property is a simple integer that represents the index number of the selected item. If an item has not been selected, the ListIndex property will be set to -1.

Add the lines of code in Listing 5.11 to the DblClick event subroutine to see how these properties work.

LISTING 5.11   Determining the Selected Item

```
Private Sub lstTitlesOut_DblClick()
    Dim sMsg As String
    sMsg = "You selected " & lstTitlesOut.Text & ";" & vbCr
    sMsg = sMsg & "Index number " & lstTitlesOut.ListIndex
    sMsg = sMsg & " out of " & lstTitlesOut.ListCount & "."
    MsgBox sMsg
    MsgBox "And a fine choice it was, too."
End Sub
```

Note that you can set the list items at design time via the Properties window. However, the other properties can be read only at runtime. These are read-only properties that have no meaning until your program is running.

 Note

> You can add items to a specific position in an existing list by using the index parameter of the AddItem method. For example, the following code inserts the tape name at the beginning of the list:
>
> lstTitlesOut.AddItem TapeName, 0

Multiselect List Boxes

So far, we've considered only single-selection list boxes. These are list boxes that enable you to select only one entry at a time. Most of the time, you'll probably find that single-selection list boxes are enough for most of your programming tasks. However, some tasks require that your users be able to select more than one entry from the list box at a time.

In our example, for instance, the rented-out list box could be used to identify the tapes that a member has returned. What would happen if a member returns more than one tape? If you used a single-selection list box, as you currently are doing, that would mean that the user would have to select one tape and then press a command button to indicate that the tape had been returned. You haven't added such a button yet, but assume for the moment that one exists. The user would then have to repeat this process for each returned tape.

The MultiSelect Property

It would be better to let the user select more than one tape and press the button once. The list box can behave in this way thanks to the MultiSelect property. By default, the MultiSelect property is set to 0 - None, but you can also set it to 1 - Simple or 2 - Extended.

Simple Versus Extended Multiselect List Box

A simple multiselect list box lets your user select more than one entry in the list box by clicking each item with the mouse or by pressing the spacebar. The user can select only individual entries, not groups of entries. This is the main difference between the simple and the extended MultiSelect types.

If you set the MultiSelect property to 2, your list box becomes an extended multiselect list box. The user can select a group of items by clicking and dragging them with the mouse or by pressing Shift and clicking the item that you want to be the last item selected. The user can also use the mouse with Ctrl depressed to select and deselect individual items.

Try experimenting with the MultiSelect property now until you are satisfied that you appreciate the differences between the simple and the extended multiselect list box styles. Before you continue, set the MultiSelect property for your list box to 2 - Extended.

The Selected Property

The list box's Text property provides you with the text of the currently selected list box item. But what if your list box is a multiselect list box and it has more than one selected item? The Selected property helps you solve this problem.

The `Selected` property is an array of Boolean values that enables you to determine whether a particular item in the list box is currently selected. The `List` property enables you to access the text of any item in the list box regardless of whether or not it is currently selected. Both of these properties are arrays, indexed from 0. You can therefore use these two properties together with the `ListCount` property to scan through the items in the list box and determine which items are selected and which are not. Listing 5.12 shows how to do this.

LISTING 5.12   Finding Selected Items

```
Dim I As Integer
For I = 0 To lstTitlesOut.ListCount - 1
    If lstTitlesOut.Selected = True Then
        Debug.Print lstTitlesOut.List
    End If
Next I
```

Remember that the `ListCount` property returns the actual number of items in the list box, whereas the `Selected` and `List` properties reference the entries from an index of 0.

Removing Items from a List Box

Let's add a button to the form for returned tapes. Add the button described in Table 5.16 below the Rent a Tape button.

TABLE 5.16   The Return Button

Object	Property	Value
CommandButton	Caption	&Return a Tape
	Name	cmdReturn

The `RemoveItem` Method

Individual items can be removed from a list box by calling the list box's `RemoveItem` method. The syntax is

```
object.RemoveItem index
```

This method requires a parameter, the index number of the item to be deleted from the list. Any item can be deleted, not just selected ones. However, the way you typically use list boxes is to first let the user select the items and then let the user issue a command to perform the deletion.

If you were using a single-selection list box, the code needed to delete the selected entry would be

```
If lstTitlesOut.ListIndex <> -1 Then
   lstTitlesOut.RemoveItem lstTitlesOut.ListIndex
End If
```

You're using the ListIndex property as a parameter to the list box's RemoveItem method.

Things get a little more complicated with multiselect list boxes. If you think about it, when you have a list box that has multiple items selected, each time you remove one item, the indexes of the other items change. In fact, they decrease by one as each item is removed. You have to use a little more care when coding multiselect list box deletion routines, otherwise your program will not work as expected.

Add the routine in Listing 5.13 to the Return Button event routine.

LISTING 5.13 Removing Selected Items from a List

```
Private Sub cmdReturn_Click()
    Dim I As Integer
    I = 0
    Do
        If lstTitlesOut.Selected Then
            lstTitlesOut.RemoveItem I
        Else
            I = I + 1
        End If
    Loop Until I > lstTitlesOut.ListCount - 1
End Sub
```

If you delete an item, you don't increment the index counter. For example, if you delete item number 2, the item that was previously index number 3 is now 2. By not incrementing the counter, you make sure to check that item's Selected property as well.

The Clear Method

Should you need to remove all the items from a list box in one step, you can use the list box's Clear method. This will completely clear the list box:

```
lstTitlesOut.Clear
```

Lesson Summary

The list box, like the check box and option button controls, limit the range of user data to discrete values. Remember that the default MultiSelect property is set to Single

`Select only`. This is useful if you're just displaying a list of items and do not want the user to do anything with the list. The most common style is `Extended Select`. This enables the user to select a single item or multiple items that are not contiguous. The next lesson will offer more insight as to how to use the list box as well as a counterpart control, the combo box.

Quiz 5

1. Which line adds the item *Apple* to the list box?

    a. `lstFruit.AddItem "Apple"`

    b. `lstFruit_AddItem "Apple"`

    c. `InputBox("Apple").AddItem = lst.Fruit`

    d. `AddItem "Apple" To lstFruit`

2. What value does the `ListIndex` property take when no items are selected in the list box?

    a. `0`

    b. `1`

    c. `-1`

    d. The number of elements in the list + 1

3. Which loop correctly prints out all the items in a list box? (Assume `Counter` is an integer with an initial value of `0`.)

    a. ```
While Counter < lstFruit.ListCount
Debug.Print lstFruit.Text(Counter)
Wend
```

    b. ```
For Counter = 1 to lstFruit.ListCount
Debug.Print lstFruit.Text(Counter)
Next Counter
```

    c. ```
For Counter = 0 to lstFruit.ListCount - 1
Debug.Print lstFruit.List(Counter)
Next Counter
```

    d. ```
.For Counter = 1 to lstFruit.ListCount
Debug.Print lstFruit.List(Counter)
Next Counter
```

4. The difference between a simple `multiselect` list box and an extended `multiselect` list box is that

    a. A simple list box lets you select only one list element

    b. A simple list box doesn't let you deselect items

    c. An extended list box lets you double-click to select the entire list

    d. An extended list box lets you select a group of items using standard Windows interface conventions

Exercise 5

Complexity: Moderate

1. Create a form with a list box. When you click a command button, an input box will enable you to add an item to the list box.

Complexity: Advanced

2. Create a form with a list of items hard coded in the Form_Load. When you double-click an item in the list, it will be removed from the list. Or when you select an item and press a Remove Item button, it item will be deleted from the list.

LESSON 6

Advanced List Box Techniques and the ComboBox Control

Before we move on to consider the combo box, consider a couple of advanced list box techniques that we did not address in Lesson 5. These are

- Using the Columns property
- Storing numbers in a list box
- Sorting list boxes
- Searching the list box at runtime

The Columns Property

The list box style that you used in Lesson 5 scrolls through a single list of items vertically. When the list box fills up, it displays a vertical scrollbar that can be used to bring the hidden items into view.

5

You can divide the list box into columns and scroll horizontally instead by setting the Columns property to the number of columns you want. By default, this property is set to 0. Each column is given the same width so, if you set Columns to 2, each column occupies half the overall width of the list box. Note that the number of columns in this property represents the number of columns displayed at one time, not the number of columns altogether.

Try setting the lstTitlesOut list box's Columns property to 2 and then rerun the project. When the first column fills up, items will display in the second column. When the second column fills up, a horizontal scrollbar will be displayed, enabling you to bring the hidden columns into view.

Storing Numbers in a List Box

As well as storing text in a list box item, the list box also can store a number alongside the text. The number is never displayed, but it can be stored and retrieved by your program. This list of numbers can be used for anything. It might be an index into a database, an index into another list box, or even a list of ages to correspond to a list of names.

The property you need for this feature is called ItemData. The ItemData property is an array of Long integers, one for each item in the list box. When you add a new item into the list box, the ItemData value starts out at zero. You could write something such as

```
lstTitlesOut.ItemData(lstTitlesOut.ListCount - 1) = MyNumber
```

which would set the ItemData value for the last entry in the list box to a Long integer called MyNumber.

Sorted List Boxes

Normally, when you enter items into a list box, they are added in the order in which you enter them (unless you use the optional index parameter in the AddItem method). However, if you set the list box's Sorted property to True, the list box automatically performs an alphabetical sort on the items, ensuring that they remain in alphabetical order.

Set Sorted to True and run the program. Notice that when you add new titles they display in alphabetical order.

By changing the order in which the items are displayed in the list box, any attempt to add a number using ItemData no longer works. What you need is a way to tell what index number the last item was added to. Another property gives you this information. It is called NewIndex and it returns the index number of the last item added to the list box. This is very useful when using sorted list boxes. Listing 5.14 provides an example of this technique.

LISTING 5.14   The NewIndex Property

```
Dim I As Integer
Dim S As String

For I = 0 To 99
    S = "Entry " & I
    lb.AddItem S
    lb.ItemData(lb.NewIndex) = I
Next I
```

Different Styles

There is an alternate way of displaying selected items within a list box. Like the References dialog box or Components dialog box, the items in the list have check boxes in front of them. When an item is selected, you either click the check box to mark and unmark the item, double-click the item's test, or move the highlight to the item and press the spacebar.

To cause the list box to display check boxes in front of each item, you use the Style Property and set it to 1 - CheckBox. The default setting is 0 - Standard. Figure 5.23 shows the difference between a list box with the Style property set to standard and checkbox. If you do decide to use the check box style, VB sets the MultiSelect property to 0 - None because you can not select more than one item at a time using this list box model.

FIGURE 5.23

Standard list box compared to check–box-style list box.

The ComboBox Control

A combo box is a combination of two other controls: TextBox and ListBox. One of the disadvantages of single selection list boxes is that they occupy a lot of real estate on your form. After you have made your selection, you rarely need to see the remaining entries that lie unselected in the list box, but they are still there and still taking up space. As you will discover when you start writing your own real-life programs, space on forms is at a premium. It would be nice if list boxes could just be folded up and set aside until they were needed again.

The combo box provides a tidy solution to this problem in that it contains a single-selection list box that remains hidden until it is needed. Instead, all that stays visible at all times is the text box portion of the control and a small drop-down button (a down arrow bitmap button), which the user can press to display the list box at runtime.

What's more, you can use a combo box where you previously used a group of option buttons. Although the code that is required to support the control would be different, a combo box can be viewed as functionally similar to a group of option buttons.

You could have used combo boxes, for example, in place of the Marital Status or Credit Card groups of option buttons. If you find yourself in a situation like this and are unsure which control to use, here are some pointers to help you make your choice:

- If you have a small, set number of options, you should use the option button.
- If you have a larger set of options, or the text for the options is not fixed, then use the combo box.

Figure 5.24 shows how the ComboBox control appears on the toolbox.

FIGURE 5.24

Adding a combo box to the form.

Add the label and combo box described in Table 5.17 to Form1. You'll use the combo box to store a list of special promotions that the store is offering at any particular time. A combo box is appropriate in this case because the names and number of promotions can vary and there could be so many that it would be impractical to use option buttons.

TABLE 5.17   The Promotions Combo Box

Object	Property	Value
Label	Caption	Promotions:
	Name	lblPromotions
ComboBox	Name	cboPromotions

Figure 5.25 shows the combo box at design time. To get everything to fit, enlarge the form and put the Rent a Tape, Return a Tape, and Titles Rented list boxes a little closer together.

FIGURE 5.25

Video Store form with Promotions combo box.

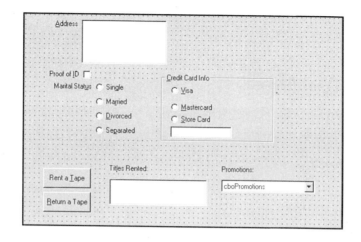

> **Note**
>
> You can select multiple controls and move them together by drawing a "rubber band" box around them by holding down the mouse button and drawing a rectangle. Selected controls are highlighted.

The Style Property

Although the combo box has now been added to Form1, you need to do a little more work before you can go ahead and start programming it. First, you need to look at its Style property. This property controls how the combo box behaves at runtime. There are three different styles for you to choose from:

- Drop-down combo
- Simple combo
- Drop-down list

The drop-down combo box consists of three areas: the edit area, the down arrow, and the list area. The edit area enables users to enter text as they would in a text box. The down arrow is displayed just right for the exit area. The list area of the drop-down combo box stays hidden from view until the user clicks the down arrow associated with the box or presses the Alt+down arrow.

Either action causes the list area to drop down below to edit area, or above the edit area if the combo box is too close to the bottom of the screen. The list area closes as soon as the user selects an item. Because the user can enter text, or choose from a list of items, this style provides a useful tool for data entry fields that may have some values that are used often. This type also enables the user not to be restricted to the list because the text area acts like a text box as well.

The simple combo box similar to the drop-down combo box with its list area open at all times. Again, its values can be set by the user input in the edit area, or by the user clicking the desired list item. The default setting for the Height property of this object will display only the edit area; therefore, it's a good idea to increase the Height property at design time in order to let the items in the list area to be viewed. Because the list area is constantly displayed, you have less form space available to you.

The drop-down list box is almost identical to the drop-down combo box with one functional difference; the text area will only allow text that is contained within the list area. While the selected item appears in the edit area, the user can type nothing there. You should use this style for data entry fields when you want to a limited number of valid values.

To see how these controls work, you first need to add some entries to the list box part of the combo box so that you've got something to select from at runtime.

Add the code in Listing 5.15 to Form1's Form_Load subroutine. The combo box has an AddItem method that you can use in the same way as a normal list box's AddItem method. If you look at the Properties window for the combo box, you'll also see that it shares many of the same properties as the ListBox control.

LISTING 5.15   Filling the Combo Box

```
Private Sub Form_Load()
    ' Initialize ComboBox
    cboPromotions.AddItem "None"
    cboPromotions.AddItem "Rent three get one free!"
    cboPromotions.AddItem "Gold star tape"
    cboPromotions.AddItem "Extra day rental free"
    cboPromotions.AddItem "New member first tape free"
End Sub
```

Now let's look at each style in turn.

Drop-Down Combo

This style is characterized by the text box part of the combo box. The text box in this style of combo box is editable, which means that your users have a choice of either selecting an entry from the list box part of the combo box or typing in their own entry into the text box part.

The combo box has a `Text` property that you should use with this style to obtain the text selected or entered in the text box. You have to use the `Text` property to determine the entered text because you cannot be certain that the text has come from the list box part of the control.

This `ComboBox` control provides a limited search facility. The user can key in the first part of the desired entry and then press Enter. If the keyed entry matches the beginning of an item in the list box portion, then that item is selected.

For instance, if you press the drop-down button, type `G`, and then press Enter, the Gold star tape promotion would be selected for you. Another way to perform the search is to key in the text that uniquely identifies the item in the list box portion and press the down arrow key on you keyboard. To select the New member first tape free promotion, key in `Ne`, to distinguish the promotion from the entry `None`. You could key in `ne` or `NE` because the search is not case sensitive. If there is no match, the combo box will display the first item in the list.

Simple Combo

The main difference between the simple combo and the other styles is that the list box portion is always displayed. Therefore, you have to be careful to set the height of the combo box at design time because the height you set determines the height of the list box portion at runtime. If you don't set the height of the combo box, you won't see the list box at all and the combo box will look just like an ordinary text box.

This combo box style also allows the user to key in the text; you can use its `Text` property to see the text the user entered. This combo box has no search facility.

Drop-Down List

This style of combo box is the one you want to use in your program. The main difference between this and the other two styles is that the text box portion of the combo box is now protected so that the user cannot type anything into it. The `Text` property is now read-only at runtime. This means you can read the `Text` property to see the text in the text box, but you cannot assign a value to it (at least without generating a runtime error).

Set this value and run the program. The combo box in action is shown in Figure 5.26.

Before you continue to the next lesson, save the sample program as `VIDEO.FRM/VIDEO.VBP`.

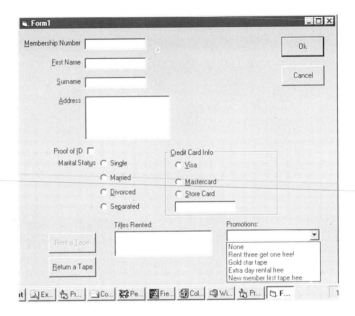

FIGURE 5.26

The combo box in action.

Lesson Summary

In this lesson, you learned that there is another way to display data in a list box, using the Column property. Using this property is useful if you want to display more information to your user without having a drastically large list box.

You also learned of an alternate style for displaying your data within a list box. This method is by having check boxes in front of each item in the list. It offers more control for a user to select desired items.

The combo box is incredibly useful if you are limited on screen real estate. You get the benefit of the list box that takes up the space of a text box.

In the next lesson, you will learn how to access controls using arrays.

Quiz 6

1. A Columns property value of 2 on a list box means
   a. Your list is broken into two columns and can be scrolled horizontally or vertically
   b. Your list is broken into multiple columns the user can scroll horizontally, two of which are visible at once

   c. The items are split into two list boxes

   d. Any nonzero value for this property splits the list into two columns

2. Which property returns the index value of the last item added to a list box?

   a. `NewIndex`

   b. `ListIndex`

   c. `ListCount`

   d. `ListCount - 1`

3. A combo box is a combination of which two controls?

   a. `ListBox` and `Label`

   b. `ListBox` and `CommandButton`

   c. `TextBox` and `OptionButton`

   d. `TextBox` and `ListBox`

4. Which type of list box would you use if you wanted a bare-bones list box that a user could use to type an item or select it and that stays the size it was given at design time?

   a. `ListBox`

   b. Drop-down combo-style combo box

   c. Simple combo-style combo box

   d. Drop-down list-style combo box

Exercise 6

Complexity: Moderate

1. Add a `ListBox`, a command button, and two text boxes with their labels:

Object	Property	Value
ListBox	Name	lstTitles
Command button	Name	cmdAdd
	Caption	"Add to List"
Label	Name	lblTitle
	Caption	"Title"

continues

Object	Property	Value
TextBox	Name	txtContent
	Text	" "
Label	Name	lblPosition
	Caption	"Position"
TextBox	Name	txtPosition
	Text	" "

The first text box will be placed in a list box. The second text box is used for position the text within the list box. If the second text box is left blank, the item in the first text box will be added at the end of the list box.

Complexity: Moderate

2. Create a simple data entry form with a combo box. If the user enters a value in the text area that's not in the list area, ask if they want to add it to the combo box's list area. If they want to add it, add that text value to the list.

LESSON 7

Control Arrays

So far, you have set about the task of designing forms in a pretty consistent way. You have always added the controls that you need to a form using the toolbox and then simply loaded the form (either implicitly or explicitly) at runtime and relied on Visual Basic to create the control objects for you.

This is fine when you know in advance how many instances of a particular control you will need. The problem is that there are many occasions when you do not have this information when you develop your project.

Let's say you want to store information on more than one credit card for each member, including the account number and expiration date. You don't know in advance how many and what types of card a member is going to want to use. One way to tackle this problem would be to design a form that allows for a theoretical maximum number of cards and to duplicate the controls required for each card that many times. Although such an approach would work, it isn't very elegant and there's bound to be one credit card junkie out there with more cards than you allowed for.

Instead, you're going to use a technique to generate any number of sets of identical controls at runtime. Load the saved VIDEO.VBP project. To make room for this lesson's example, remove the Marital Status option buttons, the Promotions combo box, and the Credit Card Info frame and its contents. You also need to remove (or comment out) the code that refers to these controls in the OK button routine. Now add a set of controls that describe a single credit card. These controls are summarized in Table 5.18. Resize and move controls around on the form so that the layout is similar to that shown in Figure 5.27. Save this version of the program as VIDEO2.VBP.

FIGURE 5.27

Credit card form at design time.

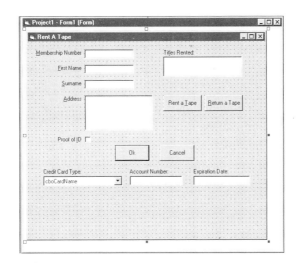

TABLE 5.18 The Credit Card Info Controls

Object	Property	Value
Label	Caption	Credit Card Type
ComboBox	Name	cboCardName
	List	Visa
		MasterCard
		Store Card
	Style	2 - Dropdown List
Label	Caption	Account Number
TextBox	Name	txtCardNumber
	Text	None

continues

TABLE 5.18   continued

Object	Property	Value
Label	Caption	Expiration Date
TextBox	Name	txtExpDate
	Text	None

Notice that the new controls have plenty of blank space beneath them. The idea is that you are going to create as many control objects as you need at runtime from these three controls.

Visual Basic always creates the first set of three controls for you. If for any reason you do not want to display the first set of controls when the form displays, you must set its Visible property to False at design time.

In this example, assume that the member has at least one credit card to register. Therefore, you always need to display at least one set of these three controls.

The Index Property

The next thing to do, and this is the key to the solution to this problem, is to set the Index property of each of these three editable controls to zero while you're still in design mode. Do this so each of these three controls becomes a control array. A control array is a mechanism for creating instances of controls at runtime.

What Is a Control Array?

A control array isn't conceptually much different from any other type of array, such as an array of integers, which you learned about in Chapter 3, "Variables, Constants, and Associated Functions." Like an array of integers, a control array is a grouping of identical variables, except that in the case of a control array, the variables are control object variables that contain references to control objects, rather than just integers. Also, like an array of integers, each individual control object is accessed by specifying its index number in parentheses after the name of the control itself.

If you have an array of, say, 10 text boxes all called Text1, you could print the contents of their Text properties to the Debug window by using the following simple For...Next loop.

```
Dim I As Integer
For I = 0 To 9
    Debug.Print Text1(I).Text
Next I
```

Other Ways to Create Control Arrays

We've just shown you one way to create a control array: by setting the control's Index property to 0. There are two other ways to create a control array: by giving two controls the same name and by copying a control using the Copy and Paste commands from VB's Edit menu.

Giving Two Controls the Same Name

This method involves creating two or more controls of the same type at design time on the same form. We'll use a TextBox control as an example.

Draw a new text box somewhere on the form. Change its Name property to txtTest. Now draw another text box on the form and change its Name property to txtTest as well. Visual Basic asks you if you want to create a control array, as shown in Figure 5.28.

FIGURE 5.28

Creating a control array at design time.

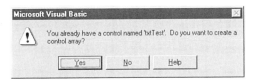

VB asks you this only the first time that you set two controls to have the same name. If you press the Yes button, Visual Basic sets the name of both controls to txtTest and sets the index of the two controls to different values. It gives one txtTest control an index of 0 and the other an index of 1.

Copying a Control

Copying a control involves placing a control on a form and then using the Copy and Paste options from Visual Basic's Edit menu to place an additional control with the same name on the form. Again, Visual Basic asks you to confirm that this is what you intend to do and, if you press the No button, it creates the new control with a unique name. Although the method to create the control array is different, Visual Basic behaves in the same way with regard to the creation of the control array itself.

Creating New Instances of Controls at Runtime

When the program runs, VB creates only as many of each control in an array as you created at design time. To create more elements in the control array than you specified at design time, you have to tell VB to do it in code.

Now that you know what a control array is and how to create one, the next problem to solve is how to create further instances of each control at runtime.

The Load Statement

In the credit card example, create five additional instances of these three controls. Use the Load statement, which creates controls at runtime. Delete the txtTest controls (if you added them in the previous example) and add the highlighted code in Listing 5.16 to the form's Load event subroutine.

LISTING 5.16 Loading Controls at Runtime

```
Private Sub Form_Load()

    Dim I As Integer

    ' Load additional control arrays.
    For I = 1 To 5
        Load cboCardName(I)
        Load txtCardNumber(I)
        Load txtExpDate(I)
        CboCardName(I).Visible = True
        TxtCardNumber(I).Visible = True
        TxtExpDate(I).Visible = True
    Next I

End Sub
```

In this example, I is the Index value for the new control object. Index 0 references the existing control object in each of your three arrays; to create subsequent controls in the array, you must start with I set to a value of 1.

 Note

Control object arrays are always indexed from 0, regardless of any Option Base that you may have set for the form.

When each new control is created, its properties are, with a few exceptions, set to the same values as the control on which it was based. The Visible property, however, is automatically set to False, so you need to change this value.

If you run the program, you still won't see the new controls, however. That's because they all occupy the same position on the form: The Top, Left, Height, and Width properties—which describe the object's position on the form—are the same as the control on which the other controls are based. As a result, you have to move each object so that you can see it at runtime.

The method used here is simply to calculate a new position for the control based on its position in the control array. The changes are highlighted in Listing 5.17. Don't worry too much about the details here; we'll cover coordinates in more detail in Chapter 8, "Using ActiveX Controls."

LISTING 5.17 The Controls So That You Can See Them

```
Private Sub Form_Load()
    Dim I As Integer

    ' Load additional control arrays.
    For I = 1 To 5
        Load cboCardName(I)
        Load txtCardNumber(I)
        Load txtExpDate(I)
        CboCardName(I).Visible = True
        TxtCardNumber(I).Visible = True
        TxtExpDate(I).Visible = True

        cboCardName(I).Top = cboCardName(0).Top _
                    + (I * cboCardName(0).Height)
        txtCardNumber(I).Top = txtCardNumber(0).Top _
                    + (I * txtCardNumber(0).Height)
        txtExpDate(I).Top = txtExpDate(0).Top _
                    + (I * txtExpDate(0).Height)
    Next I

End Sub
```

This code will move the new controls to a position relative to the original control's height and the new control's position in the array. Figure 5.29 shows you the form at runtime.

Referencing Indexed Controls in Your Code

We said earlier that the way to use an indexed control variable at runtime is to specify the Index property value of the control object that you want to access in parentheses after the variable name. Well, Visual Basic is pretty clever in that it recognizes when an event has occurred in a control object that is part of a control array and it provides you with the Index value in the event subroutine as a parameter to the subroutine.

Take a look at the GotFocus event subroutine for the txtCardNumber control:

```
Private Sub txtCardNumber_Click(Index As Integer)

End Sub
```

5

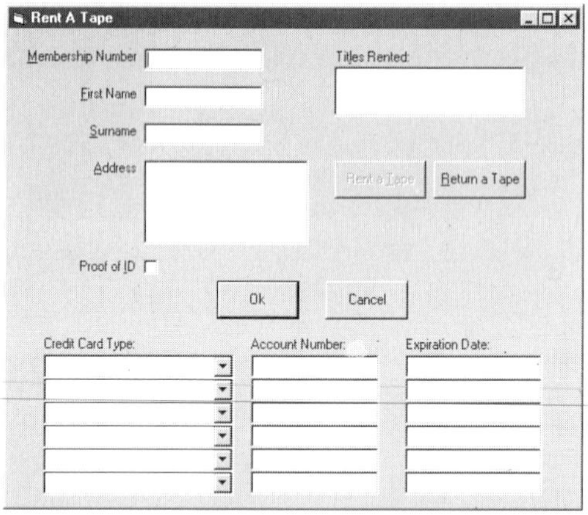

Figure 5.29

*Form with additional
controls created at
runtime.*

The subroutine has a parameter, `Index As Integer`, which it wouldn't otherwise have. The `Index` parameter contains the `Index` property value of the control that triggered the event. Try experimenting by entering the following line in this event routine:

```
txtCardNumber(Index).Text = "I'm index number " & Index
```

Now you can click a Card Number text box to see its index number. This is how you can create a single set of code that is run for all the control objects in a control array. It's a pretty powerful feature!

Lesson Summary

Up to this point, you had to access each object one by one. This is effective but very tedious if you have a lot of controls on the form. Using control arrays, you access a group of controls by using looping techniques like a `For...Next` Loop. As you get more advanced and you start linking your VB applications to databases, using control arrays can make working with data structures more efficient.

Quiz 7

1. Which of the following statements is not a reason to use a control array?

    a. A control array is useful when you don't know ahead of time how many controls you'll need during runtime

    b. A control array is useful when you are dealing with a group of nearly identical controls

    c. A control array lets you efficiently add functionality for each instance of the control

    d. A control array lets you group related controls, such as a label and the object it describes

2. Assume you created a control at design time named Text1. What do you need to do to be able to create elements of a Text1 control array at runtime?

    a. Set the `Array` property to `True`

    b. Set the `Index` property to `0`

    c. Create a second Text1 at design time and set its `Visible` property to `False`

    d. Nothing; you can create control arrays from any control

3. In the same situation as Question 2, which statement creates an element in the Text1 control array at runtime?

    a. `Create Text1`

    b. `Load Text1`

    c. `Load.Text1`

    d. `Text1 = True`

4. Finally, what additional processing do you need to do for Text1?

    a. Initialize its contents to `Null`

    b. Set the focus to the control

    c. Assign it different coordinates from Text1 and make it visible

    d. Copy all the data from Text1 into Text1

Exercise 7

Complexity: Easy

1. Create a program with a control array of 10 command buttons. When the user presses on a button, the index value of the command button will appear in a text box.

Complexity: Easy

2. Write a program that will add all the values in an array of text boxes to a list box.

Chapter Summary

This chapter presented the basic operations and techniques of a lot of the standard VB controls you will use within your VB applications. In very little time, you will master the properties and methods of these controls. Here is a recap of the important points covered in this chapter.

- The text box can be used for single or multiple-line data entry.

- In a text box, don't forget to change the ScrollBars property if you want to be able to view the information that goes beyond the left side and bottom of the control.

- The ampersand in front of a letter within Label creates an accelerator key combination.

- MsgBox is either a statement or function depending on how it is referenced in your code.

- Setting the Default property on a command button will cause this button's event to trigger if the user presses the Enter key; however, if the focus is on any command button, the Default value is ignored.

- Setting the Cancel property on a command button will cause the button's event to trigger if the user presses the Esc key.

- Check boxes, option buttons, list boxes, and combo boxes limit the range of user data to predefined values.

- The Frame control enables you to display any set of controls as a logical group. This is extremely useful when it comes to option buttons.

- Control arrays provide a way to access a set of controls with limited coding by using a looping technique like For...Next.

If you move beyond these basic intrinsic controls and start using third-party controls, such as Sheridan Software's DataWidgets, you will discover that a lot of the properties and methods are based on the these basic controls. They will, of course, have more features and functionality, but a lot of what you learned in this chapter will help you understand those controls.

In Chapter 6, "Building the GUI with Forms, Menus, and MDI Forms," you will discover how to effectively make a graphical user interface (GUI) with the controls you have become familiar with in this chapter.

CHAPTER 6

Building the GUI with Forms, Menus, and MDI Forms

Although you've been using forms since Chapter 1, "What's All That Stuff on My Screen?" you've been using them in a very simple way. Forms, like controls, have properties, events, and methods. You can customize the way the form looks and acts depending on your application's needs. Furthermore, there is more than one type of form for you to use.

In this chapter, we're going to address some of the design aspects that you need to consider when using different types of forms. As we progress, we'll build a new application based on the MDI (Multiple Document Interface) style of form, which we'll use as a platform for demonstrating the ideas that we introduce.

Learning about forms, handling form variables and properties across instances of the same forms, and studying related concepts, such as form collections, will give you the skills and confidence to build programs that look and act like professional Windows applications.

LESSON 1

Forms

In every project you have written so far, you have been using a form entitled Form1 as part of the default project. This form is actually a type of window called a *single document interface* (SDI) window.

Don't confuse the terms *window* and *form*. For our purposes, they are one and the same. You already know from experience that Windows applications work by displaying windows on your computer's screen. Well, a form is just the name given to a window in a Visual Basic project.

The word *document* in single document interface is important, because many Windows programs work with documents of one type or another.

What Is a Document?

We all know what a document is in the real world—think of legal documents, insurance documents, and don't forget tax documents. However, whereas a real-world document is an official piece of paper, we are using the word in a different sense to describe a collection of data that can be worked on as a unit by a particular application program. In fact, Visual Basic itself is an example of a program that works with documents of a particular type—in this case, your project.

How does all this affect the design of your applications? When we designed the Video Store application in Chapter 5, "Controls," we didn't have documents in mind. Instead, we designed the form around the individual data items (name, address, and so on) that the application had to process. Applications that are designed this way are data-centric applications. If you change the structure of the data, you usually have to make sweeping changes to the structure of the application.

Although there isn't anything wrong with designing data-centric applications, Windows programs are particularly suited to working in a different way—a *document-centric* way. In this chapter, we are going to look at using forms in the context of the document-centric application—but more on that in a moment.

Single Document and Multiple Document Interface

Document-centric applications can let the user work on either one document at a time (single document) or more than one document at a time (multiple document).

Windows WordPad, for example, can work on only one document at a time. If you try to create a new document or open an existing one, WordPad has to store the currently loaded document to disk or abandon it first. If you want to have two different documents loaded at the same time, you have to run two copies (we call them *instances*) of WordPad and load each document into its own copy of WordPad.

So, WordPad is a single document interface (SDI) application. However, you don't have to design your projects to work on just one document at a time; with careful preparation, you can build applications capable of working on more than one document with very little extra work. Such applications are known as *multiple document interface* (MDI) applications. Microsoft Word, for example, is an MDI application, because it can have more than one document open. Notepad is an SDI application, because it can have only one document open at a time.

You can use Visual Basic to create both styles of applications. In the next lesson, you will begin to develop an MDI application to demonstrate how this is done. For the moment, however, let's stick to finding out more about document-centric user interfaces and how such a user interface might influence application design.

A Typical SDI Application

Let's take a brief look at another document-centric application: Windows Notepad. (This application is in the Accessories folder if you're using Windows 95, or the Accessories program group of Windows 3.x.)

When you run Notepad, it displays a window, as shown in Figure 6.1.

FIGURE 6.1

Notepad running under Windows.

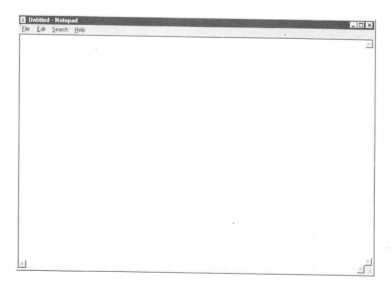

6

Notepad is basically a text editor—a kind of baby word processor. You use it to create or edit documents that contain only printable characters, such as letters and numbers, rather than any special formatting. You can't make words bold, change their font, or italicize them as you can with a proper "grown up" word processor. Notepad is a useful little application, though, and for our purposes, it's a great example of a document-centric SDI application.

Document-centric Windows applications follow certain fundamental conventions in the way their user interfaces are designed. Although those conventions are not cast in stone, it's a big help to your users if your programs work in a way that is similar to applications that they're already using.

Notepad's User Interface

Let's look at Notepad's user interface a little more closely.

First, when you started Notepad, what did it do? It created a fresh document of the type that it works on, a text document, ready for you to start editing. Visual Basic 6 also creates a fresh document, the default project, ready for you to start editing. Although the detail of the documents is different, the overall behavior of both applications is the same.

Let's now look in more detail at the window Notepad displays.

The Title Bar

At the top of Notepad's window is a title bar. Notepad uses it to display both the title of the document that it is working on and its own name. This is another convention that document-centric applications follow. In Notepad's case, it has called the new text document Untitled. Visual Basic 6 works a little differently. It gives the default project the name Project1.

The Menu

Below the title bar is the menu bar. The menu is the way in which your program's users can tell your program what to do. It's important that your programs follow a menu design similar to other document-centric applications.

Notice that both Notepad and Visual Basic have File, Edit, and Help menus and that both programs use the same accelerator keys for those menus: Alt+F, Alt+E, and Alt+H. These three menus are the minimum menus that any SDI document-centric application should have.

The File Menu

The File menu, shown in Figure 6.2, is where you put the commands that relate to your document as a whole. This is where your users can create new documents, load existing ones, and save them to disk. If you look at both Notepad and Visual Basic 6's File menus, you will see these commands under the names New, Open, Save, and Save As. Notice that the accelerators used are the same.

FIGURE 6.2

The File menu.

The Edit Menu

The Edit menu, shown in Figure 6.3, is where you put the editing commands. Both Notepad and Visual Basic share certain Edit menu commands. They both have Cut, Copy, Paste, and Delete options. These are the standard menu commands that use the Windows Clipboard. You will see how to program access to the Clipboard later in this chapter.

FIGURE 6.3

The Edit menu.

The Help Menu

The Help menu, shown in Figure 6.4, is where you would place the commands concerned with context-sensitive help for your application. You would also place a menu command to display an About box, a window that gives some basic information about your application—such as its version number or who wrote it. Again, this is something we'll do in this chapter.

FIGURE 6.4

The Help menu.

6

Lesson Summary

Now that you have a better understanding of what MDI and SDI applications are, we'll start development of an MDI application in the next lesson.

Quiz 1

1. What is the difference between a window and a form?

    a. For our purposes, they are one and the same.

    b. A window is an interface created outside of Visual Basic, and Forms are created by Visual Basic.

    c. A Form is a type of Window.

    d. A Form can hold a document, such as Notepad.

2. What are the minimal menus that any SDI document-centric application should have?

    a. Title, File, and Help

    b. Help, File, and Edit

    c. File, Edit, Cut, Copy, Paste, Delete, and Help

    d. File, Help, and About

3. Where do you put commands that relate to your document as a whole?

    a. The File Menu

    b. The Edit Menu

    c. The Help Menu

    d. The About Menu

4. Which are typical SDI applications?

    a. Visual Basic and Windows

    b. Notepad and Word

    c. Notepad and WordPad

    d. All of the above

Exercise 1

Complexity: Easy

1. Create a form called `frmDocument`. Add a `TextBox` control and name it textbox1. Add another `TextBox` control beneath the first one and name it textbox2.

Complexity: Moderate

2. Create a form called `frmDocument` and give it a `TexBox` control. Change a `textbox` property so that no text appears initially in the text box upon execution. Then change the properties of the `TextBox` control so that it can handle more than one line of text.

LESSON 2

SDI and MDI Applications

Now that you appreciate more of what's involved in the user interface of a document-centric application, you're going to use that information to develop a sort of super Notepad, one that works with multiple documents. We'll call it HyperPad!

Building HyperPad's User Interface

The major departure from what we've done before is that HyperPad is going to be an MDI application. As part of learning how to build up the user interface of such an application, you'll also learn more about defining and programming menus, and you'll learn how to use the Clipboard.

The only functions that we don't cover in this chapter are printing—the use of the CommonDialog control to provide Open, Save As, and Print dialog boxes—and toolbars. Printing is covered in Chapter 9, "Printing," and the CommonDialog controls are covered in Chapter 8, "Using ActiveX Controls."

Adding an MDI Form to Your Project

Run Visual Basic if it is not already running and start a new project. Go to the Project menu and add an MDI form to your project by selecting the Add MDI Form menu entry.

An MDI form is basically a frame inside which other windows are displayed. The advantage of having an MDI application is that the user can work on more than one document within the same application.

Although your project can have multiple SDI forms, it can have only one MDI form at a time. If you look at the Project menu, you'll find that the MDI Form entry is now disabled (grayed out).

So, MDIForm1 will become the startup form, providing the frame to display the individual document windows inside. You will use Form1 as the form for the individual documents.

Naming the Forms

The next thing you have to do is change MDIForm1's name to something more appropriate. Call it frmMain because it's the main form in your project. You should also change the name of Form1 for the same reasons. Call it frmDocument.

The Title Bars

The text in a form's title bar is determined by the text in its Caption property. Set the Caption property of frmMain to HyperPad. Similarly, set the Caption property of

6

frmDocument to Untitled, which is the default name that you want to give to new documents. That way, when the user creates a new document at runtime, the document will automatically have the caption Untitled, and you can use the text in the form's Caption property as the name of the document.

You now need to think about the type of document that you want to be able to edit. Remember that our definition of a document is any collection of information that can be treated as a unit. In this particular case, you want the user to be able to edit a text document, so your document will consist of the individual characters that make up its text. Use the standard TextBox control to display and edit the text.

HyperPad's Text Box

Select the TextBox control in the toolbox and try to drag it onto frmMain. It won't go! An MDI form is a frame for other forms. You can't drag any old control onto it. There are certain controls that you can place on an MDI form, but they are special-purpose controls used to implement toolbars and status bars. You will see how to use those controls in Chapter 7, "Building Classes: The Foundation of Visual Basic OOP." (Additionally, you'll see in Lesson 5 how to add menus, which are actually a kind of control, to an MDI form.)

The text box is going to have to sit on frmDocument, the SDI form. Add the text box described in Table 6.1 to frmDocument. It doesn't matter where you place the text box on the form or what size you make it. You will tackle the problem of changing the size of the text box shortly.

TABLE 6.1   The SDI Form's Text Box

Object	Property	Value
TextBox	Name	txtDocument
	Text	None
	MultiLine	True
	ScrollBars	2 - Vertical

The MDIChild Property

All SDI forms are capable of being displayed within the frame of an MDI form, but to enable that behavior, you have to set a property in the form first. The property is called the MDIChild property, and it is normally set to False. Set it to True now for frmDocument.

A child form is just a form that has its MDIChild property set to True. The difference is that all the child forms will be displayed within the workspace of the MDI parent form.

Taking a Look

Let's take a look at the program. When you run the program, you can see (as in Figure 6.5) that the window relationships are visually and functionally apparent. If you move the HyperPad window, the document moves with it. Similarly, you can move the document around, but not outside, its parent form. You can resize the child window, maximize it, and minimize it. If you close it, however, you will lose it, because you have not yet inserted code to create new child forms.

FIGURE 6.5

The frmDocument *inside the MDI form.*

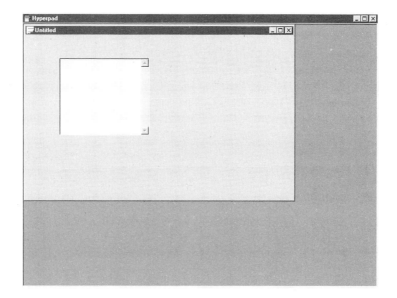

The Icon Property

When you run any Windows application, you do so by clicking its icon (from the Start button in Windows 95 or from an appropriate program group in other versions of Windows). When the user minimizes an application's main window, the program is represented by the same icon on the computer's desktop. Unless you specify otherwise, Visual Basic 6 uses default icons for both frmMain and frmDocument. These are basic icons signifying that frmMain is an MDI form and frmDocument is an SDI form. Figure 6.6 shows you how the standard icons look.

6

FIGURE 6.6

The standard form icons.

Visual Basic 6 comes complete with a library of icons. You are going to use two icons from the icons\writing directory to represent what your program does. To assign an icon to a form, simply select the Icon property for that form and then select the filename, just as you did to preload a picture into a PictureBox control. Set note03.ico for frmMain and note07.ico for frmDocument. These are shown in Figure 6.7.

FIGURE 6.7

The replacement icons.

Set the Startup Form

Now click Project1 Properties under the Project menu and select the General tab. Set the startup form to be frmMain, as shown in Figure 6.8.

FIGURE 6.8

Setting the Startup form to frmMain.

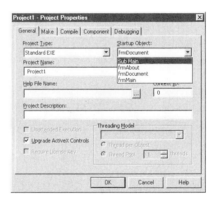

Lesson Summary

We have just completed our first MDI/SDI application, but we are nowhere near done with it yet! In the upcoming lessons, we'll give it professional functionality that other applications enjoy. Next, we'll learn how to create additional forms at runtime.

Quiz 2

1. The difference between and SDI application and an MDI application is that

    a. A user can open more than one session of an MDI application, as compared to one session with an SDI application.

    b. An SDI application uses fewer system resources overall than an MDI application.

    c. A user can work on more than one document at a time with an MDI application.

    d. An MDI application has many more options than an SDI application.

2. What does MDI stand for?

    a. Multiple Document Interface

    b. Menu Document Interface

    c. Many Document Interface

    d. Multiple Data Interface

3. An MDI form is basically

    a. A window inside which other windows are displayed

    b. A form inside which other forms are displayed

    c. A form inside which other windows are displayed

    d. A frame inside which other windows are displayed

4. The text in a form's title bar is determined by:

    a. The type of documents the form can load

    b. The type of document the form can currently load

    c. The Caption property of the MDI form

    d. The Caption property of the SDI form

Exercise 2

Complexity: Easy

1. Change the frmDocument so that it has an icon Note04.ico and place a label above the edit box titled "Document." Change both the frmMain and frmDocument so that both are maximized upon execution.

Complexity: Moderate

2. Add a second form to the HyperPad program. Name it frmDocument2 and make it a child of frmMain. Give it a multiple-line TextBox control (with no text inside) and assign it icon Note05.ico. Then make it appear in front of frmDocument upon running the program.

LESSON 3

Creating Forms at Runtime

One of the main things your program has do is to create new documents, each of which will display in a separate frmDocument window. There are three occasions when you will want to do this:

- When your application starts so that your user has a default document with which to work
- When your user uses the menu to create a new document
- When your user uses the menu to open an existing document

An AddForm Function

Place code to display a form in a function called AddForm in the frmMain module. Bring up the Code window for frmMain by selecting the frmMain form in the Project window. Then right-click and select View Code from the menu. Select Add Procedure from the Tools menu and fill out the Add Procedure dialog box to insert an AddForm function with Private scope, as shown in Figure 6.9.

FIGURE 6.9

Complete the Add Procedure dialog box as shown.

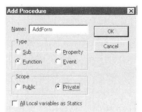

Now click the OK button on the Insert Procedure dialog box and Visual Basic 6 creates the function declaration for you. It appears as shown in Figure 6.10.

FIGURE 6.10

Code window with
AddForm *function.*

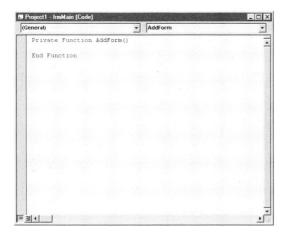

Because this function is going to add a form to the application, you need to modify its return value to return a variable of type Form:

```
Private Function AddForm() As Form

End Function
```

In case you don't quite understand how a form can be represented by a variable, think about what happens when you specify that a form should be the startup form. A variable is automatically created for you with the same name as the form, enabling you to access that form's properties and methods. You've been doing this with frmDocument for some time now, although you probably didn't think of frmDocument as a variable. When you create a form at runtime, you need to obtain a similar variable to access the new form. Listing 6.1 shows the code to do this.

LISTING 6.1   Adding a New Form at Runtime

```
Private Function AddForm() As Form
    Dim frmNewDoc As Form
    Set frmNewDoc = New frmDocument
    frmNewDoc.Show vbModeless
    Set AddForm = frmNewDoc
End Function
```

6

We'll look at this function line by line so that you see exactly what it's doing.

Form Variables

First, you declare a new variable of type Form. You're not actually creating a form at this point, just the variable where you will store the reference to the actual form.

```
Dim frmNewDoc As Form
```

The New Keyword

At this stage, frmNewDoc could be used to refer to any form in the application, even frmMain. Before you can use it, you have to assign a form to it. This is done in the second line:

```
Set frmNewDoc = New frmDocument
```

This line is doing all the hard work. It's actually doing two jobs. The code to the right of the equal sign is the part that's creating the new form. It's using frmDocument as a mold to create an identical copy of that form, complete with controls. It then assigns a reference to the form to the variable frmNewDoc so that you can access that form's properties and methods.

Showing the Form

Now that you have assigned the new form to a form variable, you can call its methods. Prior to this statement, although the form existed, it had not been displayed. To display it, you have to call its Show method. Call this method with the built-in constant vbModeless because you want the user to be able to switch between the forms in the application.

```
frmNewDoc.Show vbModeless
```

The Set Statement

Finally, you assign the form variable frmNewDoc to the name of the function AddForm with the line

```
Set AddForm = frmNewDoc
```

This is so you can return a form variable to the procedure that calls this function, so that it too can obtain a copy of the form variable.

Notice that you're using the Set statement when you assign form references, rather than just using a standard assignment operator on its own. You cannot simply write

```
AddForm = frmNewDoc
```

because frmNewDoc is a form variable, rather than a built-in data type. However, the analogy between the two types of assignments is sound.

Calling the `AddForm` Function

All that's left to do now is call this function to create a new document, a new instance of the document form. For now, add it at the point at which the application begins, in the `Load` event handler for the `frmMain` form. Add this code, as shown in Listing 6.2.

LISTING 6.2   The `MDIForm_Load` Routine

```
Private Sub MDIForm_Load()
    AddForm
End Sub
```

For the moment, you aren't doing anything with the form variable that `AddForm` returns. Although you could store it somewhere, at present you're just throwing it away. This doesn't mean that the form won't exist anymore. In fact, the form continues to exist until the user closes it. This just means that you have lost your copy of the variable that references the form. You will see that this is not necessarily as important as it may appear at first because there are techniques that you can use to obtain the form variable when you need it. We'll show you those techniques in the next lesson.

This is a good time to save the file. Save `frmDocument` as `SuperDoc.Frm` and `frmMain` as `SuperMDI.Frm`. Save the project as `HyperPad.VBP`. Run the program. HyperPad appears as shown in Figure 6.5, except this time the Editing window is opened in code instead, because it is the startup form.

Although the text box doesn't look quite right yet, you'll find that the windows behave just as you would expect them to. You can drag their borders to change their size and minimize and maximize them. When you maximize the document window, the title bar of the `frmMain` form reflects this by adding the name of the document to its title, just like Notepad and Visual Basic! This is shown in Figure 6.11.

You can even close the document window, although you can't create a new one yet.

Optimizing `AddForm`

Before you add further functionality to HyperPad, let's return to `AddForm` for a moment. The version of `AddForm` that you've written is not exactly optimized. To tell the truth, it's written in a way that helps clarify the steps involved in creating a new form at runtime. Now that you understand these steps, you can reduce that function from four lines of code to just two. Replace `AddForm` with the code in Listing 6.3. You'll find the program runs just as before.

FIGURE **6.11**

View of HyperPad with maximized document.

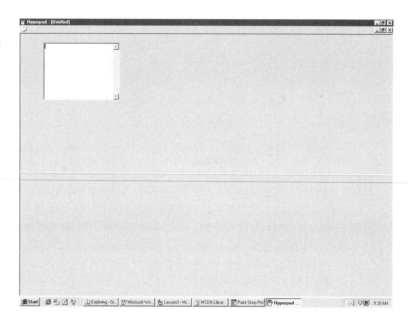

LISTING 6.3 Optimized AddForm

```
Private Function AddForm() As frmDocument
    Set AddForm = New frmDocument
    AddForm.Show vbModeless
End Function
```

Note that you changed the declaration of the function slightly. It no longer returns a variable of type Form. Now it's returning a variable of type frmDocument.

Hang on a moment, frmDocument is something you've added to the project. How can you suddenly use a form that you've added to the project as if it were a built-in data type, like an integer? Well, this is exactly what you can do. It's a pretty powerful feature. Furthermore, it means that you don't have to declare a new Form variable explicitly within the body of the function. Remember that by declaring that a function has a return value, you declare a new variable, and you can use that variable in the function by using the name of the function to refer to the variable. So, by declaring AddForm to return a frmDocument variable, you have declared a variable that you can use during the function. Of course, you still have to create the form, assign the newly created form to the AddForm return variable, and show the form. This time, however, you can use the return variable to access the form's Show method.

Lesson Summary

In this lesson we learned how create a new form at runtime. We created a procedure call `AddForm` to perform this task. In the next lesson, we'll learn to manipulate the size and position of our forms.

Quiz 3

1. What is happening when the following line of code is executed?

   ```
   Dim frmNewDoc As Form
   ```

   a. The form `frmNewDoc` is created

   b. The variable where the form will be stored is created

   c. Both a and b

   d. None of the above

2. What does the following line of code accomplish?

   ```
   Set frmNewDoc = New Form
   ```

   a. It creates the new form `frmNewDoc`

   b. It creates the new form `frmDocument`

   c. It assigns a reference to the form of the variable `frmNewDoc`

   d. Both a and c

3. Which line of code is the proper use of the `Set` statement?

   a. `Set frmNewDOc = New frmDocument`

   b. `Set frmNewDocShow(vbModeless)`

   c. `Set New frmNewDoc = frmDocument`

   d. `Set New frmNewDoc = New frmDocument`

4. After assigning a new form (`frmNewDoc`) to a form variable, how do you call its `Show` method such that the user will be able to switch between the forms in the application?

   a. `frmNewDoc.Show vbModeless`

   b. `frmNewDoc.Show(vbModeless)`

   c. `frmNewDoc.Show = vbModeless`

   d. `frmNewDoc.Show.vbModeless`

6

Exercise 3

Complexity: Easy

1. Change the non-optimized `AddForm` function so that it creates two forms upon execution instead of one.

Complexity: Moderate

2. Alter the HyperPad project such that a new form is created every time the user double-clicks `frmDocument`.

LESSON 4

Resizing and Positioning the Form

We said we'd fix that text box and show you some techniques for obtaining the form variable, so let's do both of these right now. When we obtain the form variable, we'll cover some screen resolution issues.

Prepping the Text Box for Editing

At the moment, the text box is just sitting there, looking rather sorry for itself. It's not behaving correctly. Every time the user resizes the document window, for example, the text box stays the same size.

When the new instance of `frmDocument` is created, it is displayed at first with a certain size and at a particular position. In fact, the size of the new document form is related to the size of its MDI parent form. You can prove this by changing the size of `frmMain` before you run your project. The `frmDocument` window, which is an MDI child window, is sized proportionally to the size of `frmMain`.

Also, when `frmDocument` has been created, there is nothing to stop your users from changing its size and position. In short, you can never tell how big to make the text box on the document form at design time. You have to wait until that form is running.

The `Resize` Event

The solution to this problem is to find out whenever the size of an instance of the `frmDocument` form changes and to change the size of that one form's text box at that time. Fortunately, there is an event that lets you do this: the `Resize` event.

Use the Code window to display the event subroutines for the frmDocument form. You will find the Resize event in the list of event procedures for the form in the Proc combo box.

Create a declaration for the event by clicking the Resize event in the Proc combo box. The declaration will appear as follows:

```
Private Sub Form_Resize()

End Sub
```

When you create a new form at runtime, Visual Basic 6 creates a completely fresh copy of the form you originally designed. Using the object-oriented terms you learned in Chapter 2, "Object-Oriented Programming," the runtime form is an instance of that form's class. Each instance of that form has its own copy of the form properties and any form variables that you've declared. So changing the properties of one instance of the form does not affect any other instance. However, although the data associated with each instance of the form is different each time, the program code that runs is shared between all instances of the form. This means that you have to go to only one place, the Code window for frmDocument, to program all the document forms in your running application.

Let's use the Resize event subroutine to change the size of the txtDocument text box. You want to make it the same size as the inside of frmDocument. The code to do that is shown in Listing 6.4.

LISTING 6.4   The Resize Event Routine

```
Private Sub Form_Resize()
   Me.txtDocument.Top = 0
   Me.txtDocument.Left = 0
   Me.txtDocument.Width = Me.ScaleWidth
   Me.txtDocument.Height = Me.ScaleHeight
End Sub
```

6

Run the project again just to satisfy yourself that this code works. Resize and move the document window. HyperPad now sizes its text box correctly, as shown in Figure 6.12.

Now let's take a look at the code you added.

FIGURE 6.12

View of HyperPad with the text box fixed up.

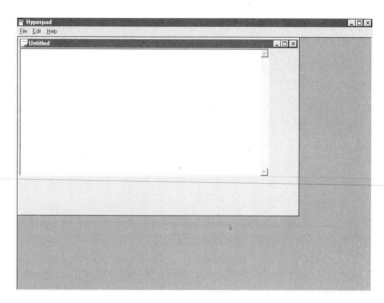

The Me Keyword

Each line of code makes some use of the keyword Me, as in

```
Me.txtDocument.Top = 0
```

The Me keyword is a reserved keyword in Visual Basic 6 that refers to a particular running instance of a form. It is equivalent to the form variable for that form. You can use Me to refer to the form that is in context. For example, Me in a line of code in frmMain refers to the frmMain form, whereas Me in a line of code in the frmDocument form refers to one instance of the frmDocument form. When you have only one instance of a form in an application, such as frmMain in this application, it's easy to tell which window Me refers to. However, imagine you have five or six frmDocument windows. How can you tell which form Me will relate to in those circumstances?

In a multiple document scenario, Me always relates to the document that triggered the event. So you can safely use Me in the Form_Resize subroutine to access the properties of any instance of frmDocument. If the first instance of frmDocument was the one resized, that form's text box would be changed, and so on. You don't have to use any other technique to obtain the form's form variable.

The Top, Left, Width, and Height Properties

So far, you haven't had to worry very much about the coordinates of controls. It's so convenient to use the mouse to draw the controls where you want them that you haven't had to think about what's going on behind the scenes. The properties that set the coordinates (and size) of an object are Top, Left, Width, and Height. All objects have these properties; when you position them with the mouse, VB figures out the coordinates and assigns the values for you.

You can see this in action very easily. In design mode, bring up the form view of frmDocument and position the Properties window so that you can see both windows at the same time. Now move the text box around on the form. Notice when you let go of the text box in a new position that the values of Top and Left change. Similarly, resize the text box and watch Width and Height change.

You can set these values manually in the Properties window at any time. You may want to do this, for example, if you're lining up controls on a form, as you did in Chapter 5, "Controls," for the Video Store program. It might be easier to set all the Left properties to the same number, rather than trying to line up the controls by sight. The Format menu lets you do this even more easily; a few mouse clicks and everything is aligned.

Similarly, you can set the values in code, just as you would any other property value, which is what you're doing in the Resize event.

Changing Object Coordinates in Code

The Top and Left property values are always relative to an object's container control. For example, use the Properties window to set frmDocument's Top property to 0. The form moves to the top of the screen. Now run the program. The form is now at the top of the MDI form because at runtime that window is the container for the frmDocument.

Similarly, the lines

```
Me.txtDocument.Top = 0
Me.txtDocument.Left = 0
```

in the Resize event above set the text box's position within the document form. The position of the form on the screen doesn't affect this.

Now let's move on to the lines

```
Me.txtDocument.Width = Me.ScaleWidth
Me.txtDocument.Height = Me.ScaleHeight
```

Here you're setting the width and height of the text box. However, the expressions Me.ScaleWidth and Me.ScaleHeight require a little explanation.

The ScaleWidth property of a form, at runtime, returns the internal width of the form. This is the width from the inside edge of the left border to the inside edge of the right border. Similarly, the ScaleHeight property returns the internal height of the form. These measurements are different from the standard Width and Height properties of a form, which measure the form to its external edges. This is important. If you tried to set the width and height of the TextBox control to the external width and height of the form, the text box would be too big for the form! This is a common mistake made by many programmers new to Visual Basic.

That's all there is to it. You'll now find that no matter how you size the document form at runtime, the text box resizes itself correctly. It's fixed!

The Move Method

Before we move on to looking at some other techniques, let's do a little optimization on the code that you've just written. It turns out you can replace the four lines of code that you've just written with a single line of code! It reads as follows:

```
Me.txtDocument.Move 0, 0, Me.ScaleWidth, Me.ScaleHeight
```

Here you are calling the text box's Move method. The four parameters are the values that will be placed into the Top, Left, Width, and Height properties of the control. You can also use this method to move an object without resizing it; the Width and Height parameters are optional.

Now you have a document form that automatically resizes its text box every time it is resized. The Resize event is triggered when the form is first displayed, so you don't need to provide the same functionality in any other event subroutine for the form.

Screen Resolution

One trap you should be careful not to fall into is using fixed-size forms. Bear in mind that although you might be working with a top-of-the-line computer monitor capable of displaying very high resolutions, your users may be running on something more down to earth. You've already seen that Visual Basic 6 faithfully reproduces the size and position of your MDI forms to the same size as you left them at design time. The same is true for ordinary (non-MDI child) SDI forms, too. Unless you're careful, you could easily end up trying to display a form that is too large for the physical screen on which it is being displayed.

One technique is to assume that your users have simple VGA resolution screens and to size all your forms accordingly. This is the "lowest common denominator" approach. A far more satisfactory solution would be to change the position and size of the main window when that window is created but before it is actually displayed. The form's Load event subroutine is ideal for implementing this.

The `Screen` Object

Visual Basic 6 supplies a built-in object, called the `Screen` object, that you can use to determine the size of the physical screen on which your application is displayed at run-time. The `Screen` object has two properties that you can use to help calculate how large to make your forms. Say you want to size `frmMain` so that it is 75 percent of the width and height of the screen so it is centered in the middle of the screen, regardless of how large the physical screen is.

The code to do this is presented in Listing 6.5.

LISTING 6.5 Centering HyperPad on Any Size Screen

```
Private Sub MDIForm_Load()
Me.Height = Screen.Height * 0.75
Me.Width = Screen.Width * 0.75
Me.Move (Screen.Height - Me.Height) / 2, (Screen.Width - Me.Width) / 2

AddForm
End Sub
```

Here you are setting the height and width of the form to 75 percent of the actual height and width of the screen. After you've done this, you can center the form on the screen by moving it as shown. All you're doing is taking the height and width of the screen, subtracting the new height and width of the form, and dividing the remaining space by 2 to center the form on the screen. HyperPad will have proportionally the same size no matter what screen resolution you run it on.

Lesson Summary

In this lesson, we learned how to position and re-size our forms, and we even took the physical screen size in consideration. In the next lesson, we'll explore how to add Menus to our application.

Quiz 4

1. The properties that set the coordinates and size of an object are
    a. `Top, Bottom, Left, Right`
    b. `Top, Bottom, Width, Height`
    c. `Top, Down, Left, Right`
    d. `Top, Left, Width, Height`

2. Which is an advantage of using the `Move` command?

   a. It can move an object without resizing it

   b. It can both move and resize and object

   c. It helps optimize code

   d. All of the above

3. Which line of code just moves an object to the corner of the screen, and does not resize it?

   a. `Me.txtDocument.Move 0,0,0,0`

   b. `Me.txtDocument.Move 0,0`

   c. `Me.txtDocument.Move 0,0,NULL,NULL`

   d. `Me.txtDocument.Move 0,0,,`

4. Which are valid properties of the `Screen` object?

   a. `Screen.Height, Screen.ScaleHeight, Screen.Width, Screen.ScaleWidth`

   b. `Screen.Height, Screen.Width`

   c. `Screen.ScaleHeight, Screen.ScaleWidth`

   d. None of the above

Exercise 4

Complexity: Easy

1. Create an empty form. Set the width and height to 5000. Using the `width` and `height` properties, write code that will prevent the user from changing the size of the form.

Complexity: Moderate

2. Set up an MDI parent form and add a child document. Set up the project so that when the program is run, no child document is displayed. Create a File menu with two options: New and Quit. Enable the options so that when the user clicks New, a new form is generated.

LESSON 5

Adding Menus to Your Project

Now it's time to look at adding menus to the project. From the earlier look at Notepad's menus, you've got a pretty good idea what menus you want to add to HyperPad. You used Menu Editor in Chapter 2, "Object-Oriented Programming," to add a rudimentary menu to the file picker. Let's take a closer look at menus, now that you're older and wiser.

What Is a Menu?

A menu in Visual Basic 6 terms is a type of control. As such, it has a lot in common with the controls that you've already used. Menus, like other controls, have properties and events. However, they don't have any methods. Also, each menu item is a separate menu control. You can set some of the properties of a menu when you add the menu item using Menu Editor. Alternatively, after you have completed adding a menu item to a form, you can use the Properties window to change the properties of an individual menu item. We'll show you how to do this later in this lesson.

Before you display Menu Editor, you have to display the form to which you want to add the menu. Display frmMain and then select Menu Editor from the Tools menu.

Learning to Use Menu Editor

The Menu Editor is shown in Figure 6.13.

FIGURE 6.13

Menu Editor window.

6

Adding Top-Level Menu Items

At the top of the window is a text box labeled Caption. This is where you enter the text that will appear on the menu bar. Initially, you want to add three top-level menus to the menu bar: the File, Edit, and Help menus. Let's deal with the File menu first.

Add the text &File to the Caption text box. You can add an accelerator to a menu as easily as you can to a Label control by prefixing the accelerator character with an ampersand.

The next thing to do is to give this menu item a name. Like a control, each individual item in the menu, from top-level items down, has to have a name. Use a naming convention similar to the one used for controls and forms and call this menu item mnuFile. Set the Name text box to mnuFile.

Menu Editor should now appear as shown in Figure 6.14.

FIGURE 6.14

Completed Menu Edit window.

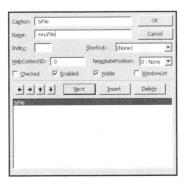

The next task is to add the Edit and Help menus to the menu bar. At the bottom of Menu Editor is a list box that currently contains one item, the File menu that you just added. This list box represents the menu hierarchy and can display every menu item, regardless of its level in the menu hierarchy.

To add a new top-level menu after the File menu (this will be the Edit menu), just click the Next button. Figure 6.15 shows the empty entry highlighted.

Enter the name mnuEdit and the caption &Edit for the Edit menu. Then add a menu for &Help/mnuHelp. Now when you click the OK button, the menu bar contains all three menus, as shown in Figure 6.16.

FIGURE 6.15

Adding a menu item to the end of the menu.

FIGURE 6.16

The design mode frmMain *with menus.*

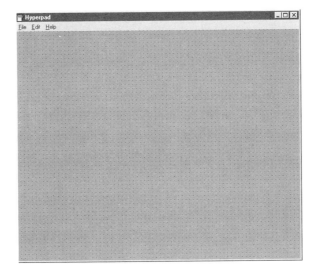

Adding Subordinate Menu Items to the Top-Level Menus

Now that you've added the top-level menus, you need to add the individual menu items that your users can select to send commands to HyperPad.

Return to Menu Editor. Select the Edit menu item on the list box and then press the Insert button. You now have a blank item you can use to add an item under the File menu, as shown in Figure 6.17. Note that Insert always inserts the new menu item above the selected menu item.

FIGURE **6.17**

Inserting a menu item.

Set the caption to &New and the name to mnuFileNew. Structuring the name in this way serves as a reminder to you that this new menu should be a submenu item of the File menu. Recall that the arrow keys above the list box in Menu Editor control the position of each menu item in the menu. You can move a menu item up or down the list by pressing the up or down arrows. Similarly, you can make an individual menu item a subordinate to the item that appears directly above it in the list box by pressing the right arrow key. This is shown for the New menu item in Figure 6.18.

FIGURE **6.18**

Making mnuFileNew *a submenu of* mnuFile.

Add the rest of the menus now. The captions and names for the menus are detailed in Tables 6.2, 6.3, and 6.4.

TABLE 6.2   mnuFile Menu Items

Caption	Name
&New	mnuFileNew
&Open...	mnuFileOpen
&Close	mnuFileClose

Caption	Name
&Save	mnuFileSave
Save &As...	mnuFileSaveAs
Print Set&up...	mnuFilePrintSetup
&Print...	mnuFilePrint
E&xit	mnuFileExit

TABLE 6.3   mnuEdit Menu Items

Caption	Name
Cu&t	mnuEditCut
&Copy	mnuEditCopy
&Paste	mnuEditPaste
De&lete	mnuEditDelete
Select &All	mnuEditSelectAll
Time/&Date	mnuEditTimeDate
&Word Wrap	mnuEditWordWrap

TABLE 6.4   mnuHelp Menu Items

Caption	Name
&About HyperPad	mnuHelpAbout

As you can see, you have quite a bit of additional functionality to add to HyperPad yet, some of which we won't tackle until later in the book.

Shortcut Keys

If you look at Notepad's menus, you will see additional *shortcut* keys that you can use to access specific menu items quickly. For instance, to add the time and date to the document, you can simply press the F5 key. You want to reproduce these types of shortcuts in HyperPad. Menu Editor assists you in this task.

Return to Menu Editor. Below the Cancel button, you will see a Shortcut combo box that you can use to add shortcuts to your menu items. Figure 6.19 demonstrates adding a shortcut, Ctrl+N, to the mnuFileNew menu item.

6

FIGURE 6.19

Adding a shortcut to a menu item

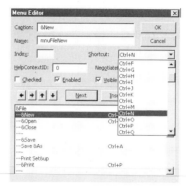

Add the shortcuts listed in Table 6.5.

TABLE 6.5 HyperPad's Shortcut Key Assignments

Menu Item	Shortcut
mnuFileNew	Ctrl+N
mnuFileOpen	Ctrl+O
mnuFileSaveAs	Ctrl+A
mnuFilePrint	Ctrl+P
mnuEditCut	Ctrl+X
mnuEditCopy	Ctrl+C
mnuEditPaste	Ctrl+V
mnuEditDelete	Del
mnuEditTimeDate	F5

Now when you select frmMain's menus, you'll see the shortcut keys displayed.

Adding Separator Bars

You'll notice that Notepad spaces out its menu items by introducing separator bars. You can do this too by using Menu Editor. Add separators between mnuFileClose and mnuFileSave, between mnuFileSaveAs and mnuFilePrintSetup, and between mnuFilePrint and mnuFileExit.

In Menu Editor, insert a blank menu item between the two menu items that you want to separate. This menu item will become the separator bar. Then give the new menu item a – caption. That's a single hyphen. Menu Editor will generate a separator bar for that menu item. You still have to give the menu item a name, so call the first one in the File menu mnuFileSep1, the second mnuFileSep2, and so on.

You can now do the same for the Edit menu. Add a separator between `mnuEditDelete` and `mnuEditSelectAll` and between `mnuEditTimeDate` and `mnuEditWordWrap`. Figures 6.20, 6.21, and 6.22 show how your three submenus should now look.

FIGURE 6.20

View of File menu.

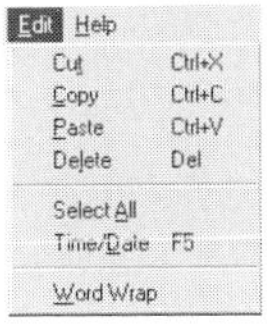

FIGURE 6.21

View of Edit menu.

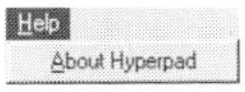

FIGURE 6.22

View of Help menu.

The Word Wrap Menu Item

Notice that we've included the Word Wrap menu in the HyperPad implementation. If you try out this menu item in the real Notepad, you'll find that a check box appears in the menu when Word Wrap is on.

Remember that each menu item is actually a control on the form. There is a property called `Checked` that you can set to `True` or `False` at runtime when the user selects that particular menu item.

You can preset the `Checked` property to `True` using Menu Editor. You can also set it using the Properties window after the menu has been added to the form. There is a check box on Menu Editor window with the caption `Checked`. If you set it for a menu item, that menu item will immediately appear with a checkmark next to it.

Context-Sensitive Menus

Finally in this lesson, we'll talk about how to make your menu items context-sensitive. If you look at Notepad's menus, you will see that some of them are disabled (grayed out). This means that you cannot select them because selecting them would be inconsistent with Notepad's current state. For instance, the Edit menu's Cut, Copy, and Paste commands remain grayed out until you select some text in the document.

6

Let's add the same feature to HyperPad. However, this time use the Properties window to set the property for the menu item because the menu item already exists.

Display the Properties window for the form. At the top of the window is a combo box. When you click it, it drops down to reveal all the controls on the form, including all the menu items that you've just added. Find the following menu items, and set their Enabled properties to False:

1. mnuFileClose
2. mnuFileSave
3. mnuFileSaveAs
4. mnuFilePrint
5. mnuEditCut
6. mnuEditCopy
7. mnuEditPaste
8. mnuEditDelete
9. mnuEditSelectAll
10. mnuEditTimeDate
11. mnuEditWordWrap

Now when you run your program, these items will be disabled by default when the program starts. You can enable and disable individual menu items at runtime by setting the Enabled property accordingly. You will write a subroutine to set up these context-sensitive menus in the next lesson.

Lesson Summary

We covered menus extensively in this lesson, and you should now be able to create professional looking menu trees, complete with shortcuts. Next, we'll add code to the menu events to complete the functionality of our menus.

Quiz 5

1. To display the Shortcut Key text

    a. In Menu Editor, position the cursor after the item and type it in

    b. It is automatically displayed when a shortcut is created

c. When you type in the Shortcut Key a name, include the desired text in quotes on the same line

d. There is no way to display Shortcut Key text

2. The line of code

```
mnuFileOpen.Enabled = FALSE
```

does the following:

a. Displays a check in front of the menu item

b. Removes a check in front of the menu item

c. Changes the menu item to gray

d. Removes the menu item from the menu

3. Which statement about the separator bars is true?

a. When they are selected, they close up the group below them

b. A single underscore character is used to create a separator

c. A separator bar does not require a name

d. A separator bar cannot be selected for any use whatsoever

4. When a menu item is disabled, it means:

a. The menu item is permanently unavailable

b. The menu item has already been selected

c. The menu item is currently unavailable

d. The menu item is currently active

Exercise 5

Complexity: Easy

1. Create a new form and then create a menu item that branches out to three sub-levels. Name the Top_Level menu TopLevel. Name the first sublevel item SubLevel1. Name the second sublevel SubLevel2.

Complexity: Moderate

2. Using the structure of the three top-level menu items introduced in this lesson, File, Edit, and Help, combine them all together to make one large menu item and call it MainMenu. Make sure File, Edit, and the Help menu all branch out to their own original menu items, and include the separator bars.

6

LESSON 6

Filling in the Blanks: Programming the File Menus

It's time to start programming!

Even though you haven't added code to the menu events, the user can still send commands to the program using Windows conventions. Just as changing the window's size generates a Resize event, double-clicking the window's Close box generates an Unload event. You've actually already used this feature. It provides a way to exit a program that doesn't have that functionality programmed in. This is because closing the last window in a program ends the program.

Confirming a Close Command

Let's add a feature to HyperPad. If the user tries to close a document before saving any changes, bring up a message box reminding the user that he or she will lose the changes.

First, you need a way to tell when the text in a document has changed since it was last saved. You can do this by adding a Boolean variable to the General Declarations section of frmDocument. Adding a variable in this way is rather like adding an additional property to the form. Go to the Code window for frmDocument and add the following declaration to the General Declarations section:

```
Dim Changed As Boolean
```

Because the default value for a Boolean variable is False, you don't have to assign anything to this variable. When a new document is created, its Changed variable will be created and initialized to False by default.

You know that the document has changed when the user types something in the text box. There is a TextBox event that you can use just for this purpose: the Change event.

The Change Event

Add the code in Listing 6.6 to the Change event subroutine for txtDocument.

LISTING 6.6 Setting the Form-Level Change Flag

```
Private Sub txtDocument_Change()
    Changed = True
End Sub
```

Look at the way that you've accessed the `Changed` form variable. Each instance of the form will have its own copy of `Changed`, and, accordingly, only that copy will be affected when the code runs. You could also have written

```
Me.Changed = True
```

Note that this is the same syntax that you would have used if `Changed` were a property of the form. Now you can see why we said earlier that form variables are like adding your own properties to a form.

You now have a way to tell if a document needs to be saved or not. You can use this variable to handle the situation of the user closing the form without saving it first.

The `Unload` Event

Let's have a look at the `Unload` event subroutine for `frmDocument`.

Visual Basic declares the `Unload` event as follows:

```
Private Sub Form_Unload(Cancel As Integer)

End Sub
```

The event is generated when a form is closed, regardless of the method used to close it. The same event is generated if you close a form by using the `Unload` statement or if your user manually closes it with the mouse. You'll notice that the subroutine includes a `Cancel` parameter. If you set that parameter to `True` in the body of the subroutine, the form will stay open and the operation to close it will be canceled. Add the code in Listing 6.7 to the `Unload` event subroutine for `frmDocument`.

LISTING 6.7   The `Unload` Event Routine

```
Private Sub Form_Unload(Cancel As Integer)
If Changed Then
    Select Case MsgBox("The text in the " & Me.Caption & _
                    " file has changed." & vbCr & vbCr & _
                    "Do you want to save the changes?", _
                    vbExclamation + vbYesNoCancel, frmMain.Caption)
        Case vbYes
            'Perform save
        Case vbNo
            'Allow form to close
        Case vbCancel
            'Cancel close form
            Cancel = True
    End Select
End If
End Sub
```

6

As you can see, you're checking the value of the form's Changed variable when the form is unloaded. If changes were made to the text in the text box, a modal message box prompts the user to decide whether to save the changes, ignore them, or cancel the close operation. Look carefully at the If statement that includes the call to the MsgBox function. It incorporates a number of techniques, including

- Returning the key pressed directly to the Select Case statement
- Forcing the message text to be displayed on more than one line by embedding a carriage return character—vbCr—in the message text
- Selecting the button combinations to display using a built-in constant
- Selecting the Exclamation Mark icon to be displayed by adding two constants together
- Specifying that the text in frmMain's title bar should be used in the title bar of the message box

The message box that is produced by this function is shown in Figure 6.23.

FIGURE 6.23

The confirmation message box.

HyperPad is beginning to behave like a professional Windows application now!

You're not going to add the code to save the text now, so you've left that option in the Select Case statement empty. If the user presses the No button in the message box, you need do nothing else. You can just allow the form to close, losing the text in the text box. Finally, if the user decides to cancel the close operation, you can handle that case by setting the Cancel variable to True.

The File New Menu Item

Now let your users create new document windows by selecting the File Newmenu item. Because you've already written the AddForm function that does this, introducing this functionality should be quite straightforward. First, display the Code window for the frmMain form. This is where the programming will take place because the menu item is part of frmMain.

Locate the mnuFileNew menu in the Object combo box. When you select the menu entry in the combo box, the Click event subroutine declaration is added to the Code window. Add the call to the AddForm function, as shown in Listing 6.8.

LISTING 6.8   The File New Routine

```
Private Sub mnuFileNew_Click()
    AddForm
End Sub
```

When you run the program now, you'll be able to create as many new documents as you can fit into your PC's memory. Go on—try it!

Context-Sensitive Menus: Using the Forms Collection

In Lesson 5, you disabled the Close, Save, Save As, and Print menu items by default. You also disabled the Edit menus. You did this for a very good reason: If you close all the documents in HyperPad, those menus go *out of context*. In other words, those menus are applicable only when there is at least one active document. To prevent users from selecting menus that are out of context, well-behaved Windows programs make sure that such menus are disabled.

Let's write a subroutine that you can use to enable or disable the context-sensitive menus accordingly. Go into the frmMain Code window and enter the subroutine in Listing 6.9. You can either type in the sub definition, as described in Chapter 3, "Variables, Constants, and Associated Functions," or click Procedure under the Tools menu and fill it out, as shown in Figure 6.24.

FIGURE 6.24

The context-sensitive menu procedure definition.

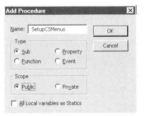

LISTING 6.9   Setting Up Context-Sensitive Menus

```
Public Sub SetupCSMenus()
Dim Found As Boolean
Dim I As Integer
For I = 0 To Forms.Count - 1
    If Forms(I).Name = "frmDocument" Then
        Found = True
        Exit For
    End If
Next I
```

continues

LISTING 6.9   continued

```
mnuFileClose.Enabled = Found
mnuFileSave.Enabled = Found
mnuFileSaveAs.Enabled = Found
mnuFilePrint.Enabled = Found
End Sub
```

You're declaring this subroutine as `Public` because you will need to call it from the `frmDocument` form.

The `Forms` Collection

One line that's interesting in this subroutine is the `For` statement:

```
For I = 0 To Forms.Count - 1
```

When you create forms in Visual Basic 6, they are automatically added to something called the forms collection. A collection is a way of grouping together similar objects in Visual Basic 6 so they can be retrieved or manipulated easily. Because Visual Basic 6 adds new forms to the `forms` collection for you, you might as well make use of this functionality.

The `Count` Method

Collections have a `Count` property that you can use to find out how many items are in the collection. The `Forms.Count` property is an integer, the total number of forms in your running application. Be careful: The count includes `frmMain`!

You can access an individual item in the collection by specifying its index in parentheses, as in the statement:

```
If Forms(I).Name = "frmDocument" Then
```

Because the indexes in the collection start at 0, it is necessary to fix the value of `I` by subtracting 1 from the number of forms returned from the `Count` method. If there are two forms in the collection, the variable `I` will take the value `0` on the first pass through the loop and `1` on the second pass.

Together, these two lines (the `For...` statement and the `If...Then` statement) enable you to cycle through each form in the collection and find out if one of them is a `frmDocument` type of form by checking the value of the form's `Name` property. The rest of the subroutine is straightforward. You're setting a `Boolean` variable to note if you found such a form and enabling or disabling the menu items accordingly.

Calling `SetupCSMenus`

All that's left to do is to find a suitable point to call this subroutine from. You need to call it from two places: once when you create a new form and again when a form is closed. When a form is created, its `Load` event is triggered; when it is closed, its `Unload` event is triggered. Listing 6.10 is the code to add to `frmDocument`'s `Load` event subroutine.

LISTING 6.10   Setting Up the Menus When a Form Is Loaded

```
Private Sub Form_Load()
    frmMain.SetupCSMenus
End Sub
```

Notice how you preceded the call to `SetupCSMenus` with the name of the form in which the subroutine is contained. Because you've declared the subroutine to be `Public`, you can call it from `frmDocument`, but if you don't prefix it with the name of the form, Visual Basic 6 will assume it is a part of `frmDocument` and, accordingly, will not be able to find it.

Before you can add the same line to `frmDocument`'s `Unload` event, there is a small hurdle to overcome.

You see, the `Unload` event subroutine is called just prior to the form being destroyed. `SetupCSMenus` will find the form that is being unloaded in the `forms` collection because it hasn't been destroyed yet. To get around this, you need a way to let `SetupCSMenus` know which form is being unloaded so it can ignore that form when it is found in the `forms` collection.

Tracking Unloading Forms

The answer to this little problem is to add an additional `Boolean` form variable to `frmDocument`. Add it now and modify the `Unload` event subroutine for `frmDocument` as shown in Listing 6.11. (Changes are in bold.)

LISTING 6.11   Calling `SetupCSMenus` from `Form_Unload`

```
Public Closing As Boolean

Private Sub Form_Unload(Cancel As Integer)
If Changed Then
    Select Case MsgBox("The text in the " & Me.Caption & _
                    " file has changed." & vbCr & vbCr & _
```

continues

6

LISTING 6.11 continued

```
                                "Do you want to save the changes?", _
                                vbExclamation Or vbYesNoCancel, frmMain.Caption)
                Case vbYes
                    'Perform save
                Case vbNo
                    'Allow form to close
                Case vbCancel
                    'Cancel close form
                    Cancel = True
        End Select
    End If
    Closing = Not Cancel
    frmMain.SetupCSMenus
End Sub
```

You're declaring Closing as Public so that SetupCSMenus can see it in the form. In Form_Unload, you're setting the Closing form variable to True after the user has confirmed that he or she wants to close the form. Then, of course, you modify SetupCSMenus as in Listing 6.12 to check this variable so it ignores that form as being an open document. Again, the changed lines are highlighted in bold.

LISTING 6.12 The Closing Variable

```
Public Sub SetupCSMenus()
Dim Found As Boolean
Dim I As Integer
For I = 0 To Forms.Count - 1
    If Forms(I).Name = "frmDocument" Then
        If Forms(I).Closing = False Then
            Found = True
            Exit For
        End If
    End If
Next I
mnuFileClose.Enabled = Found
mnuFileSave.Enabled = Found
mnuFileSaveAs.Enabled = Found
mnuFilePrint.Enabled = Found
End Sub
```

The File Close Menu

Now that HyperPad handles forms being closed correctly and the File menus are truly context-sensitive, you can add the code to close a form from the File Close menu. Use the Code window to add the Click event subroutine for the mnuFileClose menu. Then complete the subroutine as in Listing 6.13.

LISTING 6.13   The File Close Routine

```
Private Sub mnuFileClose_Click()
    Unload frmMain.ActiveForm
End Sub
```

This line of code is important. It demonstrates another way you can obtain access to a form variable.

The ActiveForm Property

The ActiveForm property is one of the MDI form's properties. It is the MDI child form that is currently active. Of course, it is the active MDI child form that you want to close.

You don't have to worry about an MDI child form not being available because the Close menu is context-sensitive. If no frmDocument forms are open, the Close menu will be disabled.

Well, we covered quite a lot of ground in this lesson, and now it's crunch time. Run HyperPad again and watch how your menus are affected when you have no documents open compared to when you have one or more open. Now is a good time to practice testing your program thoroughly. Try running the program through its paces with one window open, with no windows open, with many windows open, with some changes made to the text box, with no changes made to the text box, and so on.

Lesson Summary

In this lesson we learned how to add functionality to our menu items, as well as enable and disable menu items when the application required it, making them context sensitive. Don't worry about the Edit menus for the moment: We'll come to them next.

Quiz 6

1. Adding a variable to the General Declaration section of a form document is a lot like:

    a. Adding an additional property to the form

    b. Adding an additional event to the form

    c. Adding a Public variable to the project

    d. Adding a Private variable to the project

2. Which of the following does not generate an Unload event?

    a. When a form is closed

    b. When the user manually closes the form with the mouse

    c. When a form generates an Unload event

    d. When a form loses focus to another form

3. What is a forms collection?

    a. A way of grouping together different objects so they can be retrieved or manipulated manually

    b. A group of subordinate menu items below a single top-level menu item

    c. A group of similar top-level menu items

    d. A way of grouping together similar objects so they can be retrieved or manipulated manually

4. What is the property of an MDI form that indicates which MDI Child form is currently active?

    a. ActiveForm property

    b. CurrentForm property

    c. ChildForm property

    d. TopForm property

Exercise 6

Complexity: Easy

1. Implement a message box that pops up whenever a form is being closed. Include the name of the form being closed in the message box.

Complexity: Moderate

2. Using the HyperPad program, limit the number of forms that can be added to five. If the user tries to open more than five forms, pop up a message box telling them that no more forms can be created until some are closed.

LESSON 7

Filling in the Blanks: Programming Edit Menus

Like the File menus, you need to make the Edit menus fully context sensitive. However, doing this is more complex than you might think at first.

Enabling/Disabling Menu Options

The first point to recognize is that the Edit menu items need to be enabled and disabled at different times. Table 6.6 shows you the conditions under which each menu must be enabled or disabled.

TABLE 6.6   When to Enable and Disable Edit Menu Items

Menu	Enable When	Disable When
mnuEditCut	At least one form document is present and text in that document is selected	No forms are present or the active document has no text selected
mnuEditCopy	Same as mnuEditCut	Same as mnuEditCut
mnuEditPaste	At least one form document is present and text is present in the Windows Clipboard	No forms are present or there is no text present in the Windows Clipboard
mnuEditDelete	Same as mnuEditCut	Same as mnuEditCut
mnuEditSelectAll	At least one form document is present	No forms are present
mnuEditTimeDate	Same as mnuEditSelectAll	Same as mnuEditSelectAll
mnuEditWordWrap	Same as MnuEditSelectAll	Same as mnuEditSelectAll

Notice that all the menus require at least one form to be present before they are enabled. Some of the menus have additional requirements, but that basic requirement must be satisfied first. This can be done by adding the highlighted code in Listing 6.14 to the end of the SetupCSMenus subroutine.

6

LISTING 6.14   Adding Edit Menu to Setup Routine

```
Public Sub SetupCSMenus()
Dim Found As Boolean
Dim I As Integer
For I = 0 To Forms.Count - 1
    If Forms(I).Name = "frmDocument" Then
        If Forms(I).Closing = False Then
            Found = True
            Exit For
        End If
    End If
Next I
mnuFileClose.Enabled = Found
mnuFileSave.Enabled = Found
mnuFileSaveAs.Enabled = Found
mnuFilePrint.Enabled = Found

' enable / disable Select All, TimeDate, and WordWrap
' edit menus according to whether or not there is
' an active document
mnuEditSelectAll.Enabled = Found
mnuEditTimeDate.Enabled = Found
mnuEditWordWrap.Enabled = Found
If Found = False Then
    ' disable Copy, Cut, Delete and Paste menus
    ' when no forms are found
    mnuEditCopy.Enabled = False
    mnuEditCut.Enabled = False
    mnuEditDelete.Enabled = False
    mnuEditPaste.Enabled = False
    ' remove any check mark from the Word Wrap menu
    mnuEditWordWrap.Checked = False
End If
End Sub
```

Notice that you're also forcing the Checked property of the Word Wrap menu to False, so that any checkmark that may be set against that menu item is cleared when the menu goes out of context.

The Select All, Time/Date, and Word Wrap menu items can be enabled and disabled on the basis of whether or not a document is present. On the other hand, the Copy, Cut, Delete, and Paste menus must be disabled if no documents are present, although they have special requirements that must be satisfied before you can enable them.

The SelLength Property

The additional requirement for Copy, Cut, and Delete is that they can be enabled only when text has been selected in the active frmDocument's text box. You can determine whether text is currently selected in the text box by checking its `SelLength` property. The `SelLength` property is available only at runtime, so you won't find it in the list of properties in the text box's Property window. If `SelLength` is 0, there is no text selected. If it's greater than 0, then that many characters of text have been selected. Now modify the `If` statement that you've just added to `SetupCSMenus` so that it reads as shown in Listing 6.15.

LISTING 6.15   Special Cases for the Edit Menu

```
If Found = False Then
    ' disable Copy, Cut, Delete and Paste menus
    ' when no forms are found
    mnuEditCopy.Enabled = False
    mnuEditCut.Enabled = False
    mnuEditDelete.Enabled = False
    mnuEditPaste.Enabled = False
    ' remove any check mark from the Word Wrap menu
    mnuEditWordWrap.Checked = False
Else
    If frmMain.ActiveForm.txtDocument.SelLength > 0 Then
        ' Enable Copy, Cut and Delete menus if there is
        ' an active form and text is selected in it.
        mnuEditCopy.Enabled = True
        mnuEditCut.Enabled = True
        mnuEditDelete.Enabled = True
    Else
        ' Disable Copy, Cut and Delete menus if there is
        ' an active form and there is no text selected in it.
        mnuEditCopy.Enabled = False
        mnuEditCut.Enabled = False
        mnuEditDelete.Enabled = False
    End If
End If
```

If a form is present and text is selected in that form's text box, the Copy, Cut, and Delete menus are now enabled. Note that you still need to disable these menus expressly when there is no text selected to allow for when the focus has moved from a document form that has text selected to one that does not.

At the moment, you're calling only `SetupCSMenus` when a `frmDocument` form is loaded or unloaded. You now need to accommodate for the following events: when a user selects some text and when a user switches from one document form to another.

The `KeyUp` and `MouseUp` Events

Your program still has a small problem. No specific event is called when a user selects some text in a text box. How can you get around this? If you think about it, there are two ways that a user can select some text: either by clicking and dragging the mouse over the text or by using the keyboard equivalent of pressing the cursor keys with the Shift key depressed.

Two events signal the end of these operations: the MouseUp and KeyUp text box events. Add a call to SetupCSMenus to both these subroutines in the txtDocument control, as shown in Listing 6.16.

LISTING 6.16 Calling Setup Routine when the User Selects Text

```
Private Sub txtDocument_KeyUp(KeyCode As Integer, Shift As Integer)
    frmMain.SetupCSMenus
End Sub

Private Sub txtDocument_MouseUp(Button As Integer, Shift As Integer,
➥ X As Single, Y As Single)
    frmMain.SetupCSMenus
End Sub
```

The Activate Event

To make sure that the menus behave correctly when the user moves from one document to another, you need to add another call to SetupCSMenus, this time from frmDocument's Activate event. This code is shown in Listing 6.17.

LISTING 6.17 The Form Activate Event Routine

```
Private Sub Form_Activate()
    frmMain.SetupCSMenus
End Sub
```

A form's Activate event is called when the form becomes the active form. This happens when a form is created and the user clicks it, making it the active form when more than one MDI child document form is present. (There is a corresponding Deactivate event, which is called when a form loses the focus, but you don't need to use it.)

Before you can run HyperPad with these changes, you have to do one more thing. In SetupCSMenus, you are now making a reference to the text box on frmDocument in the line that reads

```
If frmMain.ActiveForm.txtDocument.SelLength > 0 Then
```

If you run the program now, you will get a runtime error when this statement is reached. The reason is that when a document form is created during the AddForm function, the form's Load event subroutine is called. However, although the Load event subroutine is called after the form itself has been created, the controls on that form aren't created until the Load event is completed.

The error occurs because you're making a reference to a control that doesn't yet exist.

You can use two techniques to overcome this.

1. Add a call to the form's Show method in its Load event subroutine prior to calling SetupCSMenus. This will force Visual Basic 6 to create the controls and display the form. Because the form is already loaded, the Load event isn't triggered a second time, which is just as well because otherwise you would enter an endless loop!

2. The other technique is to move the call to SetupCSMenus from the Load event subroutine to the form's Activate event subroutine. The Activate event is called first after the form and its controls have been created and the form becomes active.

Luckily, you already have a call to SetupCSMenus in the Activate event subroutine for frmDocument, so the easiest way to get around the error is to remove the call to SetupCSMenus from frmDocument's Load event subroutine.

That's it! The Cut, Copy, and Delete menus will now be context sensitive.

Try running HyperPad again and experiment with selecting text and moving from one document to another.

The Paste Menu Item and the `Clipboard` Object

You have already disabled the Paste menu if there are no document forms loaded. However, the Paste menu can be enabled only when there is text in the Clipboard. The Clipboard is a storage area available for use by all the programs running on your Windows desktop. Visual Basic 6 has a built-in Clipboard object that represents the Windows Clipboard. The Clipboard object has a number of methods that you can use. One of them, GetFormat, can tell you if there is any text on the Clipboard that can be pasted into your document.

Modify the If statement at the end of the SetupCSMenus subroutine, which should now read

```
If Found = False Then
    ' disable Copy, Cut, Delete and Paste menus
    ' when no forms are found
    mnuEditCopy.Enabled = False
    mnuEditCut.Enabled = False
    mnuEditDelete.Enabled = False
    mnuEditPaste.Enabled = False
    ' remove any check mark from the Word Wrap menu
```

6

```
        mnuEditWordWrap.Checked = False
Else
    If frmMain.ActiveForm.txtDocument.SelLength > 0 Then
        ' Enable Copy, Cut and Delete menus if there is
        ' an active form and text is selected in it.
        mnuEditCopy.Enabled = True
        mnuEditCut.Enabled = True
        mnuEditDelete.Enabled = True
    Else
        ' Disable Copy, Cut and Delete menus if there is
        ' an active form and there is no text selected in it.
        mnuEditCopy.Enabled = False
        mnuEditCut.Enabled = False
        mnuEditDelete.Enabled = False
    End If
    If Clipboard.GetFormat(vbCFText) Then
        mnuEditPaste.Enabled = True
    Else
        mnuEditPaste.Enabled = False
    End If
End If
```

You have used another of Visual Basic 6's built-in constants (vbCFText, which stands for Clipboard format text) to find out if there is any text on the Clipboard. The GetFormat method returns a Boolean value representing whether any data of the requested format was found. If there is any text on the Clipboard, you can enable the Paste menu; otherwise, disable it.

Copying Text into the Clipboard

Both the Copy and Cut edit menus need to copy the selected text from the text box to the Clipboard. The Cut and Delete menus also have to remove the selected text physically.

The SetText Method

Let's write a subroutine to copy the text from the text box to the Clipboard. Place the subroutine in frmMain. It should read as shown in Listing 6.18.

LISTING 6.18   Copying Text to the Clipboard

```
Private Sub CopyTextToClipboard()
    Clipboard.SetText frmMain.ActiveForm.txtDocument.SelText
End Sub
```

Here you're using another Clipboard method, SetText, to copy the selected text to the Clipboard. You're also obtaining that text by using the SelText text box property. The

SelText property is available only at runtime. It contains the selected text—very useful. All you need to do now is add a call to CopyTextToClipboard to both the mnuEditCopy and mnuEditCut Click event subroutines, as shown in Listing 6.19.

LISTING 6.19   The Cut Menu Item

```
Private Sub mnuEditCopy_Click()
    CopyTextToClipboard
    SetupCSMenus
End Sub

Private Sub mnuEditCut_Click()
    CopyTextToClipboard
    SetupCSMenus
End Sub
```

Deleting the Selected Text from the Text Box

Additionally, both the Cut and Delete Edit menus need to delete the selected text from the text box. Unfortunately, there isn't a single method that will do the job for you, but you can do it quite easily by using a combination of the text box's SelStart, SelLength, and Text properties. Create a new subroutine in frmMain as shown in Listing 6.20.

LISTING 6.20   The Cut Menu Item

```
Private Sub DeleteSelectedText()
    Dim Text As String
    Dim SelStart As Long
    Dim SelLength As Long
    ' Put the text in a local string variable
    Text = frmMain.ActiveForm.txtDocument.Text
    ' Get the begining and ending positions of the selected text.
    SelStart = frmMain.ActiveForm.txtDocument.SelStart
    SelLength = frmMain.ActiveForm.txtDocument.SelLength
    ' Replace text box with a string containing what's before
    ' and what's after the selection.
    frmMain.ActiveForm.txtDocument.Text = Left(Text, SelStart) & _
            Right(Text, Len(Text) - (SelStart + SelLength))
    ' Reset the cursor
    frmMain.ActiveForm.txtDocument.SelStart = SelStart
End Sub
```

At first sight, this subroutine may seem a little daunting, so let's break it down line by line.

The SelStart and SelLength Properties

The first three lines are straightforward. You're making local copies of the Text, SelStart, and SelLength text box properties to use later in the subroutine. You already know about Text and SelLength. The SelStart property gives you the offset into the text of the text box at which the selection starts. If SelLength is greater than 0, it means that some text is selected. The SelStart property tells you at which character position in the text the selected text begins.

The fourth line in the subroutine removes the selected text. It chops the text into two portions using the Left and Right string functions. The two portions are the strings to the left and right of the selected text. It then uses the string concatenation operator to join them back together, minus the selected portion, and places the result in the text box.

The final line positions the text box's text cursor to where the selection started; otherwise, it would be positioned back at the beginning of the text box, which would look strange. You can try cutting text out of the text box without the last line to see what we mean. The last line also demonstrates another use for SelStart. If SelLength is set to 0, SelStart sets or returns the position of the text cursor. This is pretty complex stuff and shows just how much you can do with a simple text box.

Finally, you need to add calls to DeleteSelectedText from the Cut and Delete menus' Click event subroutines, which now read like Listing 6.21.

LISTING 6.21   Calling the Delete Routine

```
Private Sub mnuEditCut_Click()
    CopyTextToClipboard
    DeleteSelectedText
    SetupCSMenus
End Sub

Private Sub mnuEditDelete_Click()
    DeleteSelectedText
    SetupCSMenus
End Sub
```

Lesson Summary

Okay, you now have working Cut, Copy, and Delete menus. All that's left to do is finish off the Paste and other Edit menus and add an About box. HyperPad then will be complete. We've got one more trick up our sleeve that we'll show you in the next lesson. For now, run HyperPad again and experiment with cutting and copying text to the Clipboard.

You can use the Clipboard viewer program that comes with Windows to see the text on the Clipboard if you want. You can also use the Shift+Insert key combination to paste text because that is a built-in Windows function.

Quiz 7

1. Which menu does *not* require at least one form document to be present before being enabled?

    a. mnuEditCut

    b. mnuEditDelete

    c. mnuEditPaste

    d. They all must have at least one form document that is present

2. When a user selects text in a text box, the best way to check is to

    a. Check the KeyUp event

    b. Check the MouseUp event

    c. Check if the SelLength property is greater than 0

    d. Check if the SelLength property is equal to 0

3. A form's Activate event is called when

    a. A form becomes an Active form

    b. When a form is created and the user clicks it

    c. When the Load event subroutine is called

    d. Both a and b

4. Which of the following statements is true?

    a. The SelLength property can be negative

    b. If SelLength is greater than 0, it means text was selected

    c. If SelLength is less than or greater than 0, it means text was selected

    d. The SelLength property limit value is 256

6

Exercise 7

Complexity: Easy

1. Using the HyperPad project, implement a message box that gets activated whenever the Delete menu item is selected. Have it report the number of characters that is being deleted.

Complexity: Moderate

2. Change the HyperPad project so that whenever the use releases the mouse button after making a selection, it deletes the selected text.

LESSON 8

Filling in the Blanks: Finishing Up HyperPad

All that's left to do is to wrap up the Edit menus and add an About box, but don't forget the extra trick we mentioned. We'll save that for the end. The Edit menu items that you have left to program are Paste, Select All, Time/Date, and Word Wrap. Let's consider the Paste menu.

Pasting Text from the Clipboard

The Clipboard object provides a method, called GetText, that you can use to obtain the text on the Clipboard so that you can paste it into the text box. You have already seen how to determine if there is any text on the Clipboard and how to set the context of the Edit menus accordingly. However, the fact that text was on the Clipboard at the time you enabled the Paste menu doesn't mean that it will still be there at the time you actually paste it in. For example, in the meantime the user may have switched to a graphics application and used Cut and Paste to move some graphics data around. Unfortunately, the Clipboard object has no events, so it cannot tell your program when its contents have changed.

To overcome this problem, you should double-check when you paste in the text that there is still text there to paste.

There is one other consideration as well. Although the Clipboard provides you with the basic method to obtain the text, you still have some work to do to support the paste itself.

With all that taken into consideration, the finished Paste menu's Click event subroutine for frmMain should look like Listing 6.22.

LISTING 6.22   The Paste Command

```
Private Sub mnuEditPaste_Click()
Dim Text As String
Dim ClipboardText As String
Dim SelStart As Long
```

```
If Clipboard.GetFormat(vbCFText) Then
    ' Replace selected text (if any)
    If frmMain.ActiveForm.txtDocument.SelLength > 0 Then
        DeleteSelectedText
    End If
    ' Move stuff we need to variables
    Text = frmMain.ActiveForm.txtDocument.Text
    SelStart = frmMain.ActiveForm.txtDocument.SelStart
    ClipboardText = Clipboard.GetText
    ' Concatenate new text string and replace text box
    ' contents with it.
    frmMain.ActiveForm.txtDocument.Text = Left(Text, SelStart) & _
        ClipboardText & Right(Text, Len(Text) - SelStart)
    ' Restore cursor position.
    frmMain.ActiveForm.txtDocument.SelStart = SelStart
Else
    SetupCSMenus
End If
End Sub
```

When you paste text into a document, you have to check first if any text is already high-lighted. If so, the text you are pasting in should replace the highlighted text. That's what the nested If statement is doing.

The next two lines obtain local copies of the Text and SelStart text box properties.

You are then using the Clipboard object's GetText method to obtain the text that is currently on the Clipboard. It's being assigned to another local variable, ClipboardText.

The next line is the one that is doing the job of adding the text. Note that you're adding the Clipboard text at the current position of the text cursor, which is what you expect when pasting text from the Clipboard.

Finally, the last line repositions the text cursor to the point at which you pasted in the text, as you did in the Cut menu.

The Remaining Edit Menu Items

You're through with the Clipboard functions now. Let's finish up the Edit menu items.

Select All

The Select All menu simply selects all the text in the text box. This is pretty straightforward to program using the text box's SelStart and SelLength properties. The Select All routine is shown in Listing 6.23.

LISTING 6.23   Select All the Text

```
Private Sub mnuEditSelectAll_Click()
   frmMain.ActiveForm.txtDocument.SelStart = 0
   frmMain.ActiveForm.txtDocument.SelLength = _
   Len(frmMain.ActiveForm.txtDocument.Text)
   SetupCSMenus
End Sub
```

By setting the text box's SelStart property to 0 and its SelLength property to the length
of the text in its Text property, you select all the text in the text box. Finally, don't forget
to call SetupCSMenus because text is now selected in the document and the context-
sensitive Edit menus may need to be updated. It's as easy as that!

Time/Date

When you use the Time/Date menu option in Notepad, it adds the current time and date,
in Windows short format, to the document. The routine shown in Listing 6.24 will do the
same thing.

LISTING 6.24   Adding the Date and Time

```
Private Sub mnuEditTimeDate_Click()
   Dim Text As String
   Dim SelStart As Long
   ' Replace selection (if any)
       DeleteSelectedText
   If frmMain.ActiveForm.txtDocument.SelLength > 0 Then
   End If
   ' Use our regular trick to get the text,
   ' add what we want to it, and replace the
   ' text box contents with the result.
   Text = frmMain.ActiveForm.txtDocument.Text
   SelStart = frmMain.ActiveForm.txtDocument.SelStart
   frmMain.ActiveForm.txtDocument.Text = Left(Text, SelStart) & _
   Now & Right(Text, Len(Text) - SelStart)
   frmMain.ActiveForm.txtDocument.SelStart = SelStart
   ' Menus may need to be updated.
   SetupCSMenus
End Sub
```

Again, while you're adding text to the document, you need to check if there is any selected text to be deleted first. Then you get on with the job of adding the time and date text
to the correct position in the text box.

Word Wrap

We pointed out earlier that it isn't possible to provide a word wrap facility using the standard TextBox control. The application that you're trying to emulate, Notepad, implements word wrap by removing the horizontal scroll bar. When word wrap is turned on, the text is forced to wrap at the end of each physical line of text according to the size of the document window. Unfortunately for you, the standard text box does not let you set the scrollbar's property at runtime. You can find out what the property is currently set to, but if you try to change its value, a runtime error is generated.

There are advanced techniques that you can use to overcome this problem, but they involve using the Windows API and are outside the scope of this book.

Therefore, for the moment, implement the Word Wrap menu to provide the code for implementing the checkmark in the menu itself.

The Word Wrap menu's Click event subroutine should therefore read

```
Private Sub mnuEditWordWrap_Click()
    mnuEditWordWrap.Checked = Not mnuEditWordWrap.Checked
End Sub
```

This is a straightforward way to toggle the checkmark. If there is no checkmark, the menu's Checked property will be False. Therefore, Not False is True and vice versa.

Adding an About Box

All great Windows programs have great About boxes. This is when you get the chance to put your artistic abilities to the test and try to code the most exciting About box possible. Check out the About boxes of your favorite applications. You'll find a whole range of styles used, from straightforward text to animated graphics.

The About box that you're going to add to HyperPad will contain the basic information that you need to add to any About box. You need a place to display the copyright and version information of the program, together with a copy of the icon used for frmMain.

The About box starts out life as a straightforward SDI form. So, first add a new form to the project, name it frmAbout, and set its Caption property to About HyperPad.

The BorderStyle Property

Next, set the form's BorderStyle property to 3 - Fixed Dialog. In the forms you've used so far, you haven't expressly set this property. You've always used the default setting of 2 - Sizable. However, this About box is going to be a dialog-style form. As

6

such, it must not have sizable borders. Its size has to be fixed. To do this, set its BorderStyle property to 3 - Fixed Dialog. You'll see from the Properties window that you can use a number of different styles. You will come across some of the other styles later in this book.

Set the MinButton and MaxButton properties to False. In this way, you prevent the form from being minimized or maximized, which is just what you need for the About box.

There is also a property called ControlBox that you can set to hide the ControlBox on the form's title bar. It's not doing any harm there, so leave it alone, but you can experiment with removing it if you want.

The Image Control

Previously, you added pictures to forms using a PictureBox control. Visual Basic's Image control can also contain a picture. The difference between the two controls is that the PictureBox control has more functionality. You can tell this by glancing at the list of properties for the controls. Also, the PictureBox control can double as a container for other controls, just like the frame. You can therefore use it as a captionless Frame control even without using it to display a picture. The PictureBox control is also one of the few controls that you can drag directly onto an MDI form. For these reasons, it is arguably the more flexible of the two controls.

However, the tradeoff here is that the Image control uses fewer system resources and repaints faster than the PictureBox control. If you don't need the PictureBox control's extra bells and whistles, the Image control will do the job.

Add an Image control to the form. You will use an Image control to display a copy of HyperPad's icon in the About box. Figure 6.25 shows how the Image control appears on the toolbox.

FIGURE 6.25

Adding an Image control to the About box.

You can add a copy of the note02.ico icon to the Image control by setting its Picture property to the icon file, as you did earlier for the icon properties in frmMain and frmDocument. You might also want to set the Icon property of the form to the same file. Although you can't minimize the About box, Windows 95 displays the icon in the title bar. If you don't add your own icon, you'll see the standard SDI form icon instead.

Finally, you can add Label controls as appropriate and set their Caption properties to whatever you want to say in your About box. The only control that's mandatory here is an OK button to close the form. That source code is shown in Listing 6.25.

LISTING 6.25   Dismissing the About Box

```
Private Sub Command1_Click()
    Unload Me
End Sub
```

Note how the `Me` keyword has uses for any old form, not just child forms.

Back at `frmMain`, program the About box menu option as in Listing 6.26. You could have done that without peeking!

LISTING 6.26   Calling the About Box

```
Private Sub mnuHelpAbout_Click()
    frmAbout.Show vbModal
End Sub
```

Figure 6.26 shows what the About box form looks like when HyperPad is running.

FIGURE 6.26

HyperPad's About box.

Something Up Our Sleeve!

Great, HyperPad's nearly done. But we did mention that we were holding back a final trick until the end? The trick is an extra menu, called the Window menu. All the best MDI applications have one, so HyperPad mustn't be left out. A Window menu serves two purposes. One is to hold a *window list*. This is a list of the open MDI child windows. The other is to provide the `Cascade` and `Tile` commands that your users can use to help organize the documents open in the MDI frame.

The first thing you have to do is add the Window menu itself. Do this using Menu Editor, placing it between the Edit and Help menus. When you add the Window menu, make sure you click the WindowList check box. This is a great timesaving Visual Basic feature, because Visual Basic completely manages the window list for you. Figure 6.27 shows you the completed entry in Menu Editor.

6

FIGURE 6.27

Adding a Window List menu.

When you run HyperPad, you'll see a list of the open windows in the Window menu. What's more, you can move around the open documents by selecting their entries in the Window menu, even if the document window is minimized. Figure 6.28 shows you what this looks like with five open documents.

FIGURE 6.28

The window list with six untitled documents.

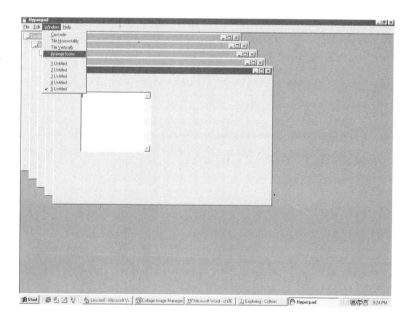

Finally, there are the menu commands to add to arrange the windows. There are a total of four different commands that you can add: Cascade, Tile Horizontally, Tile Vertically, and Arrange Icons. Add these menus to the Window menu using Menu Editor. Use the names `mnuWindowCascade` and the like. Don't worry about where the window list will go; Visual Basic always adds it to the end of the menu.

Listing 6.27 shows the code to place in each menu.

LISTING 6.27   Code to Rearrange Windows

```
Private Sub mnuWindowArrangeIcons_Click()
    frmMain.Arrange vbArrangeIcons
End Sub

Private Sub mnuWindowCascade_Click()
    frmMain.Arrange vbCascade
End Sub

Private Sub mnuWindowTileHorizontally_Click()
    frmMain.Arrange vbTileHorizontal
End Sub

Private Sub mnuWindowTileVertically_Click()
    frmMain.Arrange vbTileVertical
End Sub
```

Yes! Just one line of code per menu—we said we had a trick up our sleeve! As you can see, the MDI form has a method called Arrange that does the job for you. Now you can organize your documents with a click of the mouse.

Lesson Summary

In this lesson we put some finishing touches on HyperPad. We included such options as pasting, selecting all the text, added the time/date option, and added an About box. We can still add another nifty feature to HyperPad: popup menus. In the next lesson, we'll cover just that.

Quiz 8

1. The BorderStyle property Fixed Dialog has one main advantage. What is it?

   a. It draws a 3-D border around the form

   b. It renders the form's border unsizeable

   c. It enables the user to resize the form

   d. It draws a bold, thick border around the form

6

2. Because the Clipboard can hold graphics as well as text, the Clipboard event to check is

   a. The `GraphicsPaste` event

   b. The `TextPaste` event

   c. The `Click` event

   d. There is no event to check such an occurrence

3. The difference between an `Image` control and a `PictureBox` control is

   a. The `Image` control has more functionality than the `PictureBox` control

   b. The `PictureBox` control can double as a container for other controls

   c. The `Image` control can double as a container for other controls

   d. There is no difference—they are the same thing

4. The main advantage an `Image` control has over the `PictureBox` is

   a. The `Image` control can double as a container for other controls

   b. The `Image` control can be resized at runtime, the `PictureBox` control cannot

   c. The `Image` control repaints faster than the `PictureBox` control

   d. An `Image` control can be dragged directly onto an MDI form

Exercise 8

Complexity: Easy

1. Add a menu item called Unselect All that does the opposite of Select All: It removes the selection of all selected text.

Complexity: Moderate

2. Rewrite the Sender program (from Chapter 4, "Subroutines, Functions, and the Visual Basic 6 Language") so that the Sender forms are all child forms of `frmMDISender`. Make `frmMain` a regular form. Implement the program with the same functionality as before.

LESSON 9

Filling in the Blanks: Programming Popup Menus

Now we are going to look at another kind of menu that we can add to the project: the popup menu.

What Is a Popup Menu?

A popup menu isn't much different than the top-level menus you created in Lesson 5. They function in exactly the same way. The difference between the two is that a popup menu is hidden until the user performs an action (usually a mouse click) that causes Windows to display the menu. A top-level menu can always be found on the menu bar. A popup menu can pop up practically anywhere!

Adding Popup Menus to Your Programs

Creating a popup menu isn't much different than creating a top-level menu, other than the fact that a popup menu is displayed through the command PopUpMenu.

Before we dig deep in the PopUpMenu command, let's see it in action first (yes, it's that simple to use).

Add the code in Listing 6.28 to the Form_Click event subroutine for frmDocument.

LISTING 6.28 Implementing a PopUp Menu

```
Private Sub Form_Click()
    PopupMenu frmMain.mnuFile
End Sub
```

6

Then run HyperPad and click the form surrounding the edit box. The file menu we created earlier will appear wherever you click the mouse. Figure 6.29 shows you what it might look like when you run it. When you use it, you'll see it has the exact same functionality as a top-down menu.

FIGURE 6.29

View of a popup menu.

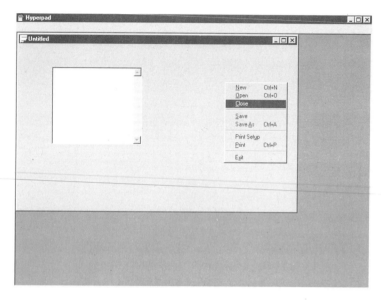

The PopUpMenu Command

We used a pretty simple example above, but there is a little more to the syntax than just the command PopupMenu and a menu object. The complete syntax is

```
[object.]PopupMenu menuname [, flags [,x [, y[, boldcommand ]]]]
```

The menuname parameter is any menu object that you have created. We'll see later how to build menus that can only be seen via popup Menu and not through menu bar.

The flags arguments further define the location and behavior of a popup menu, as well see a little later in this lesson.

The x and y arguments enable you place a popup menu in a specific coordinate on a form. If you leave them out altogether, the menu will appear wherever the mouse was clicked.

Finally, the boldcommand argument enables you to specify the name of a menu control in the popup menu that you want to show up bold. Note that you may only have one menu in the popup appear bold.

The menuname Argument

The menuname is simply the name of any menu that you have created, either through code or Menu Editor. The menu must have at least one menu item. This is because a popup menu only contains the menu items of a menu; an empty menu will result in an error. If you take a look at Listing 6.14, though, you'll notice that `frmMain` is included before the menuname. Why isn't the call simply

`PopupMenu mnuFile?`

Well, it would be if `frmDocument` had the menu `mnuFile`, but it doesn't. `frmMain` does. The `PopupMenu` command can display any menus owned by different forms. You just have to tell Windows which form, otherwise it can't find them and it will return an error. To pop up a menu that another form owns, simply include the name of the form before the `menuname` argument.

POPUPMENU Constants

The Flags parameter of `PopupMenu` can take the values summarized in Tables 6.7 and 6.8. You can combine the arguments using the Or operator.

TABLE 6.7   Location Constants for the `PopupMenu` Flags Parameter

Location Constant	Description
vbPopupMenuLeftAlign	The specified x location defines the left edge of the popup menu
vbPopupMenuCenterAlign	Centers the popup menu around the specified x location
vbPopupMenuRightAlign	The specified x location defines the right edge of the popup menu

TABLE 6.8   Behavior Constants for the `PopupMenu` Flags Parameter

Behavior Constant	Description
vbPopupMenuLeftButton	Specifies that the popup menu is to be displayed when the user clicks a menu item with the left mouse button only (default).
VbPopupMenuRightButton	Specifies that the popup menu is to be displayed when the user clicks a menu item with either the right or left mouse button.

6

Let's put some of these arguments to use. Referring to the last example, let's make the popup menu center at our specific *x* location of 100 when the user clicks a menu item with either the right or left mouse button. Our code would then look like that in Listing 6.29.

LISTING 6.29   Implementing a Popup Menu

```
Private Sub Form_Click()
    PopupMenu frmMain.mnuFile, vbPopupMenuCenterAlign +
➥ vbPopupMenuRightButton, 100, 0
End Sub
```

Figure 6.30 shows what the menu will look like when you activate the popup menu. Of course, you may be wondering why we didn't just make a popup menu for the edit box to make it work like Notepad or WordPad. Well, go ahead and right-click the edit box. You'll see that Visual Basic 6 supplies the edit control with a built-in popup menu.

FIGURE 6.30

The popup window at its new position.

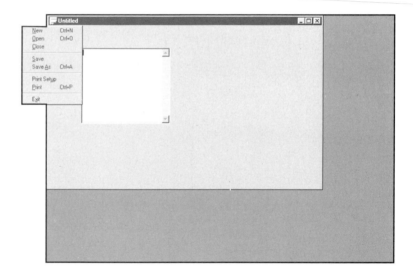

The `Boldcommand` Argument

There's one more fancy thing you can do with a popup menu, and that is specifying a menu choice to appear in bold when the menu appears. Only one menu item in the popup menu can be bold. This is a nice touch when you want a particular choice to stand out among the rest. To set a specific item, just include the menu item you want in the last argument position of the command call. Let's rewrite our command call to include just the File menu argument and our bold selection, which will be the Print menu item (see Listing 6.30). We are not interested in changing the other arguments, so we'll just leave them blank. Figure 6.31 shows the item in bold in our popup menu.

FIGURE 6.31

The popup menu with the Print command in bold.

LISTING 6.30 Implementing a Popup Menu

```
Private Sub Form_Click()
    PopupMenu frmMain.mnuFile , , , ,frmMain.mnuFilePrint
End Sub
```

Creating Menus Specifically for Popup Menus

Let's say you want your popup menu only to appear as a popup, and never as a choice from the menu bar. Simply create the menu as you would with Menu Editor, and simply uncheck the Visible box. Then refer to it as any other menu.

Lesson Summary

After completing this lesson, you should have a good feel for popup menus, and should be comfortable using them. Remember that the content of the popup menu is just as important as where and when you display it.

Quiz 9

1. What would happen if the x and y arguments were left out when PopupMenu was called?

   a. The menu would pop up wherever the mouse button was clicked.

   b. The menu would appear in the upper-left corner of the form.

   c. An error would occur.

   d. The menu would not show up.

2. The Location Constant vbPopupMenuCenterAlign does which of the following:

   a. Centers the popup menu with respect to the current form.

   b. Centers the popup menu around the specified *x* location.

    c. Centers the popup menu around the specified *y* location.

    d. Centers the popup menu using both the specified *x* location and specified *y* location.

3. The way to handle the optional arguments in the PopupMenu command that you do not want to change is to

    a. Replace the arguments with zeros.

    b. Replace the arguments with PopMenu constants.

    c. Skip the argument completely, marking its spot with a comma.

    d. Skip the argument completely, marking its spot with a space.

4. To Bold more than one item in a popup menu, simply

    a. Use the '&' character to append the menu items to be bold.

    b. Use the '+' character to append the menu items to be bold.

    c. Insert a comma after each menu item to be bold in the last argument position.

    d. More than one menu item cannot be bold.

Exercise 9

Complexity: Easy

1. Alter the popup menu that we created so that the *x* coordinate of the pop-menu is always equal to the center of the form.

Complexity: Moderate

2. Change the HyperPad program such that when the user clicks the form, the Edit menu pops up. Check to see if text is selected in the text box. If it is, make the Cut menu item bold. If it is not, make the Select All option bold.

Chapter Summary

This chapter explained the difference between an Single Document Interface (SDI) and a Multiple Document Interface (MDI), as well as creating applications to implement them both. Throughout the chapter, the application HyperPad was developed, which is a mini word processing program.

Building HyperPad involved form techniques, such as adding forms at runtime, placing forms, resizing forms, and assigning icons to forms. Three forms were used to make HyperPad. They included an MDI form, an SDI form to hold the TextBox control, and an SDI form for the About box.

A large part of developing HyperPad was developing the user interface. Menu controls were created using Menu Editor, and they were placed in the top-level menu bar or used as a popup window. The PopUpMenu command was covered thoroughly with numerous examples. Text operations were implemented that involved cutting and pasting text, selecting text, adding a time/data function, and a word wrap routine.

Window operations were also introduced, and a menu was created to execute their functions. The operations included the cascading of the documents, tiling them both horizontally and vertically, and changing their arrangement.

6

CHAPTER 7

Building Classes: The Foundation of Visual Basic OOP

For you to make the most of Visual Basic 6's object-oriented features, it is important that you have a complete understanding of classes. In this chapter, you'll see precisely what the relationship is between a class and an object. You'll learn about the classes already built into Visual Basic 6 and how to create your own classes.

You'll learn how an apparently complex problem can be simplified by applying object-oriented design techniques to it and how classes can be reused. You'll also discover how you have been using many of the object-oriented features of Visual Basic 6 since Chapter 1, "What's All That Stuff on My Screen?"

LESSON 1

Classes and Objects

A class is a category of things. An object is a thing, and each object belongs to a class. Car is a class. Your brother's '87.Honda Civic is an object of the class car.

A class is a description of a set of characteristics. An object contains specific characteristics that can change over the period of time the object is in existence. We can describe the chair class as having (at minimum) a place to sit and legs to hold it up. We can further describe the chair class as having such optional characteristics as a back, armrest, rockers, and cushion. In your house, you may have the objects stool (three legs and a seat), desk chair (with ergonomic backrest), and dining room chair (with designer cushion and armrest).

Simply put a class is a description of the object. You can even think of a class as a structured template used to define objects. The class defines the attributes and actions of the object. In the academic world a class is abstract; it doesn't really exist, an object exists and is based on a class. An architecture professor engages her students in many discussions on the house class, but these discussions are all theoretical. Not until the students graduate will they design and complete their first house object.

Class Design Techniques

Imagine you're designing a computer keyboard. You start by designing a key for the letter A; it has everything. It is beautiful with round edges. It has a spring thing and a click thing, and makes just the right clicking sound before it bounces back up. The boss loves it, but what about the rest of the keys?

In this example, it would be better to start out with a generic design—in other words, a class design. The design would have all the information you need to produce an object, in this case a key class. To create the letter B would require very little effort using the key class. If your boss comes back and says, oh, we don't want a click sound, you simply make the changes to the class design and all the key objects created from the class automatically support the new behavior.

You've already seen this approach in action in the HyperPad example in Chapter 6, "Building the GUI with Forms, Menus, and MDI Forms." In design mode, you made a document form, which you can think of as a prototype. When the program runs, the program can generate one document window after another, at the whim of the user. These objects are all based on the single design prototype. If you change any of the characteristics of the design—as indeed you'll do in Chapter 8, "Using ActiveX Controls"—these changes will be reflected in each new document object the next time the program runs.

Instances

An object is an instance of a class. The terms object and instance have similar meanings. In fact, they can often be used interchangeably. However, in programming, if you refer to an instance, you are really keeping the class in the front of your mind. You can talk about an object, on the other hand, as a fairly independent entity.

HyperPad, for example, is based on a form class designed for text entry. When the program runs, HyperPad generates one or more instances of the form class. The user can edit text in each instance independently. (In other words, the user can edit text in each window object independently.) The user can move and resize these objects, a feature found in most other Windows programs.

Classes, Classes Everywhere

Classes are intrinsic to Visual Basic 6. As an example, consider one of the most commonly used classes in Visual Basic 6: the form.

When you move the mouse over a form object at runtime, the form object reacts by generating MouseMove events. However, when you move the mouse over a form class at design time, no event is generated. The two forms that you see at design time and runtime may appear similar, but they are quite different conceptually.

Think of what happens when you add controls to a form class at design time. The controls are visually displayed on the form class, but like the form class itself, they don't work yet. This is because they, too, are classes.

When you run a project, what happens? Not only is an instance of the form class created, but an instance of each control class is created too.

You can begin to see that Visual Basic 6 is intuitively object oriented. In fact, it's difficult to think of using Visual Basic 6 without using one type of object or another.

Other Class Types

Visual Basic 6 has a number of different types of classes. Forms and controls are two of the types. The other class types that you can use fall into the following four categories:

- Single-instance classes
- User-defined classes

7

- Database classes
- Miscellaneous classes

Predefined Single-Instance Classes

Visual Basic 6 creates a few special objects based on single-instance classes when you run your project. They are special in that they represent single items in the environment in which your project runs. Because VB generates these objects automatically, they are always available to your running program.

Objects created based on single-instance classes are already familiar to you. You've used three of these objects: the Screen, Clipboard, and Debug objects.

See Table 7.1 for a list of Visual Basic 6's predefined single-instance objects.

TABLE 7.1   The Visual Basic 6 Predefined Single-Instance Objects

Object	Description
App	Represents your running application
Clipboard	Represents the Clipboard
Err	Represents an error
Debug	Represents the Debug window
Printer	Represents the printer attached to your PC
Screen	Represents the physical screen on your PC

User-Defined Classes

User-defined classes are very important, and much of this chapter is devoted to showing you how to use them. They are the real key to making your own applications object oriented. With user-defined classes, you can invent your own classes with properties and methods that you define.

Database Classes

Use of the database classes is a large topic on its own. Chapter 13, "Database Programming," is dedicated to showing you how to use databases and the classes that go with them.

Miscellaneous Classes

There are three miscellaneous classes that you might find of use in your projects. These are shown in Table 7.2.

TABLE 7.2   Miscellaneous Classes

Class Type	Description
Collection	A grouping of objects
Font	Represents a font
Picture	Represents a graphical image

Lesson Summary

In this lesson you learned that a class is a description of an object. A *class* is the template on which an object is created (based). Visual Basic 6 has many different types of classes, such as single-instance classes or user-defined classes. The form object used in many of the program examples in this book is actually based on a Visual Basic class called a *form*. Visual Basic also provides several objects for the programmer to use, such as the App or Clipboard object.

Quiz 1

1. A class is _____.

    a. an object

    b. a set of general characteristics

    c. an instance

    d. an abstract object

2. Which of the following statements about objects is false?

    a. An object is an instance of a class.

    b. An object's characteristics can never change.

    c. In many cases, you can have any number of objects based on a single class.

    d. Object is to class what "that Saturn out front" is to "car."

3. Which one of the following is NOT a single-instance class generated by Visual Basic?

    a. App

    b. Printer

    c. Window

    d. Debug

7

4. When you run a program with a form that has several controls

    a. An instance of the form class is created.

    b. An instance of each control class in the project is created.

    c. The form and other objects begin responding to events.

    d. All of the above

LESSON 2

The Form Class

Now we're going to look at how objects are actually implemented and managed in Visual Basic 6. We'll start out in this lesson demonstrating certain features that are common to all classes. We're using forms as an example because you are already familiar with them. In the next lesson, we'll turn our attention to the control classes; later in this chapter, we'll introduce user-defined classes, which are central to designing fully object-oriented applications.

Let's start out by showing you what really happens when Visual Basic creates an object from a class.

Let's start with a nice new default project and review what you already know.

The Form1 Class

When you run the default project, Visual Basic 6 starts by creating an instance of the Form1 class. After the form object has been created, you are able to access the running form object by using its name in your code, as in:

```
Form1.Show vbModeless
```

Note that in this syntax, Form1 is actually a type of variable known as an object variable.

An object variable isn't conceptually complex. It's really just a variable, and in that respect it's no different from an Integer or a String variable. However, the object variable doesn't store data in the same way that an Integer or String variable stores data. Instead, it stores something called an object *reference*. The reference is a bit like a sign-post; it tells Visual Basic 6 where the actual object is. Of course, Visual Basic 6 does all this behind the scenes so that by the time the form object's Load event subroutine is called, the object variable is ready for you to use.

Creating Your Own Form1 Object

We can show you how this works by writing a program to do what VB does automatically.

Click Add Module under the Project menu to begin a new code module. Select Module and click the Open button. Give the module the name modMain by bringing up the module's Properties window. Next, create a public subroutine called Main. Now make Sub Main the startup form. Do this by clicking Project1 Properties (you don't need to show the ellipsis on menu options) under the Project menu, and then click the General tab. Under Startup Object, select Sub Main.

After this has been done, add the code in Listing 7.1 to the Main subroutine.

LISTING 7.1   Loading a Form via Code

```
Public Sub Main()
' Create the object variable
Dim Form1Variable As Form1
Debug.Print "Created a " & TypeName(Form1Variable) _
 & " variable"
' Create an instance of Form1 and assign a reference to
' it to Form1Variable.
Set Form1Variable = New Form1
Debug.Print "Now it's a " & TypeName(Form1Variable) _
 & " variable"
' Now use the variable name to call one of the
' object's methods.
Form1Variable.Show vbModeless
End Sub
```

This piece of code does the same job Visual Basic 6 does when you specify that Form1 should be the startup form. However, we changed the name of the variable that Visual Basic 6 creates to emphasize that it is a variable that has been created.

The statement

```
Dim Form1Variable As Form1
```

creates the variable. The line is saying, *Create a variable that can contain a reference to a* Form1 *object.*

The Print command uses the TypeName function to find out what sort of object Form1Variable is connected to. Remember that at this stage, all you have done is create the variable itself. You haven't assigned a reference to a running form object to it yet. Therefore, TypeName returns the text Nothing.

7

The next line:

```
Set Form1Variable = New Form1
```

creates the new form object and completes the job of assigning its reference to
Form1Variable. (Recall from Chapter 6, "Building the GUI with Forms, Menus and
MDI Forms," that you need to use the Set statement when dealing with objects.) You
then prove that this has worked by asking for the TypeName of the object referenced by
Form1Variable again. This time, TypeName returns Form1.

To prove that the object is really there and that the connection to it works correctly, you
then call its Show method to display it on the screen.

So, objects are accessed through object variables, and different types of object variables
are used to access different types of objects. The really clever part is that you can create
your own specific form classes merely by changing the Name property of each form
module added to your project. You'll see later that the same is true for the user-defined
classes.

Referencing an Object More Than Once

If an object variable simply contains a reference to an object, does this mean that two
object variables can reference the same object?

The answer is Yes! Let's show you how this works.

Modify Main so that it reads as shown in Listing 7.2.

LISTING 7.2   Two Variables Referencing the Same Form

```
Public Sub Main()
' Create the object variables
Dim Form1Variable As Form1
Dim AnotherForm1Variable As Form1
' Create an instance of Form1 and assign a reference to
' it to Form1Variable.
Set Form1Variable = New Form1
' Assign the form to the second variable
Set AnotherForm1Variable = Form1Variable
If AnotherForm1Variable Is Form1Variable Then
   MsgBox "The two variables point to the same object."
End If
Form1Variable.Show vbModeless
AnotherForm1Variable.Left = 0
AnotherForm1Variable.Width = Screen.Width
End Sub
```

Here you're creating two object variables, both capable of storing references to instances of the Form1 class. You then go on to create a new form and assign a reference to it to Form1Variable, just like you did in the previous example. The next line takes the reference stored in Form1Variable and assigns it to AnotherForm1Variable. Now both Form1Variable and AnotherForm1Variable contain the same object reference.

The Is Statement

Just as you can't assign object references with the normal equal sign as you can with other variable types, you can't compare two object references with the equal sign. Instead, use the Is operator, as in the expression

```
AnotherForm1Variable Is Form1Variable
```

This expression returns True if the two variables point to the same object; otherwise, it returns False.

Note that you can use either the Form1Variable or AnotherForm1Variable to access the object's methods and properties:

```
Form1Variable.Show vbModeless

AnotherForm1Variable.Left = 0
AnotherForm1Variable.Width = Screen.Width
```

Form Object Types

In the previous example, you created a form based on the Form1 class. To do that, you declared an object variable of the type Form1, created the form itself (with New), and then assigned the reference to the form to the variable. Now assume you want to write a subroutine to center the form on the screen.

Listing 7.3 shows one possible solution.

LISTING 7.3   Passing a Form as a Procedure Argument

```
Public Sub CenterForm(AnyForm1Form As Form1)
AnyForm1Form.Move (Screen.Width - AnyForm1Form.Width) / 2, _
   (Screen.Height - AnyForm1Form.Height) / 2
End Sub
```

As you can see, to complete this task, the subroutine needs access to the form's Move method and its Width and Height properties. The way to do this is to pass the reference to the form that you want to center to another object variable that is a parameter of the subroutine. The code that you would use to call this subroutine from the form's Load event subroutine would be

```
CenterForm Me
```

The Me keyword provides the reference that you need to the form object that called the subroutine.

Although that solution would work, it is limited in one important way. It can be used only to center forms that are instances of the Form1 class. If you have another form class in your project, say Form2, you wouldn't be able to use the same subroutine because Visual Basic 6 would complain that you are attempting to pass a Form1 object reference to a Form2 object variable. It's a bit like trying to store a String in an Integer: The two class types are completely different as far as Visual Basic 6 is concerned, even though they are both forms.

The solution is to use a more generic class type. Visual Basic 6 has a built-in class type called Form. An object variable of type Form can be used to hold a reference to any form object, be it a Form1 object or whatever. Let's modify CenterForm so that it will work for any type of form. The final version is shown in Listing 7.4.

LISTING 7.4   Centering any Form on the Screen

```
Public Sub CenterForm(AnyForm As Form)
AnyForm.Move (Screen.Width - AnyForm.Width) / 2, _
    (Screen.Height - AnyForm.Height) / 2
End Sub
```

Now you can call CenterForm from a Form1 form, a Form2 form, or any type of form, including an MDI form.

Lesson Summary

Visual Basic forms are based on the Visual Basic form class. You can create your own forms in code with the New keyword. A single object can be referenced by more than one variable. To determine if two objects are the same use the Is statement.

Quiz 2

1. The following line of code:

```
Set Form1Variable = New Form1
```

    a. Creates a new `Form1` object and assigns the object reference to the variable `Form1Variable`.

    b. Sets the variable `Form1Variable` equal to the default property of Form1.

    c. Causes a runtime error because the function `CreateObject` is required to create a new instance of a form.

    d. The Function `New` tests if Form1 contains more then one object reference and returns the number of references to the variable `Form1Variable`.

2. How does an object variable differ from some other type of variable, such as a `String`?

    a. The names of object variables must begin with `Form`.

    b. Object variables must be written in Java.

    c. Object variables cannot be passed to subroutines.

    d. You must use the `Set` statement to assign a value to an object variable.

3. Which one of the following is True?

    a. The `Is` statement can be used to create an instance of an object.

    b. A single object can only be referenced by a single variable.

    c. A single object can be referenced by multiple variables.

    d. Variables can not contain object references.

4. The `New` statement

    a. Creates a new file

    b. Creates an object

    c. Redimensions an array

    d. Prepares an object for reuse

Exercise 2

Complexity: Easy

1. Write a few lines of code to create a new instance of a Visual Basic form using the `CreateObject` statement as opposed to the keyword `New`.

Complexity: Moderate

2. Write a program that creates a new instance of a form and assigns the object reference to two different variables. Using one of the references, modify the form's

backcolor and caption. Using the same reference, show the modified form; after the form is displayed, set the variable you have been using to Nothing. Add a button that uses the other reference to hide the form. What happens when you try to hide the form?

LESSON 3

Control Classes

Now that you appreciate what's going on behind the scenes when form objects are created, you can move on to considering the object-oriented nature of controls—or, to give them a more accurate title, control classes.

Although controls are classes, they differ from forms and the other classes in Visual Basic 6 in two important ways:

- They cannot exist on their own. They have to be contained within a form. In fact, a form class is known as a container for the control classes that appear on it. Therefore, when you delete a form class from your project, all the control classes that are contained within it are deleted, too.
- Whereas forms and other classes are implemented within Visual Basic 6 itself, controls can be implemented outside, as separate programs that conform to the ActiveX Control Extension (OCX) standard.

Through the OCX standard, third-party suppliers can produce their own specialty controls. (We'll call these controls OCX controls from now on.) This is an important way in which Visual Basic 6's functionality can be extended. If you want to add some special functionality to your project, it is likely that someone has already written an OCX that does what you need. If they haven't, you can write your own. We will cover the details of ActiveX Control creation in Chapter 17, "Advanced ActiveX and Registry API Techniques."

What Are OCX Controls?

The great thing about OCX controls is that they are as easy to use in Visual Basic as the standard controls. This is because they have properties and methods and fire off events in just the same way. The only difference is that the standard controls are permanently built in to Visual Basic 6 and cannot be removed from the toolbox, whereas OCXs are packaged as separate files. Because of this, you have to go through a small procedure to tell

Visual Basic 6 that you want to use a particular OCX in your project. This procedure is known as referencing the OCX.

Referencing OCXs

The tool that you use to reference an OCX is the Custom Controls dialog box. Display it by selecting Components from the Project menu. This dialog box is shown in Figure 7.1.

FIGURE 7.1

A Custom Controls dialog box.

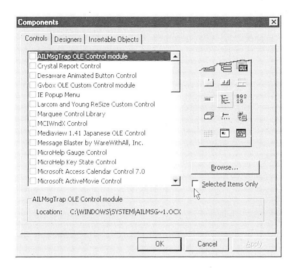

The first thing you'll want to do is find out which OCXs are available for use on your computer. To do this, make sure that the Selected Items Only check box in the lower-right corner of the dialog is not checked. This way, all the OCXs installed on your PC are displayed, rather than just the ones currently in use. Visual Basic can do this because each OCX file has already been registered with Windows. This happened when the OCX was installed. To the left of each entry in the list box is a small check box. Use it to signal to Visual Basic 6 that this is an OCX that you want to use in this project. Just click the check box with the mouse so that a check mark appears next to the description of the OCX. The full path name of the currently highlighted OCX file is displayed at the bottom of the dialog box so that you can check which OCX file is going to be used.

Each OCX file can contain more than one control class. For example, the Common Windows Control OCX (COMCTL32.OCX) contains a total of nine controls. (We'll show you these controls in Chapter 8, "Using ActiveX Controls.")

7

After you press the OK button, Visual Basic 6 loads the control classes from the OCX file and updates the toolbox with the new controls. After the controls have been added to the toolbox, you can add them to your forms in the usual way.

When you save your project to disk, the reference to the OCX is saved with it so that when you next load your project, the OCX is loaded too. Similarly, when you compile your project, the references to the OCXs are stored in the compiled program so that the correct OCX files can be found at runtime.

Object Variables for Controls

You need to be aware of one important restriction when using controls. Whereas form object variables can be declared in your code by the name you have given to the form, control classes can be referenced only by their class name.

A quick example should prove the point. Start with the default project and add a text box to it. The text box has its Name property set to Text1 by default. If this were a form, you could create an object variable of type Text1 and then assign a reference to it. Controls, however, behave slightly differently. Try running the following one-line example:

```
Private Sub Form_Load()
  Debug.Print TypeName(Text1)
End Sub
```

When you run the above code, Text1's type name is displayed as TextBox, rather than as Text1. You can still create a separate object variable and assign the text box's reference to it, however, the same way that you did with a form:

```
Private Sub Form_Load()
  Dim TextBoxVariable As TextBox
  Set TextBoxVariable = Text1
  Text1.Text = "Some text"
  Debug.Print TextBoxVariable.Text
End Sub
```

As you can see, the reference to the TextBox object in the variable Text1 is being assigned to the variable called TextBoxVariable, which you have created. You are assigning it in exactly the same way that you assigned form object variables, using the Set statement.

After the assignment, both Text1 and TextBoxVariable are left referencing the same physical TextBox control object.

Passing Control References

Control references can be passed in the parameters of a subroutine or function in a similar way to a form reference. Here's how you do it.

Using the previous example, add a subroutine to Form1 as follows:

```
Private Sub ControlRefTest (TextBoxVariable As TextBox)
  TextBoxVariable.Text = "Got here!"
End Sub
```

Call the subroutine from the form's Load event subroutine:

```
Private Sub Form_Load
  ControlRefTest Text1
End Sub
```

What's clever about this is that you can pass control references to subroutines and functions that are in code modules outside the context of the form. You can, therefore, develop common procedures that work, for example, on all of your text boxes.

This can be extremely useful. Imagine that you want to perform some special validation on the text that has been entered into a text box. The example in Listing 7.5 performs some rudimentary checking on the text in a text box to make sure that it is in a valid time format. (The code expects the time to be represented in the format hh:mm:ss.) If the text fails the validation check, a separate subroutine, called SetTextBoxError, is called to select all the text in the text box so that the entire entry can be easily retyped. The PC's speaker beeps and the focus is set back to the text box that failed the validation check.

LISTING 7.5 Using a Common Routine for Data Checking

```
Public Sub ValidateTime(MyTextBox As TextBox)
Dim Hour As Variant, Min As Variant, Sec As Variant
Dim I As Integer
If Len(MyTextBox.Text) = 8 Then
  For I = 1 To 8
  If I = 3 Or I = 6 Then
    If Mid(MyTextBox.Text, I, 1) <> ":" Then
    SetTextBoxError MyTextBox
    Exit Sub
    End If
  Else
    If Not IsNumeric(Mid(MyTextBox.Text, I, 1)) Then
    SetTextBoxError MyTextBox
    Exit Sub
    End If
  End If
```

7

continues

LISTING 7.5   continued

```
Next I
Hour = Left(MyTextBox.Text, 2)
Min = Mid(MyTextBox.Text, 4, 2)
Sec = Right(MyTextBox.Text, 2)
If Hour < 0 Or Hour > 23 Or Min < 0 Or Min > 59 _
Or Sec < 0 Or Sec > 59 Then
SetTextBoxError MyTextBox
Exit Sub
End If
Else
SetTextBoxError MyTextBox
Exit Sub
End If
End Sub

Private Sub SetTextBoxError(MyTextBox As TextBox)
MyTextBox.SelStart = 0
MyTextBox.SelLength = Len(MyTextBox)
Beep
MyTextBox.SetFocus
End Sub


Private Sub Text1_LostFocus()
ValidateTime Text1
End Sub
```

The ValidateTime routine should be called from the text box's LostFocus event subroutine. The call is also shown. Both ValidateTime and SetTextBoxError can be added to a standard code module. Then you only have to call ValidateTime from the LostFocus event subroutine of an individual text box to add this functionality to it. This will work for all text boxes, no matter which form they are contained on.

The Control Data Type

Visual Basic 6 also has a generic type called Control that you can use in place of the individual class name of a control. This is useful if you want to perform a more general operation on a control in a subroutine or function, and you want to pass a reference to more than one type of control to that procedure. The Control type is analogous to the Form type, which can be used to hold references to all types of forms.

We'll demonstrate this with a subroutine that disables a control by setting its `Enabled` property to `False`. This subroutine can be used with any control that has an `Enabled` property, which is almost all of them:

```
Public Sub DisableControl(AnyControl As Control)
  AnyControl.Enabled = False
End Sub
```

TypeName and If TypeOf

At times, it can be useful to determine what type of control a control variable is currently referencing. This is particularly true in common procedures where a reference has been passed to a Control type variable.

You can do this in the same way that you would find out the class name of a form object, by passing the reference to the `TypeName` function. For example,

```
Debug.Print TypeName(AnyControl)
```

Alternatively, you can use the `TypeOf` keyword in an `If...Then` statement. The syntax for this expression is

```
If TypeOf objectname Is objecttype Then
```

For example, to disable only `TextBox` controls, you would use

```
Public Sub DisableControl(AnyControl As Control)
  If TypeOf AnyControl Is TextBox Then
 AnyControl.Enabled = False
  End If
End Sub
```

Finally, to disable anything but `TextBox` controls, use the `Not` operator:

```
If Not (TypeOf AnyControl Is TextBox) Then
  AnyControl.Enabled = False
End If
```

Working with Objects: The With Statement

Sometimes you will want to perform multiple operations on the same object. For example, you might want to set multiple coordinates of a control, as in

```
ThatForm.txtTheBox.Left = 0
ThatForm.txtTheBox.Top = 0
ThatForm.txtTheBox.Width = 200
ThatForm.txtTheBox.Height = 200
```

7

Visual Basic provides a shorthand way to do this, without having to retype the entire object reference. This is the `With` statement, which has the syntax:

```
With object
    [statements]
End With
```

To phrase the above example more concisely, you would write:

```
With txtTheBox
    .Left = 0
    .Top = 0
    .Width = 200
    .Height = 200
End With
```

You actually get a double benefit from using `With`. First, you reduce your typing load (and the possibility of clumsy-finger mistakes) because you type the reference `ThatForm.txtTheBox` only once. Second, your program will run faster because Visual Basic has to *dereference* it only once. (*Dereferencing* is a fancy word for *figure out where it is*.) In a short demonstration program such as this, the second benefit is insignificant, but in a full-blown application, it can make a significant difference.

Lesson Summary

Just as Visual Basic forms are based on the form class, ActiveX controls are also Visual Basic classes. Using the Visual Basic control classes, you can write multiple-purpose routines to process ActiveX controls by passing a control reference into a subroutine or function. In order to determine the type of ActiveX controls being referenced by a variable, use the `TypeOf` keyword. This lesson also showed how to find out the class name of an ActiveX control using the `TypeName` function.

Quiz 3

1. What does the following code do, assuming `Text1` is a reference to an ActiveX `TextBox` control?

   ```
   With Text1
   .ToolTipText = "Hello World"
   .Text = "Hello World"
   End With
   ```

   a. Tests the control to see if it has a value that is not "".

   b. Sets the variables `ToolTipText` and `Text` to the string `"Hello World"`.

   c. Sets the ActiveX control, `Text1`, `ToolTipText` and `Text` methods to the string "`Hello World`".

   d. Sets the ActiveX control, `Text1`, `ToolTipText` and Text properties to the string "`Hello World`".

2. Visual Basic's custom control is called an ___.

   a. VBX

   b. ADO

   c. OOP

   d. OCX

3. If you have a `TextBox` control called `Text1`, what would you expect to be returned from:

`TypeName(Text1)`

   a. `TextBox`

   b. `Control`

   c. Nothing is printed unless you previously assigned it a value

   d. `Text1`

4. How would you declare a subroutine to set a Command button's caption to Click Me? The subroutine takes only a Command button as an argument.

   a. `Public Sub SetCaption(TheButton As CommandButton)`

   b. `Public Sub SetCaption(TheButton As Control)`

   c. `Public Sub SetCaption(TheButton As Command1)`

   d. `Public Sub SetCaption(Caption As Property)`

Exercise 3

Complexity: Moderate

1. Write a function that passes a `TextBox` control by reference and determines if the text string in the `TextBox` is a valid date. The function should return True for valid dates and False for invalid dates.

Complexity: Easy

2. List the situations in which you would use the `TypeName` and `TypeOf` statement.

7

LESSON 4

Introducing User-Defined Classes

User-defined classes are really the key to making the most of Visual Basic 6's object-oriented features. Without them, your project cannot be considered fully object oriented.

Although you've been using classes for some time now, the classes that you have been using to date have been limited in two important respects:

- They have been written by someone else. You have been reusing them rather than creating your own. The reusability of classes is an important feature of object-oriented programming and, of course, you have been able to customize the behavior of these classes by setting their properties, calling their methods, and programming their events. So far, however, you have been unable to develop your own classes from scratch.
- They have been mainly concerned with the user interface of your project. The single-instance classes are used for accessing operating system services, such as the Clipboard, but if you consider the two main types of classes that you have used so far (forms and controls), it should be clear that they address only the user interface of your projects.

Why You Might Implement Your Own Classes

Before we go any further, it is important that you understand why there should be a need for you to implement your own classes. The problem is that your project's user interface may account for only a fraction of the code that you have to write.

We can show you what we mean by looking back at some of the projects that you've developed so far. Take the video store project, for example. In that project, it was clear that all you were implementing was the user interface of a much larger application. Accordingly, the types of objects you were concerned with were display objects (controls) required to display information on a form.

What you didn't consider were all the other types of objects that could exist in such an application. Real-world objects, such as members, videotapes, credit cards, and accounts would all need to be represented somehow if you were going to complete that application and make it fully object oriented.

HyperPad, too, has the same problem because it should ideally introduce a new type of object to the world: a HyperPad document. It's important that you recognize that the data that HyperPad processes doesn't consist only of the characters stored in the Text property of the TextBox control. Instead, you need to think of a HyperPad document as an autonomous object independent of the text box. It just so happens that a text box was a convenient control to use for manipulating the text of the document for editing purposes. The document itself could and should be completely independent.

HyperPad's Document Object

Armed with this knowledge, let's see how we sneakily got around this problem. In Chapter 6, "Building the GUI with Forms, Menus and MDI Forms," you managed to get away without having to create a separate user-defined HyperPad document object because the TextBox control satisfied some of the requirements for the document. The form you used for the document window, frmDocument, provided the remaining functionality. Specifically, the form provided a mechanism to name the document and determine whether its contents had changed since it was last saved, and the text box contained within the form provided the capability to store and edit the text of the document.

This is, in fact, how many Visual Basic 6 programmers go about their programming: reusing forms, controls, and other classes to provide a *best-fit* approach to program design. After all, if objects that you need to create in your projects fit well into an existing class, such as a form or a control, then there's no real reason to go to the additional effort of implementing the object as a separate class.

However, there are cases in which there are benefits to going to this extra effort. If you later want to replace the TextBox control with a different control, for example, you may experience incompatibility problems between the two controls. In Chapter 8, "Using ActiveX Controls," you're going to do just that when you replace the text box in HyperPad with one of the RichTextBox control. This will enable you to change the font and color attributes of the text in your HyperPad document and make it truly a "super" document.

We're now going to look at the changes that you need to make to HyperPad to implement the document as a separate user-defined class. Open the HyperPad project as you left it at the end of Chapter 6, "Building the GUI with Forms, Menus, and MDI Forms."

The Class Module

The key to creating your own classes at runtime is the class module. HyperPad doesn't have one, so let's start by adding a class module to it. This class module will become the HyperPad document class.

The CD included with this book contains two versions of HyperPad in the directory for this chapter. The version in the OldHPad subdirectory has not been modified. The version in the HyperPad directory includes the changes described in this chapter.

7

Understanding how to create and implement classes is crucial to your success in object-oriented programming. Open the version in OldHPad so you can follow this step-by-step example.

Add a class module to the project by selecting Add Class Module from Visual Basic 6's Project menu. This brings up the Add Class Module dialog box for class modules, as shown in Figure 7.2.

FIGURE 7.2

An Add Class Module dialog box.

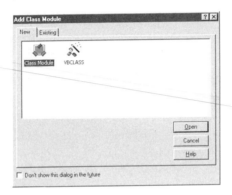

Your Add Class Module dialog box may differ, depending on the version of Visual Basic 6 you have. The Class Builder and ADDIN Builder are supplied only with the Professional and Enterprise Editions of Visual Basic 6.

The Existing tab is included with all editions of Visual Basic 5. As its name implies, it enables you to add class modules that you have already written to your project. Reusability is one of the main features of object-oriented programming; when you have a class that works correctly, you do not need to reinvent the wheel each time you need the functionality of that class.

Select Class Module in the Add Class Module dialog box. VB 6 adds the class to your project, and it appears in the Project Explorer as Class1 (Class1). This is shown in Figure 7.3.

Notice, also, that the Add Class dialog box has brought you straight to the Code window for your class. This is shown in Figure 7.4.

Going straight to the Code window for your class is important because the class module has no visual interface of its own. However, apart from this, class modules are, in all other respects, identical to forms. Because you are so used to forms now, this should come as good news. In fact, everything that you will learn about class modules in this lesson can be equally applied to form modules.

FIGURE 7.3

The class has been added to your project.

FIGURE 7.4

The Code window displayed for the class module.

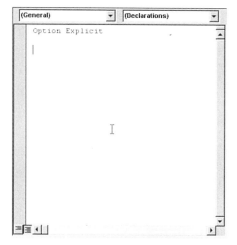

Before we continue with programming HyperPad's new document class, there are a couple of points to note:

1. A class module is a class—it doesn't become an object until an instance of it is created at runtime. Think of it as a blueprint for an object. It's up to you to decide what a class module represents in your project. It might represent a customer, an item of stock, a bank account, a currency, or anything you like. It's entirely up to you.

2. You cannot begin a project by specifying that a class module should be the startup form. If, for any reason, you need to start your project by creating an instance of a class module, you can achieve the same result by using the Sub Main startup method and creating an instance of your class module manually.

7

What Does a Class Module Contain?

A class module can contain three items:

- Subroutines and functions that you add to its General Declarations section: These become the methods of the class.

- Properties that you add to the class module: These are the variables that the class will manipulate. Some of the properties are declared as Public, accessible from any part of the supporting program, and some are Private, accessible only from within the class.

- Events that you add to the class module: Events are different from methods. *Events* are procedures that are called from within the class and have an effect on objects outside the class object. They are outgoing interfaces. *Methods* are procedures that are called from outside the class module and have an effect on the class object. They are incoming interfaces.

You should be quite familiar with adding subroutines, functions, variables, and constants by now. However, what you haven't seen is the concept of a user-defined property. By the word *property*, we don't just mean Public variables. Instead, we're talking about something much closer to the properties that you see in the Properties window. These properties are not added to the Properties window. You can make them work in the same way as "real" properties, but they remain something that you add to the class module via the Code window.

Lesson Summary

This lesson introduced you to user-defined classes, which are classes that you design and create in Visual Basic. User-defined classes are created with a Visual Basic class module. A user-defined class method is a subroutine or function declared in the class module and variables and property procedures make up the properties of a user-defined class. Private class properties are only accessible from within the class module, while public properties can be accessed by code outside of the class module. Class modules can contain events which are procedures called from within the class and can have an effect on objects outside the class object.

Quiz 4

1. A class module is used to create _____.

    a. a user-defined class

    b. a database class

    c. a library of standard procedures and functions

    d. None of the above

2. Which of the following can NOT be contained in a class module?

    a. events

    b. ActiveX controls

    c. methods

    d. properties

3. A class property declared private _____.

    a. can be accessed outside of the class module

    b. can never be modified

    c. can be accessed only from within the class module

    d. automatically generates a property procedure

4. Classes that you can create are called _____.

    a. database classes

    b. user modules

    c. user-defined objects

    d. user-defined classes

Exercise 4

Complexity: Easy

1. Create a new class called Test1. Add a function to the class called `loopback` that takes a single string parameter as input and returns the input string as the function's return parameter.

Complexity: Moderate

2. Write a program to use the class Test1 created in the previous exercise. The program should create an instance of the Test1 class and invoke the object's `Loopback` method displaying the returned string in a message box.

7

LESSON 5

Using Classes with HyperPad

Now let's make the changes needed to make HyperPad more object oriented.

Building the Class

Of course, this would all have been a lot easier if you had begun the HyperPad project as an object-oriented design. You didn't, and you will have to make several changes before you can implement clsDocument and have it work. Let's take them a step at a time.

The Class Module's Properties

The first thing to do is to give the new class module a suitable name. Call it clsDocument instead of Class1. To change the name, use the Properties window and look at the properties for the class module. The class module has only one property, Name. Any other properties that the class has are user defined. Before you go any further, save the class. Open the File menu and select Save objDocument.cls.

Now add some properties to clsDocument. In the General Declarations section of clsDocument, add the following declarations:

```
Option Explicit
Public Changed As Boolean
Public Closing As Boolean
Public DocName As String
Public DocumentForm As frmDocument
```

What you have really done here is to create four public properties for the new clsDocument object. Two of them, Changed and Closing, existed before as form-level variables. The other two are new. For now, that is all you need to do with the new class, but there is some work to be done in the original code of HyperPad.

Changes to frmDocument

Switch to the Code window of frmDocument and make the following changes listed:

1. Remove the following two lines from the Declarations section.
   ```
   Dim Changes as Boolean
   Public Closing as Boolean
   ```

2. Add the following line to the Declarations section.
   ```
   Public objDocument as New clsDocument
   ```

3. Add the following code to Sub Form_Load().

```
Private Sub Form_Load()
   Set objDocument.DocumentForm = Me
   objDocument.DocName = Me.Caption
End Sub
```

4. Change all references to Changed and Closing so that VB can access them from the class. The easiest way to make global changes such as this is to click Replace under the Edit menu from inside the frmDocument module. Visual Basic 6's Find and Replace dialog boxes let you make procedurewide, modulewide, or project-wide searches. (Additionally, you can opt to limit searches to selected text regions.)

5. Make sure the default scope of Current Module is checked, enter Changed as the string to find, and enter objDocument.Changed as the string to replace, as shown in Figure 7.5. Follow the same procedure to change Closing to objDocument.Closing. In this case, you'll need to change the occurrence of Closing in the frmMain module as well, so instead of the line in the SetupCSMenus routine that reads

FIGURE 7.5

The Replace dialog box.

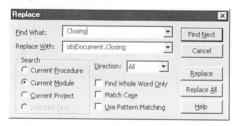

If

```
Forms.Closing = False Then
```

you will have

```
If Forms.objDocument.Closing = False Then
```

Note

Make the searches manually rather than clicking Replace All because you don't want to change occurrences of "changed" or "closing" in cases where the word is not used as a variable reference.

6. Switch to Sub Form_Unload() of frmDocument. There is a change to make here and an addition. The change is to the message displayed in the MsgBox function. It

7

changes the reference from `Me.Caption` to `objDocument.DocName`. The addition is at the end of the procedure. All new text is in bold.

```
Private Sub Form_Unload(Cancel As Integer)
If objDocument.Changed Then
  Select Case MsgBox("The text in the " & objDocument.DocName & _
    " file has changed." & vbCr & vbCr & _
    "Do you want to save the changes?", _
    vbExclamation + vbYesNoCancel, frmMain.Caption)
 Case vbYes
    'Perform save
 Case vbNo
    'Allow form to close
 Case vbCancel
    'Cancel close form
    Cancel = True
  End Select
End If
objDocument.Closing = Not Cancel
frmMain.SetupCSMenus
If Cancel = False Then
  Set objDocument = Nothing
End If
End Sub
```

7. Add the following changes to the `Change` event of `txtDocument`.

```
Private Sub txtDocument_Change()
  objDocument.Changed = True
  If Right(Me.Caption, 2) <> " *" Then
 Me.Caption = objDocument.DocName & " *"
  End If
End Sub
```

If you made the one change to `frmMain` when you ran the `Replace` function, your work is done. If not, make that change now (see Step 4).

A Look at the Code

The class you have created is the simplest of all possible classes. The properties were all declared as Public variables, and you created neither methods nor events. The `DocName` property is included so that you can remove the program's dependence on the caption of `frmDocument`. The name of the document needs to be a part of the class. The other new variable is an object variable that completes the encapsulation process by enabling you to access the document's form as a part of the class.

According to the principles of object-oriented programming, all the data for an object should be accessed only through references to that object. The class that defines the object is said to encapsulate the data. That means that the class can protect the data from changes that are not appropriate. In this case, little *protection* is necessary, but in some cases, the data must not be allowed to assume certain values. For example, a variable that counts the number of transactions on a bank account may not have a negative value. You will see how properties are protected in Lesson 7.

Creating an Object

After the blueprint is drawn, HyperPad needs to be able to create a new instance of `clsDocument` when it is opened and each time the `AddForm` function is called. The following declaration does the job:

```
Public objDocument As New clsDocument
```

It declares the object as a variable, and the `New` in the line also creates an instance of the object. This is a convenient technique, and one that you will use in the future. As an alternative, you could have used

```
Public myDocument As clsDocument
Sub Form_Load()
  Set myDocument = New clsDocument
End Sub
```

to do the same thing. Either way you do it, it is called instantiating the object.

The `Form_Load` procedure creates a reference to the new object and sets the value of `DocName`.

```
Private Sub Form_Load()
  Set objDocument.DocumentForm = Me
  objDocument.DocName = Me.Caption
End Sub
```

The change you made to `Sub txtDocument Change()` adds a Windows convention to HyperPad. It is conventional to tag document titles with an asterisk if the document has been changed. The following code performs that function for you:

```
If Right(Me.Caption, 2) <> " *" Then
  Me.Caption = objDocument.DocName & " *"
End If
```

The Events in `clsDocument`

Even though you did not add any events to `clsDocument`, Visual Basic inserted two events by default. They are shown in Figure 7.6. The `Initialize` event is fired when an object is created (instantiated) from the class, and the `Terminate` event is fired when the class is destroyed. Often there will be no code in these events, but you may need them to create or destroy class-related objects.

7

FIGURE 7.6

The default events for a class.

```
Option Explicit
Public Changed As Boolean
Public Closing As Boolean
Public DocName As String

Private Sub Class_Initialize()

End Sub

Private Sub Class_Terminate()

End Sub
```

Destroying the Object

Sounds drastic, doesn't it? Perhaps, but it is also important. Objects take up memory space, and that memory space is not relinquished by Visual Basic simply by unloading the object. When HyperPad is done using an instance of objDocument, the form Unload event contains the code

```
If Cancel = False Then
   Set objDocument = Nothing
End If
```

The Nothing keyword does remove the object from memory. If you do not do this, you will soon have all your available RAM filled up with unreferenced objects, a phenomenon called *memory leak* by old-hand programmers.

Visual Basic keeps an internal count of how many object variables are currently referencing a given object. When that count falls to zero, VB destroys the object that was referenced. This is a particularly useful feature. If Visual Basic did not keep this count for you, you would have to do it yourself to be sure you didn't pull the rug from under the feet of some code somewhere.

 Note

When you are programming with objects, do not use the End VCR button or the keyword End to exit from your programs. Both close your program abruptly, without using the form unload or query unload procedures. Similarly, don't exit from the development environment with a program running. In either case, you will generate memory leaks. Memory leaks are objects that are left in memory with no way to close them except rebooting the computer.

Running the Program

Now you are ready to run the new HyperPad. Try all the features that have been implemented to this point. About the only visible difference is the addition of .* to the end of Untitled in the caption of the form. Internally, though, it is a very different program.

Lesson Summary

In this lesson, you created your first user-defined class called clsDocument. The class is used to enhance the HyperPad application. This lesson showed how to create an object with the user-defined class, use the objects properties and how to destroy the object. The class module have events initialize and terminate were introduced and discussed. The initialize event is fired when an instance of the class is created, and the terminate event is fired when the object is destroyed.

Quiz 5

1. What events are triggered when an instance of a class is created and when an instance of a class is destroyed?

   a. Load and Unload

   b. Initialize and Terminate

   c. Add and Remove

   d. Add and Destroy

2. Which of the following is one of a class module's predefined properties?

   a. OLE

   b. Instancing

   c. Public

   d. Name

3. How do you create an instance of a user-defined class using two lines of code?

   a. `Public objSomeObject As clsSomeClass`
      `New objSomeObject = clsSomeClass`

   b. `Public objSomeObject As clsSomeClass`
      `Set objSomeObject = New clsSomeClass`

   c. `Public objSomeObject As clsSomeClass`
      `Set objSomeObject = clsSomeClass`

   d. `Declare objSomeObject As clsSomeClass`
      `Set objSomeObject = New clsSomeClass`

7

4. How do you destroy a user-defined object?

    a. Call the Unload event routine of the form that references the object.

    b. Set the object reference to a Null string (" ").

    c. Set the object reference to Nothing.

    d. Set all the references to the object to Nothing.

Exercise 5

Complexity: Easy

1. Describe the differences between creating class properties with public variables versus private variables.

Complexity: Easy

2. Describe what the class initialize and terminate events are used for.

LESSON 6

Collections

Now that HyperPad is more object oriented than it was before, you can begin to use the additional features of Visual Basic 6 that are designed to make programming with classes even easier.

One of these features is the collection. In fact, you met collections in the guise of the forms collection in Chapter 6, "Building the GUI with Forms, Menus, and MDI Forms." Remember that every form that's created in your project is automatically added to the forms collection, which provides a convenient mechanism for gaining access to all the forms in your project. You relied on it in frmMain's SetupCSMenus subroutine. Now you're going to look at collections in detail, including how you can create your own.

To get started, think of a real-world collection, such as a stamp collection. A stamp collection consists of lots of individual stamps, each of which is an object. The stamp collection as a whole can also be thought of as an object, but one that contains lots of other stamp objects.

A stamp collection might physically consist of a binder in which the stamps are stored. The binder forms an intrinsic part of the collection. It keeps the stamps clean and prevents them from getting lost. It also enables you to organize the stamps so that you can locate individual objects in the collection quickly.

A collection in Visual Basic 6 terms is similar to the real-world stamp collection. A collection is a Visual Basic 6 object in its own right and is analogous to the binder in which the stamp objects are kept. Being an object, the collection also has methods that you can call to organize the objects it contains.

This is pretty neat. You can effectively ask the binder to find the right object for you.

Creating Collections

Okay, how do we create a collection? Some collections are created and maintained for you automatically. The forms collection is one you've already seen. Others that you have yet to see include the printers collection and numerous collections used to access databases.

You're going to enhance HyperPad by adding all the clsDocument objects to a new collection. Say you want to provide a documentwide search facility. By storing all the clsDocument objects in one collection, you can search through them all with ease.

Because a collection is an object, creating one is just a matter of creating a new instance of the built-in Collection class. Add the statement in Listing 7.6 to the General Declarations section of frmMain.

LISTING 7.6   Declaring the Collection

```
Option Explicit
Public DocColl As New Collection
```

The variable is Public so that you can access it from outside frmMain.

Now when HyperPad is started and frmMain is created, the DocColl collection will be automatically created.

Destroying Collections

Now that you've created the collection, the question arises as to how to destroy it. You could rely on Visual Basic 6 to tidy up everything for you when the program terminates and do nothing explicitly. However, it's good programming practice to be tidy and destroy it yourself. Listing 7.7 presents the code to destroy the collection in frmMain's Terminate event.

7

LISTING 7.7   Destroying the Collection

```
Private Sub MDIForm_Terminate()
  Set DocColl = Nothing
End Sub
```

This is the same syntax used to destroy a user-defined object. The same rules about object destruction apply, so the DocColl collection object is destroyed only because its reference count has fallen to zero.

What Happens When You Destroy a Collection?

Destroying a collection can have far-reaching effects. Here's why. Visual Basic 6 maintains a count of how many references there are to each and every object. When that count falls to zero for an object, the object is destroyed. This is why you can use the same Set ObjectVariable = Nothing syntax both to dereference an object from a variable and to destroy the object itself.

This is important because collections don't actually store objects. (OK, we know we said they did, but we were just trying to get you to understand the idea of a collection.) In fact, collections store only object references. The object isn't physically moved into the collection. Instead, a copy of its reference is created and that is stored in the collection. In this sense, you can think of a library card catalog as a collection of books, even though the books themselves are stored elsewhere.

Storing references in a collection is efficient and it has the advantage of hooking into Visual Basic 6's object deletion behavior. When you destroy a collection, you also destroy the object references contained within it. If the reference counts for the objects that were referenced by the collection fall to zero, those objects will also be destroyed.

As a result, it is possible to destroy all the objects in the collection just by destroying the collection. If you don't want those objects to be destroyed, you must make another reference to the objects before you destroy the collection.

Adding Object References to the Collection

The objects that you're going to add to this new collection are the clsDocument objects created in frmDocument's Load event.

Keys

Before you can add more clsDocument objects, you need some way of telling one from the other. Right now, you don't know which clsDocument object reference is which in the collection. You really have no means of distinguishing them. You need a fast way to locate the correct reference, either to access it or to remove it from the collection.

The answer to this problem is to use a key when adding the reference to the collection in the first place. A key is a string you define that is a unique identifier that you associate with that particular object.

You could, for example, add a static Integer variable to frmMain's General Declarations section and increment it each time you create a new clsDocument object. You could then convert that integer number to a string and use it as a key to the object reference. You could store the key in a form variable so that you would know which key to use to obtain the correct object reference from the collection. Below are the changes needed to implement this strategy.

Adding and Incrementing a Key

In frmMain, add a new Integer variable called CollKeyIndex, as shown in the code in Listing 7.8. The CollKeyIndex variable is automatically initialized to zero when HyperPad starts.

LISTING 7.8   frmMain's General Declarations

```
Public CollKeyIndex As Integer
```

Now add a new Integer variable to frmDocument's General Declarations section, as shown in Listing 7.9. This new variable stores the key number used when adding the objDocument reference to the collection.

LISTING 7.9   frmDocument's General Declarations

```
Option Explicit
Public objDocument As New clsDocument
Dim CollKey As Integer
```

The Add Method

The easiest syntax to use to add the objects to the collection is

```
frmMain.DocColl.Add objDocument
```

Here, you're passing the object reference in objDocument to the collection's Add method. From now on, each object will be referenced by both the objDocument variable and a

7

copy of the reference in the collection. Each object will have two active references. The effect of this is that you must set the objDocument variable to Nothing and remove the reference from the collection before Visual Basic 6 actually destroys the object.

The complete syntax for the Add method is

```
object.Add item [,key] [,before¦,,after]
```

You have the option to specify before or after arguments to give the position in the collection. These values can either be integer values (indicating the position) or strings (indicating the key). You want to use only the key parameter, however. Modify frmDocument's Load event subroutine so that it appears as shown in Listing 7.10. The modified lines are highlighted.

LISTING 7.10   Assigning Keys to the Collection Members

```
Private Sub Form_Load()
frmMain.DocColl.Add objDocument, CStr(frmMain.CollKeyIndex)
CollKey = frmMain.CollKeyIndex
frmMain.CollKeyIndex = frmMain.CollKeyIndex + 1
Set objDocument.DocumentForm = Me
objDocument.DocName = Me.Caption
End Sub
```

The second parameter to the collection's Add method is the string equivalent of the current value of CollKeyIndex in frmMain. You're taking a copy of that value and storing it locally in frmDocument in the new Integer variable, CollKey, so that you can use it later when you need to find the object. You then increment CollKeyIndex in frmMain so that the next time you create an object, it will be stored with a different key.

Of course, this mechanism limits you to creating approximately 32,000 objects in one HyperPad session. This should be large enough, but you could always change CollKeyIndex and CollKey to be Long integers, in which case the limit could be extended to 4 billion objects in one session. It's just a theoretical limit, really, but you need to be aware of it. Of course, you could use a different mechanism to create the key that relies, for example, on large random numbers. That way, you could remove this limit altogether.

The Remove Method

You have to be careful to remove the object reference from the collection; otherwise, the clsDocument objects will not be destroyed. You need to add only one line to frmDocument's Unload event. The line is in bold in Listing 7.11.

LISTING 7.11 The Remove Method

```
Private Sub Form_Unload(Cancel As Integer)
If objDocument.Changed Then
   Select Case MsgBox("The text in the " & objDocument.DocName & _
   " file has changed." & vbCr & vbCr & _
   "Do you want to save the changes?", _
   vbExclamation + vbYesNoCancel, frmMain.Caption)
 Case vbYes
   'Perform save
 Case vbNo
   'Allow form to close
 Case vbCancel
   'Cancel close form
   Cancel = True
  End Select
End If
If Cancel = False Then
  objDocument.Closing = True
End If
frmMain.SetupCSMenus
If Cancel = False Then
   frmMain.DocColl.Remove CStr(CollKey)
  Set objDocument = Nothing
End If
End Sub
```

Just before the object is destroyed, you remove the reference to it from the collection.

Using the Collection to Provide a Search Facility

Now that the collection is available, here are the changes you need to make to implement a document-wide search facility.

Add a new menu item to the end of HyperPad's Edit menu, with the properties shown in Table 7.3.

TABLE 7.3 The Find Item on the Edit Menu

Property	Value
Name	mnuEditFind
Caption	&Find
Shortcut Key	Ctrl+F
Enabled	False

7

Add a new form to HyperPad with the objects and properties shown in Figure 7.7 and summarized in Table 7.4.

FIGURE 7.7

A View of frmFind
form.

TABLE 7.4   Objects and Properties for frmFind

Object	Property	Value
Form	Name	frmFind
	Caption	Find
	BorderStyle	3 - Fixed Dialog
	ControlBox	False
	MaxButton	False
	MinButton	False
Label	Name	lblFind
	Caption	&Text to find
	AutoSize	True
	TabIndex	0
TextBox	Name	txtFind
	MultiLine	True
	TabIndex	1
CommandButton	Name	cmdFind
	Caption	Find
	Default	True
	TabIndex	2
CommandButton	Name	cmdCancel
	Caption	Cancel
	Cancel	True
	TabIndex	3

Add the code in Listing 7.12 to mnuEditFind's Click event subroutine in frmMain.

LISTING 7.12   mnuEditFind's Click Event in frmMain

```
Private Sub mnuEditFind_Click()
  frmFind.Show vbModal
End Sub
```

In frmMain's SetupCSMenus subroutine, add the highlighted code shown in Listing 7.13 in the section of the routine that enables the Select All, Time/Date, and Word Wrap menu items.

LISTING 7.13   Enabling and Disabling the Find Menu Item in SetupCSMenus

```
' enable / disable Select All, TimeDate, WordWrap, and Find
' edit menus according to whether or not there is
' an active document
mnuEditSelectAll.Enabled = Found
mnuEditTimeDate.Enabled = Found
mnuEditWordWrap.Enabled = Found
mnuEditFind.Enabled = Found
```

Complete the cmdCancel button programming in frmFind, as shown in Listing 7.14.

LISTING 7.14   The Find Form's Cancel Button

```
Private Sub cmdCancel_Click()
  Unload Me
End Sub
```

The ZOrder Method

Finally, program the search routine itself in cmdFind's Click event subroutine, as shown in Listing 7.15. This routine works by bringing the form that contains the found string to the front. It does this by calling the ZOrder method on the form, which sets the position of an object within its graphical level.

LISTING 7.15   The Find Routine

```
Private Sub cmdFind_Click()
Dim DocumentObject As clsDocument
Dim FindResults As Integer
```

continues

7

LISTING 7.15   continued

```
For Each DocumentObject In frmMain.DocColl
  FindResults = InStr(DocumentObject.DocumentForm.txtDocument.Text, _
    txtFind.Text)
  If FindResults > 0 Then
 DocumentObject.DocumentForm.ZOrder
 DocumentObject.DocumentForm.txtDocument.SelStart = FindResults - 1
 DocumentObject.DocumentForm.txtDocument.SelLength = Len(txtFind.Text)
 Exit For
  End If
Next DocumentObject
Unload Me
End Sub
```

How It Works

This search routine requires a little explanation.

The first line of interest is the collection version of the For Each...Next statement.
Chapter 4, "Subroutines, Functions, and the Visual Basic 6 Language," shows how to use
the For Each...Next loop with arrays. For collections, the For Each...Next statement
has the syntax

```
For Each element In group
  [statements]
  [Exit For]
  [statements]
Next [element]
```

The For...Each...Next statement is a lot like the For...Next loop you first saw in
Chapter 4, "Subroutines, Functions, and the Visual Basic 6 Language." The difference is
that it works only with collections, and you don't need to know how many objects are in
the collection.

This statement cycles through each reference in the collection and assigns the reference
to the object variable that you name in the statement. You have declared a new object
variable, DocumentObject, that remains in scope only for the duration of this subroutine.
That variable receives a reference to each clsDocument object in the collection on each
pass through the For Each...Next loop.

The search itself is accomplished using the InStr function and by accessing the text
in the txtDocument text boxes directly. If the string is found, the document form
containing the string is brought to the front of the ZOrder and the found text is selected
so that it is visible in the document.

Other Ways to Access the Collection

Using the `For Each...Next` loop is just one way to access the collection. Remember that you have given each reference in the collection a key. Let's program an example of how to access the object through the key. Don't add this example to HyperPad, however.

The `Item` Method

To obtain an object reference for a key, you must use the collection's `Item` method. When you pass a string value to the `Item` method, it treats `Item` as the key and returns the object corresponding to that key.

```
DocColl.Item CollKey
```

To print the current value of the `clsDocument` object's `Changed` variable for a particular form, using its key to access the reference in the collection rather than its own copy of that reference in its `objDocument` variable, you would write

```
Debug.Print frmMain.DocColl.Item(CStr(CollKey)).Changed
```

The `Count` Property

You can also treat the objects in a collection as elements of an array, with `Item` corresponding to an array index. To find out the number of properties in a collection, use the `Count` property.

```
NumObjects = DocColl.Count
```

To iterate through the list, you would use

```
For I = 1 To NumObjects
  Debug.Print frmMain.DocColl.Item.Changed
Next I
```

Lesson Summary

A Visual Basic collection is an object that enables you to organize other objects and provides methods for finding, adding and removing objects. The statement `For Each … Next` provides the Visual Basic programmer with a fast and efficient way to read through the elements of a collection.

7

Quiz 6

1. A collection has methods you can call to _____.

    a. create new forms

    b. create new ActiveX controls

    c. organize the objects it contains

    d. calculate the size of objects

2. To add an item to a collection, use the _____.

    a. Add property

    b. Add method

    c. Insert method

    d. AddItem method

3. If I have a collection called oColl, what does the following code do?

    ```
    iValue = oColl.Count
    ```

    a. Adds the object Count to the collection.

    b. Uses an object called count.

    c. Sets the variable iValue with the number of items in a collection.

    d. Produces an error because the Set statement is required for the code to work properly.

4. What is the advantage of having a key associated with a reference in a collection?

    a. A key can uniquely identify a reference with a descriptive string.

    b. The key automatically corresponds to the class's Caption property.

    c. Assigning keys gives you an opportunity to keep a count of the collection members.

    d. There is no way to access members of a collection numerically via an array subscript.

Exercise 6

Complexity: Moderate

1. Create a Collection to store the months of the year. Add the month name as a data item and the string representation of the numeric month as the key. Add code to retrieve the month name based on the numeric string.

Complexity: Advanced

2. Create a form with several controls. Walk through the form's `Controls` collection displaying the name of the control using the `TypeName` statement.

LESSON 7

Using Property Procedures with Your Classes

We said earlier in this chapter that it is possible to add your own properties to classes. Let's see why you might want to do this.

The Benefits of Properties

To see how a user-definable property might work, let's have a closer look at some of the properties built into the form class and see how they differ from ordinary class variables. Take the `Top`, `Left`, `Width`, and `Height` properties, for example. When the values of those properties are changed, the size or position of the form changes accordingly. The form's `Caption` property also does something spectacular. When you assign some text to it, that text magically appears in the title bar of the form.

You might think that this is pretty intuitive, but that's the whole point. There is no magic connection between the `Caption` property of a Visual Basic 6 form and the title bar of a window. Instead, the property is able to recognize and respond to changes in its value. This capability sets properties apart from mere class variables. It's as if they have a built-in event that gets triggered when the property is set to something.

This is important because the code that you write in an object-oriented program can be simplified somewhat if the properties of a class can react when they are accessed by code in other parts of the program.

One example of this in HyperPad is the class variable `Changed`. This variable records when a change occurs to the text of a document. That information is then used to determine whether the document needs to be saved when an attempt is made to close the form. Also, when the text has changed, an asterisk is added to the caption of the form so that the user can tell at a glance which documents need to be saved.

The code to add the asterisk is implemented in the `Changed` event of the form's `txtDocument` text box. There, you set the value of the `clsDocument` object's `Changed` variable to `True`. If the caption doesn't already end in an asterisk, you add it accordingly.

7

This isn't very object oriented. It would be better if the Changed variable could react to a change in its current value and set or clear the asterisk in the caption itself. Later on, when you add the code to save the document, you will need to reset Changed to False, after the document has been successfully saved. You will need to add some more code to remove the asterisk at that time. So unless you introduce a user-defined property, you'll end up with code that adds and removes the asterisk from the form's caption in two different places in the project. This is inherently undesirable because any time you have code in two places you have to maintain (debug or make changes to) the same code twice. This is extra work, and it increases the chances of a bug slipping through.

Adding a Class Property

To make Changed a proper property, one that can react to changes in its value, go to the clsDocument module and replace Public Changed As Boolean in the Declarations section with Private DocChanged As Boolean. The declarations now look like this:

```
Option Explicit
Private DocChanged As Boolean
Public Closing As Boolean
Public DocName As String
Public DocumentForm As frmDocument
```

Now select the Add Procedure menu item from the Visual Basic 6 Tools menu. Complete the Add Procedure dialog box as shown in Figure 7.8. Be sure to check the Property option.

FIGURE 7.8

Adding a property to the clsDocument class.

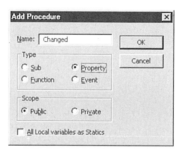

When you press the OK button, Visual Basic 6 adds the new property to the General Declarations section of the class.

The Property Get and Property Let Events

The property consists of two events: a Property Get event and a Property Let event. They appear in the Code window, as shown in Figure 7.9.

FIGURE 7.9

The Property Get *and* Property Let *events for* Changed.

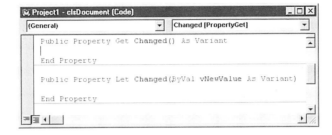

As you can see, the new Changed property has been set as a variant. The parameter in the Property Let event, vNewValue, will be a variant by default unless you change it to something else. At this stage, you have to complete the programming of these events. The way the property works is that when you set the property to a specific value in your code, the Property Let event is triggered with the new value passed in the parameter. Similarly, when you obtain the current value of the property in your code, the Property Get procedure is called. The Property Get event works like a function, so you can return a value by modifying its declaration accordingly.

Let's see how these two procedures look when the correct code has been added to make them work. The revised contents of the class module are shown in Listing 7.16.

LISTING 7.16   The Class Module

```
Private DocChanged As Boolean
Public Closing As Boolean
Public DocName As String
Public DocumentForm As frmDocument
Public Property Get Changed() As Boolean
Changed = DocChanged
End Property
Public Property Let Changed(NewValue As Boolean)
DocChanged = NewValue
End Property
```

The first thing you've had to change is the name of the variable that was previously called Changed. This is because there would be a naming clash with the new Changed property. Instead, you have changed its name to DocChanged. You are still using it to hold the value associated with the new property, it's just that you no longer give the rest of HyperPad unlimited access to that variable. From now on, all access to the DocChanged variable will pass through the Changed property. You've even declared DocChanged as Private so that only the code in the clsDocument module can access it directly.

7

Finally, you can now move the asterisk code from the `Changed` event of `txtDocument` to the `Property Let` event for the new `Changed` property. You don't need to change any of the code in the rest of HyperPad that accesses this property because the syntax to access it is the same as when it was a variable. The new `Property Let` and `Changed` events are listed in Listing 7.17.

LISTING 7.17   Updated `Property Let` and `txtDocument_Change` Routines

```
Public Property Let Changed(NewValue As Boolean)
DocChanged = NewValue
If DocChanged = True Then
  If Right(DocumentForm.Caption, 2) <> " *" Then
 DocumentForm.Caption = DocName & " *"
  End If
Else
  If Right(DocumentForm.Caption, 2) = " *" Then
 DocumentForm.Caption = DocName
  End If
End If
End Property
'    The following is in frmDocument
Private Sub txtDocument_Change()
'    Delete the If...Then
  objDocument.Changed = True
End Sub
```

Try running HyperPad again. If you have made the changes exactly as we have specified, you'll find that it runs correctly and that the new `Property Get` and `Property Let` events are triggered automatically.

Property Set

There is one further event that properties can respond to. This is the `Property Set` event. This book classifies this event as an advanced feature of Visual Basic 6, so we do not cover it in detail. The `Property Set` event is used when the variable behind a property is not just a simple variable, such as a `Boolean`, `Integer`, `Long`, or `String`, but an object variable. In other words, it is possible for a property to be a reference to another object.

In such a case, it would be necessary to use the `Set` statement to pass a reference to the object variable property. The `Property Set` event is triggered when a user-defined property is used in a `Set` statement. For example:

```
Set MyObject.MyProperty = MyObjectVariable
```

or

```
Set MyObject.MyProperty = New MyClass
```

Form Properties

There's one final point to be made about these properties. We've introduced only user-definable properties in a class context because they tend to get used primarily with class modules. However, there's nothing to stop you from adding them to form modules too.

Lesson Summary

Class properties, called property procedures, can be added to a class module to enable programmers to modify private class variables from outside of the class. The property procedure gives the class designer control over the setting and retrieving of class properties. To retrieve a private property from outside of the class, use a `Property Get` procedure. To set a private variable use a `Property Let` procedure. To set a private object variable use a `Property Set` procedure.

Quiz 7

1. To add a property procedure to a class _____.

    a. select the property procedure OCX from the toolbar.

    b. select the Add Procedure menu item from Visual Basic 6's tools menu.

    c. declare a variable in the declarations section of the class.

    d. declare a variable in the class's initialize event.

2. What event routine is triggered when another portion of the program attempts to set a value for a variant type property called `MyProperty`?

    a. `Public Property Set MyProperty(NewValue As Variant)`

    b. `Public Property Let MyProperty()`

    c. `Public Property Let MyProperty(NewValue As Variant)`

    d. `Public Property Set MyProperty()`

3. The `Property Set` routine is used _____.

    a. When the variable being modified is a variant.

    b. Interchangeably with the `Property Let` routine.

    c. When the variable being modified is an object.

    d. To retrieve an object reference from a private variable.

7

4. Which of the following is *not* true about a property procedure?

    a. Property procedures allow functions or subroutines outside of the class module a way to modify private variables of the class.

    b. Use the property `Equals` event to compare properties.

    c. Use the property `Set` event to set values of objects.

    d. Programmers can add property procedures to class modules.

Exercise 7

Complexity: Moderate

1. Add a property procedure to a form for holding the date the form was created. Make it a read-only property.

Complexity: Moderate

2. Add the `CenterForm` subroutine found in Lesson 2 to a Form. Make the Subroutine public. Use a second form to create an instance of your form and invoke the `CenterForm` method.

LESSON 8

The Benefits of Using Classes

All this seems like a lot of work, and the program seems to do just about the same thing it did before you made all these changes. You might be wondering, why bother? In this lesson, you will be reminded of the advantages of user-defined classes.

Easy Maintenance

In Lesson 7, we mentioned that if you did not use property procedures to insert and remove the asterisk from `frmDocument`'s caption, the code would have to be repeated in two different parts of the program. Properties in some programs may be changed in many more than two sections of code. That means that if the program's requirements change, the code in many different parts of the program will have to be changed.

A classic example is the renowned year 2000 problem, which is a topic of panic in newspapers and magazines. Most of the programs that suffer from the problem were written well before the advent of object-oriented programming. Programmers today are combing through hundreds of thousands of lines of code searching for any variable reference that might represent a date and making changes to each one. When they finish, they pray that they have not missed any. Had the date been handled as a date class, only a single code module would have to be changed!

Reusable Code

As you might imagine, programmers use the same routines in program after program. For years, the best programmers have maintained text files of their favorite procedures and functions and used cut-and-paste techniques to insert them into their programs. Then they had to rename variables and otherwise make the old routine fit the new program.

A big time saver? Sure, but you can save a class as a separate file and simply insert it into your program. Even if the events and properties in the class have the same name as procedures and variables in the new program, simply by referencing the class object you can invoke the correct event or change the correct property. This is known as a $5.00 word in object-oriented programming: *polymorphism.*

Sharing Code in Large Projects

Large projects are a particular nightmare to project managers. These projects may have dozens of programmers, all working on different parts of the same project. For example, Sally is handling the cash deposits portion of the code while Juan is dealing with cash balances and Jim is handling the code for withdrawals.

In the top-down model of programming, Sally, Juan, and Jim would need to know all the details of each other's code. Obviously, a deposit would affect the balance. Each person must be careful not to use a variable name that has been used by one of the others, and each must be aware of the rules that have been set for any variable in the project. A change in code written by any of the programmers has a direct impact on all of them.

Object-oriented programmers don't have these worries. Juan, handling the cash balance, needs to tell Sally and Jim only the names of the methods in his class module and the data types for the properties, the interface for the class. He does not need to know a thing about Sally's and Jim's code, and they don't need to know how his works. If Juan discovers the need to change how a property is handled, he can change the Property Get and Property Let procedures in his class module and the change will have no effect at all on the code that Sally and Jim are writing.

Data Hiding

Private properties are hidden from the rest of the program. The only way to change them is through the Property Let procedure and the only way to read them is through the

Property Get procedure. The Property Let procedure can be written to include the business rules so that improper values are not allowed.

You can even implement read-only properties, properties that are changed only inside the class module but that can be read by the rest of the code. Juan could maintain a count of the number of deposits and the number of withdrawals in a month, for example, that Sally and Jim could read but could not explicitly change. To accomplish that, Juan would delete the Property Let procedure for both properties. In VB, the BorderStyle property, for example, is read-only at runtime.

The concept of data hiding is called encapsulation in object-oriented programming circles. Generally, all properties should be encapsulated except when there are no constraints on them. If a property can legally (and safely) hold any value that may be sent by the rest of the program, it is OK to use a public property. If there must be limitations, or if the value should not be changed or should not be changed after it has been set, use a Private property with Property Let and Property Get procedures. If you are not sure, lean toward Private properties.

Improved Program Design

Some programmers do it right the first time, but most of us start coding first and thinking later. Our programs, such as Topsy, "just grow." Over the development period we make dozens of changes, most of them affecting more than one procedure. We add new procedures to *patch* what we did wrong in other procedures and soon wind up with a mishmash of code that will render us speechless when we look at it a few months down the line.

One of the side effects of object-oriented programming is that you must design the objects before you can even think of writing the code. It seems like an extra, time-consuming step, but it is really a big time saver because you will have fewer corrections to make during the testing stages. True, you could insert the think-before-you-program step into your normal program design stages, but it is so much easier just to sit down and start coding.

In other words, object-oriented programming results in better, more robust programs, not just because programming with objects is a better method (it is) but because it forces you to think before you code. In cooking, the sauce is everything; in programming, planning is everything. Let's look at the design process to get an idea of what that means.

Designing an Object-Oriented Program

For the sake of this simulation, let's say that you have finished this course and started the Handy Dandy Software Company. Pat Fixit, an appliance repairperson, has come to you for help.

"I need to keep track of the service calls I perform for my customers," Pat says. "I tried doing it on paper, but I just seem to keep getting it all tangled up."

As you question Pat further, Pat tells you of the need to keep a record of each appliance serviced for each customer, including the type of appliance, its model and serial number, and the nature of each repair. You know this will take a database, a topic we will cover in Chapter 13, "Database Programming," and you have some ideas about the screens you will need for handling each type of data entry.

Actually, you already have most of the information you need to do an object-oriented design. Look at the list of requirements that Pat gave you. Each of the nouns in that list is a potential object. We have appliance and customer as the primary nouns, and they suggest the main objects that you will need.

The nature of the object also tells you something about the properties for the object. The customer object, for example, will probably need the following:

- Name (break it down into Last_Name and First_Name)
- Address
- City
- State
- Zip code
- Phone number

The appliance object needs the following:

- Type_of_Appliance
- Make
- Model
- Serial Number
- Repair
- Repair_Date

7

The properties, in turn, suggest the `Property Let` and `Property Get` procedures. The `Type_of_Appliance` property, for example, would probably be an integer, with 1 representing a washing machine, 2 a dishwasher, and so on. The `Property Let` procedure would limit the properties' values to those that are valid. The `Repair_Date Property Let` procedure would check to be sure its parameter is a valid date.

As you progress in your coding, or in your discussion of the project with Pat, you may find other items (properties) to add to these, but adding them is simplicity itself because they are encapsulated in a single place.

Lesson Summary

This lesson discussed the many beneficial reasons to program using user-defined classes, such as providing reusable code and easier maintenance of the software. This lesson also introduced the object oriented programming the concept of data hiding, called encapsulation. Encapsulation can be achieved with Visual Basic by using private property variables and property procedures.

Quiz 8

1. If you create a class that is a business rule and the rule changes for an object in your program, you must change

    a. The code in the class module

    b. All the code in the program

    c. None of the code

    d. Create a new class

2. If you want to insert a class module you wrote for a different program into your current project, you must change

    a. All the property names in your class

    b. All the method names in your class

    c. All the event names in your class

    d. None of the above

3. If you need to share a class module with other programmers, they need to know

    a. All the inner workings of your class

    b. The names of the class methods and the names of the properties as well as the data types of the class properties

c. The names of the class methods and the names of the properties

d. All of the above

4. When non-object data in your class is hidden,

   a. It cannot be accessed from the program.

   b. It can be changed at random by the main program.

   c. It can be changed only through the Property Let procedure.

   d. It can be changed only through the Property Get procedure.

Exercise 8

Complexity: Easy

   1. List three advantages to object-oriented programming.

Complexity: Moderate

   2. List the class properties and methods for the Dog class based on the following statement: The Dog has a name, color and breed. The Dog can bark and run.

Chapter Summary

This chapter introduced the building block of Visual Basic object oriented programming, classes. Classes are a description of a set of characteristics. Several examples were used to help you understand the concept of classes and objects. Visual Basic classes and objects that you are already familiar with, such as the Form and ActiveX controls, were re-examined from an object-oriented point of view. Techniques for designing and creating user-defined classes were discussed as well adding custom properties and methods. The main points of this chapter are as follows:

- A class is a description of a set of characteristics.
- An object is an instance of a class, and each object belongs to a class.
- Visual Basic 6 has many different types of classes, such as single instance classes, user-defined classes, database classes and miscellaneous classes.
- A Visual Basic Form is a class.
- You can create your own instance of a Form.
- Objects can be referenced by more than one variable.
- ActiveX controls are Visual Basic classes.

7

- You can make multiple-purpose routines to process ActiveX controls by passing a control reference into a subroutine or function.
- In order to determine the type of ActiveX control being referenced, use the TypeOf keyword.
- To find out the class name of an ActiveX control, use the TypeName function.
- Classes that you design and create in Visual Basic are called user-defined classes.
- User-defined classes are created with a Visual Basic class module.
- A user-defined class method is a subroutine or function declared in the class module.
- Variables and property procedures make up the properties of a class.
- Private class properties are only accessible from within the class _module, while public properties can be accessed by code outside of the class module.
- Class modules can contain events which are procedures called from within the class and have an effect on objects outside the class object.
- Class modules have two standard events, initialize and terminate. The initialize event is fired when an instance of the class is created. The terminate event is fired when the object is destroyed.
- A Visual Basic collection is an object that enables you to organize other objects and provides methods for finding, adding and removing objects.
- Class properties can be added to a class module to be used to modify private class variables from outside of the class. The property procedure gives the class designer control over the setting and retrieving of class properties.
- Classes simplify code maintenance.
- In object oriented programming the concept of data hiding is called encapsulation. Encapsulation can be achieved with Visual Basic by using private property variables and property procedures.

Object-oriented programming is different, but not difficult. This chapter details some of the reason why you should use object-oriented programming over the top-down programming model. Classes will be used in example throughout the book to continue to build on the object-oriented concepts and features used in this chapter.

In Chapter 8, "Using ActiveX Controls," the HyperPad project will become greatly enhanced with several very special ActiveX controls called the CommonDialog control and the common Windows controls, such as the StatusBar control and the TabStrip control.

CHAPTER 8

Using ActiveX Controls

The end of Chapter 7, "Building Classes: The Foundation of Visual Basic OOP," left HyperPad rather unfinished. HyperPad still lacks many of the professional features that you would expect to find in a modern Windows application—features such as a toolbar, a status bar, and ToolTips. Also, HyperPad is still missing the Open and Save As dialog boxes. Luckily, with the Professional and Enterprise editions of Visual Basic 6, Microsoft provides 10 controls designed to solve just these sorts of problems:

- The CommonDialog control
- The RichTextBox control
- The ToolBar control
- The ImageList control
- The StatusBar control
- The TabStrip control
- The TreeView control
- The ListView control
- The ProgressBar control
- The Slider control

All controls are implemented as ActiveX control extensions (OCXs). This chapter begins by configuring a project to use them. The first lesson explains how to use the CommonDialog control. The remaining lessons use the other controls, using HyperPad as a demo platform.

LESSON 1

Introducing the `CommonDialog` Control

Load the HyperPad project from Chapter 7, "Building Classes: The Foundation of Visual Basic OOP." In Chapter 7, you learned how to reference OCXs to use them in your own projects. Bring up the Components dialog box now by clicking Components on the Project menu, or by pressing Ctrl+T. Add the controls listed in Table 8.1 to the toolbox.

TABLE 8.1 OCX Controls to Reference

OCX Description	Filename
Microsoft `CommonDialog` Control 6.0	COMDLG32.OCX
Microsoft `RichTextBox` Control 6.0	RICHTX32.OCX
Microsoft Windows Common Controls 6.0	COMCTL32.OCX

Figure 8.1 shows the toolbox after the controls for this chapter are loaded. The toolbox must be widened so that all the controls can be seen.

FIGURE 8.1

Toolbox with `CommonDialog` *and Windows 95 controls.*

There is also a Microsoft Common Controls 2 6.0 available that adds two more controls—an Animation control and a Spin Button control. They are not used in this chapter.

The Microsoft `RichTextBox` control and the Microsoft Windows Common Controls form the group of controls that are known as the *Windows 95 controls*.

Understanding the `CommonDialog` Control

Some years ago, Microsoft recognized that many different Windows applications needed to perform common tasks, such as loading and saving files, printing, and choosing fonts and colors. To assist programmers in these tasks and to promote standardization, Microsoft developed a group of ready-to-use dialog boxes and made them part of the Windows operating system. The Common Dialog boxes are still an intrinsic part of the various versions of Windows, and the `CommonDialog` control provides you with an easy way to use them. The toolbox icon for the `CommonDialog` control is shown in Figure 8.2.

FIGURE 8.2

The `CommonDialog`
control.

One common misconception is that the Common Dialog boxes themselves are a part of the `CommonDialog` control. They are not. The `CommonDialog` control simply acts as a go-between between your project and the dialog boxes, which are buried inside the operating system itself, in the Windows Application Program Interface.

One interesting side effect of the dialog boxes being part of the operating system is that their look and feel differs among the different versions of Windows, most notably between the 16-bit versions of Windows, Windows 3.x, and Windows 95. However, by using the `CommonDialog` control, your programming interface into the dialog boxes remains consistent.

Figures 8.3, 8.4, 8.5, and 8.6 provide you with a sneak preview of how a few of the dialog boxes look under Windows 95.

FIGURE 8.3

The Save As dialog box.

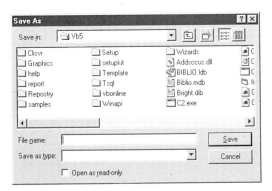

FIGURE 8.4

The Print setup dialog box.

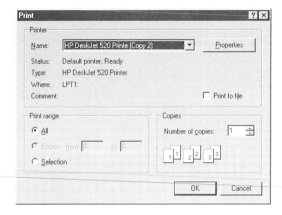

FIGURE 8.5

The Color dialog box.

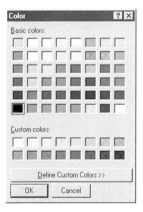

FIGURE 8.6

The Font dialog box.

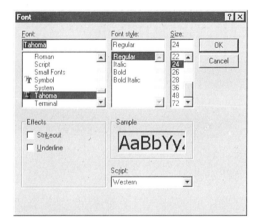

What's great about these dialog boxes is that all the underlying functionality is preprogrammed. You get a professional look to your programs, and you don't have to write a single line of code! What's more, you can even customize the dialog boxes to a certain extent.

A Control Without a User Interface

One of the features of the controls that you've used so far is that the control itself provides the graphical interface with which the users of your program interact. For example, the TextBox control is responsible for displaying a text box on the form at runtime. The CommonDialog control is different. At runtime, it is completely invisible. This is because it has no visual interface of its own. It is, in fact, one of a number of controls that do not directly interact with the user but instead provide an additional programming service. Examples of other controls that behave this way are the Timer and the MSComm (communications) controls.

A Control That Can Be Dragged onto an MDI Form

Open the HyperPad project and make frmMain the active form. You learned in Chapter 6, "Building the GUI with Forms, Menus, and MDI Forms," that you can't add just any control to an MDI form. The CommonDialog control is an exception. Select the CommonDialog control and drag it onto the form, as shown in Figure 8.7. Yes, unlike other controls, the CommonDialog control is quite happy to be added to an MDI form.

FIGURE 8.7

The frmMain *in design mode with the* CommonDialog *control added.*

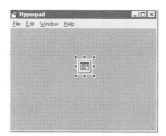

As you can see, the control appears as a small icon. It can't be resized, although you can move it around the form. It doesn't matter where you place it; it is only providing a programming interface through its properties and methods.

Learning to Program the CommonDialog Control

Now that the CommonDialog control has been added to frmMain, using it is a straightforward matter of learning how to use its properties and methods. The control has no events.

The first thing to note is that the same control can be used to access any of the Common Dialog boxes provided by Windows. This will become evident if you look at its properties, as shown in Figure 8.8.

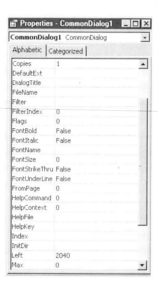

Notice how some of the properties apply to one type of dialog box, whereas others are common to all types. For instance, PrinterDefault, FromPage, and Copies obviously apply to printing, whereas those that begin with the word Font, such as FontBold and FontUnderline, apply to the Font dialog box. Others, such as CancelError and Flags, are common to all the dialog boxes.

Click Custom in the Properties window to open the Property Pages of the CommonDialog control, as shown in Figure 8.9. The separate tabs on the Property Pages provide further emphasis on the versatility of the control.

The `Flags` Property

The `Flags` property is arguably the most important property. It enables you to customize how a dialog box appears before you display it. For example, the File dialog boxes (Open and Save As dialog boxes) in Figure 8.3 contain a check box labeled Open as read only. You may not want to make this feature available in your project unless you want to give your users the capability to read a document without changing it. You can turn off the display of that particular check box by setting a flag in the `Flags` property.

In fact, you can set a large number of customizable options. The examples in this book show you how to use many of the flags, but you should consult the online Help for a full list of the options and what they can do.

The File Dialog Boxes

The two dialog boxes associated with files are the Open and Save As dialog boxes. The code you need to add to the Open menu's `Click` event to display the Open dialog box is in Listing 8.1.

LISTING 8.1   Bringing Up the listingFile Open Dialog Box

```
Private Sub mnuFileOpen_Click()
    CommonDialog1.Filter = "Text files (*.txt)¦*.txt¦All files¦*.*"
    CommonDialog1.ShowOpen
End Sub
```

The call to the `ShowOpen` method displays the Open dialog box. The dialog box is displayed modally, so the call doesn't return until the user presses either the Open or the Cancel button.

The `Filter` Property

The `Filter` property applies only to the File dialog boxes. Its purpose is to select entries for the Files of type combo box. It allows users to select the file extensions that will be listed in the combo box. This is a feature of most Windows applications. Visual Basic's common dialog box, for example, defaults to `Project Files (*.vbp, _*.mak, *.vbg)`.

The syntax for the `Filter` string is

```
object.Filter [= description1 ¦filter1 ¦description2 ¦filter2...]
```

The `Filter` string requires some explanation. Each file type (or group of file types) is represented by a two-part string: a description and the actual file specification. The description appears in the combo box, whereas the CommonDialog control uses the file spec to select the files. The two parts of the filter string are separated by the pipeline symbol, the vertical bar that represents Or in syntax diagrams. (On most keyboards, the pipeline symbol is a broken vertical bar that shares a key with the backslash.)

You can add as many Filter strings as you want, separating the Filter strings with the same pipeline symbol. Each Filter string appears as a separate entry in the combo box. The code to use in HyperPad is

```
CommonDialog1.Filter = "Text files (*.txt)¦*.txt¦All files (*.*)¦*.*"
```

The first Filter string is Text files (*.txt)¦*.txt, which selects and displays all files with the .txt extension.

Figure 8.10 shows the user selecting "Text files (*.txt)" from the available types.

FIGURE 8.10

The Text files *filter.*

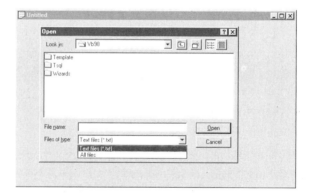

Determining Whether the User Canceled

The user has the choice of selecting a file to open and pressing the Open button (or double-clicking the file of his or her choice), or pressing the Cancel button to cancel the whole operation. Then it's up to your program to respond correctly.

There are two ways to determine which button has been pressed. The first technique works only with file dialogs, whereas the second can be used with any of the Common Dialog boxes.

The Non-Error-Trapping Method

This method applies only to the File dialog boxes because it checks the FileName property to determine whether a file name was selected. Before you call the ShowOpen method, assign an empty string to the FileName property. Then, when the method returns, check to see if the FileName property is still empty. The FileName property remains empty unless the user selected a file and pressed the Open button (or double-clicked a file). The code to implement this strategy is shown in Listing 8.2.

LISTING 8.2   Checking for Cancel Without Error Handling

```
Private Sub mnuFileOpen_Click()
CommonDialog1.Filter = "Text files (*.txt)¦*.txt¦All files (*.*)¦*.*"
    CommonDialog1.Filename = ""
    CommonDialog1.ShowOpen
    If CommonDialog1.Filename <> "" Then
    'A file was selected. Add the code to load it here
    End If
End Sub
```

Note that if a file is selected, the `FileName` property contains the full path to the file, not just the file name, so you have all the information you need to locate the selected file. If you want just the name, use the `FileTitle` property.

The `Error-Trapping` Method

The non-error-trapping technique of checking the `FileName` property works fine for the File dialog boxes. However, it doesn't work for the others. Instead, you need a sure-fire way of determining which button was pressed. That's what the error-trapping technique does.

`Error trapping` is a mechanism in Visual Basic 6 that allows your own code to be run when an error occurs at runtime. Without error trapping, a compiled EXE version of your project will terminate rather ungraciously when an error occurs. Visual Basic 6 allows you to set up something called an error handler. This is an entry point in your project that runs when an error occurs. Error handlers are covered in detail in Chapter 10, "Problem Solving: Handling Errors and Debugging Your Program." You can use it with the `CommonDialog` control to determine when the Cancel button has been pressed.

To use error trapping, set the control's `CancelError` property to `True` and install a suitable error handler. Listing 8.3 shows how the `Click` event looks using the `Error-Trapping` method.

LISTING 8.3   Checking for Cancel with `Error-Trapping`

```
Private Sub mnuFileOpen_Click()
Dim Cancel As Boolean
On Error Goto ErrorHandler
Cancel = False
```

continues

LISTING 8.3 continued

```
CommonDialog1.Filter = "Text files (*.txt)|*.txt|All files (*.*)|*.*"
CommonDialog1.CancelError = True
CommonDialog1.ShowOpen
If Not Cancel Then
    'The Open button was pressed. Add the code to load the file here
End If
Exit Sub

ErrorHandler:
If Err.Number = cdlCancel Then
    Cancel = True
    Resume Next
End If
End
End Sub
```

The line that begins On Error GoTo is the line that installs the error handler. It says that if an error occurs in this subroutine at runtime, program execution should jump to the label ErrorHandler. By setting the CancelError property to True, the CommonDialog control forces an error to occur when the user presses the Cancel button. Each runtime error has a unique number in Visual Basic, so it's easy to check whether the error that occurred was the user pressing the Cancel button on a Common Dialog box. The error code is represented by the constant cdlCancel. The constant is made globally available to your project by the CommonDialog control itself. That's why you can use it in your project without specifically declaring it.

If a user presses the Cancel button in a Common Dialog box, the dialog box closes and an error is raised upon exiting from the dialog. Because of the error, the program jumps to the error handler instead of executing the instruction immediately following the call to CommonDialog1.

Each error in Visual Basic has a unique number. The error handler checks the error number to be sure that the error was caused by the dialog box's Cancel button. If it was, the variable Cancel is set to True and the Resume Next statement is executed. If it was not, the program simply exits from the mnuFileOpen procedure.

The Resume Next statement tells the computer to resume operation at the statement following the one that raised the error. In this procedure, the line that raised the error is the call to CommonDialog1, and the next line is If Not Cancel Then.

It's a lot easier to watch this than it is to read about. Place the cursor on the line

```
On Error Goto ErrorHandler
```

and press F9. (Don't worry about what is happening, it's covered in detail in Chapter 10, "Problem Solving: Handling Errors and Debugging Your Program.") Then press F5 to run the program. When the program starts running, select Open from the File menu. The program stops running and highlights a line of code that is the next line to be executed. Press F8 and watch the highlight move to the next line. When you press F8 with `CommonDialog1.ShowOpen` highlighted, the Common Dialog File Open dialog box opens. Click the Cancel button. When the program returns to the code window, the next statement highlighted is on the first line of the error-handler code. Continue pressing F8 to watch the flow of the program. Repeat the same steps, this time selecting a file to load, and watch the flow of the program to load a file. (Because the file load procedure is not yet added, no file is actually loaded.)

What you just did is called *single stepping* through a section of code. It's a perfect way to see exactly what is happening in a program. Now, back to work.

The `Flags` Property

The Open dialog box still has the Open as read-only check box. To get rid of it, you must set a flag in the `Flags` property just before you call `ShowOpen`:

```
CommonDialog1.Flags = cdlOFNHideReadOnly
```

You can set many flags that do neat things. For instance, the flag `cdlOFNFileMustExist` prevents users from attempting to open a file that doesn't exist and cdlOFNHideReadOnly prevents read-only files from showing up. How could they do that? By typing in the name of a file that is not in the list. What's great about these flags is that they simplify your code tremendously. If it weren't for the `cdlOFNFileMustExist` flag, for example, you would have to write your own routine to check that the file actually exists.

To use more than one flag at a time, use the logical `Or` operator to combine them:

```
CommonDialog1.Flags = cdlOFNHideReadOnly Or cdlOFNFileMustExist
```

The constants are defined by the `CommonDialog` control. You don't have to declare them yourself.

Next add the code for the Save As dialog box, as shown in Listing 8.4.

LISTING 8.4 FileSaveAs Routine

```
Private Sub mnuFileSaveAs_Click()
Dim Cancel As Boolean
On Error Goto ErrorHandler
Cancel = False
CommonDialog1.DefaultExt = ".txt"
CommonDialog1.Filter = "Text files (*.txt)|*.txt|All files (*.*)|*.*"
CommonDialog1.CancelError = True
CommonDialog1.Flags = cdlOFNHideReadOnly Or _
                      cdlOFNOverwritePrompt
CommonDialog1.ShowSave
If Not Cancel Then
    'A filename was selected. Add the code to save the file here
End If
Exit Sub

ErrorHandler:
If Err.Number = cdlCancel Then
    Cancel = True
    Resume Next
End If
End Sub
```

The main difference between the Save As dialog box and the Open dialog box is in the use of the DefaultExt property. If you set DefaultExt to a file extension (we've used .txt) then if the user enters a file name without an extension, the CommonDialog control automatically adds the default extension. This way you can be certain that the file name returned in the FileName property will contain a full file name, complete with a valid extension.

We've also used a new flag, cdlOFNOverwritePrompt. This causes the dialog box to warn the user that the file already exists, preventing an accidental overwrite.

Note that when the CommonDialog control gets a file name from the user; it doesn't actually perform the Open or Save operation for you. You have to code that yourself. File I/O (that's input and output) is covered in Chapter 12, "Reading and Writing Disk Files," but the File Open and Save As menu items are completed in the next lesson, which looks at one of the Windows 95 controls, the RichTextBox control. The FileOpen and SaveAs methods are standard methods of the RichTextBox control.

Lesson Summary

In this chapter we introduced CommonDialog control and learned how to program it. We looked at dialog boxes such as the Save As dialog box, the Print setup dialog box, the

Color dialog box, and the Font dialog box. In the next lesson we'll look at the `RichTextBox` control and perform some font color operations with it.

Quiz 1

1. What `CommonDialog` control property allows you to customize how a dialog box appears before you display it?

    a. The `Flags` property

    b. The `Filter` property

    c. The `Display` property

    d. The `Form` property

2. What are the two dialog boxes associated with files?

    a. FileManager and Open dialog boxes

    b. WinMin and Open dialog boxes

    c. Save As and Open dialog boxes

    d. Save As and LoadFile dialog boxes

3. Which statement below is false about the `Filter` property?

    a. The `Filter` property applies only to the File dialog boxes.

    b. Its purpose is to select entries for the Files of type combo box.

    c. You can add as many filter strings that you want to the property.

    d. Each field in the filter string is separated by a comma.

4. What statement is true about placing a `CommonDialog` control on an MDI form?

    a. It appears as a small icon.

    b. It cannot be resized.

    c. It cannot be placed on a MDI form.

    d. Both a and b.

Exercise 1

Complexity: Easy

1. Create a form with a `CommondDialog` control that opens files. Show the `CommondDialog` control when the form loads. Include a filter in the Property Pages of the `CommondDialog` control that displays only text files in the directory listing. We are not interested in opening the file.

Complexity: Moderate

2. Create a form with a `CommonDialog` control and two command buttons placed at the bottom of the form. Label one command button Open and the other one Save As. Write a program so that when the user clicks the Open button, an Open dialog box appears that will open only text files. Set up the Save As button such that it displays a Save As dialog box. Hide the read only box for both dialogs.

LESSON 2

The `RichTextBox` Control, Font and Color Dialog Boxes

Now that you've seen how the File Common Dialog boxes work, it's time to learn how to use the Font and Color dialog boxes. However, there is a small problem. At present, HyperPad can work only with simple text, because it uses the `TextBox` control. That simplifies the storage, display, and editing of the text in a document, but it is also a limiting factor. To use the Font and Color dialog boxes, you are going to have to change the way HyperPad works so that you can apply font and color changes to text.

What you really want is a replacement for the `TextBox` control—another control that works just like it, but that also allows you to change the fonts and colors of its text. Fortunately, the `RichTextBox` control was designed to do just that. It is a direct, drop-in replacement for the `TextBox` control that fully supports all the `TextBox` control's properties, events, and methods. It also has some additional features that let you control the displayed fonts and colors.

What Is Rich Text?

The `RichTextBox` control gets its name from a Microsoft standard called *rich text format* (RTF). This is a standard for storing text with additional attributes, such as font and color. Quite a few word processors and other document editors can work with RTF, including WordPad and Microsoft Word.

RTF itself is very complex and would ordinarily require a considerable amount of programming effort to support fully. Luckily, with the `RichTextBox` control, all the hard work has been done for you. What's more, the `RichTextBox` control also provides methods to load and save RTF files, and because it's backward compatible with the `TextBox` control, you can still work with ordinary text if you want to.

Replacing the TextBox Control

To use the RichTextBox control, you must make a change to HyperPad that, at first sight, seems pretty drastic. You have to delete the TextBox control from frmDocument and replace it with a RichTextBox control. However, because the RichTextBox control has all the same properties, events, and methods as the ordinary TextBox control, it turns out that this replacement isn't as drastic as you might at first imagine. Furthermore, if you give the new RichTextBox control the same name as the control it's replacing, you actually need to make no programming changes at all and the program will work exactly as it did before!

Try the changes now:

1. Double-click frmDocument in the Project Explorer window to bring the form to the front.

2. Click the text box to select it; then press the Del key.

3. Select the RichTextBox control from the toolbox and draw it onto the form in place of the original text box.

Figure 8.11 shows the RichTextBox control icon.

FIGURE 8.11

The RichTextBox
control icon.

Change the properties of the new control to those shown in Table 8.2.

TABLE 8.2   RichTextBox Control Properties

Property	Value
Appearance	0 - Flat
BorderStyle	0 - No border
Name	txtDocument

By default, the Appearance and BorderStyle properties are set so that the RichTextBox has a 3D appearance. This isn't desirable for HyperPad, because you want the control to extend to the inner edge of the document window.

Now try running HyperPad. It works exactly as before. In fact, you won't be able to tell that you're no longer using the TextBox control.

Setting Fonts and Color

The next thing to do is to provide some additional menus in HyperPad so that the user has access to the Font and Color Common Dialog boxes. This means that the user will be able to use the Font and Color Common Dialog boxes to change the text in the rich text box.

Add two new menu items to HyperPad's Edit menu. These are specified in Table 8.3.

TABLE 8.3   Menu Items to Be Added to HyperPad's Edit Menu

Menu Name	Caption
mnuEditFont	F&ont...
mnuEditColor	Colo&r...

Ensure that both menu items are always enabled, because you will want to be able to change the current font settings as well as those of the selected text. The properties of the RichTextBox control that affect the selected text also affect the current font and colors if no text is selected.

The code for the Font menu's Click event is in Listing 8.5. Note the use of the With...End With structure to apply multiple property values to a single object.

LISTING 8.5   Letting the User Change the Font

```
Private Sub mnuEditFont_Click()
CommonDialog1.Flags = cdlCFBoth Or cdlCFEffects
CommonDialog1.ShowFont
With frmMain.ActiveForm.txtDocument
    .SelFontName = CommonDialog1.FontName
    .SelFontSize = CommonDialog1.FontSize
    .SelBold = CommonDialog1.FontBold
    .SelItalic = CommonDialog1.FontItalic
    .SelStrikeThru = CommonDialog1.FontStrikeThru
    .SelUnderline = CommonDialog1.FontUnderline
    .SelColor = CommonDialog1.Color
End With
End Sub
```

As you can see, the code uses the CommonDialog control's ShowFont method to display the Font dialog box. It sets two flags. The first, cdlCFBoth, tells the Font dialog box to display both printer and screen fonts in its list of fonts. In fact, you can display a wide range of different font types in this dialog box, limiting the display to either printer or screen fonts, and even just to TrueType fonts that work on both screen and printer. If you don't specify the font type to display, no fonts will appear in the dialog box.

The second flag, `cdlCFEffects`, indicates that you want to see the attributes for the fonts, which include the `strikethrough`, `underline`, and `color` attributes. Note that you can use this one control to set the color of the fonts as well, although you cannot define custom colors with it. You need the Color dialog box to do that.

Figure 8.12 shows you how the Font dialog box appears with the `effects` flag set. Table 8.4 lists some additional flags for you to try. For more information on these flags, refer to the online Help.

FIGURE 8.12

The Font dialog box with the `cdlCFEffects` flag set.

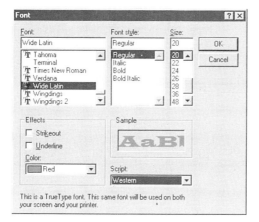

TABLE 8.4 Additional Flags for the Font Common DialogBox

Flag Constant	Description
cdlCFANSIOnly	Displays only fonts that contain a complete ANSI character set
cdlCFFixedPitchOnly	Displays only fixed-pitch fonts
cdlCFPrinterFonts	Displays only printer fonts
cdlCFScalableOnly	Displays only fonts that are scaleable
cdlCFScreenFonts	Displays only screen fonts
cdlCFTTOnly	Displays only TrueType fonts

Note that the constants shown in Table 8.4 do not provide any error handling to allow for the user pressing the Cancel button. This is purely for the sake of clarity. You should always install an error handler to check for the `cdlCancel` error code in your own code.

Applying the selected font styles is straightforward enough. You simply copy the font properties from the CommonDialog control. Note that the RichTextBox properties begin with Sel. This is because they apply only to the selected text, rather like the SelStart and SelLength properties that you saw in Chapter 6, "Building the GUI with Forms, Menus, and MDI Forms." Similarly, the changes apply to the current font settings if no text is selected.

Now add the code for the Color menu's Click event (see Listing 8.6). This will allow the user to set the Color property of the font.

LISTING 8.6   Activating the Color Dialog Box

```
Private Sub mnuEditColor_Click()
CommonDialog1.Flags = cdlCCFullOpen
CommonDialog1.ShowColor
frmMain.ActiveForm.txtDocument.SelColor = CommonDialog1.Color
End Sub
```

Again, it is the Flags setting that characterizes the way the dialog box works. The only flag the code uses is cdlCCFullOpen, which provides the full Color dialog box to allow the user to define his or her own custom colors or to select the standard colors from the prepared palette.

Figure 8.13 shows you how the full Color dialog box looks.

FIGURE 8.13

The full Color dialog box.

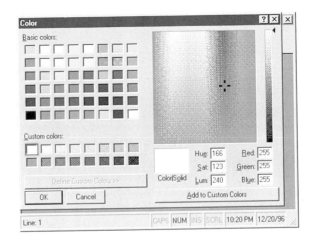

Loading and Saving Rich Text Files

All that's left now is to complete the programming of the Open and Save As dialog boxes by calling the `RichTextBox`'s methods to load and save rich text files. The methods provided by the `RichTextBox` control for this purpose are called `LoadFile` and `SaveFile`. Both methods support loading either rich text or ordinary text files, as you will see from the completed `Click` event subroutines for the Open and Save As menus. The `Open` routine is in Listing 8.7.

LISTING 8.7   Opening a Rich Text or Text File

```
Private Sub mnuFileOpen_Click()
Dim Cancel As Boolean
    On Error GoTo ErrorHandler
    Cancel = False
    CommonDialog1.Filter = _
      "Text files (*.txt)¦*.txt¦All files (*.*)¦*.*" & _
      "RichText files (*.rtf)¦*.rtf¦" CommonDialog1.CancelError = True
    CommonDialog1.Flags = cdlOFNHideReadOnly Or _
      cdlOFNFileMustExist
    CommonDialog1.ShowOpen
    If Not Cancel Then
    ' Load a File
        If UCase(Right(CommonDialog1.filename, 3)) = _
          "RTF" Then
          ' It is an RTF file
            frmMain.ActiveForm.txtDocument.LoadFile _
              CommonDialog1.filename, rtfRTF
        Else
          ' It is a text file
            frmMain.ActiveForm.txtDocument.LoadFile _
              CommonDialog1.filename, rtfText
        End If
        ' Set the document name
        frmMain.ActiveForm.objDocument.DocName = _
          CommonDialog1.filename
        ' Set FileChanged parameter
        frmMain.ActiveForm.objDocument.Changed = False
    End If
    ' All done here
    Exit Sub

ErrorHandler:
    If Err.Number = cdlCancel Then
        Cancel = True
        Resume Next
    End If
End Sub
```

What's Happening Here?

The new code adds a filter string for RTF files to the Common Dialog File Open list. When a file is selected, the file name is passed to the load file routine. The load file routine uses the `LoadFile` method of the `RichTextBox`. The syntax of the `LoadFile` method is

```
object.LoadFile pathname, filetype
```

The components of the `LoadFile` method are as follows:

- `object` is the name of the `RichTextBox` object.
- `pathname` is the full path and file name of the file to load.
- `filetype` is either `rtfRTF`, which means the file must be a valid rich text file, or `rtfText`, which means the file can be any text file.

The code in Listing 8.7 contains an `If...Then...Else` to handle either case. The `SaveAs` routine is shown in Listing 8.8.

LISTING 8.8   The SaveAs Routine

```
Private Sub mnuFileSaveAs_Click()
Dim Cancel As Boolean
On Error GoTo ErrorHandler
Cancel = False
CommonDialog1.DefaultExt = ".rtf"
CommonDialog1.Filter = "RichText files (*.rtf)|*.rtf|" & _
                       "Text files (*.txt)|*.txt|All files (*.*)|*.*"
CommonDialog1.CancelError = True
CommonDialog1.Flags = cdlOFNHideReadOnly Or _
                      cdlOFNOverwritePrompt
CommonDialog1.ShowSave
If Not Cancel Then
    With frmMain.ActiveForm
        If UCase(Right(CommonDialog1.filename, 3)) = "RTF" Then
            .txtDocument.SaveFile CommonDialog1.Filename, rtfRTF
        Else
            .txtDocument.SaveFile CommonDialog1.Filename, rtfText
        End If
        .objDocument.DocName = CommonDialog1.Filename
        .objDocument.Changed = False
    End With
End If
Exit Sub

ErrorHandler:
```

```
If Err.Number = cdlCancel Then
    Cancel = True
    Resume Next
End If
End Sub
```

The changes to the Save As menu's Click event are similar to those you made to open a file. Again, an RTF entry is added to the Filter property and the code distinguishes between rich text and ordinary text files by means of the file extension.

To complete this lesson, you must also provide the code to go into the Save menu's Click event (see Listing 8.9). The Save menu should determine whether the current document has been saved to disk. If the document has not, the menu item should perform the same task as the Save As menu item. It does that by calling the Save As menu's Click event directly. If the document has already been saved, then the Click event just resaves the document using the current file name.

LISTING 8.9 The Save Routine

```
Private Sub mnuFileSave_Click()
With frmMain.ActiveForm
    If .objDocument.DocName = "Untitled" Then
        mnuFileSaveAs_Click
    Else
        If UCase(Right(.objDocument.DocName, 3)) = "RTF" Then
            .txtDocument.SaveFile .objDocument.DocName, rtfRTF
        Else
            .txtDocument.SaveFile .objDocument.DocName, rtfText
        End If
        .objDocument.Changed = False
    End If
End With
End Sub
```

As you can see, the code determines if the document has been saved by checking whether its name is still the default Untitled. If it is, the Save As menu's Click event is called directly; otherwise, the RichTextBox control's SaveFile method is called. The If...Then...Else to determine the file type parameter is the same as that in the SaveAs method.

Figure 8.14 shows how HyperPad now looks with a rich text document loaded.

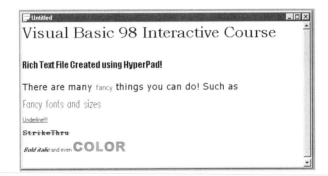

FIGURE 8.14

HyperPad displaying rich text.

Lesson Summary

In this lesson we replaced the TextBox control with the more powerful RichTextBox control. This allowed us to work with Rich Text files, as well as add font and color functionality. In the next lesson we'll add a toolbar to HyperPad.

Quiz 2

1. What does RTF stand for?

    a. Rough Text Format

    b. RichTextForm

    c. RadicalTextFormat

    d. RichTextFormat

2. Which property below does NOT belong to RichTextBox conrol?

    a. Appearance

    b. Enabled

    c. BorderStyle

    d. Name

3. Which attribute below is NOT a font attribute?

    a. strikethrough

    b. underline

    c. effects

    d. color

4. Which statement below is False?

   a. The RichTextBox control fully supports all the TextBox control's properties.

   b. You can replace a TextBox control with a RichTextBox control just by deleting the TextBox control and replacing it with a RichTextBox control with the same name.

   c. The RichTextBox control can display different fonts.

   d. Both the RichTextBox control and TextBox control can display colors.

Exercise 2

Complexity: Easy

1. Create a form with a CommonDialog control and two command buttons placed at the bottom of the form. Label one command button "Font" and the other one "Color." Have the Font dialog appear when the Font button is clicked, and have the Color dialog box appear when the Color button is clicked.

Complexity: Moderate

2. Create a form with a CommondDialog control. Place a label in the center with the text Change Me. Create three command buttons, one with the caption Font, one with the caption Fore Color, and one with the caption Back Color. Write a program such that when the user clicks Font, the user can change the font in the label control. Allow the user also to change the fore color and back color of the label control using the appropriate buttons.

LESSON 3

The ToolBar and ImageList Controls

Now to add a toolbar to HyperPad. A toolbar usually appears at the top of a program's main window and consists of a bar containing small buttons and, possibly, other controls. The idea of the toolbar is to give the user direct access to the most commonly used features of the program. Most of the time, toolbar buttons are used as direct replacements for equivalent functions on the program's menu. Toolbars are popular, because the user can point and click at a toolbar button a lot more quickly and much more conveniently than navigating through a menu structure.

Toolbars also have another important function. They make your applications look a little friendlier. However, their little buttons just cry out to be pressed, so you should make sure that you disable them, as you do their menu equivalents, when the buttons go out of context.

Adding a Toolbar to Your Project

Adding a toolbar to your project involves using two Windows 95 controls. The first of these is called the ToolBar control. You use it to create the toolbar and the basic toolbar buttons. The second control is the ImageList control. The image list's job is to store the images displayed on the toolbar button tops. In fact, you can use an image list to store any images you like, not just the ones destined for a toolbar's buttons. Your only limitation is the amount of available memory. Remember that images are memory hogs!

Once the images are loaded into the image list, the toolbar buttons can be linked to the images. From that point on, the ToolBar control does the rest, automatically repainting its buttons in the down position when they get pressed and graying them out when they become disabled, so you need only one bitmap per button.

Figure 8.15 shows how the ToolBar and ImageList controls appear on the toolbox.

FIGURE 8.15

The ToolBar *and* ImageList *controls.*

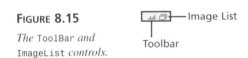

Image List

Toolbar

Add these two controls to frmMain. Like the CommonDialog control, the ImageList control will quite happily sit on the MDI form because it has no visual interface of its own and will be invisible at runtime. The ToolBar control automatically aligns itself to the top of the form, although you can change its alignment by setting its Align property. Leave it at the top of the form, where convention dictates a toolbar should be.

Figure 8.16 shows frmMain in design mode with both controls added.

The ImageList MaskColor Property

The MaskColor property affects the way the images contained in the image list are displayed. The purpose of this mask is to facilitate situations where an image is going to be displayed on top of an existing graphic. This is exactly what you are about to do in displaying an image on top of a button. The mask is a black-and-white image created from the original image in the image list. The MaskColor value determines which color in the image is going to be used as the "background" (and therefore which color will be transparent when the image is finally displayed). All other colors will be opaque. As a rule of thumb, the most predictable results occur when you use the button face color for the mask. The button top that the image is to be displayed on is gray, and you should use the same gray color as the mask color for this image list. Follow Figure 8.17 to set the MaskColor correctly.

FIGURE 8.16

HyperPad in design mode with the ImageList *and* ToolBar *controls added.*

FIGURE 8.17

Applying a MaskColor *property to the image list.*

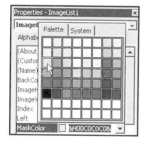

At this stage, the toolbar doesn't look too exciting. For a start, it has no buttons. Your job: to add some.

Adding Buttons to the Toolbar

If you check out the toolbar's properties, you'll find one at the top of the Properties Windows called (Custom). Notice that the property name is in parentheses. This is because it isn't a property itself, but a link to a Properties Pages dialog box inside the OCX. Many of the Windows 95 controls have this (Custom) entry in their Properties windows. The reason it's there is that many of the properties of the control are too complex to be programmed directly from the Properties window. Some properties are interrelated and require a more structured editing tool than the ordinary Properties window. The Property Pages dialog box provides this additional structure.

When you select the (Custom) entry, a small button with ellipses on it appears. Press that button to display the Property Pages dialog box for the control. Use the dialog box to create three new toolbar buttons. These three buttons will be used

- To create a new document
- To open an existing document
- To save the current document to disk

The dialog box that is displayed contains three tabs: General, Buttons, and Pictures. The first thing to do is to add the buttons themselves. Select the Buttons tab and press Insert Button three times. This is shown in Figure 8.18.

FIGURE 8.18

The ToolBar *control Property dialog.*

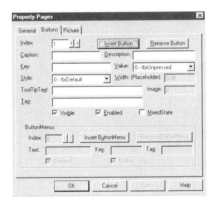

Each time you press the Insert Button, a new button is added to the toolbar. What's actually happening here is quite interesting. The buttons you are creating at design time will be added to a Buttons collection at runtime. That's why this dialog box has a Key field. Just like any other collection, you can associate a key with the button object itself so that you can locate that button in the collection at runtime.

Note that you cannot rely on a button occupying the same index position in the collection when your program is run. This is because the toolbar is potentially customizable by the user, a feature that is covered at the end of this lesson.

Use the Spin button to set the Index to 1 and type New in the Key field. You can optionally add a caption that will appear beneath the button, but for this exercise leave the Caption field blank. (It is not conventional to have captions on toolbars.) Set the Key for Index 2 to Open, and set the Key for Index 3 to Save.

You can also set styles for the buttons. The standard toolbar button is `tbrDefault`, but you can select from other styles:

- `tbrCheck`
- `tbrButton Group`
- `tbrSeparator`
- `tbrPlace Holder`

Check Style

The Check style changes the way the button operates at runtime. Instead of emulating a standard Command button, this style makes the button work like a check box. The button stays in its down position when it is first pressed. It then has to be pressed once again to be released. For example, the bold, italic, and underline buttons in Word are Check Style buttons.

Button Group

When you set two or more buttons to be a button group, they behave just like Option buttons. In other words, when you push one, and another in the group is already pressed, it pops back up. You can create more than one group of buttons on the toolbar by adding separator buttons to act as spacers between the groups.

Separator

A Separator button is not displayed as a button at all, but as a small gap between buttons. You can use separators to help group buttons together, both visually and functionally.

Placeholder Style

The Placeholder style allows a button to be used as a container for another control. This is how you can add other controls to the toolbar.

By using button groups, separators, and place holders, you can add all the features of a professional word processor to HyperPad's toolbar, such as a group of buttons to make text bold, italic, underlined, or strikethrough. You can also add combo boxes to allow the user to select the font and font size without having to use the Font `CommonDialog` boxes.

Adding Images to the Buttons

Now that you have three buttons to play with, here's how to add bitmaps to the button tops. If you have Visual Studio, the bitmaps are located in the VB home directory under COMMON\GRAPHICS\BITMAPS\TLBR_W95.

The bitmaps to use are shown in Figure 8.19.

FIGURE 8.19

Bitmaps for the buttons.

These three bitmaps must be loaded into the ImageList control. To do this, select the (Custom) properties of the ImageList control to display the ImageList Property Pages dialog box, and select the Images tab. On that tab is the Insert Picture button, which you can use to load the images into separate index positions in the image list. Figure 8.20 shows you this dialog box with the three bitmaps loaded. Bitmaps in the ImageList control can be referred to by index, or you can add a key, if you want. For larger collections of images, keys are easier to remember; use the same key name for the bitmap as for the button.

FIGURE 8.20

Loading images into the ImageList control.

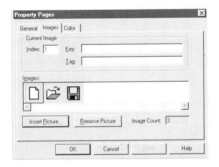

You now have bitmaps that correspond to each of the three buttons. Each button is a Button object in the toolbar's Buttons collection and, correspondingly, each image is a ListImage object in the image list's List Images collection. Now all you have to do is link the images to the buttons.

At design time, the index numbers of the ListImage objects and the Button objects are fixed. In other words, the Button object with an index of 1 will always be the new button at design time. Similarly, the ListImage object with an index of 1 will always be the bitmap that is associated with that button.

To link the two together, return to the Custom Properties dialog box of the ToolBar control and display its General tab. The ImageList combo box allows you to link the toolbar to an image list. This is shown in Figure 8.21. When you open the combo box, it displays all the ImageList controls on the form.

FIGURE 8.21

Linking the image list with the ToolBar dialog box's General tab.

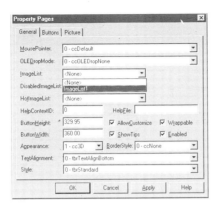

Once the toolbar knows which image list to use, it has access to the List Images collection in that control. All that's left to do then is to specify which ListImage object in the collection to use for each button.

To do this, select the Buttons tab. A text box labeled Image is at the bottom of the displayed dialog box. In the text box, enter the index number of the ListImage object that you want on that button. (If you used keys for the images, you can add a key instead of an index number.) So, for button index one, enter a 1 in the Image text box. For button index two, enter a 2, and so on.

A word of warning: Once you have connected the image list to the toolbar, you cannot add new images to the image list unless you remove all references to it from the toolbar. That can be a lot of work if you have a large toolbar. As always, the best strategy is to plan ahead.

That's all there is to it. Now when you run HyperPad, it will have a toolbar, as shown in Figure 8.22, although the toolbar isn't fully functional yet.

Disabling the Save Button

On the Buttons tab is an Enabled check box that you can use to enable or disable a button at startup. You should disable the Save button at startup for the same reasons that you disabled the Save menu item. Like the menu, you'll have to add a line to the SetupCSMenus subroutine to enable or disable the button at runtime. This is shown in Listing 8.10.

FIGURE 8.22

*HyperPad running
with the toolbar.*

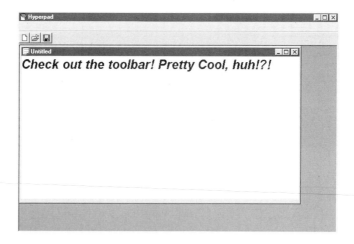

LISTING 8.10   Making the Toolbar Context Sensitive

```
mnuFileClose.Enabled = Found
mnuFileSave.Enabled = Found
mnuFileSaveAs.Enabled = Found
mnuFilePrint.Enabled = Found
Toolbar1.Buttons("Save").Enabled = Found
```

As you can see from the single new line,

```
Toolbar1.Buttons("Save").Enabled = Found
```

that it's easy to access the Save button at runtime using the key you set up at design time.

What Happens When the Button Is Pressed?

When a toolbar button is pressed, it generates a `ButtonClick` event. Listing 8.11 shows how to program the three buttons.

LISTING 8.11   Programming the Toolbar

```
Private Sub Toolbar1_ButtonClick(ByVal Button As Button)
Select Case Button.Key
    Case "New"
        mnuFileNew_Click
    Case "Open"
        mnuFileOpen_Click
    Case "Save"
```

```
            mnuFileSave_Click
End Select
End Sub
```

The `ButtonClick` event's `Button` parameter is a reference to the `Button` object that was pressed. All you have to do is check the `Key` property of that particular object to tell which of the three buttons generated the event. If you're finding the use of the word "Button" confusing, it's probably because the `ToolBar` control gives the `Button` object variable the same name as the `Button` class. That's why the declaration reads `Button As Button`. There's nothing to stop you from changing the name of the variable, so you could write the subroutine shown in Listing 8.12 instead.

LISTING 8.12   Same Routine, Different Variable Name

```
Private Sub Toolbar1_ButtonClick(ByVal TheButton As Button)
Select Case TheButton.Key
    Case "New"
        mnuFileNew_Click
    Case "Open"
        mnuFileOpen_Click
    Case "Save"
        mnuFileSave_Click
End Select
End Sub
```

Additional Toolbar Features

The toolbar has some nice additional features that you might want to use. These include ToolTips and the capability to let the user reorganize the toolbar at runtime.

ToolTips

You know what ToolTips are—those little pop-ups that appear when you point at something. ToolTips contain a small piece of text that describes what the object to which you're pointing to does. This is a particularly helpful feature for your users, because some toolbar button graphics can be rather obscure. Your users will want to know what that button with the little flying polygons on it does without having to press it.

The toolbar has support for ToolTips built in, so adding ToolTips is a trivial exercise. Just return to the Buttons tab on the toolbar's Custom Properties dialog box. In there, you'll find a field labeled `ToolTip Text`. Just add the text that you want to appear in the ToolTip to this field, and set the toolbar's `ShowTips` property to `True`, and the ToolTip will be displayed at runtime. The text to add to your three buttons is New file, Open file, and Save file.

Figure 8.23 shows you HyperPad running with ToolTips.

FIGURE **8.23**

HyperPad with ToolTips.

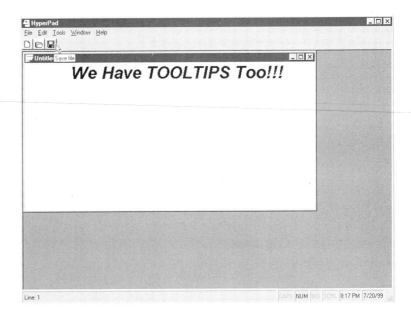

Reorganizing the Toolbar's Buttons at Runtime

Did you know that your users can reorganize the toolbar at runtime? Try double-clicking the background of the toolbar (any place other than a button) when HyperPad is running. The Customize Toolbar dialog box shown in Figure 8.24 appears. Your users can use this dialog box to move the buttons around. If you don't want your users to have this facility, you should set the toolbar's AllowCustomize property to False.

FIGURE 8.24

The toolbar's Customize Toolbar dialog box.

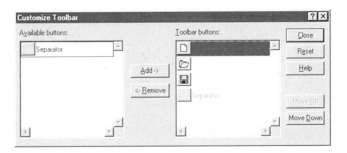

8

The text that appears next to each bitmap is a description of the button. However, this text is not picked up from the ToolTip Text field on the Buttons tab. Instead, it comes from the Description field on the same tab. You'll have to add some text to that field, or your dialog box will display just the buttons without the descriptive text.

Lesson Summary

In this lesson we added a toolbar to HyperPad and showed you how to add buttons to it. ToolTips were introduced, as well as reorganizing a toolbar's buttons at runtime. The next lesson introduces the StatusBar control.

Quiz 3

1. Which style allows a button to be used as a container for another control?

   a. Check Style

   b. Separator Style

   c. Frame Style

   d. Placeholder Style

2. A Button Group most closely resembles which type of control?

   a. OptionButton control

   b. Radiobuttons

   c. The Checkbox control

   d. Both a and b

3. The Check Style changes the way the button operates at runtime in what way?

   a. When the user clicks the button, it stays depressed.

   b. When the user clicks the button, a check mark is displayed on the left of the button.

   c. When the user clicks the button, all other buttons in its group is disabled.

   d. When the user clicks the button, it stays depressed until pressed again.

4. To add ToolTips to the toolbar, you must

   a. Add the text that you want to appear in the ToolTip Text field

   b. Double-click the object you want to have the tool tip, and type the text you want to appear in the text box that appears, and set the ShowTips property to True

c. Add the text that you want to appear in the `ToolTip Text` field, and set the `ShowTips` property to `True`

d. Either b or c

Exercise 3

Complexity: Easy

1. Create a form with a `CommonDialog` control, an `ImageList` control, and a toolbar. Create two buttons on the toolbar. Setup the first button to display the Font dialog box and the second to display the color dialog box. Choose any bitmaps you see fit for the toolbar buttons.

Complexity: Moderate

2. Create a form with a `ToolBar` control and an `ImageList` control. Create three buttons with the key "ButtonOne," "ButtonTwo," and "ButtonThree," respectively. Assign any three bitmaps to them. Then create three `CommandButtons` with the captions "Hide buttons," "Show buttons," and "Set Tool Tip Text." Write the program such that when the user clicks "Hide buttons," all the buttons disappear, when "Show buttons" is clicked, they all reappear, and when "Set Tool Tip Text" is clicked, each button will have the tip text "ButtonOne Tool Tip Text," and so on.

LESSON 4

The `StatusBar` Control

One feature that's missing from HyperPad is a status bar. This is a horizontal bar that sits at the bottom of the main window of an application. Its purpose is to display useful information about what's going on in the application. In HyperPad, this could include the current position of the cursor in the document and any other relevant information. Figure 8.25 shows you how the `StatusBar` control appears on the toolbox.

FIGURE 8.25

The `StatusBar` *control.*

First, add the `StatusBar` control to `frmMain` in the usual way. Like the toolbar, the status bar knows where it is supposed to go, so it aligns itself to the bottom of the form. It has an `Align` property, just like the toolbar, so you can vary the alignment if you like.

Figure 8.26 shows you how frmMain now looks with the status bar added.

FIGURE 8.26

frmMain *in design mode with a* StatusBar *control added.*

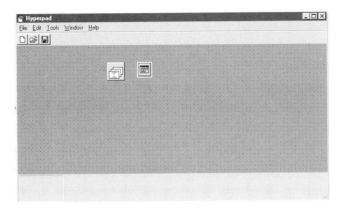

Take a closer look at the bar itself. It consists of three distinct regions. To the left is an indented panel that, at the moment, is empty. At the far right is a Windows 95-style sizing handle that can be used at runtime to resize the main window with the mouse. The remaining part of the bar is unused at present, and so it is empty. Try running HyperPad now. You can use the new resizing handle, although nothing appears yet in the indented panel.

What Do I Use the Status Bar For?

The first thing to work out is what information you want to display in the status bar. Typically, this will dictate how many panels you will need. The Style property controls whether the bar has just one panel or is capable of showing multiple panels. You are going to need multiple panels for this example. The panels we are going to add will show information regarding text, caps lock, num lock, the insert key, scroll lock, the time, and the date.

Adding Panels

The StatusBar control stores each Panel object in a Panels collection, just like the ToolBar stores each Button object in a Buttons collection. You should realize now that Microsoft has designed the Windows 95 controls to be used in very similar ways.

You can define the number of panels and the properties of each Panel object by selecting (Custom) from the control's Properties window. Figure 8.27 shows the StatusBar's Panels Property dialog box.

FIGURE 8.27

The Panels Property dialog box.

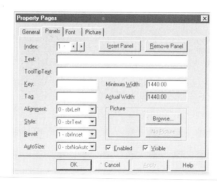

Panels can be added to and removed from the status bar using this dialog box.

Panel Properties

Add six more panels with properties set according to Table 8.5.

TABLE 8.5 Panels to Add to the Status Bar

Index	Key	Alignment	Style	Bevel	AutoSize
1	Text	0 - Left	0 - Text	1 - Inset	1 - Spring
2	Caps	1 - Center	1 - CAPS	1 - Inset	2 - Content
3	NumLock	1 - Center	2 - NUM LOCK	1 - Inset	2 - Content
4	Ins	1 - Center	3 - INS	1 - Inset	2 - Content
5	Scroll	1 - Center	4 - SCROLL	1 - Inset	2 - Content
6	Time	1 - Center	5 - Time	1 - Inset	2 - Content
7	Date	1 - Center	6 - Date	1 - Inset	2 - Content

The Key Property

The Key property defines the key that will be used to identify a Panel object in the Panels collection at runtime.

The Alignment Property

The Alignment property determines how the text in the panel will be positioned. You can choose Justified, Left, Center, or Right.

The Style Property

The Style property is an important property. It determines what is to be stored in a panel. The first panel is used to store some text. However, the other panels display the states of the Caps Lock Numlock, Ins, and Scroll keys. The last two panels display the current time and date.

The `Bevel` Property

The `Bevel` property determines whether the panel is displayed inset into the status bar, raised from it, or flat with no bevel at all.

The `AutoSize` Property

The `AutoSize` property determines how large a panel is. The first panel is set to `Spring`, which means that it shrinks and grows according to the size of the status bar at runtime. The rest are sized according to their content. There is no need to set their sizes manually. Alternatively, you could set `AutoSize` to `None`, in which case you would have to set the minimum size of the `Panel` object at design time and then manually control its size at runtime by setting its `Width` property in your code.

Adding Text to a Text Panel

All that's left for you to do now is to add some text to the first panel to tell the user which line of the document contains the cursor. The `RichTextBox` assists in this task, because it has a couple of nice features that the ordinary `TextBox` lacks. One of these is the `GetLineFromChar` method and the other is the `SelChange` event.

The `GetLineFromChar` Method

Listing 8.13 shows the code for a new `Public` subroutine to add to `frmMain`. The `GetLineFromChar` method returns the line number of a character. To return the line number of the cursor, the program sends the selection `SelStart` as an argument.

LISTING 8.13 Routine to Display a Line Number

```
Public Sub DisplayLineNumber()
Dim LineNum As Integer

With frmMain.ActiveForm.txtDocument
    If .SelStart > 0 Then
        LineNum = .GetLineFromChar(.SelStart)
    End If
    frmMain.StatusBar1.Panels("Text").Text = "Line: " & CStr(LineNum + 1)
End With
End Sub
```

This subroutine needs to be called whenever a document form becomes the active form or whenever the position of the insertion point changes. One place to call it from is the `Activate` event in the `frmDocument` form, as shown in Listing 8.14.

LISTING 8.14   Calling `DisplayLineNumber`

```
Private Sub Form_Activate()
frmMain.SetupCSMenus
frmMain.DisplayLineNumber
End Sub
```

As you can see, all you need to do is to call the subroutine.

The `SelChange` Event

The `RichTextBox`'s `SelChange` event is triggered whenever the value of the `SelPos` property is changed. This occurs, of course, whenever the insertion point is moved; the `SelChange` event is a convenient event to use for this purpose. This is shown in Listing 8.15.

LISTING 8.15   Calling `DisplayLineNumber` When the Cursor Moves

```
Private Sub txtDocument_SelChange()
frmMain.DisplayLineNumber
End Sub
```

Don't forget to clear out the text from the panel when a form is destroyed. You can implement this by making a small change to the `If Cancel = False Then...End If` statement block at the end of `frmDocument`'s `Unload` event, as shown in Listing 8.16.

LISTING 8.16   Update to the `Unload` Event

```
If Cancel = False Then
    frmMain.DocColl.Remove CStr(CollKey)
    Set objDocument = Nothing
    frmMain.StatusBar1.Panels("Text").Text = ""
End If
```

Just a few simple changes, and you now have a working status bar that tells you on which line of your document you are working.

Lesson Summary

In this lesson we added the `StatusBar` control to the HyperPad project and explored the relevant properties. In the next lesson, we look at the `TabStrip` control.

Quiz 4

1. Which property is not valid for a Panel object?

    a. Key

    b. AutoSize

    c. Level

    d. Bevel

2. Which property determines what is stored in a Panel object?

    a. Key

    b. Style

    c. Type

    d. Bevel

3. Of the following listed which is a valid Alignment property?

    a. Justified

    b. Top

    c. Bottom

    d. Both b and c

4. When is the SelChange event triggered?

    a. When the contents of a panel change

    b. When a panel is resized

    c. When the value of the SelPos property has changed

    d. When the value of the SelCount property has changed

Exercise 4

Complexity: Easy

1. Create a form with a CommandButton label. Add Click and a StatusBar control. Place the StatusBar control on the left side of the form. Write a program such that whenever the user clicks the Add Click button, the number of clicks is displayed in the StatusBar control.

Complexity: Moderate

2. Add a new Panel to the `StatusBar` control in HyperPad that displays the current contents of the clipboard. It doesn't have to display the entire contents, just the first 20 characters or so. Make sure it is updated every time text is copied to the clipboard.

LESSON 5

The `TabStrip` Control

You already know what the `TabStrip` control looks like. It's the same control that you've seen in some of Visual Basic's own dialog boxes. The Project Options dialog box and the Windows 95 controls' Properties dialog boxes all make use of this versatile control to separate option screens into separate but related "tabs," much like a card index tab.

To see the features of the `TabStrip` control (and the remaining Windows 95 controls), add a new form to HyperPad. Call the form `frmOptions` and set its properties according to Table 8.6. The purpose of the new form is to provide an Options dialog box, rather like the one in Visual Basic itself. Actually, this lesson uses this form as a vehicle for demonstrating the remaining Windows 95 controls, but you could extend all manner of user-configurable settings to this dialog box if you want.

TABLE 8.6   `frmOptions` Properties

Property	Value
BorderStyle	3 - Fixed Dialog
Caption	Options
ClipControls	False
ControlBox	False
MaxButton	False
MinButton	False
Name	frmOptions

Two new menu items to add to `frmMain` that give you a way to display the dialog box are defined in Table 8.7.

TABLE 8.7   Menus to Add to `frmMain`

Name	Caption	Menu Type
mnuTools	&Tools	Top level between `mnuEdit` and `mnuWindow`
mnuToolsOptions	&Options...	Submenu to `mnuTools`

Add the code in Listing 8.17 to the `mnuToolsOptions` `Click` event subroutine to display the new dialog box.

LISTING 8.17   Bringing Up the `frmOptions` Dialog Box

```
Private Sub mnuToolsOptions_Click()
frmOptions.Show vbModal
End Sub
```

You're now ready to add a `TabStrip` control to `frmOptions`. Figure 8.28 shows you how the `TabStrip` control appears on the toolbox.

FIGURE 8.28

The `TabStrip` *control.*

Drag a `TabStrip` control onto the form and add two Command buttons, as shown in Figure 8.29. Set the `Name` of these three controls to `tabOptions`, `cmdOK`, and `cmdCancel`. Set the `Default` and `Cancel` properties of the two buttons accordingly.

FIGURE 8.29

`frmOptions` *form with* `TabStrip` *control and Command buttons added.*

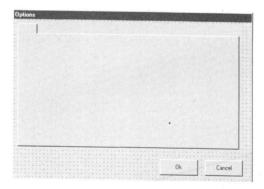

Finally, add the code in Listing 8.18 to the Command buttons' `Click` events, so that the form gets unloaded when either button is pressed.

LISTING 8.18 Unload the Form

```
Private Sub cmdOK_Click()
Unload Me
End Sub

Private Sub cmdCancel_Click()
Unload Me
End Sub
```

How Does the `TabStrip` Control Work?

The `TabStrip` control has a lot in common with the other Windows 95 controls you have seen. It consists of a `Tabs` collection that contains individual `Tab` objects. Each `Tab` object relates to one tab on the `TabStrip` control. As with the `ToolBar` and the `StatusBar`, you can define how many `Tab` objects should be created and how their properties should be set at design time.

When you first add the tab strip to a form, the `Tabs` collection already contains one default `Tab` object. You can add more `Tab` objects to the `Tabs` collection by using the control's Properties dialog box. Display this dialog box the same way the other Windows 95 controls are displayed, by selecting the (Custom) entry in the control's Properties window. As you can see from Figure 8.30, the dialog box allows you to define everything that you would associate with each `Tab` object in the collection, including its `Key`, `Caption`, and `ToolTip Text`.

FIGURE 8.30

The Tabs tab.

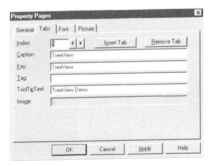

There's even an image index that you can enter if you want to add an image to the tab. This works in exactly the same way as adding pictures to toolbar buttons. You have to add an `ImageList` control to the form first. The General tab allows you to tie in the correct `ImageList` control from those that may already be on the form. The General tab is shown in Figure 8.31.

FIGURE 8.31

The General tab.

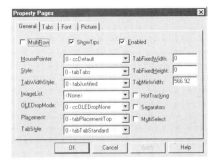

The project needs four tabs, one for each of the remaining Windows 95 controls. Use the Tabs tab in the Properties dialog box to add three more tabs. Set the properties for each tab to the values shown in Table 8.8.

TABLE 8.8 Tab Object Properties

Index	Caption	Key	ToolTip Text
1	TreeView	TreeView	TreeView Demo
2	ListView	ListView	ListView Demo
3	ProgressBar	ProgressBar	ProgressBar Demo
4	Slider	Slider	Slider Demo

After you press the Properties dialog box's OK button, the changes you made are reflected in the onscreen tab strip.

Tabs or Buttons

The `Style` property allows you to choose between the standard Tab style or a Button style. Figure 8.32 shows you the tab strip using the Button style.

FIGURE 8.32

`tabOptions` *using Button style instead of Tab style.*

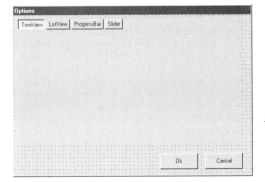

The Tab style is more intuitive than the Button style and is the accepted convention, but you can use buttons if you prefer. For this example, switch back to the Tab style.

Defining the Control Groups

The next stage is to define the groups of controls that appear when the tabs are selected. This is where things get a little complicated. The tab strip was not designed to be a container for other controls. Therefore, you cannot create the control groups by themselves using the TabStrip control alone. You're probably wondering why you can't simply click a tab and display the group that goes with that tab. Unfortunately, the TabStrip control really knows nothing about the control groups it is meant to display.

Creating the groups of controls themselves is easy. You can use any control that is capable of being a container for other controls. If you remember from Chapter 6, "Building the GUI with Forms, Menus, and MDI Forms," the PictureBox control supports this feature.

There are four Tab controls, so you need to add four PictureBox controls to frmOptions.

Now for the tricky part. You must make the four picture boxes a control array by giving them the same name and setting their index values to 0, 1, 2, and 3, respectively. The array of picture boxes simplifies selecting the correct picture box at runtime. Here's how:

1. Draw a picture box on top of the TabStrip control. Size it so it fills the tab strip without covering the tabs.
2. Click the picture box to select it, then press Ctrl+C to copy it onto the clipboard.
3. Click the form (not on the picture box!).
4. Press Ctrl+V to paste the copy of the picture box onto the form.
5. Visual Basic asks if you want to start a control array. Answer Yes and click OK.
6. Drag the new picture box so it is a little below and a little to the right of the first picture box.
7. Click the form.
8. Press Ctrl+V to paste another copy of the picture box onto the form.
9. Drag the new picture box so it is a little below and a little to the right of the second picture box.
10. Click the form.
11. Press Ctrl+V to paste another copy of the picture box onto the form.

12. Drag the new picture box so it is a little below and a little to the right of the third picture box.

13. Add a label to each picture box. Use Figure 8.33 as a guide.

FIGURE 8.33

frmOptions *with*
PictureBox *controls*
added.

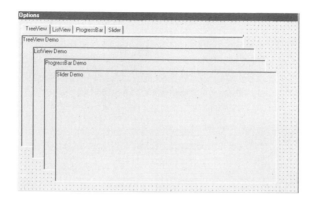

Be careful when you add the picture boxes to the form. It's easy to make one picture box a child of another accidentally. You must click the form before adding each picture box to ensure that the new picture box is contained by the form and not by the previous picture box. Figure 8.33 shows the design-time form with picture boxes added.

Note that the picture boxes occupy slightly different positions on the form. That is a design-time strategy that makes it easier to add other controls to the correct picture box. Once the design is completed, the four picture boxes must be moved so that they are superimposed on each other in the correct position on the tab strip.

Picture Box ZOrder

Recall from Chapter 7, "Building Classes: The Foundation of Visual Basic OOP," that the ZOrder method sets the position of an object within its graphical level. Each picture box occupies a different position in the ZOrder of controls on the form. In other words, the four picture boxes appear to be stacked on top of each other. This is important because it is the key to using the tab strip.

The tab strip must have the lowest ZOrder so that all other controls appear to sit on top of it. To see why, click the tab strip to select it and press Ctrl+J to move it to the top of the ZOrder. That makes it hard to work, doesn't it? Press Ctrl+K to move the tab strip back to the rear, where it belongs.

Click the first picture box to select it. Look at the Properties window to be sure you have selected `Picture1`. Press Ctrl+J to move it to the top of the ZOrder. Figure 8.34 shows the design-time `frmOptions` with `Picture1` at the top of the ZOrder.

FIGURE 8.34

`frmOptions` *with*
rearranged picture box
ZOrder.

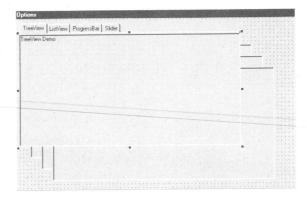

Linking the `TabStrip` Tabs to the Correct Picture Boxes

When the form is loaded, the picture box at the top of the ZOrder is the one that is visible and associated with the first tab. All that's left to do now is to make sure that when a different tab is pressed at runtime, the correct picture box is brought to the top of the ZOrder.

This is accomplished through the `TabStrip`'s `Click` event. Add the code in Listing 8.19 to that event.

LISTING 8.19   Selecting the Correct Tab Option

```
Private Sub TreeViewDemo()
End Sub

Private Sub ListViewDemo()
End Sub

Private Sub ProgressBarDemo()
End Sub

Private Sub SliderDemo()
End Sub

Private Sub tabOptions_Click()
Picture1(tabOptions.SelectedItem.Index - 1).ZOrder
```

```
Select Case tabOptions.SelectedItem.Index
    Case 1 'Run the TreeView demo
        TreeViewDemo
    Case 2 'Run the ListView demo
        ListViewDemo
    Case 3 'Run the ProgressBar demo
        ProgressBarDemo
    Case 4 'Run the Slider demo
        SliderDemo
End Select
End Sub
```

When you click a tab, the SelectedItem property of the TabStrip indicates which tab you selected. The SelectedItem property is an integer that ranges from 1 to the number of tabs on the TabStrip—in this case, 4. Recall that the indexes of Picture1 range from 0 to 3. All you need to do is associate a tab with a picture box by subtracting one from the SelectedItem property. Thus, the line:

```
Picture1(tabOptions.SelectedItem.Index - 1).ZOrder
```

sets the ZOrder of the correct picture box and brings it to the front.

The Select Case statement is a piece of advanced planning. Note that the code also creates the four demonstration procedures at this stage, although they are empty for now. Empty procedures such as this are called *stubs* or *program stubs*. They are a convenience, allowing you to design your program without having to write all of it at once.

Run the program and select Options from the Tools menu to display the form at runtime. You can select the tabs and see the correct picture box displayed. Later, when you complete the four demonstration subroutines, each of the tabs will demonstrate a different ActiveX control.

After you've seen the way this works, return to design mode and move the four picture boxes into the same position, so that they are positioned within the borders of the tab strip itself. Then set their BorderStyle properties to None and run HyperPad again. The result is shown in Figure 8.35.

You can, of course, add whatever controls you like to the picture boxes.

Working with Multiple Picture Boxes

Working with multiple picture boxes at design time can be a bit confusing. Probably the least confusing method is to resize and position the controls as shown in Figure 8.36.

FIGURE 8.35

The completed tab strip.

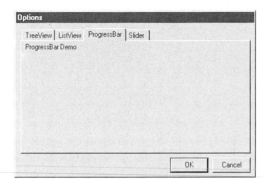

FIGURE 8.36

One approach to working with multiple picture boxes.

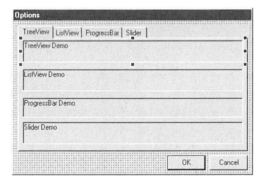

This keeps all four picture boxes visible and easy to find. To add controls to one of the picture boxes, click it and press Ctrl+J to bring it to the top of the ZOrder. Then drag it to the top of the tab strip and size it to fill the tab strip while you add controls. When you are done with that picture box, make it smaller and drag it back to its original position.

This does require additional code, but it makes working with the picture boxes so much easier that it is worth more code. The changes in the code are shown in Listing 8.20.

LISTING 8.20   Using the Move Method to Position the Picture Boxes

```
Private Sub tabOptions_Click()
' Move the picture
Picture1(tabOptions.SelectedItem.Index - 1).Move _
  tabOptions.ClientLeft, tabOptions.ClientTop, _
  tabOptions.ClientWidth, tabOptions.ClientHeight
' Bring it to the top
Picture1(tabOptions.SelectedItem.Index - 1).ZOrder
' Give it time to draw
DoEvents
```

```
Select Case tabOptions.SelectedItem.Index
    Case 1 'Run the TreeView demo
        TreeViewDemo
    Case 2 'Run the ListView demo
        ListViewDemo
    Case 3 'Run the ProgressBar demo
        ProgressBarDemo
    Case 4 'Run the Slider demo
        SliderDemo
End Select
End Sub
```

The new code uses the Move method to reposition and size the correct picture box, then uses the ZOrder method to bring it to the top. The ClientLeft, ClientTop, ClientWidth, and ClientHeight properties define the inner dimensions of the tab strip and ensure that the picture box fills the entire tab strip without covering the tabs and without overlapping the edges. The DoEvents command is needed because of the time it takes to draw the picture box in its new size and position.

Another approach to using multiple picture boxes is to size and position all of them to their final position and use Ctrl+J and Ctrl+K to change the design-time ZOrder. Try both techniques and use the one you prefer.

The BeforeClick Event

The TabStrip also has a useful event called BeforeClick. This event gets called when the user clicks a tab but before the focus has moved away from the previous one.

The BeforeClick event is particularly useful for running "cleanup" code between tabs. The code in the next two lessons takes advantage of BeforeClick. You can also use this event to prevent the focus from moving from one tab to another. The BeforeClick event is issued with a Cancel parameter. You can set this parameter to False to cancel the Click event.

How to Display a Tab Programmatically

Another useful feature of the TabStrip control is that it allows you to select a tab from within your code. Each Tab object has a Selected property. Your code can read the Selected property or it can write it. Therefore, the following code will work for the tabstrip example. Try executing it from the Debug window when any tab is displayed other than the ProgressBar tab.

```
? tabOptions.Tabs("ProgressBar").Selected
```

This returns False. Alternatively:

```
tabOptions.Tabs("ProgressBar").Selected = True
```

makes the ProgressBar tab the selected one.

There is a perfectly good reason why you might want to use this feature in frmOptions. At present, the tab strip in frmOptions is dependent on the top-level picture box being the one for the TreeView demo. If the picture boxes on your form are arranged as shown in Figure 8.36, all four of them are visible in their reduced size when the form opens. Only after you click a tab does the form arrive at its desired appearance. If you are using full-size picture boxes, the one that shows will depend on the design-time ZOrder—if you have the Slide demo on top when you start the program, that is the picture box that is on top at runtime. Add the code in Listing 8.21 to make the Form Load event "click" a tab for you.

LISTING 8.21   Setting the Tab Control's Initial Value

```
Private Sub Form_Load()
Me.Move (Screen.Height - Me.Height) / 2, (Screen.Width - Me.Width) / 2
DoEvents
tabOptions.Tabs("TreeView").Selected = True
End Sub
```

By setting the TreeView's Selected property to True, the TabStrip's Click event is triggered and the TreeView's picture box is brought to the top of the ZOrder. However, if you don't display the form first, the picture box generates an error.

DoEvents

The DoEvents command tells Windows to finish processing any other events in its queue. In this example, DoEvents gives the form time to display. If you leave out DoEvents, you run the risk of trying to display the picture box before the form has had time to display itself.

Lesson Summary

In this lesson we introduced the TabStrip control. We implemented this control using picture boxes, and showed you how to display the tab programmatically. In the next lesson we'll introduce the TreeView control.

8

Quiz 5

1. Which are valid styles for a TabStrip control?

   a. Tabs and Boxes

   b. Tabs and Buttons

   c. Tabs

   d. Tabs and Menus

2. Which property value is NOT valid for a Tab object property?

   a. TreeView

   b. ListView

   c. ReportView

   d. Slider

3. What event gets called when the user clicks a tab but before the focus has moved away from the previous one?

   a. Cleanup

   b. PreviousClick

   c. BeforeClick

   d. PrevClick

4. What command tells Windows to finish processing any other events in it queue?

   a. FlushAll

   b. FlushEvents

   c. CompleteEvents

   d. DoEvents

Exercise 5

Complexity: Easy

1. Create a form with a menu option entitled MyTab that opens a TabStrip control with two tabs. Write the program such that whenever the user switches tabs, a Msgbox appears reading Just left Tab #[index] with index being the tab just left.

Complexity: Moderate

2. Create a form with a menu option entitled PictureTab that opens a `TabStrip` control that displays four bitmaps of all the same size. Make sure that when the `TabStrip` control opens, the first picture tab is displayed.

LESSON 6

The `TreeView` Control

The Windows 95 user interface implements lists in a variety of styles. Frequently, the lists are hierarchical. The Windows Explorer is a typical example: It is a list of files and folders. This lesson explains how to program lists with the same look and feel. You can use them in file browsers and in many other applications.

Introducing the `TreeView` and `ListView` Controls

The `TreeView` and `ListView` controls are closely related. They are meant to be used together. A good example of the use of these two controls is in the Windows 95 Explorer, as shown in Figure 8.37.

FIGURE 8.37

Windows Explorer makes use of the `TreeView` *and* `ListView` *controls.*

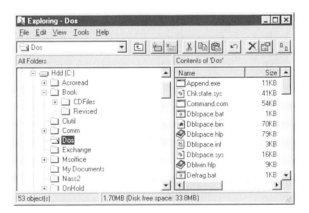

The `TreeView` control makes up the left pane of the Explorer. The `ListView` control is on the right.

The `TreeView` control is used to display a high-level chart of information. When a user selects an item from the `TreeView` control, the item is expanded and displayed in more detail in the `ListView` control. Although most people are familiar with the control combination for viewing directory and file hierarchies, you can use this combination for any hierarchical data. For example, you can use the TreeView control to display a company's list of accounts and the ListView control to display detai!s about a selected account.

Adding a TreeView Control

Bring Picture1 to the front and size it to fill the tab strip's interior. Click the TreeView icon in the toolbox and draw it in the picture box. The TreeView icon is shown in Figure 8.38.

FIGURE 8.38

The TreeView icon.

After you've added the control, size it so that it fills the area underneath the label. It should look like Figure 8.39.

FIGURE 8.39

Initial appearance of the TreeView control.

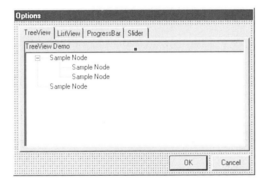

The Sample Node entries that you see do not actually exist. They are merely there to give you an idea how the TreeView will look at runtime. This is a nice feature. It saves you the effort of running your code every time you want to change the properties that affect the TreeView control's appearance.

How Does the TreeView Control Work?

A good way to start thinking about the TreeView control is as a tree-structured list box. As with a list box, you can add and remove individual lines of text. Each line can respond to the user clicking it with the mouse. However, this is about as far as the similarity extends.

Instead of adding lines of text to the TreeView, you add Node objects to its Nodes collection. A Node object is an item in a TreeView control that can contain images and text. Furthermore, you can establish relationships between Node objects when the objects are added to the collection. A number of different relationships can be established, including parent/child, which is the key relationship in constructing a tree structure of nodes within the TreeView.

In some respects, the concept of adding Node objects to a Nodes collection is similar to the way the TabStrip, ToolBar, StatusBar, and ImageList controls work. Each of those controls contains a collection of objects of a specific type. However, the difference with the TreeView control is that it assumes that you will want to add Node objects to the Nodes collection at runtime only. Compare that to the other Windows 95 controls. They provide a special tab in their Properties dialog box that allows you to specify the objects to be added to their internal collections at design time. This is how you added Button objects to the toolbar, Panel objects to the status bar, and Tab objects to the tab strip.

Take a quick look at the TreeView control's Property dialog box. You get to it in the same way as with the other controls, through the (Custom) entry in the Properties window. The dialog box is shown in Figure 8.40. As you can see, it has no Nodes tab, which is a giveaway that you're going to have to do this work programmatically.

FIGURE 8.40

The TreeView *control's Property dialog box.*

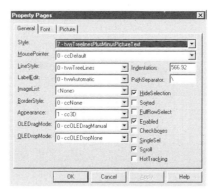

Adding a Node to the Nodes Collection

The following example shows you how to add a node to the TreeView control.

The first thing you must know is the text you want the node to display. The text may come from a database, a text file, or a directory listing. In this example, the text is hard coded into the program. As your knowledge of Visual Basic increases through the use of this book, you can explore other sources.

Add the code in Listing 8.22 to the `TreeViewDemo` subroutine.

LISTING 8.22   Adding Nodes to a Tree

```
Private Sub TreeViewDemo()
Dim MyNode As Node
Dim I As Integer
Dim Text As String

'Clear out any objects from the TreeView
TreeView1.Nodes.Clear

For I = 1 To 100
    Text = "Node " & CStr(I)
    Set MyNode = TreeView1.Nodes.Add(, , , Text)
Next I
End Sub
```

Note that the first thing the code in this example does is clear any preexisting Node objects from the `Nodes` collection with `TreeView.Nodes.Clear`. This is because this demo subroutine will be run every time you click the `TreeView`'s tab on the tab strip. If you don't clear out preexisting nodes, the code will attempt to add the new ones with the same key. As you remember from Chapter 7, "Building Classes: The Foundation of Visual Basic OOP," keys must be unique.

This example adds 100 Node objects to the `Nodes` collection. The text for each node is made up of the word `Node` and a number from 1 to 100. The line that does all the work is the call to the `Nodes` collection's `Add` method. Here, the `Add` method returns a reference to the newly created Node object. The code is not doing anything with that reference, but it's coded this way to show you that the method is capable of returning the reference should you need it.

You can also code the `Add` method so that it doesn't return anything. Just treat the method as if it were a subroutine rather than a function, as follows:

```
TreeView1.Nodes.Add , , , Text
```

Figure 8.41 shows you how the `TreeView` looks when this example is run.

FIGURE 8.41

TreeView with 100 nodes.

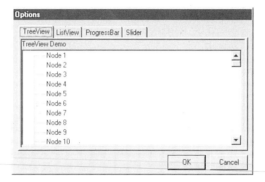

What Are All Those Commas?

Remember that the Nodes collection is a collection. Pretty obvious, isn't it? The syntax of the Add method for a TreeView Nodes collection is

```
object.Add(relative, relationship, key, text, image, selectedimage)
```

The components of the Add method are as follows:

- object is the TreeView Nodes collection.
- relative is an optional parameter that is the node number or key of an existing Node object.
- relationship is an optional parameter that specifies the placement of the new object.
- key is an optional unique string that can be used to identify the Node object.
- text is the string that appears in the node.
- image is an optional parameter that is the index of an image in an image list.
- selectedimage is an optional parameter that is the index of an image list image to be shown when the node is selected.
- The relationship parameter controls where the new node will be placed. The options are
  - tvwLast: The node is placed after all other nodes and at the same level as the node named in relative.
  - tvwNext: The node is placed immediately after the node named in relative.
  - tvwPrevious: The node is placed immediately before the node named in relative.

- tvwChild: The node becomes a child node of the node named in relative. This is the default value.
- If no Node object is named in relative, the new node is placed in the last position of the top-node hierarchy and relationship has no effect.

So what about the commas? You assign each node a text string, and you probably should assign a key. But, if you just want the new node to be added to the end of the list, you can omit relative and relationship. If you used a line such as:

```
TreeView1.Nodes.Add Key, Text
```

the compiler would assume that your key was really relative because it is first in the list, and your test would be seen as (an incorrect) relationship.

When you leave out a parameter that precedes a parameter that you include, the empty space in the list must be marked by commas. So,

```
TreeView1.Nodes.Add , , , Text
```

has three empty spaces preceding the Text parameter. Note that the code leaves off the last two parameters, too. No commas are needed (or allowed) following the last parameter you include.

Displaying Images in the TreeView Control

The TreeView control is capable of displaying a small bitmap next to the text in a node. It can do this because it can optionally reference images that are stored in an ImageList control.

Obviously, to add images you must also add an ImageList control. Add it to frmOptions so it can also be used by other controls on the form. Leave it with its default name of ImageList1.

Modify the code in Listing 8.21 so that it reads as shown in Listing 8.23.

LISTING 8.23   Adding Nodes with Images

```
Private Sub TreeViewDemo()
Dim MyImage As ListImage
Dim MyNode As Node
Dim I As Integer
Dim Text As String

'Clear out any objects from the TreeView and ImageList
TreeView1.Nodes.Clear
```

continues

LISTING 8.23   continued

```
ImageList1.ListImages.Clear

'Add the closed file image to the ImageList
Set MyImage = ImageList1.ListImages.Add(, "closed", _
            LoadPicture("graphics\bitmaps\outline\closed.bmp"))

'Link the TreeView to the ImageList
Set TreeView1.ImageList = ImageList1

For I = 1 To 100
    Text = "Node " & CStr(I)
    Set MyNode = TreeView1.Nodes.Add(, , , Text, "closed")
Next I
End Sub
```

Before you run this code, make sure to set the ImageList's MaskColor property to white, as shown in Figure 8.42. If you don't do this, the images might not display correctly for the reasons described in Lesson 4.

FIGURE 8.42

Setting the image list's MaskColor to the background color of the TreeView.

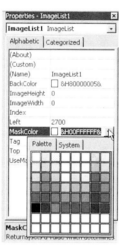

As you can see, after you have cleared the nodes and List Images collections, you have to load the appropriate image into the image list. You can do this manually, using the ImageList control itself at design time, but here you're doing the same thing programmatically. The reason is to demonstrate using a single image list for multiple purposes. Bear in mind that the single image list on this form is going to be used to demonstrate both the TreeView and the ListView controls. Therefore, each time you click the

TreeView or ListView tabs, you need to clear out any images that were left in the image list from the previous demonstration.

The image that you are adding to the image list is an image of a closed folder. The path is relative to Visual Basic 6's home directory.

The second parameter to the ImageList's List Images collection's Add method is the key for the ListImage object. The key is simply closed. Later, when you need to retrieve this image to use it in the TreeView's node, you can use the same key to locate the correct ListImage object.

Note that there's nothing to prevent you from adding more than one image to the image list. Although each node that you add to the TreeView can have only one image associated with it, different Node objects can reference different ListImage objects from the same ImageList control.

At this stage, you need to link the ImageList control to the TreeView. Again, this can be done at design time through the TreeView's General tab in its Properties page. However, this code is doing the job programmatically.

The only difference in your use of the Node collection's Add method this time is that you're now telling the TreeView control to create the node with the image that has the key closed. When you run the example, the node text is displayed next to the image of a closed folder, as shown in Figure 8.43.

FIGURE 8.43

The TreeView control displaying images in each node.

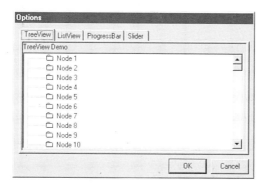

Node Relationships

You learned earlier that it is possible to establish relationships between Node objects. There are, in fact, four different relationships that you can establish:

- Previous
- Next

- Last
- Child

Consider that we created a new node relative to an existing node, which will be referred to as a relative node. The Previous relationship would place a new node immediately before the relative node. The Next relationship would place the new node immediately after the relative node. The Last relationship would position the new node at the end of the level in which the relative node was positioned. The child node would add the new node in the level beneath the relative node. The relationship that you'll probably want to use most is child, so try that one first. Type in the example in Listing 8.24.

LISTING 8.24   Child Nodes

```
Private Sub TreeViewDemo()
Dim MyImage As ListImage
Dim MyNode As Node
Dim I As Integer
Dim J As Integer
Dim ParentKey As String
Dim ChildKey As String
Dim Text As String

'Clear out any objects from the TreeView and ImageList
TreeView1.Nodes.Clear
ImageList1.ListImages.Clear

'Add the closed file image to the ImageList
Set MyImage = ImageList1.ListImages.Add(, "closed", _
      LoadPicture("graphics\bitmaps\outline\closed.bmp"))
'Add the leaf image to the ImageList
Set MyImage = ImageList1.ListImages.Add(, "leaf", _
         LoadPicture("graphics\bitmaps\outline\leaf.bmp"))

'Link the TreeView to the ImageList
Set TreeView1.ImageList = ImageList1

For I = 1 To 10
   ParentKey = "Node" & CStr(I)
   Text = "Parent node " & CStr(I)
   Set MyNode = TreeView1.Nodes.Add(, , ParentKey, Text, "closed")
   For J = 1 To 3
      ChildKey = "Node" & CStr(I) & "\" & CStr(J)
      Text = "Child node " & CStr(I) & "\" & CStr(J)
      Set MyNode = TreeView1.Nodes.Add(ParentKey, _
tvwChild, ChildKey, Text, "leaf")
```

```
      Next J
   Next I
   End Sub
```

8

The `TreeView` control that results from Listing 8.24 is shown in Figure 8.44.

FIGURE 8.44

TreeView *control with*
child nodes.

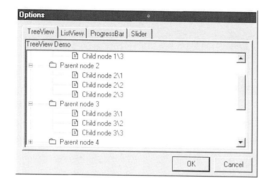

Double-click a node to expand it to show its children.

This exercise starts by adding two bitmaps to the image list. The second bitmap (which is given a key of `leaf`) represents a leaf node, which is a node that has no children.

The program adds 10 top-level (parent) nodes, each of which has three children.

Look at the differences between the two `TreeView Add` methods. The outer one, which adds the parent node, is virtually the same as the call made earlier, except that this time it is added to the `Nodes` collection with a key. The key is specified in the third parameter. This is important, because you need to know the parent's key when you later add the nodes that are children.

The inner `Add` method adds the child nodes. Here, for the first time, the code specifies values in the first and second parameters of the `Add` method. The first parameter identifies the parent node. This is known as the relative node. The second parameter is a constant that specifies what the relationship is going to be. In this case, the relationship is a child relationship. The constant `tvwChild` is predefined by the `TreeView` control, so you don't have to declare it yourself.

Other Relationships

The other three constants of the relationships `Last`, `Next`, and `Previous` are described in Table 8.9.

TABLE 8.9 Other Node Relationships

Constant	Relationship
tvwLast	The new node is positioned at the end of the level in which the relative node is positioned.
tvwNext	The new node is positioned immediately after the relative node.
tvwPrevious	The new node is positioned immediately before the relative node.

Deleting Nodes

To delete a single node from the TreeView control, just specify the node to be deleted in the Node collection's Remove method. You can specify either the index or the key of the node to be deleted. For example:

```
TreeView1.Nodes.Remove 1
```

will remove the Node object that has an index of 1, or

```
TreeView1.Nodes.Remove "Fred"
```

will remove the Node object that has a key of Fred.

If you remove a node that is the parent of child nodes, the child nodes will be removed also.

Sorting Nodes

If a node contains child nodes, the children can automatically be sorted alphabetically by setting the parent Node object's Sorted property to True. Try the example in Listing 8.25, which demonstrates this.

LISTING 8.25 Sorting Demo

```
Private Sub TreeViewDemo()
Dim MyImage As ListImage
Dim MyNode As Node

'Clear out any objects from the TreeView and ImageList
TreeView1.Nodes.Clear
ImageList1.ListImages.Clear

'Add the closed file image to the ImageList
Set MyImage = ImageList1.ListImages.Add(, "closed", _
Loadpicture("graphics\bitmaps\outline\closed.bmp"))
```

```
'Add the lead image to the ImageList
Set MyImage = ImageList1.ListImages.Add(, "leaf", _
Loadpicture("graphics\bitmaps\outline\leaf.bmp"))

'Link the TreeView to the ImageList
Set TreeView1.ImageList = ImageList1

Set MyNode = TreeView1.Nodes.Add(, , "Parent key", "Parent", "closed")
MyNode.Sorted = True
Set MyNode = TreeView1.Nodes.Add("Parent key", _
tvwChild, "Child J", "J", "leaf")
Set MyNode = TreeView1.Nodes.Add("Parent key", _
tvwChild, "Child I", "I", "leaf")
Set MyNode = TreeView1.Nodes.Add("Parent key", _
tvwChild, "Child H", "H", "leaf")
Set MyNode = TreeView1.Nodes.Add("Parent key", _
tvwChild, "Child G", "G", "leaf")
Set MyNode = TreeView1.Nodes.Add("Parent key", _
tvwChild, "Child F", "F", "leaf")
Set MyNode = TreeView1.Nodes.Add("Parent key", _
tvwChild, "Child E", "E", "leaf")
Set MyNode = TreeView1.Nodes.Add("Parent key", _
tvwChild, "Child D", "D", "leaf")
Set MyNode = TreeView1.Nodes.Add("Parent key", _
tvwChild, "Child C", "C", "leaf")
Set MyNode = TreeView1.Nodes.Add("Parent key", _
tvwChild, "Child B", "B", "leaf")
Set MyNode = TreeView1.Nodes.Add("Parent key", _
tvwChild, "Child A", "A", "leaf")
End Sub
```

The order in which you add the 10 child nodes doesn't matter; the TreeView always displays them in alphabetical order, as shown in Figure 8.45.

FIGURE 8.45

Using the node's Sorted *property.*

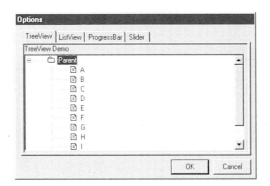

The `ExpandedImage` Property

In the previous examples, the parent node always displays the closed folder bitmap, even when you double-click it to expand it. Wouldn't it be better if, when you expanded the node, the bitmap changed to show that the node was now expanded? You can achieve this effect by using the node's `ExpandedImage` property. Modify the parent/child example from Listing 8.23 so that it reads as shown in Listing 8.26 (added lines in bold).

LISTING 8.26   The `ExpandedImage` Property

```
Private Sub TreeViewDemo()
Dim MyImage As ListImage
Dim MyNode As Node
Dim I As Integer
Dim J As Integer
Dim ParentKey As String
Dim ChildKey As String
Dim Text As String

'Clear out any objects from the TreeView and ListView
TreeView1.Nodes.Clear
ImageList1.ListImages.Clear

'Add the closed file image to the ImageList
Set MyImage = ImageList1.ListImages.Add(, "closed", _
        LoadPicture("graphics\bitmaps\outline\closed.bmp"))

'Add the open file image to the ImageList
Set MyImage = ImageList1.ListImages.Add(,"open", _
        LoadPicture("graphics\bitmaps\outline\open.bmp"))

'Add the lead image to the ImageList
Set MyImage = ImageList1.ListImages.Add(, "leaf", _
        LoadPicture("graphics\bitmaps\outline\leaf.bmp"))

'Link the TreeView to the ImageList
Set TreeView1.ImageList = ImageList1

For I = 1 To 10
    ParentKey = "Node" & CStr(I)
    Text = "Parent node " & CStr(I)
    Set MyNode = TreeView1.Nodes.Add(, , ParentKey, Text, "closed")
    MyNode.ExpandedImage = "open"
    For J = 1 To 3
        ChildKey = "Node" & CStr(I) & "\" & CStr(J)
        Text = "Child node " & CStr(I) & "\" & CStr(J)
```

```
        Set MyNode = TreeView1.Nodes.Add(ParentKey, _
    tvwChild, ChildKey, Text, "leaf")
        Next J
    Next I
    End Sub
```

Now when you run this example and double-click a closed folder, the node expands and changes its bitmap to the open folder. Double-click the node to close it, and the bitmap reverts to the closed folder. This is shown in Figure 8.46.

FIGURE 8.46

TreeView *using the* ExpandedImage.

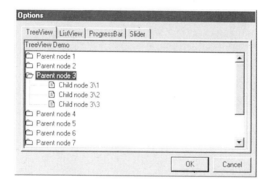

Specifying a Selected Image

You can also display an image when a node is selected. There is a sixth parameter to the Add method that you haven't used. You can specify another image key in this parameter and that image displays when the node is selected, regardless of whether it is expanded or not.

Style and LineStyle Properties

These two properties control how the information in the Nodes collection is presented when the TreeView is displayed. Try running the previous example again, but this time try different combinations of these two properties. You'll find that you can get the TreeView to display a small Plus/Minus box, which indicates whether a node is expanded, by setting LineStyle to 1 - RootLines. You can also control which visual components of the node are displayed by setting the control's Style property to different values. Figure 8.47 shows the previous example running with root lines instead of tree lines. It is accomplished by adding the line.

FIGURE 8.47

TreeView *displaying root lines instead of tree lines.*

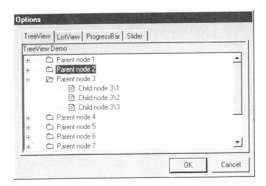

```
TreeView1.LineStyle = tvwRootLines
```

You can add that line almost anywhere in the `ListViewDemo` code.

Tables 8.10 and 8.11 define the constants to use for each value.

TABLE 8.10 LineStyle Property Constants

Constant	Value	Description
tvwTreeLines	0	Displays lines between sibling nodes and their parents
tvwRootLines	1	Displays lines between root nodes and a small Plus/Minus box to indicate if a node is currently expanded

The `Style` property determines the graphical appearance of the `TreeView` control. Table 8.11 lists the constants you can use.

TABLE 8.11 Style Property Constants

Constant	Value	Description
tvwTextOnly	0	Displays text only
tvwPictureText	1	Displays picture and text
tvwPlusMinusText text	2	Displays the Plus/Minus box and only
tvwPlusPictureText	3	Displays the Plus/Minus box and picture and text
tvwTreelinesText	4	Displays tree lines and text only
tvwTreeLinesPictureText	5	Displays tree lines, picture, and text

Constant	Value	Description
tvwTreelinesPlusMinusText	6	Displays tree lines, picture, and text
tvwTreelinesPlusMinusPictureText	7	Displays all the components

Editing the Text in a Node

The LabelEdit property controls whether or not the text in the TreeView's nodes is editable. This property can be set to two values, lvwAutomatic and lvwManual. If the property is set to lvwAutomatic (which is the default setting), clicking the text of a selected node displays a text box, allowing the user to edit the node's text. At this point, the TreeView's BeforeLabelEdit event is triggered, allowing you to perform any preparation work for the impending change. When the edit is completed, the control's AfterLabelEdit event is called. You can use this event to pick up the changed text and act on the change if required.

Alternatively, if the LabelEdit property is set to lvwManual, you have to call the control's StartLabelEdit method before any editing can begin. The Windows 95 Explorer uses this feature to allow you to rename folders and files easily.

Detecting When a Node Is Clicked

Two events can be triggered when the user clicks a Node object. These are Click and NodeClick.

The NodeClick event supplies a reference to the node that was selected. Also, the NodeClick event is called whenever a node is selected, by whatever means (mouse or keyboard).

The Click event, however, is triggered specifically by a mouse click any part of the node's entry in the TreeView. This means that a Click event is fired when you click a Plus box to expand a node, whereas the NodeClick is not. Try the example in Listing 8.27. It will use the debug method to print out a message when the NodeClick event is fired and when the Click event is fired.

LISTING 8.27 Testing the Node's Click Events

```
Private Sub TreeView1_NodeClick(ByVal MyNode As Node)
Debug.Print "NodeClick event: "; MyNode.Key, MyNode.Text
End Sub

Private Sub TreeView1_Click()
Debug.Print "Click event"
End Sub
```

The NodeClick and Click events are often triggered by the same physical event, in which case the NodeClick event is always triggered first. By running the previous code, you'll see that the NodeClick event is always performed before the Click event.

Programmatically Selecting a Node

The Node object has a Selected property that you can both read and set. If you set a node's Selected property to True, it will become the selected node.

Locating the Parent of a Child Node

To obtain a reference to a child's parent node, use the child node's Parent property. Be aware, however, that a top-level node will have no parent, and attempting to read its Parent property generates a runtime error.

Expanding and Collapsing a Node

You can both expand and contract individual nodes in the collection by setting their Expanded property accordingly. The example in Listing 8.28 will expand every node in the collection. Add the code to the end of the TreeViewDemo subroutine.

LISTING 8.28   Expanding the Nodes

```
For Each MyNode In TreeView1.Nodes
    MyNode.Expanded = True
Next MyNode
```

Similarly, to contract them all, use

```
For Each MyNode in TreeView1.Nodes
    MyNode.Expanded = False
Next MyNode
```

Other TreeView Features

The TreeView control has a number of additional features. For instance, to find out if a node has any children, you can check its Children property. This will return the number of children that the node currently has. You could combine this property with the Expanded property to ensure you expand only Node objects that have children, as shown in Listing 8.29.

LISTING 8.29   Expanding Selected Nodes

```
For Each MyNode in TreeView1.Nodes
    If MyNode.Children > 0 Then
        MyNode.Expanded = True
    End If
Next MyNode
```

8

Another useful property is FullPath. This returns the fully qualified path of a node. The full path will consist of the text in each node from the root down to the target node. Each text component is separated by the character that is set in the TreeView's PathSeparator property (which is a \ character by default).

Lesson Summary

We covered the TreeView control in this lesson. We learned about Node objects and their properties, and we even displayed images in the TreeView control. Next up is a look at the closely related ListView control.

Quiz 6

1. Which is not a relationship you can establish with Nodes?

    a. Before

    b. Parent

    c. Child

    d. Last

2. Which line of code below correctly removes a Node object with an index of 1?

    a. TreeView1.Nodes.Remove "One"

    b. TreeView1.Nodes.Remove 0

    c. TreeView1.Nodes.Remove 1

    d. TreeView1.Nodes.Delete 1

3. What property determines whether or not the text in the `TreeView`'s nodes is editable?

    a. The `TextEdit` property

    b. The `Caption` property

    c. The `LabelEdit` property

    d. The `NodeEdit` property

4. The difference between a `NodeClick` and a `Click` event is

    a. The `Click` event is fired when you click a Plus box to expand a node, whereas the `NodeClick` is not.

    b. The `NodeClick` event is called by either the mouse or keyboard, whereas the `Click` event is called by only the mouse.

    c. There is no difference between the `NodeClick` and `Click` event.

    d. The `NodeClick` is effective only at design time, whereas the `Click` event is at runtime.

Exercise 6

Complexity: Easy

1. Alter the Options form in the HyperPad project and add two buttons at the bottom. Set the caption to the first button to Number of Nodes and the caption of the second button to Node Path. When the user clicks the first button, bring up a message box displaying the number of nodes. When the user clicks the second button, display the full path of the node. All the information returned should be relative to the parent.

Complexity: Moderate

2. Alter the Options form in the HyperPad project and add a Label and two Command Buttons. Clear the text in the label, and set the caption of the two Command Buttons to Display Text Only and Display All Components. Write code such that the current node selected will be displayed in the label, and make the two buttons change the display property of the `TreeView` to display text only and display all the components respectively.

LESSON 7

The ListView Control

Now that you've mastered the TreeView control, you'll be happy to know that the ListView control works in a remarkably similar way. However, there is one major difference. The ListView control contains two collections instead of just one. They are

- ListItems
- ColumnHeaders

The ListItems Collection

ListItems is the main collection in this control. It stores the individual ListItem objects displayed in the List view. You can view the items in one of four different ways:

- Large icons
- Small icons
- List
- Report

Figures 8.48, 8.49, 8.50, and 8.51 show each of the four different views using the List view in the Windows 95 Explorer.

FIGURE 8.48

The large icon view.

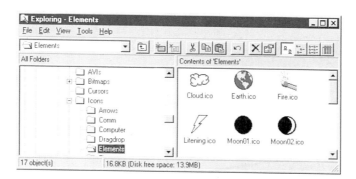

8

FIGURE 8.49

The small icon view.

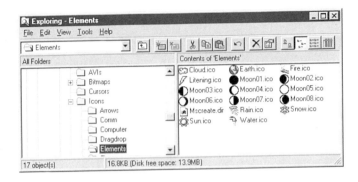

FIGURE 8.50

The list view.

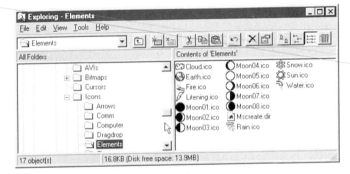

FIGURE 8.51

The report view.

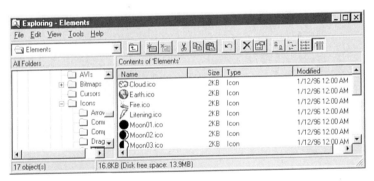

The `ColumnHeaders` Collection

Look at the report view in Figure 8.51. Note that it's fundamentally different from the others. Not only does it display more information about each `ListItem` object, but that information is presented in a series of columns. What's more, each column has a header. This header is provided by the `ColumnHeaders` collection.

The header isn't just for presentation purposes. It is functional, too. If you click any of the headers, the items will be sorted by that column.

Adding `ListItems` Objects to the List View

In this example, you are going to add a `ListView` control to HyperPad's `frmOptions` form and then simply add some `ListItem` objects to it.

Start by resizing `Picture1`, which you used in the previous lesson, so it is out of the way. Then resize the List view picture box, `Picture1`, to fill the tab strip and press Ctrl+J to bring it to the top of the `ZOrder`.

Add a `ListView` control to `Picture1` and size it to fill the picture box. Figure 8.52 shows the icon for the `ListView` control. Figure 8.53 shows you how `frmOptions` should appear with the `ListView` added.

FIGURE 8.52

The `ListView` *control icon.*

FIGURE 8.53

`frmOptions` *with* `ListView` *added.*

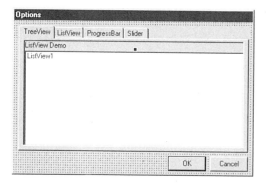

Now add the code in Listing 8.30 to the `ListViewDemo` subroutine.

LISTING 8.30 The `ListView` Demo

```
Private Sub ListViewDemo()
Dim I As Integer
Dim MyItem As ListItem
Dim MyImage As ListImage
Dim ImageKey As String
Dim Key As String
Dim Text As String

ListView1.ListItems.Clear
```

continues

LISTING 8.30 continued

```
ImageList1.ListImages.Clear

For I = 1 To 18
    ImageKey = "note" & CStr(I)
    Set MyImage = ImageList1.ListImages.Add(, ImageKey, ‹
    LoadPicture("graphics\icons\writing\note" & Format(I, "00") & ".ico"))
Next I

Set ListView1.Icons = ImageList1

ListView1.View = lvwIcon ' Set to large icons view

For I = 1 To 18
    ImageKey = "note" & CStr(I)
    Key = "ListItem" & CStr(I)
    Text = "List item " & CStr(I)
    Set MyItem = ListView1.ListItems.Add(, Key, Text, ImageKey)
Next I
End Sub
```

This example loads the 18 note icons (note01.ico to note18.ico) from the icon library into the image list. It then sets the List view's Icons property to reference the ImageList control on the form so that the List view can obtain the icons from the image list by key. Figure 8.54 shows how the List view appears with Listing 8.30 running.

FIGURE 8.54

An example of ListView *running in large icon view.*

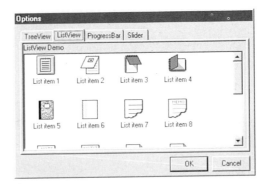

As you can see from the code, the ListItems collection's Add method performs the task of creating the ListItem objects and adding them to the collection. Like the other Add methods you have used, you can obtain a reference to the newly created list item, as the code is doing here, or you can discard the reference by treating the Add method as a subroutine.

Disassociating the Image List from a Control

At this point, we need to demonstrate a technique for reusing an ImageList control. In these examples, we've tried to simplify matters by using and reusing a single image list (ImageList1). However, unless you are very careful, you can run into a problem. To see this problem for yourself, try switching between the ListView and TreeView demonstrations by clicking their respective tabs. This generates a runtime error, as shown in Figure 8.55.

FIGURE 8.55

A runtime error caused by reusing the ImageList.

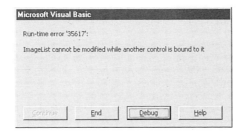

This error is caused when the TreeView demonstration attempts to clear the ListImages collection in the ImageList control after the ListView demonstration has been run. This happens because the ListView was set to reference the ImageList in the line that reads

```
Set ListView1.Icons = ImageList1
```

In other words, the ImageList has been told that the ListView still needs the images it contains and is raising the error when the TreeView demonstration attempts to clear the ListImages collection.

You need a way to disassociate the ListView from the shared ImageList when the demonstration is over.

It is here that the TabStrip's BeforeClick event comes into its own. Stop HyperPad by pressing the error dialog box's End button and then add the code in Listing 8.31 to the TabStrip's BeforeClick event.

LISTING 8.31   Disassociating the Shared ImageList

```
Private Sub tabOptions_BeforeClick(Cancel As Integer)
Select Case tabOptions.SelectedItem.Index
    Case 1 'TreeView cleanup code
        Set TreeView1.ImageList = Nothing
    Case 2 'ListView cleanup code
        Set ListView1.Icons = Nothing
```

continues

LISTING 8.31 continued

```
      Case 3 'ProgressBar cleanup code
      Case 4 'Slider cleanup code
   End Select
   End Sub
```

As you can see, this code uses the BeforeClick event to remove the association between the ImageList and the TreeView or ListView when the tab focus moves from one of these demonstrations. Now that the ImageList is not associated with any control, you are free to reuse it however you want, and no error is generated.

Note that we've allowed a place for some additional cleanup code for both the ProgressBar and the Slider demonstrations in the next lesson.

Small Icon View

If you look at Figures 8.48 and 8.49, you can be forgiven for thinking that the ListView somehow automatically converts large icons to small ones. Unfortunately, it does not. The feature as demonstrated by the Windows 95 Explorer is part of the Explorer and is not part of the ListView control itself.

This means that you have to create the images that you want to use for small icons.

The ListView distinguishes between large and small icons by means of its SmallIcon property. This performs the same function as the Icon property, except that the ImageList referenced by SmallIcon is used when displaying the ListView in small icon, list, or report view. The Icon property is used only for displaying large icons.

There is nothing to prevent you from using the same ImageList control for both Icon and SmallIcon, provided you use different images within that control for the large and small icons. Any type of image can be used. You aren't restricted to purely icon files.

Listing 8.32 modifies the previous example to add an additional image to ImageList1. This contains a small bitmap to display instead of the note icons when the ListView is switched to small icon view.

LISTING 8.32 Small Icon View

```
   Private Sub ListViewDemo()
   Dim I As Integer
   Dim MyItem As ListItem
```

```
Dim MyImage As ListImage
Dim ImageKey As String
Dim Key As String
Dim Text As String

ListView1.ListItems.Clear
ImageList1.ListImages.Clear

For I = 1 To 18
    ImageKey = "note" & CStr(I)
    Set MyImage = ImageList1.ListImages.Add(, ImageKey, _
      LoadPicture("graphics\icons\writing\note" & _
      Format(I, "00") & ".ico"))
Next I
Set MyImage = ImageList1.ListImages.Add(, "small", _
    LoadPicture("graphics\bitmaps\bitmaps\assorted\w.bmp"))

Set ListView1.Icons = ImageList1 'large icon ImageList
Set ListView1.SmallIcons = ImageList1 'small icon ImageList

ListView1.View = lvwSmallIcon ' Set to small icons view

For I = 1 To 18
    ImageKey = "note" & CStr(I)
    Key = "ListItem" & CStr(I)
    Text = "List item " & CStr(I)
    Set MyItem = ListView1.ListItems.Add(, Key, _
      Text, ImageKey, "small")
Next IEnd Sub
```

The small icon's key is provided in the fifth parameter to the `ListItems` collection's `Add` method. The program did not provide anything for this parameter last time.

You must also make a change to the `BeforeClick` event. Add the line in bold.

```
Case 2 'ListView cleanup code
        Set ListView1.Icons = Nothing
        Set ListView1.SmallIcons = Nothing
```

Now the `ListView` has enough information to work out which image should be displayed in both large and small icon views. To change between views, set the `ListView`'s `View` property to the appropriate constant.

Figure 8.56 shows the List view displaying small icons.

FIGURE 8.56

The small icon view.

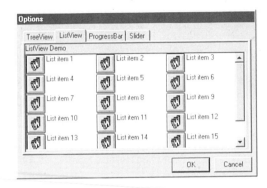

List View

No additional coding is required to display the ListView control in List view (apart from setting the View property to lvwList). Figure 8.57 shows the previous example running in List view. As you can see, the only difference between small icon view and list view is that the icons are arranged horizontally in small icon view and vertically in List view. The List view still displays the small icons.

FIGURE 8.57

The list view.

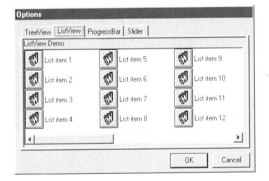

Report View

Before you can display the List view in Report mode, you have to add some ColumnHeader objects to the ColumnHeaders collection. The objects in this collection can be defined at design time, however.

To begin with, display the Column Headers tab in the ListView's Custom Properties dialog box by selecting the (Custom) entry from the Properties window. This appears as shown in Figure 8.58.

FIGURE 8.58

The Column Headers tab.

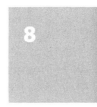

Insert three columns as shown in Table 8.12.

TABLE 8.12 Column Header Definitions

Index	Text	Alignment	Width	Key
1	Name	0 – Left	1440	Name
2	Size	1 – Right	722	Size
3	Type	2 – Center	1440	Type

Now modify the previous example so that the code reads as shown in Listing 8.33. The lines that are added or amended are shown in bold.

LISTING 8.33 Report View Demo

```
Private Sub ListViewDemo()
Dim I As Integer
Dim MyItem As ListItem
Dim MyImage As ListImage
Dim ImageKey As String
Dim Key As String
Dim Text As String

' In case this tab is clicked twice
Set ListView1.Icons = Nothing
Set ListView1.SmallIcons = Nothing
'
' Clear the ListView and the ImageList
ListView1.ListItems.Clear
ImageList1.ListImages.Clear
```

continues

LISTING 8.33   continued

```
For I = 1 To 18
    ImageKey = "note" & CStr(I)
    Set MyImage = ImageList1.ListImages.Add(, ImageKey, _
      LoadPicture("graphics\icons\writing\note" & _
      Format(I, "00") & ".ico"))
Next I
ImageKey = "small"
Set MyImage = ImageList1.ListImages.Add(, ImageKey, _
  LoadPicture("graphics\bitmaps\assorted\w.bmp"))

Set ListView1.Icons = ImageList1
Set ListView1.SmallIcons = ImageList1

ListView1.View = lvwReport ' Set to report view

For I = 1 To 18
    ImageKey = "note" & CStr(I)
    Key = "ListItem" & CStr(I)
    Text = "List item " & CStr(I)
    Set MyItem = ListView1.ListItems.Add(, Key, Text, _
      ImageKey, "small")
    MyItem.SubItems = CStr(CInt(Rnd * 10000))
    MyItem.SubItems = Key
Next I
End Sub
```

As you can see from the example, each ListItem object contains an array of SubItem strings. The first element in this string array (element 0) refers to the text contained in the ListItem object. This is why we named the first ColumnHeader object Text. Element 0 is already populated with the text of the object, so there is no need for you to set it. Elements 1 and 2, however, relate to the second and third ColumnHeader objects that you defined at design time. All we're doing is setting the size to a random number and the type to the key name for the ListItem object. Figure 8.59 shows how the ListView control appears in Report view.

Sorting the Report View

To sort the report view, you must respond to the user clicking a header of the report. The ListView generates a ColumnClick event when this occurs. Listing 8.34 shows you how to program the ListView to sort the three columns correctly.

FIGURE 8.59

The ListView *control in Report view.*

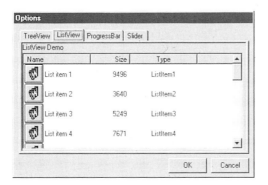

LISTING 8.34   Sorting the Report

```
Private Sub ListView1_ColumnClick(ByVal MyColumnHeader As ColumnHeader)
ListView1.SortKey = MyColumnHeader.Index - 1
ListView1.Sorted = True
End Sub
```

The minimum amount of information you need to supply is the SortKey by which the list will be sorted. This is always the ColumnHeader Index less one because the Index values run from 1 to 3 (in our example), whereas the SortKey is always indexed from 0.

You can additionally specify whether the list should be sorted in ascending or descending order by setting the SortOrder property. For example, to specify that the list should be sorted in descending order, you would set SortOrder to the constant lvwDescending (lvwAscending is the other constant). Again, these constants are provided by the ListView control itself.

Lesson Summary

In this lesson we implemented the ListView control and added ListItem objects to the ListView control. We showed the four different views that the ListView control could perform, such as the Large icon view, the Small icon view, the List view, and the Report view. The next lesson covers the ProgressBar control and the Slider control.

Quiz 7

1. Which way can you not view items with the `ListView` control?

    a. Large Icons

    b. List

    c. Report

    d. Images

2. How does `ListView` distinguish from large and small icons?

    a. It does not have to since it converts them automatically.

    b. `ListView` cannot distinguish them. It must be done manually.

    c. It does so by means of the `SmallIcon` property.

    d. It does so by means of the `LargeIcon` property.

3. Which event is used to disassociate the image list from a control?

    a. `BackClick`

    b. `BeforeClick`

    c. `PrevClick`

    d. `UndoClick`

4. To specify whether a list should be sorted in ascending or descending order, you must

    a. set the `SortOrder` property

    b. set the `Order` property

    c. set the `lvwDescending` property

    d. set the `lvwAscending` property

Exercise 7

Complexity: Easy

1. Alter the Options form in the HyperPad project and add two buttons at the bottom. Set the caption to the first button to Icon View and the caption of the second button to Report View. When the user clicks the first button, set the List view to the large icon view style. When the user clicks the second button, change the List view to the Report view style.

Complexity: Moderate

2. Alter the Options form in the HyperPad project and add three Command Buttons. They should be labeled Background Color, List View, Small Icon View, respectively. Have the first Command Button allow the user to change the background color of the ListView display. The second and third button should change List view to the list style and to the small icon style.

LESSON 8

The ProgressBar and Slider Controls

Finally, it's time to consider how to program the ProgressBar and Slider controls.

The ProgressBar Control

The ProgressBar control provides a graphical display that gives your users a rough estimation of the progress of a lengthy operation within your software. You might be saving a file to disk, for example, or printing a document. The icon for this control is shown in Figure 8.60.

FIGURE 8.60

The ProgressBar
control icon.

To show how the ProgressBar control works, enlarge Picture1 and bring it to the top of the runtime ZOrder. Add a ProgressBar control to the picture box. Size the control so that it appears as in Figure 8.61.

FIGURE 8.61

The ProgressBar
control added to
frmOptions.

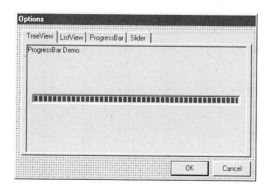

Whatever the operation that you're programming is, the first thing you need to do is decide the minimum and maximum numbers that the progress bar will represent. For example, if you want the progress bar to represent the percentage of how complete the operation is, the minimum is 0 and the maximum is 100. Alternatively, assume that you are printing a document with 10,000 characters in it. You might then select a scale from 0 to 10,000, updating the progress bar after each character is printed. (Not a very practical example, but you get the idea.) Indeed, you can establish any minimum and maximum values for the progress bar to use by setting its Min and Max properties accordingly. You can even use negative numbers. The only restriction is that the Max property must be greater than the Min property, which is pretty self-explanatory. Min and Max are set to 0 and 100, respectively, by default.

Listing 8.35 shows you the how to use the ProgressBar.

LISTING 8.35   ProgressBar Demo

```
Private Sub ProgressBarDemo()
Dim Min As Single
Dim Max As Single
Dim I As Integer
Dim SaveTime As String
Min = 0
Max = 10
ProgressBar1.Min = Min
ProgressBar1.Max = Max
SaveTime = Time
For I = Min To Max
    Do While Time = SaveTime
    Loop
    SaveTime = Time
    ProgressBar1.Value = I
Next I
End Sub
```

This demonstration code simply increments the ProgressBar's Value property by 1 each second. (Remember the Time function returns the current time in a String variable.) That's all there is to it!

The Slider Control

The Slider control is a useful control that gives you the sort of functionality you would expect from a volume control or something similar. You can use it to control changes in any value. It also establishes minimum and maximum values for the value being set.

To learn how to use it, enlarge Picture1 and bring it to the top of the design-time ZOrder. Add a Slider control to the picture box. The Slider control icon is shown in Figure 8.62.

FIGURE 8.62

The Slider *control icon.*

Add a TextBox called txtSliderValue and clear its Text property. Arrange the two controls so that they appear as shown in Figure 8.63.

FIGURE 8.63

The Slider *control on* frmOptions.

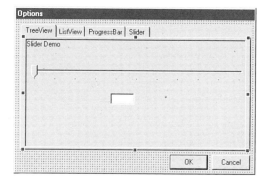

Note the setting of the Slider control's Min and Max properties. Set them to 0 and 10, the same values you used for the corresponding properties in the ProgressBar.

The SmallChange and LargeChange properties control how far the slider will move in the event of a small or large movement. A small movement is achieved by dragging the slider handle to the next tick (the small dots underneath the slider itself). A large movement is achieved by clicking the slider bar rather than dragging the slider handle. Leave these values set to 1 and 5, respectively, which are suitable for your purposes.

The slider provides two events that you can use to monitor its value. These are

- Scroll
- Change

The Scroll Event

The Scroll event is triggered whenever the Value property of the Slider control changes, whether you are in the process of dragging the slider handle or using the cursor keys to control the slider.

The Change Event

The difference between the Change event and the Scroll event is that Change is generated when the change to Value is completed. Therefore, if you drag the slider's handle with the mouse, the Change event will not occur until you release the mouse.

Populate the txtSliderValue TextBox, as shown in Listing 8.36. This should give you a clear idea of how the control works.

LISTING 8.36   Slider Demo

```
Private Sub SliderDemo()
txtSliderValue.Text = Slider1.Value
End Sub

Private Sub Slider1_Change()
txtSliderValue.Text = Slider1.Value
End Sub

Private Sub Slider1_Click()
txtSliderValue.Text = Slider1.Value
End Sub
```

Lesson Summary

In this lesson we showed you how to use both the ProgressBar control and the Slider control, and we demonstrated the difference in each.

Quiz 8

1. When setting the values for the Min and Max properties of a ProgressBar control, the values must be

    a. Both values must be positive

    b. Min may be negative, but Max must be positive

    c. Min must start at zero, Max must be positive

    d. Both can be either positive or negative

2. Which Slider control property determines the maximum change affected by dragging the slider's handle?

    a. SmallChange

    b. LargeChange

8

    c. `MinChange`

    d. `MaxChange`

3. If you were told to design a volume control for a music application, which control would be best to use?

    a. The `ProgressBar` control

    b. The `Slider` control

    c. Either one would be appropriate

    d. Neither one would be appropriate

4. If you were told to design a percentage indicator for formatting a disk, which control would be best to use?

    a. The `ProgressBar` control

    b. The `Slider` control

    c. Either one would be appropriate

    d. Neither one would be appropriate

Exercise 8

Complexity: Easy

1. Create a form and add a `Slider` control, a Command Button, and a Text Box control. Write a program that displays the current value of the `Slider` control when it is clicked. When the user clicks the Command Button, increase the max value of the `Slider` control by five.

Complexity: Moderate

2. Alter the HyperPad project by include three additional toolbar buttons: Date/Time, Font, and Color. The three buttons will insert the date/time in the edit box, bring up the Font Dialog, and bring up the Color Dialog respectively. Add ToolTip text as well.

Chapter Summary

This chapter presented various approaches and techniques that can be used to put ActiveX controls to work. The first lesson introduced the `CommonDialog` control and how to implement it with an MDI form. The `CommonDialog` control to acts as a go- between for Windows operating system dialog boxes of Open/SaveAs, Print, Color, and Font. The second lesson replaced the `TextBox` control with the modern `RichTextBox` control, and shows how a `RichTextBox` control uses the standard rich text format, which can handle various fonts, sizes, and colors.

HyperPad was changed so that these rich text properties can be selected using the `CommonDialog` control. Lesson 3 introduced the toolbar, and this was implemented into the HyperPad project. Buttons were created on the toolbar that created a new file, opened a file, and saved a file, each with their own symbolic bitmap. The `StatusBar` control was placed on the bottom of HyperPad in Lesson 4. Now the line number, time, and date are displayed at the bottom of HyperPad as well as the status of the Caps, Num Lock, Insert, and Scroll Lock keys. The `TabStrip` control was introduced in Lesson 5, and such topics as Zorder and working with Multiple Picture boxes were covered. The `TreeView` control was added to the `TabStrip` control in Lesson 6, as well as the different display styles that could be implemented.

The `ListView` control was added to HyperPad in Lesson 7. All the different display styles of the `ListView` were covered, such as the Large icon style, Small icon style, List style, and Report style, and sorting the Report view. Finally, Lesson 8 covered the `ProgressBar` control and `Slider` control and how to add these as well to the `TabStrip` control in the HyperPad project. This chapter covered the Active X controls extensively, and one should feel quite comfortable in adding these controls to their programs to give any application a professional look and feel.

CHAPTER 9

Printing

The *paperless office* has been a dream of computer manufacturers for years, but it's not likely to become reality any time soon. Businesses need hard copies of certain documents as permanent, legal records. There are people who still write letters, books are still being published, and a lot people don't like reading documents off a monitor screen. Chances are that your programs will also need printed output.

Under DOS, adding print capabilities to a program has traditionally been one of the most tedious and difficult programming tasks. This was due to the fact that developers needed to be concerned with what type of printer support to add, what printer drivers were needed, and a lot of unknown factors. With the adoption of Windows as an operating system interface, printer support became easier to add to a program, because a developer only had to be concerned with one set of printer rules—those of the operating system. Adding printer support is an intrinsic part of Visual Basic and is simple to learn. Its simplicity belies the complexities of the work that Visual Basic is doing behind the scenes to manage your print job.

LESSON 1

Introducing Printing

The key to printing from Visual Basic is learning how to use the Printer class, the Printer object, the Printers collection, and the printer itself. Sound confusing? Don't worry, each one is quite distinct from the other in spite of the similarity of their names.

The Printers Collection

When your VB project starts, it automatically creates the Printers collection. The Printers collection consists of a collection of Printer objects, one Printer object for each printer that is connected to your computer.

To see this for yourself, make sure that you have at least two printers available within your Windows environment. If not, add some. Follow your Windows documentation to add printers. Don't worry if you don't have the specified printer actually connected; Windows won't care. Windows is just installing a driver program that will convert standard printer commands into commands that the specified printer can understand. (Be sure to delete the extra printers when you finish these exercises, though, to avoid confusion.)

Figure 9.1 shows a typical Printers window. The first icon in the Printers window lets you add additional printers (well, printer drivers) to the system. The second icon is an HP DeskJet printer, and the third is the computer's fax modem. In case you're wondering how a fax modem can be a printer, the software driver for the modem looks like a printer driver to Windows, and you can select the fax modem "printer" to send any printable document via facsimile. If you have a fax modem, your Visual Basic programs will be able to do the same thing.

FIGURE 9.1

The Windows Printers window.

Now that you know about the Printers collection, take a look at it. Start a new project and enter the code in Listing 9.1.

LISTING 9.1   Viewing the `Printers` Collection

```
Private Sub Form_Load()
    Dim oPrinter As Printer
    For Each oPrinter In Printers
        Debug.Print oPrinter.DeviceName
    Next oPrinter
End Sub
```

As you can see, the program creates an object variable, `oPrinter`, based on the `Printer` class. The `For Each...Next` loop assigns each `Printer` object in the Printers collection to that variable and displays the `DeviceName` property in the Debug window. On the computer shown in Figure 9.1, the Debug window would contain

```
HP DeskJet 520 Printer
WINFAX
```

The `Port` Property

Several printers of the same type might be connected to a computer, especially on networked computers. The `Port` property of the `Printer` object offers the only way to identify a printer uniquely. Although Windows 95 and Windows NT strongly discourage you from writing directly to a port rather than through a driver, you might need to know the port number so you can be sure which printer will be used for a job. Change the code from Listing 9.1 to that of Listing 9.2 (changes are in bold).

LISTING 9.2   Uniquely Identifying a Printer

```
Private Sub Form_Load()
Dim oPrinter As Printer
For Each oPrinter In Printers
    Debug.Print oPrinter.DeviceName; " On "; oPrinter.Port
Next oPrinter
End Sub
```

The output will change. On the example computer, it now looks like this:

```
HP DeskJet 520 Printer On LPT1:
WINFAX On COM2:
```

The Print Job

Before you get too involved in trying to print, it is important to understand the concept of the print job. Whether you are printing text, graphics, or a mixture of both, the printing assignments that you give through Visual Basic are organized into print jobs. Visual Basic buffers the information you send to the printer in memory until your program signals that the print job has ended. Then the Windows Print Manager takes over. It waits until any earlier print jobs complete, then it sends your print job to the printer as a unit.

This idea is critical to the operation of a printer in a multitasking system such as Windows. It is the only way the computer can keep print jobs from different programs separated. If not for print jobs, the printed output of two different operations could get jumbled together. Consider the effect of having a love letter mixed in with a business contract!

The point to understand here is that printing is a two-step process. You begin the process by using the print output methods (coming up soon) for the Printer object that you want to receive your print job. There is no need to specify where the print job begins; Visual Basic handles that automatically. When you use the first print output methods, VB starts the print job for you. After that, all further printer output will be buffered for you until you tell Visual Basic to end it.

The EndDoc Method

When you start a document to print, how do you end it? There are two ways. You can explicitly use the EndDoc method or you can exit from the program. Exiting from a program with a print job pending automatically calls the EndDoc method. It's a clumsy way to end a print job and not a recommended approach, but it will get the job stop.

The NewPage Method and the Page Property

If your print job requires more lines of text on a page than will fit, the Printer object automatically adds a new page and the Printer object's Page property will be incremented by one.

Rather than let the Printer object determine your page breaks, you can print multiple-page documents completely under your control. The NewPage method ends the current page, increments the Page property, and sets up the next page for subsequent output. You will have to count lines or otherwise determine when you are about to reach the end of the page to control this, however. Lesson 6 covers this in detail.

The Default Printer and the Printer Object

One of the printers connected to your computer is designated as the default printer, which means that it will receive all print jobs that are not specifically sent to another printer. Visual Basic's Printer object initially points to the default printer.

The TrackDefault Property

If you start a program running and then change the default printer, the VB program will point to the new default printer. On occasion, you might not want that behavior. Perhaps, for example, you are sending a fax with Word and want to print hard copy from your VB program. You sure don't want the VB output to go to the fax, too!

The `TrackDefault` property offers the solution. The `TrackDefault` property is a Boolean quantity. When it is set to `True`, VB's `Printer` object always points to the default printer. Set it to `False` and VB's `Printer` object will not change when the default printer changes. You won't need this often, but when you do, you'll be glad that you have this capability. The syntax is

```
Printer.TrackDefault = False
```

Or, if you have set it to `False` and want to change it back

```
Printer.TrackDefault = True
```

Changing the Printer

What if you want to print to another printer? Preferably, you will let the user choose the printer. If you want to change the printer in code, though, remember that Visual Basic prints to a `Printer` object rather than to a physical device. All you need to do is change the device that the object references. The following code will print to each of your printers in succession.

```
Private Sub Form_Load()
    Dim oPrinter As Printer
    Printer.TrackDefault = False
    For Each oPrinter In Printers
        Set Printer = oPrinter
        Printer.Print "Printing to " & Printer.DeviceName
        Printer.EndDoc
    Next
    Printer.TrackDefault = True
End Sub
```

The `Print` Method

You have been using the `Print` method almost from the first page of this book. How many times have you typed `Debug.Print`? Actually, there are four possible recipients of the `Print` method's efforts. The syntax for the `Print` method is

```
object.Print outputlist
```

The components of the syntax are as follows:

- `object` is any one of the Debug window, a form, a picture box on a form, or the `Printer` object.
- `outputlist` is an optional expression or list of expressions to be printed. If `outputlist` is omitted, the `Print` method prints a blank line.

Try it out, using the code in Listing 9.3.

LISTING 9.3   The `Print` Method and the `Printer` Object

```
Private Sub Form_Load()

    Dim A As Integer
    Dim B As Double
    Dim S As String
    A = 20
    B = 3.14159
    S = "This is a test"
    Printer.Print A
    Printer.Print B
    Printer.Print S
    Printer.Print
    Printer.Print "And the test has ended"
    Printer.EndDoc

End Sub
```

This will print the following on your printer:

```
20
3.14159
This is a test

And the test has ended
```

Note that the `Printer` object interpreted the variables correctly. `Printer.Print A` did not print the letter `A` on your page.

Formatting the Output

You don't always want to print each variable on a separate line, nor do you always want to print right at the left edge of the page. And you don't have to. Visual Basic offers several ways to position your printed output.

For starters, you can use concatenation, which you learned in Chapter 4, "Subroutines, Functions, and the Visual Basic 6 Language." The ampersand works as well on the printer as it did in a text box. After all, you are printing strings either way. You could write

```
Printer.Print A & " " & B & " " & S
```

and the printer will print

```
20 3.14159 And the test has ended Concatenation works with any two-string
expressions.
```

Another technique is to use either a comma or a semicolon between variable names at the end of a line. Add a semicolon to the end of each of the `Printer.Print` lines from Listing 9.3. Run the program and see what happens. Replace the semicolon with a comma and run it again. Here's what the symbols do:

Symbol	Action
;	Does not use a linefeed. The next variable or string literal is printed in the next print position.
,	Moves to the next print zone.

Note
Print zones are spaced 14 fixed-width print positions apart. Chances are that you are printing with proportionai fonts, in which a "w" takes more space than an "i". If you use print zones or spaces to align text, be sure you leave enough space.

Two functions help you position your text: the `Spc` function and the `Tab` function. As you might guess, `Spc` moves n spaces to the right and `Tab` moves to column n. You can also use Tab by itself to move to the next print zone. It is easier to see than it is to describe. (If you want to save paper, use `Debug.Print` instead of `Printer.Print` for the following demonstration.) Enter the code in Listing 9.4 and try it out.

LISTING 9.4   Using `Tab()` and `Spc()`

```
Private Sub Form_Load()
    Dim A As Integer
    Dim B As Long
    Dim S As String
    A = 20
    B = 3.14159
    S = "This is a test"
    Debug.Print A; Tab; B; Tab; S
    Debug.Print A, B, S
    Debug.Print A; Spc(20); B; Spc(10); S
End Sub
```

In the Immediate window, you will see the following results:

```
20              3               This is a test
20              3               This is a test
20                      3               This is a test
```

As you can see from the output, the keyword, Tab, and the comma have the save effect on tab positioning. The keyword, Spc, on the other hand moves the text with a bit more precision. If the length of the text was within the next tab zone, you might have difficulty lining your columns up by relying on the Tab or comma. Using the Spc keyword, you can write a function to determine how many spaces are needed to make your columns line up.

In the early days of printing, all characters took up exactly the same space on a line. It was common to refer to a printer as an 80-column printer, which meant that there were 80 character spaces across the page. Publishers and printers, meanwhile, used proportional fonts, where the actual space a character takes on a page depends on the character.

The letter *W*, for example, takes up more than one fixed-width column, whereas the letter *I* takes less. Proportional fonts are prettier to look at and easier to read, but they make life hard for programmers, especially when they are trying to print columnar data. If the exact print position is important, be sure to test extensively before releasing a program. This issue is covered in more depth later in this chapter.

Lesson Summary

In the past, trying to get anything printed through Visual Basic was a very difficult task. A lot of developers would rather rely on third-party report tools, but there are still some diehard programmers who like to take printer matters into their own hands. Through the use of the Printer methods, you have the power to take control of how your printout will look.

This lesson dealt with simple printing to your printer with very basic formatting. In the next lesson, you'll learn how to use fonts as part of your output to augment any sort of printing you have planned.

Quiz 1

1. In the code
   ```
   Dim MyPrinter As Printer
   MyPrinter is
   ```

   a. A Hewlett-Packard InkJet

   b. The printer connected to LPT1

   c. The default printer

   d. An object based on the Printer class

2. How do you tell Windows to start a print job?

    a. `Printer.StartJob`

    b. `Printer.Print`

    c. `Set PrinterJob as New PrintJob`

    d. Use any of the printer output methods

3. How do you end a print job?

    a. `Printer.EndJob`

    b. `Printer.EndDoc`

    c. `Printer.Quit`

    d. Windows knows when the job ends

4. How does Visual Basic set the default printer?

    a. With the `TrackDefault` property

    b. With the `Printer.Change` method

    c. The default printer is set by Windows

    d. None of the above

Exercise 1

Complexity: Easy

1. Write a program that will print five lines of text on one page and five lines of text on another page.

Complexity: Easy

2. Write a program that displays all the printers you have installed on your computer and to which port they are connected.

LESSON 2

Using Fonts

Typesetters argue that different styles of print are typefaces and that a font is a collection of all of the characters in a typeface of any single size. Typesetters are, of course, correct; they are experts of their own field. Sometime in the early days of computers, however, the term "font" came to mean typeface, and the name has stuck. So, at least while you are working with computers, fonts refer to typefaces.

This lesson teaches you how to work with different fonts in printing. You don't have to settle for your printer's default fonts. In fact, you don't have to settle for your printer's fonts at all!

Fonts, Fonts, and More Fonts

Early computers and printers offered little in the way of fonts. They didn't really have the capability of displaying and printing anything finer than 5_7 dot-matrix letters and numbers, which are quite crude compared to today's standards. The EGA display and nine-pin printers brought some improvements. The SVGA display and lower-cost laser and InkJet printers have brought a revolution.

Windows supports TrueType fonts, which are the revolution. TrueType fonts are *scalable*, which means that the font can be displayed (and printed) in any desired size. (Well, there are limits.) Windows itself comes with a good variety of TrueType fonts, and if you want more they are available from other vendors at low cost, and from the Internet at no cost. Having TrueType fonts means that Windows can use the same typefaces to display a document as it prints. From the viewpoint of printing, it means that you can print in almost any typeface you want.

Most TrueType fonts are proportional fonts, which means that each character takes up a different (proportional) amount of space. Windows supports some fixed-width fonts, which are easier to display and require fewer resources. Compare the differences between the main text in this book and the listings. The listings are printed in a fixed-width typeface, whereas the balance of the book is printed in a proportional font.

The effect of all this is that you get a wide choice of fonts and font sizes to use in your printing projects. Start a new project, the Font Demo project, or load the completed project from the CD that comes with this book. Add a label and three Command buttons to the form as shown in Figure 9.2. Set the properties according to Table 9.1.

FIGURE 9.2

The Font Demo form at design time.

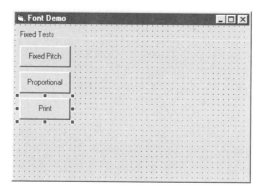

TABLE 9.1 The Font Demo Project's First Controls

Object	Property	Value
Form	Name	frmFontDemo
	Caption	Font Demo
Label	Name	Label1
	Caption	Fixed Tests
CommandButton	Name	cmdFixed
	Caption	Fixed Pitch
CommandButton	Name	cmdProportional
	Caption	Proportional
CommandButton	Name	cmdPrint
	Caption	Print

Listing 9.5 shows the code for the two Command buttons.

LISTING 9.5 The Code for cmdFixed and cmdProportional

```
Private Sub cmdFixed_Click()
    Printer.Print ;
    With Printer
        .Font.Name = "Courier"
        .Font.Size = 12
        .Font.Bold = False
        .Font.Italic = False
        .Font.Underline = False
    End With
    Printer.Print "Fixed"
    Printer.Print "WWWWWWWWWWWWWWWWWWWW"      ' 20 of them
    Printer.Print Tab; "^"
    Printer.Print "iiiiiiiiiiiiiiiiiiii"      ' 20 of them
    Printer.Print Tab; "^"
End Sub

Private Sub cmdProportional_Click()
    Printer.Print ;
    With Printer
        .Font.Name = "Times"
        .Font.Size = 12
        .Font.Bold = False
        .Font.Italic = False
        .Font.Underline = False
    End With
```

continues

LISTING 9.5   continued

```
    Printer.Print "Proportional"
    Printer.Print "WWWWWWWWWWWWWWWWWWWW"     ' 20 of them
    Printer.Print Tab; "^"
    Printer.Print "iiiiiiiiiiiiiiiiiiii"     ' 20 of them
    Printer.Print Tab; "^"

End Sub

Private Sub cmdPrint_Click()
    Printer.EndDoc
End Sub
```

A Look at the Code

The code in Listing 9.5 introduces several new concepts. The first thing to notice is that the first line of each procedure is `Printer.Print` ;. It isn't necessary to start a print job explicitly, but one of the tricky vagaries of the `Printer` object is that when you want to change a font, you have to start by getting the `Printer` object's attention with `Printer.Print`. (The semicolon keeps the printer in the same row on the page.)

The `With...End With` structure shows that `Font` is a property of the `Printer` object. Use `With...End With` to change several of the `Font` property's attributes at once. If you want to change only one, for example, all you need to do is make the font bold, use `Printer.Font.Bold = True`. In the code for this program, you are setting five different properties; the `With...End With` structure is more efficient.

Even though `Font` is a property, it also has properties. Table 9.2 lists the font's properties.

TABLE 9.2   The Attributes of the `Font` Property

Attribute	Type	Definition
Name	String	Selects the font to use. Examples are Times (for Times New Roman) and Arial.
Size	Number	Sets the point size of the font. See note below.
Bold	Boolean	Turns bold print on or off.
Italic	Boolean	Turns italic on or off.
Underline	Boolean	Turns underline on or off.
Strikethrough	Boolean	Turns strikethrough on or off.
Weight	Number	Another way to handle bold. Numbers less than 550 are set to 400, which is normal weight. Numbers greater than 550 are set to 700, which is bold.

The cmdPrint button ends the print job with EndDoc.

Running the Program

When you run the Font Demo program, click cmdFixed, then on cmdProportional, and finally on cmdPrint. The program demonstrates the proportional font problem by printing 20 W's and 20 i's in a fixed-width font and a proportional font. Under each row of letters, the program prints a caret at the beginning of the second print zone.

Notice that the caret is under letter number 15 for both letters in the fixed-width font. Then look at the proportional font, and you will have a good idea of what the problem is. Twenty W's certainly take up a lot more room than 20 I's!

 Note

> When you are setting fonts to sizes lower than eight points, you have to get tricky. First set the font size, then set the font name, and then set the size again. Windows will most likely not use the font you selected, but will substitute a similar font that is easier to read in the smaller size. The font Small Font was created for just this purpose.

More Fonts

Now to improve the project. Add the objects listed in Table 9.3 to the form.

TABLE 9.3 Additional Objects for Font Demo

Object	Property	Value
Label	Name	Label2
	Caption	Available Fonts
Label	Name	Label3
	Caption	Selected Tests
Label	Name	Label4
	Caption	Size
Label	Name	Label5
	Caption	Attributes
CommandButton	Name	cmdArial
	Caption	Arial
CommandButton	Name	cmdTimes
	Caption	Times New Roman
	Style	Graphical

continues

TABLE 9.3 continued

Object	Property	Value
CommandButton	Name	cmdWingDings
	Caption	WingDings
CommandButton	Name	cmdSelected
	Caption	Click to Accept Selected Font
CommandButton	Name	cmdPrint
	Caption	Print
ListBox	Name	lstFontName
	Sorted	True
ListBox	Name	lstFontSize
CheckBox	Name	chkBold
	Caption	Bold
	Font	MS SansSerif Bold
CheckBox	Name	chkItalic
	Caption	Italic
	Font	MS SansSerif Italic
CheckBox	Name	chkUnderline
	Caption	Underline
	Font	MS SansSerif Underlined

Arrange the objects as shown in Figure 9.3.

FIGURE 9.3

The finished version of Font Demo.

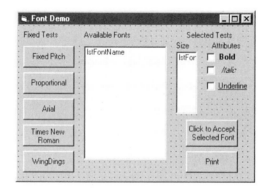

Note — The Command Button `cmdTimes` style is set to graphical. This is so that the wrapped text will be centered within the button.

Now add the code from Listing 9.6 to the project.

LISTING 9.6 Completing the Font Demo Program

```
Option Explicit
Public sFontName As String
Public sngFontPoints As Single
Public bFontBold As Boolean
Public bFontItalic As Boolean
Public bFontUnderLine As Boolean

Private Sub Form_Load()
    Dim x As Integer
    Dim y As Integer
    ' Fill FontName listbox with fonts installed
    ' on system
    For x = 0 To Printer.FontCount - 1
        lstFontName.AddItem Printer.Fonts
    Next
    lstFontName.ListIndex = 0
    sFontName = lstFontName.List(lstFontName.ListIndex)
    ' Fill FontSize listbox with point sizes
    For y = 8 To 16 Step 2
        lstFontSize.AddItem y
    Next
    lstFontSize.ListIndex = 0
    sngFontPoints = lstFontSize.List(lstFontSize.ListIndex)
End Sub

Private Sub chkBold_Click()
    bFontBold = chkBold.Value
End Sub

Private Sub chkItalic_Click()
    bFontItalic = chkItalic.Value
End Sub

Private Sub chkUnderline_Click()
    bFontUnderLine = chkUnderline.Value
End Sub

Private Sub cmdArial_Click()
    Printer.Print ;
```

continues

LISTING 9.6 continued

```
    With Printer
        .Font.Name = "Arial"
        .Font.Size = 12
        .Font.Bold = False
        .Font.Italic = False
        .Font.Underline = False
    End With
    Printer.Print "Testing the Arial font"
End Sub

Private Sub cmdPrint_Click()
    Printer.EndDoc
End Sub

Private Sub cmdTimes_Click()
    Printer.Print ;
    With Printer
        .Font.Name = "Times"
        .Font.Size = 12
        .Font.Bold = False
        .Font.Italic = False
        .Font.Underline = False
    End With
    Printer.Print "Testing Times New Roman"
End Sub

Private Sub cmdSelected_Click()
    Printer.Print ;
    With Printer
        .Font.Size = sngFontPoints
        .Font.Name = sFontName
        .Font.Bold = bFontBold
        .Font.Italic = bFontItalic
        .Font.Underline = bFontUnderLine
    End With
    Printer.Print "Printing with " & sFontName; _
        " at "; sngFontPoints; " Point Size"
    Printer.Print "Attributes: Bold = "; bFontBold; _
        " Italic = "; bFontItalic; " Underline = "; bFontUnderLine
End Sub

Private Sub cmdWingDings_Click()
    Printer.Print ;
    With Printer
        .Font.Name = "WingDings"
        .Font.Size = 12
        .Font.Bold = False
```

```
        .Font.Italic = False
        .Font.Underline = False
    End With
    Printer.Print "Testing WingDings:
End Sub

Private Sub lstFontName_Click()
    sFontName = lstFontName.List(lstFontName.ListIndex)
End Sub

Private Sub lstFontSize_Click()
    sngFontPoints = lstFontSize.List(lstFontSize.ListIndex)
End Sub
```

A Look at the New Code

The Declarations section declares five formwide variables for font attributes.

The first For...Next loop in the Form_Load procedure reads the available fonts from the Printer object and fills lstFontNames with them. The second loop fills lstFontSize with the numbers 8, 10, 12, 14, and 16. Both list boxes have their ListIndex property set to 0 and a default value is assigned to sFontName and sngFontSize. The default value prevents an error if you attempt to print without having designated a font or a font size.

Visual Basic really makes your work easy here. You don't need to be concerned with what fonts are installed on a given system. VB reads and lists them for you.

The code in the Click events of all except the cmdSelected Command button prints a brief message to the print job identifying the font that is selected by the button. The Click event for cmdSelected is more complicated because it has more work to do. It builds a message that includes the font name, size, and attributes and prints it to the print job.

The Click events for the list boxes set the appropriate variable for font name and font size. The Click events for the check boxes set the variables for font attributes in the same way.

Running the Program

When you run the program this time, click each of the buttons once on the Fixed Tests side of the form. Then select a font and one or more attributes and click Selected. Select fonts and attributes several times, clicking Selected after each set of choices. Finally, close the print job by clicking Print.

The running program is shown in Figure 9.4.

FIGURE 9.4

The running Font Demo program.

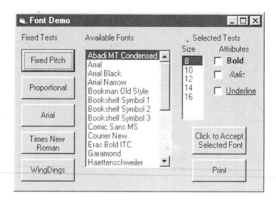

This time you get a more varied printout. Some of it might be surprising. Not all the fonts give you letters! The Symbols and WingDings fonts let you do some pretty interesting things, especially when you change font sizes to go with them.

Lesson Summary

Every system has their own set of fonts at their disposal, so when you develop reports, you will need to keep that in mind. There are about eight base fonts that all Windows systems have. You should try not to deviate from them, otherwise, your output might not come out the way you planned.

In this lesson, you learned how to apply formatting styles to your output. In your next lesson, you'll be covering how to use the Common Dialog box's Printer options. This will help you add functionality like multiple copies of a report, printer settings, and so on.

Quiz 2

1. Because TrueType fonts are _____, they can be printed and displayed in any reasonable size.

    a. scalable

    b. resizable

    c. proportional

    d. portable

2. Proportional fonts give a different amount of _____ to different characters.

   a. ink

   b. space

   c. points

   d. tabs

3. Which command makes the printer's font 16 points?

   a. `Printer.Font.16`

   b. `Set Font.Size = 16`

   c. `Printer.Font.Size = 16`

   d. `Let FontSize = 16`

4. Which of the following is not a valid attribute for a font?

   a. `Size`

   b. `Bold`

   c. `UnderLine`

   d. `Color`

Exercise 2

Complexity: Easy

1. Write a program that will print a typeface sample sheet for the font Arial. The first line should be in regular, then italic, then bold, and then bold italic. Use any sentence you want.

Complexity: Moderate

2. Write a program that will list all the fonts installed on your system and print a sample of a selected font.

LESSON 3

The Printer and the `CommonDialog` Control

The best way to handle printers, as with many other features of the computer, is to let your user have control. It might be that on Monday, Jane User wants to send her print output to a laser printer, on Wednesday she wants to send it to an InkJet printer, and on

Friday she prefers her fax. In Chapter 8, "Using ActiveX Controls," you learned about
the Windows `CommonDialog` control and used it for file management. Now it is time to
use the printer control features of the `CommonDialog` control.

The Printer Common Dialog Boxes

The `CommonDialog` adds two dialog boxes to your arsenal. They are the Print Setup dialog box and the Print dialog box. Use the `CommonDialog` control to add the user interface
to let your users change printer settings in HyperPad. Load HyperPad as you left it in
Chapter 8, "Using ActiveX Controls." New code added in this lesson demonstrates the
two printer Common Dialog boxes and improves the printer functions in HyperPad.

In case you skipped Chapter 8's lesson, adding the `CommonDialog` box control to your
program, select the Components item from the Project menu item. Mark the component
item, Microsoft Common Dialog Control 6.0, from the Controls list box. To find the
HyperPad project, you can load it from the CD found in Chapter 8's directory under
HyperPad.

The Print Setup Dialog Box

The Print Setup dialog box is shown in Figure 9.5. From the Print Setup dialog box, the
user can select the default printers, set the printer orientation, and select the paper size
and the source of the paper (if there is more than one paper tray for the printer). By
clicking the Properties button, the user can also set the printer's properties.

FIGURE 9.5

*The Print Setup dialog
box.*

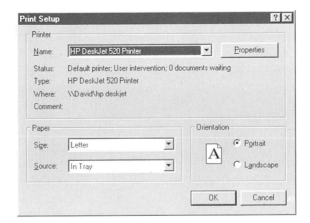

Different printers have different capabilities. The Print Setup dialog box will,
for the most part, reflect those capabilities.

The key to the appearance and function of the common dialog box is in the Flags property. In the code of Listing 9.7, the Flags property is set to show the Printer Setup dialog box. Setting the PrinterDefault property to True enables you to print to the selected printer with the Print method, and the printer that you select in the Printer Setup dialog box becomes the default printer.

LISTING 9.7   Displaying the Print Setup Dialog Box

```
Private Sub mnuFilePrintSetup_Click()
    ' Set Flags to show the print setup dialog
    CommonDialog1.Flags = cdlPDPrintSetup
    ' Set Selected printer = default printer
    CommonDialog1.PrinterDefault = True
    ' Show the dialog
    CommonDialog1.ShowPrinter
End Sub
```

The last line in the listing calls the Print dialog box's only method: ShowPrinter.

The Printer Setup dialog box does not return the name of the selected printer, nor does it inform you in any way that the user has changed the printer. You can detect this quite easily with code, however, by storing Printer.DeviceName in a variable before calling the dialog box and comparing it with Printer.DeviceName after the dialog box is exited.

The Print Dialog Box

Now that Jane User can select which printer to use, it is time to allow her to specify how the printed output should be handled. Opening the Print dialog box is a matter of calling the ShowPrinter method without setting the Flag property to cdlPDPrintSetup. That does not mean that you won't set any flags, though. The Print dialog box is extremely flexible. You can allow (or disallow) a large array of features. Table 9.4 lists the flags and their meaning.

TABLE 9.4   The Printer Dialog Box Flags

Flag	Description
cdlPDAllPages	Returns or sets the state of the All Pages option button.
cdlPDPageNums	Returns or sets the state of the Pages option button.
cdlPDNoPageNums	Disables the Pages option button and the associated edit control.
cdlPDSelection	Returns or sets the state of the Selection option button. If neither cdlPDPageNums nor cdlPDSelection is specified, the All option button is in the selected state.

continues

TABLE 9.4   continued

Flag	Description
cdlPDNoSelection	Disables the Selection option button.
cdlPDPrintToFile	Sets or returns the state of the Print to File check box.
cdlPDDisablePrintToFile	Disables the Print to File check box.
cdlPDHidePrintToFile	Hides the Print to File check box.
cdlPDCollate	Returns or sets the state of the Collate check box.
cdlPDReturnDefault	Returns the default printer's name.
cdlPDUseDevModeCopies	If the printer does not support multiple copies, setting this flag disables the Number of Copies spinner control in the Print dialog box. If the printer does support multiple copies, the requested number of copies is stored in the Copies property.
cdlPDHelpButton	Causes the Print Dialog box to show the Help button.
cdlPDPrintSetup	Causes the system to display the Print Setup dialog box instead of the Print dialog box.
cdlPDNoWarning	Disables the No Default Printer warning message.
cdlPDReturnIC	Returns an information context for the printer selection made in the dialog box. The information is returned in the dialog box's hDC property.
cdlPDReturnDC	Returns a device context for the printer selection made in the dialog box. The information is returned in the dialog box's hDC property. To use more than one flag, which is the usual case, OR together all the flags that you want to use.

The Print dialog box for HyperPad is called by selecting Print from the File menu. The code for mnuFilePrint is shown in Listing 9.8.

LISTING 9.8   Bringing Up the Print Dialog Box

```
Private Sub mnuFilePrint_Click()
    Dim bCancel As Boolean
    Dim nCopy As Integer
    On Error GoTo ErrorHandler
    bCancel = False
    CommonDialog1.Flags = cdlPDHidePrintToFile Or _
                          cdlPDNoSelection Or _
                          cdlPDNoPageNums Or _
                          cdlPDCollate
```

```
    CommonDialog1.CancelError = True
    CommonDialog1.PrinterDefault = True
    CommonDialog1.Copies = 1
    CommonDialog1.ShowPrinter
    If oCancel = False Then
        'Add actual print routines here
        For nCopy = 1 To CommonDialog1.Copies
            'PrintDocument
        Next nCopy
    End If
    Exit Sub

ErrorHandler:
    If Err.Number = cdlCancel Then
        oCancel = True
        Resume Next
    End If
End Sub
```

The code in Listing 9.8 creates the Print dialog box shown in Figure 9.6.

FIGURE 9.6

HyperPad's Print dialog box.

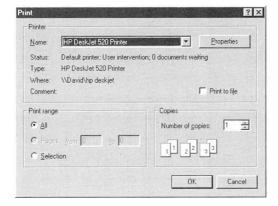

A Look at the Code

You can see the effects of the code in Figure 9.6. The code that sets the `Flag` property,

```
CommonDialog1.Flags = cdlPDHidePrintToFile Or _
                      cdlPDNoSelection Or _
                      cdlPDNoPageNums Or _
                      cdlPDCollate
```

- Hides the Print to File check box
- Disables the Selection option button

- Disables the Pages option button and the edit boxes for it (Note that this automatically selects the All option button.)
- Enables the Collate check box

Multiple Copies

Rather than rely on the iffy proposition that Jane User's printer driver supports multiple copies, the flag `cdlPDUseDevModeCopies` is not used. Instead, the common dialog's `Copies` property is used in a `For...Next` loop to print the file `Copies` times.

Although most laser and inkjet printers support multiple copies, there is still a crop of dot-matrix printers that do not. Because there is no way to be sure what kind of printer Jane User has, the `For...Next` loop offers multiple copies at the expense of speed. That is because each copy is a separate print job. If you use the `cdlPDUseDevModeCopies` flag and do not select Collate, printers that support multiple copies can make multiple copies as a part of the same print job, which is much faster. Printers that do not support multiple copies require that you open the Print dialog box for each copy you want.

Collating Copies

If the Collate check box is selected, each copy of a multiple-page document will be printed as a unit. For example, if you have a three-page document and print two copies with Collate checked, you will get pages 1, 2, 3 and pages 1, 2, 3. With Collate turned off, you would get pages 1,1 ,2,2 ,3,3. Collating copies is a great convenience, but it does slow the printing process, because each copy becomes a separate print job. The overall job, especially for large documents, might still be faster because if the printer doesn't collate the pages, someone will have to do it by hand.

Print to File

With the Print to File option, you can send the printer output to a file on disk instead of to a printer. You can print the file at a later time. Note that if you later print the file to a different type of printer than the one selected during the Print to File operation, the page breaks and font spacing might be incorrect. The Print to File option is not enabled for HyperPad.

Selection and Pages Options

The Selection option and the Pages option are disabled in HyperPad. Enabling Selection allows you to print only selected text. Enabling Pages allows you to print a specified page or range of pages instead of the entire document. Many users consider these to be important options, and you might want to include them.

Printing

The Print dialog box does not print your document. As you can see from the code in Listing 9.8, you are responsible for using the properties to format and control your print job. What the `CommonDialog` control does for you with the Print dialog box is provide you with a standard, professional user interface for collecting the print job's parameters. The common interface, the same one that most commercial programs use, gives your users a familiar and comfortable way to work with the printer.

Lesson Summary

In this lesson, you learned about the two printing dialog boxes that are part of the `CommonDialog` control, Printer and Print Setup. Both of these dialog boxes should look familiar to you, because they are common through all Windows applications. By using these in your application, you provide a common look and feel that is consistent with other Windows applications. The most important thing to remember is that every printer is different and they all have various capabilities; therefore, not all features are available.

Speaking of different printer functions, the next lesson is going to focus on different Printer object properties that might be available to you, provided your printer supports those features.

Quiz 3

1. Where do you change the printer's orientation from Portrait to Landscape?

   a. The Print dialog box

   b. The Print Setup dialog box

   c. The Properties dialog box of Print Setup

   d. It can be changed only by pushing a button on the printer

2. Where do you change the paper size?

   a. The Print dialog box

   b. The Print Setup dialog box

   c. The Properties dialog box of Print Setup

   d. It can be changed only in code

3. Where do you change the number of copies to be printed?

   a. The Print dialog box

   b. The Print Setup dialog box

    c. The Properties dialog box of Print Setup

    d. The printer can print only one copy

4. The `cdlPDUseDevModeCopies` flag

    a. Disables multiple copies for all printers

    b. Enables multiple copies for all printers

    c. Disables multiple copies for printers that do not have built-in copies support

    d. Creates multiple copies for printers that do not have built-in copies support

Exercise 3

Complexity: Easy

1. Add Printer support to a program's menu item. One menu item should be Print Setup and the other should be Print.

Complexity: Moderate

2. Adding to Exercise 3.1, set the properties to the Print dialog box to hide/disable the Print to File and Print Range Selection.

LESSON 4

Printer Capabilities

You're getting close to being able to write some practical print routines now. However, it's important that you understand something about the printer that your software is going to use and the dimensions of the paper that it is going to print on. You might wonder why this is necessary. After all, if the `Print` method simply sends text to the printer, isn't that enough to get on with, well, printing text? Although the `Print` method is all you need to know to print text, you can make your software far more intelligent and, therefore, produce more professional-looking reports and other printed output by determining the capabilities of the printer itself and taking the time to ensure that, for instance, the user isn't trying to print a report on envelopes.

Printer Driver

There are literally thousands of different makes and models of printers out there. You have no way of knowing in advance which printers the users of your software are going to have installed.

Windows uses a subprogram called a printer driver so that application software doesn't have to concern itself with the intricacies of each printer's software interface. For example, many printers expect to receive instructions coded in the Postscript printer language of what to print. Other printers use their own proprietary languages. Many dot-matrix printers use escape sequences instead of a defined language. The bottom line is that the actual sequence of instructions sent to each printer is different for each printer.

The printer driver translates your software's requests for print output into the low-level commands or character sequences needed to produce the desired effects.

The effect of the printer driver goes much further than this, however. You can also find out quite a lot of information about the capabilities of the printer by using a combination of `Printer` class programming and error handling, using the following `Printer` class properties:

- `ColorMode`
- `Duplex`
- `Orientation`
- `PaperBin`
- `PaperSize`
- `PrintQuality`

Each of these properties can be set to a range of different values, as described in the Visual Basic online Help. However, not all printers support the full range of settings. If you try to set, for example, the `Duplex` property to `vbPRDPVertical`, which indicates double-sided printing with a vertical page turn, on a printer that supports only one-sided printing, an error will occur. The error is code 380 (`Invalid property value`). The fact that an error occurs when you select an invalid property setting might seem inconvenient, but you can use this feature and trap the errors so that you can identify the capabilities of a particular printer.

Error handling is covered in detail in Chapter 10, "Problem Solving: Handling Errors and Debugging Your Program." Listing 9.9 provides an example of how to implement this technique. It identifies the paper sizes the default printer supports. This code is on the CD that comes with this book as `Sizes.VBP`.

LISTING 9.9   Checking Supported Paper Sizes

```
Private Sub Form_Load()
    Dim OldPaperSize As Integer
    OldPaperSize = Printer.PaperSize 'Save original paper size
```

continues

LISTING 9.9 continued

```
        CheckPaperSizeSupported vbPRPSLetter
        CheckPaperSizeSupported vbPRPSLetterSmall
        CheckPaperSizeSupported vbPRPSTabloid
        CheckPaperSizeSupported vbPRPSLedger
        CheckPaperSizeSupported vbPRPSLegal
        CheckPaperSizeSupported vbPRPSStatement
        CheckPaperSizeSupported vbPRPSExecutive
        CheckPaperSizeSupported vbPRPSA3
        CheckPaperSizeSupported vbPRPSA4
        CheckPaperSizeSupported vbPRPSA4Small
        CheckPaperSizeSupported vbPRPSA5
        CheckPaperSizeSupported vbPRPSB4
        CheckPaperSizeSupported vbPRPSB5
        CheckPaperSizeSupported vbPRPSFolio
        CheckPaperSizeSupported vbPRPSQuarto
        CheckPaperSizeSupported vbPRPS10x14
        CheckPaperSizeSupported vbPRPS11x17
        CheckPaperSizeSupported vbPRPSNote
        CheckPaperSizeSupported vbPRPSEnv9
        CheckPaperSizeSupported vbPRPSEnv10
        CheckPaperSizeSupported vbPRPSEnv11
        CheckPaperSizeSupported vbPRPSEnv12
        CheckPaperSizeSupported vbPRPSEnv14
        CheckPaperSizeSupported vbPRPSCSheet
        CheckPaperSizeSupported vbPRPSDSheet
        CheckPaperSizeSupported vbPRPSESheet
        CheckPaperSizeSupported vbPRPSEnvDL
        CheckPaperSizeSupported vbPRPSEnvC3
        CheckPaperSizeSupported vbPRPSEnvC4
        CheckPaperSizeSupported vbPRPSEnvC5
        CheckPaperSizeSupported vbPRPSEnvC6
        CheckPaperSizeSupported vbPRPSEnvC6
        CheckPaperSizeSupported vbPRPSEnvB4
        CheckPaperSizeSupported vbPRPSEnvB5
        CheckPaperSizeSupported vbPRPSEnvB6
        CheckPaperSizeSupported vbPRPSEnvItaly
        CheckPaperSizeSupported vbPRPSEnvMonarch
        CheckPaperSizeSupported vbPRPSEnvPersonal
        CheckPaperSizeSupported vbPRPSFanfoldUS
        CheckPaperSizeSupported vbPRPSFanfoldStdGerman
        CheckPaperSizeSupported vbPRPSFanfoldLglGerman
        Printer.PaperSize = OldPaperSize 'restore original paper size
    End Sub

    Private Sub CheckPaperSizeSupported(PaperSize As Integer)
        Dim Supported As Boolean
        On Error GoTo ErrorHandler
        Supported = True
        Printer.PaperSize = PaperSize
```

```
    If Supported = True Then
        Debug.Print "This printer supports paper size: "; PaperSize
    Else
        Debug.Print "This printer does not support paper size: "; PaperSize
    End If
    Exit Sub

ErrorHandler:
    If Err.Number = 380 Then
        Supported = False
        Resume Next
    End If
End Sub
```

9

The code in the CheckPaperSizeSupported procedure begins by initializing the Boolean variable Supported to True. The routine then tries to change the paper size. If the change is successful, Supported is still True. If the change triggers an invalid property error (code 380), the error routine sets Supported to False. If some other error occurs (which it shouldn't), this example ends the subroutine. In this example, the code prints out each printer constant and whether or not it is supported. It would be a simple exercise to rewrite the routine as a function that returns either True or False, and then the calling routine could decide what to do if the paper size isn't supported. Note that this code will work only when using the Printer variable. When accessed via the Printers collection, Printer object properties are read-only.

Lesson Summary

The important tip for this lesson is that not all printers are created equal. Unless you know your application is going to output to a particular printer, you should not rely on a lot of the fancier Printer object functions. If you do, you should write procedures that verify the target printer is capable of the functions you want to use before you send anything to the printer.

In the next lesson, you'll learn how to incorporate simple line graphics and text together.

Quiz 4

1. Windows' printer capabilities can make your software

     a. Complex and unreliable

     b. Into a flight simulator

     c. Far more intelligent

     d. Into a duplex color mode orientation

2. You identify the paper size that the default printer supports with

    a. `Printer.PaperSize`

    b. `CheckPrinterSizeSupport`

    c. `vbPRPSLetterSmall`

    d. `If Supported = True Then`

3. A simple way to send text to the printer is by using

    a. `Printer.PaperBin`

    b. `Debug.Print`

    c. `Printer.Print`

    d. `Printer.PrintQuality`

4. To set double-sided printing with a vertical page orientation

    a. Set the `Simplex` property to `vbVertical`

    b. Set the `Simplex` property to `OldPaperSize`

    c. Set the `Duplex` property to `vbPRPSFanfoldUS`

    d. Set the `Duplex` property to `vbPRDPVertical`

Exercise 4

Complexity: Easy

1. Write a program that will look at all the printer drivers installed on your system, and generate a report whether or not they are capable of supporting the following properties:

`ColorMode`

`Duplex`

Complexity: Moderate

2. Write a program that will look at all the printer drivers installed on your system and print a report showing the support that it has for various `PaperSize` properties.

LESSON 5

Combining Text and Graphics

Although Visual Basic's graphics methods are covered more fully in Chapter 11, "Adding Pizazz with Graphics," this lesson demonstrates how to add certain graphics features to your printed output. The basic principles outlined in this lesson can be combined with the more advanced features of Chapter 11 to create elaborate printed forms.

The Virtual Page

When you print from a Visual Basic program, you are actually printing to a virtual page, a page that exists only in the computer's memory. The physical page does not get printed until you use the EndDoc method to send the print job to the printer. When you grasp this idea, you can change the way you think about printing. The concept that printing begins at the top-left corner of a page and continues in sequential order to the bottom-right corner no longer has to limit the way you handle your print jobs. Right up to the moment of Printer.EndDoc, you can *print* anything you want, anywhere at all on the page!

The Coordinate System

The key to locating printed items on the page is the coordinate system. If you have ever played MineSweeper or located a street on a map of your city, you already understand the coordinate system. The Visual Basic coordinate system for your virtual page sets the origin, that is, the starting point, at the top-left corner of the page. This is the point where X = 0 and Y = 0. (*X* is the horizontal location and *Y* is the vertical location.)

CurrentX and CurrentY

Visual Basic keeps track of the next print location in two variables. The exact location of the next thing to be printed is at Printer.CurrentX and Printer.CurrentY. You can read this information with your code. Better yet, you can change CurrentX and CurrentY to move your text and graphics to any point on the virtual page.

ScaleMode

The default measuring system for Visual Basic is in *twips*. A twip is 1/20 of a point. (Points are typesetters' measurements. A point is 1/72 of an inch.) There are 1,440 twips in an inch, which allows incredibly precise positioning for your output—much more precise, in fact, than you probably need.

Measuring in twips means that you have to calculate positions in twips. If you want something at 1.25 inches from the left edge of the page, for example, you would need to calculate the position as `Printer.CurrentX = 1.25 * 1440`. No, it isn't hard, but it is extra code and extra work. This is where `ScaleMode` comes into play. You can change the measurements to points, pixels, characters, inches, millimeters, or centimeters. You can even create your own measurement system! Table 9.5 lists the available `ScaleMode` values.

TABLE 9.5   The `ScaleMode` Property

Constant	Meaning
vbUser	0 User-defined
vbTwips	1 Twips
vbPoints	2 Point
vbPixels	3 Pixel
vbCharacters	4 Character
vbInches	5 Inch
vbMillimeter	6 Millimeter
vbCentimeter	7 Centimeter

You can set the `ScaleMode` property for forms and objects on forms in the Properties window, but you must set it with code for the `Printer` object. Try the code in Listing 9.10.

LISTING 9.10   Using the `ScaleMode` Property

```
Private Sub Form_Load()
    Printer.ScaleMode = vbInches
    Printer.CurrentX = 1
    Printer.CurrentY = 1
    Printer.Line -(2, 1)
    Printer.EndDoc
End Sub
```

This code starts by setting the printer's `ScaleMode` property to 5, for inches. It then sets the next print position at one inch from the left edge of the page and one inch from the top of the page, and uses the `Line` method to draw a one-inch-long horizontal line. (The `Line` method is covered in more detail later in this lesson.) Try it out and measure the line's length and position on the page.

What happened? If your printer is typical, the line is one inch long, all right, but it isn't in the right place, because most printers can't start printing at the edge of the paper.

ScaleWidth and ScaleHeight

The ScaleWidth and ScaleHeight properties are the useable dimensions of your page. Try the code below:

```
Private Sub Form_Load()
    Printer.ScaleMode = vbInches
    Debug.Print Printer.ScaleWidth
    Debug.Print Printer.ScaleHeight
    End
End Sub
```

With the HP 520 printer, this code displays

```
8
10
```

in the Debug window. You know you have 8 1/2_11-inch paper in the printer, but the printable width is eight inches and the printable height is 10 inches. The difference is the built-in printer margins, that part of the page that the printer cannot use. Change the code from Listing 9.10 to that of Listing 9.11 (changes are in bold).

LISTING 9.11 Improved Code for Drawing a Line

```
Option Explicit
Public dXOffSet As Double
Public dYOffSet As Double

Private Sub Form_Load()
    Printer.ScaleMode = vbInches
    dXOffSet = (Printer.Width / 1440 - Printer.ScaleWidth) / 2
    dYOffSet = (Printer.Height / 1440 - Printer.ScaleHeight) / 2
    Printer.CurrentX = 1 - dXOffSet
    Printer.CurrentY = 1 - dYOffSet
    Printer.Line -(Printer.Currentx + 1, Printer.Currenty)
    Printer.EndDoc
End Sub
```

Run this program and again measure the line's position and length. The line's length, of course, didn't change. The position from the left of the page is now correct, but the position from the top is still incorrect! Take a look at the code, in particular the assumptions that it makes.

The two public variables, dXOffSet and dYOffSet, are calculated to be half the difference between the page's actual size and the ScaleWidth and ScaleHeight sizes. (Note that the values of Printer.Width and Printer.Height are still in twips, which is why they are divided by 1,440.) The assumption is that the printer divides that difference equally, which is true for width but apparently false for height.

In fact, most printers need a little more margin on the bottom to grip the paper while it prints. Hewlett-Packard's manual says that the top margin is 0.4 inches, but experimental data shows that even that is incorrect. Change Printer.CurrentY = 1 - dYOffSet to Printer.CurrentY = 0 and run the program again. The line will be printed at the top edge of the printable page. If you measure the distance from the top edge, you now have the Y margin offset for your printer. (On the HP 520, that distance is 5/16 of an inch.)

The problem with this, of course, is that you have no idea what printer the user will be using. If you write all your code based on your printer's Y margin offset, your measurements will be wrong more often than not. There is no absolute solution. You could provide your users with a setup section in your code that would save their Y margin offset to the system registry, which is probably the only way to get precision printing. (Using the system registry is covered in Chapter 17, "Advanced ActiveX and Registry API Techniques.") Fortunately, you rarely have to go to this extreme because most of your print jobs can use less precise vertical positioning. The idea is to get the text and graphics to print correctly relative to each other rather than relative to the top edge of the page.

The Line Method

The most common requirement for mixing text and graphics calls for text to be placed either just above a line or inside a box. Both requirements use the same method, the Line method. The correct syntax for the Line method is

```
object.Line Step (x1, 1) Step (x2, y2), color, BF
```

The components of the syntax are as follows:

- object is an optional expression that evaluates to a form, the Printer object, or a picture box. If object is omitted, the form with the focus is assumed to be object.

- Step is an optional keyword specifying that the starting point coordinates are relative to the current graphics position given by the CurrentX and CurrentY properties.

- (x1, y1) are optional single values indicating the coordinates of the starting point for the line or rectangle. The ScaleMode property determines the unit of measure used. If omitted, the line begins at the position indicated by CurrentX and CurrentY.

- Step is an optional keyword specifying that the end-point coordinates are relative to the line starting point.

- (x2, y2) are required single values indicating the coordinates of the end point for the line being drawn.

- color is an optional long integer value indicating the RGB color used to draw the line. If color is omitted, the ForeColor property setting is used. You can use the RGB function or QBColor function to specify the color.

- B is an optional parameter. If it is included, it causes a box to be drawn using the coordinates to specify opposite corners of the box.

- F is an optional parameter. If the B option is used, the F option specifies that the box is filled with the same color used to draw the box. You cannot use F without B. If B is used without F, the box is filled with the current FillColor and FillStyle. The default value for FillStyle is transparent.

For output to the printer, the two most common implementations of the Line method are shown in Listing 9.12. The code is available as Lines.VBP on the CD that comes with this book.

LISTING 9.12   Using the Line Method with the Printer

```
Option Explicit
Public dXOffSet As Double
Public dYOffSet As Double

Private Sub Form_Load()
    Printer.ScaleMode = vbInches
    dXOffSet = (Printer.Width / 1440 - Printer.ScaleWidth) / 2
    dYOffSet = 5 / 16
    Printer.CurrentX = 1 - dXOffSet
    Printer.CurrentY = 1 - dYOffSet
    Printer.Line -(Printer.CurrentX + 2, Printer.CurrentY)
    Printer.CurrentX = 1 - dXOffSet + 1 / 16
    Printer.CurrentY = Printer.CurrentY - _
        Printer.TextHeight("I")
    Printer.Print "Atop the Line"
    Printer.CurrentX = 1 - dXOffSet
    Printer.CurrentY = 2 - dYOffSet
    Printer.Line -(Printer.CurrentX + 2, _
        Printer.CurrentY + 5 / 16), , B
    Printer.CurrentX = 1 - dXOffSet + 1 / 16
    Printer.CurrentY = Printer.CurrentY - _
        Printer.TextHeight("I")
    Printer.Print "Inside the Box"
    Printer.EndDoc
    End
End Sub
```

A Look at the Lines Program Code

Note that the variable dYOffSet is set here for the HP 520 printer. You can adjust it to suit your own printer. There are a couple of new ideas in the code, and two practical uses of the Line method.

The line Printer.Line

```
(Printer.CurrentX + 2, Printer.CurrentY)
```

draws a two-inch horizontal line. Because the Line method changes CurrentX and CurrentY to the end point of the line that it draws, the following line in the code

```
Printer.CurrentX = 1 - dXOffSet + 1 / 16
```

resets CurrentX. Note that it adds 1/16 of an inch to the original CurrentX so that the text will begin slightly inset from the start of the line. The tricky part of the code comes next. The CurrentY property for text is the top of the text. To print text on top of the line, you must move the CurrentY position above the line by the height of the characters. Rather than use a constant for this—a technique that fails when the font size changes— the code uses another property of the Printer object, the TextHeight property.

```
Printer.CurrentY = Printer.CurrentY - Printer.TextHeight("I")
```

Printer.TextHeight("I") returns the height of the tallest letter in the font. The code line subtracts that from the existing CurrentY to position the text above the line.

Drawing a box on the screen uses more of the parameters of the Line method. The code

```
Printer.Line -(Printer.CurrentX + 2, Printer.CurrentY + 5 / 16), , B
```

starts at the printer's current X and Y positions and draws a two-inch box that is 5/16 of an inch high. Note the , , B at the end of the line. It is required because the code leaves out the color parameter, which precedes the B in the syntax of the Line method. The following code sets the printer's CurrentX and CurrentY parameters to position the text inside the box.

 Note   To position text inside a box, you must draw the box first. If you do it the other way, the box will cover the text.

These techniques enable you to reproduce fill-in forms with Visual Basic. With care and attention to detail, you can reproduce them almost exactly. Chapter 10, "Problem Solving: Handling Errors and Debugging Your Program," shows how to add other graphics, including company logos, to the virtual page.

Lesson Summary

Understand the coordinate system for printing is not that different than understanding the coordinate system for drawing graphics on the screen. It's just another linear system. By becoming familiar with this system, you can really take advantage of VB's printing capabilities and really make some effective reports, as you'll learn more about in the next lesson.

Quiz 5

1. To change the printer's measurements to inches, use the line

   a. `Printer.ScaleMode = 0`

   b. `Printer.ScaleMode = 2`

   c. `Printer.ScaleMode = 5`

   d. `Printer.ScaleMode = 6`

2. The parameter `Printer.CurrentX` represents

   a. The next print position relative to the left edge of the page

   b. The next print position relative to the left edge of the printable area

   c. The next print position relative to the top edge of the page

   d. The next print position relative to the top edge of the printable area

3. The code `Printer.Line - (CurrentX + 2, CurrentY)` draws

   a. A box

   b. A vertical line

   c. A horizontal line

   d. Nothing because no color is specified

4. When printing text, the `Print` method places the text

   a. Above the `CurrentY` position

   b. Below the `CurrentY` position

   c. Centered on the `CurrentY` position

   d. None of the above

Exercise 5

Complexity: Easy

1. Write a program that will print "Microsoft" on the top line of the page, "Visual" on the center of the page, and "Basic" on the bottom of the page.

Complexity: Easy

2. Write a program that will print "Microsoft Visual Basic Rules!" centered on the page vertically and horizontally. The font to be used is bold Times New Roman, and its font size is 18 points.

LESSON 6

Printing Reports from Visual Basic

In this lesson, we will concentrate on the type of issues that arise specifically when printing reports. Everything that you have learned so far about printing from Visual Basic still applies. However, some additional techniques will help you print betterlooking reports than you might be able to achieve otherwise.

Printing Headers and Footers

Headers and footers often appear in printed reports. Typically, the sort of information that you might include in a header would be

- Report title
- Date and time
- Column headings (if you are printing a tabular report)

Typical footers might include

- Date and time
- Author
- Page number

Whatever you decide to include in your report headers, the first thing you need to determine is how to structure the report programming so that you can detect when the report needs to print a header. The best way to do this is to write a subroutine that does some basic checking on the CurrentY property before anything is printed.

For example, Listing 9.13 checks to see if CurrentY is within an inch of the bottom of the printed page. If it is, then a footer is printed. After the footer has been printed, it's then necessary to check whether the CurrentY is at the top of page, which it will be because you will have advanced to the next page after the footer was printed. In this case, the header is printed. You can put what you like into the subroutines to print the headers and footers, but we have provided you with some simple routines to get you going. The code is on the CD as HeadFoot.VBP.

LISTING 9.13   Routines to Print Headers and Footers

```
Private Sub CheckHeaderAndFooter()
    If Printer.CurrentY + 1440 > Printer.ScaleHeight Then
        PrintFooter
    End If
    If Printer.CurrentY = 0 Then
        PrintHeader
    End If
End Sub

Private Sub PrintFooter()
    Dim Footer As String
    ' setup the font for the footer
    Printer.Print ;
    Printer.Font.Name = "Arial"
    Printer.Font.Size = 10
    Printer.Font.Bold = False
    Printer.Font.Italic = False
    Printer.Font.Strikethrough = False
    Printer.Font.Underline = False
    'Create the text to be printed
    Footer = "Page - " & CStr(Printer.Page)
    'Print the footer in the center of the page, three quarters of an inch
    'from the bottom of the page
    Printer.CurrentX = (Printer.ScaleWidth - Printer.TextWidth(Footer)) / 2
    Printer.CurrentY = Printer.ScaleHeight - 1080
    Printer.Print Footer
    'Print a line across the page, one inch from the bottom
    Printer.Line (0, Printer.ScaleHeight - 1440)-(Printer.ScaleWidth,
    Printer.ScaleHeight‹ - 1440)
    'Advance to the next page
    Printer.NewPage
End Sub

Private Sub PrintHeader()
    Dim Header As String
    'Set the font for the header
```

continues

LISTING 9.13 continued

```
        Printer.Font.Name = "Arial"
        Printer.Font.Size = 10
        Printer.Font.Bold = False
        Printer.Font.Italic = False
        Printer.Font.Strikethrough = False
        Printer.Font.Underline = False
        'Set the text to be printed
        Header = "My application"
        'Print the text at the top of the page, in the center
        Printer.CurrentX = (Printer.ScaleWidth - Printer.TextWidth(Title)) / 2
        Printer.CurrentY = 0
        Printer.Print Header
        'Print a line one inch down the page
        Printer.Line (0, 1440)-(Printer.ScaleWidth, 1440)
        'Set the CurrentX and Y up ready for printing the text to go on this page
        Printer.CurrentX = 0
        Printer.CurrentY = 1800 '1 and a quarter inches down the page
    End Sub
```

Detecting the End of the Page

In Listing 9.13, you need to detect the end of the page about one inch prior to getting there. That's why CheckHeaderAndFooter checks that there is at least one inch left. Of course, the CurrentY value is being tested before any printing actually gets done, so you are assured of trapping this condition before it's too late.

If you are about to print into the area that is defined as the footer margin, the program prints the footer. The subroutine that prints the footer makes sure that the end of the page is marked by calling the NewPage method. This will cause the printer to throw a new page and move CurrentX and CurrentY back to 0.

Finally, the header print subroutine ensures that the CurrentX value is reset to 0 (the left of the page) and that CurrentY is left at a position below the header. If it didn't do this, the text would end up printing in the space allocated to the header.

Lesson Summary

By combining what you already learned in the last lesson and what you learned in this lesson, you can really make some effective reports. You can also use these last two lessons to help you figure out just how much text can fit on a page, so you can properly word wrap text from a memo-type field. The next lesson will cover how to convert the format of raw numbers into something more presentable for printouts and reports.

Quiz 6

1. When printing headers and footers

   a. Use `Printer.SectionMode = vbPRNTExtra`.

   b. Use the same print methods you've learned in previous lessons to output the header/footer information.

   c. It's necessary to adjust the virtual page height to exclude the header (and footer).

   d. All of the above.

2. Typically, the sort of information you might include in a header would include

   a. Report title

   b. Date and time

   c. Column headings

   d. All of the above

3. To check whether you need to print a header or a footer

   a. Look at the value of `Printer.SectionMode`

   b. Interactively query the user

   c. Check the specifications in your printer manual for the dimensions of the printable section of the page

   d. Look at the value of `Printer.CurrentY`

4. A twip is approximately

   a. 1/1,440th of an inch

   b. 11 1/2 inches

   c. 2 millimeters

   d. None of the above

Exercise 6

Complexity: Easy

1. Write a program that will print "Microsoft Visual Basic 6" on the header of each page that is printed.

Complexity: Moderate

2. Building on Exercise 6.1, add a footer that prints the current date and page that is flush right.

LESSON 7

Formatting Numeric Output

This lesson and the next explore the Format function. This versatile function converts and formats dates, numbers, strings—anything you like. Unlike some of the other formatting functions provided by Visual Basic (such as Str and Val), Format gives you a much greater degree of control over how your data is presented. You can choose from Format's predefined named formats, such as Currency or Fixed, or insist on finer control by creating your own user-defined format.

The Format function returns a string, which you can use for either screen or printer output. This lesson covers Format's options for numeric formatting; Lesson 8 covers date formatting.

The Format Function

The syntax for Format is

```
Format(Expression [, Format [, FirstDayOfWeek [, FirstWeekOfYear]]])
```

The Format function always returns a String data type. The idea is that you are formatting one of the built-in data types and producing a string formatted in a particular way.

Let's look at each data type in turn that can be formatted using Format.

Numeric Formatting

Numbers (whatever their type: integers, longs, singles, doubles, or currencies) can be formatted using the Format function. The simplest way to use Format is to provide the numeric expression without providing any formatting characters in the second parameter.

For example:

```
Private Sub Form_Load()
    Dim MyInteger As Integer
    MyInteger = 5
    Debug.Print Format(MyInteger)
    Debug.Print Str(MyInteger)
End Sub
```

This code outputs

```
5
 5
```

Note that both functions return a number formatted as a string. However, positive values formatted by Format do not have a leading space. The Str version has an extra space at the beginning. (Recall that this space is the position that would be occupied by a minus sign if the number were negative.)

Named Numeric Formats

One of Format's predefined numeric formats might suffice for your needs. Format makes nine different named numeric formats available. These are summarized in Table 9.6.

TABLE 9.6 Named Numeric Formats

Format Name	Description
General number	Displays the number without any thousands separators.
Currency	Displays the number depending on the settings for currency formatting currently configured in the control panel.
Fixed	Displays a minimum of one digit to the left and two to the right of the decimal place.
Standard	The same as fixed, except that the number is also formatted with thousands separators.
Percent	Displays the number as a percentage by multiplying it by 100 first. The number is always displayed with two digits to the right of the decimal point and with the trailing percent sign.
Scientific	Uses standard scientific notation.
Yes/No	Displays No if the number is zero; otherwise displays Yes.
True/False	Displays False if the number is zero; otherwise displays True.
On/Off	Displays Off if the number is zero; otherwise displays On.

Try out these predefined formats. Enter the example in Listing 9.14. The code is available on the CD that accompanies this book as Format1.VBP.

LISTING 9.14 The Named Formats

```
Private Sub Form_Load()
Dim MyInteger As Integer
Dim MySingle As Single
MyInteger = 12345
MySingle = 1.54321E-2
```

continues

LISTING 9.14   continued

```
Debug.Print Format(MyInteger, "General Number")
Debug.Print Format(MyInteger, "Currency")
Debug.Print Format(MyInteger, "Fixed")
Debug.Print Format(MyInteger, "Standard")
Debug.Print Format(MySingle, "Percent")
Debug.Print Format(MySingle, "Scientific")
Debug.Print Format(False, "Yes/No")
Debug.Print Format(50, "True/False")
Debug.Print Format(True, "On/Off")
End Sub
```

This code produces the following output:

```
12345
$12,345.00
12345.00
12,345.00
1.54%
1.54E-02
No
True
On
```

As you can see, these predefined named formats are extremely useful and might suffice for your needs when it comes to formatting numbers for display.

User-Defined Numeric Formats

There are occasions, however, when these named formats will not suffice and you will require more control over your number formats. In these situations, you can use a combination of a series of special formatting characters to control exactly how the Format function formats your numbers. These formatting characters are summarized in Table 9.7.

TABLE 9.7   Characters for User-Defined Formatting

Character	Name	Description
0	Digit placeholder	Forces Format to display a zero or a digit if the number passed contains a digit in that position. If the number passed contains more digits to the right of the decimal point than are specified in the format string, the number is rounded to as many decimal places as there are 0s in the format string.

Character	Name	Description
#	Digit placeholder	Works in a similar way to 0 except that if the number does not contain a digit in the position specified by the format string, Format will display nothing in that character position.
.	Decimal point position	Fixes the position of the decimal point. Depending on your locale settings, Format might display a comma instead of a decimal point.
%	Percentage	The number passed to Format is multiplied by 100 and the percent sign is displayed at the position given in the format string.
,	Thousands separator	If the number is large enough to extend to the left of the decimal point past the position of this character in the format string, a comma will be displayed as a thousands separator. The actual character displayed as the thousands separator depends on your locale settings in the control panel. In some locales a decimal point is displayed instead of a comma.
E-, E+, e-, e+	Scientific	Causes Format to display the number in scientific format. The use of lowercase or uppercase E determines whether the exponent character will be displayed with a lower- or uppercase E. The minus sign indicates that numbers with a negative exponent will be displayed with a negative sign next to the exponent. Numbers with a positive exponent will be displayed with a space. The + sign indicates that numbers displayed with a positive exponent will be displayed with a plus sign next to the exponent.
\	Literal character Display	To display a literal character, just precede it with a \ (backslash).

For example, type in Listing 9.15. The code is available on the CD as Format2.VBP.

LISTING 9.15   The User-Defined Formats

```
Private Sub Form_Load()
Dim MySingle As Single
    Dim MyInteger As Integer
    Dim MyCurrency As Currency
    MySingle = 0.23
    MyInteger = 123
    MyCurrency = 123456.78
    Debug.Print Format(MyInteger, "00000")
    Debug.Print Format(MyInteger, "#####")
    Debug.Print Format(MySingle, "###%")
    Debug.Print Format(MyCurrency, "###,###,##0.00")
    Debug.Print Format(0, "###,###,##0.00")
    Debug.Print Format(MyCurrency, "\$###,###,##0.00")
End Sub
```

This code outputs

```
00123
123
23%
123,456.78
0.00
$123,456.78
```

Note the backslash in Listing 9.15. It allows the computer to interpret the next character literally instead of as a format character.

Lesson Summary

As you can see, the range of options is extremely flexible. Experiment with the Format function yourself with the numeric formatting characters so that you are satisfied that you understand how they can be used. This next lesson will explore how to format date strings.

Quiz 7

1. The Format function

    a. Is used to initialize the virtual page

    b. Always returns a number

    c. Provides less control than the Str function

    d. Provides a great degree of control over how your data is presented

2. Which of the following types of numbers can be used with the `Format` function?

    a. Integer

    b. Currency

    c. Single

    d. All of the above

3. Which of the following is not a named numeric format?

    a. Yes/No

    b. Percent

    c. Dollars

    d. Standard

4. What is the output of the following code?

```
Debug.Print Format(1.02,"True/False")
```

    a. True

    b. 1.02

    c. 1

    d. <1>

Exercise 7

Complexity: Easy

1. Write a program that will print out the following series of numbers as currency on the form. Display the raw number and currency formatted number in a column next to the raw number.

```
186232
302010
5551212
-8679305
```

Complexity: Moderate

2. Write a program that will add five numeric values from text boxes and print all five values and their sum in Standard notation when the user presses a Print button.

LESSON 8

Formatting Dates for Output

The `Format` function has a number of predefined formats for displaying dates and times as well as numbers.

Named Date Formats

The named date formats are summarized in Table 9.8.

TABLE 9.8   The Named Date Formats

Format Name	Description
General Date	This is the most flexible date/time format. If the Date expression passed has only an integer portion, only the date is displayed. Similarly, if it has only a decimal portion, only the time is displayed. The format of the date and time displayed depends on your system's locale settings.
Long Date	This format will display a date in the format specified by your system locale's long date setting.
Medium Date	This format will display a date in the format specified by your system locale's medium date setting.
Short Date	This format will display a date in the format specified by your system's short date setting.
Long Time	This format will display a time only in your system locale's long time format.
Medium Time	This format displays the time in 12-hour format using only hours and minutes and the AM/PM indicator.
Short Time	This format displays the time in 24-hour format.

Try the examples in Listing 9.16 to see how these formats work. You could even try changing your locale settings in the control panel to see how this affects the displayed dates and times. The code is available on the CD as `Format.vbp`.

LISTING 9.16   The Named Date Format Examples

```
Private Sub Form_Load()
    Debug.Print Format(Now, "General Date")
    Debug.Print Format(Now, "Long Date")
    Debug.Print Format(Now, "Medium Date")
```

```
      Debug.Print Format(Now, "Short Date")
      Debug.Print Format(Now, "Long Time")
      Debug.Print Format(Now, "Medium Time")
      Debug.Print Format(Now, "Short Time")
   End Sub
```

The output on your system is

```
1/25/98
Sunday, January 25, 1998
25-Jan-98
1/25/98
10:52:28 PM
10:52 PM
22:52
```

User-Defined Date and Time Formatting Characters

If one of the above built-in formatting types is insufficient for your needs, Format has a range of date and time formatting characters that you can use to build up your own date and time formats. These are summarized in Table 9.9.

TABLE 9.9   The Characters for User-Defined Date Formatting

Character	Description
:	Time separator.
/	Date separator.
c	Displays date and time information only.
d	Displays the day of the month as a number (1–31).
dd	Displays the day of the month with a leading zero (01–31).
ddd	Displays the day of the week as an abbreviated name (Sun–Sat).
dddd	Displays the day of the week as a full name (Sunday–Saturday).
ddddd	Displays the date according to your locale's short date settings.
dddddd	Displays the date according to your locale's long date settings.
w	Displays the day of the week as a number (1–7), starting at the day specified in FirstDayOfWeek (defaults to Sunday).
ww	Displays a number representing the week of the year (1–53).
m	Displays the month as a number without a leading zero (1–12). If m immediately follows h or hh, Format displays the minute rather than the month.

continues

TABLE 9.9　continued

Character	Description
mm	Displays the month as a number with a leading zero (01–12). If m immediately follows h or hh, Format displays the minute rather than the month.
mmm	Displays the abbreviated name of the month (Jan–Dec).
mmmm	Displays the full name of the month (January–December).
q	Displays the quarter of the year as a number (1–4).
y	Displays the day of the year as a number (1–366).
yy	Displays the year as a two-digit number (00–99).
yyyy	Displays the year as a four-digit number (100–9999).
h	Displays the hour as a number without leading zeros (0–23).
hh	Displays the hour as a number with leading zeros (00–23).
n	Displays the minute as a number without leading zeros (059).
nn	Displays the minute as a number with leading zeros (00–59).
s	Displays the second as a number without leading zeros (059).
ss	Displays the second as a number with leading zeros (00–59).
ttttt	Displays a complete time depending on your system's locale settings.
AM/PM	Displays the time in 12-hour format, using the text AM or PM.
am/pm	Displays the time in 12-hour format, using the text am or pm.
A/P	Displays the time in 12-hour format, using the text A or P.
a/p	Displays the time in 12-hour format, using the text a or p.
AMPM	Displays the time in 12-hour format, using your locale's AM or PM text setting.

The range of different formats available is quite broad, but Listing 9.17 gives you some examples to get you going. The code is on the CD as Format4.VBP.

LISTING 9.17　The User-Defined Date Format Examples

```
Private Sub Form_Load()
    Debug.Print Format(Now, "dddd  d mmmm yyyy")
    Debug.Print Format(Now, "AM/PM")
    Debug.Print Format(Now, "hh:mm:ss")
    Debug.Print Format(Now, "ttttt")
End Sub
```

The output of this program, of course, depends on the current date and time. It will look something like the following:

```
Sunday  25 January 1998
PM
22:55:13
10:55:13 PM
```

Experiment some more yourself with these settings.

Lesson Summary

This lesson explained how to use the format function to manipulate the presentation of dates. As you become more advanced and start moving into database development and financial system, both this lesson and Lesson 7 will play a big role.

Quiz 8

1. How can you display the current time in the format `hh:mm:ss`?

   a. `Debug.Print Format(Now, "hh:mm:ss")`

   b. `Debug.Print Format(Now, "Short Time")`

   c. `Debug.Print Format(Now, "Medium Time")`

   d. `Debug.Print Now`

2. What is the output from the following program?

   ```
   Dim SomeDate As Date
   SomeDate = "Dec 31, 1999"
   Debug.Print Format(SomeDate, "Short Date")
   ```

   a. The last day of 1999 in a short format, suitable for the country and control panel settings

   b. `12/31/99`

   c. `12-31-99`

   d. `99DEC31`

3. Which code fragment displays the current day of the week?

   a. `Debug.Print Format(Now,"Weekday")`

   b. `Debug.Print Format(Now,"dddd")`

   c. `Debug.Print Format(Weekday)`

   d. None of the above

4. Assume the following declaration:

```
Dim LastDay As Date
LastDay = "Dec 31 1999 23:59:59"
```

How would you format this date to produce the following output?

`23:59:59 12/31/1999`

a. `Format(LastDay,"Long Date")`

b. `Format(Lastday,"hh:mm:ss mm/dd/yyyy")`

c. `Format(LastDay,"q")`

d. `Format(LastDay,"hh:mm:ss mm/dd/yy")`

Exercise 8

Complexity: Easy

1. Write a program that will print the current date and time in two different columns. The date should display the day of the week, month, day, and year. The time should be displayed in Military time.

Complexity: Easy

2. Write a program that has text boxes for Your Birthday, your spouse's (or significant other's) birthday, and anniversary (any one will do). When the user presses the Print button, the program should print the day of the week for each date entered.

Chapter Summary

This chapter describes how to use the Printer Object and Printer Collection to effectively output information through VB. Some of the formatting functions are not specific to the use Printer Object, so don't think you can't use them elsewhere in your VB code. The following is a recap of the important points covered in this chapter:

- Outputting the printer is as simple as saying `Printer.Print`.

- By adding the `CommonDialog` control to your application, you are adding elements of the Windows environment that everyone is familiar with. This provides a consistent look and feel between your application and other Windows products with hardly any coding.

- The usage of `CurrentX` and `CurrentY` enable you place your text and graphics on a page with precision.

- Not all printers are created equal so your mileage will definitely vary.

- Experiment with the Format function for both numbers and date/time values. Understanding how it works will help with financial and scientific applications.

- There are a lot of Printer Object methods available that couldn't be covered here. If you look in the VB Help, you can get a better grasp of what methods are available to you.

9

CHAPTER **10**

Problem Solving: Handling Errors and Debugging Your Program

In order to make your programs run flawlessly, you must learn how to properly handle errors in your Visual Basic programs. As your applications become more complex, you will also have to learn how to debug your applications to make sure that they are working properly. In this chapter, you will learn about the many different types of errors that can occur in a Visual Basic program and how to write code that can properly react to error conditions. You will also learn how to use the various features built into Visual Basic 6 to enable you to debug your programs.

LESSON 1

Errors in Visual Basic 6 Programs

Errors? There are errors in my program? Impossible! Unfortunately, errors creep (sometimes gallop!) into programs. Often they show up where you least expect them, for instance, in that really simple piece of code you did not test thoroughly. This chapter explains what kinds of errors there are, how to deal with them, and how to avoid them.

Types of Errors

It may seem like there are many different types of errors, but only three kinds of errors show up in Visual Basic programs.

Syntax Errors

They can be very taxing, but syntax errors are not taxes. Syntax is defined as the rules for making meaningful phrases out of words. In programming, it's pretty much the same thing. As clever as your computer may seem, it has a rigid set of rules about how and when things must be done. You can violate syntax in speech or writing and still convey some meaning, but your computer won't even try to understand you if you key something in incorrectly.

First, deliberately create a few syntax errors so you can get an idea of what they are and how Visual Basic 6 responds to them. Start a new project and enter the following code in the Form_Load event:

```
Private Sub Form_Load()
Dim i As Integer

If i = 0

End Sub
```

It's hard to miss Visual Basic's reaction when you hit Enter after that zero! The message box jumps right out and tells you all about it: Compile Error: Expected: Then or GoTo. Just to make sure you know where your problem is, it even paints the line red! The error, of course, is that If requires either Then or GoTo in order to make sense.

Now delete the offending line and put a Command button on your form. Put the following code in the Click event:

```
Private Sub Command1_Click()
Dim i As Integer
For i = 1 To 3

Debug.Print i
End Sub
```

Run the program and click the Command1 button. The For...Next loop is incomplete without the Next. Visual Basic can't detect this one as easily, because Next is not expected to be on the same line as For.

You can generate hundreds of syntax errors such as these. Ideally, you will never forget a Then or a Next, but until you are perfect, just grin and bear it. Your program won't make it out the door with syntax errors, and you are the only one who knows about them.

Runtime Errors

Runtime errors are more insidious: They might not show up the first time you execute your program. Runtime errors are errors that appear only when you run your program, and often only when a certain sequence of events takes place. Change the code in the `Click` event of Command1 to the following:

```
Private Sub Command1_Click()

Dim A As String, B As Integer
A = "a"
B = A

End Sub
```

Now what happens when you click the Command1 button? This runtime error does not appear until you click that button, but it shows up the first time you do. Replace that code with the following for a less obvious runtime error:

```
Private Sub Command1_Click()

Dim i As Integer, j As Integer
j = 6
For i = 6 To 0 Step -1

Debug.Print j / i
Next

End Sub
```

This code actually runs—for a while. You probably would never write this code into a program because you know that division by zero is not allowed. And that is exactly what happens when the loop steps down to zero. What is probable, though, is that a variable you expect to be nonzero somehow becomes zero. It can happen. Worse yet, it can happen months after you release the program to your customer. When it happens in a running program, outside the development environment, the program displays a message box and then shuts down with no chance for recovery.

Obviously, runtime errors are dangerous to your well-being. Most of this chapter is about how to deal with them.

Logic Errors

Some runtime errors, including the examples above, are caused by logic errors, which are really thinking errors. A *thinking* Visual Basic programmer, for example, would not attempt to assign a string value to an integer. (It is legal in C and C++, but that's a different book.) Having a variable unexpectedly become zero is a bit different; even the best programmers can't anticipate everything that might happen.

Logic errors do not necessarily cause runtime errors. Sometimes a logic error may "just" cause data corruption or generate incorrect results. The only way to avoid logic errors is to plan your program carefully before you begin writing code.

How Visual Basic 6 Helps You Avoid Errors

Visual Basic 6 has several features that can help you avoid the most common errors. Take a look at them before you move on. Click the Tools menu and select Options. The five check boxes on the left of the Code Settings frame help you detect and prevent errors in your code. Figure 10.1 shows the Editor tab with all five of the check boxes selected.

FIGURE **10.1**

The Editor tab of the Options dialog box.

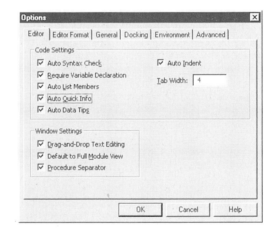

Auto Syntax Check

The automatic syntax check is on by default. It was the syntax checker that warned you about the missing Then in the first example in this chapter. The only mystery about automatic syntax checking is why Visual Basic lets you turn it off. In a word, don't. But if you did want to turn this feature off, uncheck the check box for Auto Syntax Check from the Editor tab in the Options dialog box shown in Figure 10.1.

Require Variable Declaration

One of the most common sources of runtime errors is mistyped variable names. For example, you may have something like the following:

```
Private Sub Form_Load()

Dim iNumber As Integer
```

```
iNumber = 47
Debug.Print iNmber

End Sub
```

With Require Variable Declaration disabled, this code runs just fine, but `iNmber` shows as zero in the Immediate window. That is, after all, the value of `iNumber` because it was never declared.

If Require Variable Declaration is disabled in your Code Settings frame, enable it now. That simple option places Option Explicit in the General Declarations section of every part of your program. That requires that all variables must be declared, and it detects typing errors such as this. With Option Explicit enabled, Visual Basic 6 provides you with a warning, as shown in Figure 10.2.

FIGURE 10.2

The error message for undefined variables.

Auto List Members

The Auto List Members option tells Visual Basic to help you complete a statement as you are writing it. If the feature is disabled in your IDE, enable it by checking the Auto List Members check box in the Editor tab of the Options dialog box, shown in Figure 10.1. Enter the following code:

```
Private Sub Form_Load()

Dim iNumber As

End Sub
```

As soon as you press the space bar after `As`, you see the drop-down list shown in Figure 10.3.

FIGURE 10.3

The Auto List Members drop-down list.

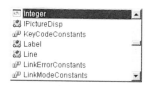

As you continue typing, the word Integer appears in the drop-down menu. Press Enter when the integer is highlighted, and VB 6 completes the statement for you.

You might or might not consider Auto List Members a desirable feature. You have to wait a moment before the drop-down box appears, which may be an annoyance. On the other hand, this feature reduces the number of errors your typing skills inject into your program, which is, of course, a benefit. Remember that you can always change the setting.

Auto Quick Info

Quick Info provides you with a pop-up box that tells you the correct syntax for any function you use in your code. Visual Basic 6 is loaded with functions you can call. Even as brilliant as you are, it is not likely that you will remember the correct syntax for all of them. Figure 10.4 shows the Quick Info pop-up box.

FIGURE 10.4

The Quick Info pop-up box.

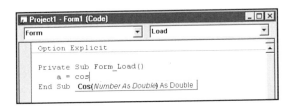

Like Auto List Members, Auto Quick Info adds a brief delay to your programming. You may prefer to bring up Quick Info only when you really need it; it is always only a keystroke away. You can view Quick Info by pressing Ctrl+I while the cursor is on the function name.

Auto Data Tips

The Auto Data Tips option helps during the debugging and testing stages of your program. Take a look at Auto Data Tips at work. If Auto Data Tips is not enabled, enable it first. (Enabled means there is a checkmark in the check box.) Then enter the following code:

```
Private Sub Form_Load()

Dim dAngle As Double, dSine As Double
dAngle = 90 * 3.14159 / 180
dSine = Sin(dAngle)

End Sub
```

Place the cursor on the line `dSine = Sin(dAngle)` and press F9 to set a breakpoint there; then run the program. When the program enters the Break mode, place your mouse pointer over the variable `dAngle`. A text box pops up and shows you the current value of the variable. Now place the mouse pointer over `dSine`. Its value is zero because it has not yet been assigned a value. If you press F8 and place the mouse pointer over `dSine` again, the variable's new value appears.

You can see that Auto Data Tips can be most helpful for finding unexpected values. Later in this chapter, you will see some other useful ways to uncover them.

Lesson Summary

In this lesson you learned that there are many different type of errors that you can encounter while writing a Visual Basic program; for example, a syntax error. Syntax errors are caused by code the compiler does not understand and thus cannot run and compile. A runtime error occurs while the programming is executing and will cause your program to invoke an error handler. Logic errors do not invoke an error handler but produce erroneous results.

Visual Basic also has several built-in features to simplify coding, such as the Auto Syntax Check, the Auto List Members, and the Auto Quick Info feature. Visual Basic's Auto Syntax Check looks for invalid Visual Basic syntax during design time. Visual Basic's Auto List Members helps you code by displaying valid methods and properties of the object being used. Visual Basic's Auto Quick Info provides a pop-up box that displays the correct syntax for any function you use in your code.

Quiz 1

1. Syntax errors are detected

    a. At design time

    b. At runtime

    c. Only when specific conditions are met

    d. When your program crashes

2. What type of error allows a variable to assume an unexpected value?

    a. A runtime error

    b. A syntax error

    c. A logic error

    d. It can never happen

3. What Visual Basic 6 feature helps you complete a statement that you have begun typing?

   a. Auto Data Tips

   b. Auto Syntax Check

   c. Auto List Members

   d. Auto Quick Info

4. What Visual Basic 6 feature helps you with the syntax of a function call?

   a. Auto Data Tips

   b. Auto Syntax Check

   c. Auto List Members

   d. Auto Quick Info

Exercise 1

Complexity: Easy

1. Describe the differences between runtime errors and logic errors.

Complexity: Easy

2. Using the Auto Quick Info function, write a line of Visual Basic code to display the string "Hello World" in a critical message box.

LESSON 2

Writing Error Handlers

Whaddaya mean, error handlers? I don't need no stinking error handlers! The fact is, though, that Visual Basic makes errors, and it does it on purpose! Remember the error that the CommonDialog generates when you cancel a save? It isn't really an error, but it is a convenient mechanism that VB 6 uses to signal that the save is canceled.

Realistically, all programs generate errors, some on purpose, but most unexpectedly. Being ready for the unexpected separates a great program from an okay program, and a great programmer from an ordinary programmer. This lesson explains how to expect the unexpected.

What Happens When an Error Occurs

Visual Basic 6 provides a rich tapestry of error-handling power. You can, and should, draw upon it to handle any errors that may crop up in your program. Take a look at the object that makes it all possible.

The err Object

VB 6 contains a built-in object for error handling. The Err object has six properties and two methods, which are listed in Table 10.1.

TABLE 10.1   Error Object (Err) Properties and Methods

Property/Method Name	Type
Clear	Method
Description	Property
HelpContext	Property
HelpFile	Property
LastDLLError	Property
Number	Property
Raise	Method
Source	Property

When an error occurs, VB 6 sets the err object's properties to reflect the nature of the error. You can determine the exact error by reading those properties. Most programmers use two of the Err object's properties: Number and Description. As you hone your skills, the others will become useful as well.

The Number property contains the number of the last error. VB 6 has reserved error numbers 1 through 1,000 for its own use, although it does not yet use all of them. Additionally, error numbers above 31,000 are reserved. You can use numbers between 1,000 and 31,000 to create your own error numbers.

The Description property contains a text string that describes the error. The description is most useful to programmers while they are testing a program. Your program's users are likely to be confused by some of the cryptic messages in Err.description.

The Raise method lets you generate errors on purpose. Why would you want to do that? For starters, you can use the Raise method to test error handlers in your application. You can also raise an error in a function or component that is passed back to the calling program's error handler to let the caller know an error has occurred.

10

The Error Function

The Error function returns the error message that corresponds to a specific error number. If you do not supply a number, it returns a message corresponding to the last error that occurred. The error message is the Description property of the err object. If no error has occurred, the Error function returns an empty string.

The Error Handler

Your program should anticipate errors. Actually, the best programmers attempt to prevent errors by allowing only valid inputs and by disabling menu options and buttons that are not valid at a specific time. For example, Microsoft Word does not let you use Save or Save As if there is no file to be saved. Nevertheless, some things sneak past us and are impossible to prevent, such as the Cancel error in the CommonDialog File controls. So you must prepare for errors, and the way to do that is to include error handlers in your code. Take a look at the special statements and functions that Visual Basic provides to create error handlers.

On Error

The On Error statement is a conditional branching statement, such as If...Then. It says, "If there is an error, here is where to go." There are several choices about where to go.

The GoTo line statement causes program execution to branch to a line number or label in the same procedure. Line number is a misnomer, because it must also be a label. (A label is a word or number followed by a colon. See the code in Listing 10.1 for an example.)

The GoTo 0 statement turns off error trapping in your subroutine or function. If there is no On Error GoTo statement in your subroutine or function, this is the default condition. This doesn't mean that the computer does not respond to errors, but that your On Error GoTo statement has been turned off, and Visual Basic's default error handling is turned on. In some cases, the default error handling might be okay, but in many cases it displays a message and then unceremoniously dumps you from the program.

The On Error statement affects only the subroutine or function in which it appears. When End Sub is executed, the error trapping that was effective for that subroutine is turned off. It is said *to go out of scope*.

Resume

If the On Error statement is anything other than On Error GoTo 0, there must be a Resume statement. The Resume statement tells Visual Basic what to do after it has noticed and dealt with the error. The choices are simple:

- The Resume statement tells Visual Basic to continue execution on the same line that caused the error in the first place. If you are clever, your program has fixed the error condition before it resumes. If not, it generates an infinite loop. Your program goes 'round in circles like a dog chasing its tail!
- The Resume Next statement tells the program to continue execution on the next line. That may seem reckless, but sometimes it is exactly the right thing to do.
- The Resume Line statement sends the program off to another line number or label.

Try It Out

Enough of this talk. It's time to try out some code to see how error handlers work. Create a new directory called Goofs. Create a new project in Visual Basic or copy Goofs.vbp from the CD that comes with the book.

The project needs two Command buttons, a label, and a text box on the form, but there is nothing special here, so you can leave them with their default names and labels (see Figure 10.5).

FIGURE 10.5

The Code for
Goofs.vbp.

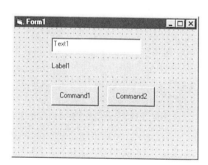

Add code to the project, as shown in Listing 10.1.

LISTING 10.1   The Code for Goofs.vbp

```
Option Explicit

Private Sub Form_Activate()

' Clear the label
Label1.Caption = ""
' Clear the textbox
Text1.Text = ""
' set the focus on the textbox
Text1.SetFocus

End Sub

Private Sub Text1_GotFocus()

Text1.SelStart = 0
Text1.SelLength = Len(Text1.Text)

End Sub

Private Sub Command1_Click()

Dim iNum1 As Integer, iNum2 As Integer
On Error GoTo Error_Handler
iNum2 = 22
iNum1 = Val(Text1.Text)
Label1.Caption = iNum2 / iNum1

Exit_Command1_Click:
Text1.SetFocus
Exit Sub

Error_Handler:
MsgBox "Error Number " & Err & vbCrLf & Error, 48, "Whoops!"
Resume Exit_Command1_Click

End Sub

Private Sub Command2_Click()

Dim iError As Integer
On Error GoTo Error_Handler
iError = Int(Val(Text1.Text))
Err.Raise iError

Exit_Command2_Click:
Text1.SetFocus
Exit Sub
```

```
Error_Handler:
MsgBox "Error Number " & Err & vbCrLf & Err.Description, 48, "Whoops!"
Resume Exit_Command2_Click

End Sub
```

Running Goof

Now run the program. Start by clicking both Command buttons without entering anything into the text box. Then enter various numbers, clicking Command1 and Command2
to see the results. Try numbers that are beyond the correct range for integers, too.

Note | Note that many of the error messages you get from Command2 say the same thing: `Application-defined` or `object-defined error`. That is because Microsoft has not yet assigned a meaning to that specific error number.

10

A Look at the Code

Notice that the initialization code for this project is in the form's `Activate` event instead
of the `Load` event. The main reason is that the `SetFocus` method does not work until the
form has been loaded and `Text1` exists. The `Activate` event clears the text box and the
label and sets the focus in the text box. (Real tough stuff!)

Take a look at the `GotFocus` event of `Text1`. The code sets the beginning position for text
selection at the beginning of any text that is in the text box. Then it sets the length of the
selection the same as the length of the string. In other words, it selects all the text that is
in the text box whenever the text box receives focus. That way you can simply type new
numbers in the text box without having to erase the old ones manually.

The code that is most interesting here is that for Command1 and Command2.
Command1's `Click` event contains a typical `On Error` statement: `On Error GoTo`
`Error_Handler`. The label `Error_Handler:` appears at the end of the procedure. In this
case, it simply displays a message box and sends program flow off to the label
`Exit_Command1_Click`. The `Exit_Command1_Click:` label and code are necessary to
keep the program from running into the error handler when there are no errors. The code
for Command2 uses the `Raise` method to generate an error in the program as well as
`Err.Description` instead of the `Error` function to display the error message. The effect
is the same; however, use of the `err` object is recommended, because it is an object-
oriented approach.

A more sophisticated error handler might use a Select-Case statement to deal with specific errors. For example, an effort to open a file can generate error numbers 52 through 76. A well-written error handler would deal with many of them specifically. Instead of displaying the Error string Disk not ready for error 71, for example, you might display a less cryptic message that suggests that your user should insert a disk in the drive.

The error strings you get from the err object are not always very informative to people who are not computer geeks. Error 6, for example, simply states Overflow. You know that that means you entered a value that is outside of the maximum range for the variable type, but you should give your user more information so they can correct the problem. Replace the error handler code for Command1 with the code in Listing 10.2, and try the program again.

LISTING 10.2 An Improved Error Handler

```
Select Case Err
Case 6
MsgBox " Values must be between +32767 and -32768", 48, " Please Note:"
Case 11
MsgBox " Division by 0 is not allowed", 48, " Please Note:"
Case Else
MsgBox "Error Number " & Err & vbCrLf & Err.Description, 48, "Sorry."
End Select
Resume Exit_Command2_Click
```

True, it seems like a lot of work to deal with every possible error, and it is. It also makes the difference between a program that is frustrating to use and one that your users are happy to double-click through.

Lesson Summary

To handle properly and trap errors that may occur in your program, you need to use error handlers. Using the Visual Basic statement On Error GoTo creates an error handler. Use the Visual Basic built-in error object, Err, to retrieve the number of the error that occurred as well as display the associated error message. To return control back to the program after an error has occurred, use the Resume statement. With Resume, you can issue the line that cause the error, resume at the line of code after the line that caused the error, or resume to a specific label.

Quiz 2

1. _____ is the Visual Basic error object.

   a. `VB.Object.Error`

   b. `Error`

   c. `VB_Err`

   d. `Err`

2. What does the following line do?

   `On Error Goto exit0`

   a. It jumps program execution to line 0 if an error occurs.

   b. It jumps program execution to line 0.

   c. It jumps program execution to a label called exit0.

   d. It disables error handling.

3. In the following code, which one of the following is true?

   `MyDay()`

   ```
   On Error GoTo First_Exit
   On Error GoTo Second_Exit
   A = C/D
   ```

   a. You can only have a single error handler in the same procedure.

   b. The first error handler is the active error handler when `A=C/D` is executed.

   c. Neither error handler is activated.

   d. If the statement `A=C/D` fails, program execution transfers to `Second_Exit`.

4. Error handlers go out of scope when

   a. Program flow exits the procedure containing the error handler.

   b. Never, if you declare a global handler.

   c. The form in which the handler is declared is unloaded.

   d. You receive the message `On Error GoTo -1`.

Exercise 2

Complexity: Easy

1. Write a program that uses the Visual Basic `err` object to raise user defined errors 1 and 2.

Complexity: Moderate

2. Modify the above program to use an error handler in a command button click event that issues a `Resume Next` statement if error 1 occurs. The line of code that follows the raise error method should display a message box that states the code was executed. If error 2 occurs, jump to a label called `exit_command` and exit the subroutine.

LESSON 3

The Noble Art of Debugging

You've written your program and it works. Okay, it works most of the time. Or worse yet, it doesn't work most of the time, even though you know the code is perfect. What to do?

Now comes the part of programming that separates the programmers from the dabblers: the noble (and sometimes not so noble) art of debugging. It is a form of puzzle solving that explains why programmers are known to stay up all night and consume anything at all that contains caffeine.

What's All This Business About a Bug, Anyhow?

The story goes that one of the earliest computers—built with electromagnetic switches called *relays* in the days before transistors—failed one day. The technicians labored until they found the cause: A moth had become trapped between a pair of relay contacts. Since that day, any failure in computer hardware or software is called a *bug*. There is some debate about the veracity of the story, although the grand dame of computing, Admiral Grace Hopper, swears it is true, and if you search the Internet, you can find a picture of the moth.

The Visual Basic 6 Debugging Tools

Visual Basic 6 has a wealth of tools to help us debug and test our programs. You'll learn how to use them in this lesson. Open the View menu and select Toolbars. From the Toolbars popup menu, select Debug. The Debug toolbar appears, as shown in Figure 10.6.

FIGURE 10.6

The Debug toolbar.

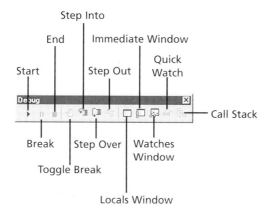

> **Note**
>
> You can quickly open any of the toolbars by right-clicking any other toolbar or on the menu bar. A popup window offers you access to all the available toolbars.

Let's take a quick look at each of the items on the Debug toolbar and then try a few exercises to practice using them.

Start

The first three buttons are called VCR buttons because they look and behave exactly like the buttons on your VCR. The first button is the Start button, which starts executing (that is, running) your program.

Break

The second button is the Break button. It acts like the pause button on a VCR. The program stops running when you click it. You can view and work in the Immediate window, the Code window, and all the other Visual Basic windows while your program is paused. The Break button is also a good way to get out of an infinite loop condition. You can also break your program by pressing Ctrl+Break, which is helpful if you don't have the Debug toolbar open.

While your program is in Break mode, the Start button becomes a Continue button that you can use to restart the program.

End

The End button stops the running program. In VCR terms, it is a stop and rewind button, because you cannot pick up where you left off after you click End.

Set Breakpoints

Now you are getting to the real goodies! A *breakpoint* is a line in the code where the program automatically goes into Break mode. That means that if you are having problems, you can run your program to a given point, then stop it, and check and even change the values of your variables. It is a great way to watch the progress of a program as it executes.

To set a breakpoint, put your cursor on the line where you want to stop the program, and click the Set Breakpoint button, or press F9. To clear a single breakpoint, put the cursor on the line containing the breakpoint and click Set Breakpoint or press F9. On the Debug menu is an item that enables you to clear all your breakpoints at the same time.

Baby Steps

When your program has hit a breakpoint, the fun really begins. Now you can make the program continue for a single step at a time or for a whole group of steps. There are four step commands, shown in Table 10.2.

TABLE 10.2   The Step Commands

Command	Action	Shortcut
Step Into	Single-steps: Each time you click Step Into, the program executes a single line of code and stops again. It is a wonderful way to watch the flow of a program, one step at a time. Between steps, you can check the values of the variables in the program, and even change them.	F8

Command	Action	Shortcut
Step Over	A great convenience when the program branches to a procedure or to a function that you already know works. Rather than single stepping your way through the procedure, you click Step Over. The program branches to the procedure, carries out the instructions there, and returns to the next line. It is especially nice when the procedure contains a lengthy For...Next loop. If the current line of the program is not a function or procedure call, Step Over acts the same as Step Into.	Shift+F8
Step Out	Handy if you happen to forget to use Step Over or if you have seen all the execution necessary in a function. When you click Step Out, the program completes execution of all the code in the current function and stops at the line following the function call.	None
Run to Cursor	Lets you skip through part of your code. Imagine, for example, that you need to see what is happening in a function that also contains a lengthy For...Next loop. Single stepping through the loop takes forever and accomplishes nothing. After you almost run through the loop have once, put your cursor on the line after the loop and click Run To Cursor. The program completes the loop and stops where the cursor is waiting.	None

Watch This

Now that you have all these ways to stop your program, single step through your program, and skip over parts of your program, what good is it all? Just what can you do with it? Simply put, you can use the rest of your debugging features to test and validate your program's operation. You can watch what is happening through several windows that Visual Basic makes available to you.

It's time to put your knowledge of the Debug tools to work. Create a new directory called Debug Demo, then open a new project in Visual Basic or load debugging.vbp from the CD that comes with this book. The components of the project are described in Table 10.3.

TABLE 10.3 Controls for the debugging.vbp Project

Control	Property	Value
Form	Name	frmDebug
	Caption	Debug Demo
Label	AutoSize	True
	Caption	X
Label	Autosize	True
	Caption	Y
Label	AutoSize	True
	Caption	Y
Label	AutoSize	True
	Caption	Select Operation
OptionButton	Name	optOperation
	Caption	&Add X + Y
	Index	0
	Value	True
OptionButton	Name	optOperation
	Caption	&Subtract X - Y
	Index	1
OptionButton	Name	optOperation
	Caption	&Multiply X * Y
	Index	2
OptionButton	Name	optOperation
	Caption	&Divide X/Y
	Index	3

Control	Property	Value
OptionButton	Name	optOperation
	Caption	&Raise X ^ Y
	Index	4
OptionButton	Name	optOperation
	Caption	Yth Roo&t of X
	Index	5
CommandButton	Name	cmdCalculate
	Caption	&Calculate
CommandButton	Name	cmdQuit
	Caption	E&xit

10

Arrange the controls as shown in Figure 10.7.

FIGURE 10.7

The Debug Demo project.

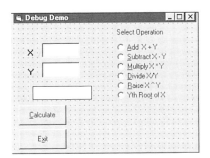

Listing 10.3 shows the code for this project.

LISTING 10.3   The Debug Demo Project

```
Private Sub subAdd()

lblAnswer = txtOpX + txtOpY

End Sub

Private Sub subDivide()

lblAnswer = txtOpX / txtOpY

End Sub
```

continues

LISTING 10.3   continued

```
Private Sub subMultiply()

lblAnswer = txtOpX * txtOpY

End Sub

Private Sub subSubtract()

lblAnswer = txtOpX - txtOpY

End Sub

Private Sub cmdCalculate_Click()

Select Case iOperation
  Case 0: subAdd
  Case 1: subSubtract
  Case 2: subMultiply
  Case 3: subDivide
  Case 4: subRaise
  Case 5: subRoot
End Select

End Sub

Private Sub cmdQuit_Click()

Unload Me
End

End Sub

Private Sub optOperation_Click(Index As Integer)

iOperation = Index

End Sub

Private Sub txtOpX_GotFocus()

txtOpX.SelStart = 0
txtOpX.SelLength = Len(txtOpX)

End Sub

Private Sub subRoot()
```

```
        lblAnswer = dOpX ^ (1 / dOpY)

End Sub


Private Sub subRaise()

Dim iCounter As Integer
Dim dCumulator As Double
dCumulator = 1
For iCounter = 1 To dOpY
    dCumulator = dOpX * dCumulator
Next iCounter
lblAnswer = dCumulator

End Sub

Private Sub txtOpY_GotFocus()

txtOpY.SelStart = 0
txtOpY.SelLength = Len(txtOpY)

End Sub
```

You should be aware that there is at least one serious flaw in this code (this is a debugging lesson!). The flaw is a logic error, and one that causes some consternation. Take a brief look at the code so you can get an idea of what is happening before you explore the debugging process.

What It Does

The program is a crude calculator. It handles only two numbers at a time, without accumulation, and it lacks the sophistication of a real calculator.

Enter the operands into the text boxes, select an operation from the Option button array, and press the Calculate command button. The result appears in lblAnswer.

When you click an Option button, the global variable iOperation is set to the value of the optOperation index. The Select-Case structure in cmdCalculate's Click event uses iOperation to select a procedure that performs the selected operation. One of the operations has a bug in it, and the procedure for raising a number to a power uses a For...Next loop to multiply X by itself Y times when the code X^Y would have done the job in a single step. This example uses that to demonstrate the value of Step Over and Step Out.

Running and Debugging the Debug Demo Program

If you do not have the Debug toolbar showing, right-click the menu bar and select Debug now. Click the Run button to run the program. Move everything around so that you have full access to the program window, the Debug toolbar, and the Immediate window that pops up every time you run a program in the IDE. Your screen should look something like that shown in Figure 10.8.

FIGURE 10.8

The Debug Demo program ready to be tested.

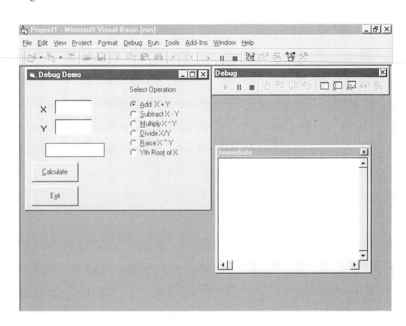

> **Tip**
>
> When you select the Debug toolbar or the Immediate window to move them, the program window may disappear. The Alt+Tab combination lets you bring it back.

Now type a 2 in the X text box and a 3 in the Y text box. The Add X + Y option is on by default, so click Calculate to perform the calculation.

What's this? 2 + 3 does not equal 23! (If you think it does, you are reading the wrong book.) It's time for some debugging, but first check out the other operations, just to evaluate how wide ranging the debugging process needs to be. Select each of the other operations in turn and click cmdCalculate after each one. Hmmm, they seem to be working okay. But what is the bug in the addition routine?

Click Break. The program window disappears, but don't worry about that. It is typical behavior, and you don't need it for the moment. You need the Immediate window.

The Immediate Window

The Immediate window shows up every time you run your program from the IDE. You've been using it all along to receive information from your programs to help you in debugging. It is the window that gets the results from a `Debug.Print` operation. What you may not know is that you can also type commands into it while your program is in Break mode. You can use the Immediate window to check the values of your variables or even to change them.

Select the Immediate window now by clicking the window. To check your values, enter `?` `txtOpX` and press Enter. Okay, it shows you the 2 that you know is in there, so the X value has not changed. Try the Y value by entering `? txtOptY` and pressing `Enter`. Well, it seems to be okay, too. Try `? txtOpX + txtOpY`. Darn! There's that 23 again! Try `? txtOpY + txtOpX`. Interesting: Now the answer is 32. Change one of the variables. Type `txtOpX = 3` in the Edit window and press Enter. Now move your cursor back to the line `? txtOpX + txtOpY` and press Enter again. This time you get 33! There's a clue here somewhere. See if you can figure it out before you read the next paragraph.

Note

> To quickly and easily view values of variables during Break mode, don't forget about the Visual Basic 6.0 Auto Data Tips. Auto Data Tips, discussed in Lesson 1, show you the current value of a variable in Break mode when you simply hold the mouse pointer over the variable.

Yep! You got it! The operands in the expression are strings, not numbers, and the plus sign concatenates the strings. Visual Basic is clever enough with all the other operations to convert the strings into numbers, because there is no way to subtract or multiply strings. But when the arguments are strings, the plus sign performs concatenation, just like the ampersand does. Fixing this is going to take some serious work!

Click the Stop button and bring up the Code window. In the Declarations section of General, add the following line to create some numeric variables to use:

```
Public dOpX As Double, dOpY As Double
```

Now the program must convert the string values of `txtOpX` and `txtOpY` into doubles and replace every instance of `txtOpX` and `txtOpY` that involves a calculation with `dOpX` and `dOpY`. The process is simple enough, but tedious. After you read through the description of how to do this in your own projects, the example shows you a shortcut for this project. Under the Edit menu, select Replace, or press Ctrl+H to bring up the Replace window. The Replace window is shown in Figure 10.9.

FIGURE 10.9

The Replace window.

Enter txtOpX in the Find What box and dOpX in the Replace With box, then click Find Next. (Do not click Replace All! That really makes you have to work hard!) Replace each instance of txtOpX where it is used in a calculation with dOpX. When the Replace routine gets to the Click event of txtOpX, click Find Next to skip each instance of txtOpX in that procedure. Repeat the same process to replace txtOpY with dOpY for the calculations.

Now go to the Click event for cmdCalculate and add the following code just before the Select statement:

```
dOpX = Val(txtOpX)
dOpY = Val(txtOpY)
```

That wasn't all that bad, was it? Now for the shortcut. If you do not want to make the changes by hand, open the Project menu and select Remove frmDebug.frm. Open the Project menu again and select Add File. Find the file frmDebug2.frm on the CD that came with the book and add it to your project. Open the Project menu again. Select Project 1 Properties and change the Startup Object to frmDebug2.

All done. Run the program again and try the same two numbers. This time 3 + 2 really does equal 5. Much better. Now, back to the debugging tools. You've seen how to use the Immediate window to check a variable's value, but there is another, more automatic way. You can set up watches to keep an eye on your variables for you!

The Watch Window

The Watch window shows you the value of your program variables. Stop your program and click the Watch Window icon on the Debug toolbar or select it on the Debug menu. Close the Immediate window for now so the screen doesn't get too cluttered, and drag and size the Watch window so it is out of the way of your program.

Now select Add Watch and type d0pY in the Expression box and select All Procedures in the Context frame. Click OK and the variable is added to your Watch window. Figure 10.10 shows how it looks.

FIGURE **10.10**

Adding a variable to the Watch window.

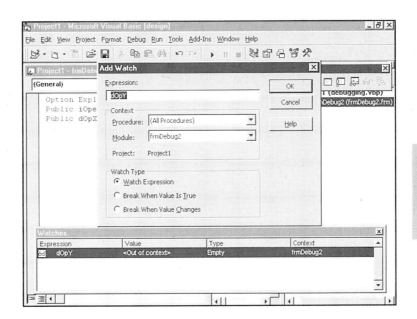

Add d0pY to the Watch window, too, and click Run to start the program. Enter some numbers and do a calculation. Nothing happened? Yep, that's the way it works. Click Break. There are the watches, plain as day.

Now add some power to the watch. Put your mouse pointer on d0pY and right-click. Select Edit Watch from the popup that appears. In the Edit Watch window, click Break When Value Changes, then click OK. Now press F5 to continue your program, and enter 22 for X and 66 for Y. Select the Raise X ^ Y option this time and then click Calculate.

What happened? The Watch Manager noticed the change in d0pY and the program entered Break mode.

While you are in Break mode, take a moment to explore some of the other debugging features.

Quick Watch

You are not watching the variable iOperation, but you may be curious about its value just the same. Click the variable name and then click Quick Watch on the Debug toolbar. The Quick Watch window shown in Figure 10.11 comes up.

FIGURE **10.11**

*The Quick Watch
window.*

Pretty slick! But Visual Basic 6 is even slicker than that. Close the Quick Watch window, and just hold the mouse pointer over the variable name dOpY for a second. There is the value right before your eyes! Now it's time to explore the single-step operation.

Single step through the program by pressing F8 repeatedly. Each time you press F8, Visual Basic executes the next command in your program. Watch it work its way through the Select-Case structure until it gets to Case 4:, when it jumps to the call to subRaise. Press F8 again and watch the program jump to the new procedure.

It is interesting to watch the For...Next loop operate for a while. For that, use the Locals window.

The Locals Window

Click the Locals Window icon on the Debug toolbar. The new window covers up the Watch window, but don't worry about it, because dOpX and dOpY are not going to change. The Locals window creates a watch on all the local variables—those that are declared in the current procedure. The first item in the window even tells you what procedure you are in. The Locals window is shown in Figure 10.12.

FIGURE **10.12**

The Locals window.

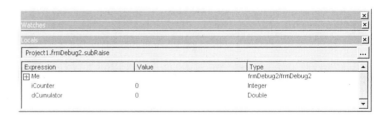

Continue pressing F8 for a while and watch the values change. The iCounter value increases by 1 each time, while dCumulator increases exponentially. Remember, though, that dOpY = 66. You probably don't want to sit there pressing F8 for 66 times—it would get terribly boring. In a moment you will see the quick way out, but first, you need a brief side trip.

> **Tip**
>
> A simple way to view the contents of a variable is to hold the mouse pointer over the variable while in Break mode. The current value of the variable will be displayed below the mouse pointer.

Don't Blow Your Stack!

Sometimes you find yourself single-stepped into a procedure without really being sure of how you got there. Never fear, Visual Basic can even tell you that. Click Call Stack and watch what happens. Figure 10.13 shows the Call Stack window. It lists the current procedure on top, followed by the calling routines. In this simple demo program, there is only a single calling routine; in more complex programs, the stack might contain several other procedures or functions.

FIGURE 10.13

The Call Stack window.

Now for the quick escape from the 66-step loop. Click the Step Out icon on the Debug toolbar. Visual Basic completes the loop and returns you to the `End Select` statement back in the `cmdCalculate_Click` procedure.

Here is one more demonstration before you finish. Change the number in `txtOpY` again and click the Calculate button. Single step to the call to `subRaise`, but do not press F8 to branch to that procedure. Instead, click the Step Over icon on the Debug toolbar. Program flow drops to the `End Select` statement. Click Continue and note that the calculation has been done. Visual Basic ran the `subRaise` procedure without stopping there.

But Wait—There's More!

Click Break and open the Watch window if it is not visible. Select the first item in the Watch window by clicking the Eyeglass icon next to the variable name. Remove the item from the Watch window by pressing Delete. Delete all items in the Watch window in the same way, and close the Watch window.

Now place your cursor on the statement `Select Case iOperation` and click Toggle Breakpoint on the Debug toolbar. Note what happens in the Code window.

Click Continue (or press F5). When the program's screen comes back up, click Calculate. The program enters Break mode on the line where you inserted the breakpoint. Now move the cursor to the End Select statement. Open the Debug menu and click Run To Cursor. The program runs through all the steps before that line and enters Break mode again. Click Continue to complete the operation.

Enter new values for both X and Y. Pick a different operation if you want, and click Calculate again. When the program hits the breakpoint, place your cursor on End Select and click Set Next Statement on the Debug menu. The current statement marker jumps to the End Select statement. Click Continue and note that the program skipped all the steps between Select Case iOperation and End Select and the calculation did not get done.

The Set Next statement is a convenient way to skip over statements that you do not want to execute. It may seem frivolous to you at the moment, but it will become invaluable as you gain more programming practice.

When you close the project, do not save the changes you have made. The project is used again later in this chapter, and you want the old, defective version.

Debug Object Revisited

In previous chapters, you have used the Debug object and the Print method to display variable values and track your application's progress. As a refresher, the Debug object is used to print messages to the Debug window. The Debug statements you embed in your code are ignored when an executable is created. One other useful Debug object method that can be used to help you debug your applications is the Assert method. The Assert method enables you to test an assumption you have made in your code; if the assumption is incorrect, your program will enter Break mode. For example, the following code is an example of using the Assert method:

```
Debug.Assert strName = " Interactive Course"
```

In the code example, if the variable strName does not equal the string "Interactive Course", your program will enter Break mode. The Assert method causes your program to enter Break mode when the assertion is false.

Lesson Summary

Visual Basic provides a useful debugging environment for testing and debugging your application and the variables you are using in your application. Using the Visual Basic debugging environment, you can easily set breakpoints, step through programs, and view variables.

Quiz 3

1. A _____ is a spot in the code where the program automatically goes into Break mode.

   a. Stop line

   b. Breakpoint

   c. Break line

   d. Stop over

2. The _____ creates a watch on all local variables.

   a. Watch Window

   b. Immediate Window

   c. Locals Window

   d. Variable Window

3. During a debug session, while in Break mode, you can use the _____ to change values of variables.

   a. Immediate Window

   b. BreakPoint

   c. Quick Watch

   d. All the above

4. To skip over a portion of code in the current procedure, use

   a. Run to Cursor

   b. Step Into

   c. Step Out

   d. Step Over

Exercise 3

Complexity: Moderate

1. Use the single-step `Debug` command to start the project Debug Demo, and single step through the entire application, including closing the form.

Complexity: Easy

2. List three ways to view the value of a variable during Break mode.

LESSON 4

Debugger Limitations

Bugs in the Debugger? Not really, but there are some things that will surprise you if you are not aware of them. For example, imagine that you are building a mission-critical application, and you think you have it working. Before you ship it out the door, you decide to walk through the application using the debugger one last time.

After several hours of testing, you click a button and nothing happens. What's going on? An event procedure should have been fired! You end the debug session and click the button to make sure the code is still there; it is. You try again with the debugger and the same thing happens. What's going on? A few hours and a call to tech support later, you learn that there is nothing wrong with your code; an event was lost while in Debug mode! Visual Basic is an event-driven programming environment and, in some instances, using the debugger and Break mode can alter the way your application behaves, causing lost events, timing problems, or lost Windows messages.

There are not many cases where the debugger changes behavior, but you need to be aware of them. Take a look.

KeyDown

Load `debugging.vbp` again if you closed it between lessons. Add the code `Debug.Print "Keydown Event Fired"` in the `txtOpX` KeyDown event, and add the code `Debug.Print "KeyUp Event Fired"` to the `txtOpX` KeyUp event.

Run the program and enter a few characters in the `txtOpX` text box. As you might expect, the two phrases appear in the Immediate window for each keystroke.

Now break the program and put a breakpoint on the line `Debug.Print "Keydown Event Fired."` Run the program again and watch what happens. For one thing, the `KeyUp` event is never fired. Because of the break in `KeyDown`, the computer's `KeyUp` event takes place outside the program. As a result, the text box's `KeyUp` event is not fired. Another event that is skipped is the `KeyPress` event, which normally would have followed the `KeyDown` event. As a result, the keyboard character never gets placed in the text box.

If you must test something that takes place in the `KeyDown` event, use `Debug.Print` to display values rather than setting breakpoints.

MouseDown

Delete the code from `txtOpX`'s `KeyDown` and `KeyUp` events. Be sure to toggle the breakpoint off, too. Select `cmdCalculate` in the Code window. Place `Debug.Print "MouseDown fired."` in the `cmdCalculate MouseDown` event and `Debug.Print "MouseUp fired."` in the `cmdCalculate MouseUp` event.

You know what's going to happen, don't you? Run the program, enter some numbers for X and Y, and click Calculate. Just as it should, the program dutifully reports both events in the Immediate window. Place a breakpoint in the `MouseDown` event and try again with some new numbers. The break in `MouseDown` prevents all the Command button's subsequent events from being fired. Not only did the program miss the `MouseUp` event, it missed the `Click` event, too; the calculation was never performed.

Use `Debug.Print` statements to monitor changes in the `MouseDown` event.

Moving the Mouse

Putting breakpoints in `MouseMove` events won't cause any lost events; however, it makes it awfully hard to do anything with the mouse! If you put a breakpoint in a `MouseMove` event, you will constantly enter Break mode as you move the mouse pointer over the object (especially fatal in a form's `MouseMove` event). Try to avoid it, especially for controls that take up a lot of space on your form.

Expect the Unexpected

You have a powerful instrument in the Visual Basic debugging tools. You can walk through programs a step at a time or skip through (or past) several steps or whole procedures. You can break out of programs when a variable changes, or when a `Boolean` variable assumes a `True` condition, or when the program reaches a certain line. And you can dynamically display variable values in the Immediate window while the program runs full speed. A wealth of tools, indeed.

On the other hand, in some cases the debugger causes problems with event sequences and timing. If you suspect that the debugger is causing your problems (that is, missing events) use a `Debug.Print` statement to prove that the event is being fired.

Beware, too, of background events that might cause your program to change expected program flow. A `Timer` event is a classic example of something that can send your program off in an unanticipated direction during debugging.

In short, expect the unexpected while debugging. Use your knowledge of event-driven programming to help you understand why the program is behaving in such a strange way. And, as always, when in doubt, read the instructions.

Lesson Summary

It is important to remember that for the majority of your applications, you can safely use Visual Basic's debugger without worrying about its impact on the flow of your program. However, beware that in a few circumstances, using the debugger can cause lost events, such as breakpoints in the `KeyDown` and `KeyUp` events. Also, there are times when using breakpoints can be cumbersome, such as in a Form `MouseMove` event.

Quiz 4

1. If I have a breakpoint set in a `KeyDown` event and I begin to single step once in Break mode, which event will not be executed because of the breakpoint in the `KeyDown` event?

    a. `KeyUp`

    b. `Activate`

    c. `OnClick`

    d. `KeyDown`

2. Putting a `BreakPoint` in the `MoveMouse` event will _____.

    a. cause lost events

    b. make debugging difficult

    c. have no real effect, especially when used in a form or large ActiveX control

    d. None of the above

3. Which of the following events do not cause debugger problems?

    a. `MouseDown` and `MouseUp`

    b. `KeyDown` and `KeyUp`

     c. `Load` and `UnLoad`

     d. `GotFocus` and `LostFocus`

4. Use _____ to view values in executing code without halting the program in the debugger.

     a. `Print.Value`

     b. `Debug.Value`

     c. `Debug.Display`

     d. `Debug.Print`

Exercise 4

Complexity: Easy

1. Create a program that has a single for with a command button. Place `Debug.Print` code in the `MouseDown`, `MouseUp` and `click` events of the command button. Run the program and click the button. Place a breakpoint in the `MouseDown` event. Run the program again and see which events are lost.

Complexity: Easy

2. Using the same program as above, add `Debug.Print` code to the `MouseMove` event of the form. Place a breakpoint on the `Debug.Print` code in the form's `MouseMove` event. Run the program—now try to use the mouse to click the command button.

LESSON 5

Advanced Debugging Techniques

There's more? You have already learned a lot of debugging techniques in this chapter; however, this lesson looks at a few more concepts that make debugging even easier. To prepare for the lesson, load the `debugging.vbp` project again.

Fixing Code in Break Mode

As you test your projects, you often wind up in Break mode because of an error. Open the Code window for the debugging project and change the code in the `subAdd` procedure by adding an e in the variable name `txtOpX`. Make the line read `lblAnswer = textOpX + txtOpY`. Check the Declarations section, and if the line `Option Explicit` is not there, type it in.

Now run the program. Enter numbers for X and Y, select Add X + Y, and click Calculate. The program enters Break mode with a message box, as shown in Figure 10.14.

FIGURE 10.14

Variable not defined error.

Click OK to close the message box. Visual Basic opens the Code window with the procedure name highlighted and the error selected, as shown in Figure 10.15.

FIGURE 10.15

The error is selected for editing.

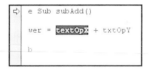

The good news is that you can edit the variable name while you are in the Break mode. There is no need to exit, edit, and restart the program. Click the letter e in the variable name and delete it, then click the Continue button or press F5 to continue the program.

You can make a lot of changes in the Edit mode, but once in a while you will make one that does not allow a simple continue. In that case, Visual Basic warns you that the program must be reset.

Getting Error Numbers and Descriptions

Back in the bad old days, when your program generated an error, it delivered a cryptic message. Often all you got was an error number. The next step was to pick up the programmers' manual and look it up, and often the message from the book was no more meaningful than the number! With Visual Basic, you get a better shot at figuring out exactly what the error means. Recall that the message box shown in Figure 10.14 offers two buttons, OK and Help. Put the error back into the subAdd procedure and run the program again. This time, click the Help button.

Pretty clear, isn't it? The last paragraph that reads: "Explicitly declare the variable, or change the spelling of the variable to match that of the intended variable," tells you exactly how to fix the problem.

You can even learn about specific errors without actually generating one in your program. In the Immediate window, type Error 10 and press Enter. Bingo! Up pops the message box for the error, along with that handy Help button. Too bad it can't find logic errors, too.

Testing Procedures and Functions

During development, you can test procedures, code segments, and functions using the debugger. From the Break mode, you can enter the name of a function or procedure in the Immediate window and press Enter to run it.

If your debugging project is not running, start it. Enter numbers for X and Y and then press Ctrl+Break to enter Break mode. Click in the Immediate window, type subMultiply, and press Enter. Use Alt+Tab to get back to the program's window and there is your answer, displayed in the proper place.

You can also type Visual Basic commands and function calls in the Immediate window. Enter the Break mode, type `MsgBox "Testing", vbOKCancel, "Gee!"` in the Immediate window, and press Enter.

Use the Immediate pane to test your own functions and procedures or to experiment with the functions and procedures that come with Visual Basic.

Conditional Compilation

You learned how to use the `Debug.Print` statement in code to help monitor applications and get information without using the debugger. A part of Visual Basic called the *compiler* converts Visual Basic source code (what you write) into executable code that the computer can read and understand. When the compiler creates an executable for the application, the `Debug` statements are ignored. When the program is run from a compiled executable, there is no Immediate window and `Debug.Print` has no effect.

Sometimes you might want to use special routines or lines of code, such as message boxes, to help provide even more information during debugging. You might also want to give your users an executable with debugging code for user testing. You cannot use `Debug.Print` statements, because they are deactivated when running from an executable. You can use conditional compilation statements.

Conditional compilation statements work similarly to Visual Basic `If...Then` blocks, except they are compiler `If...Then` blocks. The format for conditional compilation statements is:

```
# If conditional directive Then
    Visual Basic Code
# End If
```

The compiler uses the conditional directive to determine if the Visual Basic code in the
#If...#End If block is included in the running application. If the conditional directive
is True, the statement is included in the executable code. The conditional directive is a
constant defined by you in code or in a compilation flag to include or exclude the code
block. The following example:

```
#Const Debug_Flag = True

#If Debug_Flag Then
  MsgBox "Debug App"
#End If

MsgBox "Debug App
```

is included in the application. If the flag is set to False, the code is not included. Give it
a try. Place the example code in a CommandButton click event and toggle the value of the
constant Debug_Flag from True to False. Conditional compilation is a very powerful
tool that has been used by C programmers for years.

Break On...

You can control when Visual Basic enters the Break mode. Open the Tools menu and
select Options. Select the General tab. The General tab is shown in Figure 10.16.

FIGURE **10.16**

The General tab.

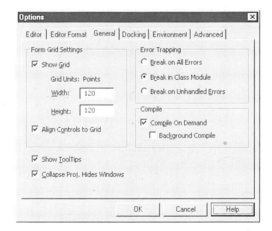

The choices are as follows:

- *Break on All Errors:* Any error causes the project to enter Break mode, whether or not an error handler is active and whether or not the code is in a class module.

- *Break in Class Module:* Any unhandled error produced in a class module causes the project to enter Break mode at the line of code in the class module that produced the error.

- *Break on Unhandled Errors:* If an error handler is active, the error is trapped without entering Break mode. If there is no active error handler, the error causes the project to enter Break mode. An unhandled error in a class module, however, causes the project to enter Break mode on the line of code that invoked the offending procedure of the class.

While you are learning, Break on All Errors is probably the safest. By now, though, Break on Unhandled Errors would be a good choice. These settings are not part of your project, but are set as a default condition that is active in all your VB projects until you change it.

Another Break On choice is available. Recall that you can select two different Break conditions in the Add Watch window:

- *Break When Value Is True:* Breaks when a variable becomes True, which can also be defined as Not Zero.

- *Break When Value Changes:* Lets you keep a check on a variable's value. If you have a variable that mysteriously seems to become something other than what you expected, this is the way to find it.

These settings are valid only for the individual Watch items. They are not persistent: When you remove the Watch, the setting is gone.

Lesson Summary

This chapter examined several advanced debugging features available in Visual Basic 6.0, for instance fixing code while in Break mode. This lesson showed how to use Visual Basic's error object, Err, to retrieve error numbers and descriptions. Several other advanced topics covered include using conditional compilation to remove debugging code from your test build to production builds, and how to use the Break On feature of Visual Basic's debugger.

Quiz 5

1. Entering the following line of code in the Immediate Window while in Break mode and pressing the Enter button causes the following to happen:

   Error 10

   a. nothing

   b. the error object property number is set to 10

   c. a message box with the error message description is displayed

   d. the program halts

2. Break On All Errors:

   a. automatically adds error handling to your compiled applications.

   b. breaks on errors where an error handler is not enabled.

   c. breaks on any error for which the code #ALLErrors is at the top of the form or module.

   d. breaks on any error that causes the project to enter Break mode regardless on the status of error handlers.

3. A Break On option is set on the variable, iCount. The program begins execution and iCount is set to 1 causing the program to enter Break mode. Which Break On option has been set?

   a. Break When Value is zero

   b. Break On All Errors

   c. Break When Value is True

   d. None of the above

4. Use _____ when you need to create executable code in different environments or to include Debug statements in executables that can easily be removed later.

   a. Debug.Print

   b. Conditional compilation

   c. Comments

   d. Print statements

Exercise 5

Complexity: Easy

1. Write a program that sets an integer value to some number and multiplies that number by another number. Use the debugger and the Watch options Break When Value Changes and Break When Value Is True to cause the program to enter Debug mode when the value of one of the integer values changes or is set to a number greater then 0.

Complexity: Moderate

2. In the previous program add an error handler, and use conditional compilation to enable and disable the error handler code.

LESSON 6

Writing Code That Is Easy to Maintain

In Lesson 4, you learned how to solve problems by using the debugging tools and about some of the problems the debugging tools introduce into the debugging process. This lesson looks at a different kind of debugging problem. Not problems caused by the debugging tools, but problems caused by bad coding techniques. (We are not talking about you; after all, you have perfect coding techniques.)

Coding is a lot like maintaining a tool shed or a garage. Everyone knows somebody who has an immaculate garage. The floor is clean and everything is either hung on pegboards or neatly stowed in a toolbox or drawer. If you want to find a bolt or a hammer or a saw—no problem! Then there is the other garage. You know, the one most of us own. The tools are there, all right; scattered on the floor, dropped behind a cabinet, thrown in heaps, and haphazardly stowed wherever it was convenient when they were last used. Find a hammer? Not in your lifetime! You get the point. Writing well-organized code makes maintaining and debugging code easier, such as finding tools in a well-organized garage.

One of the main benefits of object-oriented programming is the organization of code into classes so that everything that affects a specific piece of data is all in the same place. To appreciate the benefits of well-organized code, it will be helpful to see an example of really bad coding technique.

Spaghetti Code

Before Visual Basic, programmers used languages such as C, FORTRAN, COBOL, and assembly language. (They are all still in use, and they all have their place and purpose. Try not to get involved in the "religious wars" over which is the best programming language.) In all these languages, programmers have to write many lines of code to accomplish tasks that a Visual Basic programmer does easily. In fact, just creating a simple form, something Visual Basic programmers don't even have to do, takes a few hundred lines of carefully crafted code.

With all that code to write, some programmers fell into the habit of writing inline code instead of using more structured programming. It is not unusual to find programs so loaded with branching and conditional branching statements that it is impossible to follow the program flow. No, the programmers were not taught to do that, but they fell into the habit and it was hard to break. It was also hard to maintain that code.

You can read about coding problems in the news. The year 2000 problem is made worse by this kind of coding technique. A recent news item described a team of programmers who were searching through more than 25,000 lines of code looking for references to dates. To make it worse, they reported that there were dozens of different variable names all representing dates, not including the ubiquitous names temp and tmp! Imagine how much easier it would have been if object-oriented programming had existed when the original code was written. There would have been a few classes to change—maybe only one. The job would have been done in a few hours by a single programmer.

Code such as this, that seems to have no clear beginning, no clear end, and no clear path, is called *spaghetti code*. Program flow is as clear as the path through a bowl of spaghetti.

Sadly, you can write spaghetti code in Visual Basic, too. This example gives you an idea of what NOT to do. After you have seen that, you can learn what to do.

Create a new directory called Spagh. Start a new project, also called Spagh. The project requires only a single form and a single Command button. The properties are shown in Table 10.4.

TABLE 10.4   Object and Property Settings for Project Spagh

Object	Property	Setting
Form	Caption	Debug Spaghetti
	Height	3435
	Name	frmSpagh
	Width	5070

Object	Property	Setting
CommandButton	Caption	Start
	Height	915
	Left	1185
	Name	cmdStart
	Top	885
	Width	2205

Enter the code from Listing 10.4 in the Command_Click event.

LISTING 10.4   Spaghetti Code

```
Private Sub cmdStart_Click()
Dim A As Integer, I As String, DN As Integer

GoTo I_V

S_T:
If DN > 1 Then GoTo G_N
DN = 2
GoTo I_V

T1:
If A > 5 Then GoTo I_V
Exit Sub

G_N:
Randomize
A = Int((10 * Rnd) + 1)
DN = 0
GoTo T1

I_V:
A = 0
I = "one"
DN = 2
GoTo S_T

End Sub
```

Set a breakpoint on the line GoTo Init_Var and run the program. Click the Start button and then press F8 repeatedly until you finally exit from the procedure. Wasn't that fun? Were you able to follow the sequence of steps? The application jumps around the code until variable A contains an integer greater than 5. The variable is set using Visual Basic's random number generator, Rnd.

This application is a very brief and simple example of code that is hard to maintain. There are no comments, the variable names are meaningless, the logic is poor, and the organization is worse. Imagine a program such as HyperPad written in code such as this! Decide to make one change and you have a lifetime career.

Writing Clear and Maintainable Code

It doesn't have to be that way. You can write code that you or any other programmer can modify and maintain with minimum effort. The following hints and tips make your code look professional and your programming life a lot easier:

- *Find a naming convention and stick with it.* Use a convention that tells you the type of object represented by a variable name. For example, start all form names with the three-letter code frm. Start all text box names with the three-letter code txt and Command buttons with cmd. There is a long list of naming conventions in the VB Books On Line file that comes on the CD with Visual Basic 6. Use that or devise your own, but be consistent.

- *Use meaningful names for variables.* For example, you have little trouble deciding what curCar_Payment represents. Compare that with something such as CP, which might represent the same thing, or perhaps it means current price, or perhaps, well, who knows what it means?

- *Comment your code! Comment your code! Comment your code!* Comments make it easier for you and others to maintain your code. You may find yourself making changes to code you wrote over a year ago. What is perfectly clear when you write it can become obscure over a period of time.

- *Organize your code into classes, procedures, and functions.* If the functions and procedures become too long, consider breaking them into smaller functions and procedures. Consider placing your procedures and functions in separate code modules, just as classes are in class modules. Even then, organize: Put collections of procedures and functions that deal with financial calculations in one code module, those that handle strings in another.

- *Avoid GoTo as much as possible.* When you must use it, in error handlers, for example, make the GoTo label names meaningful. Don't even consider using numbers as GoTo labels.

- *Use space to separate your code into logical groupings.* For example, separate all of a For...Next loop from the other code in a procedure so you can see where it begins and ends. Most programmers like to use indentation to group their code. That is usually a good technique if the code lines aren't too long and there aren't too many levels of indentation. In fact, it is our preferred grouping method. The code in this book is grouped using blank lines because of typesetting considerations.

Now it's time to rewrite the Spagh program, this time using good coding techniques. Create a directory named GoodCode and start a project with the same name. Table 10.5 lists the objects in the project.

TABLE 10.5 Object and Property Settings for Project GoodCode

Object	Property	Setting
Form	Caption	-Spaghetti Code Redone—Good Coding Techniques
	Height	3435
	Name	frmGood
	Width	5070
CommandButton	Caption	Start
	Height	915
	Left	1185
	Name	cmdStart
	Top	885
	Width	2205

The code for GoodCode.vbp is in Listing 10.5.

LISTING 10.5 The Code for the GoodCode Project

```
Private Sub cmdStart_Click()

Dim iRandom_Value As Integer
'Initialize variables
iRandom_Value = 10

'Repeat until we generate a value less then or equal
'to five.

While iRandom_Value > 5
```

continues

LISTING 10.5 continued

```
'Call function GetNew
iRandom_Value = GetNew
Wend

End Sub

Public Function GetNew() As Integer

'Generate a random number
Randomize
GetNew = Int((10 * Rnd) + 1)

End Function
```

Compare the code in GoodCode to the code from the Spagh project. Notice the good code follows many of the items listed in writing clear and maintainable code, such as variable naming standards, meaningful variable names, and good code organization (not to mention comments in the code!). Which would you rather meet in a dark alley?

Lesson Summary

This lesson examined a very important aspect of writing professional Visual Basic programs—code that is easy to read and maintain. To help make this topic clear to the reader, a program was written in a very bad coding style. The program was then rewritten following several rules to make reading and maintaining the code easier, for instance variable naming standards and avoiding the GoTo statement.

Quiz 6

1. _____ code is a nickname for hard-to-maintain, unorganized code.

   a. Spaghetti

   b. Noodle

   c. Good

   d. Excellent

2. Writing easy-to-maintain code means taking advantage of Visual Basic's _____ features.

   a. Procedure

   b. Forms

    c. Object-oriented

    d. Function

3. _____ your code to make it more readable and easier to maintain.

    a. Save

    b. Comment

    c. Uncomment

    d. Debug

4. Avoid using the following statement except with error handlers:

    a. `GoTo`

    b. `Jump`

    c. `BPT`

    d. `Stop`

10

Exercise 6

Complexity: Easy

1. What would be good names for the following variables?

    User name (`datatype` string)

    Address (ActiveX Control text box)

    Function to compute an employee's salary

Complexity: Moderate

2. Design a code header made up of Visual Basic comments that could be used in your routines to describe what the routine does, as well as parameters used.

Chapter Summary

In this chapter you learned about one of the most valuable tools to a Visual Basic programmer: the debugger. Understanding and learning how to use the debugger successfully will make you a top-notch programmer. You also learned about the different types of errors that can occur, as well as how to write error handlers to trap and handle program errors in an orderly fashion. The main points of this chapter are as follows:

- Syntax errors are caused by code the compiler does not understand and cannot run and compile.

- Runtime errors occur while the programming is executing and will cause your program to invoke an error handler.
- Logic errors do not invoke an error handler but produce erroneous results.
- Visual Basic's Auto Syntax Check looks for invalid Visual Basic syntax during design time.
- Visual Basic's Auto List Members helps you code by displaying valid methods and properties of the objects being used.
- Visual Basic's Auto Quick Info provides a popup box that displays the correct syntax for any function you use in your code.
- While in Break mode, hold the mouse pointer over a variable to display the current value of the variable. This feature is known as Auto Data Tips.
- `Err` object is the Visual Basic built-in error object. Use `Err` to retrieve the number of the error that occurred as well as display the associated error message.
- To trap errors in Visual Basic, use the `On Error Goto` statement.
- To return control back to the program after an error has occurred, use the `Resume` statement. With Resume you can issue the line that caused the error, resume at the line of code after the line that caused the error or, resume to a specific label.
- Visual Basic provides the developer with many easy to use and advanced debugging tools. Learn how to use the debugger!
- Programmers should always practice good coding techniques and methods. Always comment your code and use object-oriented design methodologies if possible.

Now that you know how to handle errors, you can go back and add error handlers to your code. Practice using the debugger in the remaining sections of this book. Not only will you become more familiar with the Visual Basic debugging environment, but you will also become more familiar with what is going on behind the scenes with events, functions, and procedures.

Chapter 11, "Adding Pizazz with Graphics," looks at some of the graphics capabilities of Visual Basic 6.

CHAPTER 11

Adding Pizazz with Graphics

What is the first thing that comes to mind when you think about graphics? Drawing shapes like circles, lines, or squares? Or do you think of a computer animation application, or perhaps a picture displayed in an application? In this chapter, you learn how to use graphics in Visual Basic to draw shapes and display pictures. You will develop a simple drawing application and create an application that performs animation. You learn how to include pictures in your applications, add shapes at design time, and create graphics at runtime, using Visual Basic code and methods. But first, here is a discussion of coordinates.

LESSON 1

Understanding Coordinates

Sitting at the heart of all of the VB 6 visual elements (forms, controls, and so on) is something called a coordinate system. The first thing to understand is what it is and why it's there at all.

Start by drawing a picture of a house on a piece of paper. Make it a simple line drawing, a standard house, with a roof, chimney, four windows, and a door. You'll probably draw something like Figure 11.1.

FIGURE 11.1

Line drawing of a house.

You thought that was easy. The truth is that you just performed a very complex task. Try doing it again, but this time, write a program in Visual Basic to draw the house rather than using a pencil and paper. Not as easy a task after all, is it?

What made the task appear simple at first was that you made some very important assumptions before you carried it out. One of those assumptions was how big a piece of paper you were going to use. You assumed that you would use a small piece of paper in relation to the real size of the object, for example. It wouldn't have made sense to use a house-size piece of paper! That meant you had to use some sort of scale to which your drawing would adhere. Again, it wouldn't have made sense to draw two different windows to different scales. You could have ended up with something that looks like Figure 11.2.

Another thing you assumed was how big your drawing was going to be in relation to the size of the paper you were using. After all, if you made it too big, half of your drawing would have ended up on the table and not on the paper at all. Similarly, if you made it too small, the picture would look out of proportion to the piece of paper on which it was drawn.

One final assumption you made was which way was up, down, left, and right, as shown in Figure 11.3. This is pretty useful when drawing a house, particularly if you're going to give your drawing to a builder and tell him or her to build it for you.

FIGURE 11.2

Effect of incorrect scaling.

Now you're beginning to understand why a coordinate system is needed.

Your Computer's Screen and the Screen Object

The place to start understanding Visual Basic's coordinate system is your computer's screen itself. Your computer's screen is made up of a large grid of very small dots. Each dot is called a *pixel* (taken from the words *picture element*). Just how many pixels there are physically across and down your computer's screen depends on the hardware in your computer. There are a number of different resolutions available, anything from 640 pixels across and 480 down, to 1280 across and 1024 down. There are even higher resolutions available at a price.

You can find out about your computer's screen characteristics by using Visual Basic's built-in Screen object. You learned in Chapter 7, "Building Classes: The Foundation of Visual Basic OOP," about some objects that Visual Basic provides by default. One example is the Printer object. The Screen object is another, which represents your computer's physical screen.

You can use the Screen object to find out the resolution of your computer's screen by querying the Screen object's Width and Height properties. For instance, you could set

11

the width and height of a form to half the width and height of the screen with the following code:

```
Private Sub Form_Load ()
Form1.Width = Screen.Width / 2
Form1.Height = Screen.Height / 2
End Sub
```

FIGURE 11.3

It's important to know which way is up!

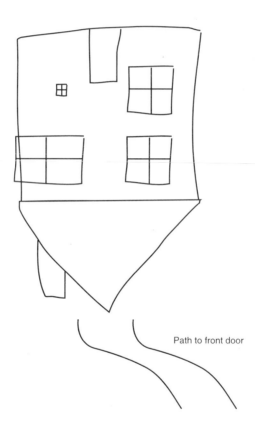

Path to front door

You can use the information to position the form in the same relative position on the screen, again independent of the physical size of the screen. The following code centers a form on a screen:

```
Private Sub Form_Load ()
    Form1.Width = Screen.Width / 2
    Form1.Height = Screen.Height / 2
    Form1.Top = (Screen.Height - Form1.Height) / 2
    Form1.Left = (Screen.Width - Form1.Width) / 2
End Sub
```

You could actually do this in one statement using the form's `Move` method, but the previous "broken down" version helps to explain the concept of coordinates.

Device-Independent Measurement

Knowing and being able to use information about the physical size of the screen is only part of the picture, however. What you really need is a measurement system that is fully device independent. In other words, you need a way to tell how big an inch is regardless of the physical size of the screen.

Luckily, Visual Basic comes to the rescue with the *twip*. That's not a typo. A twip is a unit of measurement that is approximately a 567th of a centimeter (or a 1440th of an inch, depending on how old you are!). The name comes from typesetting terms; it means a twentieth of a point. In typography, there are 72 points in an inch. You may already be familiar with the term point. It is common in computers. The print on your screen is probably 10 points high. A twip is a tiny unit of measurement, much smaller than one pixel on your screen. But, because it is a device-independent measurement, it has the same size regardless of whether your screen has 640 pixels across or 1,280.

To see twips in action, size a form to be two inches square:

```
Private Sub Form_Load ()
    Form1.Width = 2880    '440 twips per inch
    Form1.Height = 2880 'regardless of physical size of screen
End Sub
```

If the number of twips per inch is always the same regardless of the screen resolution, this must mean that the number of twips per pixel changes with different screen resolutions. After all, two inches requires a different number of pixels in different screen resolutions. This information is available, again, through the `Screen` object. You can use the `TwipsPerPixelX` and `Y` properties to determine just how many twips one physical screen pixel represents.

```
Private Sub Form_Load
    Debug.Print Screen.TwipsPerPixelX
    Debug.Print Screen.TwipsPerPixelY
End Sub
```

`TwipsPerPixelX` gives the number of twips per pixel across the screen, whereas `TwipsPerPixelY` gives the number per pixel down the screen.

Screen Origin

Remember we said it is important to know which way is up, down, left, and right. Well, Visual Basic enables you to determine the direction and distance on a form by placing the origin of the x and y-axes (the points where x and y are both zero) at the top-left corner of the form. So assume you want to draw a line from the top-left corner diagonally down the screen so that the end point is one inch to the right and two inches down the form. You could simply write

```
Form1.Line (0,0) - (1440, 2880)
```

The coordinates that are given (0,0) and (1440,2880) are scaled in *twips*. The first number within each set of parentheses is the *x* position (the horizontal axis), and the second relates to the *y* position (the vertical axis). Therefore, the start position of the line (0,0) relates to the top-left corner of the form, while the end position of the line (1440,2880) relates to a point one inch to the right on the x-axis and two inches down on the y axis. The Line method draws a line between these two points, as shown in Figure 11.4. To display the line, place this statement in the Click event subroutine for Form1, and then click the mouse button on the form.

FIGURE 11.4

Using coordinates to draw a line.

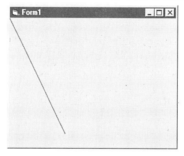

Using Other Coordinate Systems

Using twips is all well and good, but it gets rather tedious converting all of your measurements to and from the actual scale you want. Here's how to get Visual Basic to do some of the work.

One of the properties of a form (ignored up to now) is the ScaleMode property. If you look at its possible values, you find that you can set the scaling to inches, centimeters, and millimeters, as well as to some other types of ScaleModes, as shown in Table 11.1.

TABLE 11.1 ScaleMode Property Settings

Value	Description
0	User defined
1	Twip
2	Point

Value	Description
3	Pixel
4	Character
5	Inch
6	Millimeter
7	Centimeter

Try setting the ScaleMode for Form1 to inches, but don't forget that you are only changing the ScaleMode for this one form, not for all of the forms in your project. Tell Visual Basic to draw a line as before. Because you're now using inches as your ScaleMode, you don't have to convert inches to twips. So the Line method now reads

```
Form1.Line (0, 0) - (1, 2)
```

That's much simpler!

The user-defined ScaleMode property (value 0) enables you to define your own coordinate system. You can set the ScaleMode property to 0 and then create your own coordinate system by setting the ScaleWidth, ScaleHeight, ScaleLeft, and ScaleTop properties.

Spend a little time experimenting with the other ScaleModes. You may find them useful in your own graphics programs.

Lesson Summary

In this lesson the Visual Basic Screen object was introduced. Using the Screen object you can determine the characteristics of the screen your application is running on. For example, you can use the Screen object in the Load event of a form to center the form on a user's screen regardless of the computer's screen resolution. Visual Basic's default unit of device-independent measurement is called a twip. There are approximately 1440 twips per inch or 567 twips per centimeter. You can change the different coordinate systems of a form, say from twips to centimeters, by using the ScaleMode property.

Quiz 1

1. A pixel is

   a. the default Visual Basic ScaleMode

   b. a dot on the computer screen

   c. 1440th of an inch

   d. a method of the `Form` object

2. In order to find out information about your computer's display (monitor), use the Visual Basic _____ object.

   a. `Screen`

   b. `Monitor`

   c. `Display`

   d. `CRT`

3. The default Visual Basic `ScaleMode` is

   a. Inches

   b. Millimeters

   c. Twips

   d. Pixel

4. The code

```
Form1.Line (0,0) - (1440, 2880)
```

   a. Draws a line starting at coordinates (0,0) to coordinates (1440,2880)

   b. Draws a dot

   c. Draws a line starting at (0,1440) to (0,2880)

   d. Draws a line starting at (1440,2880) to (0,0)

Exercise 1

Complexity: Moderate

1. In this section the code to center a form by setting individual properties was shown. Write a single line of code using the Form's `Move` method that will also center the form.

Complexity: Moderate

2. Write a program that uses the Form `Line` method to draw a line. Make it easy to toggle the `ScaleMode` property of the form so you can view the effects of changing scale.

LESSON 2

Using Graphical Controls

In the last lesson, you learned about the coordinate system. Now take a look at the simplest way to add graphical shapes to your Visual Basic program. It uses some special custom controls referred to as the graphical controls.

Graphical Controls

The graphical controls that come with Visual Basic 4, shown on the tool bar in Figure 11.5, are the following:

FIGURE **11.5**

Graphical controls.

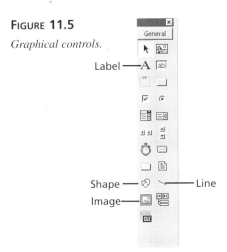

- Shape control
- Line control
- Image control
- Label control

The graphical controls enable you to create graphics at design time. Better yet, they require fewer Windows resources than the average custom control. The graphical controls are known as light controls because, unlike other custom controls, they are not true windows. The advantage of a light control is it takes up fewer system resources, but with the good news comes a few restrictions. For example, the graphical controls cannot receive focus at runtime, they cannot act as a container control, and they cannot appear on top of other controls unless they are inside a container such as a PictureBox control.

Examine each of the graphical controls except for the Image control and the Label control. You will learn more about the Image control later, and you have already made wide use of the Label control in previous applications.

Line Control

The Line control enables you to draw lines on your forms at design time. Use the Line control for special visual effects. Consider using the Line control to place borders around controls instead of using a Panel or Frame control. Try out the Line control. Start a new project with a single form. To draw a line using the Line control, perform the following steps:

1. Click the Line control on the Visual Basic toolbar shown in Figure 11.5. The mouse cursor changes into a crosshair.

2. Select a point on the form to start your line and then left-click, holding the mouse button down.

3. Drag the cursor, while holding the left mouse button down, to the line's ending point, and then release the mouse button.

Congratulations, you have just created a line, as shown in Figure 11.6. Press F4 and take a brief look at some of the properties of the Line control that you may need from time to time.

FIGURE 11.6

Creating a line using the Line control.

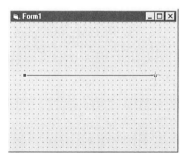

BorderStyle **Property**

Use the BorderStyle property to change the style of the line. For example, you can change the line from being solid to being dashed or dotted.

BorderWidth **Property**

Increasing the BorderWidth property increases the thickness of your line.

X1, X2, Y1, and Y2 **Properties**

The X and Y properties are (you guessed it) the coordinates for the starting and end points of your line. This comes in handy if you happen to draw the line a little cockeyed. If X1 and X2 are the same, the line is vertical; if Y1 and Y2 are the same, the line is horizontal.

You can change the X and Y properties or the BorderWidth property in your program to create animation.

Shape Control

The Shape control, shown in Figure 11.5, enables you to create the following shapes at design time:

- Oval
- Circle
- Square
- Rectangle
- Rounded rectangle
- Rounded square

Create a new project with a single form. Don't worry about saving the project because you are only adding Shape controls to a form to experiment with them. Adding a Shape control is similar to adding a Line control. When you click the Shape control, the mouse cursor changes to a crosshair. As with the Line control, place the crosshair on the form where you want the corner of the shape to begin, and then, while holding down the left mouse button, drag the cursor until you have the correct size. Then release the mouse button.

Set the following properties for your form, and add the six Shape controls. When you draw a Shape, the default shape is a rectangle. Add six Shape controls to the form. Don't worry about the size of your shapes; just make sure they all fit on the form. Set the properties for the form and for each Shape control, as shown in Table 11.2.

TABLE 11.2 Object and Property Settings for the Shape Control Demo

Object	Property	Setting
Form	Height	3480
	Name	frmShape
	Width	5295
Shape1	Shape	0 - Rectangle
Shape2	Shape	1 - Square
Shape3	Shape	2 - Oval
Shape4	Shape	3 - Circle
Shape5	Shape	4 - Rounded Rectangle
Shape6	Shape	5 - Rounded Square

Figure 11.7 shows a form similar to the one you have just created.

FIGURE 11.7

Form with each possible shape using the
Shape *control.*

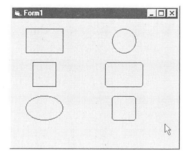

Take a look at the properties of the Shape control.

BorderWidth and BorderColor Properties

The Shape control has a BorderWidth property, similar to the Line control. It was increased on each of the shapes on the form in this project, from 1 to 3, shown in Figure 11.7, to add line thickness. Of course, the border can be drawn in any color you want.

BorderStyle Property

The BorderStyle property has the same meanings for the Shape control that it had for the Line control. The BorderWidth property affects how well BorderStyles other than solid work. For best results, use BorderWidth = 1 for BorderStyles other than solid.

Style Property

The Style property of the Shape control determines the shape of the control. It can be set to any of the six shapes displayed on the form shown in Figure 11.7.

FillStyle Property

The Shape control can be displayed as an outline, as you did in the exercise, or it can have any of eight different fill styles. Actually, you were using the transparent fill style in the exercise.

FillColor Property

If you use a FillStyle other than 1 (transparent), then the fill pattern is displayed in the FillColor. By default, that color is black, but it is easily changed.

BackStyle and BackColor Properties

The Shape control can be either transparent, which is the default, or solid. If it is solid, the color of the shape is set by the BackColor property. If the BackStyle is transparent, then the BackColor property has no effect.

DrawMode Property

The DrawMode property is used to create special effects, but its effects are rather unpredictable. Perhaps the less said about it the better! The DrawMode property affects how Visual Basic combines the Pen Color, which is the BorderColor, with the background color. The default DrawMode is Copy Pen, which ignores the background color. Even Microsoft declines to predict the results of changes in the DrawMode property. The only way to tell what happens is to experiment.

Lesson Summary

The Shape and Line controls are powerful custom controls that enable you to add graphics to your applications at design time. Using the Shape control you can create an oval, circle, square, rectangle, rounded rectangle, and rounded square. Experiment with the two controls. Try using a rounded rectangle for looks instead of a Frame control to group buttons or text boxes together. In the next lesson, you will learn how to draw shapes using coding methods instead of custom controls. Experiment also with the BackStyle and FillStyle properties of the Shape control.

Quiz 2

1. Which one of the following shapes cannot be created with the Shape control?

    a. Oval

    b. Line

    c. Circle

    d. Rounded Square

2. The BorderStyle property _____.

    a. changes the style of a line

    b. increases the thickness of a line

    c. changes the color of a line

    d. is used to create special effects

3. Which one of the following is *not* a valid property of the Shape control?

    a. ShapeColor

    b. Style

    c. DrawMode

    d. BorderStyle

4. Which one of the following is *not* considered a Visual Basic graphical control?

    a. Shape control

    b. Line control

    c. Image control

    d. PictureBox control

Exercise 2

Complexity: Easy

1. Draw a square using Line controls.

Complexity: Moderate

2. Write a program that uses a single Shape control. Add radio buttons to allow a user to select an oval, square or rectangle. Have the Shape control change to the selected shape.

LESSON 3

Using Graphical Methods

In the last lesson, you learned to use the graphical custom controls. In this lesson, you will learn how to create graphical images using Visual Basic commands called graphical methods. Use the graphical methods when the custom controls would require too much work, or the graphical effects you require cannot be done with the custom controls.

Do you remember when you got your first box of crayons or paint brush set? Well, this section is similar to that experience. You will learn how to use various methods in Visual Basic to create your own graphics and drawings. The fundamentals of drawing that you learned as a kid are similar to the fundamentals of computer drawing. To program with graphical methods requires a general understanding of the coordinate system, which was covered in Lesson 1. Then you need tools to draw with and something to draw on.

With Visual Basic, you can create graphics using graphical methods by drawing on a form, a picture box, or the Printer object. As for the drawing tools, in this lesson you will examine the following graphical methods:

- Cls
- Pset
- Line

Graphical Methods

Let's examine all the graphical methods and use them in an application.

Cls Method

The Cls method is like a chalkboard eraser. Invoking the method on a Form, PictureBox, or Image control erases all graphics or text on the form or in the control. Cls is short for *clear screen*. The syntax for the Cls method is as follows:

```
object.Cls
```

Pset Method

The PSet method is used to set a specific point on a form or picture box to a specified color. The syntax is as follows:

```
object.PSet (x,y) [color]
```

The components of the syntax are as follows:

- (x,y) are coordinates.
- color is an optional parameter that specifies the color of the point.

Line Method

The Line method is used to draw lines on an object and can be used to create many different shapes. Line has the following syntax:

```
[Object].Line [Step][(x1,y1)] [-] [Step][(x2,y2)], [color], [BF]
```

The components of the syntax are as follows:

- Step is an optional keyword to specify the starting point relative to the current x and y coordinates.
- x1, y1 are optional parameters indicating the starting point of the line (otherwise, the current x and y position is used).
- x2, y2 are required and are the end point for the line.
- color sets the color of the line.
- B is used to draw a box using the coordinates.
- F specifies that the box be filled in with the same color the box was drawn in.

That's a lot of parameters! A few examples are in order to help clarify the issue. Start a new project. Set the form's WindowState to Maximized and add the following code to Form_Click:

```
Private Sub Form_Click()
' Set ScaleMode to inches
Form1.ScaleMode = 5
' Draw a one inch horizontal line
Form1.Line (0.5, 0.5)-(1.5, 0.5)
' Draw a one inch vertical line down from the end of the first line
Form1.Line -(1.5, 1.5)
' Change form's forecolor property
Form1.ForeColor = QBColor(1)
' Draw a box
```

```
Form1.Line (2, 2)-(2.5, 2.5), , B
' Draw another box, using line color
Form1.Line (3, 3)-(3.5, 3.5), QBColor(0), B
' Draw a filled box, using line color
Form1.Line (3, 2)-(3.5, 2.5), QBColor(0), BF
End Sub
```

The comments in the code explain what each of the Line method statements is doing when you click the form.

Chalkboard

Now create an application using some of the commands you have just learned. For your first graphics method application, you will create a chalkboard. Using your mouse, you can draw pictures on the chalkboard. If you don't like the picture, you can erase the board. The drawing area for the chalkboard is a picture box. Start a new Visual Basic project called chalkbrd. Add the controls and set the properties as shown in Table 11.3.

TABLE 11.3 Object and Property Settings for the Chalkboard Project

Object	Property	Setting
Form	Caption	Chalkboard
	Height	3930
	Name	frmDraw
	Width	5295
PictureBox	BackColor	&H00FFFFFF&
	DrawWidth	2
	Height	2295
	Left	90
	Name	Picture1
	ScaleMode	3 - Pixel
	Top	60
	Width	4965
TextBox	Height	285
	Left	1155
	Name	txtWidth
	Top	2430
	Width	885

11

TABLE 11.3   continued

Object	Property	Setting
CommandButton	Caption	Change Draw Width
	Height	480
	Left	705
	Name	cmdWidth
	Top	2880
	Width	1755
Label	Caption	DrawWidth
	Height	255
	Left	225
	Name	lblWidth
	Top	2475
	Width900	
CommandButton	Caption	Clear the Board
	Height	480
	Left	2865
Name	cmdClear	
	Top	2880
	Width	1755

The completed project is on the CD that comes with this book.

Now give the user a way to change the line width by setting the DrawWidth property. Add the following code to the Click event of the Command button, cmdWidth, to change the DrawWidth property of the picture box.

```
Private Sub cmdWidth_Click()
    '
    'If valid number change the width of the point
    If IsNumeric(txtWidth.Text) Then
        Picture1.DrawWidth = Val(txtWidth)
    End If
End Sub
```

Now add the code to perform the actual drawing in the picture box. To draw the line while the mouse is moving, use the PSet command and the MouseMove event. A flag that prevents points from being drawn while a mouse button is down allows the mouse to move without drawing. Define the following variable in the form's general declaration section:

```
Dim bDrawFlag As Boolean
```

Set the variable DrawFlag to True when a mouse button is clicked over the picture box in the MouseDown event, as shown in the following code:

```
Private Sub Picture1_MouseDown(Button As Integer, Shift As Integer,
➥ X As Single, Y As Single)
    'set flag to start drawing
    bDrawFlag = True
End Sub
```

To stop drawing when the user releases the mouse button, set the variable DrawFlag to False in the picture box's MouseUp event as follows:

```
Private Sub Picture1_MouseUp(Button As Integer, Shift As Integer,
➥ X As Single, Y As Single)
    'Set flag to Stop Drawing
    bDrawFlag = False
End Sub
```

Use the PSet method and the current x and y coordinates to draw a line as the user moves the mouse by adding the following code to the picture box's MouseMove event:

```
Private Sub Picture1_MouseMove(Button As Integer, Shift As Integer,
➥ X As Single, Y As Single)
    'Only draw if the mouse button is being
    'held down.
    '
    If bDrawFlag = True Then
        Picture1.PSet (X, Y)
    End If
End Sub
```

Add the following code to the Click event of the Command button, cmdClear, to clear the picture box:

```
Private Sub cmdClear_Click()
    Picture1.Cls
End Sub
```

To finish the application, add the following code in the form's Load event:

```
Private Sub Form_Load()
    bDrawFlag = False
    txtWidth = Picture1.DrawWidth
End Sub
```

11

You are now ready to test the application. Start the application, click the picture box, and hold down the right or left mouse button. Move the mouse around. What happens? Change the DrawWidth property using the text box and the Command button, as shown in Figure 11.8. What do you think? Just like a real chalkboard (except for the "artist")!

FIGURE 11.8

Chalkboard applica-tion.

You have now created your first application using graphical methods. In the next lesson, you will use graphical methods to create various shapes.

Lesson Summary

This lesson introduced you to Visual Basicís graphical methods, which enable you to create lines and shapes using code instead of an ActiveX control. A form, PictureBox control, and the Printer object all support graphical methods. Using the CLS method erases all the graphics on the object. To plot a single point on the object, use the Pset method. To draw a line, use the Line method.

Quiz 3

1. The Shape control and the _____ control do not support graphical methods.

    a. Form

    b. Image

    c. PictureBox

    d. Printer object

2. A PictureBox control has the following line of code in the form activate event:

    Picture1.Cls

The code does one of the following:

    a. Closes a picture box named Picture1

    b. Clears (erases) the contents of the `PictureBox` control for Picture1

    c. Initializes the picture box Picture1 for graphical methods

    d. Will not work; it should be `Picture1.Cls(x1,y1)`

3. The graphical method `Pset` does the following:

    a. Sets a specific point on a form or picture box to a specified color

    b. Draws a line

    c. Clears the picture box or form

    d. Sets the mouse cursor to a point on the form

4. The following line of code

```
Picture1.Line -(100,200),,B
```

    a. Will not work because the statement is missing a set of coordinates

    b. Draws a line from the current x and current y position to the coordinates (100,200)

    c. Draws a box

    d. Draws a bold line from the current x and current y position to the coordinates (100,200)

Exercise 3

Complexity: Easy

1. Write a line of code that will clear all graphical methods from form.

Complexity: Moderate

2. Modify the chalkboard program to draw a red line instead of the default.

LESSON 5

Drawing Shapes

You will build on the different graphics methods you learned in the last lesson to create various shapes like squares and rectangles, and use a new method that enables you to create circles. This is an interactive lesson with a lot of code samples, so start up Visual Basic and get going. Create a new project so you can use it to test graphical methods code. Name the project TstShape, and add a form, three text boxes, a picture box, and three labels. Set the properties as shown in Table 11.4. The completed project is on the CD that comes with this book.

TABLE 11.4 Object and Property Settings for the TstShape Project

Object	Property	Setting
Form	Caption	Test Shapes
	Height	4545
	Name	frmTestShapes
	Width	6810
PictureBox	BackColor	&H00FFFFFF&
	DrawWidth	2
	Height	2685
	Left	1800
	Name	Picture1
	ScaleMode	3 - Pixel
	Top	90
	Width	4590
TextBox	Height	285
	Left	820
	Name	txtX
	Top	180
	Width	900
TextBox	Height	285
	Left	820
	Name	txtY
	Top	540
	Width	900
TextBox	Height	285
	Left	820
	Name	txtSize
	Top	930
	Width	900

Object	Property	Setting
Label	Caption	X coord
	Height	285
	Left	180
	Name	lblX
	Top	210
	Width	630
Label	Caption	Y coord
	Height	285
	Left	180
	Name	lblY
	Top	585
	Width	675
Label	Caption	Size
	Height	285
	Left	315
	Name	lblSize
	Top	945
	Width	375

11

Your test application is now complete. Well, almost. You have to write some code to draw various shapes. Start with a box.

Drawing Boxes

Think about how you would draw a box if you had a pencil, paper, and a ruler. You would draw one side of the box, draw another side starting where the line just finished, and continue on around until your box is drawn. You can use the same drawing technique using the Line method. The following code draws a box that starts at coordinates (100,100) and measures 200 pixels on each side:

```
Picture1.Line (100,100) - Step (200,0)
Picture1.Line - Step(0,200)
Picture1.Line -Step(-200,0)
Picture1.Line -Step(0,-200)
```

Take a look at the code. The first line uses the keyword Step. As a matter of fact, Step is used in all the code lines with the Line method. Step enables you to use a relative position instead of figuring out exact coordinates for each ending point. Relative coordinates means that the coordinates you use are based on the current x and y position of the cursor. For example, using exact coordinates, the first line of code could be rewritten without the Step keyword as

```
Picture1.Line1 (100,100) - (300,100)
```

Using the keyword Step prevents you from having to figure out the ending coordinates. For example:

```
Picture1.Line (100,100) - Step (200,0)
```

The Step command adds 200 units to the x position of 100 and 0 units to the y position of 100. The line still ends at (300,100), but all you did was give the width of the line instead of the exact coordinates using relative position. Notice that you can leave the first set of coordinates out of the Line method, and the line starts using the current x and y coordinates.

 Tip You can set the current x and y coordinates of a form or PictureBox control by setting the CurrentX and CurrentY properties.

Now add a Command button to draw a box in your application. Add the Command button, and set the properties as shown in Table 11.5.

TABLE 11.5 Box CommandButton Property Settings for the TstShape Project

Object	Property	Setting
CommandButton	Caption	Box
	Height	555
	Left	2400
	Name	cmdBox
	Top	3150
	Width	1470

Add the following code shown in Listing 11.1 to the Command button Click event.

LISTING 11.1 Draw Box Command Button Click Event Code

```
Private Sub cmdBox_Click()
Dim iX As Integer, iY As Integer, iSize As Integer
```

```
      If (IsNumeric(txtX) And IsNumeric(txtY) _
        And IsNumeric(txtSize)) Then
          iX = Val(txtX)
          iY = Val(txtY)
          iSize = Val(txtSize)
          '

          'Draw the Box
          Picture1.Line (iX, iY)-Step((iX + iSize), (iY + iSize)), , B
      End If

End Sub
```

Examine the code you used to create a box:

```
'Draw the Box
 Picture1.Line (X, Y)-Step((X + Size), (Y + Size)), , B
```

Instead of using the Line method four times to draw each line of the box, you used the special option B, to create boxes of the given size and starting points. The IsNumeric function is used to validate that the points in the text boxes are numeric. Run the application and enter an x coordinate, a y coordinate, and the size, and then click the Box Command button. The box drawn by the code is shown in Figure 11.9.

FIGURE 11.9

Box drawn using graphical methods.

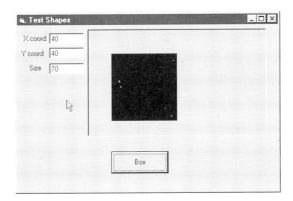

Drawing Triangles

Think about how you would draw a triangle. Do you think you could put it into code? Unfortunately the Line method does not have a draw triangle switch. To draw shapes like triangles, stars, or octagons requires you to write the functions and subroutine that enable you to create these various shapes. Add a Command button and set the properties as shown in Table 11.6.

TABLE 11.6   Triangle `CommandButton` Property Settings for the TstShape Project

Object	Property	Setting
CommandButton	Caption	Triangle
	Height	555
	Left	2400
	Name	cmdTriangle
	Top	3150
	Width	1470

Add the code to draw a triangle, as shown in Listing 11.2.

LISTING 11.2   Code to Draw a Triangle

```
Private Sub cmdTriangle_Click()
Dim iX As Integer, iY As Integer, iSize As Integer
    If (IsNumeric(txtX) And IsNumeric(txtY)) Then
        iX = Val(txtX)
        iY = Val(txtY)
        iSize = Val(txtSize)
        '
        'Get the X and Y coordinates to draw
        'the triangle. Set the starting
        'coordinates.
        '
        Picture1.CurrentX = iX
        Picture1.CurrentY = iY

        'Draw Right Triangle
        '
        Picture1.Line -(iX + iSize, ((iY + iSize) / 2))   'Hypotenuse
        Picture1.Line -(iX, ((iY + iSize) / 2)) ' Bottom
        Picture1.Line -(iX, iY) 'Straight line up - back

    End If

End Sub
```

Run the application, and enter 150 for the x coordinate, 50 for the y coordinate, and 150 for the size; then, click the Triangle button. A right triangle appears in your drawing area, as shown in Figure 11.10.

FIGURE 11.10

Box drawn using graphical methods.

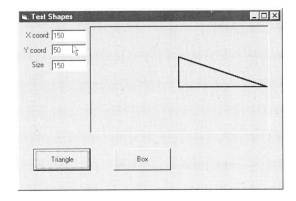

Drawing Circles

The Circle method enables you to draw circles, arcs, and ellipses. It has the following format:

```
[object].Circle [Step](x,y), radius, [color], [start], [end], [aspect]
```

where radius is a required field and specifies the length of the radius of the circular shape. Color is an optional field used to set the background color of the circular shape. The start and end variables are used to create arcs and ellipses. The aspect parameter is the aspect ratio of the circular shape and defaults to 1.0 for a perfect circle. Add a Command button to draw circles, and set the properties as shown in Table 11.7.

TABLE 11.7 Circle CommandButton Property Settings for the TstShape Project

Object	Property	Setting
CommandButton	Caption	Circle
	Height	555
	Left	4455
	Name	cmdCircle
	Top	3150
	Width	1470

Add the code in Listing 11.3 to the Command button's Click event.

11

LISTING 11.3   Adding a Button to Draw Circles

```
Private Sub cmdCircle_Click()
Dim iX As Integer, iY As Integer, iSize As Integer

    If (IsNumeric(txtX) And lsNumeric(txtY) _
      And IsNumeric(txtSize)) Then
        iX = Val(txtX)
        iY = Val(txtY)
        iSize = Val(txtSize)
        '
        '
    ' '         '

        'Set the Fill color on the Picture box
        If chkFillColor = vbChecked Then
            Picture1.FillColor = lColorValue
            Picture1.FillStyle = vbSolid
        Else
            Picture1.FillStyle = vbTransparent
        End If
        '
        'Draw the Circle
        Picture1.Circle (iX, iY), iSize
    End If

End Sub
```

In the code, the Size parameter is used to create the radius of the circle. Try the circle
function. Run the application, enter some parameters, and click the Circle Command button. A perfect circle displays in the drawing area of the application, as shown in Figure
11.11.

FIGURE 11.11

*Circle drawn using
graphical methods.*

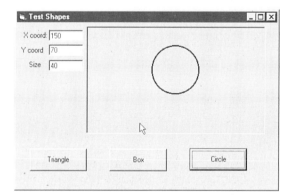

Lesson Summary

This lesson expanded on the graphical methods introduced in Chapter 10, "Problem Solving: Handling Errors and Debugging Your Program." A program was created that enabled you to display a circle, box or triangle, all created in code using graphical methods. You now have all the tools required to create complex shapes with Visual Basic. Try to draw other shapes not covered in this lesson, like ellipses, arcs, polygons, and stars. In the next lesson, you will learn how to spice up the looks of your graphical applications using colors.

Quiz 4

1. Executing the following code

   ```
   Picture1.Line (100,100) - (250,150)
   ```

   is equivalent to

   a. `Picture1.PSet (250,150)`

   b. `Picture1.Line (100,100) - Step (150,0)`

   c. `Picture1.Line (100,100) - Step(150,50)`

   d. `Picture1.Line (100,100) + Step(150,50)`

2. The code

   ```
   Picture1.Line - (50, 25)
   Picture1.Line - (0, 25)
   Picture1.Line - (0,0)
   ```

   a. Draws a triangle

   b. Draws a series of lines

   c. Draws a semicircle

   d. Draws two lines

3. To draw a circle on a `PictureBox` control, use the

   a. `Circle` property

   b. `Pset`

   c. `Ellipse` method

   d. `Circle` method

11

4. What does the aspect parameter value of 1.0 do when using the `Circle` method?

    a. Creates an ellipse

    b. Creates a semicircle

    c. Creates an arc

    d. Creates a perfect circle

Exercise 4

Complexity: Easy

1. Write code that uses the `Line` method to create a box.

Complexity: Moderate

2. Modify the chalkboard program to draw a red line instead of the default.

LESSON 5

Colors

In this lesson, you will examine several different ways to add colors to your applications. Visual Basic supports 256 colors on properly configured computer systems. Colors in Visual Basic are represented by a long integer (4 bytes), as shown in Figure 11.12.

FIGURE 11.12

Visual Basic byte color representation.

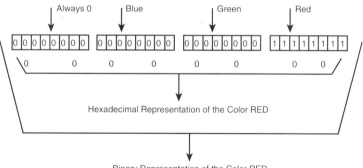

The high byte is set to 0; and the next three bytes contain the amount of red, green, and blue associated with the color. Colors are represented by hexadecimal numbers in the control and form properties, and they can be set directly using a hex number. For example, the hex number for the color red shown in Figure 11.12 is `&H000000FF&`. Note that the arrangement of digits in the hexadecimal numbers is the reverse of what you might expect. It is `00BBGGRR`.

Setting Colors on Forms and Controls Using Properties

Throughout this book, you have changed the colors of forms and controls such as the `PictureBox` and the `Label` by setting certain properties at design or runtime. Properties of forms and controls can be set by selecting the property in the Properties window and assigning a hex number to the property, or by clicking the property and selecting from the color palette displayed. Here is a quick review of some of the properties you can use to change the colors of a form or control.

BackColor Property

The `BackColor` property determines the background color of the form or control. You have used this property several times throughout this book to change the background color of a form.

BorderColor Property

BorderColor is the color used to paint the border of a control.

ForeColor Property

ForeColor is used to create the graphics or text drawn on an object such as a form or control.

FillColor Property

FillColor is the color used to fill the inside of boxes created with the `Line` method and circular shapes created with the `Circle` method.

Color Functions

Visual Basic offers two functions that return valid color numbers to set colors of objects during runtime. They are the `RGB` function and the `QBColor` function.

RGB Function

The `RGB` function is used to return a valid number that represents a color value. The syntax of the `RGB` function is as follows:

```
RGB (red, green, blue)
```

The components `red`, `green`, and `blue` are numbers between 0 and 255; 0 represents none of the colors and 255 represents the maximum possible amount of the color. These numbers correspond to the binary numbers in the byte color representation shown in Figure 11.12, but notice that the three colors are listed in reverse order. That is not particularly significant to you unless you choose to use the hexadecimal number for a color instead of the simpler RGB representations. Recall that a Byte type variable can hold numbers between 0 and 255.

To create a color using RGB you need to specify the color component values for your color. A value of 0 excludes the color and a value of 255 uses the maximum amount of the color. Here are some examples of using the RGB function to return some well known RGB color numbers:

```
Black = RGB(0,0,0)
Red = RGB(255,0,0)
Yellow = RGB(255,255,0)
```

 Tip

It may seem odd using red, green, and blue as the primary colors, when you learned in grade school to use red, yellow, and blue. The reason for the difference is that video displays are working with *transmitted* light instead of the *reflected* light from your water color paints.

QBColor Function

Trying to get the correct color value using the RGB function may be difficult, even when trying to use standard colors. Visual Basic provides a function called QBColor that enables you to select the color by name instead of toggling different RGB values to create the correct color number.

 Note

The function gets its name from a previous version of Microsoft Quick Basic. You can use the QBColor function to return an RGB color value based on a color constant value. QBColor has the following syntax:

QBColor(color)

The color parameter is one of the constant values listed in Table 11.8.

TABLE 11.8   QBColor Constants

Number	Color
0	Black
1	Blue

Number	Color
2	Green
3	Cyan
4	Red
5	Magenta
6	Yellow
7	White
8	Gray
9	Light blue
10	Light green
11	Light cyan
12	Light red
13	Light magenta
14	Light yellow
15	Bright white

Visual Basic Constants

Visual Basic also has predefined constants specifying RGB number values for a few standard colors. You can use these values, shown in Table 11.9, to set the color of an object instead of using either the RGB or QBColor functions.

TABLE 11.9 Visual Basic Color Constant Values

Constant	Description
vbBlack	Black
vbRed	Red
vbGreen	Green
vbYellow	Yellow
vbBlue	Blue
vbMagenta	Magenta
vbCyan	Cyan
vbWhite	White

It is safer to use the QBColors than the RGB colors because almost any computer that runs your programs responds correctly to them. The RGB colors do not show up correctly on computers that are not set up for 256 color displays. It may seem odd that, in this day of SVGA monitors, someone would not have it set up to handle 256 colors, but it happens.

Now, add some color to the TstShape project by adding code that fills the circles and boxes drawn with a selected color using the QBColor function. Add a combo list box and a check box to the form, frmTstShape, and set the properties shown in Table 11.10.

TABLE 11.10   Color Objects and Properties for the TstShape Project

Object	Property	Setting
ComboBox	Height	315
	Left	105
	Name	cmbColor
	Style	2 - Dropdown List
	Top	1485
	Width	1530
CheckBox	Caption	Fill Color
	Height	255
	Left	135
	Name	chkFillColor
	Top	1980
	Value	0 - UnChecked
	Width	1140

In the form frmTstShape Load event, add the code shown in Listing 11.4 to load the possible QBColor codes into the ComboBox.

LISTING 11.4   Loading Possible QBColors into a Combo Box During Form Load

```
Private Sub Form_Load()
    cmbColor.AddItem "Black"
    cmbColor.AddItem "Blue"
    cmbColor.AddItem "Green"
    cmbColor.AddItem "Cyan"
    cmbColor.AddItem "Red"
    cmbColor.AddItem "Magenta"
    cmbColor.AddItem "Yellow"
    cmbColor.AddItem "White"
    cmbColor.AddItem "Grey"
    cmbColor.AddItem "Light Blue"
```

```
      cmbColor.AddItem "Light Green"
      cmbColor.AddItem "Light Cyan"
      cmbColor.AddItem "Light Red"
      cmbColor.AddItem "Light Magenta"
      cmbColor.AddItem "Light Yellow"
      cmbColor.AddItem "Bright White"
      cmbColor.ListIndex = 0

End Sub
```

Add a new function to frmTestShape that uses the color in the combo box to get an RGB value using the QBColor function. Add the following function, shown in Listing 11.5, to frmTestShape.

LISTING 11.5 GetColor Function

```
Public Function GetColor() As Long
Dim sColor As String, lColorValue As Long
'
'Return the proper Color code
'for the color selected in the list.
'
 sColor = cmbColor
 Select Case sColor
    Case "Black"
        lColorValue = QBColor(0)
    Case "Blue"
       lColorValue = QBColor(1)
    Case "Green"
       lColorValue = QBColor(2)
    Case "Cyan"
       lColorValue = QBColor(3)
    Case "Red"
       lColorValue = QBColor(4)
    Case "Magenta"
       lColorValue = QBColor(5)
    Case "Yellow"
       lColorValue = QBColor(6)
    Case "White"
       lColorValue = QBColor(7)
    Case "Grey"
       lColorValue = QBColor(8)
    Case "Light Blue"
       lColorValue = QBColor(9)
    Case "Light Green"
       lColorValue = QBColor(10)
```

continues

11

LISTING 11.5   continued

```
    Case "Light Cyan"
        lColorValue = QBColor(11)
    Case "Light Red"
        lColorValue = QBColor(12)
    Case "Light Magenta"
        lColorValue = QBColor(13)
    Case "Light Yellow"
        lColorValue = QBColor(14)
    Case "Bright White"
        lColorValue = QBColor(15)
  End Select
  GetColor = lColorValue
End Function
```

Now that you have created a mechanism to select different colors, add the code that fills the boxes and circles with the selected color. Add the code shown in Listing 11.6 to the Click event of the Circle Command button. The new code is shown in bold.

LISTING 11.6   Circle Command Button Click Event with Color-Changing Code

```
Private Sub cmdCircle_Click()
Dim iX As Integer, iY As Integer, iSize As Integer
Dim lColorValue As Long
    If (IsNumeric(txtX) And IsNumeric(txtY) _
      And IsNumeric(txtSize)) Then
        iX = Val(txtX)
        iY = Val(txtY)
        iSize = Val(txtSize)
        '
        '
        'Get the Color
        '
        lColorValue = GetColor
        '
        'Set the Fill color on the Picture box
        If chkFillColor = vbChecked Then
            Picture1.FillColor = lColorValue
            Picture1.FillStyle = vbSolid
        Else
            Picture1.FillStyle = vbTransparent
        End If
        '
        'Draw the Circle
        Picture1.Circle (iX, iY), Size, lColorValue
    End If
End Sub
```

For the Box Command button `Click` event, add the code shown in Listing 11.7.

LISTING 11.7   Box Command Button `Click` Event with Color-Changing Code

```
Private Sub cmBox_Click()
Dim iX As iInteger, iY As Integer, iSize As Integer
Dim iColorValue As Long
    If (IsNumeric(txtX) And IsNumeric(txtY) _
      And IsNumeric(txtSize)) Then
        iX = Val(txtX)
        iY = Val(txtY)
        iSize = Val(txtSize)
        '
        'Get the Color
        '
        lColorValue = GetColor
        'Draw the Box
        Picture1.Line (iX, iY)-Step((iX + iSize), (iY + iSize)), lColorValue, BF
    End If
End Sub
```

Now you are ready to test the application. Select a color from the combo box, enter coordinates and size, and click the Box Command button. What happens? A box is drawn and filled with the selected color. To create the color effect, the `Line` method used to draw the box was modified to specify a color using the color parameter, and the `F` option was added to fill the box with the same color used to draw the box.

Now try to create a circle. What happened? The circle does not fill with the selected color. In order to fill a circle, you must set the `FillStyle` and `FillColor` properties of the object on which you are drawing the circle, in this case, the picture box. Check the check box Fill Style, and try again. Figure 11.13 shows a filled circle.

FIGURE 11.13

Circle filled with a selected color.

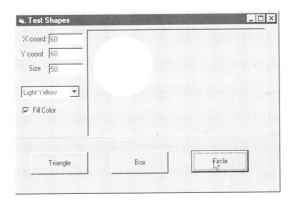

Note The graphics methods also work with the `Printer` object. `Printer.Line (0,0)-(1444,2888)` has the same effect on the printer as it did on the form. Of course, if you don't have a color printer, the colors are rendered as gray scales.

Lesson Summary

Visual Basic supports 256 colors. Visual Basic represents colors using a long integer. The color value is represented as a hexadecimal number. The RGB function can be used to return a valid number that represents a color. Visual Basic also supplies several constants for predefined colors like Red or Green. The `QBColor` function can be used to obtain a valid numeric representation of a color using the color name.

Quiz 5

1. To change to background color of a form:
   a. Set the `BackColor` property
   b. Set the `BackGround` property
   c. Invoke the `RGB Form` method
   d. Invoke the `BackGround Form` method

2. RGB stands for
   a. Red Green Blue
   b. Raster Graphical Bits
   c. Red Green Black
   d. Real Graphical Bits

3. The `FillColor` property is the
   a. Background color in forms and text boxes
   b. Color used to fill shapes created with `Line` and `Circle` methods
   c. Foreground color for custom controls
   d. Value which combines with the background property to blend special colors when using graphical methods

4. Which one of the following functions, methods or properties does not deal with color?

   a. RGB

   b. QBColor

   c. QBRGB

   d. ForeColor

Exercise 5

Complexity: Easy

1. Use the RGB function to create gray.

Complexity: Moderate

2. What is the binary representation of the color yellow? (See Figure 11.12 for hints.)

LESSON 6

Picture Control Versus Image Control

Nothing adds as much flair to an application as a well-placed picture or company logo displayed on a form or splash screen. Everyone loves pictures, and Visual Basic provides you with two custom controls that enable you to display pictures and images in your applications:

- PictureBox
- Image

The PictureBox and Image controls, shown in Figure 11.14, enable you to load pictures into your application at design time or runtime. Before you examine the two controls, review the types of picture files available.

Picture Files

The bitmap is a picture file with a .BMP file extension in which the image is stored with a pixel representation; each bit represents a pixel. An icon is a bitmap that is usually used to represent pictures on buttons, minimized windows, or the graphical representation of the application in a windows folder. Icons have an .ICO extension and have a size of 32 by 32 pixels.

FIGURE 11.14

PictureBox *and* Image *controls on the Visual Basic toolbar.*

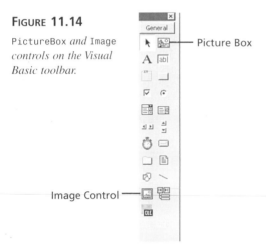

Picture Box

Image Control

A metafile stores the picture as a collection of graphical objects such as lines, circles, and squares instead of pixels. Metafiles have a .WMF file extension and are usually smaller than bitmaps. GIF and JPG files are industry standard file formats for pictures, either of which is suitable for Internet applications.

Where can you find pictures for your applications? Visual Basic comes with several icons, metafiles, and bitmaps. These files can be found on the CD that comes with this book or off of the Visual Basic CD located in the directory (\Common\Graphics\) in the subdirectories' metafiles, bitmaps, and icons. You can also download images from electronic bulletin boards, purchase clip art pictures, scan pictures into a PC, or create your own pictures using tools such as Microsoft Paintbrush or an icon editor. There is also a wide assortment of images in all formats available for download to be found on the Internet.

Loading a Picture

Take a short walk through the steps required to a load a picture into a PictureBox control or an Image control. Start Visual Basic and create a new project. Don't worry about saving the project. The examples here are to help you learn how to load pictures:

1. Place a PictureBox control and an Image control, shown in Figure 11.14, onto the form. Make the PictureBox about an inch square and make the Image control about twice the size of the PictureBox.

2. Click the `PictureBox` control, and press F4 to bring up the control's properties window.

3. Set the `AutoSize` property to `True`.

4. Scroll to the `Picture` property and click the ... button. A file dialog box is displayed.

5. Use the file dialog box to find a picture. For this example, go to the Visual Basic icons folder.

6. Go into the folder labeled Misc.

7. Select the file `misc39a.ico` and click the Open button on the file dialog box.

8. Select the `Image` control. Set its `Stretch` property to `True`.

9. Using the same steps you used for the `PictureBox`, load `Misc39b.ico` into the `Image` control.

The picture is now loaded in your `PictureBox`. You should see the firecracker icon in the `PictureBox` control, and the exploded firecracker in the `Image` control, as shown in Figure 11.15.

FIGURE 11.15

Firecracker icon displayed in a picture box.

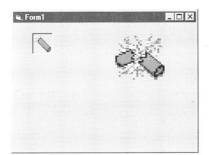

Sometimes you may want to load your pictures at runtime instead of design time, for instance, if you are trying to keep the size of your executable file small. (Pictures loaded at design time become part of the application size; thus, a large picture can substantially increase the size of your executable.)

To Load a Picture at Runtime

Use the `loadpicture` command that has the following syntax:

`LoadPicture(image file)`

where *image file* is the name and path name of the picture to load in the control.

The code in Listing 11.8 loads the Visual Basic icon `misc39a.ico` into the `Image` control.

LISTING 11.8   Loading an Icon at Runtime

```
Private Sub Form_Load()
Dim IconPath As String
    IconPath = App.Path & "\icons\misc\misc39b.ico"
    Image1.Picture = LoadPicture(IconPath)

End Sub
```

If you want to share the same image between two controls, you do not need to reload the picture. Instead, you can use the picture properties, as follows:

```
Image1.Picture = Picture1.Picture
```

Sharing images between controls conserves Windows resources. When you no longer need a picture, unload it to free up the resources by using the `LoadPicture` command as follows:

```
Image1.Picture = LoadPicture("")   'Clear out picture
```

Differences Between the `Image` and `PictureBox` Controls

You may be asking yourself, why have two controls to display pictures? After all, they seem to perform the same function. They both are used to display pictures. But the two controls have different features that distinguish them from each other. For one thing, the `Image` control, as mentioned earlier, is a lightweight control. This means it is not a window, so it uses substantially fewer resources than a `PictureBox` control. However, you cannot use the `Image` control to contain other controls; you have to use the `PictureBox`. If you want to use the graphical methods you learned earlier, such as `Line`, `Circle`, or `Pset`, you have to use the `PictureBox` control. Finally, if you want to transfer pictures in a DDE exchange, you must use the `PictureBox` control.

Lesson Summary

This lesson discussed the various uses of the `PictureBox` control versus the `Image` control. So when should you use the `Image` control? If you want to display pictures or use pictures as buttons, then use the `Image` control. If you need a `Container` object or need to perform DDE operations use the `PictureBox` control. You may also need to make your choice based on how the two controls handle images of different sizes (that is, how the control responds to pictures that are larger or smaller than the Image control or PictureBox control).

The PictureBox has a property called AutoSize. When AutoSize is set to True, the control automatically resizes the control to display the picture. Image controls do not have an AutoSize property because they are automatically resized to fit the image. There is one last important difference between the two controls. The Image control can be used to stretch an image (that is, make it larger or smaller). To stretch an image, set the Stretch property on the Image control to True. Picture boxes cannot stretch images! Experiment with the AutoSize property of the PictureBox control and the Stretch property of the Image control.

Quiz 6

1. Which one of the following is not a characteristic of the Image control?

   a. Use more Windows resources then a PictureBox control

   b. Displays pictures

   c. Considered a Windows "light control"

   d. Stretch property

2. A _____ is a picture with a size of 32×32 pixels.

   a. Bitmap

   b. Metafile

   c. Icon

   d. GraphicRaster

3. To add a picture to a PictureBox or Image control at runtime, use the

   a. PictureLoad property

   b. AddPicture method

   c. LoadPicture command

   d. LoadPicture method

4. What does the following code do if Image1 is an Image control?

   `Image1.Picture = LoadPicture("")`

   a. Loads a picture

   b. Produces a syntax error because LoadPicture is a method, not a command

   c. Loads the characters " and " into the Image control

   d. Unloads a picture and frees up Windows' resources used by the picture

Exercise 6

Complexity: Easy

1. Describe the differences between the `Image` control and the `PictureBox` control.

Complexity: Moderate

2. Create a program that enables you to stretch an image's height.

LESSON 7

Simple Animation

In this lesson, you will learn about animation, which is making objects on the screen appear as if they are moving. You will develop a simple animation program to help you understand several graphical methods and techniques. The example is based on the old bouncing-ball animation. Instead of a ball moving from side to side and up and down, the application uses a smiley face icon; as the icon moves, the facial expressions of the icon change. Before you get started, take a look at the method that is used to move the icon. The `Move` method has the following syntax:

```
object.Move left, [top], [width], [height]
```

The components of the syntax are as follows:

- `Left` is the only required parameter and indicates the direction you want to move the object.

- `Top` is the up or down direction to move the object.

- `Width` and `Height` values enable you to change the size of the object.

Here's how to use the `Move` method to move an object using absolute movement or relative movement. Using absolute movement, you specify the destination x and y coordinates to move the object inside of its container. For example, the following code moves the object to the coordinates (50,20):

```
Image1.Move 50,20
```

Relative movement specifies how far to move the object relative to its current position. For example the following code moves the `Image` control 50 units to the left and 20 units up:

```
Image1.Move Image1.Left - 50, Image1.Top - 20
```

Notice that the code uses the current position of the Image control to determine the destination coordinates. To move left using relative position, subtract from the object's Left property; to move right, add; to go up, subtract from the object's Top property; and to move down, add.

The Animation Program

Now for a quick look at how the animation program works. An Image control displays an icon, in this case, the smiley face icon. The form acts as the container for the Image control to move around. For simplicity, the Image control only goes from side to side. The image itself changes appearance as it moves across the screen. Do this by changing the icon each time the Image control is moved.

Start by creating a new project called Animate that has a single form and a Timer control. The Timer control is the control that looks like a stopwatch on the toolbar. The Timer control is covered in detail in Chapter 14, "Advanced Features." For now you only need to understand that the Timer control periodically runs the code required to move the images across the screen. Set the properties as shown in Table 11.11. The completed project is on the CD-ROM that comes with this book.

TABLE 11.11 Form and Timer Control Property Settings for the Animate Project

Object	Property	Setting
Form	Caption	Simple Animation
	Height	4545
	Name	frmAnimation
	Top	1485
	Width	1530
Timer	Enabled	True
	Interval	250
	Name	Timer1

In order to scroll through a series of icons, create an Image control array with four Image controls in the array (0–3). Only the first Image control in the array requires additional properties set. The others only need the Picture property. Set the Picture properties for each image in the image array accordingly. The images to use are the face01.ico, face02.ico, and face03.ico files located in Common\GRAPHICS\ICONS\MISC. Set the Image control properties shown in Table 11.12.

TABLE 11.12 Image Control Array Property Settings for the Animate Project

Object	Property	Setting
Image1	Height	480
	Left	75
	Picture	face01.ico
	Top	645
	Width	480
Image1	Height	480
	Left	75
	Picture	face01.ico
	Top	1290
	Width	480
Image1	Height	480
	Left	75
	Picture	face02.ico
	Top	1890
	Width	480
Image1	Height	480
	Left	75
	Picture	face03.ico
	Top	2475
	Width	480

The completed form with the images is shown in Figure 11.16.

FIGURE 11.16

Animation form with icons at design time.

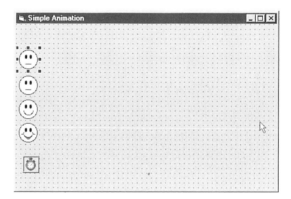

Declare the following variables and constants in the form's general declaration section:

```
Dim iImageIndex As Integer, iDirection As Integer
Const ImageRight = 1
Const ImageLeft = 2
```

The variable ImageIndex is used to toggle through the Image control array and display each image in the control array. The Direction variable determines the direction the Image control is moving and is set to one of the constants: ImageRight or ImageLeft. Add the code in Listing 11.9 to the form Load event to initialize the ImageIndex and Direction variables.

LISTING 11.9   Form Load Event Initialization Code

```
Private Sub Form_Load()
    '
    'Set up the Image control array
    '
    iImageIndex = 1
    '
    'Start in the right iDirection
    '
    iDirection = ImageRight
    '
    '
    Slider1.Value = Timer1.Interval
End Sub
```

11

Now to add the code that actually performs the animation. In the Timer control's Timer event, add the code shown in Listing 11.10.

LISTING 11.10   The Timer Control's Timer Event Code to Perform Animation

```
Private Sub Timer1_Timer()
    '
    'Move the Graphic
    '
    If iDirection = ImageRight Then
        'Move the Image 75 twips to the right
        'Don't move the image up
        '
        Image1.Move Image1.Left + 75
        '
        'Check to see if the image is of the edge of the form
        '
        If Image1.Left >= (frmAnimation.Width - Image1.Width) Then
```

continues

LISTING 11.10   continued

```
            iDirection = ImageLeft ' Change iDirection
        End If
    ElseIf iDirection = ImageLeft Then
        'Move the Image 75 twips to the left
        'Don't move the image up
        '
        Image1.Move Image1.Left - 75
        '
        'Check to see if the image is off the edge of the
        ' form
        If Image1.Left <= 0 Then
            '
            'Change the iDirection
            '
            iDirection = ImageRight
        End If
    End If
    '
    'Change the picture to give us that
    'stop motion picture animation
    '
    Image1.Picture = Image1(iImageIndex).Picture
    '
    ' Bump to the next frame
    iImageIndex = iImageIndex + 1
    '
    'Check to see if we have exceeded
    'The max number of images
    If iImageIndex = 4 Then
        iImageIndex = 1 'Reset
    End If

End Sub
```

For the finishing touch, add a Windows 95 control to enable the user to control the speed of the smiley face as it bounces across the screen. Add a Slider control, and set the properties, as shown in Table 11.13.

TABLE 11.13   Slider Control Property Settings for the Animate Project

Object	Property	Setting
Slider	Height	375
	Max	100
	Min	5

Object	Property	Setting
	Name	Slider1
	Top	3360
	Width	4575

In the `Form Load` event, add the following code:

```
Slider1.Value = Timer1.Interval
```

In the `Slider Scroll` event, add the following code:

```
Private Sub Slider1_Scroll()
    Timer1.Interval = Slider1.Value
End Sub
```

Run the application shown in Figure 11.17.

FIGURE 11.17

Animation application in action.

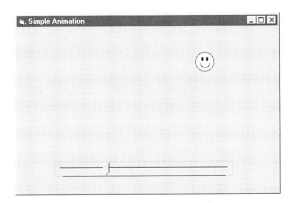

The smiley face is moving across the screen, changing facial expressions along the way. You have created a simple animation application! To change the speed of the smiley face's movement, adjust the `Interval` property of the `Timer` control by using the `Slider` control. As an exercise, enhance the application to include up and down movement. Before you show off the application, don't forget the quiz!

Lesson Summary

In this lesson, you created an application that demonstrates simple animation using the `Move` method of an object (in the example the `Image` control). Using several different icons, the `Image` control and the `Timer` control the running application produces a smiley face animation program.

Quiz 7

1. The following line of code

   ```
   Image1.Move 50,20
   ```

   is an example of

   a. Relative movement

   b. Absolute movement

   c. Direct movement

   d. Coordinate movement

2. What does the following code do?

   ```
   Image1.Move Image1.Left - 50, Image1.Top - 20
   ```

   a. Moves a form to the right 50 units and down 20 units

   b. Moves an Image control to the right 50 units and up 20 units

   c. Moves an Image control to the left 50 units and up 20 units

   d. Moves an Image control to the right 50 units and down 20 units

3. The following code

   ```
   If Image1.Left >= (frmAnimation.Width - Image1.Width) Then
   ```

   is used to determine

   a. If the image is at the top of the form

   b. If the image is off the left edge of the form

   c. If the image is off the bottom of the form

   d. If the image is off the right edge of the form

4. To make the smiley face in your program change expressions, you used

   a. A control array of Image controls

   b. A control array of PictureBox controls

   c. Separate Image controls

   d. Separate PictureBox controls

Exercise 7

Complexity: Easy

1. Explain what *relative movement* is and give an example.

Complexity: Easy

2. Explain what *absolute movement* is and give an example.

LESSON 8

Miscellaneous Graphics Issues

In this lesson, you will take a close look at the effect of the `AutoRedraw` property. You will learn how to print high resolution graphics from a `Picture` control to the printer, and you will also examine a custom control that is included in all of the editions of Visual Basic except for the standard edition. The Graph custom control enables you to display graphs and charts in your applications.

AutoRedraw Property

Run the chalkboard application you created during Lesson 3. Draw a line or a picture on the chalkboard, and then bring up the debug window. Overlay the chalkboard application with the debug window. Now, close the debug window; notice your drawing's gone! Next, set the `AutoRedraw` property on the picture box to `True`, and try the same experiment. The drawing is still there!

So what is the `AutoRedraw` property up to? When a window is overlaid with another window and then redisplayed, Microsoft Windows automatically redraws the window and all of the controls. But Windows does not redraw the graphics you created with graphical methods unless the `AutoRedraw` property for the form or picture box is set to `True`. When the `AutoRedraw` property is set to `True`, Windows applies the graphical methods to your form or picture box and to a copy of the form or picture box in memory. If another window overlays your graphics, then Windows uses the copy of the image in memory to re-create the graphics.

PictureBox Property

The default value for the `AutoRedraw` property is `False`. You may be thinking to yourself, no problem. I'll just set `AutoRedraw` to `True` all the time and then I won't have to worry about graphical methods being erased. However, remember that setting `AutoRedraw` to `True` causes Windows to keep a copy of the image in memory. This increases the application's consumption of memory. Only set `AutoRedraw` to `True` when you are using graphical methods; otherwise, your forms and controls are repainted normally by Windows.

If possible, minimize the amount of memory `AutoRedraw` eats up by using a picture box instead of a form. The amount of memory required to maintain a picture box is normally less than the amount required to maintain the entire form or screen. If you are working on a system without a lot of memory, consider redrawing the graphics yourself instead of using the `AutoRedraw` property.

Hard Copy

When you want to print your pictures to paper, Visual Basic comes to the rescue. Not only will VB 6 send the bitmap from a picture box to the printer, but you can locate it anywhere you want on the page, and you can scale it to any size you want. The latter is important, as you will see.

When you program for businesses, they like to see their logo on the forms, and they also like it on their printed output. It is not hard to scan a logo into the computer using a full-page scanner or a hand scanner. The images you get, though, are often far too large to use on printed pages. Graphics programs can reduce images in almost any format, but the reduced image tends to get pretty ugly. Parts that were once round grow jagged edges, and angled lines look more like staircases than straight lines. The solution is the `PaintPicture` method.

The `PaintPicture` Method

The syntax of `PaintPicture` is enough to frighten almost anyone. It is

```
object.PaintPicture picture, x1, y1, width1, height1, x2, y2, width2, height2,
opcode
```

The components of the syntax are as follows:

- `object` is an optional object expression that evaluates to a `Form`, a `PictureBox`, or a `Printer`. If `object` is omitted, the Form with the focus is assumed to be `object`.
- `Picture` is the source of the graphic to be drawn onto the object. This must be the `Picture` property of a Form or a PictureBox.
- `x1, y1` are single-precision values indicating the destination coordinates (x-axis and y-axis) on the object for the picture to be drawn. The `ScaleMode` property of the object determines the unit of measure used.
- `width1` is an optional single-precision value indicating the destination width of the picture. The `ScaleMode` property of the object determines the unit of measure used. If the destination width is larger or smaller than the source width (width2), the picture is stretched or compressed to fit. If it is omitted, the source width is used.

- `height1` is an optional single-precision value indicating the destination height of the picture. The `ScaleMode` property of the object determines the unit of measure used. If the destination height is larger or smaller than the source height (height2), the picture is stretched or compressed to fit. If it is omitted, the source height is used.

- `x2, y2` are optional single-precision values indicating the coordinates (x-axis and y-axis) of a clipping region within the picture. The `ScaleMode` property of `object` determines the unit of measure used. If omitted, 0 is assumed.

- `width2` is an optional single-precision value indicating the source width of a clipping region within the picture. The `ScaleMode` property of `object` determines the unit of measure used. If omitted, the entire source width is used.

- `height2` is an optional single-precision value indicating the source height of a clipping region within the picture. The `ScaleMode` property of `object` determines the unit of measure used. If omitted, the entire source height is used.

- `opcode` is an optional long value or code that is used only with bitmaps. It defines a bit-wise operation that is performed on the picture as itís drawn on `object`.

If you use negative numbers for the destination height, your picture prints upside down. If you use negative numbers for width, your picture prints as a mirror image.

It seems a bit overwhelming, doesn't it? Fortunately, you can leave out most of the parameters and still get exactly the results you want.

Time to put together a little demo program. Assume that John and Lisa have started their own programming business, named Mythical Programming Company. They paid a graphic artist to create a logo, which is on the CD with the name `Mythical.GIF`. Now they want to use that logo when they print their invoices.

Start a new project called PixLogo. The completed project is on the CD that accompanies this book. Place a picture box, two command buttons, and an array of three option buttons on the form. The properties are shown in Table 11.14.

TABLE 11.14 Properties for the PixLogo Project

Object	Property	Value
Form	Name	frmPixLogo
PictureBox	Name	pixLogo
	AutoSize	True
	Picture	Mythical.GIF

continues

TABLE 11.14   continued

Object	Property	Value
Command Button	Name	cmdPrint
	Caption	Print
Command Button	Name	cmdDone
	Caption	Done
Option Button	Name	optScale
	Index	0
	Caption	Full
	Value	True
Option Button	Name	optScale
	Index	1
	Caption	Half
Option Button	Name	optScale
	Index	2
	Caption	Quarter

The layout of the form is shown in Figure 11.18.

FIGURE 11.18

The PixLogo project.

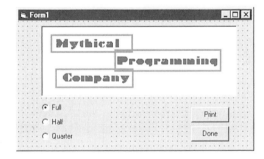

Now add the code from Listing 11.11.

LISTING 11.11   The Code for PixLogo

```
Option Explicit
Private Sub cmdDone_Click()
'    Finished - Close the print job and exit
     Printer.EndDoc
```

```
        End
End Sub


Private Sub cmdPrint_Click()
 Static lPrintY As Long
       '   Paint the picture to the correct scale
       '   and reset the picture's currency so
       '   the next picture will not overprint it
      If optScale Then
       '   Full scale
           Printer.PaintPicture pixLogo.Picture, 0, lPrintY
           lPrintY = lPrintY + pixLogo.Height + 722
      ElseIf optScale Then
       '   half scale
           Printer.PaintPicture pixLogo.Picture, _
               0, lPrintY, pixLogo.Picture.Width / 2, _
               pixLogo.Picture.Height / 2
           lPrintY = lPrintY + pixLogo.Height / 2 + 722
      Else
       '   neither of above, must be quarter scale
           Printer.PaintPicture pixLogo.Picture, 0, _
               lPrintY, pixLogo.Picture.Width / 4, _
               pixLogo.Picture.Height / 4
           lPrintY = lPrintY + pixLogo.Height / 4 + 722
      End If
End Sub
```

A Look at the Code

There is nothing spectacular here. To save paper (and time), the logo can be printed repeatedly on the same sheet of paper. To keep them from all being printed in the same place, a static variable is used in cmdPrint's Click event. Each time a logo is printed, 722 twips (0.5 inches) are added to the variable.

The code for full scale printing,

```
Printer.PaintPicture pixLogo.Picture, 0, lPrintY
```

uses only the picture and the X1 and Y1 coordinates for printing the logo. The code for half-scale and quarter-scale printing also requires Width1 and Height1. In this case, the program simply divides the actual picture's width and height by the correct factor. So the code for half scale is

```
Printer.PaintPicture pixLogo.Picture, _
        0, lPrintY, pixLogo.Picture.Width / 2, _
        pixLogo.Picture.Height / 2
```

and the code for quarter scale divides the picture's dimensions by four.

Note that none of the `PaintPicture` routines includes the `EndDoc` method, which is in `cmdDone`'s `Click` event instead.

Running the Program

When you run the program, have it print one copy of the logo at full scale, one at half scale, and one at quarter scale, and then click Done. It takes a while before the program finishes processing the print job and sends it to the printer; high resolution graphics take a lot more "thinking time" than text.

The `Chart` Control

Say you have an application that is tracking several data points, and you would like to create a chart to graphically display them. You could use OLE and Microsoft Excel to create a chart and display the data in your program, or if you have the Professional or Enterprise edition of Visual Basic, you can use the special `MSChart` custom control.

The `MSChart` custom control, shown in Figure 11.19, enables you to create different types of graphs such as pie charts, bar charts, Gantt charts, 3D charts, and area graphs. You can access these features and define the graph by setting property values. First, we'll provide a brief review of some of the important `MSChart` control properties, and then a simple application to exercise the `MSChart` control.

FIGURE 11.19

The MSChart *custom control.*

MS Chart

`Row` and `Column` Properties

In order to build a chart or graph with data, you must treat each data item as a point in the graph or chart. To modify a specific data item in the graph or chart, you must point to the data point on the graph using the `Row` and `Column` properties. Setting the `Row` and

`Column` properties identifies a specific point in the chart so you can add or modify data for that point.

AutoIncrement Property

The `MSChart` control has a feature called the `AutoIncrement` property that enables you to automatically increment to the next data point in the graph when adding data. Set the `AutoIncrement` property to `True` when adding several data points to a graph. When the `AutoIncrement` property is set to `True`, the `Column` value is automatically incremented by one when a data point is added.

Data Property

To add data to the graph, set the `GraphData` property to your data after you have set the `ThisPoint` property. The data is added to the `Graph` control at the location pointed to by the `ThisPoint` property.

ChartType Property

The `ChartType` property determines the type of chart displayed, for example, pie charts or bar charts.

TitleText Property

Use the `TitleText` property to assign a label the chart.

ChartData Property

Use the `ChartData` property to load an array of data points. For example, you may retrieve several cells from an Excel spreadsheet and want to chart the values. Place the values in an array and set `ChartData` to the array. The data points will automatically be graphed.

Using the Properties Together

The properties that were just reviewed are used together to graph data points. The simplest way to add data points to a graph is to set the `Column` and `Row` properties to the starting point and then set the `AutoIncrement` property to `True`. With `AutoIncrement` set to `True`, each time a data value is assigned to the `Data` property, the `Column` property is automatically incremented.

Using the MSChart Control

Start a new Visual Basic project with a single form, a combo box, three command buttons, and a `MSChart` control. Set the properties as shown in Table 11.15.

TABLE 11.15 Object Property Settings for the Chart Project

Object	Property	Setting
Form	Caption	Example of the Graph control
	Name	frmGraph
ComboBox	Height	315
	Left	960
	Name	cmbType
	Style	2 - Dropdown List
MSChart	DrawMode	0 - vtChDrawModeDraw
	ChartType	1 - vtChChartType2DBar
	Name	MsChart1

See Figure 11.20 for the layout of the form.

FIGURE 11.20

The Chart project.

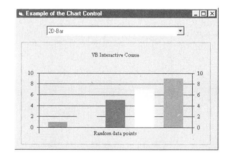

ComboBox Control

Now add the code in Listing 11.12 to the project.

LISTING 11.12 Code for the Graph Project

```
Option Explicit
Private Sub cmbType_Click()
  Dim sSelectedGraph As String
    sSelectedGraph = cmbType.Text

    ' Change the graph to the type selected
    Select Case sSelectedGraph
        Case "3D-Bar"
            MSChart1.chartType = VtChChartType3dBar
        Case "2D-Bar"
            MSChart1.chartType = VtChChartType2dBar
```

```
        Case "2D-Pie"
            MSChart1.chartType = VtChChartType2dPie
        Case "Line"
            MSChart1.chartType = VtChChartType2dLine
        Case "3D-Area"
            MSChart1.chartType = VtChChartType3dArea
        Case Else
            MSChart1.chartType = VtChChartType3dLine
    End Select
    MSChart1.Refresh
End Sub


Private Sub Form_Load()
  Dim iX As Integer
    '
    'Add 5 data points to the Chart
    'Make the difference between each point 2.
    '
    'Turn the Auto increment property on
    MSChart1.AutoIncrement = True

    'Set the number of Rows and Columns

    MSChart1.Column = 1

    For iX = 1 To 9 Step 2
        With MSChart1
            .Data = iX  'Set the data point to graph
                End With
    Next iX
    '
    'Add a Title to the graph
    '
    MSChart1.TitleText = "VB Interactive Course"

    'Set the row label
    MSChart1.RowLabel = "Randomn data points"


    '
    'Add some different graph selections to the ComboBox control
    '
    cmbType.AddItem "2D-Bar"
    cmbType.AddItem "2D-Pie"
    cmbType.AddItem "3D-Bar"
    cmbType.AddItem "Line"
    cmbType.AddItem "3D-Area"
    cmbType.AddItem "3D-Line"
    cmbType.ListIndex = 0
End Sub
```

A Look at the Code

The `Form_Load` event initially sets up the chart to have five data points, assigns values to the data points and assigns a title. The `autoincrement` property must be `True`, or all of the data will be assigned to the same point. (Not much of a graph then!)

The code in `cmbType_Click` sets the type of graph, and it redraws the graph with `MSChart1.Refresh`. There are several types of graphs that were not included because they are more suited to scientific applications than business graphing. If you need one of the other types, it can be added in.

Running the Program

Try the program out. You should be able to view and print six different styles of graph. Once more, you can add the other styles as needed.

Lesson Summary

This lesson covered many different miscellaneous graphics issues. The `AutoDraw` property of a `PictureBox` control can be used to have shapes created with graphical methods redrawn automatically if overlaid by another form. To send a graphic to the printer use the `Printer`'s object `PaintPicture` method. To create charts and graphs using Visual Basic use the `MSChart` control. The `MSChart` control enables you to create professional looking charts and graphs via code.

Quiz 8

1. A box is drawn using graphical methods on a form. Another application overlays the form and is then minimized. The box on the form is missing. Why?

    a. It's a Windows screen paint problem.

    b. The form's `AutoRedraw` property is `True`.

    c. The form's `DrawMode` property is `manual`.

    d. The form's `AutoRedraw` property is `False`.

2. To print an image or picture in a `PictureBox` control use the

    a. `Print` method

    b. `PaintPicture` method

    c. `PrintPicture` method

    d. `SendToPrinter` method

3. To change a chart from a pie chart to a bar chart, set the

   a. `ChartStyle` property

   b. `ChartStyle` method

   c. `DataChart` property

   d. `ChartType` property

4. The property to add data a single point of data at a time to a chart is

   a. `ThisPoint`

   b. `Data`

   c. `Value`

   d. `ChartData`

Exercise 8

Complexity: Easy

1. Write a program that uses the `MSChart` control and the `ChartData` property to create a chart using an array.

Complexity: Moderate

2. Write a program that uses the `MSChart` control and the `ChartData` property to create a chart that uses multiple data sets (that is, more than one array).

Chapter Summary

Now you have the tools to dress up your programs with slick looking graphics. You can draw pictures, use and print high-resolution graphics, and put well-designed graphs in your project. In Chapter 12, "Reading and Writing Disk Files," you will learn to use disk files so you can save that data you have been generating, and call it up and use it again. The main points of this chapter are as follows:

- Visual Basic uses a coordinate system to determine the size of forms, controls, and other graphics.

- The `Screen` object enables you to determine the resolution of the computer's screen your application is executing.

- Using the `Screen` object you can readjust the size of a form or control or center the form on the screen regardless of the size or resolution of the screen.

- Visual Basic's default unit of measurement is the twip.

- Visual Basic contains many different ActiveX controls that can be used to create lines and various other shapes with little or no code.

- The `Form`, `Printer` object, and `PictureBox` control all support graphical methods.

- Graphical methods enable you to draw or create your own shapes and lines via code.

- Visual Basic supports up to 256 colors.

- Visual Basic stores color values in a long integer. The color values are represented by hexadecimal numbers.

- To easily obtain the hexadecimal color values, Visual Basic supplies several color functions like RGB and QBColor. Visual Basic also supplies several constants for standard colors.

- To display bitmaps or images use the `PictureBox` control or the `Image` control.

- If you want to display pictures or use pictures as buttons, then use the `Image` control. If you need a `Container` object or need to perform DDE operations use the `PictureBox` control.

- To create charts or graphs use the `MSChart` ActiveX control.

CHAPTER 12

Reading and Writing Disk Files

This chapter shows how to use Visual Basic's File controls to let your users browse through files on their systems. It also shows how to perform various file input and output operations. It explains the different terms used to describe the file system and the different types of file input and output access methods. Best of all, it puts all this knowledge to work by showing you how to create several applications. For instance, it shows you how to develop a file-browsing application and an object-oriented Notepad application. Get started by reviewing the Windows file system.

LESSON 1

Using File System Controls

This lesson explains how to use the file system controls provided by Visual Basic 6. The file system controls enable you to add file system navigation functionality to your application. The following are the file system controls:

- `DriveListBox`
- `DirListBox`
- `FileListBox`

The File controls are shown in Figure 12.1.

FIGURE **12.1**

The File controls.

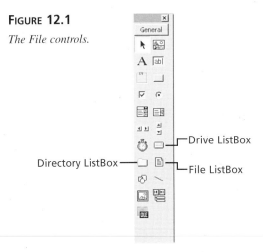

The best way to learn about these controls is to create an application that uses them. Create a new project called Browse. Add the objects and set the properties shown in Table 12.1.

TABLE 12.1   Browse Project Object and Property Settings

Object	Property	Setting
Form	BackColor	&H0FFFFFF&
	BorderStyle	1 - Fixed Single
	Caption	File Browser
	Height	5010
	Icon	face02.ico
	Name	frmBrowse
	Width	6810
DriveListBox	Height	315
	Left	1560
	Name	drvBrowse
	Top	120
	Width	2295
DirListBox	Height	2055

Object	Property	Setting
	Left	1560
	Name	dirBrowse
	Top	480
	Width	2295
FileListBox	Height	1620
	Left	1560
	Name	filBrowse
	Top	2640
(i)	Width	2295

DriveListBox Control

The DriveListBox control is a drop-down list box used to present a list of available computer drives. No code is required to get the list or to determine which drives are on the computer. The DriveListBox control gets the drive information for you from the operating system. Let's add some code to the DriveListBox Change event.

```
Private Sub drvBrowse_Change()
  MsgBox "The following drive has been selected: " _
  & drvBrowse.Drive
End Sub
```

Run the application. The drive letter displayed in the list box is your current drive. Select a new drive by clicking the list box and changing the drive. The message box, shown in Figure 12.2, appears.

FIGURE 12.2

Message box with the selected drive.

Selecting a different drive from the list box does not change your current directory, it only changes the Drive property for the DirListBox control. The new drive information could be used to change your current working directory using code or to provide information to other controls. Remove the code you added to the DriveListBox Change event. (The code was used for demonstration purposes only and is not part of the application.)

DirListBox Control

The DirListBox control works a lot like the DriveListBox control. The DirListBox control displays a list of the current directories and subdirectories for the current drive. (Remember that a directory and folder are the same thing. Visual Basic 6 uses the same name for the control as Visual Basic 3, Visual Basic 4, and Visual Basic 5.)

Run the project. The top folder in the list box is your current folder (the Visual Basic folder) and is contained on your current drive. Select a new folder by double-clicking any folder. Notice how the control automatically updates the list box for you to represent the newly selected folder and subfolders.

FileListBox Control

Files are displayed using the FileListBox control. The FileListBox control displays all the files in the current drive and folder. The FileListBox control has properties that enable you to set up search criteria to limit or expand the filenames displayed in the list box. The Pattern property provides a filter to set up file-specific search criteria. For instance, if you want to see all the files in a folder, use the default *.* setting of the property. Suppose you want to see only files with an EXE extension. The following code limits the files displayed, in the list box to only those files with an EXE extension:

```
File1.Pattern = "*.EXE"
```

The search criteria for a FileListBox control can be further fine-tuned to exclude or include files with specific file attributes. Table 12.2 contains a list of properties associated with file attributes. Setting any of the properties to True includes the file type as part of the file search criteria. Setting the property to False prevents the file type from being displayed, even if it matches the search criteria set in the Pattern property.

TABLE 12.2   File Control Properties and File Attributes

Property	Description
ReadOnly	Read-only files
Archive	Files with Archive attribute
Normal	All files without system or hidden attributes
System	System files
Hidden	Hidden files

Run the application. If you change the drive, the DirListBox control does not display the folders for the new drive. If you change the DirListBox control, the FileListBox control does not display the files in the new directory. The File controls are not working together! The next lesson demonstrates how to synchronize them.

Lesson Summary

Visual Basic has three ActiveX controls that enable you to easily add drive selection capabilities (DriveListBox), folder selection capabilities (DirListBox) and file selection capabilities (FileListBox).

Quiz 1

1. The best way to display only a list box of folders is to:

   a. Write code to scan a drive and populate the list box

   b. Use the CommonDialog custom control

   c. Read an initialization file of the folder structure and populate a list box

   d. Use the DirListBox custom control

2. How would you view only files with a .DOC file extension with a FileListBox control?

   a. Set the Filter property to *.DOC.

   b. Set the Pattern property to *.DOC.

   c. This cannot be done.

   d. Set the FileFilter property to "*.DOC".

3. To get the string value of the current drive in a DriveListBox control, you would get the value from the

   a. Text property

   b. Drive property

   c. String property

   d. Value property

4. To view folders (directories), use the

   a. DirListBox control

   b. DriveListBox control

   c. FolderListBox control

   d. None of the above

12

Exercise 1

Complexity: Easy

1. Write a line of code that sets the default directory of a `DirListBox` control to be C:\Windows.

Complexity: Moderate

2. Write a program that uses the `FileListBox` control with a Pattern property set to `*.*`. The program should have two check boxes, one to show hidden files and one to show system files.

LESSON 2

Making the File System Controls Work Together

You have created a form with `DriveListBox`, `DirListBox`, and `FileListBox` controls. If you run the application, you quickly find that these are not very useful because they show file information for the current drive and folder only. Each control should provide information for the next control in the hierarchy list. In other words, the `DriveListBox` control should provide information to the `DirListBox` control and the `DirListBox` control should provide information to the `FileListBox` control.

Figure 12.3 shows the chain reaction scenario in which changes in one control trickle down immediately to the next control in the chain.

FIGURE 12.3

Control chain reaction.

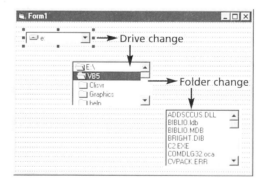

Chaining the `DriveListBox` Control to the `DirListBox` Control

The Visual Basic 6 event-driven programming model makes it possible to create a chain reaction among the File controls, automatically updating any lower control in the hierarchy if an upper-level control is changed. The first chain reaction is the `DriveListBox` control providing drive information to the `DirListBox` control. To chain the `DirListBox` control to the `DriveListBox` control, add the code shown in Listing 12.1 to the `DriveListBox` Change event.

LISTING 12.1 Setting the Directory List Box Drive

```
Private Sub drvBrowse_Change()
    'Set the directory list box to the new drive
    dirBrowse.Path = drvBrowse.Drive
End Sub
```

Chaining the `DirListBox` Control to the `FileListBox` Control

When you click a new folder in the `DirListBox` control, or when the folder in the box changes because the drive changed, the change needs to be relayed to the file list box. Add the code shown in Listing 12.2 to the `DirListBox` Change event.

LISTING 12.2 Setting the File List Box

```
Private Sub dirBrowse_Change()
    'If the folder changes - update the file list box
    filBrowse.Path = dirBrowse.Path
End Sub
```

Rounding Out the File Browser

To finish the File Browser project, add three labels to the form and set the properties for the labels shown in Table 12.3.

TABLE 12.3 File Browser Label Property Settings

Object	Property	Setting
Label	Caption	Select a Drive
	Height	255
	Left	120

continues

TABLE 12.3 continued

Object	Property	Setting
	Name	lblDrive
	Width	1335
Label	Caption	Select a Folder
	Height	255
	Left	120
	Name	lblFolder
	Width	1335
Label	Caption	Files
	Height	255
	Left	870
	Name	lblFile
	Width	600

Add a frame and five check boxes inside the frame and set the properties shown in Table 12.4.

TABLE 12.4 Frame and Check Box Property Settings

Object	Property	Setting
Frame	Caption	Select File Attributes
	Height	1650
	Left	3930
	Name	frmAttributes
	Width	2295
CheckBox	Caption	Read Only
	Height	195
	Name	chkRead
	Left	90
	Top	285
	Value	1-Checked
	Width	1350
CheckBox	Caption	Archive
	Height	195
	Name	chkArchive

Object	Property	Setting
	Left	90
	Top	510
	Value	1-Checked
	Width	1350
CheckBox	Caption	Normal
	Height	195
	Name	chkNormal
	Left	90
	Top	780
	Value	1-Checked
	Width	1350
CheckBox	Caption	System
	Height	195
	Name	chkSystem
	Left	90
	Top	1035
	Value	0-UnChecked
	Width	1350
CheckBox	Caption	Hidden
	Height	195
	Name	chkHidden
	Left	90
	Top	1305
	Value	0-UnChecked
	Width	1350

Add a label and text box and set the properties shown in Table 12.5.

TABLE 12.5 Text Box and Label Property Settings

Object	Property	Setting
Label	Caption	Search Filter
	Height	225
	Name	lblFilter

continues

TABLE 12.5   continued

Object	Property	Setting
	Top	1800
	Width	990
TextBox	Height	330
	Name	txtFilter
	Text	*.*
	Top	1770
	Width	1260

The form is completed, as shown in Figure 12.4.

FIGURE 12.4

*Completed File
Browser form.*

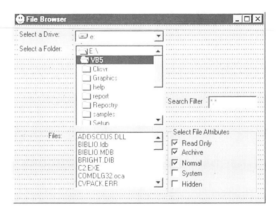

Time to add code! The CheckBox controls added to the form control the type of files
viewed in the FileListBox control. Each check box is named for a corresponding property on the List Box control. The text box added to the project sets the Pattern property
for the FileListBox control. By using the check boxes and the text box, you can use the
application to view different file types and to use filter criteria. Add the code in Listing
12.3 to the corresponding check boxes.

LISTING 12.3   Setting Search Criteria

```
Private Sub chkRead_Click()
   'Set search criteria to disable or enable
   'viewing of Read Only Files
   '
   If chkRead.Value = Checked Then
```

```
    filBrowse.ReadOnly = True
    Else
    filBrowse.ReadOnly = False
    End If
End Sub


Private Sub chkSystem_Click()
    'Set search criteria to disable or enable
    'viewing of System Files
    '
    If chkSystem.Value = Checked Then
    filBrowse.System = True
    Else
    filBrowse.System = False
    End If
End Sub


Private Sub chkArchive_Click()
    'Set search criteria to disable or enable
    'viewing of Archive Files
    '
    If chkArchive.Value = Checked Then
    filBrowse.Archive = True
    Else
    filBrowse.Archive = False
    End If
End Sub


Private Sub chkHidden_Click()
    'Set search criteria to disable or enable
    'viewing of Hidden Files
    '
    If chkHidden.Value = Checked Then
    filBrowse.Hidden = True
    Else
    filBrowse.Hidden = False
    End If
End Sub


Private Sub chkNormal_Click()
    'Set search criteria to disable or enable
    'viewing of Normal Files
    '
    If chkNormal.Value = Checked Then
    filBrowse.Normal = True
    Else
```

12

continues

LISTING 12.3   continued

```
    filBrowse.Normal = False
      End If
End Sub
```

Add the following code to the text box Change event:

```
Private Sub txtFilter_Change()
    '
    'Assign search criteria to the file list box control
    '
    filBrowse.Pattern = txtFilter.Text
End Sub
```

The running application should resemble Figure 12.5.

FIGURE 12.5

*File Browser
application.*

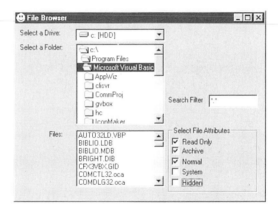

Test the File Browser application by selecting different drives and folders. Notice how
the FileListBox control changes when you click a folder. Insert a disk in your floppy
drive and select the floppy drive in the DriveListBox. The folder and FileListBox control automatically update to reflect the files and folders on the floppy disk. Use the check
boxes to view different file types. Modify the search filter criteria in the text box to view
only certain files or extensions. Notice that the browser application serves the same purpose as the CommonDialog control used in Chapter 8, "Using ActiveX Controls."

Lesson Summary

This lesson builds upon the previous lesson by showing you how to chain together the
File System controls to browse the Windows file system. By using the change event of

the different controls and various properties, you built a simple application that allows a user to select a drive and see all of the folders. Select a folder and see all of the files. The next lesson begins the process of opening, reading, and closing a file.

Quiz 2

1. A `DriveListBox` control supplies information to a `DirListBox` control. In what event should code be placed to tie the controls together?

   a. `Click`

   b. `Dbl_Click`

   c. `Change`

   d. `Validate`

2. A `DriveListBox` control supplies information to a `DirListBox` control when a new drive is selected. What property on the `DirListBox` control should be set to reflect the change in the `DriveListBox` control?

   a. `CurrentDrive`

   b. `Drive`

   c. `Path`

   d. `Text`

3. Setting the `Archive` property to `False` on a `FileListBox` control:

   a. Archives the files in the folder

   b. Does not display files with the `Archive` bit set from the `FileListBox` control

   c. Displays all files with the `Archive` bit set in the `FileListBox` control

   d. Does nothing

4. What control can be used instead of the File controls to present the user with a window to enable the user to browse the file system to select a file to open in an application?

   a. Data Access control

   b. Grid control

   c. File Explorer control

   d. `CommonDialog` control

12

Exercise 2

Complexity: Easy

1. List a few application examples where you could use the file system controls.

Complexity: Moderate

2. You have `DirListBox` control called Dir1 and `FileListBox` control called File1. Write the event procedure and the required code to displays the files in the selected folder when the folder is changed.

LESSON 3

Opening, Reading, and Closing a File

Using the File custom controls enables you to create applications to browse through the file system. The next logical step is file input/output, or file I/O. This term is used to represent the many different input and output operations that can be performed on a file, such as reading from the file or writing to the file. Accessing data via file I/O is like reading a book.

File I/O follows the same sequence of events. The first step is to locate the file you want to use. In the first part of this chapter, you learned how to locate files, using the File control; in Chapter 8, "Using ActiveX Controls," you learned to use the `CommonDialog` control. When the file has been located, the next step is to open the file. File I/O operations such as reading or writing can be done only on an open file. When you are done with the file, you close it. Let's take a look at some of the basic file I/O commands.

Opening a File

The `Open` command opens a file in Visual Basic 6. The `Open` command is covered in more detail in Lesson 4, "Sequential and Random Access Files." For the time being, assume that a sequential file is nothing more than a file that consists of ASCII characters. The `Open` statement has the following syntax:

```
Open pathname For Input As [#]filenumber
```

The following are the components of the syntax:

- `pathname` is the full path and filename of the file to open.
- `Input` specifies to open the file for reading.

- `filenumber` is an integer number between 1 and 511. The `Open` command allocates a buffer to perform the file I/O and determines the type of access to use with the buffer. A buffer is a block of memory the computer sets aside for input and output operations. The file number is used to identify the open file to other file I/O commands. For example, assume you want to open a file named VB.TXT in C:\VB using the file number 1. The code required to perform this task looks like the following:

```
Open "C:\VB\VB.TXT" For Input As #1
```

If you do not specify the path of the file, Visual Basic will assume that the file you are opening is in the current directory, usually the directory from which your application is executing.

```
Open "VB.TXT" For Input As #1
```

You can open more than one file at a time. However, you must use different file numbers for each open file. For instance, you might want to open a file called VB.TXT and copy the contents to another file, called BACKUP.TXT. If you try to use a file number currently in use by another file, an error occurs. Keeping track of file numbers can be a problem if you have to write applications that require using many different files simultaneously. Fortunately, Visual Basic provides a function called FreeFile that returns an available file number. The FreeFile syntax is as follows:

```
FreeFile[(rangenumber)]
```

The component `rangenumber` is an optional parameter. If `rangenumber` = 0 (the default), FreeFile returns file numbers between 1 and 255. If `rangenumber` = 1, FreeFile returns file numbers between 256 and 511.

The code below shows how to use FreeFile.

```
Dim iFileNum As Integer
iFileNum = FreeFile
Open "TEST.TXT" For Input As #FileNum
```

You must save the file number in a variable so you can read from the file, write to it, or close it. A line such as `Open "TEST.TXT" For Input As #FreeFile` would leave you with an orphan file that you could not use for anything.

Closing a File

When you are finished with the open file, you must execute code that will close the file. Closing the file releases the file buffer and returns the file number to the unused pool. It also flushes the buffer so that all new data for the file is saved. The Close statement has the following syntax:

```
Close [filenumberlist]
```

`filenumberlist` is a list of file numbers to close. If no file number list is provided, then all open files are closed.

The following code example closes an open file with the file number 1:

```
Close #1
```

Determining the Size of the File

Before you attempt to read a file, it is a good idea to know when to stop. Attempting to read past the end of a file will generate an error. Reading less than an entire file may also prove troublesome, depending on your program's needs.

Visual Basic has two functions that you can use to determine how much to read and when to stop reading:

- LOF returns the size in bytes of an open file.
- EOF returns True when the end of the file is reached.

The syntax for LOF is as follows:

```
FileSize = LOF(filenumber)
```

`filenumber` is the file number of the open file for which you want to obtain the size in bytes.

To determine when you have reached the end of a file, use the EOF function, which has the following format:

```
EOF(filenumber)
```

where `filenumber` is the file number of the open file. The EOF function returns True when the end of the file is reached.

Reading a File

Reading a file means extracting the characters that are in the file into a memory buffer. To a read a file, you must

- Determine how many characters to read
- Provide variables to receive the data

Visual Basic 6 provides several functions and statements to read a sequential file:

- Input
- Input #
- Line Input #

Input **Function**

The Input function has the following syntax:

```
Input(number, [#]filenumber)
```

The following are the components of the syntax:

- number is the number of characters to read.
- filenumber is the file number of the open file to read.

The Input function is used to read any number of bytes from a file into a Visual Basic variable. For instance, the following example uses the Input function to read 10 characters into the string variable LastName:

```
LastName = Input(10, #1)
```

Input # **Function**

The Input # statement provides an easy way to read a list of numbers or strings from a file and assign them to variables. The syntax for the Input # function is

```
Input #filenumber, varlist
```

The following are the components of the syntax:

- filenumber is the file number of the open file to read.
- varlist is a list of variables to receive the data.

Assume that a file contains the following: Mark, Wednesday. Using the Input function, Mark and Wednesday could be read into local variables Name and DayOfWeek.

```
Input #1, Name, DayOfWeek
```

Line Input # **Statement**

The Line Input # statement reads a single line of data at a time. The statement will read all the characters until it encounters a carriage return-linefeed sequence and returns all the data up to the carriage return. The syntax for Line Input # is

```
Line Input #filenumber, varname
```

The following are the components of the syntax:

- filenumber is the file number of the open file.
- varname is the variable to hold the line of data.

For example:

```
Line Input #1, OneLine
```

12

Sequential Read Example

The example program puts it all together and uses Open, Close, and all three input commands to read a sequential file. It reads the seq.txt file located on the CD that comes with the book. To read the text file, make sure seq.txt is located in the same directory as the project files. The general format of the seq.txt file is as follows:

```
Name, DayOfWeek.
```

Each line contains two comma-delimited variables and ends with a carriage return and linefeed.

The application opens the text file, reads the entire file, and displays it in a picture box. To experiment with the different formats of the Input command, the application can read the file using any of the methods covered so far: Input, Input #, or Line Input #.

Creating a New Project Called Seq

The new project Seq consists of a single form, a Command button, a picture box, a Frame control, and three option buttons. The completed project is on the CD that comes with this book. Set the properties for each of the controls, as shown in Table 12.6.

TABLE 12.6 Form frmSequential Objects and Property Settings

Object	Property	Setting
Form	Caption	Sequential Read
	Height	3810
	Name	frmSequential
	Width	6855
OptionButton	Caption	Input
	Height	195
	Name	optInput
	Left	90
	Top	240
	Value	True
	Width	990
OptionButton	Caption	Input #
	Height	195
	Name	optInNum

Object	Property	Setting
	Left	120
	Top	525
	Value	False
	Width	990
OptionButton	Caption	Input Line #
	Height	195
	Name	optLine
	Left	1230
	Top	240
	Value	False
	Width	1245
PictureBox	Height	195
	Name	Picture1
	Left	180
	Top	195
	Width	6630
CommandButton	Caption	Test Sequential Read Method
	Height	705
	Name	cmdInput
	Left	240
	Top	2640
	width	2520
Frame	Caption	Read Method
	Height	810
	Name	Frame1
	Left	3885
	Top	2565
(i)	Width	2610

The option buttons are used to determine which sequential Read command to use to read the text file. Complete the project by adding the code shown in Listing 12.4 to the Click event of the Command button.

LISTING 12.4   Sequential I/O Read Code in the Command Button Click Event

```
Private Sub cmdInput_Click()
Dim Read_Buffer As String   ' Buffer to read the file
Dim File_Length As Integer  ' Integer to store file size
    On Error GoTo File_Error ' Set up the error handler
    ' Clear the Picture Box
    Picture1.Cls
    '
    ' Open the text file seq.txt
    '
    Open App.Path & "\seq.txt" For Input As #1 ' Open the file
    File_Length = LOF ' Get the size of the file
    If optInput.Value = True Then
        Picture1.Print "Input Command" ' Display Command in Picture Box
        ' Input Command
        ' Read the entire file into the string
        Read_Buffer = Input(File_Length, #1)
        ' Display the contents of the file in the picture box
        Picture1.Print Read_Buffer

    ElseIf optInNum.Value = True Then
        Picture1.Print "Input # Command" ' Display Command in Picture Box
        ' Input # Command
        ' Read the entire file into the strings - Note use of EOF
        Do While Not EOF
            Input #1, Read_Buffer
            ' Display the contents of the file in the picture box
            Picture1.Print Read_Buffer
        Loop
    Else
        Picture1.Print "Line Input # Command" ' Display Command in Picture Box
        '
        ' Line Input # Command
        ' Read the entire file into the strings - Note use of EOF
        Do While Not EOF
            Line Input #1, Read_Buffer
            ' Display the contents of the file in the picture box
            Picture1.Print Read_Buffer
        Loop
    End If

    Close #1 ' Close the File
Exit_Input:
    Exit Sub ' Exit
' Basic Error Handler
File_Error:
    MsgBox Err.Description, vbCritical, "File Error"
    Resume Exit_Input
End Sub
```

The best way to see how each of the commands differs from the others is to use the Debug mode:

1. Open the Tools menu and select Options. Be sure that Auto Data Tips is checked.

2. Set a breakpoint on the following line:

```
Open App.Path & "\seq.txt" For Input As #1 'Open the file
```

3. Press F5 or click the Start button to start the program. The first option, Input, is already selected.

4. Click the Command button.

5. When the program reaches the breakpoint, single step through the rest of the cmdInput_Click function. Hold the cursor on each of the variables before and after the program has assigned it a value. Figure 12.6 shows what this looks like.

FIGURE 12.6

Single stepping through Seq.vbp.

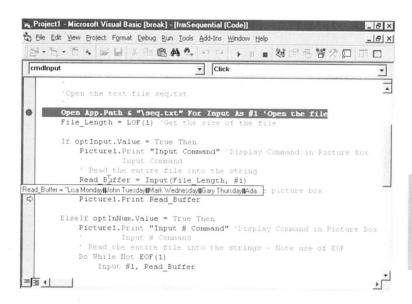

6. Repeat the single-step process for each of the Read options.

The two dark vertical bars you see between items in Read_Buffer during the Input function are the CR-LF characters that delimit (separate) the items in the text file. They are referred to as the *unprintable characters.*

Note that the Input # statement reads the name and the day in two separate operations, whereas the Line Input # statement reads the entire line at once. The Input # statement reads single data items, up to the delimiter, whereas Line Input # reads the entire line, up to the CR-LF.

You can read more than one variable with Input # by changing the varlist parameter. The new line for Seq.VBP would look like this:

```
Input #1, Name, DayOfWeek
```

You also must change the following line to

```
Picture1.Print Name, DayOfWeek
```

Try it!

Lesson Summary

This lesson covered a lot of information so to recap the main features of the lesson, you learned how to

- Open a sequential ASCII file using the Open command.
- Read data from the file using three different commands: Input, Input # and Line Input #.
- Close the file using the Close command.
- To obtain an available file number, use the FreeFile command.

The next lesson covers random access files.

Quiz 3

1. What does the following code do?

   ```
   Open "Quiz.txt" For Input As #23
   ```

   a. Opens the file Quiz.txt to write characters to
   b. Opens a file called #23 with an identifier of Quiz.txt
   c. Opens the file Quiz.txt with file number 23 for reading
   d. Opens the file called Quiz.txt and writes the number 23 to the file

2. The FreeFile function:

   a. Frees all open files by closing them
   b. Returns a free file number
   c. Deletes a file
   d. Creates a new file and places it in the Windows 95 free file pool

3. When you are done with a file, execute the _____ command to free the I/O buffer, release the file number, and close the file.

a. Terminate

b. FileClose

c. Close

d. ReturnHandle

4. What does the following code do?

```
Do While Not EOF(1)
    Line Input #1, Read_Buffer
Loop
```

a. Reads an open file a line at a time until the end of the file is reached

b. Reads an open file a character at a time until the end of the file is reached

c. Reads an open file one line at a time until an error occurs when it reads beyond the end of the file

d. Reads an open file one character at a time until an error occurs when it reads beyond the end of the file

Exercise 3

Complexity: Easy

1. Write the line of code that signals the end of file has been reached for a open file with a file number of 4.

Complexity: Moderate

2. Write a program that opens a text file and reads the first line of the text box and displays it using a message box.

12

LESSON 4

Sequential and Random Access Files

A file is nothing more than a group of related bytes, bunched together and stored on a drive. A file can contain ASCII text characters, fixed-length records, or binary data. When designing an application to read and write data to a file, you must take into consideration the type of data your application expects to read and write. With Visual Basic, you select the data type when you open a file by setting the access mode of the file.

The possible file access modes are

- Sequential
- Random
- Binary

The examples you have completed so far used sequential file access functions and statements. In this lesson, you will learn about sequential access files, random access files, and binary files.

Sequential Access

Sequential file access is used for data files comprising ASCII text characters. Figure 12.7 represents an example of an ASCII sequential text file—an application initialization file. This figure shows how the file would look if you were to open it with a file Text Editor such as Notepad and how the data in the file is stored. Each box in the drawing represents one byte of data in the disk file. To parse the initialization file, use the `Line Input #` statement, reading a line at a time until you find the correct parameter. Use sequential access for reading and writing files that contain ASCII characters.

FIGURE 12.7

Sequential file example.

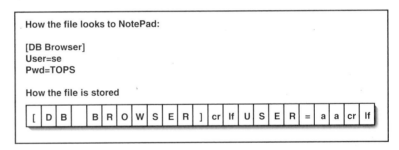

But what if you have a non-ASCII file with a fixed-length record?

Random Access

A fixed-length record is a data structure that always has the same length. That is, each record takes up exactly the same number of bytes in the disk file. The record may have a single data member or it may have several members. Table 12.7 represents a data structure called `EmployeeName`. If you fill the data structure with data and write the structure to a file, you have a fixed-length record file. For instance, the first 15 bytes in the file would always contain the value of the field named `First`, the next 15 bytes would always contain the value of the field named `Last`, and the last 2 bytes would contain the value of the field named `Count`.

TABLE 12.7 `EmployeeName` Data Structure

Name	Size
First	15 bytes
Last	15 bytes
Count	2 bytes
Total record length	32 bytes

What happens if you want to put a four-byte name in the `First` field, rather than a 15-byte name? Because the record is of fixed length, you would use a fill character for the remaining 11 bytes. A fill character is a character selected to pad or fill fields in fixed-length records when the data is not large enough to fill the field. In this example, the `First` and `Last` fields use a space for a fill character so that when the `First` and `Last` fields are displayed, the fill character is not seen. What happens if you have a last name that is longer than 15 characters and try to write it to the `Last` field? Because the record is fixed length, the `Last` field cannot be larger than 15 characters; any characters past the 15th character would be dropped (truncated).

The file access mode for fixed-length records is the random access mode. Random access enables you to take advantage of fixed-length records by retrieving records by record number rather than one character at a time. A sequential access CD player requires you to listen to songs 1 and 2 before you can listen to song 3. A random access CD player allows you to listen to song 3 while skipping the other songs. Random access mode works by using the fixed-length record size and the file size to skip over records, compute the correct record offset, and go to the record you specify.

For example, if 100 names were written to a file using the `EmployeeName` structure defined in Table 12.7, the file opened in random access mode would be able to read the 50th name in the file by specifying record number 50. Instead of reading character by character, the `Read` command would seek to the 50th record and read it. File access mode is specified in the `Open` statement. Take another look at the syntax for the `Open` statement. This time the command contains the `FileMode` parameter.

```
Open pathname [For FileMode] As [#]filenumber [Len=length]
```

The following are the components of the syntax:

- `pathname` is the full filename.
- `FileMode` can be `Input` for sequential access, `Random` for random access, and `Binary` for binary access.
- `Len` is the length for sequential access or the record length for random access.

The code shown in Listing 12.5 opens a file named `Random.dat` in random mode containing the data structure in Table 12.7.

LISTING 12.5   Opening the File `Random.dat` in Random Access Mode

```
Type Name
  First * 15 string
  Last * 15 string
  Count Integer
End Type
Dim RecordSize as Integer
RecordSize = Len(Name)
Open "Random.dat" For Random As #1 Len = RecordSize
```

This code creates a *user-defined type* (UDT) for the record `Name`. UDTs are similar to arrays, except that the elements can be of different data types. The one in the code contains two strings and an integer. Note the use of fixed-length strings for `First` and `Last`.

To read a random access file, use the `Get` statement. The `Get` statement has the following syntax:

```
Get [#]filenumber, [recnumber], varname
```

The following are the components of the syntax:

- `filenumber` is the file number of the open file to read.
- `recnumber` is the record number to read.
- `varname` is the storage variable for the record being read.

The following code example retrieves the 50th record from an open file:

```
Get #1, 50, HoldRecord
```

If you leave off the record number, `Get` returns the next record. Closing a random file uses the same syntax as the sequential file `Close` command.

Random Access Project, Part I

Begin a new project that uses random access to read a fixed-length record. This is a two-part project. This part shows how to add the code to read a fixed-length record and how to step through the file when a user clicks a Next or Previous button. The next part shows how to add the code that creates a random access file. Create a new project called Random. Add the objects and set the properties shown in Table 12.8. The completed project is on the CD that comes with this book.

TABLE 12.8 Objects, Properties, and Settings for the frmRandom Form

Object	Property	Setting
Form	Caption	-Random File - Reading and Writing
	Height	2970
	Name	frmRandom
	Width	4425
CommandButton	Caption	<<
	Height	330
	Name	cmdPrevious
	Left	330
	Top	2100
	Width	1380
CommandButton	Caption	>>
	Height	330
	Name	cmdNext
	Left	2475
	Top	2100
	Width	1380
Label	Caption	First
	Height	345
	Left	615
	Name	label1
	Top	195
	Width	705
Label	Caption	Last
	Height	345
	Left	615
	Name	label2
	Top	825
	Width	705
Label	Caption	Count
	Height	345
	Left	615

continues

TABLE 12.8   continued

Object	Property	Setting
	Name	label3
	Top	1455
	Width	705
TextBox	Height	360
	Left	1455
	Name	txtFirst
	Top	210
	Width	1995
TextBox	Height	360
	Left	1455
	Name	txtLast
	Top	810
	Width	1995
TextBox	Height	360
	Left	1455
	Name	txtCount
	Top	1455
(i)	Width	1995

The completed form is shown in Figure 12.8.

FIGURE 12.8

Project Random File form frmRandom.

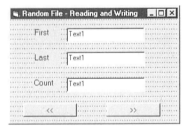

The project uses the record structure `EmployeeName`, shown in Table 12.7. Insert a new module called `random.bas` in the project and add the following record structure definition in the Declarations section of the module:

```
Type EmployeeName ' Define user-defined type.
    First As String * 15
    Last As String * 15
```

```
        Count As Integer
End Type
```

Add the code to read a record from an open random file and place data from the record into the text boxes on the form. Add a new procedure to the form. Name the procedure GetRecord and add the code shown in Listing 12.6.

LISTING 12.6   GetRecord Procedure

```
Public Sub GetRecord(RecNum As Integer)
'
'Read the specified record from the file and display on the form
'
Dim RecBuf As EmployeeName
    'Read the first record and place in the form
    Get #1, RecNum, RecBuf
    txtFirst = RecBuf.First
    txtLast = RecBuf.Last
    txtCount = RecBuf.Count
End Sub
```

Now add the code to manage stepping through the file. The two Command buttons enable the user to step through the file one record at a time. The Command button with the caption >> moves to the next record in the file until the end of the file is reached. The Command button with the caption << moves to the previous record in the file until the beginning of the file is reached. Add the code shown in Listing 12.7 to the Click event of the Command button cmdNext.

LISTING 12.7   cmdNext Click Event Code

```
Private Sub cmdNext_Click()
    'Get the next record in the file
    '
    If CurrentRec <> MaxRec Then
        '
        'Increment the record Number
        CurrentRec = CurrentRec + 1

        'Retrieve and display
        GetRecord (CurrentRec)
    Else
        MsgBox "End of file. No next record."
    End If

End Sub
```

In the `Click` event of the Command button `cmdPrevious`, add the code shown in Listing 12.8.

LISTING 12.8   `cmdPrevious Click` Event Code

```
Private Sub cmdPrevious_Click()
    'Get the previous record in the file
    '
    If CurrentRec > 1 Then
        '
        'Decrement the record Number
        CurrentRec = CurrentRec - 1

        'Retrieve and display
        GetRecord (CurrentRec)
    Else
        MsgBox "Start of file. No previous record."
    End If

End Sub
```

You may have noticed the two new variables in Listing 12.7 and Listing 12.8, `CurrentRec` and `MaxRec`. The variable `CurrentRec` is used to determine which record number in the file is currently being displayed. The `MaxRec` variable is used to determine how many records are in the file so the program does not try to read past the end of the file. Add the two variables to the Declarations section of the form, as shown below.

```
Dim CurrentRec As Integer 'Current Record
Dim MaxRec As Integer 'Max Record
```

Writing

It is time to round out your file I/O skills by learning how to write to a file. First, consider an example to help you understand the decisions you must make when writing to files.

You decide to go on a diet and want to write down everything you eat. You purchase a nice blue notebook with 200 pages. The first day of your diet, you open the notebook and begin to write on the very first page. The day slowly passes by; at the end of the day, you have filled up half a page with your meals for the day. The next day, when you write your first meal in the notebook, you decide to start the day's meal at the end of the previous day's meals, using the same sheet of paper instead of starting on a new sheet. At lunch time, you begin to enter your meal and realize that you made an error entering breakfast. You erase the entry (because you made it in pencil) and add the correction.

The decisions and actions you take when writing your diet diary are very similar to the decisions and actions you make when writing to a file in sequential access mode. The first time you write to a newly opened file, the data is placed at the beginning of the file. If you open a file with existing data, you must decide whether you want to write new data after the existing data, such as writing a new day's meals at the end of the existing day, or whether you want to write over existing data, like erasing the mistake in the diet log and writing a new entry.

Writing to Sequential Files

How do you write to a sequential file? Once again, reexamine the Open command. Take a look at the full syntax for the Open command for sequential access.

```
Open pathname For [Input Output Append] As [#]filenumber [Len=length]
```

In Lesson 2, you learned how to use the Input option to read a sequential file. The Output and Append options are used to open a file for writing. The Append option differs from the Output option in that any data written to the file is appended to the end of the file. If a file that does not exist is opened with Output or Append, a new file is created. Existing files opened with the Output option are overwritten. The command to write to a sequential file is the Print # command, which has the following syntax:

```
Print #filenumber, [outputlist]
```

The following are the components of the syntax:

- filenumber is the file number of the open file to which to write.
- outputlist is a list of strings or a variable to write to the text file. Use a space or semicolon to separate multiple items.

The following example uses the Print # statement to write a variable to a file.

```
Dim strCount as String
strCount = "one two three four five"
Print #1, strCount
```

The Print # statement makes writing to a sequential file very simple and is similar to other commands you have used, like the Debug.Print statement. The results go out to a file instead of to a screen or a printer.

Writing to Random Files

After a file has been opened for random access, use the Put command to write fixed-length records to the file. The Put statement has the following syntax:

```
Put [#]filenumber, [recnumber], varname
```

The following are the components of the syntax:

- `filenumber` is the file number of the open file to write.
- `recnumber` is the offset to write the fixed-length record (`recnumber` starts with the number 1).
- `varname` is the variable to write to the file.

To write a record at the end of the file, set the `recnumber` parameter to one more than the last record. The following example shows how to write a record at the end of the file by setting the `recnumber` parameter to one more than the last record (for this example, assume the last record is number 10):

```
Put #1, (10+1), MyRec
```

Random Access Project, Part II

Now that you know how to write data to a random file, it's time to finish the random access project. So far, you have added the code required to read and scroll through a file of fixed-length records, but you don't have a file to read. Add the code shown in Listing 12.9 to the `Form_Load` event.

 Note   This program will load correctly from the CD because it writes over the existing text file and creates a new one. Copy the program and all the associated files from the CD to your hard drive. Make sure that the text file, random.txt does not have the read-only or archive attribute set (do this by using the Windows Explorer; select the file, right-click, and select properties).

LISTING 12.9   Form `frmRandom` Load Event

```
Dim MyRecord As EmployeeName   'Declare the fixed length record
Dim FileName As String   'Filename and path
Dim RecNum As Integer   'Record Number Counter
    On Error GoTo rand_err
    '
    'Set up filename
    FileName = App.Path & "\random.txt"
    ' Open sample file for random access.
    Open FileName For Random As #1 Len = Len(MyRecord)
    'Write some records to the file
    '
    MyRecord.First = "John"
    For RecNum = 1 To 8
        MyRecord.Last = "Doe" & Str$(RecNum)
        MyRecord.Count = Str$(RecNum)
        '
        'Write the record to the file
        Put #1, RecNum, MyRecord
```

```
    Next RecNum
    '
    'Determine the number of records in the file
    '
    MaxRec = LOF / Len(MyRecord)
    'Read the first record and place in the form
    GetRecord
    'Initialize the Current Record
    CurrentRec = 1
rand_exit:
Exit Sub
'Error handler
rand_err:
    MsgBox Err.Description, vbCritical, "File I/O Error"
    Resume rand_exit
End Sub
```

Note

This code is for the sake of example. A functional program would enable the user to enter the data to be saved to the file.

What the Code Does

Listing 12.10 shows the correct method of opening the data file.

LISTING 12.10 Creating and Opening the File random.txt

```
'Set up filename
    FileName = App.Path & "\random.txt"
    ' Open sample file for random access.
    Open FileName For Random As #1 Len = Len(MyRecord)
```

If the file does not already exist, the Open statement creates a new file.

The code in Listing 12.11 shows how to write records to a random access file.

LISTING 12.11 Writing Random Records to File random.txt

```
MyRecord.First = "John"
    For RecNum = 1 To 8
        MyRecord.Last = "Doe" & Str$(RecNum)
        MyRecord.Count = Str$(RecNum)
        '
        'Write the record to the file
        Put #1, RecNum, MyRecord
    Next RecNum
```

To make the example simple, this code artificially generates eight different John Doe entries. It adds RecNum to the end of each last name to make them all different.

Random access files let you change the data stored in any record simply by writing directly to the record. Changing a sequential file requires storing the data from the entire file in an array, changing the data in the array, and writing the file back to disk. Clearly, if your data may change, it is preferable to use random access files.

To manage the scrolling through the file using the Next and Previous Command buttons, the value of the form variables CurrentRec and MaxRec must be set. The following code uses the LOF function (which means Length Of File) to determine the size of the open file and divides by the size of the fixed-length record to get the number of records in the file.

```
'Determine the number of records in the file
'
    MaxRec = LOF(1) / Len(MyRecord)
```

To set the value of the current record, set the variable to the record number. The example below sets it to the first record.

```
CurrentRec = 1
```

You are now ready to test the application. Run the Random application. Use the Next and Previous Command buttons to scroll through the different records in the file. The running Random application is shown in Figure 12.9.

FIGURE 12.9

Running the Random application.

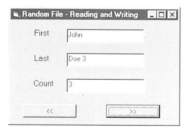

You have now learned the commands to read and write a file! The next lesson explains binary access files.

Lesson Summary

Visual Basic allows you to perform file I/O using fixed length records. The file I/O mode to perform fixed-length record operations is called the random access mode. When opening a file for sequential access mode or random access mode, use the Open statement. To read an random access file use the Get statement and to write a random access file use the Put statement. Writing to a sequential file is done via the Print statement.

Quiz 4

1. The ___ command is used to read random access files.

    a. `Read`

    b. `Write`

    c. `Get`

    d. `Input`

2. Reading or writing a fixed-length record is an example of ____ file access.

    a. Sequential

    b. Normal

    c. Random

    d. Read_Write

3. `Open "C":\VB.TXT" For Random as #1 Len=20`

    a. Opens the file `C:\VB.TXT` in random access mode with a fixed-length record size of 20

    b. The syntax is incorrect

    c. Opens the file `C\VB.TXT` in binary mode

    d. Opens the file `C\VB.TXT` with 20 records in random access mode

4. To write a record past the last record in a random access mode file:

    a. Use `Seek` to go to the end of the file and the `Print` command

    b. Use the `Put` command, where the record number is one more than the current total in the file

    c. Use the `Put` command with the last record number in the file

    d. Use the `Print` command

Exercise 4

Complexity: Easy

1. When would you use sequential file access? When would you use random file access?

Complexity: Moderate

2. Write a line of code that determines the total number of records in a random access file with a file number of 1 and a fixed record called UserRecord.

LESSON 5

Binary File Access

Random access files are convenient and easy, but they do have their drawbacks. This lesson explains the ins and outs of binary file access. Many programmers avoid binary access because it is a bit complicated. But the advantages of binary access make it worth considering when you must deal with large amounts of data.

Why Use Binary Access?

Random access records are fixed-length records. Consider the record structure in Listing 12.12.

LISTING 12.12   Fixed-Length Customer Record

```
Type Customer
    ID As Integer
    FirstName As String * 20
    LastName As String * 20
    Title As String * 15
    Address As String * 30
    City As String * 20
    State As String * 2
    ZipCode As String * 11
    Phone As String * 13
End Type
```

This data structure requires 137 bytes of disk space for each record. The string for FirstName is always 20 characters long, whether the customer's first name is Ed or Rumpelstiltskin. The customer who lives at 1 D St. requires as much space for the address as the customer who lives at 2786 Wilkinshire Boulevard. In other words, random access records take a lot of disk space.

Binary access files do not use fixed-length records, which are their strength and their weakness. Look at the type declaration in Listing 12.13.

LISTING 12.13   A Customer Type for Binary Files

```
Type Customer
    ID As Integer
    FirstName As String
    LastName As String
```

```
        Title As String
        Address As String
        City As String
        State As String
        ZipCode As String
        Phone As String
End Type
```

Note that the strings are no longer declared as having a fixed length. Each record requires exactly as many bytes as there are characters in the strings, plus 2 bytes for the integer variable. It is this economy of space that makes binary files attractive.

Reading a Binary Access File

You read a binary access file the same way you read a random access file, with the Get statement. As a reminder, the syntax of Get is

```
Get [#]filenumber, [recnumber], varname
```

The difference is that recnumber for binary access is really the number of the first byte of the variable in the file. How do you know what that number is? For the first variable, it is obviously 1. When that variable has been read, you can find exactly where you are in the file by using the Seek function. The syntax is

```
Seek(Filenum)
```

Filenum is the number of the open file. The function returns the file position, that is, the number of the first byte of the next variable in the file.

Writing a Binary Access File

Write to a binary access file with the Put statement. As a refresher, the syntax is

```
Put [#]filenumber, [recnumber], varname
```

For binary access files, recnumber is the byte position where you want to write the file. If you leave recnumber out, the data will be written at the current file position. The statement without recnumber would look like

```
Put #1, , varname
```

A Programming Example

Start a new project in Visual Basic. Name the project fBinary.vbp. Place the objects in Table 12.9 on the form. The completed project is on the CD that comes with this book. This project is rather complicated, so you might want to copy it from the CD rather than

12

type it in. If so, because the program writes data to disk, you must copy it to your hard disk. (Follow the explanations of the code!)

TABLE 12.9   Starting the Binary Project

Object	Property	Value
Form	Name	Form1
	Caption	Binary Files
	Height	3855
	Width	6600
PictureBox	Name	Picture1
	Enabled	False
	Height	3195
	Width	6315
	Left	120
(i)	Top	60

Draw 11 text boxes inside the picture box. Set their properties according to Table 12.10.

TABLE 12.10   Adding Text Boxes to Picture1

Object	Property	Value
TextBox	Name	txtFirst
	Top	345
	Left	300
	Width	2055
	Height	285
	TabIndex	0
	Text	(None)
TextBox	Name	txtLast
	Top	345
	Left	2400
	Width	2155
	Height	285
	TabIndex	1
	Text	(None)

Object	Property	Value
TextBox	Name	txtRecNum
	Top	60
	Left	460
	Width	735
	Height	285
	Text	(None)
	TabStop	False
	Locked	True
TextBox	Name	txtTitle
	Top	960
	Left	300
	Width	2055
	Height	285
	TabIndex	2
	Text	(none)
TextBox	Name	txtPay
	Top	960
	Left	2460
	Width	2055
	Height	285
	TabIndex	3
	Text	(none)
TextBox	Name	txtAddress
	Top	1515
	Left	300
	Width	4215
	Height	285
	TabIndex	4
	Text	(none)
TextBox	Name	txtCity
	Top	2115
	Left	300
	Width	2355

12

continues

TABLE 12.10   continued

Object	Property	Value
	Height	285
	TabIndex	5
	Text	(none)
TextBox	Name	txtState
	Top	2155
	Left	2700
	Width	375
	Height	285
	MaxLength	2
	TabIndex	6
	Text	(none)
TextBox	Name	txtZip
	Top	2115
	Left	3120
	Width	1395
	Height	285
	TabIndex	7
	Text	(none)
TextBox	Name	txtPhone
	Top	2700
	Left	300
	Width	2235
	Height	285
	TabIndex	8
	Text	(none)
TextBox	Name	txtID
	Top	2700
	Left	3780
	Width	2235
	Height	285
	TabIndex	9
(i)	Text	(none)

Add labels for each text box. Rather than using a table to place the labels, use Figure 12.10 as a guide.

FIGURE 12.10

The Binary project at design time.

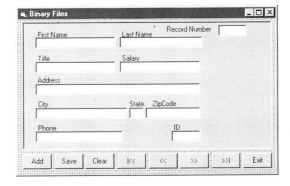

From Figure 12.10, you can see that you also need to add eight Command buttons. Use Table 12.11 to place the Command buttons.

TABLE 12.11 The Command Buttons for Binary

Object	Property	Value
CommandButton	Name	cmdAdd
	Caption	Add
	Height	375
	Left	120
	TabIndex	10
	Top	3360
	Width	735
CommandButton	Name	cmdSave
	Caption	Save
	Height	375
	Left	925
	TabIndex	11
	Top	3360
	Width	735
CommandButton	Name	cmdClear
	Caption	Clear
	Height	375

continues

TABLE 12.11   continued

Object	Property	Value
	Left	1730
	TabIndex	12
	Top	3360
	Width	735
CommandButton	Name	cmdFirst
	Caption	¦<<
	Height	375
	Left	2535
	TabIndex	13
	Top	3360
	Width	735
CommandButton	Name	cmdPrev
	Caption	<<
	Height	375
	Left	3340
	TabIndex	14
	Top	3360
	Width	735
CommandButton	Name	cmdNext
	Caption	>>
	Height	375
	Left	4145
	TabIndex	15
	Top	3360
	Width	735
CommandButton	Name	cmdLast
	Caption	>>¦
	Height	375
	Left	460
	TabIndex	16
	Top	3360
	Width	735

Object	Property	Value
CommandButton	Name	cmdQuit
	Caption	Exit
	Height	375
	Left	5760
	TabIndex	17
	Top	3360
(i)	Width	735

Take a deep breath, and then add a module to the project. Use the Properties window to name the module Binary. Add the declarations in Listing 12.14 to the Declarations section of the module.

LISTING 12.14   Global Declarations for Binary

```
Option Explicit
Public udtPlayer As Player
Public arrRecPos() As Long
Type Player
    ID As Integer
    FirstName As String
    LastName As String
    Title As String
    Salary As Currency
    Address As String
    City As String
    State As String
    ZipCode As String
    Phone As String
End Type
```

The declarations create a user-defined data type, Player, as a template for the data. They also declare a global variable of type Player and set up a dynamic array for storing the file positions of each record. Unlike random access files, binary access files do not store records in fixed-length blocks. To move to anything other than the next record, the program must keep track of the byte position of each record in the file.

Add a procedure to the module and enter the code from Listing 12.15.

12

LISTING 12.15   The FillText Procedure

```
Public Sub FillText()
    With udtPlayer
    With Form1
            .txtID = .ID
          .txtFirst = .FirstName
          .txtLast = .LastName
          .txtTitle = .Title
          .txtPay = .Salary
          .txtAddress = .Address
          .txtCity = .City
          .txtState = .State
          .txtZip = .ZipCode
          .txtPhone = .Phone
    End With
    End With
End Sub
```

When the program reads a record from the file, this procedure is used to copy data from the record into the text boxes. Because this procedure is in a module, each text box must be referenced to its parent form.

Checking for Valid Data

Often certain parts of a record are allowed to be empty, whereas other parts are required fields. That means that a record that does not have data in those fields is invalid and should not be saved to disk. This program does not allow data to be saved unless there is a first name, a last name, and a salary.

Add a new function to the module and enter the code from Listing 12.16.

LISTING 12.16   The CheckValidData Function

```
Public Function CheckValidData() As Boolean
    CheckValidData = True
    If Form1.txtFirst = "" Or _
        Form1.txtLast = "" _
        Or Form1.txtPay = "" Then
      CheckValidData = False
      MsgBox "Empty data", vbOKOnly, "Note!"
    End If
End Function
```

This function is an example of how to handle required fields. If any of the three required fields is empty, a message box warns the user, and the Save operation (the procedure that calls this function) is aborted. A more sophisticated example would point out which field needs to be fixed and place the focus on that field.

That is all the code for the module. Close the module's Code window and open the Code window for Form1.

Opening the File

The code in Listing 12.17 is in three parts. The first part is the formwide variable declarations. The second part is the Form_Load procedure. It opens the data file when the form is loaded. The third part is the Form_Unload procedure, which closes the file before unloading the form.

LISTING 12.17 The Declarations and the Form_Load Procedure

```
Option Explicit
Public lFileLen As Long
Public iRecNum As Integer
Public lFilePos As Long
Private Sub Form_Load()
Dim sFileName As String
'    Build the filename
     sFileName = App.Path & "\Player.dat"
'    open the file
     Open sFileName For Binary As #1
'    get length of file
     lFileLen = LOF(1)
End Sub


Private Sub Form_Unload(Cancel As Integer)
     Close #1
End Sub
```

The formwide variables are used to keep track of the file's length, the file position, and the record number. All three change as data is added to the file.

The first thing the code in Form_Load does is build the string for the filename. Note that it uses App.Path; the data file Player.dat must be in the same directory as the executable file. The Open statement opens the file for binary access. Finally, the LOF() function returns the file length to the variable lFileLen. This is used to determine when the Read operation reaches the end of the file.

12

The Form_Unload event explicitly closes the file. Always remember the three steps for file handling:

1. Open the file.
2. Manipulate the file (read or write or both).
3. Close the file.

When you write data to a file, it is buffered in memory until a large enough block of data has been prepared to make writing to that disk efficient. If you do not close the file, the data that is buffered in memory will be lost.

Reading the File

The data from the file is read by the Form_Activate procedure. The code for Form_Activate is in Listing 12.18.

LISTING 12.18   Reading the File

```
Private Sub Form_Activate()
    '    initialize to starting position
    iRecNum = 0
    lFilePos = 1
    '    read in the data file to get position information
    '    and number of records
    Do
        Get #1, lFilePos, udtPlayer
        iRecNum = iRecNum + 1
        '    add position to array
        ReDim Preserve arrRecPos(iRecNum)
        arrRecPos(iRecNum) = lFilePos
        '    get file position for next record
        lFilePos = Seek
    Loop Until lFilePos >= LOF(1)
    '    display next blank record number
'   disable data entry
    Picture1.Enabled = False
    '    enable/disable command buttons
    cmdSave.Enabled = False
    cmdClear.Enabled = False
    cmdNext.Enabled = True
    cmdPrev.Enabled = True
    cmdFirst = True
End Sub
```

The reading begins at file position (byte) 1. After the data has been read, the file position is stored in the dynamic array so it can be found again. The array index for each record is the record number of that record. The line `ReDim Preserve arrRecPos(iRecNum)` adds a new element to the array for each record that is read. Note the use of `Redim Preserve` to save the existing array data.

When the old file position has been saved, the current file position is saved in `lFilePos` by calling the `Seek` function. The loop checks to be sure that `lFilePos` is less than the length of the file. If it is not, the program has finished reading.

When all the records have been read in, the program sets you up to view them. `Picture1` is disabled to prevent typing new data into the text boxes, and the Navigation buttons `cmdFirst`, `cmdNext`, `cmdPrev`, and `cmdLast` are enabled.

Because you need at least those Navigation buttons to be operational before you can view the file, they are next. The code for all four Navigation buttons is in Listing 12.19.

LISTING 12.19 The Navigation Buttons

```
Private Sub cmdFirst_Click()
'   Goes to first record
'     disable data entry
    Picture1.Enabled = False
'     enable/disable command buttons
    cmdSave.Enabled = False
    cmdClear.Enabled = False
    cmdNext.Enabled = True
    cmdPrev.Enabled = True
'     First record
    iRecNum = 1
    lFilePos = 1
    Get #1, lFilePos, udtPlayer
    txtRecNum = iRecNum
'     Fill in the textboxes from the udt
    Call FillText
'     cmdNext is logical focus
    cmdNext.SetFocus
End Sub

Private Sub cmdLast_Click()
'     disable data entry
    Picture1.Enabled = False
'     enable disable command buttons
    cmdSave.Enabled = False
    cmdClear.Enabled = False
    cmdNext.Enabled = True
    cmdPrev.Enabled = True
'     find last file position
    lFilePos = arrRecPos(UBound(arrRecPos))
    Get #1, lFilePos, udtPlayer
```

12

continues

LISTING 12.19   continued

```
'   get record number
iRecNum = UBound(arrRecPos)
txtRecNum = iRecNum
'   fill in the textboxes
Call FillText
'   cmdPrev is logical focus
cmdPrev.SetFocus
End Sub


Private Sub cmdNext_Click()
'   test for last record
If Val(txtRecNum) + 1 > UBound(arrRecPos) Then
    MsgBox "This is the last record", vbOKOnly, "End of File"
    cmdPrev.SetFocus
    Exit Sub
End If
'   get file position
lFilePos = arrRecPos(Val(txtRecNum) + 1)
Get #1, lFilePos, udtPlayer
iRecNum = iRecNum + 1
txtRecNum = iRecNum
'   Fill in the textboxes
Call FillText
cmdNext.SetFocus
End Sub


Private Sub cmdPrev_Click()
'   text for first record
If Val(txtRecNum) - 1 < 1 Then
    MsgBox "This is the first record", vbOKOnly, "Beginning of File"
    cmdNext.SetFocus
    Exit Sub
End If
'   get file position
lFilePos = arrRecPos(Val(txtRecNum) - 1)
Get #1, lFilePos, udtPlayer
iRecNum = iRecNum - 1
txtRecNum = iRecNum
'   fill in the textboxes
Call FillText
cmdPrev.SetFocus
End Sub
```

With the exception of cmdFirst, the Navigation buttons use the array to find the file position of the record. Of course, cmdFirst need only read from byte 1 of the file. The cmdNext code checks to be sure it is not going beyond the last record, and cmdPrev, checks to be sure it does not go beyond record number one.

Adding Data

While you are reading the existing data, you cannot edit the fields. The text boxes are disabled by the simple trick of putting them all in a picture box and disabling the picture box. Data in the records cannot be changed in this program because new data may overwrite the next record with variable-length fields. The program will let you add new data only at the end of the file.

Adding data begins with the Add button, which clears all the text boxes and moves the file position to the end of the file. It also enables the picture box so you can enter text into the text boxes and enables the Save and Clear buttons so you can save your changes or clear the text boxes. The code for cmdAdd, cmdClear, and cmdSave is in Listing 12.20.

LISTING 12.20 Adding Data and Writing to the File

```
Private Sub cmdAdd_Click()
'   Prepare to add a new record
    '   Clear all textboxes
    cmdClear = True
End Sub

Private Sub cmdClear_Click()
'   Clears all text boxes
    txtID = ""
    txtFirst = ""
    txtLast = ""
    txtTitle = ""
    txtPay = ""
    txtAddress = ""
    txtCity = ""
    txtState = ""
    txtZip = ""
    txtPhone = ""
    iRecNum = UBound(arrRecPos)
    txtRecNum = iRecNum
    '   enable data entry
    Picture1.Enabled = True
    '   enable/disable command buttons
    cmdSave.Enabled = True
    cmdClear.Enabled = True
    cmdNext.Enabled = False
    cmdPrev.Enabled = False
    txtFirst.SetFocus
```

continues

LISTING 12.20   continued

```
End Sub

Private Sub cmdSave_Click()
    '   Check to be sure the key data is filled in
    If CheckValidData = False Then Exit Sub
    '   Put data from textboxes into udt
    With udtPlayer
        .ID = Val(txtID & "")
        .FirstName = txtFirst
        .LastName = txtLast
        .Title = txtTitle
        .Salary = Val(txtPay)
        .Address = txtAddress
        .City = txtCity
        .State = txtState
        .ZipCode = txtZip
        .Phone = txtPhone
    End With
    '       Calculate File Postion
        lFilePos = lFileLen + 1
    '   Save it to disk
    Put #1, lFileLen + 1, udtPlayer
    '   update record number
    iRecNum = UBound(arrRecPos) + 1
    '   Add the record position to array
    ReDim Preserve arrRecPos(iRecNum)
    arrRecPos(iRecNum) = lFilePos
    '   update record number
    txtRecNum = iRecNum + 1
    '   Clear textboxes for next new entry
    cmdClear = True
    '   update file length
    lFileLen = LOF(1)
End Sub
```

Note that cmdAdd calls on cmdClear to do all its work. You can "click" a Command button in code by setting it to True, as in cmdClear = True. It's a convenient way to avoid writing the same code twice. The main reason for having two buttons that do the same thing is to avoid confusing the user. Add and Clear have two, apparently different, meanings.

The code in cmdSave calls the CheckValidData function to assure that the required fields are filled in. If they are, it next copies data from the text boxes into the UDT to prepare it for saving. The file position is calculated as 1 byte past the end of the file. Finally, it writes the data to the end of the file with

```
Put #1, lFileLen + 1, udtPlayer
```

To finish off the process, cmdSave puts a reference to the new data in the array and recalculates lFileLen and iRecNum.

And Now, the Rest of the Code

The balance of the code adds restrictions to some of the text boxes so that only certain keystrokes will be recognized. The code is in Listing 12.21.

LISTING 12.21 The Rest of the Code

```
Private Sub txtPay_KeyPress(KeyAscii As Integer)
    '    only numbers and backspace and decimal point allowed
    If KeyAscii <> Asc(".") And KeyAscii <> 8 And _
        (KeyAscii < Asc("0") Or KeyAscii > Asc("9")) _
    Then KeyAscii = 0
End Sub


Private Sub txtState_KeyPress(KeyAscii As Integer)
    '    only letters and backspace allowed
    If KeyAscii <> 8 And (UCase(Chr(KeyAscii)) < "A" Or _
        UCase(Chr(KeyAscii)) > "Z") Then KeyAscii = 0
End Sub

Private Sub txtState_LostFocus()
    txtState = UCase(txtState)
End Sub
```

The code for txtPay allows only numbers, a decimal point, and the backspace key (KeyAscii = 8). All other keystrokes are converted to KeyAscii = 0.

The code for txtState allows only letters and the backspace key. When the text box loses focus, the letters are converted to uppercase letters.

Running the Program

You've studied all the code, so running Binary should be simple. When the program starts, it reads in the data from Player.dat. If the file does not exist, it is created.

Scan through the records with the Navigation buttons, then add a couple of records. Be sure to try adding a record with one of the required fields empty.

Use Notepad to view the way the data is actually stored in Player.dat. Notice that the plain ASCII data is still readable, but the text is interspersed with some unrecognizable characters. When you store numeric data in binary form, you cannot read it with an

12

ordinary text viewer. There is a minor benefit from this: The average snoop will not be able to learn Freddy Kruger's salary just by viewing the file!

In fact, one of the major space savings with binary access is in the storage of numeric data. Saving an integer such as 32333 in text requires 5 bytes of storage. Saving the same number in binary requires only 2 bytes. It doesn't sound like much, but with a large collection of data, the savings in disk space can be significant.

The price to pay is the inconvenience in changing data. It's easy enough to add to the end, but to change something in the middle requires reading all the data into an array or a temporary disk file and then rewriting it all, one record at a time, inserting the changed record in place of the original. Perhaps that is why so many programmers avoid binary access files.

Lesson Summary

To handle variable length records use the binary access mode. To read a binary access file use the Get statement. To write to a binary access file use the Put statement. To help you get a handle on using binary files, you created a Visual Basic application that works very much like a standard database application. The application enables you to add new records to the file and navigate through the file.

Quiz 5

1. Records saved in binary access files are:
    a. Fixed length
    b. Variable length
    c. Completely unreadable
    d. Encrypted

2. The variable iNumber is declared as an integer. If it is assigned the value 23,456, how much disk space will it take in a binary access file?
    a. 6 bytes
    b. 5 bytes
    c. 8 bytes
    d. 2 bytes

3. What is the main advantage of using binary access files?
    a. They save space on the disk
    b. They are easier to use than random access

    c. They make you look smart

    d. The files are more secure

4. What is the main disadvantage of using binary access files?

    a. The files take too much disk space

    b. It is difficult to edit data in existing records

    c. Put and Get are too confusing to use

    d. All of the above

Exercise 5

Complexity: Easy

1. When would you use binary file access?

Complexity: Easy

2. Define a variable length record that consists of the following members:

UserName

Address

Age

LESSON 6

Building a File Class

In this lesson, you will create a simple application that can create, read, or write text files: a Notepad application. So why write another Notepad application when Windows already comes with a Notepad application and you have seen Notepad applications elsewhere (like HyperPad)? Well, the important part of this Notepad application is the object-oriented approach taken for file I/O to create the Notepad, using a File class.

Figure 12.11 shows the design for the File class. The File class consists of three private properties: FileHandle, fMode, and Status. The file handle stores the file number returned from FreeFile and used in file I/O commands. The fMode property stores the file access mode to use when opening the file (that is, read or write). The Status property stores the current error status of the File object.

FIGURE **12.11**

The File class.

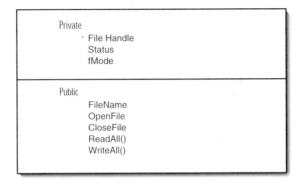

The class also has two public properties: `FileName` and `Mode`. The `FileName` member is the path and name of the file. The `Mode` property uses a property procedure to create a public property that enables you to set the private variable `fMode` to read or write. The class has four methods: `OpenFile`, `CloseFile`, `ReadAll`, and `WriteAll`. The `OpenFile` method is used to open a file, and `CloseFile` is used to close a file. The `ReadAll` method reads the entire contents of the file, and the `WriteAll` method writes a string to a file.

Create a new project called CNotepad. The completed project is on the CD that accompanies this book.

Before you set any form properties, insert a class module by selecting Add Class Module on the Project menu. Use the Properties window to name the class `CFile`.

Now add the private and public properties shown in Figure 12.11. In the Declarations section of the class module, add the following variables and constants:

```
Private FileHandle As Integer 'Private File Number
Private Status As Integer 'Error Flag - True = OK
Private fMode As Integer ' Mode to Open the file
Public FileName As String 'File Name
'
'File Mode Constants
'
Const FInput = 0 'Input Sequential Mode
Const FOutput = 1 'Output Sequential Mode
```

The variables defined as private can be modified only by functions or subroutines in the class module. To allow code outside of the class to modify a private variable (property), use a property procedure. For example, add the `Mode` property, which enables users to set the private property `fMode`. To create the public property, add the `Get` and `Let` property procedures, shown in Listing 12.22.

LISTING 12.22 Public Property Procedures for the Property Mode

```
Public Property Get Mode() As String
    'Return the current value of mode
    If fMode = FInput Then
        Mode = "read"
    Else
        Mode = "write"
    End If
End Property


Public Property Let Mode(vNewValue As String)
    'set the mode
    If vNewValue = "read" Then
        fMode = FInput
    Else
        fMode = FOutput
    End If
End Property
```

The Get and Let procedures allow code (or applications when compiled as and ActiveX component) outside of the class to make changes to the class private properties. The class properties have been added. It's time to create the class methods. There are four procedures in the class module that translate to the four methods of the class. Start with the OpenFile method.

OpenFile Method

The OpenFile method opens the file contained in the public member FileName. The file handle, a private member, contains the next available file number, returned from the FreeFile function. A simple error-handling routine is installed that sets the private member status to False if an error occurs. Other member methods will not execute during an error condition. The application using the file object does not have to check for file errors because errors are handled in the object. Add a new procedure called OpenFile to the class module and add the code shown in Listing 12.23.

LISTING 12.23 OpenFile Method

```
Public Sub OpenFile()
    'Set up the error handler
    On Error GoTo Open_Error
    '
    ' Get a free file handle and store in private area
    FileHandle = FreeFile .
```

continues

LISTING 12.23   continued

```
        '
        'Open the file in Sequential Mode
        '
        '  Check the status of the private property and
        '  open the file for input or output.
        '
        Select Case fMode
            Case FOutput
                Open FileName For Output As #FileHandle
            Case Else
                Open FileName For Input As #FileHandle
        End Select
        'Set the Status property for other member functions
        Status = True
Exit_Open:
    Exit Sub

    '
    'Error Handler
    '
Open_Error:
    MsgBox "OpenF()- Error opening file. " _
        & Err.Description
    'Set the Status property to failure
    Status = False
    Resume Exit_Open
End Sub
```

CloseFile Method

The CloseFile method closes the open file and resets the private properties of the class.
Create the method by adding a procedure named CloseFile to the class and then adding
the code shown in Listing 12.24.

LISTING 12.24   CloseFile Method

```
Public Sub CloseFile()
    '
    'Close the FileHandle and set to 0
    '
    Close #FileHandle
    FileHandle = 0 'Reset the file handle
    Status = False 'Reset the Status
End Sub
```

ReadAll Method

The ReadAll method takes a single parameter, TextBuffer, and reads the entire file into the string. Add the ReadAll procedure to the class module, and add the code shown in Listing 12.25.

LISTING 12.25   ReadAll Method

```
Public Sub ReadAll(TextBuffer As String)
Dim OneLine As String
    '
    'Check Private member for errors and exit if False
    If Status = False Then GoTo Exit_Read
    '
    'Setup the error handler
    On Error GoTo Read_Error
    '
    'Read data into
    'the OneLine variable and
    'store in the TextBuffer
    'until the end of the File
    '
    While Not (EOF(FileHandle))
        Line Input #FileHandle, OneLine
        TextBuffer = TextBuffer + OneLine + Chr(13) + Chr(10)
    Wend
    Status = True
Exit_Read:
    Exit Sub
    '
    ' Error Handler
    '
Read_Error:
    MsgBox "ReadAll()- Error reading file. " _
        & Err.Description
    Status = False   'Set the status property to error condition
    Resume Exit_Read
End Sub '
```

WriteAll Method

The WriteAll method writes the TextBuffer passed into the method to the open file. Add the WriteAll procedure to the class module, and add the code shown in Listing 12.26.

LISTING 12.26   WriteAll Method

```
Public Sub WriteAll(TextBuffer As String)
  If Status = False Then GoTo Write_Error
  On Error GoTo Write_Error
  '
  'Write the String
  '
  Print #FileHandle, TextBuffer
  Status = True
Exit_Write:
  Exit Sub
  '
'Add some simple Error Handling code
  '
Write_Error:
  MsgBox "WriteAll()- Error writing text to file. " _
 & Err.Description
  Status = False
  Resume Exit_Write
End Sub
```

The CFile class is now complete. Add the objects to the form and set the properties as shown in Table 12.12.

TABLE 12.12   Objects, Properties, and Settings for the Notepad Application

Object	Property	Setting
Form	Caption	NotePad
	ClipControls	False
	Height	4560
	Top	1395
	Width	5730
TextBox	Height	3210
	Left	60
	MultiLine	True
	Name	txtBuffer
	ScrollBars	3 - Both
	Top	15
	Width	5490
CommonDialog	DialogTitle	Select Text File
	Filter	Text (*.txt)¦*.txt

Object	Property	Setting
	Left	0
	Name	cmdlgFile
	Top	3225
CommandButton	Caption	&Open
	Height	465
	Left	105
	Name	cmdOpen
	Top	3360
	Width	1290
CommandButton	Caption	&New
	Height	465
	Left	1500
	Name	cmdNew
	Top	3360
	Width	1290
CommandButton	Caption	&Save
	Height	465
	Left	2865
	Name	cmdSave
	Top	3360
	Width	1290
CommandButton	Caption	E&xit
	Height	465
	Left	4230
	Name	cmdExit
	Top	3360
	Width	1290

Add the menu items shown in Table 12.13.

TABLE 12.13   Menu Properties for `frmNotePad`

Caption	Name
&File	mnuFile
&New	mnuNew
&Open	mnuOpen
&Save	mnuSave
sep1	-
E&xit	mnuExit

Add the following code to the `Form_Terminate` event:

```
Private Sub Form_Terminate()
  End
End Sub
```

Now add the code shown in Listing 12.27 to the `cmdOpen_Click` event.

LISTING 12.27   Open Button `Click` Event Code

```
Private Sub cmdOpen_Click()
Dim ReadBuffer As String
    On Error GoTo Open_Cancel
    cmdlgFile.ShowOpen
    If cmdlgFile.FileName <> "" Then
        'Clear Buffer
        txtBuffer.Text = ""
        'Create a File Object
        Set MyFile = New CFile
        'Set the FileName
        MyFile.FileName = cmdlgFile.FileName
        'Set the Mode to read
        MyFile.Mode = "read"
        'Open the File
        MyFile.OpenFile
        'Read the file into a buffer
        MyFile.ReadAll ReadBuffer
        'Close the file
        MyFile.CloseFile
        'Place the file contents in the textbox
        txtBuffer.Text = ReadBuffer
        '
        'Enable the Save button
        '
        cmdSave.Enabled = True
        mnuSave.Enabled = True
```

```
          'Release the object
          Set MyFile = Nothing
      End If
Open_Exit:
      Exit Sub

Open_Cancel:          'Assume Cancel was pressed
      Resume Open_Exit
End Sub
```

Add the code shown in Listing 12.28 to the cmdNew_Click event.

LISTING 12.28   New Button Click Event Code

```
Private Sub cmdNew_Click()

      On Error GoTo New_Cancel 'Enable the error handler
      txtBuffer.Text = ""        'Clear the text
      cmdlgFile.FileName = "NewFile" 'Set Default Name
      cmdlgFile.ShowOpen  'Show the File Window
      cmdSave.Enabled = True 'Enable command buttons
      mnuSave.Enabled = True '
New_Exit:
      Exit Sub
      '
      'Error Handler
New_Cancel:
      cmdlgFile.FileName = ""
      Resume New_Exit

End Sub
```

The code in Listing 12.29 is for the cmdSave_Click event.

LISTING 12.29   Save Button Click Event Code

```
Private Sub cmdSave_Click()
      '
      'Check if File Name is Valid
      '
      If cmdlgFile.FileName <> "" Then
          'Create a File Object
          Set MyFile = New CFile

          'Set the FileName
          MyFile.FileName = cmdlgFile.FileName
```

continues

LISTING 12.29   continued

```
            'Set the Mode to write
            MyFile.Mode = "write"

            'Open the File
            MyFile.OpenFile

            'Write the buffer to the file
            MyFile.WriteAll txtBuffer

            'Close the file
            MyFile.CloseFile
            MsgBox "File " & MyFile.FileName & " saved.", _
                MB_ICONINFORMATION, "File Saved"
            '
            'Release the Object
            '
            Set MyFile = Nothing
        End If
End Sub
```

The cmdExit_Click event is shown in Listing 12.30.

LISTING 12.30   Exit Button Click Event Code

```
Private Sub cmdExit_Click()
    Unload Me
End Sub
```

The code for the menus is shown in Listing 12.31. Each menu item calls the corresponding Command button. For example, the code for mnuNew_Click calls the procedure cmdNew_Click. The line Call cmdNew_Click is equivalent to cmdNew = True, which you learned in the last lesson.

LISTING 12.31   Menu Items Click Event Code

```
Private Sub cmdExit_Click()
  Unload Me
End Sub


Private Sub mnuNew_Click()
  Call cmdNew_Click
End Sub
```

```
Private Sub mnuOpen_Click()
  Call cmdOpen_Click
End Sub


Private Sub mnuSave_Click()
  Call cmdSave_Click
End Sub


Private Sub mnuExit_Click()
  Call cmdExit_Click
End Sub
```

Run the application. Press the New button, enter a filename, and click OK. Enter text in the text box, as shown in Figure 12.12. Press the Save button or use the menu selection to save the text to the file. Click the Open button and select the file you have just created. The text you saved will appear in the text box. To cut and paste text, highlight the text and use the Windows shortcut keys Ctrl+X to cut, Ctrl+C to copy, and Ctrl+V to paste.

FIGURE 12.12

CNotepad application.

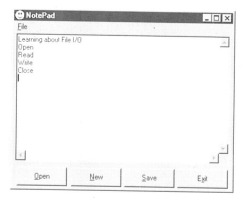

The File class is a base template you can use to build a more complex File class with more members and methods to shield you from the many different file I/O access modes. The File class can be modified to work with binary and random files as well as sequential files.

The Visual Basic File System Object

So far in this lesson, a File class was created to make File I/O simpler and more intuitive however, Visual Basic 6 includes a new object called the File System Object which can be used to work with sequential files. The File System Object is part of the Visual Basic scripting library. To use the File System Object requires you to add the Microsoft Scripting Runtime to your project's references.

The File System Object provides a simple interface to open, read write to sequential text files. It cannot be used to open, read or write binary or random files. However, you can use the File System Object's copy, delete and move methods on any file type. Let's see how to use the File System Object to open and read a text file.

Creating a File Using the File System Object

Before you can create a file with the File System Object, you must create an instance of the File System Object as follows:

```
Dim oFSO as New FileSystemObject
```

Don't forget to select the scripting object in your project reference! When you have an object instance of the File System Object, you are ready to begin working with sequential files. To create a new file, use the CreateTextFile method which has the following syntax:

```
FileSystemObject.CreateTextFile(FileName[,OverWrite[,Unicode]])
```

The following are the components of the syntax:

- FileName is the full path and filename of the file to open.
- OverWrite is an optional parameter that when set to True will create a new file or overwrite an existing file.
- UniCode is an optional parameter that if set to True creates a Unicode file.

The CreateTextFile method returns a TextStream object that can be used to read or write to the sequential file. The following code is an example of creating a new file with the File System Object:

```
Dim oFSO as New FileSystemObject
Dim MyFile as TextStream
Set MyFile = oFSO.CreateTextFile(App.Path & "\myfile.txt",True)
```

Opening a File Using the File System Object

To open a sequential file using the File System Object, use the OpenTextFile method. The OpenTextFile method has the following syntax:

```
FileSystemObject.OpenTextFile(FileName[,IOMode[,Create,[Format]]])
```

The following are the components of the syntax:

- `FileName` is the full path and filename of the file to open.
- `IOMode` specifies to open the file for reading or appending.
- `Create` creates a new file if set to `True`.
- `Format` specifies to ASCII, UniCode or system default.

The `OpenTextFile` method also returns a `TextStream` object.

Closing a File Using the File System Object

To close an open file using the File System Object, use the `Close` method that has the following syntax:

```
FileSystemObject.Close
```

Reading and Writing to a File Using the File System Object

The File System Object includes methods that enable you perform the same type of file access as the `Input` command. The following is a list of the methods:

- `Read` reads a specified number of characters.
- `ReadLine` reads up to the new line character.
- `ReadAll` reads the entire file contents.

The File System Object also provides several methods to write text to a file:

- `Write` writes text out to a file.
- `WriteLine` writes text to a file and adds the new line character.

Of course the best way to learn about the File System Object is to look at some code that uses the File System Object to manipulate a text file. The code for the File System Object example is shown in Listing 12.32.

LISTING 12.32 Example of the File System Object

```
'Get an Instance of the File System Object
Dim oFSO As New FileSystemObject
'Declare a reference for the Text Stream object
Dim MyFile As TextStream
'Place to store file text
Dim strBuffer
    'Create the File and over write if it already exist
    Set MyFile = oFSO.CreateTextFile(App.Path & "\vbich12.txt", True)
```

continues

LISTING 12.32   continued

```
'First let's write a single line out to the text file
MyFile.Write ("VB 6 Interactive Course. ")

' Now write some text but end with a newline character.
MyFile.WriteLine ("Web Based Training!")

'Close the File
MyFile.Close

'Open the File back up
Set MyFile = oFSO.OpenTextFile(App.Path & "\vbich12.txt", ForReading)

'Read the entire file into a string
strBuffer = MyFile.ReadAll

'Close the file and display the file contents
MyFile.Close

MsgBox strBuffer
```

The File System Object makes sequential file access much easier and provides the programmer with the familiar object model found throughout Visual Basic. Because the File System Object only supports sequential file access, you can modify the CFile class to create your own object model for binary and random file access.

Lesson Summary

Building on the class/object foundation of Visual Basic 6, a user-defined class was created to make file I/O simpler. The CFile class enables someone not familiar with the many Visual Basic file I/O commands and statements to quickly build an application that uses file I/O. The user-defined class used properties and methods to shield the developer from the details of the Visual Basic Open and Input statements. The File System Object, new for Visual Basic 6.0, was also introduced as a simple way to use an object to perform sequential file I/O.

Quiz 6

The following questions are based on the code you have just completed.

1. `MyFile.OpenFile` is an example of:

    a. Using the `File` object's method `OpenFile`

    b. Referencing the `File` object's property `OpenFile`

    c. Referencing the `File` object's member `OpenFile`

    d. Invalid syntax

2. What is wrong with the following code?

```
Set MyFile = New File
MyFile.FileName = cmdlgFile.FileName
MyFile.Mode = "read"
MyFile.OpenFile
MyFile.WriteAll txtBuffer
Set MyFile = Nothing
MyFile.CloseFile
```

    a. There is nothing wrong with the code.

    b. `MyFile.Mode = "read"` should be `Set MyFile.Mode = "read"`.

    c. The object tries to execute the `CloseFile` method after `MyFile` has been set to nothing.

    d. `MyFile.FileName = cmdlgFile.FileName` is incorrect; use the `Name` property on `cmdlgFile` instead.

3. If you wanted to change the name of the class from `File` to `MyFile`, you would:

    a. Change the public member `FileName` to `MyFile`

    b. Change the class property `Name` to `MyFile`

    c. Change the project name to `MyFile`

    d. Change the class `ClassName` property to `MyFile`

4. The following code:

```
Select Case Mode
 Case FOutput
   Open FileName For Output As #FileHandle
 Case Else
   Open FileName For Input As #FileHandle
 End Select
```

    a. Opens two files, one for input and one for output

    b. Opens a single file, based on the value of `Mode`

    c. Will cause an error by opening two files with the same file number

    d. Opens a file for output; if the file exists, it will open it for input

Exercise 6

Complexity: Easy

1. If you wanted to modify the CFile class to support copying files or deleting files would you add properties to the class or methods? Explain your answer.

Complexity: Moderate

2. Write the code required to open a text file called MyText.txt and read a single line of text from the file using the File System Object.

Chapter Summary

In this chapter you learned all about file I/O such as reading and writing from and to files. You learned about the different access modes and file types such as sequential, random, and binary. You learned how to use the various file ActiveX controls that ship with Visual Basic 6. You also continued to build on your Visual Basic OOP skills by creating and using a File class. The main points of this chapter are as follows:

- Visual Basic has several ActiveX controls that can be used to view and select drives, folders and files.
- The DriveListBox ActiveX control is used to display and select available drives.
- The DirListBox ActiveX control is used to display and select folders on a selected drive.
- The FileListBox ActiveX control is used to display and select files in a selected folder.
- It is easy to chain the file system ActiveX controls so that they work together.
- To display a dialog box to enable users to select a file, use the CommonDialog ActiveX control.
- Sequential files are text or ASCII files that can be read with such utilities like Notepad.
- To open a file, use the Open command.
- To close a file, use the Close command.
- To obtain an available file number, use the FreeFile command.
- LOF command returns the size in bytes of an open file.
- EOF returns True when the end of a file is reached.
- To read a sequential file use the Input command.

- To read a single line from a sequential file, use the `Line Input` command.
- Use random file access to read or write to files that use fixed-length records.
- Use the `Get` command to read a random file and the `Put` command to write to a random file.
- Use binary access to work with file records that have variable lengths.
- To read a binary file, use the `Get` command; to write to a binary file, use the `Put` command.
- Binary file access is very efficient with disk space, but it is difficult to add records if they are not placed at the end.
- You can create your own classes to make using standard Visual Basic operations, such as file I/O, easier.
- Visual Basic 6 includes an object that can be sued with sequential file access called the File System Object, which is part of the scripting library.

In this chapter, you created a simple database application using a file to store the information. Storing information in a file has its limitations, as you will see in Chapter 13, "Database Programming," when you learn about databases and how to create database applications using Visual Basic.

12

CHAPTER 13

Database Programming

This chapter introduces data access. *Data access* describes the different methods available to store, retrieve, add, delete, and update information in a database. This chapter provides an introduction to databases, database design, and ADO (Active Data Objects). Finally, this chapter describes how to create classy-looking custom reports from database files.

Visual Basic is a convenient way to create front-end programs for database access. Front-end programs insulate the ordinary user from the complexities of database management systems (DBMS) and protect the data from accidental (or malicious) deletion and alteration.

LESSON 1

What Is a Database?

You have probably heard the term *database* used before. In very general terms, a database is an object that stores information and provides methods for managing the data, adding new information, or editing or retrieving existing information. A database can be a single file or a complex, full-scale client/server relational database management system.

There are many types of databases and access methods. Examples include x-base, ISAM, relational databases, and object databases. Each of the different types of databases mentioned has different internal database structures and query languages. The database and access methods we will concern ourselves with are the database that ships with Visual Basic 6, the Microsoft Access database and the ADO object model. Previous versions of Visual Basic used the Jet database engine and the DAO (Data Access Object model) with the Microsoft Access Database.

ADO is the newest Microsoft Data Access Object model that will enable you to use the methods and techniques you learn with the Access database with many of the databases described above through the magic of OLE DB. Before you get into the details of the Access database and the ADO, consider an everyday example of a database a loose-leaf recipe book.

A recipe book contains information for many recipes and is organized into different categories, such as meat, poultry, fish, bread, or desserts, to speed up the search for specific recipes. The main food categories in a recipe book can be broken down further into subcategories. For example, the dessert recipes can be broken into subcategories such as ice cream, cakes, and pies. Recipes in each subcategory are ordered alphabetically to make recipe searches easier.

If you wanted to make an apple pie, you could quickly go to the dessert category, look in the pie subcategory, and search for recipes that start with the letter A. Using categories in a recipe book makes finding a recipe much faster than scanning through all the recipes. Some recipe books provide a table of contents where you can look up apple pie and quickly get the page number. You can also add new recipes to the book or change existing recipes in the book by writing in new ingredients. If you find a recipe you do not like, you can remove it from the book.

A database is much the same. It provides the means to retrieve existing data quickly, to add new data, and to remove data. A database lets you go a step or two further than any type of book, though. Consider trying to list all the recipes that use salt as an ingredient. With a cookbook, that would be a major chore. With a database and a program, it is child's play.

Visual Basic comes with built-in support for the Microsoft Access database program and for the database files that are created by Access. You can distribute database files with your VB programs and your users do not need to have Access on their computers to use the files. (Actually, that is true of all the different database files that Visual Basic supports.)

Access Database

The Access database is a relational database shared by Visual Basic 6 and Microsoft Access. A relational database is a database that structures the data by breaking them into logical objects that have relationships between them. Using relationships reduces the amount of redundant data and makes comprehension easier. Relational databases also provide mechanisms to correctly maintain the relationships between objects; this function is called referential integrity. Referential integrity assures, for example, that if you substitute Equal for sugar in one part of a recipe, the same substitution is made throughout the recipe.

Relational databases support SQL (Structured Query Language) to manipulate and retrieve data. The Access database consists of a single file, with a file extension of MDB, to store the many parts of the database. To manipulate the information in the Access database, the Visual Basic 6 application developer uses a new Microsoft Data Access Object model called ADO (Active Data Objects).

ADO and OLE DB

In previous versions of Visual Basic, database access was done using DAO (Data Access Objects) and the Jet engine to access Microsoft Access databases. To get to information stored on remote databases such as Microsoft SQL Server or Oracle, a Visual Basic developer would use RDO (Remote Data Objects) and ODBC (Open Database Connectivity standard). DAO and RDO provided developers with powerful and easy to use object models to access databases but they were far from perfect.

For starters, it was quite confusing to have two different objects models to access database information. Developers were not always sure which object model to use and the two object models were quite different. ODBC proved to be a very valuable standard; however, ODBC was designed for accessing relational database information. Microsoft wanted a data access standard that would provide developers the same programming interface when accessing all types of data, such as relational database information, email, files or even data stored in a spreadsheet. To this end, Microsoft created OLE DB. OLE DB is an API (Application Programming Interface) that provides a universal data access specification so developers can access many types of information such as relational database information and email using the same API.

To make OLE DB available to Visual Basic programmers, Microsoft developed the Active Data Objects (ADO). ADO provides Visual Basic developers with a single data access model that is simpler than DAO or RDO. ADO also provides a data access interface that can be used with all types of data, such as relational databases, email, or spreadsheets.

Database Terms

Before covering the how to's of database programming with Visual Basic 6, some often used database terminology needs to be covered.

SQL

SQL stands for Structured Query Language. Most books tell you that *SQL* is pronounced *Sequel*, but most database programmers just say "Ess Cue Ell." SQL is a language that enables you to perform operations such as retrieving data, sorting data, adding new data, deleting data, or updating data in relational databases.

Tables

Tables are the storage areas for specific types of information. A table is made up of columns, which describe each attribute of an item stored in the table, and of rows, which are individual records in the database. Columns have names, data types, and sizes. A single record in a table is made up of one row containing all the columns in the table. A table named Authors is shown in Figure 13.1.

FIGURE **13.1**

Authors table in BIBLIO.MDB.

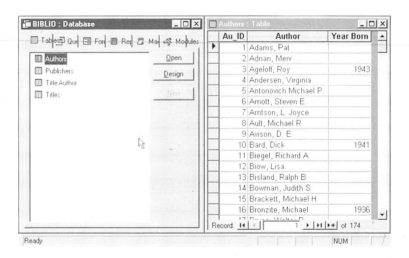

A good way to visualize a table is to think of a telephone book. The listings in the white pages have three columns, Name, Address, and Phone Number. Each line in the book is equivalent to a row in the database; it is a single record.

Primary Key

Primary key is a database term used to signify the column or columns that uniquely identify a single row in a table. In Figure 13.1, the AU_ID column is the primary key of the Authors table.

Foreign Key

Foreign key is a database term that refers to a column in a secondary table that is related to a column in a primary table. For example, an Owner table has a column and primary key called owner_name. The Address table has a column also called owner_name and every person in the Address owner_name table must exist in the Owner table.

Indexes

The idea of an index is similar to the categories and subcategories contained in the recipe book example. An index is built on table columns and is used to speed up the retrieval of data from an executing query. Indexes are used to order (sort) the data in specific ways. In the phone book database, one could have a Last Name index (such as the real phone book is ordered) and a Phone Number index, which would make it easy to, say, count all the numbers in a given exchange.

Queries

A query is an SQL statement used to retrieve rows of information from one or more tables. A query can also have search criteria to limit the amount of data returned from the tables. For example, you could create a query to return only cake recipes.

RecordSets

A *recordset* is a Microsoft ADO object that represents the data in a table or a query. You can use a RecordSet to view, update, or delete data in a table or query.

Relational Database Example

Figure 13.2 shows an example of two database tables, one called Employee and the other called Skills. The employee table has information about a particular person who works for a company. The Skills table has information about the job skills that are important to the company. The company president decides that they would like to be able to review each employee and the employee's job skills. He asks you to create a database that will enable him to view that information. Well, how do you do that? First, take a look at solving the problem with a non-relational method, by creating a single table that contains the employee information and the employee skills information in a single table.

Figure 13.3 shows the new table. But what if an employee has more than one skill? You would have to repeat all the employee information to show each employee skill. For example, if Fred has three skills, you must repeat his ID, name, department and phone number three times. That doesn't seem very efficient, does it?

Now look at how it could be done using a relational database model. Look at the tables from a relational viewpoint. First examine the relationship between employees and job skills: A single employee can have more than one job skill. The employee could be a programmer and a tester. What about the skills? A single skill can belong to more than one employee; for example, there could be more than one programmer. The relationship between the employee and skills is said to be a many-to-many relationship because a single employee can have more the one job skill, and a single job skill can be possessed by more than one employee.

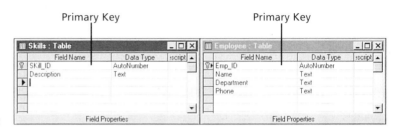

FIGURE 13.2

Employee and Skills tables.

Field Name	Data Type
SKill_ID	AutoNumber
Description	Text

Field Name	Data Type
Emp_ID	AutoNumber
Name	Text
Department	Text
Phone	Text

SKill_ID	Description
1	Programmer
2	Tester
3	Manager
(AutoNumber)	

Emp_ID	Name	Department
1	Mark	MIS
2	Lisa	Management
(AutoNumber)		

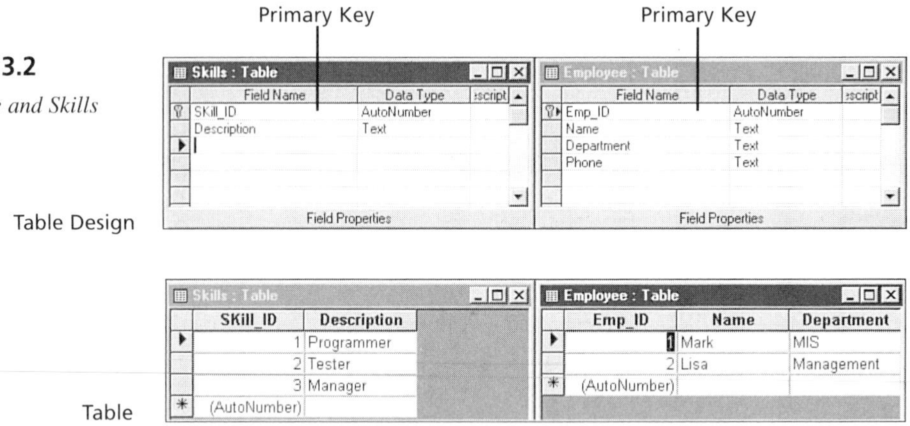

FIGURE 13.3

Employee table design and a data query.

Field Name	Data Type
Emp_ID	Number
Name	Text
Department	Text
Phone	Text
Skills Description	Text

Emp_ID	Name	Department	Phone	Skills Descripti
1	Mark	MIS	555-5555	Programmer
1	Mark	MIS	555-5555	Tester
2	Lisa	Management	555-5555	Manager
0				

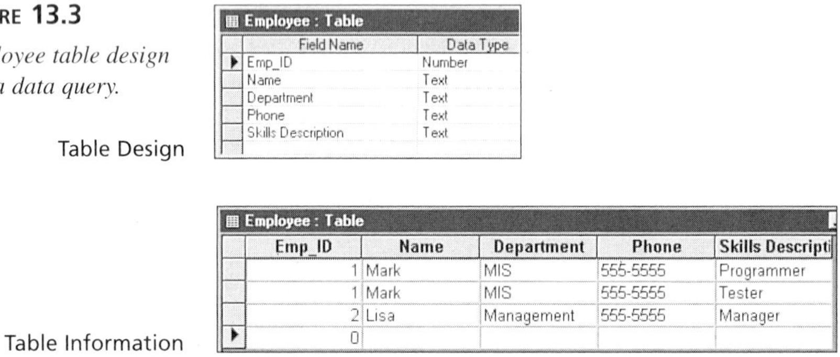

To solve our problem, let's create another table that establishes one-to-many relationships with the Employee and Skills tables, called the Employee_Skills Table, as shown in Figure 13.4.

The employee Skills table contains two fields: the employee_id and the skill_id. To add a skill to an employee, you add one entry to the Employee_Skills Table. You do not repeat all the information in the Employee Table or the Skills Table: Only the primary keys of each table are repeated. To find all the skills for a single employee, you start with the Employee Table and find the primary key of the specific employee. You then use the employee_id and search the Employee_Skills Table for all entries with the specific employee_id. You then use each of the skill_ids to retrieve the specific skill.

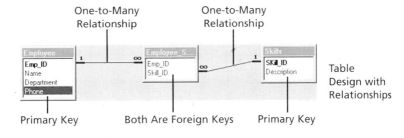

Figure 13.4

Employee Skills Table.

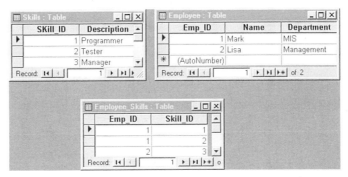

Table Information

One of the biggest advantages of organizing data this way is that it avoids duplication of data. Not only does that save disk space, but it helps avoid errors. For example, are Fred Prinznettle and fred Prinznettle the same person?

Note that the primary keys of the Employee Table and the Skills Table become foreign keys to the Employee_Skills Table.

The process of using information from many tables in a relational database is called joining the tables. You could join the three tables to find all the employees who were programmers or testers. You could display a single column from one table or several columns from multiple tables. From this, you can begin to see the flexibility and power of relational databases.

13

Lesson Summary

This lesson introduced the basic elements of a database and the terminology used in the remainder of this chapter. A database is an object that stores information and provides methods for managing the data. The Access database is a relational database shared by both Visual Basic and Microsoft Access.

SQL stands for Structured Query Language and is the standard language used to manipulate data in a relational database. Tables are specific storage areas within a database and are made of columns and rows. A query is a SQL Statement that is used to retrieve information. A recordset is a Microsoft ADO object that represents the data in a table or a query. You can use a recordset to view, update, or delete data in a table or query. Lesson 2, which discusses database design, covers relationships more fully.

Quiz 1

1. An Access database is a _____ shared by Visual Basic 6 and Microsoft Access.

   a. Relational database

   b. Flat file

   c. Client/server database

   d. X-base database

2. _____ is a database mechanism to correctly maintain the relationship between objects.

   a. Index

   b. Table

   c. Referential integrity

   d. Recordset

3. A _____ is built on table columns and is used to speed up data retrieval from an executing query.

   a. Primary key

   b. Index

   c. SQL

   d. Recordset

4. A consumer can have accounts with many banks. Banks can have more than one consumer. This type of relationship is a _____.

   a. One-to-one

   b. Many-to-many

   c. Many-to-one

   d. Master detail

Exercise 1

Complexity: Moderate

1. A user queries a database table called Jobs. The user always searches on the column job_description. What should the user check on the Jobs table to make sure the query is running as fast as possible?

Complexity: Easy

2. If an employee has one and only one employer and an employer has one or more employees, what is the relationship between employer and employee?

LESSON 2

Designing a Database

To further enhance your database abilities, this lesson covers some basic concepts of database design. A well designed database makes programming and tuning the application much easier. In this lesson, you learn a simple design methodology for relational databases and a standard relational database technique called normalization.

The lesson also examines logical database design issues. A logical database design is typically a block diagram of entities and relationships referred to as an E-R (Entity_Relationship) diagram. Relational databases use the term entities to represent an object in the logical design, and attributes to represent the properties of the entity. For example, the tables in BIBLIO.MDB are entities, and the fields in each table are the attributes of each entity.

Logical design is creating all the entities in a database and establishing relationships between the entities. Logical design does not take into account the type of database or the system on which the database will reside. Physical database design is taking the logical database design and creating a database and database objects to represent the entities and relationships in the logical database design. In the physical database design, each entity becomes a table, and the attributes of the entity become the columns of the table.

13

Database Design Goal

Before you begin the process of designing a database, it is important to understand some of the goals. The design goals for logical database design are to

- Establish database purpose
- Support all queries

- Produce all reports
- Be able to perform all calculations
- Process all transactions
- Enforce restrictions and defaults

Database Design Process

Where do you start the database design process?

Retrieving Information and Analyzing Information

The first step in designing a database is to talk to the people who will use it. Gather all the information to be represented in your database. Gather all the reports generated by hand that you expect to generate with the database. Add in the new reports that the users want. Gather any information sheets and any available information on the data and their characteristics. This is an important step because it will answer the following questions: What is in the database, and why is it in the database?

Break Down Information into Separate Entities

Get a piece of paper or a database design tool and break down the collected data items collected into separate entities. An entity is a distinct object in the database. Each entity becomes its own table. For example in the BIBLIO.MDB database, entities are the Publishers, Authors, and Titles tables.

Assign Attributes to Each Entity

When you have created separate entities for each object, assign attributes to each entity. An attribute is a property or characteristic of the object, such as its name, address, or amount. Each attribute becomes a field in the table.

Identify a Unique Identifier for Each Entity

A row in a relational database needs to be uniquely identified so you can retrieve that row and only that row. Select one or more attributes that uniquely identify a single row in the entity. This unique identifier is referred to as the primary key. For example, if you live in the United States, your Social Security number is an attribute that uniquely identifies you to the IRS at tax time. So your Social Security number is your primary key in the IRS database.

Establish Relationships Among the Entities

Determine the types of relationships that exist among your entities. There are three types of relationships in relational database design:

- One-to-one
- One-to-many
- Many-to-many

One-to-One

A one-to-one relationship is one in which each row in one table is represented by a single row in another table.

One-to-Many

A one-to-many relationship is one in which a row in one table may be represented by many rows in another table.

Many-to-Many

A many-to-many relationship is one in which a row from one entity may be represented by one or many rows in another table, and a row from the second table may be represented by one or many rows in the first table. Many-to-many relationships should not exist in a relational database design because many-to-many relationships cannot be properly joined to represent a single row correctly. To resolve the problem, create another table that has a many-to-one relationship with the first table and a many-to-one relationship with the second table. For example, the TitlesAuthors table in the BIBLIO.MDB database is a table created to solve the problem of the many-to-many relationship between Authors and Titles.

Normalize the Logical Design

When you have established relationships for your logical design, it is time to normalize the design. Normalization involves a set of rules used to test the soundness of your database design. Each rule is applied to the logical database design; then, the logical design is said to be in rule# form, for which rule# is first, second, and so on, to fifth. There are five normalization rules.

For most database designs and for the methodology used in this book, you will apply only the first three rules, leaving the database in Third Normal Form. Normalization will not fix inaccuracies or missing data items in your logical design. However, normalization will help point out possible problems with a logical database design. The following are the first three rules of normalization:

First Normal Form

No columns (attributes) may be multivalued columns or repeating groups. In other words, each column in a row can have only one value.

13

Second Normal Form

When the primary key consists of more than one column (attribute), all the nonprimary key columns (attributes) must depend on the entire primary key and not a part of the key. Note that a primary key that is made up of more than one attribute is called a composite key.

Recall the BIBLIO.MDB database. It contains a table named Authors, a table named Titles, and a table named TitlesAuthors which links the two together. If you attempt to combine Authors and Titles into a single table, the only key for uniquely identifying a row is a composite key made up of Au_ID and ISBN. But the information about the author, the fields Author and Year Born, depend only on Au_ID, which is only part of the primary key.

The combined table would be in First Normal Form, but not in Second Normal Form. Splitting the table into two, even at the cost of adding a third table to link them, is more efficient. Note that the two attributes of the Authors table are entered only once. Note that, in a First Normal Form, if an author had more than one title, the same data about the author would be repeated for each title.

Third Normal Form

Non-key attributes must not depend on other non-key attributes. Consider the Titles table, as an example. Imagine that someone added the publisher's phone number to that table. The primary key of the table is ISBN, but the publisher's phone number is dependent on PubID and not on ISBN. The table would be in Second Normal Form.

Design Exercise

Design a simple database using the methodology described in this lesson, starting from the beginning.

Retrieving Information and Analyzing Information

For this exercise, you have been given the task of creating a simple database for a local school. The following reports are required:

- A list of the students and their local addresses
- A list of the students and the teachers they have
- A list of teachers and the students they teach
- A list of the teacher's names and the subjects they teach

During the fact-finding mission, you find the following:

- Several students have the same first and last name. There are two John Smiths and a pair of twins named Billy and Bobby Johnson.
- Each student has a unique student ID number assigned by the school.
- No teachers have the same first and last name, but no teachers have ID numbers. There is a temptation to use the teachers' last names as the key, but the possibility exists that new teachers might be hired. A single duplicate last name would ruin the whole system.
- The most subjects taught by a single current teacher is two, but the most subjects any teacher has ever taught at the school is three.

Break Down Information into Separate Entities

Study the information gathered and think for a few minutes about the types of entities (objects) you need in your school database to provide the types of reports and requirements defined in the analysis stage. Remember, entities become tables in your physical database design. Jot down the separate entities you have come up with on a sheet of paper, and go to the next step.

Assign Attributes to Each Entity

Assign attributes to each of the entities on your paper. Remember, attributes are like object properties and, in the physical database design, are the columns to your tables.

Identify a Unique Identifier for Each Entity

Assign the primary key status to one or more attributes in each entity. Remember, the primary key must uniquely identify each entry. For example, for any value of the primary key in the Authors table in BIBLIO.MDB, only a single author is returned. If the entity does not have a unique identifier, create an identity attribute for the entity. Identity attributes (contrived columns or counters in the physical database) are system-generated numbers used to uniquely identify a record.

Let's take a look at the entity design created so far for our exercise. Your design should be similar. Don't worry if you have more attributes or entities than shown in Figure 13.5. For the exercise, the smallest number of attributes was used, and some attributes have been added to help you understand normalization.

FIGURE 13.5

The Teachers and Students tables.

The primary key selected for the Students entity is the unique student number Student ID. For the Teachers entity, the primary key is a contrived key because the Teachers had no unique identifier. Notice the attributes in each entity. The non-key attributes of the Students entity are Name and Address. The non-key attributes of the Teachers entity are Name, Subject1, Subject2, and Subject3. The attributes Subject1, Subject2, and Subject3 will hold the different subjects taught by a teacher. Three subject fields were selected because the maximum number of subjects ever taught by a teacher is three. At this time, there is nothing to establish relationships between the Teachers and Students tables.

Establish Relationships Between the Entities

The next step is to determine the relationships between the tables.

The relationship can be created with a third table that establishes the connections between the two. For example, teacher A teaches students B and C. The new table is shown in Figure 13.6.

FIGURE 13.6

Connecting the tables.

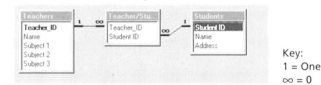

Key:
1 = One
∞ = 0

Normalize

Begin to apply the rules of normalization to your design.

First Normal Form

Look at the logical database design shown in Figure 13.6, and make sure that no attributes are multivalued columns (repeating groups). Wait a minute—look at the Teachers table. Subject1, Subject2, and Subject3 are repeating groups. The design does not meet First Normal Form. So fix the logical design by removing the subject attributes, and then create another table called Subject, plus a table called Teacher/Subject to link the Subject table to the Teachers table. Now your logical design is said to be in First Normal Form. This new design is better because it might not always be true that no teacher teaches more than three courses. With this design, adding extra courses for a teacher is a matter of adding a record. Remember that it is always easier to add records than it is to add fields.

Second Normal Form

The second rule of normalization is applied to only entities that have composite primary keys (a primary key with more than one attribute). The only entities that meet this requirement are Teacher/Student and the new link table, Teacher/Subject. Because both tables are link tables, there are no non-key fields that do not depend on the primary key, so our database is already in Second Normal Form.

Third Normal Form

The third and final rule says all non-key attributes must not depend on other non-key attributes. Study the logical design. What do you think? No problem, right? Now your logical design, as shown in Figure 13.7, is in Third Normal Form. The logical design process is complete.

FIGURE 13.7

Normalized logical database design.

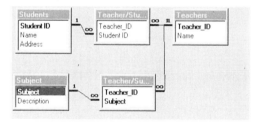

It is rare that a design is carried beyond Third Normal Form. There's such a thing as going too far. Using this design in a Visual Basic program will involve a lot of INNER JOIN clauses in SQL statements. Adding a higher level of normalization only increases the complexity of data retrieval.

Lesson Summary

In this lesson you learned about taking user requirements, analyzing the requirements, and creating a logical database design. When the logical design was created, you learned about Normalization. Normalization is a set of rules applied to your logical database design that test the soundness of your design. After you have normalized, you can use a tool like Microsoft Access or the Visual Basic Data Manager to create the database and tables (physical design).

Each entity becomes a table and each attribute becomes a column. Where you have key relationships, set up referential integrity to maintain the relationships correctly. The next lesson introduces the Visual Basic Data control that uses ADO to connect to databases. But first it's time for a quiz.

13

Quiz 2

1. Which one of the following is not one of the primary goals of database design discussed earlier?

    a. Support all queries.

    b. Produce all reports.

    c. Create small tables.

    d. Be able to perform all calculations.

2. The first step in the database design process discussed in this section is

    a. Retrieving information and analyzing information

    b. Breaking down information into separate entities

    c. Normalization

    d. Assigning attributes to each entity

3. Allowing no columns (attributes) that are multivalued columns repeating groups is the rule for

    a. Third Normal Form

    b. Second Normal Form

    c. Normalization

    d. First Normal Form

4. When converting the logical design into the physical design, each entity becomes a

    a. Column

    b. Table

    c. Attribute

    d. Database

Exercise 2

Complexity: Moderate

1. Design a table with the following attributes (columns):

    Name (size 25)

    City (size 40)

    State (size 2)

    Age

LESSON 3

Using the ADO Data Control

In this lesson, you will begin to create database applications using Visual Basic. You may be wondering how complex the code must be for database applications. The programming can be tricky, but luckily for you, Visual Basic provides a custom control called the ADO Data control that enables you to create database applications without writing a single line of code.

The ADO Data control icon is shown in Figure 13.8.

ADO Data control icon

ADO Data Control

The best way to understand the ADO Data control and how it works is to write a single form application that uses the ADO Data control. Because you have not yet learned how to design and create your own database, this program uses the example database that comes with Visual Basic, BIBLIO.MDB. BIBLIO.MDB is located in the Visual Basic home directory and is an Access database that contains information on database books. The database contains several tables and SQL queries. For an example, you will use only the Authors table, which has the structure shown in Table 13.1.

TABLE 13.1 Authors Table in BIBLO.MDB

Column	Data Type	Description
Au_ID	Long Integer	Primary key
Author	Text	Author's name
Year Born	Integer	Year author was born

Now start a new data project named Authors, add an ADO Data control, and set the properties for the objects, as shown in Table 13.2. The completed project is on the CD that accompanies this book.

TABLE 13.2   Object and Properties Settings for the Authors Project

Object	Property	Setting
Form	Caption	Authors Table
	Height	2910
	Width	5100
Data control	Align	2 - Align Bottom
	Caption	Authors
	Name	datAuthors

How do you tie a database to the ADO Data control on the form? First, you need to determine the type of database you are going to use. Click the ADO Data control, bring up the Properties window for the ADO Data control, and find the ConnectionString property.

ConnectionString Property

The ConnectionString property can be set at design time or at runtime. The ConnectionString tells the ADO Data control the type of connection and how to make a connection to a database. For our application, we will use the OLE DB ODBC data provider, which enables us to use any database that has an ODBC data source setup on our machine. One big advantage of using the ODBC data provider is that you will be using essentially the same code whether or not you are using a local database like Access or a relational database management System like Microsoft SQL Server.

Double-click the ConnectionString property to bring up the property page. Notice the many options that are displayed as possible choices for the ConnectionString property. In this chapter, the examples will use the Use ODBC Data Source Name option of the ConnectionString property. Because the ODBC OLE DB provider is being used, an ODBC DSN (Data Source Name) for the Microsoft Access database Biblio.mdb needs to be added.

Adding an ODBC Data Source

An ODBC data source is a name that references a particular ODBC database and is used by applications to specify the database. The data source is also referred to as a DSN, for data source name. You must setup a DSN for a database before applications can use ODBC to retrieve information from that database. The DSN is used by ODBC to look up specific database information in the ODBC.INI file or the Windows registry, such as the type of database, the location of the database, and the ODBC driver used. An ODBC data source is added by using the ODBC option that is located in the Windows control panel shown in Figure 13.9.

FIGURE 13.9

ODBC Driver manager in the Windows control panel.

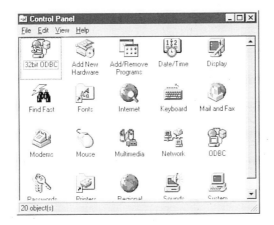

To add an ODBC source, perform the following steps:

1. Double-click the ODBC icon shown in Figure 13.9. The ODBC Data Source Administrator, as shown in Figure 13.10, appears.

FIGURE 13.10

ODBC Data Source Administrator.

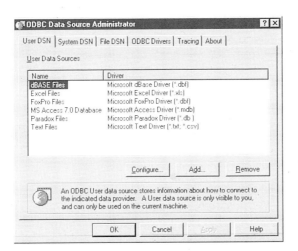

2. Click the Add button. The Create New Data Source dialog box, as shown in Figure 13.11, appears. The Create New Data Source dialog box displays all the installed

ODBC drivers on your PC. An ODBC driver is a dynamic link library that processes ODBC function calls from the application and translates them to the native
database language. The driver also receives information from the database and
translates the information to an ODBC format if required. For this example, select
the Microsoft Access ODBC driver installed on your PC. If you do not have any
installed ODBC drivers, refer to your Visual Basic documentation about installing
ODBC drivers.

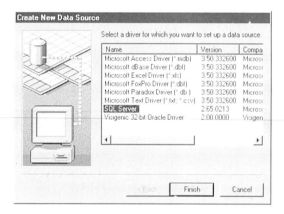

FIGURE 13.11

*Create New Data
Source dialog box.*

When you have selected an ODBC driver, click the Finish button. The ODBC
Microsoft Access Setup dialog box, as shown in Figure 13.12. appears.

FIGURE 13.12

*ODBC Microsoft
Access Setup dialog
box.*

3. Fill in the Data Source Name text box. Remember that you will use this name in
   your applications to refer to the database you are accessing. You can use any name
   you desire, but you should use a descriptive name that gives you information on

the type of database or the database server the DSN represents. For our example, use `Biblio` for the Data Source Name. `Biblio` represents our Microsoft Access database name `Biblio.mdb`.

4. The Description text box provides more information about the database. In the Description text box, enter `Interactive VB ODBC example`.

5. Click the Select button shown in Figure 13.12. A standard file selection dialog box is displayed. Select the Biblio.mdb file, which is located in your Visual Basic root directory.

6. Click the OK button to add the ODBC data source. To close the ODBC Data Source Administrator, click the OK button. You have now added an ODBC source that can be used with Visual Basic to create database programs.

ConnectionString Property

Next, set the `ConnectionString` property to the value Biblio (the ODBC DSN you just added for BIBLIO.MDB located in the Visual Basic home directory), by clicking on the data control's `ConnectionString` property. The General Property page dialog box appears. Select the Use ODBC Data Source Name radio button and then select Biblio in the combo box.

RecordSource Property

Click the `RecordSource` property. The `RecordSource` property is the table or query used by the `Data` control to create a recordset object. Set the `RecordSource` property to `Authors`.

CommandType Property

The `CommandType` property tells the data provider the type of command in the `RecordSource` property object. There are several possibilities:

- The `adCmdTable` type indicates a table name in the `RecordSource` property.
- `adCmdText` indicates a SQL statement in the Source property.
- `adCmdStoredProcedure` indicates a stored procedure in the Source property. Stored Procedures are a set of SQL statements stored in a RDBMS system such as Oracle or Microsoft SQL Server.
- `adCmdUnknown` is the default and means that the command in the `RecordSource` property is not known and the data source provider will be queried before the command is executed to determine the type of command.

For this application, set the `CommandType` property to `adCmdTable`.

13

BOFAction and EOFAction Properties

The BOFAction property controls what happens when you move to the beginning of the recordset—to the first record. The EOFAction property controls what happens when you reach the end of the recordset.

For BOF, you get two choices:

- adDoMoveFirst keeps the Data control pointing to the first record.
- adStayBOF moves beyond the first record. Of course, there is no record before the first record. The action causes the Data control to execute the Validation event on the first record, then disables the Move Previous button on the Data control.

adDoMoveFirst is the most logical setting, and it is the default for the Data control.

For EOF, you get three choices:

- adDoMoveLast keeps the Data control pointing to the last record. This is the default mode.
- adStayEOF moves the Data control beyond the last record. This triggers the Data control's Validation event on the last record, then disables the Move Next button on the Data control.
- adDoAddNew adds a new record to the recordset. It sounds good, but a user can unknowingly add a huge number of empty records to the recordset that way.

CursorType Property

Setting the CursorType property to set the type of recordset created. The choices are as follows:

- AdOpenKeySet provides a recordset that supports full navigation and can be updated. New records added by other users after the recordset was created do not appear as part of the recordset.
- AdOpenDynamic provides a truly dynamic recordset that supports full navigation and can be updated. New records added by other users after the recordset was created do appear as part of the recordset.
- AdOpenStatic provides a recordset that supports full navigation and can not be updated.

Navigating the Recordset with the Data Control

A recordset created with the Data control can be navigated without writing any code by using the arrow buttons on the Data control. Figure 13.13 shows the Data control and the action taken when the navigation arrows in the Data control are pressed.

FIGURE 13.13

ADO Data *control navigation.*

move first   move last

move previous   move next

Run the Authors application and press the Data control navigation arrows. What happens? Nothing. So far you have created a recordset on the Authors table, but you have not told Visual Basic what information in the Authors table to display and where to display the information. To display information in the recordset, you must bind a control to a column in the recordset. Binding a control associates a column in the recordset with the control. When the application runs, the data in the selected row is displayed automatically in the bound control. The following standard Visual Basic controls can be bound to a database column:

- TextBox
- ListBox
- CheckBox
- ComboBox
- ImageControl
- Label
- PictureBox

How do you bind a control to a database column? To find out, add a TextBox to frmAuthors and set the properties, as shown in Table 13.3.

TABLE 13.3 Property Settings for TextBox txtAu_ID

Object	Property	Setting
TextBox	Height	330
	Left	840
	Name	txtAu_ID
	Top	465
	Width	1305

To bind the TextBox control to a database column, perform the following steps:

1. Click the TextBox and bring up the Properties window.
2. Click the DataSource property in the Properties window, and a list of Data controls on the form will be displayed.

3. Set the `DataSource` property to `datAuthors`. This binds the control to the recordset of the selected `Data` control, in this case, the Authors table recordset.

4. Click the `DataField` property. A list of columns defined in the table or query specified in the `RecordSource` property of the `Data` control is displayed.

5. Set the `DataField` property to `Au_ID`. The `TextBox` control, `txtAu_ID`, is bound to the Author's table, column `Au_ID`.

Run the application. What happens now? The `TextBox` has a number in it. This is the `Au_ID` of the first record in the recordset.

Press the `Data` controls navigation bars. See the information in the `TextBox` change. Let's finish the project. Add the following controls to the form and set the properties, as shown in Table 13.4.

TABLE 13.4 Objects and Property Settings for the Authors Project

Object	Property	Setting
Label1	Caption	Id
	Height	255
	Left	90
	Name	lblAu_ID
	Top	465
	Width	710
Label2	Caption	Name
	Height	255
	Left	90
	Name	lblName
	Top	945
	Width	710
Label3	Caption	Year Born
	Height	255
	Left	90
	Name	lblBorn
	Top	1425
Text1	DataSource	datAuthors
	DataField	Author
	Height	330
	Left	840

Object	Property	Setting
	Name	txtAuthor
	Top	945
	Width	3420
Text2	DataSource	datAuthors
	DataField	Year Born
	Height	330
	Left	840
	Name	txtYearBorn
	Top	1425
	Width	1050

Run the project, as shown in Figure 13.14.

FIGURE 13.14

Author application.

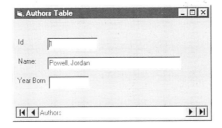

Use the navigation controls to step through the different records in the database. Congratulations. You have just created an application to navigate the Authors table without writing a single line of code.

Lesson Summary

In this lesson, you learned how to set up an ODBC (Open Database Connectivity) data source to use with Visual Basic. An ODBC data source is a name that references a particular ODBC database and is used by applications to specify the database. This lesson introduces a new ActiveX control, called the ADO (Active Data Objects) Data control. Using the Data control, you can easily build database applications that enable you to navigate through a recordset, update, add, or delete with little or no code. This is made possible by the capability to bind recordset columns to other ActiveX controls, such as the TextBox control, using the Data control. The next lesson explains how to manipulate the data in the database with code and how to quickly generate database entry forms.

Quiz 3

1. The _____ property, set at design time or runtime, tells the ADO Data control the type of data provider being used and how to make a connection to the database.

    a. Database

    b. ConnectionString

    c. Connect

    d. DatabaseName

2. Which one of the following is not a valid CursorType setting?

    a. adOpenKeyset

    b. adOpenDynamic

    c. adOpenStatic

    d. adOpenTable

3. The ____ property is the table or query used by the ADO Data control to create a recordset object.

    a. Database

    b. RecordSource

    c. Connect

    d. Source

4. Which one of the following cannot be bound to an ADO Data control?

    a. TextBox

    b. ListBox

    c. CheckBox

    d. CommandButton

Exercise 3

Complexity: Easy

1. Using the authors example, replace the TextBox controls with label controls. Bind the Label controls to the different database fields.

Complexity: Easy

2. Using the same form used in the example earlier (Authors), change the CursorType property of the ADO Data control to all possible options. Run the application with each option. Which options enable you to modify records?

LESSON 4

Using the Data Controls

The applications you have created so far in this chapter have used the standard Visual Basic controls in conjunction with the Data control to display and manipulate the data in recordsets. Quickly review the standard controls that can be bound to a column in a recordset to display data:

- TextBox
- ListBox
- CheckBox
- ComboBox
- ImageControl
- Label
- PictureBox

Note

If the Data controls do not appear in your toolbox, right-click the Toolbox and select Components. The Data controls are Microsoft DataGrid, Microsoft DataList controls and Microsoft FlexGrid. In the interest of creating smaller programs, select only those that you need for a project.

You have bound a TextBox control to a database field to display the data in the recordset, but you could have easily used a Label control in cases where you did not want the user to be able to modify the data fields. The CheckBox control can have the value True or False; it should only be used for database Boolean fields. The PictureBox and Image controls are used to display graphical data from the database: bitmaps, icons, and metafiles. Visual Basic provides several other special *data-aware* custom controls:

- DataList
- DataCombo
- DataGrid
- MSFlexGrid
- DataRepeater (Professional and Enterprise Editions)
- MSHFlexGrid

13

The special `Data` controls shown in Figure 13.15 are tightly integrated with the `Data` control to offer you more flexibility and functionality. Let's examine how to use these new controls.

FIGURE 13.15

Data controls.

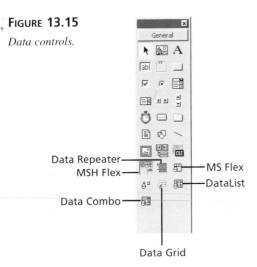

Data Repeater
MSH Flex
MS Flex
DataList
Data Combo
Data Grid

DataList and DataCombo

The `DataList` and `DataCombo` are very similar to the standard `ListBox` and `ComboBox`. However, there are some key features that make these two controls a better choice for database applications:

- The controls automatically fill up with a selected field from the recordset. The normal `ListBox` and `ComboBox` must be populated with the recordset using the `AddItem` method.

- The controls can pass a value to a second `Data` control, making these two `Data` controls ideal for lookup tables when entering foreign key information from another table.

Filling a ComboBox with the Results from a Query

Let's look at the first key feature by filling a `ComboBox` with publisher names from the Publishers table. Start a new Visual Basic project called LookUp. The completed project is on the CD that comes with this book. Add the objects and set the properties for the LookUp project, as shown in Table 13.5.

TABLE 13.5 Object and Property Settings for the LookUp Project

Object	Property	Setting
Form	Caption	Publisher Look Up
	Height	3480
	Name	frmLook
	Width	6195
ADODataControl	CommandType	1 - adCmdText
	ConnectionString	Biblio
	Height	300
	Left	90
	Name	datPublisher
	RecordSource	Select Name from Publishers
	Top	90
	Visible	False
	Width	2280
DataCombo	Height	315
	Left	315
	Name	dbcPublisher
	Style	2 - dbcDropdownList
	Top	1050
	Width	3255

The Data control above is tied to the SQL query Select Name from Publishers. The query returns a single column from the Publishers table Name. It's time to set the two properties that will fill the DataCombo with the query information. Set the RowSource property of the DataCombo to the Data control datPublisher. The RowSource property specifies the recordset to use to fill the ListBox. Set the ListField property to Name. The ListField property specifies the field from the recordset that is displayed in the combo ListBox.

Run the application and click the ComboBox shown in Figure 13.16 to see the publisher names in the Publishers table. The list is automatically populated with information. Close the ComboBox and type the letter W in the TextBox portion of the ComboBox. The TextBox automatically fills with Waite Group Press.

13

FIGURE 13.16

DataCombo *displaying a list of publishers.*

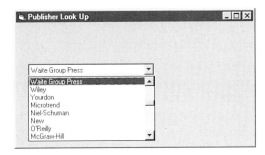

Styles of the DBCombo

The DataCombo has three different styles that affect the way the control looks and behaves on the form:

- dbcDropdownCombo: Includes a text box and a drop-down list. The list drops down when the user clicks the drop-down arrow. Clicking one of the items in the list copies it to the TextBox portion of the DBCombo. The user can also type in an entry that is not in the list.

- dbcSimpleCombo: Includes a text box and a list which doesn't drop down. This must be resized so that the user can see the list. Clicking one of the items in the list copies it to the TextBox portion of the DBCombo. The user can also type in an entry that is not in the list. Typing in the text box also causes the list to scroll to the first matching entry.

- dbcDropdownlist: Includes a text box and a drop-down list. The list drops down when the user clicks the drop-down arrow. Clicking one of the items in the list copies it to the TextBox portion of the DBCombo. Typing in the text box also causes the list to scroll to the first matching entry. The user cannot type in an entry that is not in the list.

Note that these same styles are available for the ComboBox control you used in Chapter 5, "Controls." Choosing the correct style is important for making your programs behave the way you want. Change the Style property of the DataCombo and experiment with all three styles until you are satisfied that you understand the differences.

Passing a Value to Another Data Control

Why would you want to pass a value from a DataList or DataCombo to another Data control?

To help find the answer, examine Table 13.6, the Titles table, which contains the titles of database books. If you were creating a data entry screen for the Titles table, how would you display the foreign keys coming from other tables such as PubID from the

Publishers table? After all, the `PubID` field is a system identity field used to uniquely identify a publisher and has no meaning outside of our database. In a data entry screen for the Titles table, you would want to display the publisher's name and, when the record was saved, store the field `PubID` in the Titles table. The `DataList` and `DataCombo` enable you to do this by passing a value back to another `Data` control.

TABLE 13.6 Partial Column Listing of the Title Table in `BIBLIO.MDB`

Column	Data Type	Description
`Title`	TextBook	Title
`Year Published`	Integer	Year the book was published
`ISBN`	Text	Primary key, uniquely identifies a book
`PubID`	Long Integer	Foreign key to the Publishers table

Save the LookUp project, and start a new project called Titles. Instead of using the Application Wizard, create a data entry screen the old-fashioned way: by hand. The project uses seven `TextBoxes`, a `DataCombo`, eight `Labels`, two `ADO Data` controls, and five Command buttons. Use Table 13.7 and Figure 13.17 as guides for positioning and naming the controls.

FIGURE 13.17

The Titles project at design time.

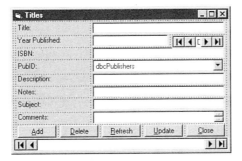

TABLE 13.7 The Titles Project

Object	Property	Value
Form	Name	`frmTitle`
	Caption	`"Titles"`
	Height	3270
	Left	160
	Top	2400
	Width	5520

13

continues

TABLE 13.7 continued

Object	Property	Value
ADO Data control	Name	datPublishers
	Caption	"Data2"
	CommandType	1-adCmdText
	ConnectionString	Biblio
	RecordSource	"Select PubID,Name from Publishers"
	Top	375
	Visible	0 'False
CommandButton	Name	cmdClose
	Caption	"&Close"
	Height	300
	Left	4440
	TabIndex	19
	Top	2610
	Width	975
CommandButton	Name	cmdUpdate
	Caption	"&Update"
	Height	300
	Left	3360
	TabIndex	18
	Top	2610
	Width	975
CommandButton	Name	cmdRefresh
	Caption	"&Refresh"
	Height	300
	Left	2280
	TabIndex	17
	Top	2610
	Width	975
CommandButton	Name	cmdDelete
	Caption	"&Delete"
	Height	300

Object	Property	Value
	Left	1200
	TabIndex	16
	Top	2610
	Width	975
CommandButton	Name	cmdAdd
	Caption	"&Add"
	Height	300
	Left	120
	TabIndex	15
	Top	2610
	Width	975
ADO Data control	Name	Data1
	Caption	
	ConnectionString	Biblio
	Height	345
	Left	0
	CommandType	2 adCmdTable
	RecordSource	"Titles"
	Top	2925
	Width	5520
TextBox	Name	txtComments
	DataField	"Comments"
	DataSource	"Data1"
	Height	310
	Left	2040
	MultiLine	1 'True
	ScrollBars	2 'Vertical
	TabIndex	14
	Top	2270
	Width	3375

continues

13

TABLE 13.7   continued

Object	Property	Value
TextBox	Name	txtSubject
	DataField	"Subject"
	DataSource	"Data1"
	Height	285
	Left	2040
	MaxLength	50
	TabIndex	12
	Top	1954
	Width	3375
TextBox	Name	txtNotes
	DataField	"Notes"
	DataSource	"Data1"
	Height	285
	Left	2040
	MaxLength	50
	TabIndex	10
	Top	1640
	Width	3375
TextBox	Name	txtDescription
	DataField	"Description"
	DataSource	"Data1"
	Height	285
	Left	2040
	MaxLength	50
	TabIndex	8
	Top	1326
	Width	3375
TextBox	Name	txtISBN
	DataField	"ISBN"
	DataSource	"Data1"
	Height	285
	Left	2040

Object	Property	Value
	MaxLength	20
	TabIndex	5
	Top	668
	Width	3375
TextBox	Name	txtYearPub
	DataField	"Year Published"
	DataSource	"Data1"
	Height	285
	Left	2040
	TabIndex	3
	Top	354
	Width	1935
TextBox	Name	txtTitle
	DataSource	"Data1"
	Height	285
	Left	2040
	MaxLength	255
	TabIndex	1
	Top	40
	Width	3375
DataCombo	Name	dbcPublishers
	DataField	"PubID"
	DataSource	"Data1"
	Height	315
	Left	2040
	TabIndex	20
	Top	960
	Width	3360
	Style	2
	ListField	"Name"
	BoundColumn	"PubID"
	Text	"dbcPublishers"

13

Use Figure 13.17 to place the labels and enter their captions.

Fortunately, for all the controls on frmTitles, there is surprisingly little code. Add the code in Listing 13.1 to the project.

LISTING 13.1   Code for the Titles Project

```
Private Sub cmdAdd_Click()
    Data1.Recordset.AddNew
End Sub

Private Sub cmdDelete_Click()
    Data1.Recordset.Delete
    Data1.Recordset.MoveNext
End Sub

Private Sub cmdRefresh_Click()
    Data1.Refresh
End Sub

Private Sub cmdUpdate_Click()
    Data1.UpdateRecord
    Data1.Recordset.Bookmark = Data1.Recordset.LastModified
End Sub

Private Sub cmdClose_Click()
    Unload Me
End Sub

Private Sub Data1_Error(ByVal ErrorNumber As Long, Description As String,
ByVal Scode As Long, ByVal Source As String, ByVal HelpFile As String,
ByVal HelpContext As Long, fCancelDisplay As Boolean)
    MsgBox "Data error event hit err:" & Description

End Sub

Private Sub Data1_Reposition()
    Screen.MousePointer = vbDefault
    On Error Resume Next
    Data1.Caption = "Record: " & (Data1.Recordset.AbsolutePosition + 1)
End Sub
```

The keys to the operation of this project lie in the two Data controls and the DataCombo. The ADO Data control Data1 creates a recordset from the Titles table of BIBLIO.MDB. Each of the text boxes on the form draws its data from one of the fields in the table. The ADO Data control datPublishers creates a recordset from the query "Select PubID, Name from Publishers". The recordset contains only two fields, the PubID field and the Name field from the Publishers table of BIBLIO.MDB.

Now that there are two `Data` controls, each with its own RecordSet, the bulk of the work is done by the `DataCombo`. The following steps explain how it works:

1. The `DataSource` property is set to `Data1`. That binds the `DataCombo` to the `RecordSource` from the Titles table.

2. The `RowSource` property is set to `datPublishers`. That means that the list will be filled with data from the `datPublishers` `Data` control.

3. The `ListField` property is set to `Name`, which means that the `Name` field from the snapshot will display in the `DataCombo` list.

4. The `BoundColumn` property is set to `PubID`. This is the `PubID` field from the `RowSource` RecordSet, the recordset of `PubId` and `Name` from `datPublishers`.

5. The `DataField` property is set to `PubID`. This is the `PubID` column from the `DataSource` RecordSet, the RecordSet of `Data1`.

Steps four and five link the two recordsets together. The `PubID` field in the Publishers table is the primary key of that table. It is a foreign key in the Titles. That means it is a reference to the record in the Publishers table that has the same `PubID` value. (That is what referential databases are all about.)

Now that the two recordsets are linked together in the `DataCombo`, when you scroll through the list of titles, the correct publisher's name is shown in the `DataCombo`. The `PubID` from the Titles table is passed to the `DataCombo` and it instantly scrolls to the correct record.

Better yet, if you add a new record, you can now select a publisher from the `DataCombo` list and the correct `PubID` is passed back to the Titles table.

Try it out. Run the program. After you have stepped through a few titles, click Add and add in the information from this book. Be sure to select the correct publisher. The running program is shown in Figure 13.18.

FIGURE 13.18

The Titles project at runtime.

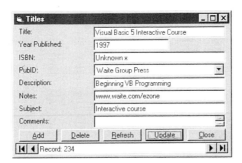

13

The `DataGrid` Control

The `DataGrid` enables you to quickly display data from a table or query in a spreadsheet fashion and allows you to update the data in the grid. The `DataGrid` ties directly to the `ADO Data` control so the information in the recordset is automatically loaded into the grid. The `DataGrid` is one of the easiest `Data` controls to use. Getting the `DataGrid` up and running only requires setting the grid `DataSource` property. Save the Titles project, and start a new project called `DataGrid`. Add the objects and set the properties for the `DataGrid` project, as shown in Table 13.8.

TABLE 13.8 Object and Property Settings for the `DataGrid` Project

Object	Property	Setting
Form	Caption	Testing DataGrid
	Height	4410
	Name	frmGrid
	Width	8895
ADO DataControl	Caption	Titles
	CommandType	2 adCmdTable
	ConnectionString	Biblio
	Height	300
	Left	75
	Name	datTitles
	RecordSource	Titles
	Top	285
	Visible	False
	Width	2025
DataGrid	DataSource	datTitles
	Height	2610
	Left	210
	Name	dbgTitles
	Top	975
	Width	8455

Run the application shown in Figure 13.19. Scroll the grid and resize the columns. Try modifying a record. The `DataGrid` makes displaying information easy. You can add any of the same Command buttons for the `DataGrid` that you used with other data forms. The `AddNew` and `Delete` methods don't really care how you are displaying the data.

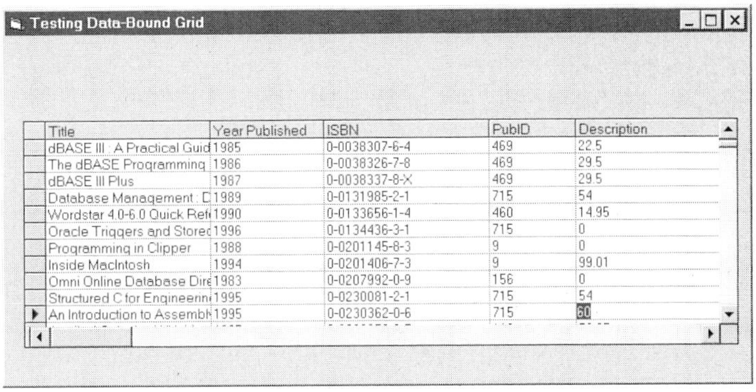

FIGURE 13.19

`DataGrid` *displaying information from BIBLIO.MDB.*

The `DataGrid` control example is deceptively simple. Actually, there are many properties, events, and methods to be used with the `DataGrid`, and many complications can develop from its use. But the `MSHFlexGrid` control can do all the same things, and it offers greater flexibility in the process.

The `MSHFlexGrid` Control

The `MSFlexGrid` control is one of the most versatile controls in your database arsenal. (It is also quite useful in applications that are not database oriented.) `MSFlexGrid` does everything that the `DataGrid` can do, and then some. An important difference is that when the `MSHFlexGrid` is bound to a `Data` control, it is read-only. The control adds a collection of capabilities in data management and appearance that will keep you amazed and pleased for a long time to come. This section contains two projects, and it is only an introduction.

Introduction to `MSHFlexGrid`

Start a new project named flxGrid.VBP. Put an `MSHFlexGrid`, a `Data` control, and five Command buttons on the form. Set the properties according to Table 13.9. The completed project is on the CD that comes with this book.

13

TABLE 13.9   The flxGrid Project

Object	Property	Value
Form	Name	frmFlexGrid
	Caption	FlexGrid One
	Height	3945
	ClientWidth	5595
CommandButton	Name	Command5
	Caption	"BackColor"
	Height	555
	Left	4440
	Top	3360
	Width	1035
CommandButton	Name	Command3
	Caption	"ForeColor"
	Height	555
	Left	3360
	Top	3360
	Width	1035
CommandButton	Name	Command4
	Caption	"Font"
	Height	555
	Left	2280
	Top	3360
	Width	1035
CommandButton	Name	Command2
	Caption	"Grid Lines Fixed"
	Height	555
	Left	1200
	Top	3360
	Width	1035
CommandButton	Name	Command1
	Caption	"Grid Lines"
	Height	555
	Left	120

Object	Property	Value
	Top	3360
	Width	1035
ADO DataControl	Name	datAuthors
	Caption	Authors
	CommandType	2-adCmdTable
	ConnectionString	Biblio
	RecordSource	Authors
	Visible	False
MSHFlexGrid	Name	MSHFlexGrid1
	DataSource	datAuthors
	Height	3075
	Left	120
	Top	60
	Width	5295
	AllowBigSelection	0 'False
	GridLines	0
	GridLinesFixed	0
	AllowUserResizing	1

This project shows you what some of the property settings mean and how they affect the overall appearance of the MSHFlexGrid. Add the code from Listing 13.2.

LISTING 13.2 The Code for the FlexGrid Project

```
Private Sub Command1_Click()
    If MSHFlexGrid1.GridLines < 3 Then
        MSHFlexGrid1.GridLines = MSHFlexGrid1.GridLines + 1
    Else
        MSHFlexGrid1.GridLines = 0
    End If
End Sub

Private Sub Command2_Click()
    If MSHFlexGrid1.GridLinesFixed < 3 Then
        MSHFlexGrid1.GridLinesFixed = MSHFlexGrid1.GridLinesFixed + 1
    Else
        MSHFlexGrid1.GridLinesFixed = 0
    End If
End Sub
```

13

continues

LISTING 13.2   continued

```
Private Sub Command3_Click()
    Static iClicks As Integer
    Select Case iClicks
        Case 0: MSHFlexGrid1.CellForeColor = &HFF&
        Case 1: MSHFlexGrid1.CellForeColor = &HFF00&
        Case 2: MSHFlexGrid1.CellForeColor = &HFF0000
        Case 3
            MSHFlexGrid1.CellForeColor = 1
            iClicks = -1
    End Select
    iClicks = iClicks + 1
End Sub

Private Sub Command4_Click()
    Static iClicks As Integer
    Select Case iClicks
        Case 0: MSHFlexGrid1.CellFontBold = 1
        Case 1: MSHFlexGrid1.CellFontItalic = 1
        Case 2: MSHFlexGrid1.CellFontBold = 0
        Case 3
            MSHFlexGrid1.CellFontItalic = 0
            iClicks = -1
    End Select
    iClicks = iClicks + 1
End Sub

Private Sub Command5_Click()
    Static iClicks As Integer
    Select Case iClicks
        Case 0: MSHFlexGrid1.CellBackColor = &HFF&
        Case 1: MSHFlexGrid1.CellBackColor = &HFF00&
        Case 2: MSHFlexGrid1.CellBackColor = &HFF0000
        Case 3
            MSHFlexGrid1.CellBackColor = &HFFFFFF
            iClicks = -1
    End Select
    iClicks = iClicks + 1
End Sub
```

Command1 and Command2 show you the meaning of the GridLines and FixedGridLines properties. They step through the four choices for each one, giving you a live chance to see the effects of changing the properties. Command3 cycles you through four choices of ForeColor which, you may recall, is the color of the text. Command5 does the same for BackColor. There is an anomaly in the ForeColor and BackColor properties: Setting them to 0 does not give you black. Instead it gives you the system colors. To get black, set the color to 1. Command4 gives you a selection of font effects.

Run the program and click each of the buttons several times. As you do, watch the effects and take note of the ones you like. Note that you can resize the cells so that you can read all the text in them. The running program is shown in Figure 13.20.

FIGURE 13.20

The MSHFlexGrid *in action.*

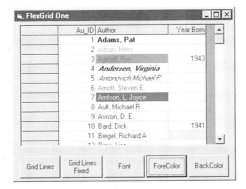

And Now for Something Completely Different

When you were learning about the ideas behind the relational databases, you considered an employee skills database. Recall that Mark had more than one skill. If you were to view that database with a DataGrid control, Mark's name would be listed once for each skill he had. That isn't bad, but it would be nice to find a way to merge the rows so that Mark's name appeared in a larger block beside his group of skills. Well, guess what the MSFlexGrid can do? You've got it!

Start a new project named flxMerge.prj. The finished project is on the CD that comes with this book. Place an MSFlexGrid control, a Data control, and a check box on the form. Use Table 13.10 to position and name the objects.

Note

This project requires a new ODBC Data Source that you must add, called Skills for the SKILLS.MDB database that is included on the CD.

13

TABLE 13.10 Objects for the flxMerge.prj Project

Object	Name	Property
Form	Name	frmMerge
	Caption	"Skills"
	Height	3195
	Width	6870

continues

TABLE 13.10 continued

Object	Name	Property
CheckBox	Name	chkMerge
	Caption	"Merge Cells"
	Height	255
	Left	5640
	Top	120
	Width	1215
ADO Data control	Name	datSkills
	CommandType	1-adCmdText
	ConnectionString	Skills
	RecordSource	"Select * from employees"
	Visible	0 'False
MSHFlexGrid	Name	flxSkills
	DataSource	datSkills
	Height	2535
	Left	180
	Top	120
	Width	5415
	MergeCells	1

Now add the code from Listing 13.3 to the Code window.

LISTING 13.3 Code for flxMerge

```
Option Explicit

Private Sub Form_Load()
    Dim sSQL As String
    sSQL = "SELECT DISTINCTROW Employees.Name, "
    sSQL = sSQL & "Employees.Department, Skills.Skill "
    sSQL = sSQL & "FROM ([Emp Skills] "
    sSQL = sSQL & "INNER JOIN Employees "
    sSQL = sSQL & "ON [Emp Skills].EmpID = Employees.EmpID) "
    sSQL = sSQL & "INNER JOIN Skills "
    sSQL = sSQL & "ON [Emp Skills].SkillID = Skills.SkillID "
    sSQL = sSQL & "ORDER BY Employees.Department;"
    datSkills.RecordSource = sSQL
    datSkills.Refresh
```

```
    DoInitialSettings
'    flxSkills.Refresh
End Sub

Sub DoInitialSettings()
    Dim i As Integer
    flxSkills.Row = 0
    For i = 0 To flxSkills.Cols - 1
        flxSkills.Col = i
        flxSkills.CellFontSize = 8
        flxSkills.CellAlignment = 1
        ' Allow merge on all Columns
        flxSkills.MergeCol = True
    Next i
    flxSkills.ColWidth = 1.5 * 1444
    flxSkills.ColWidth = 1.5 * 1444
    flxSkills.MergeCells = 0
End Sub

Private Sub chkMerge_Click()
    flxSkills.MergeCells = chkMerge
End Sub
```

A Look at the Code

It builds an SQL query that returns the employee names and departments from one table and the employee skills from another, based on the information in yet a third table. The SQL query looks like this:

```
SELECT DISTINCTROW Employees.Name, Employees.Department, Skills.Skill
FROM ([Emp Skills] INNER JOIN Employees ON [Emp Skills].EmpID =
Employees.EmpID) INNER JOIN Skills ON [Emp Skills].SkillID =
Skills.SkillID ORDER BY Employees.Department;
```

Don't get too excited by this complicated-looking query. The SQL query language is covered in the next lesson.

When the query is built, the Form_Load procedure assigns it to the RecordSource property of the Data control, and then it refreshes the Data control so that it returns the selected recordset.

The MSHFlexGrid control's DataSource property is datMerge, the Data control on the form. When the Data control is refreshed, the MSHFlexGrid expands to accommodate the recordset's three fields, and the Form_Load procedure calls the DoInitialSettings procedure.

The key to the behavior of the MSFlexGrid is to set the control's properties before you do anything fancy. The DoInitialSettings procedure does that. It starts by making row 0

13

the active row. The For...Next loop then cycles through all the columns in the MSHFlexGrid and sets the properties for each column in the grid. The CellAlignment property has 10 options, from 0 through 9. Try all of them to select the one that you like best.

The feature that this demonstration emphasizes is the MergeCells property. Before a column's cells can merge, its MergeCol property must be set to True. This is also done in the For...Next loop. Finally, the MergeCells property is set to 0, which disables the MergeCells action.

Run the program now. The initial screen is shown in Figure 13.21.

FIGURE 13.21

The flxMerge *screen at runtime:*
MergeCells = 0.

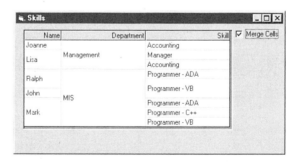

Skills

Name	Department	Skill	☐ Merge Cells
Joanne	Management	Accounting	
Lisa	Management	Manager	
Lisa	Management	Accounting	
Ralph	MIS	Programmer - ADA	
Ralph	MIS	Programmer - VB	
John	MIS	Programmer - VB	
Mark	MIS	Programmer - ADA	
Mark	MIS	Programmer - C++	
Mark	MIS	Programmer - VB	

Note that several of the employees are listed more than once in the Name column because they have more than one skill. Click the Merge Cells check box. Pretty neat, isn't it? The screen with MergeCells = 1 is shown in Figure 13.22.

FIGURE 13.22

The flxMerge *screen at runtime:*
MergeCells = 1.

Skills

Name	Department	Skill	☑ Merge Cells
Joanne		Accounting	
Lisa	Management	Manager	
		Accounting	
Ralph		Programmer - ADA	
John	MIS	Programmer - VB	
		Programmer - ADA	
Mark		Programmer - C++	
		Programmer - VB	

The code for the CheckBox simply sets the MergeCells property to match the value of the CheckBox, either 0 or 1.

Lesson Summary

Visual Basic ships with many data ActiveX controls that use the ADO Data control to provide data aware functionality with little or no programming. Examples of these controls are the DataGrid or the DataCombo. You learned how to tie one recordset to another recordset to display proper values in a combo box, as well as writing application using the MSHFlex grid and the DataGrid.

Quiz 4

1. To automatically populate a DataCombo, you must

    a. Set the RowSource property of the DataCombo to a properly configured Data control.

    b. Set the DataSource property of the DataCombo to a properly configured Data control.

    c. Use the AddItem method of the DataCombo.

    d. Set the Source property of the DataCombo to a properly configured Data control.

2. When passing a value from a DataCombo to another Data control, the value for the properties DataField and _____ must be the same, but from different RecordSets.

    a. DataSource

    b. Source

    c. BoundColumn

    d. Database

3. What ADO Data control property should you set with the following SQL statement to return the Name column from the Publishers table into a DataList?

    Select Name from Publishers.

    a. Database

    b. RecordSource

    c. DataField

    d. SQLStatement

13

4. The _____ enables you to quickly display data in a table or query in a spreadsheet fashion.

    a. DataGrid

    b. Data Bound spreadsheet

    c. DataList

    d. Data TextBox

Exercise 4

Complexity: Easy

1. What are some benefits to using the DataGrid?

Complexity: Moderate

2. Create a Visual Basic project that uses and ADO Data control and a DataGrid. Use a text box to enter in any valid Biblio table name and a command button to refresh the grid.

LESSON 5

Using the Data Objects

In the last lesson you learned how to use the ADO Data control to create database applications without writing any code, but sooner or later you need to perform functions that are not provided by the Data control. For example, the Data control does not provide a search facility. Imagine searching through several thousand records looking for a specific one. Not to worry. You can write code to manipulate the recordset in the ADO Data control to perform this type of function.

To learn how to manipulate the database recordset using code, start a new project. The following examples use an Access database that comes with Visual Basic, BIBLIO.MDB. The table for the following example is the Publishers table, which has the format shown in Table 13.11.

TABLE 13.11   Publishers Table in BIBLIO.MDB

Column	Data Type	Description
PubID	Long integer	Primary key used to uniquely define a Publisher
Name	Text	Publisher's name
CompanyName	Text	Name of the company
Address	Text	Publisher's address
City	Text	Publisher's city
State	Text	Publisher's state
Zip	Text	Publisher's zip code
Telephone	Text	Publisher's telephone number
Fax	Text	Publisher's fax number
Comments	Text	Free form description area

An Easier Way

Visual Basic 6 provides a quick and easy way to create forms based on database tables, called the Data Form Wizard. Before you can use the Data Form Wizard, it must be available as an add-in. To check this, open the Add-Ins menu. If the Data Form Wizard is not in the list of add-ins, select Add-In Manager. The window for the Add-In Manager is shown in Figure 13.23.

FIGURE 13.23

Add-In Manager.

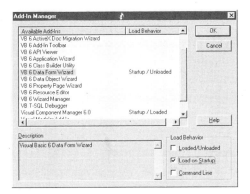

Make sure there is a checkmark on Loaded/Unloaded for the Data Form Wizard. If there is no checkmark in the box next to the Data Form Wizard, click the check box; then click OK.

Building the Form

When the Data Form Wizard Add-In is available, you are ready to go. Although the completed program is on the CD that accompanies this book, you should follow these steps instead of simply loading it from the disk:

1. Select the Data Form Wizard from the Add-Ins menu.

2. On the opening screen, take the default setting of None; then click Next.

3. The Database Type screen appears. Select Access; then click Next.

4. The Data File Selection screen appears. Use the Browse button to find and select the BIBLIO.MDB as your database. Then click Next. The Data Access Form screen is shown in Figure 13.24.

FIGURE 13.24

The wizard's Data Access screen.

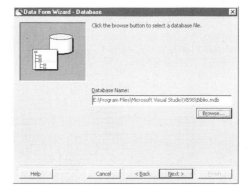

5. The next screen enables you to set the name of the form and the form layout. For the name of the form, enter Publisher. Select a form type of Single Record and a binding type of ADO Data control. Click Next.

6. The Record Source Selection screen, shown in Figure 13.25, appears. In the drop-down box, select Publishers. Include all the columns on the form. You can also reorder the columns on the form if you like. Click Next.

7. Finally. The Control Selection screen appears. This screen enables you to determine what type of database capabilities your form will have. For example, update, delete or add. Take the default, which is all the check boxes selected. Then click Finish.

Now sit back and watch while Visual Basic 6 builds your data form. Pretty spectacular, right? But there are probably some things you will want to change, at least for this project.

13

FIGURE 13.25

The wizard's Record Source Selection screen.

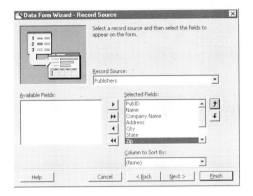

If you try to run it now, it will protest mightily. Time to fix it. Select Publishers Properties from the Project menu and change the Startup Object to frmPublishers. Click OK, and it is all fixed. To clean up the project, remove Form1 (which is not used).

Manipulating the Recordset with Code

Examine the code generated by the Application Wizard. The ADO Data control on the form is named ADODC1 and has a recordset based on the table Publishers. (Remember, a recordset is an object that represents the records in a database table or query.)

Add Button

In design mode, double-click the button labeled Add. The code in the button click event is

```
Private Sub cmdAdd_Click()
On Error GoTo AddErr
  datPrimaryRS.Recordset.AddNew

  Exit Sub
AddErr:
  MsgBox Err.Description
End Sub
```

The AddNew method creates a new record in the recordset. When the AddNew method is invoked, all the bound controls are cleared and an empty record is placed in the recordset. One thing missing is that when you click Add, the focus remains with the button. Change the code to look like this:

```
Private Sub cmdAdd_Click()
 On Error GoTo AddErr
  datPrimaryRS.Recordset.AddNew
```

```
      txtFields.SetFocus
Exit Sub
AddErr:
  MsgBox Err.Description
End Sub
```

When you click Add, you can enter data into the bound TextBoxes and save the new record by using the Update method or by moving to a different record with one of the navigation buttons on the Data control.

Update Button

The code behind the Update button is

```
Private Sub cmdUpdate_Click()
  On Error GoTo UpdateErr

  datPrimaryRS.Recordset.UpdateBatch adAffectAll
  Exit Sub
UpdateErr:
  MsgBox Err.Description
End Sub
```

The Update method saves the values of the current bound controls.

Delete Button

The code in the click event of the Delete button is

```
Private Sub cmdDelete_Click()
  On Error GoTo DeleteErr
  With datPrimaryRS.Recordset
    .Delete
    .MoveNext
    If .EOF Then .MoveLast
  End With
  Exit Sub
DeleteErr:
  MsgBox Err.Description
End Sub
```

Examine the error handler of course—except the Data control added by the Data Form Wizard:

```
Private Sub datPrimaryRS_Error(ByVal ErrorNumber As Long, Description As
String, ByVal Scode As Long, ByVal Source As String, ByVal HelpFile As
String, ByVal HelpContext As Long, fCancelDisplay As Boolean)
  'This is where you would put error handling code
  'If you want to ignore errors, comment out the next line
  'If you want to trap them, add code here to handle them
  MsgBox "Data error event hit err:" & Description
End Sub
```

As it turns out, the Publishers table is linked to other tables in BIBLIO.MDB by referential integrity, so deletions are not allowed on anything except new entries you might add.

Now, back to the Delete button. The `Delete` method deletes the current record in the recordset object. Then the current record no longer exists, so the `MoveNext` method is used to move to the next record. The `MoveNext` method is the same as clicking the > arrow on the navigation bar of the `Data` control. Other recordset methods that perform the same functions as the `Data` control navigation bar are `MovePrevious`, `MoveLast`, and `MoveFirst`.

Refresh Button

The code in the click event of the Refresh button is

```
Private Sub cmdRefresh_Click()
  'This is only needed for multi user apps
  On Error GoTo RefreshErr
  datPrimaryRS.Refresh
  Exit Sub
RefreshErr:
  MsgBox Err.Description
End Sub
```

The `Refresh` method rebuilds the current recordset. The `Refresh` method can be used in multiple-user environments to update the recordset a user is working on, with new records and changes made by other users. Using it in a single-user environment doesn't accomplish much unless you are fond of the hourglass icon.

Start the Publish application, as shown in Figure 13.26.

FIGURE 13.26

The Publishers project.

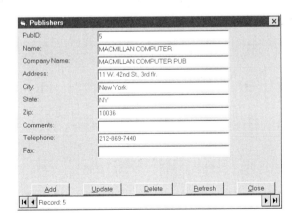

13

Move **Method and** BookMark **Property**

You can use the Move method of the recordset to move a number of records in any direction. For instance the following code moves forward two records from the current position:

```
ADODC1.RecordSet.Move 2
```

The following code moves back five records from the current position:

```
ADODC1.RecordSet.Move -5
```

To mark a record in the database that we can come back to latter use a bookmark. To use a bookmark, save the BookMark property into a variable and then set the bookmark property with the saved value to return to the record, for example, the following code saves a bookmark:

```
vMark = ADODC1.Recordset.Bookmark
```

The code saves the position of the current record in the variable vMark. To return to the record later using the bookmark, set the Bookmark property with saved value. For example:

```
ADODC1.Recordset.Bookmark = vMark
```

Lesson Summary

The Data control enables you to build database applications with little or no code. This lesson examined how to enhance the Data control using code. To add a new empty record to the recordset use the Data control's recordset object's AddNew method. After you add the values for each column, use the Data controls UpdateRecord to save the values to the recordset or to update any values that have been modified. To delete a record from the recordset use the Data control's recordset's Delete method. The next lesson introduces you to the SQL language.

Quiz 5

1. The Visual Basic Add-In _____ can generate a data entry form to manipulate a database table or query using the ADO Data control.

   a. Table Wizard

   b. Form Wizard

   c. Data Form Wizard

   d. Data Manager

2. The recordset method _____ creates a new record in a recordset.

    a. `AddNew`

    b. `Insert`

    c. `InsertNew`

    d. `Update`

3. To remove a record from a recordset, use the _____ method.

    a. `Delete`

    b. `Remove`

    c. `Kill`

    d. `RemoveCurrent`

4. Use the _____ method of an `ADO` `Data` Control to rebuild the recordset.

    a. `Rebuild`

    b. `Run`

    c. `Search`

    d. `Refresh`

Exercise 5

Complexity: Moderate

1. Using the publisher's project, add a button and a text box to the form. When the button is clicked, add code to take a numeric value from the text box and move the recordset that number from the current record.

Complexity: Easy

2. What is a bookmark?

13

LESSON 6

Managing Your Data with SQL

The early days of computer database programming were a nightmare. There were a dozen different database management programs, and each one had its own language and its own techniques for retrieving data. Programmers became expert in one or another of the languages, or they became jack-of-all-trades programmers, subject to interference from all the different techniques they had to remember. Relational database systems, for all their advantages, performed poorly because of the extra work required to maintain relationships.

The first commercial SQL product was released by IBM in 1961. It was quickly followed by products from Oracle and several other vendors. A standard was proposed to the American National Standards Institute (ANSI) in 1968, which had the effect of stabilizing the SQL language. Currently there are more than 70 DBMS products that use SQL. There are slight differences, true, but a programmer who knows SQL can adapt readily. This lesson serves as your introduction to SQL.

SQL is built around two concepts: Data Definition Language (DDL), which is used for creating databases, and Data Manipulation Language (DML), which is used for retrieving and editing data. DDL is available in the Professional and Enterprise editions of Visual Basic, but is not covered in this book.

Data Manipulation Language (DML) is built around a few statements and operations. It is really a simple language, although it can create very complex "sentences." This lesson takes you from the simplest of SQL statements into more elaborate (and, thus, more selective) statements. Each new statement is introduced in its simplest form. Then, modifying clauses are added to refine the statement.

Trying Out the Examples

The project to try out the SQL examples is deliberately simple. Start a new project named SQL.vbp. Maximize the form and add an ADO Data control, a DBGrid, and a Command button. Use Table 13.12 as a guide.

TABLE 13.12   Objects for SQL.vbp

Object	Property	Value
Form	Name	frmSQL
	Caption	"SQL Demo"
	WindowState	2 'Maximized
CommandButton	Name	cmdQuit
	Caption	"E&xit"
	Height	435
	Left	180
	Top	5880
	Width	1095

Object	Property	Value
ADO Data control	Name	ADODC1
	CommandType	1- adCmdText
	ConnectionString	Biblio
	RecordSource	"Select * from Publishers"
	Visible	0 'False
DataGrid	DataSource	ADODC1
	Name	dbgSQL
	Height	5535
	Left	120
	Top	120
	Width	9315

Now add the code from Listing 13.4.

LISTING 13.4   Code for the SQL Demo Project

```
Option Explicit
Public sSQL As String

Private Sub cmdQuit_Click()
    Unload Me
End Sub

Private Sub Form_Load()
    BuildSQL
    ADODC1.RecordSource = sSQL
    ADODC1.Refresh
End Sub

Public Sub BuildSQL()
    sSQL = "SELECT *"
    sSQL = sSQL & " FROM Publishers"
End Sub
```

13

The secret of this project is the BuildSQL procedure. You will have to revise this procedure to try out each new SQL statement. The procedure builds the sSQL string using concatenation. For each change, you have to rewrite the code in this function, and you must
follow specific guidelines to avoid errors. For example, the second SQL statement is

```
SELECT Publishers.[Company Name], Publishers.State
FROM Publishers;
```

To build the `sSQL` string from this statement, change the procedure to

```
Public Sub BuildSQL()
    sSQL = "SELECT Publishers.[Company Name], Publishers.State"
    sSQL = sSQL & " FROM Publishers;"
End Sub
```

Add `sSQL = "` in front of the first line of the SQL statement, and add `sSQL = sSQL & "` in front of all the other statements.

Note the space between the quotation mark and the first character in the line that adds the second string to the first. It is very important that you add that space as the first character of every line except the first. If you do not, the concatenated statement will be wrong because the words on separate lines will be smashed together to form a single, indecipherable word. The Code window including this new version of the `BuildSQL` procedure is shown in Figure 13.27.

FIGURE 13.27

The Code window with the second SQL statement.

The running program is shown in Figure 13.28.

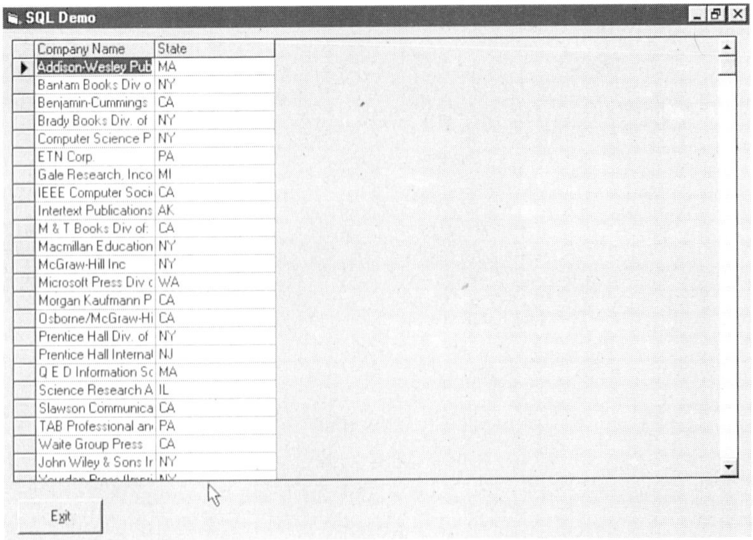

FIGURE 13.28

The SQL demo program at runtime.

The Select Statement

The Select statement returns selected data to a recordset. You've seen several examples of the Select statement already. In its simplest form it looks like

```
SELECT * FROM Publishers
```

If you make that statement in the RecordSource of a Data control, it returns all the fields from all the records from the Publishers table. The * is a wildcard that tells SQL to select every field in the table. The FROM clause defines the table.

Narrowing the Field

What if you don't want all the fields? Suppose you only want Company Name and State? You would modify the Select statement to read

```
SELECT Publishers.[Company Name], Publishers.State
FROM Publishers;
```

There are two items of interest in this new statement. The first is the list of fields to select. Like any list in programming, the items in the list are separated (delimited) by commas. Note that each field is qualified by the table name; that is, the State field is listed as Publishers.State. You could have used State in this query because the query is based on a single table. However, it is a good idea to reference the table name in all your queries so that you can avoid the mistake of not referencing it when you should.

The second new idea is the use of brackets around the Company Name field. These are required because of the space in the field's name. Some programmers avoid the space by using the underline character, as in Company_Name, but SQL provides you with a tool for resolving spaces in the field name, and the brackets do improve readability. If you get to design your own tables, the choice is yours. You may use spaces or underbars. Note that Company Name and Company_Name are not the same.

The WHERE Clause: Becoming More Selective

What happens if you only want the names of publishers from California? The WHERE clause lets you be as selective as you want. The query for California publishers looks like this:

```
SELECT Publishers.[Company Name], Publishers.State
FROM Publishers
WHERE Publishers.State="CA";
```

The runtime screen is shown in Figure 13.29.

13

FIGURE 13.29

Publishers from California.

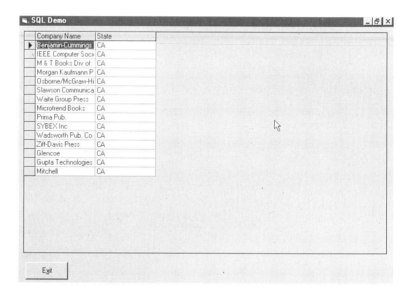

You must handle queries with the WHERE clause a bit differently. The line

```
WHERE Publishers.State="CA"
```

requires special handling in the VB code. Change it to read

```
sSQL = sSQL & " WHERE Publishers.State=" & chr(39) & CA  & Chr(39)
```

The string CA must be delimited before it is sent to the database in an SQL statement. Different data types require different delimiters. The requirements are listed as follows:

- String: Quotation marks. Example:

  ```
  sSQL = sSQL &  Chr(34) & sVar & Chr(34)
  ```

- String: Single Quotation marks—"'" or Chr(39). Example:

  ```
  sSQL = sSQL &"'" & sVar & "'"
  ```

- Date: Pound Sign—"#" or Chr(35). Example:

  ```
  sSQL = sSQL & "#" & datVar & "#"
  ```

- Number: No delimiter. Example:

  ```
  sSQL = sSQL & nVar
  ```

The first string example uses Chr(39) instead of a quotation mark because we have to pass a quote symbol to the SQL engine, but we don't want VB to think we're ending the string literal. Therefore, we use an alternate way of specifying the quote symbol, CHR(39).

The WHERE clause specifies the Selection Criteria for the query. You can refine the WHERE clause with other qualifiers. For example:

```
SELECT Publishers.[Company Name], Publishers.State
FROM Publishers
WHERE (((Publishers.State)='CA')) OR (((Publishers.State)='NY'));
```

selects publishers from California or New York.

Putting Things in Order

The query that returns California and New York publishers might display them in almost any order. Access displays them in the order in which they were entered, but some database engines do not guarantee an order without the ORDER BY clause. The result is that publishers from both states are intermixed. You can have them sorted, if you want, by adding the ORDER BY clause.

```
SELECT Publishers.[Company Name], Publishers.State
FROM Publishers
WHERE (((Publishers.State)="CA")) OR (((Publishers.State)='NY'))
ORDER BY Publishers.State;
```

By default, ORDER BY sorts in ascending order. Add DESC to the end if you want them in descending order. Refine it one more step with

```
SELECT Publishers.[Company Name], Publishers.State
FROM Publishers
WHERE (((Publishers.State)="CA")) OR (((Publishers.State)="NY"))
ORDER BY Publishers.State, Publishers.[Company Name] ;
```

This sorts the publishers alphabetically as well. The first item in the ORDER BY list is the priority item. That is, the data is sorted first by State and then by [Company Name]. If you reverse the order, the query returns a list that is sorted first on [Company Name], with the State field sorted second.

Change the ORDER BY clause to

```
ORDER BY Publishers.State DESC, Publishers.[Company Name] ;
```

and the states will be sorted into descending order.

Using a Variable in a Statement

Database front-end programs often have to make a selection based on user input. Add two more controls to frmSQL to see how this is done. You will need a TextBox and a Command button. Use Table 13.13 to set the properties.

13

TABLE 13.13   Adding User-Defined Selection

Object	Property	Value
TextBox	Name	txtVariable
	Height	315
	Left	3060
	Text	"NJ"
	Top	5940
	Width	675
CommandButton	Name	cmdGo
	Caption	"Find"
	Height	435
	Left	4320
	Top	5880
	Width	1155

Add the following code in `cmdGo_Click`:

```
Private Sub cmdGo_Click()
    sSQL = "SELECT Publishers.[Company Name], Publishers.State"
    sSQL = sSQL & " From Publishers"
    sSQL = sSQL & " Where Publishers.State = "
    sSQL = sSQL & Chr(39) & txtVariable & Chr(39)
    ADODC1.RecordSource = sSQL
    ADODC1.Refresh
End Sub
```

Type any two-letter state postal code in the text box, and click GO. The `DataGrid` is updated to list the publishers from that state. (Some states will not return anything. Guess why?)

The runtime screen is shown in Figure 13.30.

Queries on More Than One Table

The key word in relational database is *relational*. It means, as you know, that tables are related to each other via a key. You might guess that you can create queries to select items from more than one table, and you would be correct. In fact, you saw just that when you worked with the `MSHFlexGrid`'s `MergeCells` property. The following query:

```
SELECT Publishers.[Company Name], Titles.[Year Published]
FROM Publishers
INNER JOIN Titles ON Publishers.PubID = Titles.PubID
ORDER BY Publishers.[Company Name], Titles.[Year Published] DESC;
```

returns a sorted list of the publishers and the years in which they have published books. What makes it all work is the INNER JOIN, which links the key in Publishers with the foreign key in Titles.

FIGURE 13.30

Selection based on user input.

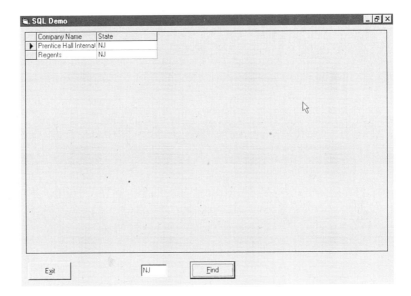

What About Duplicates?

Sometimes a query returns duplicate records. The INNER JOIN query above is an example. If a publisher has more than one book for a given year, each one will get its own record in the recordset. If all you wanted to know was whether a publisher has published a book in a specific year, you must add a predicate to the query. The query would change to

```
SELECT DISTINCT Publishers.[Company Name], Titles.[Year Published]
FROM Publishers
INNER JOIN Titles ON Publishers.PubID = Titles.PubID
ORDER BY Publishers.[Company Name], Titles.[Year Published] DESC;
```

The DISTINCT predicate assures that only records that are different from one another will be returned.

Aggregate Queries

Sometimes you need to know details about a database that cannot be found using a standard SELECT query. For example, you might want to know how many titles each publisher has produced. That calls for an aggregation of the data, a grouping and counting. Queries that do this are called, not surprisingly, aggregate queries.

The following query solves the problem:

```
SELECT DISTINCTROW Publishers.Name,
Count(Titles.Title) AS Count,
Titles.[Year Published]
FROM Publishers
INNER JOIN Titles ON Publishers.PubID = Titles.PubID
GROUP BY Publishers.Name, Titles.[Year Published];
```

The SQL statement has a few new wrinkles. The second item in the select list is
`Count(Titles.Title) AS Count`. Count is one of the aggregate functions. As you might
expect, it counts all the records that meet the criteria, which in this case is all the titles.
There is no field in the database that includes the count, so an alias must be created for
it—something to call it in the recordset the query generates. That alias is created by the
AS clause. The column in the grid is titled Number.

Finally, the GROUP BY clause combines all records that have identical values into a single
record in the recordset. It isn't likely that this particular recordset will return identical
records, but every item that is returned from an aggregate query must have an aggregate
function. Table 13.14 lists the aggregate functions.

TABLE 13.14   The Aggregate Functions

Function	Action
GROUP BY	Combines all identical records into a single record. Each row in the result table will be unique on whatever this clause is. It also defines the summing level of the aggregate functions.
SUM	Finds the total of the values in a field.
AVG	Finds the average of the values in a field.
MIN	Finds the lowest value in a field.
MAX	Finds the highest value in a field.
COUNT	Finds the number of values in a field.
STDev	Finds the standard deviation of the values in a field.
VAR	Finds the variance of the values in a field.
FIRST	Returns the first record.
LAST	Returns the last record.
EXPRESSION	Creates a calculated field.

Computer books often go out of print. Generally, a five-year-old book is out-of-date because most of the information it contains is no longer meaningful. Change the SQL query to

```
SELECT DISTINCTROW Publishers.Name,
Count(Titles.Title) AS Count
FROM Publishers INNER JOIN Titles
ON Publishers.PubID = Titles.PubID
WHERE (((Titles.[Year Published])>1991))
GROUP BY Publishers.Name;
```

This WHERE clause is no different from the WHERE clause in a regular SELECT query.

 Note

> The aggregate function lets you gather or create an aggregation of useless data, too. Avoid the temptation. Your user doesn't really need to know the average or the standard deviation of the year of publication.

More SQL

SQL is a simple language that provides database programmers with tremendous power to manipulate databases and tables. Because the Data control does not support them, this book does not include Action statements that can create new tables, delete tables, add new records to a table or delete records from a table. The Data control also does not support the Data Definition Language (DDL) that lets you create a whole new database.

Lesson Summary

This lesson examined how to use SQL DML (Data Manipulation Language) to return database records to a recordset. The SQL Select statement retrieves records from one or more SQL tables to a Data control recordset. The Where clause in the select statement enables you to add conditions to the statement to filter the results. The Order By clause orders the recordset by the column specified. You can also use several aggregate functions in SQL to find out specific details about the data in the database. Examples of aggregate functions are Min (returns the lowest value) or Sum (sums all the values in the selected column). If you want to expand your knowledge of database programming after you have completed this course, read *Visual Basic 6 Database How-To* from Waite Group Press, or point your Web browser to www.mcp.com for a list of the latest and best books in the field.

13

Quiz 6

Use the following SQL statement for questions 1 and 2:

```
SELECT Publishers.[Company Name], Publishers.State

FROM Publishers
WHERE (((Publishers.State)="CA")) OR (((Publishers.State)="NY"))
ORDER BY Publishers.State;
```

1. This query will return

    a. All the records in the Publishers table

    b. Only the records where State = CA

    c. Only the records where State = NY

    d. All the records where State = CA or State = NY

2. The ORDER BY clause

    a. Places orders for books in the Titles list

    b. Sorts the RecordSet into alphabetical order on the publishers.name field

    c. Sorts the RecordSet into alphabetical order on the publishers.state field

    d. None of the above

3. To use user-supplied data in a SELECT statement:

    a. Delimit it with quotation marks.

    b. Delimit it with the double quotes.

    c. Delimit it with a pound sign.

    d. No delimiters are needed.

4. The line

```
INNER JOIN Titles ON Publishers.PubID = Titles.PubID
```

    a. Links two tables together on the PubID field

    b. Adds the PubID field to the Titles table

    c. Merges the Publishers table and the Titles table into a single table

    d. Contains a syntax error and will not work

Exercise 6

Complexity: Easy

1. What does the SQL statement do?

```
SELECT DISTINCTROW Publishers.Name
FROM Publishers
WHERE (((Publishers.State)="CA")) OR (((Publishers.State)="NY"))
```

Complexity: Moderate

2. Using the BIBLIO database, write the SQL statement required to return the following columns:

Table	Column
Titles	Title
Titles	ISBN
Authors	Author
Titles	Year Published
Publisher	Company Name

LESSON 7

Using the Data Environment and Creating Reports

Imagine you have developed a great Visual Basic database application that stores information about all your customers, invoices, and orders. How do you get the information out of the database and onto a sheet of paper so you can mail your customers their invoices for the month? The answer is to use a report.

Visual Basic enables you to create professional looking reports using the Visual Basic report writer. The Visual Basic report writer is new to Visual Basic 6, previous version used a report writer call Crystal Reports. Using the Visual Basic report writer you can create customized reports, form letters, mailing lists, invoices, summary sheets, and orders. You can use the Visual Basic report writer to generate reports from many different databases.

13

To make large scale report writing and database application development simpler, Visual Basic 6 includes and ActiveX Designer called the Data Environment. ActiveX Designers are controls you use at design time that produce runtime objects and code to simplify your coding. The Data Environment enables you to store database connections, queries and stored procedures (for RDBMS that support them). Using the Data Environment you can create a report or a data entry form by dragging and dropping table columns on to the form or report.

Installing the Data Environment and Report Designer

Before continuing, you need to make sure that the Data Environment and Report Designer are registered and configured. Both ActiveX Designers ship with the Professional and Enterprise editions of Visual Basic 6. To register and install the designers, perform the following steps:

1. From Visual Basic's main menu, select Project and then select Components.
2. Click the Designers tab.
3. Select Microsoft Data Environment and Microsoft Data Report.
4. Click OK.

The ActiveX Designers are now installed!

The Data Environment

Before you can create a report, you must first add a Data Environment to the project. To add a Data Environment, perform the following steps:

1. From the Visual Basic main menu, select Project and then select More ActiveX Designers and then Data Environment. The dialog box shown in Figure 13.31 appears.

FIGURE 13.31

Data Environment design window.

2. Right-click the connection object and select Properties. The Data Link Properties dialog box appears. Select the Connection tab shown in Figure 13.32.

3. The Use Data Source Name radio button is selected by default. Select Biblio in the drop-down combo box. Click the Test Connection button; a message box stating that Test Connection Succeeded appears.

4. Click the OK button.

FIGURE 13.32

Data Link Properties dialog box.

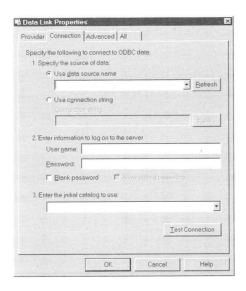

Now that we have a database connection in our Data Environment, let's add a command. A command is a table or SQL statement that is stored in the Data Environment. The command can then be used later to create a report or bind columns to a data form using drag and drop. Perform the following steps:

1. Click the Add Command toolbar button located on the Data Environment design window, shown in Figure 13.32. A command object is added to the connection. Right-click the command object and select Properties. The Command Properties dialog box, shown in Figure 13.33, appears.

2. In the Command Name text box, shown in Figure 13.33, enter qryPublishers.

3. In the Database Object combo box, select Table.

4. In the Object Name combo box, select Publishers. Note that if you wanted to, you could use a SQL statement. Click OK.

The qryPublishers command is added to the Data Environment, shown in Figure 13.34. Let's see how to use the qryPublishers command to create a report.

13

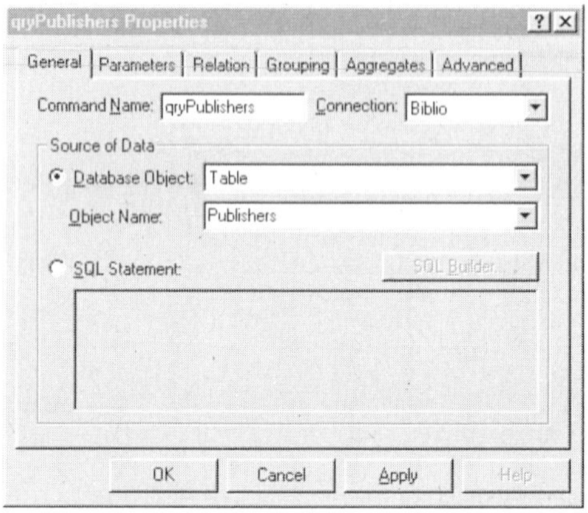

FIGURE 13.33

Command Properties dialog box.

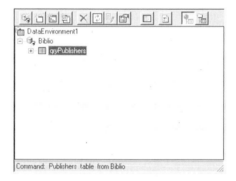

FIGURE 13.34

Data Environment design window with the qryPublishers *command.*

Report Designer

From the Visual Basic menu, select Project and then select Data Report. The Data Report Designer, shown in Figure 13.35, is displayed.

Design a report that prints out some selected fields from the Data Environment command qryPublishers. To design the report, perform the following steps:

1. Click the Report Header section, shown in Figure 13.35. Right-click and select Insert Control and then Report Title from the pop-up window.

2. Set the report title to "List of Publishers". Perform this action by setting the Caption property in the properties window. Make the Caption bold by clicking the Font property and checking the Bold check box.

3. Tile the Data Environment window and the report designer window. From the Visual Basic main menu, select Window and Tile Vertically.

FIGURE 13.35

Data Report design window.

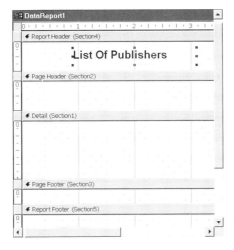

4. Expand the qryPublishers to show the columns, by clicking the plus sign by the qryPublishers name in the Data Environment design window. Your project should look similar to Figure 13.36.

FIGURE 13.36

Data Environment design window and Report design window.

5. To add a column to the report, drag a column from the Data Environment window and drop into on to the detail section of the report designer. For this report, drag and drop the columns Company Name, City, and State.

6. Move the report Label controls for each column in to the Page Header section of the report. Leave the report text boxes for each column in the detail section.

7. Shrink the detail section to show as little white space as possible. The amount of room between the detail section and the page footer section, is the amount of space between rows.

8. Add a page number to the report by right-clicking the Page Footer selection and selecting Insert Controls and Current Page Number.

9. The last step is set the `DataSource` property of the report Design window to DataEnvironment1 and the `DataMember` property to qryPublishers. The completed report in Design mode is shown in Figure 13.37.

FIGURE 13.37

Completed report in Design mode.

You are done. To run the report, add a Form to the project and place a single command button on the form. In the `click` event of the command button, add the following line of code:

```
DataReport1.Show
```

The finished report is shown in Figure 13.38.

You can see that the finished report provides you with a toolbar to print the report or to export the report to a file such as an HTML page. Notice the code to show the report is quite simple, you only have to invoke the `Show` method. The `DataReport` object contains several methods and properties that make customizing the report quite easy. For instance to export the report to an HTML file use the `ExportReport` method.

FIGURE 13.38

Completed report.

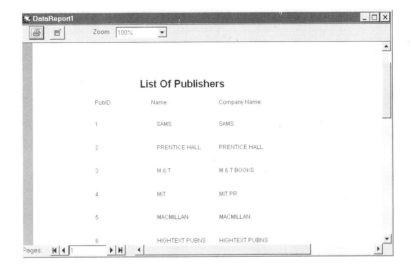

Lesson Summary

Visual Basic provides a Data Environment that enables you to store connection information as well as queries. Using the Data Environment, you can create data-bound forms
and reports by dragging and dropping columns onto the form or report. The Report
Designer works in conjunction with the Data Environment to allow a user to quickly and
easily create reports from a database using drag and drop.

Quiz 7

1. You can print information in a database to a printer by creating a

    a. Query

    b. Recordset

    c. Snapshot

    d. Report

2. The ActiveX Designer used to create a report is the

    a. Form Designer

    b. Data Report Designer

    c. Query/Report/Form Builder

    d. Report Builder

13

3. Which one of the following is not stored in the Data Environment?

    a. Form

    b. Tables

    c. Connection

    d. Query

4. To save a query in a Data Environment, you add a

    a. Connection

    b. Form

    c. Command

    d. Data control

Exercise 7

Complexity: Easy

1. Create a form that displays the qryPublishers from the Data Environment used in this section by dragging and dropping columns onto the form.

Complexity: Easy

2. Add a button to export the report used in this lesson to HTML.

Chapter Summary

In this chapter you learned all about using databases with Visual Basic 6. You learned what a database is as well as how to design your own databases and tables. You also learned how to use the ADO Data control to easily create database applications with Visual Basic. The main points of this chapter are as follows:

- *SQL* stands for Structured Query Language and is the standard language for accessing relational database information.

- A *relational database* is a database that structures the data by breaking it into logical objects that have relationships between the objects.

- *Tables* are storage areas for specific types of information.

- A *primary key* is a database term used to signify the column or columns that uniquely identify a single row in a table.

- A *query* is a SQL statement used to retrieve rows of information from one or more tables. The SQL statement used to retrieve information is the Select statement.

- A *recordset* is a Microsoft ADO object that represents the data in a table or a query. You can use a recordset to view, update, or delete data in a table or query.

- A *logical database design* is one that creates all the entities in a database and establishes relationships between the entities.

- A *physical database design* is one that takes the logical database design and creates a database and database objects to represent the entities and relationships in the logical database design.

- A *one-to-one relationship* is one in which each row in one table is represented by a single row in another table.

- A *one-to-many relationship* is one in which a row in one table is represented by many rows in another table.

- A *many-to-many relationship* is one in which a row from one entity may be represented by one or many rows in another table, and the row from the second table may be represented by one or many rows in the first table.

- *Normalization* of a database design involves a set of rules used to test the soundness of your database design.

- The ADO Data control provides an easy database access method that enables you to create database applications with little or no code.

- The ConnectionString property of the ADO Data control enables you to specify the OLE DB provider and defines how you establish your connection in your application. The ODBC provider enables you to use the ADO Data control with any ODBC source.

- The recordset object of the ADO Data control is the primary object used to manipulate the data in the Source (query, table, or stored procedure) property.

- Binding an ADO Data control to existing ActiveX controls enables you to automatically set the control value with columns from the recordset without writing any code.

- Visual Basic ships with many data ActiveX controls that use the ADO Data control to provide data aware functionality with little or no programming. Examples of these controls are the DataGrid or the data ComboBox.

- You can manipulate data in a database using the ADO recordset object model or by using the SQL language. You can also create ADO recordset's by setting the Source property of the ADO Data control to a SQL Statement.

- Visual Basic provides a Data Environment that enables you to store connection information as well as queries. Using the Data Environment you can create data-bound forms and reports by dragging and dropping columns onto the form or report.

13

- Visual Basic ships with its own Report Designer. The Report Designer works in conjunction with the Data Environment to allow a user to quickly and easily create reports from a database.

In Chapter 14, "Advanced Features," you will look at numerous advanced Visual Basic topics, such as creating an executable for distribution, the `Timer` control, and DDE, as well as methods and techniques to optimize your applications.

CHAPTER 14

Advanced Features

This chapter covers many different topics. It teaches you how to use the Timer Control to perform background processing, DDE implementation, and how to create setup programs to distribute your applications using the Setup Wizard. It teaches you how to use functions in dynamic link libraries to increase your application's performance time or to perform applications that are not normally part of Visual Basic.

Do you wonder what it means to be multitasking? This chapter gives you the answer as you examine Visual Basic and the Windows architecture. You'll learn the difference between cooperative multitasking and preemptive multitasking, as well as how to create applications that can communicate with each other using DDE.

Finally, it teaches you how to create an executable, distribute your applications, and optimize the code you write.

LESSON 1

The Timer Control

Throughout this book, we have been covering user event-driven programming, where events are triggered as a result of a user action. What if you wanted to check every 10 minutes to see if a file existed, or your application was required to take some action every few seconds without any user input?

The `Timer` control in Visual Basic 6 keeps track of time intervals and fires a `Timer` event whenever a certain amount of time has elapsed. Timer controls can be used for background processing or to take some sort of action at regular intervals. Before you jump into the specifics of the control, consider how timers are used in everyday life.

Timers are found everywhere in the real world. The most obvious example is an alarm clock. You set your alarm clock to wake you up at a specified time. Another good example is a VCR. Assume you can actually figure out how to program your VCR, and you set it to record a half-hour TV show at 8:00 p.m. on one channel, and then to record another half-hour TV show at 10:00 p.m. on a different channel. So what happens? At 8:00 p.m., an event is triggered to start recording a TV show on the specified channel. Somehow, the VCR checks to see if the recording interval of half an hour has elapsed, and if so, it stops recording. When 10:00 p.m. arrives, the whole process starts over.

Using `Timer` Controls

To understand the `Timer` control, create a new project that displays the current time in a status bar at the bottom of the form. Start a new project called timerapp. Add the `Timer` control shown in Figure 14.1 to the form.

FIGURE 14.1

`Timer` *control on the Visual Basic toolbar.*

Timer control ——

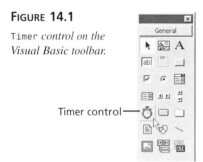

It's no mistake that the icon looks like a stopwatch!

Now take a look at the two most important `Timer` control properties: `Enabled` and `Interval`.

The `Enabled` Property

The `Enabled` property has two possible settings, `True` or `False`. If the `Enabled` property has a value of `True`, the timer is operational and counting down the time interval. If the property is set to `False`, the timer is not operational and is not counting down any time interval.

The `Interval` Property

The `Interval` property is the number of milliseconds between `Timer` events. Let's say we want to do some task every 10 seconds. A millisecond is one thousandth of a second. Setting the `Interval` property to represent a 10-second time period, we divide 10 seconds by .001 to get 10,000. A value of `1000` would be every one second, and a value of `500` every half second. The minimum value for a timer interval is `0` and the maximum value is `65,536`, which is just over a minute. You can set the `Interval` property and the `Enabled` property at design time or at runtime.

You want the time in the status bar to update every second, so using the previous formula to compute the interval value, set the value of the `Interval` property to `1000` (1/.001 = 1000) and set the `Enabled` property to `True`.

Add the objects shown in Table 14.1, and set the properties.

TABLE 14.1 Application timerapp Objects and Property Settings

Object	Property	Setting
Form	Caption	Example of Background Processing
	Height	2790
	Name	frmTimer
	Width	6390
Timer	Enabled	True
	Interval	100
	Left	15
	Name	Timer1
	Top	45
StatusBar	Height	615
	Name	StatusBar1

Add three panels to the status bar, and then place the following code into form frmTimer's load event:

```
Private Sub Form_Load()
    StatusBar1.Panels.Text = "Grey"
    StatusBar1.Panels.Text = Date$
    StatusBar1.Panels.Text = Time$
End Sub
```

The code sets the text of each of the three panels on the `StatusBar` control. The first panel of the status bar represents the current background color, the second panel displays the date, and the third panel displays the time. The line

```
StatusBar1.Panels.Text = Date$
```

uses the `Date$` function to return a string value of the current date, and it displays the
date in the second panel of the status bar. The line

```
StatusBar1.Panels.Text = Time$
```

uses the `Time$` function to return a string value of the current time, and it displays the
time in the third panel of the status bar.

Add the following line of code in the `Timer` event subroutine:

```
Private Sub Timer1_Timer()
    StatusBar1.Panels.Text = Date$
    StatusBar1.Panels.Text = Time$
End Sub
```

Okay, it's time to run the application to see what it does. The application looks like that
in Figure 14.2.

Notice when the application is running that the time in the third panel is being updated
every second. What's happening? The timer interval counts down and executes the code
in the `Timer` event. Change the `Interval` property to `5000`, and run the program again.
Now the time is being updated at five-second intervals instead of one-second intervals.

As it turns out, displaying the date and time in the `StatusBar` control can be done without a timer control by setting the `Style` property of the panel. Now take a look at a more
complex problem.

Background Processing

The `Timer` control is limited in that the maximum interval allowed is 65,535 milliseconds. What do you do if you need to load a file into a database at 10-minute intervals
or you want to do some other background task while the user is idle? Simple. Just keep
an internal count of the number of time intervals that have passed. Modify the current
project to change the background color of the form every 10 seconds. Reset the
`Interval` property setting to `1000` so that it fires the `Timer` event every second. Add the
following to the declarations in the form `frmTimer` module:

```
Dim iTimeToChange as Integer
```

The `iTimeToChange` variable is used to keep track of the number of intervals that have passed since the last time the background color of the form was changed. Add the following code to the form's load event:

```
Private Sub Form_Load()
    StatusBar1.Panels.Text = "Grey"
    StatusBar1.Panels.Text = Date$
    StatusBar1.Panels.Text = Time$
    iTimeToChange = 0
End Sub
```

Next, add the code shown in Listing 14.1 to the `Timer` event.

LISTING 14.1 Timer Event Code

```
Private Sub Timer1_Timer()
    StatusBar1.Panels.Text = Time$
    iTimeToChange = iTimeToChange + 1
    If iTimeToChange = 10 Then

        ' Case Statement to check the Text in the first panel and
        ' then change the  background color based on the
        ' current color

        Select Case StatusBar1.Panels
        Case "Red"
            Me.BackColor = RGB(0, 255, 0)
            StatusBar1.Panels = "Green"
        Case "Green"
            Me.BackColor = RGB(0, 0, 255)
            StatusBar1.Panels = "Blue"
        Case Else
            Me.BackColor = RGB(255, 0, 0)
            StatusBar1.Panels = "Red"
        End Select
        iTimeToChange = 0 'Reset the Back color counter
    End If

End Sub
```

The following lines increment the `iTimeToChange` variable and check to see if the variable is equal to 10:

```
iTimeToChange = iTimeToChange + 1
If iTimeToChange = 10 Then
```

They change the background color every 10 intervals, in this case every 10 seconds. If you set the timer `Interval` to `60000`, or 60 seconds, the background color would change every 10 minutes.

14

Run the application. Notice how the time changes in the status bar every second and how the background color changes only every 10 seconds.

Now that you are an expert with the `Timer` control, it is time (no pun intended) to bring up a few limitations of the control:

- Even though the timer `Interval` property is measured in milliseconds, the system only generates 18 clock ticks per second, so the actual precision of a timer interval is no more than 1/18th of a second, which is a little over 55.5 milliseconds.

- If your application is performing intensive computing such as querying a database, accessing a network, or performing file input or output, your application may not get the `Timer` events as often as the `Interval` property specifies. Also, the interval is not guaranteed to fire the event exactly on time. If you need precision timing, use the `GetSystemTime` API function.

- Using a small timer interval can slow system performance, because the `Timer` events are continuously triggered. Do not use a small interval unless you really need one.

Despite the `Timer` control's limitations, it is a very useful control for taking action at specific intervals. You, the programmer, must take its limitations into account and set the `Interval` property accordingly, based on your application's needs.

Lesson Summary

In this lesson we created a new project to demonstrate the capabilities of the Timer control, and showed how to use it with regard to background processing. We also covered some of the limitations of the control. In the next lesson, we'll introduce the concept of multitasking.

Quiz 1

1. The `Timer` control is limited to _____ milliseconds.

   a. 100,000

   b. 1,000,000

   c. 65,535

   d. There is no limit to the number of milliseconds to which the `Timer` control can be set.

2. When you set the timer Interval to 60,000, it is equal to _____ seconds.

    a. 6 seconds

    b. 60 seconds

    c. 600 seconds

    d. 6 minutes

3. If you need precision timing, use the _____.

    a. `Time` Control

    b. `GetSystemTime` API function

    c. `iTimeToChange` variable

    d. `GetIntervalTime` API function

4. Which can slow system performance regarding the use of a `Timer` control?

    a. Using a small timer interval

    b. Using a large timer interval

    c. Setting the timer Interval property to 18 clock ticks per second

    d. Using more than one Timer control.

Exercise 1

Complexity: Easy

1. Change the exercise in Lesson 1 by cutting the interval in half to 500. Change the program so that it still changes the color of the background every 10 seconds.

Complexity: Moderate

2. Change the `Timer` Control exercise in Lesson 1 so that a second timer is used. Set the interval of the second timer to one second, and have it change the background color every 15 seconds. Keep the first timer running as usual. Also, add a fourth panel to the status bar to display the current interval of the second timer.

LESSON 2

Understanding the Architecture

You have almost made it to the end of the book, and by now you should have a good grasp of the things Visual Basic can do. This lesson briefly examines some key Windows

14

and Visual Basic architecture issues in order to enhance your abilities as a programmer. Start by considering the different types of multitasking environments available to the Visual Basic programmer.

Cooperative Multitasking Versus Preemptive Multitasking

In order to help you understand the different types of multitasking, imagine you work at a day-care center and are in charge of three seven-year-old children. It's recess time, so you take the children outside to play. The three children want to ride bicycles; the problem is that you only have one bicycle, so the children have to share. You tell the children to share the bicycle and just take turns so that everyone gets to ride. You have some work to do so you leave the children. They begin to ride the bike, sharing and taking turns. But it's not too long before one child decides that the other kids have ridden the bike longer than they should have, forgets sharing, and keeps the bike.

The example of the children voluntarily sharing the bicycle is the premise of cooperative multitasking. Applications execute and share the computer's processor with the other applications. It is up to the applications to decide when to give up the system processor and allow another application to run. Like the child who decided not to give up the bicycle, there are many applications that perform such tasks as file I/O and database access that do not free up the processor. Windows 3.x is an example of a cooperative multitasking operating system.

Now back to our story. The two children who are not getting a chance to ride the bike run in to tell you that the third child refuses to share. You grab your work and an alarm clock and head outside to enforce the shared bike policy. You tell the three children that they each get to ride the bike for 10 minutes. You use the alarm clock to let them know their turn is over. You decide to stay outside with the children to make sure they relinquish the bike every 10 minutes. You are now operating on the same premise as preemptive multitasking.

With preemptive multitasking, the operating system allows each application to execute for a certain amount of time. If the application does not give up the processor voluntarily, when the time slice expires, the operating system gives the processor to another application. This is a simplistic explanation, for there are other factors such as task priority and interrupts that this book does not go into. Windows 95 and Windows NT are examples of preemptive multitasking systems.

Single or Multithread

What does it mean when someone says they have a single-threaded application, and what the heck is a thread? A *thread* is simply executing code. Every application in a Windows environment has at least a single thread of execution. An application is said to be multi-threaded when it can create more than one thread of execution.

Suppose you have a database application and you have a query that executes for a long time. Your application also needs to enable your user to edit some data in another table. If your application is multithreaded, you can start your query by creating a thread to perform the query and then, while the query thread is executing, begin to edit the table using another thread. Multitasking preemptive operating systems allocate separate time slices to each thread (that is, the query thread and the edit table thread).

In Windows 3.x, applications can only be single threaded. Windows 95 and Windows NT enable applications to use multiple threads, which can all run at the same time.

Visual Basic Applications

Let's examine briefly the architecture of a Visual Basic application. Visual Basic 6 applications will run only in a 32-bit Windows environment such as Windows 95 or Windows NT. When you compile a Visual Basic project, Visual Basic produces an executable file composed of P-code rather than machine instructions that can be directly executed by the system processor.

P-code stands for *pseudo-code*. It is an intermediate step between the instructions in your Visual Basic project and the low-level native code or machine code that your microprocessor actually executes. At runtime, `VBRUN300.DLL` converts the P-code into native code. If you have the Professional or Enterprise editions of Visual Basic, you can compile directly into native code. Compiling to native code is covered in Lesson 6.

Take a look at some important limitations of a Visual Basic application.

Stack Size

The program stack is a limited area of memory used to store various types of information in a running application. The stack stores return addresses of calling functions and procedures, arguments, and local variables in procedures, and is used in many other ways. The stack has a limited amount of space available to your application; 32-bit Visual Basic applications have a stack size of 1MB.

14

Maximum Number of Controls per Form

There is a limit of 254 controls on a single form. You can get around this limitation by using control arrays, which count as only one control.

Form, Class, and Module Limitations

A Visual Basic module cannot exceed 64K in code. If the 64K limit is exceeded, you will get an error during compilation. To fix the error, remove some of the code in the module and place it in another module. The maximum number of code lines in a form, class, or module is 65,534 lines.

Data Limitations

A *data segment* is an area of memory allocated to an application to store data. In a Visual Basic application, each form, class, and module is allocated a 64K data segment. This segment stores all static local variables, module level fixed strings, module level variables other than arrays, and variable length strings. Arrays and variable length strings are treated differently. Each variable length string is allocated its own data segment. Variable length strings can have up to four gigabytes of characters. There is no limit to the size of arrays, which are limited only by the amount of available memory. Array indexes, however, must be in the range of -2147483648 to +2147483648.

Lesson Summary

You should have a general understanding of some key features and terms of the Visual Basic and Windows architectures. Understanding the terms and concepts will come in handy, especially in the following section where you can learn about programming with idle loops.

Quiz 2

1. Which of the following statements about Threads is not true?

    a. A thread is executing code.

    b. Every application in Windows has at least one thread of executing code.

    c. Multitasking threads allocate the same time slice.

    d. Multi-threaded application is one that can create more than one thread of execution.

2. P-code stands for

    a. Project-code

    b. Psuedo-code

      c. Program-code

      d. Pre-code

3. The code your program actually executes is

      a. Machine code

      b. P-code

      c. Psuedo-code

      d. Project-code

4. The limit to the size of Arrays are

      a. 254k

      b. Only limited by the amount of available memory

      c. 64k

      d. 2,147,483,648 bytes

LESSON 3

Idle Time

In this lesson, you will build on the concepts of preemptive and cooperative multitasking by introducing the concept of idle time. To understand idle time, think about a word processing application. You create a new document, and suddenly you get writer's block and can't think of anything to write. You just sit there being idle. Well you're not the only one being idle; you're not doing anything, so the word processing application is also doing nothing.

Application idle time is the time when nothing is happening in the application between events. For some applications, you might want to use this idle time by creating a background process using a Timer control, as described in Lesson 1.

Other applications may present you with a different problem. For instance, you probably wouldn't want a process performing iterations that would tie up the application for an extended period of time. In a preemptive multitasking system, such as Windows 95 or Windows NT, you could still use your PC while the application performs the iterations thanks to the preemptive time slice, but you would not be able to interact with the application.

On a cooperative multitasking system such as Windows 3.1, a process performing a large number of iterations not only locks up the executing application, but the PC as well,

14

because there is no time for any other process to run. What happens if you accidentally started the process and wanted to stop it? You would have to let the process complete or kill the application, which sounds severe! Happily, there is a way to momentarily halt your application and return control to the operating system to enable other applications the chance to run and allow other events in your application to be processed. This technique is called an *idle loop*.

Idle Loops

To create an idle loop, use the Visual Basic command `DoEvents`.

DoEvents returns control momentarily to the operating system so that other events can be processed. `DoEvents` has the following syntax:

```
DoEvents
```

With preemptive multitasking systems, such as Windows 95 or Windows NT, use `DoEvents` in any case where you need to enable your application to process events during a long process. For instance, in the case of a process performing a lot of iterations or calculations in a loop, you can use `DoEvents` to provide a way to give the user a chance to cancel the operation.

In the past, programmers have been very creative in the use of `DoEvents` and idle loops. For example, idle loops make sure graphics and status bars are being updated correctly. Try an experiment with `DoEvents` and idle loops. Create a new project called idleloop. Add the objects and set the properties shown in Table 14.2.

TABLE 14.2   Application `idleloop` Objects and Property Settings

Object	Property	Setting
Form	Caption	Testing Idle Loops
	Height	2985
	Left	1920
	Name	frmIdle
	Top	2010
	Width	5235
CommandButton	Caption	Start
	Height	585
	Left	1665
	Name	cmdStart
	Top	1770
	Width	1620

Object	Property	Setting
TextBox	Height	435
	Left	1350
	Name	txtCount
	Text	none
	Top	960
	Width	2400

Add the code in Listing 14.2 to the Click event of the Command button.

LISTING 14.2   Start Button Click Event

```
Private Sub cmdStart_Click()
Dim iLoopCount As Integer, iCounter As Integer

  iCounter = 0
  Me.MousePointer = Hourglass
  For iLoopCount = 0 To 500
    'Increment the Counter value
    iCounter = iCounter + 1
    'Display the count in the TextBox
    txtCount = Str$(iCounter)
  Next iLoopCount
  Me.MousePointer = Default
End Sub
```

When the user clicks the Command button labeled Start, the Counter variable in the Click event procedure is incremented by 1, and the value is displayed in the text box until the variable LoopCount exceeds 500. Run the application and click the Start button.

What happened? The text box did not display every value, only the final value 501. Why? The repaint event for the text box was not allowed to process during the loop, so only the final result was displayed. Now add a DoEvents after the line of code txtCount = Str$(iCounter):

```
For iLoopCount = 0 To 500
    'Increment the Counter value
    iCounter = iCounter + 1
    'Display the count in the TextBox
    txtCount = Str$(iCounter)
    DoEvents
  Next iLoopCount
```

14

Run the application and click the Start button. See the difference? DoEvents halts execution in the loop and transfers control to the operating system. This allows other events and messages in the application to be processed, so you see the numbers incrementing in the text box.

If you are having problems with screen repaints—for instance, if a status bar display is not being updated or a text box is not displaying incremental values—consider using the Refresh method of the control or form instead of DoEvents. In the previous example, remove the DoEvents statement and put the following code in its place:

```
txtCount.Refresh
```

Now run the application. This gives the same results, but it uses the correct method. Because there are better ways to refresh displays, use DoEvents to enable your user to exit the counter loop in the application. Modify the code in the command Click event as shown in Listing 14.3.

LISTING 14.3   New Start Button Click Event

```
Private Sub cmdStart_Click()
Static iLoopCount As Integer 'Save Value
Dim iCounter As Integer
Const Max_Loop = 1500
  iCounter = 0
  '
  'Check if already processing
  ' (i.e. Caption on button says Cancel)
  ' If so set iLoopCount to the max
  ' Reset the Caption on the button
  ' and Exit
  If cmdStart.Caption = "Cancel" Then
    iLoopCount = Max_Loop
    cmdStart.Caption = "Start"
    Exit Sub
  Else
    cmdStart.Caption = "Cancel"
  End If
  Me.MousePointer = Hourglass
  For iLoopCount = 0 To Max_Loop
    'Allow events to be processed
    DoEvents
    'Increment the Counter value
    iCounter = iCounter + 1
    'Display the count in the TextBox
    txtCount = Str$(iCounter)
    'Repaint
    txtCount.Refresh
```

```
   Next iLoopCount
   Me.MousePointer = Default
   cmdStart.Caption = "Start"
End Sub
```

The procedure was modified so the `iLoopCount` variable is static, and a `DoEvents` was
added in the loop to allow the process to be interrupted. If the `Caption` property of the
`CommandButton` reads `Start`, the process is started and the `Caption` property is set to
`Cancel`. If the `Caption` property is set to `Cancel`, the routine variable `iLoopCount` is set
to the maximum value in the loop, which terminates the loop on the next iteration and
resets the `Caption` property to `Start`. Run the application and click the Start button. Now
click the Cancel button to stop processing. Figure 14.3 shows the program at runtime.

FIGURE 14.3

*An Idleloop
application.*

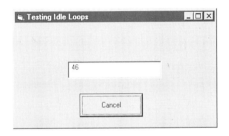

You have now written an idle loop that enables you to interrupt a lengthy process.
Remember, if you are having trouble with screen repaints, use the `Refresh` method of the
form or control. Use Timer controls for background processing and `DoEvents` to interrupt
lengthy tasks. Avoid using `DoEvents` with global data, and remember that `DoEvents` will
not return control to your application when performing blocking I/O instructions, such as
a file read or a database query.

Lesson Summary

In this lesson we learned about idle time and idle loops and how to use them effectively
in our programs. Much of this was made possible using the Visual Basic command
`DoEvents`. In the next lesson we'll learn about a new type of form called a DDE form.

Quiz 3

1. The technique used to momentarily halt an application to allow other events to be
   processed is called

   a. `DoEvents`

   b. Idle loop

    c. `ProcessEvents`

    d. Wakeup

2. The correct syntax of `DoEvents` is

    a. `DoEvents`

    b. `DoEvents([interval])`

    c. `DoEvents [interval]`

    d. None of the above

3. An idle loop can be used to allow

    a. the updating of status bar displays

    b. A database query

    c. A file read

    d. Both b and c

4. An idle loop will not return control to your application when

    a. performing blocking I/O instructions

    b. a file read

    c. a database query

    d. All of the above

Exercise 3

Complexity: Easy

1. Add a second textbox to the exercise in Lesson 4. Call it txtCount2, and place it above `txtCount`. Make sure txtCount2 displays the same information as the original `txtCount`, and refresh it properly.

Complexity: Moderate

2. Add a second control button to the exercise in Lesson 4. Let it perform the same function as the first button. Place it on the left of the first button. Add an additional line of code to each `Click` event. For the button on the left, increment the left property of the text box by −1. For the right button, increment the left property of the textbox box by +1. Run the program and click between the two buttons.

LESSON 4

DDE

DDE stands for `dynamic data exchange` and is a form of *interprocess* communications supported by the Windows operating system. Interprocess communication is two or more applications exchanging data with each other. OLE (object-linking and embedding) is another form of interprocess communications. OLE is covered in the lessons in Chapter 15, "Doing the Impossible (and More) with the Windows API." OLE is the preferred method of Microsoft Windows interprocess communication. However, OLE is not supported by all Windows applications, so DDE is still very important.

Source and Destination

Data exchange in DDE is referred to as a conversation between a source application and a destination application. As an analogy, say you have a friend you would like to call. You dial the phone number and, if your friend is there, he or she picks up the phone and begins to talk. The two of you are now engaging in a conversation. When the conversation is complete, you both hang up the phone.

DDE is similar: An application makes a call to another application; if the other application is available and can establish the link, then the DDE conversation can begin. The application that initiates the DDE exchange is called the destination, while the application responding to the request is called the source. Applications can be both DDE sources and destinations.

Figure 14.4 shows a DDE example where Microsoft Excel is the source application and is sending data from spreadsheet cells to text boxes in a Visual Basic application.

FIGURE 14.4

A DDE conversation with a Microsoft Excel source and a Visual Basic destination.

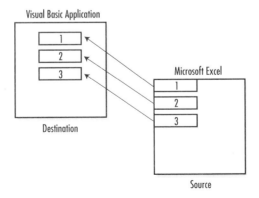

14

Establishing DDE Links

Establishing DDE links between a Visual Basic application and another application requires setting properties on controls or forms to establish the link and exchange the data. A form is the only Visual Basic object that can act as a DDE source. TextBox, Label, and PictureBox custom controls can be DDE destinations. To set up a form to be a DDE source requires setting the following properties in order.

To set up a DDE destination on a TextBox, PictureBox, or Label control, set the following properties in order:

- LinkTopic
- LinkItem
- LinkMode
- LinkTimeout

LinkTopic

The LinkTopic property consists of string, which declares the application and topic. The application could be an Excel workbook for example, and the topic is simply the fundamental data grouping used in that application, such as Sheet1. In a destination control, the LinkTopic property has the following format: application¦topic, where application is the name of the source application the destination wants to converse with, and topic is the topic of the conversation. For example, to start a DDE conversation with Microsoft Excel using the spreadsheet DDE.xls, the LinkTopic property would be set as follows:

```
LinkTopic = "Excel¦c:\spreadsheets\[DDE.xls]Chart1"
```

In a source application, LinkTopic is set to the topic that can respond to a DDE conversation; for example; a form name.

```
LinkTopic = Form1
```

LinkMode

The LinkMode property specifies the type of DDE link to be established between a source application and a destination application.

For a DDE source, a form, the LinkMode property can be set to None or Source. None is the default value for both the source and the destination. When a DDE source's LinkMode is set to None, no applications can start a DDE conversation with the source topic (form). Also, if the LinkMode property is set to None at design time, then the property cannot be modified at runtime. However, if the property is set to Source, then the LinkMode property can be toggled between Source and None at runtime. Setting the LinkMode property to Source allows the form to be a topic of DDE conversation with other applications.

For destination controls, LinkMode determines how the data is exchanged between the source application and the destination control. Valid settings are None, Automatic, Manual, or Notify. In Automatic mode, if the data in the source changes, the destination control automatically receives the data. In Manual mode, the destination control only receives data when it asks for the data. In Notify mode, the destination control receives notification that data has changed, but then must manually ask for the data.

LinkItem

The LinkItem property applies only to a destination, such as a text box, label, or picture box, and is the item that is exchanged during the DDE conversation. For example, in a DDE conversation between two Visual Basic applications, the LinkItem property could be Text1 or, if the source application is a spreadsheet, the LinkItem property could be R1C1, the coordinates of a spreadsheet cell.

LinkTimeout

The LinkTimeout property applies only to destinations, and is the amount of time Visual Basic waits for a response in a DDE conversation before raising an error. If there is no response within the LinkTimeout period, an error is raised. This prevents VB from getting hung up waiting for a response that might never come. The value of LinkTimeout is measured in tenths of a second. The default value is 50 (5 seconds).

Let's take a look at the events and methods of a DDE.

Events and Methods

LinkOpen Event

The LinkOpen event occurs when a DDE link is established.

LinkNotify Event

LinkNotify is triggered when a DDE conversation is in Notify link mode, and the data in the source changes.

LinkError Event

The LinkError event is triggered if an error occurs during a DDE conversation.

LinkClose Event

The LinkClose event occurs when the DDE link is broken.

14

LinkRequest Method

The LinkRequest method is invoked by a destination control to retrieve data from a source in Manual or Notify link modes.

LinkPoke Method

The LinkPoke method enables the destination control to send data to the source application.

LinkSend Method

The LinkSend method is used to transfer the contents of a picture box from the source to the destination.

DDE Application

To test DDE, you are going to create two projects, one for the DDE source and another for the DDE destination. Creating and testing the applications requires running two instances of Visual Basic. Start with the source project. Create a new project named VBSrc. It is important that you name the project before running the application, because the DDE destination application must use the Visual Basic project name or executable name to establish a DDE link. Add a single form to the project, add the objects, and set the properties as shown in Table 14.3.

TABLE 14.3 Application VBSrc Objects and Property Settings

Object	Property	Setting
Form	Caption	Source DDE
	Height	2175
	LinkMode	1 - Source
	LinkTopic	frmSource
	Name	frmSource
	Width	3930
TextBox	Height	300
	Left	675
	Name	txtItem
	Text	" "
	Top	540
	Width	2175

The DDE source application is complete, with no code! Run the project from Visual Basic and leave it running. Start a new instance of Visual Basic to create the DDE destination project. Start a new project named VbDest with a single form. Add the objects and set the properties, as shown in Table 14.4.

TABLE 14.4 Application VbDest Objects and Property Settings

Object	Property	Setting
Form	Caption	Destination Application
	Height	2175
	LinkMode	0 - None
	Name	frmDest
	Width	4665
TextBox	Height	330
	Left	1560
	Name	txtReceive
	Text	" "
	Top	450
	Width	2505
Frame	Caption	Link Mode
	Height	1110
	Left	195
	Name	Frame1
	Top	345
	Width	1230
OptionButton	Caption	Manual
	Height	315
	Left	90
	Name	optManual
	Top	240
	Width	1020

continues

14

TABLE 14.4 continued

Object	Property	Setting
OptionButton	Caption	Automatic
	Height	315
	Left	90
	Name	optAutomatic
	Top	465
	Width	1020
OptionButton	Caption	Notify
	Height	315
	Left	90
	Name	optNotify
	Top	975
	Width	1020
CommandButton	Caption	Conversation
	Height	465
	Left	1530
	Name	cmdConversation
	Top	990
	Width	1185
CommandButton	Caption	Get Data
	Height	465
	Left	2760
	Name	cmdGetData
	Top	990
	Width	1185

Add the code shown in Listing 14.4 to the Click event of the Command button
cmdConversation.

LISTING 14.4 Command Button cmdConversation Click Event

```
Private Sub cmdConversation_Click()

    'Start DDE conversation

```

```
cmdGetData.Enabled = False
' Set DDE link to None
txtReceive.LinkMode = vbLinkNone
'Establish Topic to Source
txtReceive.LinkTopic = "VBSrc¦frmSource"
'Establish the item of conversation
txtReceive.LinkItem = "txtItem"
'Set Timeout to 10 seconds
txtReceive.LinkTimeout = 100
'
'Determine the type of link
'
If optManual.Value = True Then
  cmdGetData.Enabled = True
  txtReceive.LinkMode = vbLinkManual
ElseIf optAutomatic.Value = True Then
  txtReceive.LinkMode = vbLinkAutomatic
ElseIf optNotify.Value = True Then
  txtReceive.LinkMode = vbLinkNotify
End If

End Sub
```

Add the code shown in Listing 14.5 to the `Click` event of the `cmdGetData` Command button.

LISTING 14.5 Command Button `cmdGetData` Click Event

```
Private Sub cmdGetData_Click()
  'Get data from the source
  txtReceive.LinkRequest
End Sub
```

Add the code shown in Listing 14.6 to the `LinkNotify` event of the `txtReceive` TextBox.

LISTING 14.6 TextBox `txtReceive` LinkNotify Event

```
Private Sub txtReceive_LinkNotify()
  MsgBox "Link Notify Event Received"
  cmdGetData.Enabled = True
End Sub
```

Run the destination application from Visual Basic. You should now have both applications running. To test the applications, select a conversation mode by using the option buttons on the destination application. After you have selected a mode, press the Command button Conversation. Switch to the source application and enter text.

14

If you have established a DDE automatic link, when you enter text in the text box of the source application, you will see the text appear in the destination application's TextBox control. For Manual and Notify modes, you must click the button Get Data to retrieve the data from the source. Try the different modes. Remember, after you select a new mode with the option buttons, you must click the Conversation button to establish the new DDE mode. The two applications are shown in Figure 14.5.

FIGURE 14.5

DDE test applications.

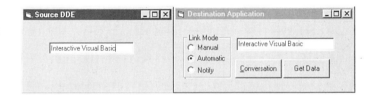

Lesson Summary

In this lesson we learned about DDE (dynamic data exchange) forms and wrote programs to establish DDE links. We also wrote an application that covered the necessary properties, events, and methods that DDE applications require. In the next lesson, we'll learn how to create an executable.

Quiz 4

1. Interprocess communications is

   a. Two or more applications exchanging data with each other

   b. Two or more hardware components exchanging data with each other

   c. The transfer of a file from one device to another

   d. Two or more threads being executed at the same time

2. The _____ responds to the request of a DDE exchange.

   a. Source application

   b. Destination application

   c. LinkMode application

   d. LinkItem application

3. The _____ event occurs when the DDE link is broken.

   a. LinkNotify

   b. LinkBroke

   c. LinkError

   d. LinkClose

4. The _____ method enables the destination control to send data to the source application.

   a. `LinkSend`

   b. `LinkPoke`

   c. `LinkTransfer`

   d. `LinkOpen`

Exercise 4

Complexity: Easy

1. Change the example in Lesson 5 and replace the textbox control on both the destination application and Source DDE with a label control. Set the caption of the label on the Source DDE to y 'Label.' Now when you run the program, the contents of the destination label should match that of the Source DDE.

Complexity: Moderate

2. Change the example in Lesson 5 and add a second textbox to the Destination Application so that it also receives the text from the Source DDE form.

LESSON 5

Creating an Executable

You have written many different applications while working with this book. In this lesson you will learn the various options available to create an executable for your applications. Creating an executable file enables you and your user to run your applications from the Windows environment without having to be in Visual Basic.

Generating an Executable

What happens when you generate an executable for an application? Visual Basic builds a Windows file that can run outside of the Visual Basic design environment by compiling the forms and code in the project. The file created has an `.EXE` extension and is called an executable file. The executable file can be run from the Windows desktop by clicking its icon or by running the executable from the Run task bar in Windows.

14

Compiling NotePad.EXE

To create an executable for the Notepad application, perform the following steps:

1. Open the Notepad project from the Chapter 12 files.

2. Select Make EXE File from the File menu.

3. The Make Project dialog box, shown in Figure 14.6, appears. The default name for the executable is the same as the Visual Basic project name. If you want to use another name for your executable file, modify the text in the FileName text box. For this exercise, do not change it.

FIGURE 14.6

Make Project dialog box.

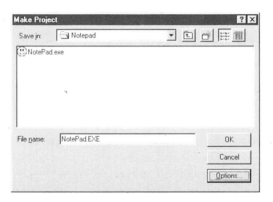

4. Click the Options button to bring up the dialog box shown in Figure 14.7.

FIGURE 14.7

Project Properties dialog box.

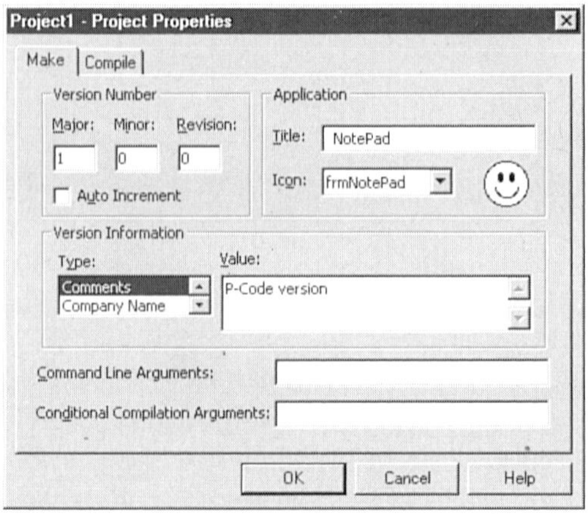

5. Use the Project Properties dialog box to customize your executable file.

Let's examine some of the options found on the EXE Options dialog box.

Version Number

The options in the Version Number are used to assign version release numbers to your executable files. An example might be Notepad Version 3.1.2, where 3 is the major revision number, 1 the minor revision number, and 2 the revision number of the project. If the Auto Increment check box is selected, the Revision number is increased every time you create an executable file for the project. Increment the Major revision number when the application goes through a large number of changes or you add major new functionality. The Minor revision number is for small changes and bug fixes to the application.

Application

The frame labeled Application contains a Title text box and drop-down combo box to add an icon to the executable file. The Title text box is the name of the executable file to create; it has the same effect as the FileName option on the Make EXE dialog box. The Icon drop-down combo box enables you to choose an icon to assign the application. The list of icons is taken from the icons assigned to forms in the project. In the example, the form frmNotePad has the smiley face icon assigned to it. Selecting the icon in the drop-down list box assigns it to the executable file.

Version Information

The version information frame enables you to enter values for various types of information. The Type list box contains the following values:

- Comments
- Company Name
- File Description
- Legal Copyright
- Legal Trademarks
- Product Name

Click Comments and add P-Code version to the Value box. Then click Company Name and add Interactive VB5 to the Value box. These values will become part of the executable file's properties. You can see them in Windows Explorer by right-clicking the file icon and selecting Properties.

14

Now, finish making the EXE file.

1. After you have set the values on the EXE Options dialog box, click the OK button
   and return to the Make EXE dialog box.

2. Click the OK button in the Make EXE dialog box. Visual Basic begins to compile
   the application. It's not very exciting to watch: It's only the Hourglass icon and the
   blinking of your hard disk activity light.

You can use the Windows Explorer to verify that the executable file has been created by
going to the appropriate folder and searching for a NotePad.EXE file.

Find the executable file you just created and execute the application by double-clicking
the file.

Compiling NativePad.EXE

By default, Visual Basic 6 compiles its executables to P-code, but you can also compile
to native code. Programs compiled into native code run faster than programs compiled
into P-code because they don't need to be interpreted.

Repeat steps one through five. Change the filename from Notepad to NativePad. In the
Project Properties window, change the comment to Native code version. Then click
the Compile tab and select Compile to Native Code. Select Optimize for Small Code and
click the OK button. The Compile tab is shown in Figure 14.8.

FIGURE **14.8**

The Compile tab.

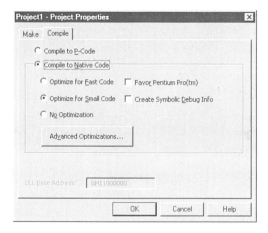

After you click OK, click the OK button on the Make Project dialog box. The compiler
has to work harder to compile native code, so the process is not as fast.

When it is all done, use Windows Explorer to view both files. The `NativePad.EXE` file is slightly larger than the `NotePad.EXE` because some of the things that were done by DLL files in Notepad are now built in to NativePad. If you run the two programs side by side, you will not notice a lot of difference in their speed. Why not? Mainly because it is a small program that doesn't really do much. If it were a large program filled with number crunching and data access, you would see a big difference.

You can also create an executable file from the command line. This comes in handy if you use batch programs to recompile several projects at once.

To create an executable from the command line, go to a DOS window and enter the following:

```
vb /make project_name [exename] [switches]
```

where

- `project_name` is the name of the Visual Basic project to build the executable.
- `exename` is an optional parameter if you want to select a different filename for the executable.
- `switches` are any compile switches to use while creating the executable file for the project.

See the help file for more information.

Now you can create executables for all of your applications and run them in the Windows environment without having to be in Visual Basic. What do you do if you want to give your application to someone else? That's covered in the next lesson.

Lesson Summary

In this lesson we showed you how to generate an executable from your Visual Basic applications. In the next lesson, we'll introduce the Setup Wizard to show you how to distribute your application.

Quiz 5

1. Which is not a value of the version information frame?

    a. Comments

    b. Legal Trademarks

    c. Date of Executable

    d. Product Name

14

2. Programs compiled into native code run faster than programs compiled into P-code because

    a. They don't have to be interpreted

    b. They are compiled in a condensed manner

    c. The program is automatically optimized

    d. Both a and b

3. An advantage of creating an executable from the command line is

    a. The overall process is faster than doing it through Windows

    b. The resulting executable is faster

    c. It is the only way to create an executable into native code

    d. Comes in handy if you use batch programs to recompile several projects at once

4. Which of the following statements is true?

    a. You can create executables for all of your applications and run them in the Windows environment without having to be in Visual Basic.

    b. Native code is faster than both machine code and P-code.

    c. Creating an executable with the command line produces the fastest possible executable.

    d. No two executables can have the same icons.

LESSON 6

Using the Setup Wizard

In the last lesson, you learned how to create executable files for your Visual Basic projects. This lesson teaches you how to distribute your application to other users. Unfortunately, this may not be as easy as creating an executable file, copying the executable file to a disk, and then running your application from another PC.

When Visual Basic creates a P-code executable file, the P-code requires the file VBRUN300.DLL to interpret the P-code. Even if the .EXE file were truly compiled and did not require the VBRUN300.DLL, your application still might not be able to run. Any OCXs and DLLs you used must be on the end user's PC or the application will not be able to execute properly. The OCXs and DLLs can also require a lot of storage space to distribute on your application's floppy disks.

To distribute your application, you will need to install the application `.EXE` file, `VBRUN300.DLL`, and any `.OCX` and `.DLL` files that your project uses.

Fortunately, Visual Basic comes with a utility to enable you to create distribution floppies for your applications with ease. The utility is called the Setup Wizard. The Setup Wizard performs the following functions:

- Creates a setup program
- Builds the executable file
- Compresses files (EXEs, DLLs, OCXs, and so on)
- Determines the number of disks required to distribute your application
- Copies all the files required for distribution to blank floppy disk
- Optionally copies the necessary files to hard disk for network distribution or makes Disk Image files that make it easy to make many copies of your distribution disks

The Setup Wizard is an application distributed with Visual Basic and is not invoked from the Visual Basic design environment. You will find it in the Visual Basic program group on the Startup menu.

Walking Through the Setup Wizard

The Setup Wizard guides you through the steps required to create a program to distribute your application by asking you questions about your application and by examining your project file. This exercise will walk you through each step of the Setup Wizard. Start the Setup Wizard. If this is the first time you have run it, you will see an introduction screen, as shown in Figure 14.9. Click the Next button to begin.

FIGURE 14.9

Application Setup Wizard introduction screen.

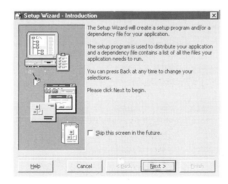

14

1. Figure 14.10 shows the Setup Wizard. The first question is the name and location of the project you want to distribute. You can use the Browse button shown in Figure 14.10 to select a project, or you can enter the path and project name in the

Project File box. Check the Rebuild Project's EXE option if you want the Setup Wizard to recompile your application and generate a new executable; otherwise, the Setup Wizard will use the existing EXE file. Select the Notepad project that you just compiled, cNotePad.vbp, which was originally created in the Chapter 12 files. Other options that you may need from time to time are as follows:

FIGURE 14.10

Application Setup Wizard, step 1.

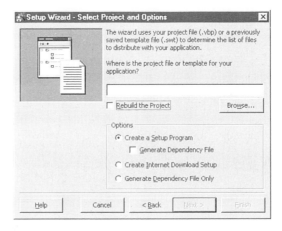

Generate Dependency File: Generates a file that contains dependency information and includes it in the setup. Dependency files are used for any object of an .OCX, .DLL, or .EXE, ActiveX component, or a project that could be used as a component in other projects. The dependency file is included with your setup program.

Create Internet Download Setup: Enables you to create an Internet download setup for only ActiveX Control projects, ActiveX EXE, and ActiveX DLL projects that have public classes, including projects that contain UserDocuments. If you have the Learning Edition of Visual Basic, you will not see this choice.

Generate Dependency File Only: Generates a dependency file with the same name as your project and a .DEP extension, and places it in the same directory as your project.

Create a Setup Program: Select this, and click the Next button. The Setup Wizard will move to the next step in the distribution process.

2. The next window offers you a choice of distribution media. You can choose:

Floppy Disk if you just want to make a single set of distribution disks.

Single Directory for distribution over a network or by compact disk.

Disk Directories, which creates an image of floppy disk distribution files. You can copy the disk images to floppy to make multiple copies of the distribution set.

If you have a couple of floppy disks on hand, select Floppy Disk. If not, select Disk Directories. The Distribution Method dialog box is shown in Figure 14.11. When you have made your selection, click Next.

FIGURE **14.11**

The Distribution method dialog box.

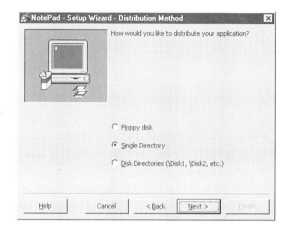

3. If you selected Floppy Disk distribution, the dialog box shown in Figure 14.12 enables you to select the disk drive and the disk size for the distribution disks. Make the selections that match your system, and click Next.

FIGURE **14.12**

Choosing the floppy disk.

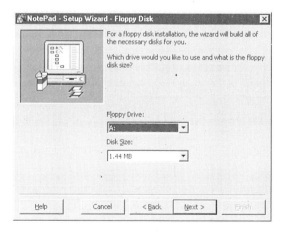

While you were answering questions, the Setup Wizard has been busy analyzing your VBP file and its components. Among other things, it has checked your project for its use of ActiveX components. The dialog box shown in Figure 14.13 reports the ActiveX components that were found and enables you to add any that were missed. Notepad does not use any ActiveX components. Click Next.

14

Figure 14.13

*The Setup Wizard's
ActiveX component
dialog box.*

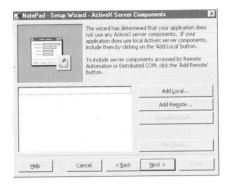

4. The Setup Wizard also detects dependencies, which are the `.DLL` and `.OCX` files that your project requires beyond the ones that are always included. The Confirm Dependencies dialog box shown in Figure 14.14 lists the dependencies that were found. You can remove any file from the list, but be aware that your distributed program probably will not run if the file is not already on the target platform (your user's computer, that is). You can get more information by clicking the File Details button. Click Next when you are done.

Figure 14.14

*The Dependency
dialog box.*

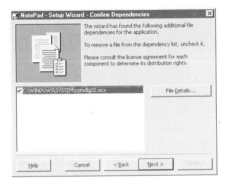

5. The next dialog box is the File Summary dialog box. It is a list of the standard `.DLL` and `.OCX` files that must be distributed with your application. The dialog box is shown in Figure 14.15.

If there are additional files that your application needs—Help files, database files, or any others—use the Add button to include them as well. The Summary Details button tells you how many files must be distributed, and totals their size.

FIGURE 14.15

*The File Summary
Wizard.*

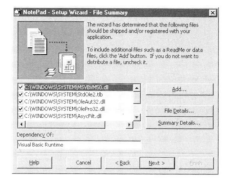

6. Finished! The only choice left on the dialog box shown in Figure 14.16 is whether or not to save a template for your project. The template simplifies the creation of another set of setup disks if you make changes in your project. You won't need them for this one. Click Finish.

FIGURE 14.16

Finished!

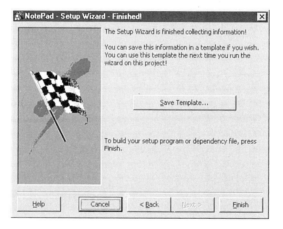

7. The Setup Wizard then sets about collecting and compressing the files for your very own Setup.exe program. The files are all compressed and packed into as small a space as possible. The compressed set of files for CNOTEPAD.EXE only take about two megs of disk space.

Testing the Distribution Floppies

Try out the distribution floppies you just created by placing the first floppy disk in the drive and running setup.exe. The setup application created by the Setup Wizard installs the CNotepad application. Follow the installation steps and install the application on your PC. If possible, find a PC that has never had Visual Basic installed.

14

One of the hardest parts of creating an application for distribution is to make sure that all the DLLs, OCXs, and other files are all in the right places. Installing on a PC that lacks Visual Basic or the application you're testing helps you locate the missing files so you can add them to the setup process. After you have installed the application, make sure you test it. The Setup Wizard is a good utility to speed up application development!

Lesson Summary

In this lesson we showed you how to use the Setup Wizard to generate a setup program to help distribute your application. Next, we'll cover some optimization topics and techniques that may help your Visual Basic programs run faster and more efficiently.

Quiz 6

1. Which of the following is not a function of the Setup Wizard?

    a. Creates a setup program

    b. Determines the number of disks required to distribute your application

    c. Builds the executable file

    d. Sets the version information

2. If you want the Setup Wizard to generate a new executable, you must

    a. Generate a dependency file

    b. Delete your old EXE file

    c. Select the Rebuild Project's EXE option

    d. The Setup Wizard cannot generate a new executable

3. Which of the following is not a choice of distribution media?

    a. Floppy Disk

    b. Single Directory

    c. Tape Drive

    d. Disk Directories

4. Which of the following statements below is true?

    a. The entire setup program must all fit on one disk.

    b. Each setup program can only install one executable file.

    c. All executable files are automatically converted to native code.

    d. You will need to install any .OCX and .DLL files that your project uses.

LESSON 7

Application Optimization

Optimizing is the process of tweaking your code so that it runs better or faster, or uses less memory. One aspect of optimization is to make your program seem to run faster even though it doesn't. This lesson introduces optimization, but you should keep in mind that optimization is an ongoing process that should begin before you write the first line of code.

Optimization Goals

If you compile a project to native code, the Compile tab on the Project Properties dialog box offers a choice of optimization techniques: Optimize for Small Code and Optimize for Fast Code. (There are a couple of specialized check boxes, too, but they require machine code techniques that are meaningless at the Visual Basic code level.) The suggestion is that you can have one or the other, and that is essentially true. But many of the techniques that generate small code also enhance a program's speed, if only because they create better organized programs.

Getting Started: The Appearance of Speed

If your programs are going to be used by other people, one of the first things you want to do is make them at least appear to load faster. How many times have you sat in front of your computer, drumming your fingers and waiting for a program to load? The first thing to do is add a splash screen, that fancy little gizmo that pops up and keeps your mind occupied for a while until the real program loads.

Even the splash screen can be optimized:

- Keep it simple. The fewer controls, the better. If it has a picture, use an `Image` control instead of a `PictureBox` (more on that later).

- Use the `Show` method in the form `load` event. Use code like the following:

```
Sub Form_Load ()
'    Make it paint
     Show
'    Give it a chance to paint
     DoEvents
'    Load the main form
     Load frmMain
'    Get rid of this memory hog
     Unload Me
'    Bring up frmMain
     frmMain.Show
End Sub
```

14

When a form is loaded, all of the code in the load event is executed before the form is shown. The Show method forces the form to be painted before the event is completed, and the DoEvents gives the processor the time to do the paint job. The splash form stays on the screen until frmMain has been completely loaded. After that is done, there is no need for it, and it is unloaded to free the memory that it used. As a final act, it invokes the Show method on frmMain. Because frmMain is already loaded, the Show method brings it up instantly.

More Appearance Issues

If your project has more than one modeless form, consider loading all of them at startup while your user is enjoying the splash screen. You will take a memory hit for this, but it may be worth it. To switch from frmMain to frmSecondChoice requires only

```
frmSecondChoice.Show
frmMain.Hide
```

and the form snaps onto the screen. It can be impressive!

If there is data that you know your application will need, preload it. Get it into memory while your splash screen is still up. It will add a slight delay to your startup time, but the data will be there when you need it. No need to wait for that slow, slow hard drive. (Remember when you thought it was fast?)

Loading the forms and data may seem to take an uncomfortably long time. So add a progress bar to your splash screen. It really does create enough distraction to keep your user's mind occupied.

Get rid of everything you don't need. There's no way to write a program that doesn't use any DLL files or any OLE files. Actually, it would be a pretty dull program if you could! But Visual Basic includes some controls by default that you may not be using. And you may have added some custom controls to your project that you never used, but never deleted, either. If a custom control is on the toolbar, it will be included in your project, and it will be loaded into memory along with the ones you are using.

Open the Components dialog box before you compile your program, and unselect everything that VB will allow. Do the same with the References dialog box. For example, by default VB always includes OLE Automation in your project references. It adds a considerable overhead that you may not need. (If it is actually in use, you won't be allowed to delete it.)

Optimizing Display Speed

Because Windows is so graphical, the display speed contributes to the perceived speed of your application. Keep the following in mind:

- Turn off `ClipControls` unless you are using graphical methods.
- If you can spare the memory, set `AutoRedraw` to `True` for complicated forms.
- Use the `Image` control instead of a `PictureBox` control. The `Image` control is always faster.
- Make controls invisible when you are resizing or moving them with code. When you resize a control, Windows must erase it from the screen, repaint the background where it was, and repaint it at its new size. When you move a control, Windows must erase it from the screen, repaint the background where it was, and repaint it in its new location. Both take time. Making the control invisible reduces the number of repaints and improves the speed greatly.
- If you have to move a lot of controls, put them in a picture box and set its `Visible` property to `False`. Then you can move the picture box, or move the controls within the picture box. When you make the picture box visible again, one repaint does the whole job.

Optimizing Real Speed

Following just a few rules can enhance your program's actual operating speed. Unless you are doing major calculations, the improvement might not be apparent. More than likely, the video speed of the computer, network delays, and disk I/O will affect the program's speed more than anything you can do in code. Still, try the following:

- Avoid variant variables. This is important from a size viewpoint, too. Be sure that you `Dim` every variable in your program. You might have noticed `Option Explicit` throughout your reading of this book. That simple declaration forces all variables to be declared. While you are declaring them, give them a type.
- Use integers where you can, using long integers as a second choice.
- Use `Double` in preference to `Currency` for calculations.
- Use variables rather than properties. Using a property in an expression always triggers an event. For example, to align an array of text boxes with another text box

```
For i = 0 to 10
    txtData.Left = txtOther.Left
Next i
```

is slow, while

```
iLeft = txtOther.Left
For i = 0 to 10
    txtData.Left = iLeft
Next I
```

is much faster.

14

- Use `For...Each` rather than `For...Next` where applicable.
- Use `With...End With` to resolve object references.
- Reduce what you do inside your loops.

Optimizing Size

- Avoid variants. (Heard that before?) They take up too much overhead, in both space and processing time.
- Reclaim memory space used by global arrays and strings that are no longer needed. Use code such as `sString = ""` to reclaim string space. And use `Erase arrLongArray` to get rid of the space used up by an array.
- Unload forms you no longer need. Hiding a form only makes it invisible.
- If you no longer need a picture, get rid of it with `Image1.Picture = Loadpicture()` or `Set Image1.Picture = Nothing`.
- Use `Image` controls instead of `PictureBox` when you can. `Image` controls are lightweight controls that use far fewer resources.
- Share your picture. If you need the same picture in several different places, don't load it into each place. Using the following code requires that the picture only be in memory once. That saves loading time and memory.

```
pixStored = LoadPicture("C:\Windows\Arches.BMP")
Image1.Picture = pixStored
Picture1.Picture = pixStored
```

- Use RLE or WMF pictures instead of bitmaps.
- Take out the trash. Chances are your program has been through a lot of false tries. You have added controls to a form, then changed your mind and removed them. If you added code to their events, did you get rid of that, too? When you delete a control, its code moves from its normal position into the General section of the code, where your user-defined procedures and functions are placed. While you are at it, get rid of those variables you added and never used. Take out the trash!

Lesson Summary

This lesson provides a beginning look at optimization. As your skills and knowledge improve, you will find more optimizing techniques. The important thing to remember about optimizing is that you must begin optimizing with the first line of code, not after it is all written.

Quiz 7

1. To make your application appear to load faster, use a _____ screen to keep your mind occupied while the program loads.

    a. Popup

    b. Splash

    c. Paint

    d. Pow

2. Which below is not a way to optimize display speed?

    a. Turn on `ClipControls` unless you are using graphical methods

    b. Use the `Image` Control instead of a `PictureBox` control

    c. If you can spare the memory, set `AutoRedraw` to True for complicated forms

    d. If you have to move a lot of controls, put them in a picture box and set its `Visible` property to `False`

3. Which of the following can help enhance your program's actual operating speed?

    a. Use integers where you can, using long integers as a second choice

    b. Use `For...Next` rather than `For...Each` where applicable

    c. Use Currency in preference to Double for calculations

    d. Increase what you do inside your loops

4. Which of the following can help optimize the size of your program?

    a. Hide a form you no longer need

    b. Use a `PictureBox` control instead of an `Image` control where you can

    c. If you no longer need a picture, remove it with Image1.Picture = ""

    d. Avoid variants

Chapter Summary

This chapter covered many different topics. In the first lesson, the `Timer` Control was discussed, along with a small program to demonstrate its features and usefulness. The next lesson examined some key Windows and Visual Basic architecture issues in order to enhance your abilities as a programmer. The next lesson, the idle time concept, was introduced, and this helped build upon the concepts of preemptive and cooperative multitasking. The main project of the lesson was a program that enables a user to interrupt a lengthy process.

14

Lesson 4 covered data exchange using DDE links, and an application was written so that two applications could communicate to each other using a DDE link. Lesson 5 showed you how to create an executable from a Visual Basic program, and Lesson 6 showed you how to distribute it professionally using the Setup Wizard. The final lesson provides a beginning look at optimization. The important thing to remember about optimization is that you must begin optimizing with the first line of code, not after it is all written.

CHAPTER 15

Doing the Impossible (and More) with the Windows API

In the past, in order for you to develop any application for the Windows environment, you needed the Microsoft Software Developers Kit (SDK) and a good understanding of C, Pascal, or even (gasp!) Assembler. Within the SDK, you learned all about this mystic component called the Windows API. *API* stands for Application Programmer's Interface, and it's not really a new concept. Almost all operating systems have API library functions that you can call so you don't have to keep recreating the wheel.

In this chapter, you learn the mysticism behind the Windows API and how simple it is to use them in your applications.

LESSON 1

Using the Windows API

Dynamic link libraries, commonly referred to as DLLs, are code libraries that contain functions and procedures. The word *dynamic* is a reference to the fact that, unlike traditional code libraries that are linked into your application during compile time, DLLs are loaded while the application is executing. When the application calls a function in a DLL, the DLL is loaded into memory, the function executes, and returns information to the application, just like a standard compiled call.

DLLs were created to help reduce the size of Windows applications by providing a common set of functions and procedures. In the past, the creation of DLLs was reserved for people who programmed in C/C++, Pascal, or (gasp) Assembler. Starting in Visual Basic 4, you now have the ability to create your own DLLs with Visual Basic. In this section, you will examine the more traditional DLLs that are written in other programming languages such as C or C++. You will examine a particular set of DLLs (User, GDI, and Kernel) that contain Windows functions and procedures commonly referred to as the Windows API (application programming interface) functions.

The great news for the Visual Basic programmers is that you can call Windows API functions and procedures easily from Visual Basic. Suddenly, you have hundreds of functions and procedures already written, sitting on your PC just waiting to be used! Using the Windows API, you can perform tasks that normally cannot be done in Visual Basic or have improved processing speed over standard Visual Basic programming methods.

Using Non-Visual Basic Dynamic Link Libraries

To call a routine in a DLL from Visual Basic, perform the following steps:

1. Declare the function or procedure.
2. Call the function or procedure.

DLL functions and procedures are external, not part of a module, class, or form, but part of another file. The operative word here is *library*. The library is set up so all Windows applications can call on it and use its functions and procedures. By following the steps listed above, you can take advantage of the functions and procedures in the DLL. Let's walk through the example shown in Figure 15.1.

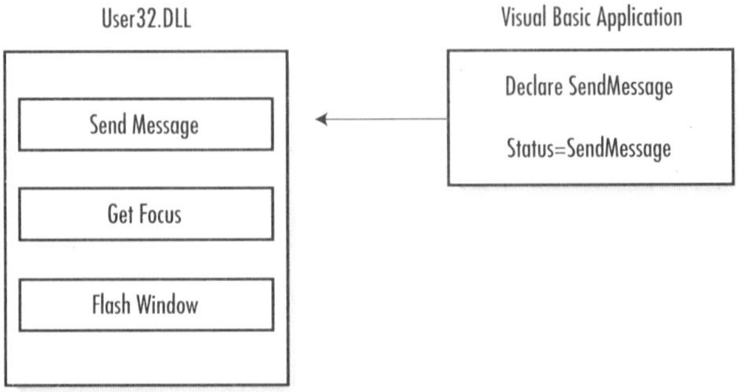

FIGURE 15.1

The Visual Basic application calling a DLL function

Figure 15.1 shows one of the Windows API DLLs: USER32.dll. Three of the many functions contained in USER32.DLL are listed in Figure 15.1. Notice how the Visual Basic application shown in Figure 15.1 is using the SendMessage function that is located outside of the Visual Basic application. Let's see what is required for the Visual Basic application to call an API function. The first step is to tell Visual Basic where the function or procedure can be found. Use the Declare statement, which has the following syntax:

- Procedures

  ```
  Declare Sub name Lib "libname" [Alias "aliasname"][([arglist])]
  ```

- Functions

  ```
  Declare Function name Lib "libname" [Alias "aliasname"][([arglist])][ As
  type]
  ```

Where name is the procedure or function to call and libname is the DLL library name where the function is located.

Alias is an optional entry. When present, it indicates that the function being called by name has another name, aliasname, within the DLL. It is used when the name in the DLL is the same as a VB keyword or when you have already used that name for another purpose in your program.

The Visual Basic code to declare the function SendMessage is

```
Declare Function SendMessage Lib "user32" _
    (ByVal hWnd As Long, ByVal wMsg As Long, _
     ByVal wParam As Long, lParam As Any) As Long
```

When you have declared an API procedure, you can use it within your Visual Basic programs just as you would any other one. If the API is declared a Sub, it is a procedure that performs a test but does not return any values. With an API that is declared a function, such as SendMessage, a return code value is expected.

By Value or By Reference

In order to use DLLs effectively, you need to understand what is meant by passing *by value* and passing *by reference*. When a parameter is passed by value, the actual value of the parameter is passed to the function or procedure. If a parameter is passed by reference, the address of the parameter is passed to the function, not the value.

The example shown in Figure 15.2 may help explain the difference. Figure 15.2 depicts a chunk of memory that starts at address 0000 and goes to address FFFF. (Addresses are traditionally given in base 16, or hexadecimal form.) At address 9100 is a variable called MyVal which contains the string "Hello". In the example, the function MyFunc is called with the variable MyVal. When MyVal is passed by a value, the string "Hello" is passed to the function. When `MyVal` is passed by reference, the address of `MyVal`, 9100, is passed to the function. By default, Visual Basic passes parameters by reference. In many cases, a DLL requires the value of the parameter and not the address.

FIGURE 15.2

The memory map of variable `MyVal`.

• To pass the

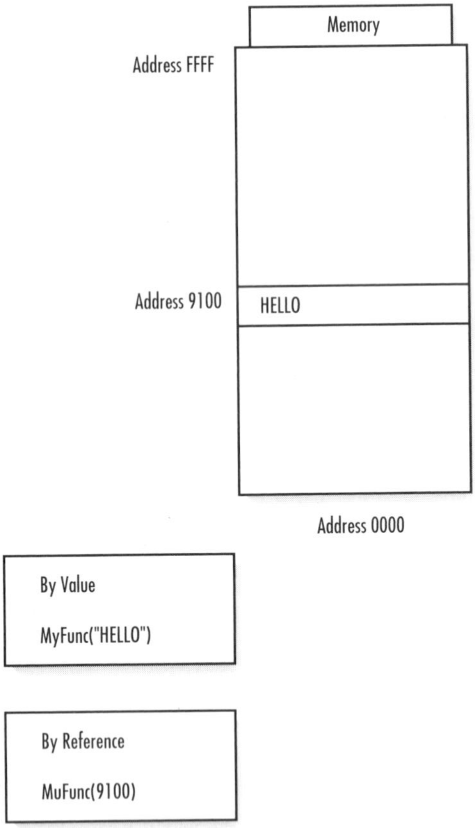

value of the parameter, use the `ByVal` keyword in the `Declare` statement. For example:

Passing by Value

```
Declare Function MyFunc Lib "MyStuff" (ByVal MyVal As String)
```

Passing by Reference

```
Declare Function MyFunc Lib "MyStuff" (MyVal As String)
```

hWnd and hDC Properties

Many of the Windows API calls require a Windows *handle*, which uniquely identifies a window or device handle. If you want to use a Window API call to modify a form or control, use the hWnd property. The hWnd property contains the Windows handle for the form or control. The property hDC gives you the device context handles of a form, PictureBox, or printer object. A device context is a Windows object that allows drawing to a window or device. A handle is always declared as a long integer data type.

Converting Data Types

Calling a DLL is very similar to calling a regular procedure or function, except for setting up the parameters. Earlier you learned that DLLs not created by Visual Basic were written in other programming languages, such as C and C++. Visual Basic data types are different from C or C++ data types, however, so you need to use caution when calling a DLL and make sure the data types for the parameters are correct.

Table 15.1 helps you convert C language declarations into the proper Visual Basic declarations. The table is important because reference materials for some DLLs show only the C++ declarations. When you run into that, use the table to substitute the correct VB variable types for the C variable types in the declaration.

TABLE 15.1   DLL Data Conversion

C	Visual Basic
BOOL	ByVal variable As Boolean
INT32-bit	ByVal variable As Long
Float	ByVal variable As Single
Double	ByVal variable As Double
Pointer to a string	ByVal variable as String
Pointer to a Long	ByVal variable As Long
NULL Pointer	vbNullString
Void Pointer	variable As Any
Char	ByVal variable As String

In case you are not familiar with the term "pointers", they are used in developing applications in C/C++. A pointer is a special variable that holds a memory address. In many ways, it's treated like standard variables, but "special" also means that they can behave slightly different in some operations. They can be used in data constructs for which no other standard variables can be used. Careless use of pointers can easily result in a program anomaly that could result in completely unexpected results and even more difficulty figuring out.

Finding a List Item

You are ready to write an application that calls a DLL. This example calls a Windows API function called SendMessage. SendMessage enables you to send messages to controls to change the control's appearance or to get information back from the control. For instance, you can use SendMessage to add a horizontal scroll bar to a list box control. This example uses SendMessage to search a list box and return the index value of the search string. Code that uses the Windows API to search a list box for a string runs much faster than the following Visual Basic code that searches a list box:

```
For iX = 1 to List1.ListCount -1
   If List1.ListIndex(iX) = "Fifty" Then
      Exit For
   End If
Next iX
```

Start a new project named test_dll. Add a form, and then add a list box, a text box, and a Command button to the form. Set the properties as shown in Table 15.2.

TABLE 15.2   Object and Properties Settings for Project `test_dll`

Object	Property	Setting
Form	Name	frmMain
	Caption	"Test DLL"
	Height	4500
	Width	3800
TextBox	Name	txtSearch
	Height	285
	Left	1560
	Text	"
	Top	100
	Width	1815
CommandButton	Name	cmdQuit
	Caption	"E&xit"
	Height	495
	Left	1200
	Top	3360
	Width	1215

Object	Property	Setting
ListBox	Name	lstData
	Height	2595
	Left	840
	Sorted	True
	Top	600
	Width	1935
Label	Name	Label1
	Caption	"Enter search text:"
	Height	255
	Left	120
	Top	120
	Width	1455

Add the code shown in Listing 15.1 to the Form_Load event.

LISTING 15.1   Code to Fill ListBox in Form_Load Event

```
Private Sub Form_Load()          '
    'Fill The List Box
    lstData.AddItem "One"
    lstData.AddItem "Two"
    lstData.AddItem "Three"
    lstData.AddItem "Four"
    lstData.AddItem "Five"
    lstData.AddItem "Six"
    lstData.AddItem "Seven"
    lstData.AddItem "Eight"
    lstData.AddItem "Nine"
    lstData.AddItem "Ten"
End Sub
```

Add the following line to the Form_Activate event:

```
Private Sub Form_Activate()
    ' Set the focus in the TextBox
    txtSearch.SetFocus
End Sub
```

Add the following line to the cmdQuit_Click event:

```
Private Sub cmdQuit_Click()
    End
End Sub
```

The first step in using a dynamic link library is to declare the function. Visual Basic comes with a utility that enables you to cut and paste Windows API declarations and constants called the *API Text Viewer*. The API Text Viewer is shown in Figure 15.3. The API Text Viewer is accessible through an add-in in Visual Basic's IDE (Integrated Development Environment). Its use is covered more fully in Chapter 18, "Using Visual Basic for Communications."

FIGURE 15.3

The Windows API Text Viewer.

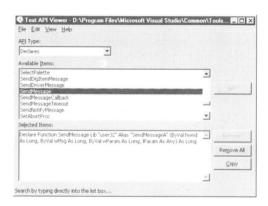

The API Text Viewer lets you copy the declarations for all of the API functions, procedures, and constants so you can paste them directly into the Code window of your VB application. This can be a great time saver.

Create a new module for the sample project. Name the module `TestDLL.bas`. Use the API viewer to find the SendMessage API. Then copy and paste the definition into the module's General Declarations section, or type the following code in the module's general declaration section:

```
Option Explicit
Declare Function SendMessage Lib "user32" _
    Alias "SendMessageA" _
        (ByVal hwnd As Long, _
         ByVal wMsg As Long, _
         ByVal wParam As Long, _
         ByVal lParam As Any) As Long
'    Message for ListBox
Public Const LB_FINDSTRING = &H18F
```

If you pasted the declaration into the program, it was pasted as a single, very long string in the Code window. Improve readability by adding line continuation characters. It is worth the extra time! There is a catch in the pasted-in code too. The last parameter in the API Text Viewer version is `lParam As Long`. The parameter sent to `SendMessage` when you are searching for a string, however, is a `string`. The declaration must be changed to allow for that. It should read, as it does above, lParam As Any. (It's these little tricks that keep programming interesting.) Now the DLL function is declared. Add the code in Listing 15.2 to the change event for the TextBox.Command button. It is the code that calls the API function.

LISTING 15.2   Calling API Function in Text_Change Event Command Button

```
Private Sub txtSearch_Change()
    Dim sTempStr        As String
    Dim lResult         As Long
    ' If nothing in list then don't search
    If lstData.ListCount < 1 Then Exit Sub
    ' Save the text contents to a temporary string
    sTempStr = txtSearch.Text
    If Len(sTempStr) = 0 Then
        ' There is no text or it is blank
        ' Set ListIndex to first item in list
        lstData.ListIndex = 0
    Else
        ' There is text so send the message to look for it
        ' and reposition to the list to the matching entry
        lstData.ListIndex = SendMessage((lstData.hwnd), _
            LB_FINDSTRING, -1, sTempStr)
    End If
End Sub
```

Now you're ready to try out the application. Run the application and enter any part of one of the text strings that shows in the ListBox.TextBox. What happens? The list box cursor moves to the number you enter. The running application is shown in Figure 15.4.

FIGURE 15.4

The Application TestDLL.

Lesson Summary

You now have a basic understanding of how to call a DLL and the Windows API. There are many reference books available to help you determine which API functions to use.

The one that most Visual Basic developers flock to is Dan Appleman's book, *Dan Appleman's Visual Basic Programmer's Guide to the Win32 API* (Ziff-Davis Press, 1997). Calling DLLs and the Windows API can enhance your program greatly! In the next lesson, you will learn how to use APIs to affect the properties of a form.

Quiz 1

1. DLL stands for

    a. Data Linked List

    b. Dynamic Link Library

    c. Windows API

    d. Dynamic Linked List

2. To use a non-Visual Basic created DLL, you must first _____ the function or procedure.

    a. call

    b. pass by reference

    c. declare

    d. execute

3. Passing the address of a variable is called passing

    a. by value

    b. by memory

    c. by variable

    d. by reference

4. To use many of Windows API routines requires a Windows handle, which can be obtained from the _____ property of most forms or controls.

    a. WindowHandle

    b. hWnd

    c. APIHandle

    d. hAPI

LESSON 2

Doing Fancy Windows, Part I

15

There are a lot of different APIs at your disposal. There are APIs that affect controls, forms, or the operating system itself. In this lesson, you will learn about one API that affects how a window behaves. The API you will use for this lesson is called *FlashWindow*, and it looks like the following:

```
Declare Function FlashWindow Lib "user32" (ByVal hWnd As Long, _
    ByVal bInvert As Long) As Long
```

The two parameters that are passed to this function are hWnd and bInvert. hWnd refers to the handle of the windows you want to cause the flash. bInvert is a Boolean value that toggles the window's caption to appear active or inactive. By default, this value is set to True. If an application is minimized and running on Windows NT, the bInvert parameter is ignored. If an application is minimized under Windows 95, the bInvert parameter is not ignored and the minimized title bar flashes.

If you take the name of the API literally, you would think it might cause the entire window to flash. In reality, it only affects a form's title or caption bar. When the bInvert argument is set to true, the caption bar's color will invert from its normal color to gray and then back to its normal color. With the Windows 95 Explorer desktop, a minimized application's caption bar appears on the taskbar. If the bInvert argument is set to true, the portion of the caption bar that appears on the taskbar flashes.

So where can this be used? There are at least two different uses for this function. One method is to deactivate the window while a process is occurring. This method will offer the user immediate feedback about the process they just initiated. It will give them the feedback that they cannot use any part of the system until the process is complete. This is helpful if a process is going to take a long time and you don't want your user to start clicking other buttons in your application. Needless clicking might fire off an event that could cause the process that is executing to abort prematurely.

The other way this function can be used is to give feedback to the user that something important has just occurred. Take any science fiction story, for example. Imagine how dull a *red alert* would be if there were no flashing red lights and sirens going off. You can simulate something similar in your application with this function.

The example for this lesson will illustrate the latter usage. Create a new directory called FlashWindow. In that new directory, create a new Standard EXE project and name the project Flash.VBP. On Form1, add two Command Buttons to the form and use the values in Table 15.3 to set the properties.

TABLE 15.3 Object and Properties Settings for Form1

Object	Property	Setting
Form	Name	frmMain
	Caption	"Flashing Titlebar"
Command Button	Name	cmdAlarm
	Caption	"Set off Alarm"
Command Button	Name	cmdEnd
	Caption	"End"

Save the form and name it FlashMain.frm. Add the following code from Listing 15.3 to the Command Button cmdAlarm.

LISTING 15.3 Code for the cmdAlarm Command Button

```
Private Sub cmdAlarm_Click()
    frmAlarm.Show
End Sub
```

When you click this button, it will cause the second form to be displayed. The contents of the second form will be described shortly. Add the following code from Listing 15.4 to the command button cmdEnd.

LISTING 15.4 Code for the cmdEnd Command Button

```
Private Sub cmdEnd_Click()
    End
End Sub
```

Add another form by selecting Add Form from the Project menu item. On this form, add a Command Button and use the values in Table 15.4 to set the properties.

TABLE 15.4 Object Properties for the Alarm Form

Object	Property	Setting
Form	Name	frmAlarm
	BorderStyle	3 - Fixed Dialog
	Caption	"Danger, Will
		Robinson, Danger!"
	ControlBox	False
Command Button	Name	cmdEnd
	Caption	"End"
Timer	Name	Timer1
	Interval	250

Save the form and name it `FlashAlarm.frm`. Add the following code from Listing 15.5 in the General Declaration section of the form. This is to set up a few module level variables for the application. Add the following code from Listing 15.5 in the General Declarations section of the form.

LISTING 15.5 General Declarations Code

```
Option Explicit
Private Declare Function FlashWindow Lib "user32" _

    (ByVal hwnd As Long, ByVal bInvert As Long) As Long

Dim rc As Long
Dim bToggle As Boolean
```

Add the following code from Listing 15.6 to the `cmdEnd` Command Button. This will close the form when the button is pressed.

LISTING 15.6 End Button's Event Code

```
Private Sub cmdEnd_Click()
    Unload Me
End Sub
```

In the `Timer` object, `Timer1`, enter the code found in Listing 15.7.

LISTING 15.7 Timer Event Code

```
Private Sub Timer1_Timer()
    If bToggle Then
        bToggle = False
        rc = FlashWindow(Me.hwnd, btoggle)
        Beep
    Else
        bToggle = True
        rc = FlashWindow(Me.hwnd, btoggle)
    End If
End Sub
```

Save the project and press F5 to run the application. When you press the Set Off Alarm button, the FlashAlarm form will be displayed, as illustrated in Figure 15.5. Timer1's Interval property was set to 250. This means that every quarter of a second, the procedure in Timer1_Timer gets executed. If the caption bar is True, the procedure will deactivate the caption bar and invoke the Beep command. If its property is False, it will reactivate the caption bar. This will continue until you press the End button.

FIGURE 15.5

The FlashAlarm shown on top of the FlashMain.

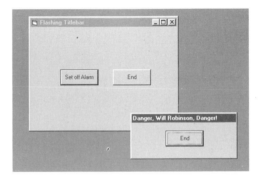

Lesson Summary

This is just one example of many that illustrate the types of things you can do with Windows API functions. The FlashWindow API is a great function to use when you want to alert the users of your application that something terrible has gone wrong and they need to do something about it. The next lesson will continue to show what a simple API function can do to a Form window.

Quiz 2

1. What parameter refers to the Windows Handle?

    a. `hWindow`

    b. `wHandle`

    c. `hWnd`

    d. `wHnd`

2. If an application is minimized on Windows NT, what happens to the `bInvert` parameter in the FlashWindow API?

    a. It falls into the Recycle Bin

    b. It affects all minimized applications

    c. It's ignored and you would never know something happened

    d. The API uses it

3. If an application is minimized on Windows 95, what happens to the `bInvert` parameter in the FlashWindow API?

    a. It falls into the Recycle Bin

    b. It affects all minimized applications

    c. It's not ignored and the minimized caption flashes

    d. The API uses it

4. The FlashWindow API requires what two parameters?

    a. `bInvert` and `hWnd`

    b. `hWnd` and `bInvert`

    c. Form Name and Boolean value

    d. None of the above

Exercise 2

Complexity: Easy

1. Write an MDI application that will cause the active MDI child form's title bar to flash.

Complexity: Easy

2. Write an application with an About box. When the About box is displayed, have its title bar flash.

LESSON 3

Doing Fancy Windows, Part II

As demonstrated in the last lesson, an API was used to modify the caption bar of a form to provide feedback to your user. In this lesson, we will use a different API to change a different part of the form. This time, the API you will use is the RealizePalette function. This function will enable you to select a logical palette for a form window. This allows you to use a larger number of colors in your application without interfering with the colors used by other forms in your program. After you call this function, all you need to do is select the colors you want the gradient to consist of.

The RealizePalette function looks like the following:

```
Declare Function RealizePalette Lib "gdi32" _
    (ByVal hDC As Long) As Long
```

The argument that is used for this function is hDC. hDC is the handle of the context device. In this function, it identifies which logical palette has been selected.

In this lesson, you will learn how to use this API to change the background pattern of your form to a gradient fill background, similar to the background you see when you install an application on your system. To display a form window gradient background, you will use the Form's Line method to draw different colors on the form.

Create a new directory called Gradient. In that directory, create a new Standard EXE project and name it Gradient.VBP. On Form1, add two Command Buttons, and use Table 15.5 to set up the properties for the objects.

TABLE 15.5   Gradient.FRM Objects' Properties

Object	Property	Name
Form	Name	frmGradient
	Caption	"Gradient Fill"
Command Button	Name	cmdLeftRight
	Caption	"Left to Right"
Command Button	Name	cmdTopBotton
	Caption	"Top to Bottom"

Save the form and name it Gradient.frm. Add the following code found in Listing 15.8 to the General Declaration section of this form.

LISTING 15.8   General Declarations Section

```
Option Explicit
Private Declare Function RealizePalette Lib "gdi32" _
   (ByVal hdc As Long) As Long

Dim RedColor(256) As Integer
Dim GreenColor(256) As Integer
Dim BlueColor(256) As Integer
```

Add the following code in Listing 15.9 to the Form_Load event.

LISTING 15.9   Code for the Form_Load Event

```
Private Sub Form_Load()

   Dim i As Integer

   ' Initialize the RGB range for color range
   For n = 1 To 256
       RedColor = 1
       GreenColor = 1
       BlueColor = n
   Next n

End Sub
```

All colors are based on three primary colors: red, green, and blue. Table 15.6 lists the color ranges for the 16 basic colors available in Windows.

TABLE 15.6   Standard Color Range of Red, Green, and Blue

Color	Red Value	Green Value	Blue Value
Black	0	0	0
Blue	0	0	255
Green	0	255	0
Cyan	0	255	255
Red	255	0	0
Magenta	255	0	255
Yellow	255	255	0
White	255	255	255

Add the following code in Listing 15.10 to the cmdLeftRight command button. The logical palette in this procedure event is the Form window.

LISTING 15.10   Code for the Command Button cmdLeftRight

```
Private Sub cmdLeftRight_Click()

    Dim rc As Long
    Dim i As Integer

    rc = RealizePalette(Me.hdc)
    Me.Scale (0, 0)-(256, 1)
    For i = 0 To 255
        Me.Line (i, 0)-(i + 1, 1), RGB(RedColor(i + 1), _
            GreenColor(i + 1), BlueColor(i + 1)), BF
        Me.ForeColor = RGB(RedColor(i + 1), GreenColor(i + 1), _
            BlueColor(i + 1))
    Next i

End Sub
```

Add the following code in Listing 15.11 to the cmdTopBottom command button. The logical palette in this procedure event is the Form window.

LISTING 15.11   Code for the Command Button cmdTopBottom

```
Private Sub cmdTopBottom_Click()

    Dim rc As Long
    Dim i As Integer

    rc = RealizePalette(Me.hdc)
    Me.Scale (0, 0)-(1, 256)
    For i = 0 To 255
        Me.Line (0, i)-(1, i + 1), RGB(RedColor(i + 1), _
            GreenColor(i + 1), BlueColor(i + 1)), BF
        Me.ForeColor = RGB(RedColor(i + 1), GreenColor(i + 1), _
            BlueColor(i + 1))
    Next i

End Sub
```

Save the program and run it by pressing F5. When you click the Left To Right command button, the program draws the black to blue gradient background horizontally across the form. When you click the Top to Bottom command button, the program draws the black to blue gradient background vertically down the form. Figure 15.6 illustrates the form with the gradient fill left to right. Figure 15.7 illustrates the form with a gradient fill from top to bottom.

FIGURE 15.6

A gradient filled horizontally across the form.

FIGURE 15.7

A gradient filled vertically on the form.

Lesson Summary

Using the `RealizePalette` function can help you add more zip to your application's form. Like all changes to the user interface, though, it should be done in moderation. In the next lesson, you will learn how API functions can affect more than just an element of a project. The next lesson will introduce you to the Windows' System Registry.

Quiz 3

1. What does hDC stand for?

    a. Handle for a Device Color

    b. An element on the periodic table

    c. Handle for a Device Context

    d. Nation's capital

2. What are three primary colors?

    a. Black, white and gray

    b. Red, white, and blue

    c. Red, green, and blue

    d. Black, white, and red

3. What is the number range of any primary color?

    a. 3

    b. 42

    c. 256

    d. 186,232

4. What kind of object will the `RealizePalette` work on?

    a. Forms only

    b. Any object that has a handle to the device context

    c. Any object that is in Visual Basic

    d. None of the above

Exercise 3

Complexity: Moderate

1. Using the Gradient example program, make the gradient fill something other than Blue to Black.

Complexity: Advanced

2. Make both the horizontal and vertical gradient available as a procedure so any form can call them.

LESSON 4

Using the Registry API

The built-in VB registry settings are convenient but limited. By using the Windows APIs, you can save your data in a more powerful way.

Create a new directory, named `Registry Program`. Start a new project, or load `RegAPI.vbp` from the CD that comes with this book. Add a command button to the main form and make five copies of it as a control array. Set the properties according to Table 15.7.

TABLE 15.7 The Property Values for the Registry API Project

Object	Property	Value
Form	Name	frmRegistry
	Caption	"Registry API Project"
Command button	Name	Command1
	Index	0
	Caption	"Create Key"
Command button	Name	Command1
	Index	1
	Caption	"Set Key Value"
Command button	Name	Command1
	Index	2
	Caption	"Query Value"
Command button	Name	Command1
	Index	3
	Caption	"Delete Value"
Command button	Name	Command1
	Index	4
	Caption	"Delete Key"
Command button	Name	Command1
	Index	5
	Caption	"E&xit"

You will not use all these command buttons in the first part of this project. You will add functionality as you move along to demonstrate the flexibility of the registry APIs.

Use Figure 15.8 as a guide for placing the controls on the form.

Now add a frame to your main form, and put two option buttons inside it. The option buttons will be part of a control array. Add a text box and a label to your form, as well. Set the properties for the new controls according to Table 15.8.

FIGURE 15.8

The completed RegAPI
form.

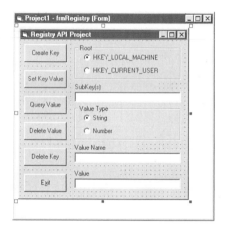

TABLE 15.8 More Properties for the RegAPI Form

Object	Property	Value
Frame	Name	fraRoot
	Caption	"Root"
Option Button	Name	optKey
	Index	0
	Caption	"HKEY_LOCAL_MACHINE"
	Value	True
Option Button	Name	optKey
	Index	1
	Caption	"HKEY_CURRENT_USER"
	Value	False
Label	Name	lblSubKey
	Caption	"SubKey"
TextBox	Name	txtSubKey
	Text	"
Frame	Name	fraValueType
	Caption	"Value Type"
Option Button	Name	optValueType
	Index	0
	Caption	"String"
	Value	True

Object	Property	Value
Option Button	Name	optValueType
	Index	1
	Caption	"Number"
	Value	False
Label	Name	lblValueName
	Caption	"Value Name"
TextBox	Name	txtValueName
	Text	"
Label	Name	lblValue
	Caption	"Value"
TextBox	Name	txtValue
	Text	"

There are controls on the form that are not yet included in this project. Like the unused command buttons, these are components you will add in a later part of the overall project for this chapter.

Add a module to the project by opening the Project menu and selecting Add Module. With the module Code window active, press F4 and name the module RegAPI. You can use this module in other programs as well, which will be a big timesaver.

Using the API Text Viewer

As mentioned in Lesson 1, Visual Basic comes with a program called API Text Viewer that you can use to view information about the Windows API. Better yet, you can copy and paste the declarations from the API Text Viewer into your programs, which can save hours of debugging time. Click Start and select Visual Studio Component Tools, then select API Text Viewer from the pop-up menu that appears. The program's opening screen is shown in Figure 15.9.

When the program opens, open the File menu and select Load Text File.

Note

The API Text Viewer offers to convert the text file to a database. It is really better if you do that, but if you elect to do it now, go have a cup of coffee while it does the conversion. It will take awhile.

FIGURE 15.9

The API Text Viewer's opening screen.

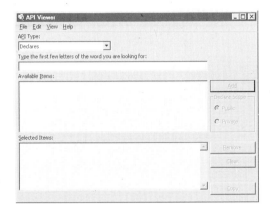

Switch the API Type to Constants. Search through the list box for `Public Const ERROR_SUCCESS = 0&`. When you find it, click it to select it, and then click the `Add` button. In the same way, select and add all of the constants in the following list:

```
Public Const ERROR_SUCCESS = 0&
Public Const HKEY_CLASSES_ROOT = &H80000000
Public Const HKEY_CURRENT_USER = &H80000001
Public Const HKEY_DYN_DATA = &H80000006
Public Const HKEY_LOCAL_MACHINE = &H80000002
Public Const STANDARD_RIGHTS_ALL = &H1F0000
Public Const KEY_QUERY_VALUE = &H1
Public Const KEY_CREATE_LINK = &H20
Public Const SYNCHRONIZE = &H100000
Public Const KEY_SET_VALUE = &H2
Public Const KEY_CREATE_SUB_KEY = &H4
Public Const KEY_ENUMERATE_SUB_KEYS = &H8
Public Const KEY_NOTIFY = &H10
Public Const KEY_ALL_ACCESS = ((STANDARD_RIGHTS_ALL Or _
 KEY_QUERY_VALUE Or KEY_SET_VALUE Or KEY_CREATE_SUB_KEY _
 Or KEY_ENUMERATE_SUB_KEYS Or KEY_NOTIFY Or KEY_CREATE_LINK) _
 And (Not SYNCHRONIZE))
Public Const REG_DWORD = 4
Public Const REG_OPTION_NON_VOLATILE = 0
Public Const REG_SZ = 1
```

Now switch the API Type to Declares, and select and add the following declarations:

```
RegCreateKeyEx
RegCloseKey
```

Finally, press Copy to copy the declarations to the clipboard. Now go back to your project and paste them all into the Declarations Section of the RegAPI module. Put the cursor on the line following Option Explicit, and select Paste from the Edit menu, or press

Shift+Ins. This creates some very long lines in your declarations section. I have a personal bias against lines that go off the edge of the screen, so my declaration section looks like this:

```
Option Explicit

Public Const ERROR_SUCCESS = 0&
Public Const HKEY_CLASSES_ROOT = &H80000000
Public Const HKEY_CURRENT_USER = &H80000001
Public Const HKEY_DYN_DATA = &H80000006
Public Const HKEY_LOCAL_MACHINE = &H80000002
Public Const STANDARD_RIGHTS_ALL = &H1F0000
Public Const KEY_QUERY_VALUE = &H1
Public Const KEY_CREATE_LINK = &H20
Public Const SYNCHRONIZE = &H100000
Public Const KEY_SET_VALUE = &H2
Public Const KEY_CREATE_SUB_KEY = &H4
Public Const KEY_ENUMERATE_SUB_KEYS = &H8
Public Const KEY_NOTIFY = &H10
Public Const KEY_ALL_ACCESS = ((STANDARD_RIGHTS_ALL Or _
    KEY_QUERY_VALUE Or KEY_SET_VALUE Or KEY_CREATE_SUB_KEY _
    Or KEY_ENUMERATE_SUB_KEYS Or KEY_NOTIFY Or KEY_CREATE_LINK) _
    And (Not SYNCHRONIZE))
Public Const REG_DWORD = 4
Public Const REG_OPTION_NON_VOLATILE = 0
Public Const REG_SZ = 1

Declare Function RegCreateKeyEx Lib "advapi32.dll" _
    Alias "RegCreateKeyExA" _
    (ByVal hKey As Long, ByVal lpSubKey As String, _
    ByVal Reserved As Long, ByVal lpClass As String, _
    ByVal dwOptions As Long, ByVal samDesired As Long, _
    lpSecurityAttributes As Any, _
    phkResult As Long, lpdwDisposition As Long) As Long

Declare Function RegCloseKey Lib "advapi32.dll" _
    (ByVal hKey As Long) As Long
```

Never fear. It does look intimidating, but it isn't really all that hard to work with. There is one change you must make to RegCreateKey. As it is pasted from the API Text Viewer, it contains the line:

```
lpSecurityAttributes As SECURITY_ATTRIBUTES,
```

This line should be changed to read

```
lpSecurityAttributes As Any,
```

In the program you will send a 0& (long) to the API as a signal to use the default security attributes for your registry entries; if you do not make this change, you will have to work extra hard to accomplish the same thing.

Adding the Code

Now it is time to add some code to the form events. Double-click one of the command buttons and add the code shown in Listing 15.12.

LISTING 15.12   The Code for the Form

```
Private Sub Command1_Click(Index As Integer)
    ' Decodes command button array
    Dim sType As String

    ' Selects command action

    Select Case Index
    Case 0 ' Create new key
        If optKey Then
            CreateNewKey HKEY_LOCAL_MACHINE, "SOFTWARE\" & txtSubKey
        Else
            CreateNewKey HKEY_CURRENT_USER, "SOFTWARE\" & txtSubKey
        End If

    Case 1  ' Create new value or set value
        If optKey Then
            SetNewValue HKEY_LOCAL_MACHINE, _
                "SOFTWARE\" & txtSubKey, _
                sType, _
                txtValueName, _
                txtValue
        Else
            SetNewValue HKEY_CURRENT_USER, _
                "SOFTWARE\" & txtSubKey, _
                sType, _
                txtValueName, _
                txtValue
        End If

    Case 2 ' Read a value
    Case 3 ' Delete value
    Case 4 ' Delete Key

    Case 5 ' Quit
        Form_Unload

    End Select

End Sub
```

And in Form_Unload add the following:

```
Private Sub Form_Unload(Cancel As Integer)

    Unload Me
    End

End Sub
```

Close the form Code window, and open the Code window for RegAPI.Bas.

Insert a procedure named CreateNewKey, and add the code shown in Listing 15.13.

LISTING 15.13 The CreateNewKey Sub

```
Public Sub CreateNewKey(lRoot As Long, sSubKey As String)

    ' Creates a new key in registry
    ' Parameters:
    ' lRoot is one of HKEY_CURRENT_USER or HKEY_LOCAL_MACHINE
    ' sSubKey is the subkey name (requires leading \)

    Dim lResult As Long
    Dim hKeyHandle As Long
    Dim sMsg As String
    Dim lType As Long
    Dim lValue As Long

    ' error checks
    If Len(sSubKey) = 0 Then
        sMsg = "Bad input to create key" & vbCrLf
        sMsg = sMsg & "Key = " & sSubKey
        MsgBox sMsg
        GoTo Exit_subCreateKey
    End If

    ' Create the key
    lResult = RegCreateKeyEx _
        (lRoot, _
        sSubKey, _
        0&, _
        vbNullString, _
        REG_OPTION_NON_VOLATILE, _
        KEY_ALL_ACCESS, _
        0&, _
        hKeyHandle, _
        lResult)

    ' check to be sure function created a key
    If lResult <> ERROR_SUCCESS Then
        sMsg = "Could not create key"
```

continues

LISTING 15.13   continued

```
        MsgBox sMsg
        GoTo Exit_subCreateKey
    End If

    ' Key was created, now close it
    lResult = RegCloseKey(hKeyHandle)
    If lResult <> ERROR_SUCCESS Then
        sMsg = "Could not close key"
        MsgBox sMsg
        GoTo Exit_subCreateKey
    End If

Exit_subCreateKey:
    Exit Sub

Error_subCreateKey:
    MsgBox Error
    Resume Exit_subCreateKey
End Sub
```

A Look at the Code

This is getting pretty involved! Take a look at the code before you get lost. Start with the code for the form. The command buttons are part of an array. When you click one of them, the only way to know which button was clicked is to look at the array index. That is the purpose of the Select-Case structure. The following code reads the value of the optKey option buttons and sends the correct key and subkey information to the CreateNewKey sub, which is part of the RegAPI.Bas module:

```
If optKey Then
    CreateNewKey HKEY_LOCAL_MACHINE, "SOFTWARE\" & txtSubKey
Else
    CreateNewKey HKEY_CURRENT_USER, "SOFTWARE\" & txtSubKey
End If
```

At this time, the only other command button that does anything is the Exit button, which switches to Form_Unload.

The work is done in the RegAPI.Bas module's CreateNewKey sub. The code starts with an error check. A message box warns if there is no subkey specified. Then the following code creates the key.

```
lResult = RegCreateKeyEx _
    (lRoot, _
    sSubKey, _
    0&, _
```

```
vbNullString, _
REG_OPTION_NON_VOLATILE, _
KEY_ALL_ACCESS, _
0&, _
hKeyHandle, _
lResult)
```

Microsoft defined the third parameter as lpReserved, which means that they may find a use for it in the future. Meanwhile, it must be a long integer 0.

The next parameter is a constant, vbNullString, provided by Visual Basic for use when calling external procedures where the external procedure requires a string whose value is zero.

The parameter REG_OPTION_NON_VOLATILE enables you to save the new subkey to the registry. Changing it to REG_OPTION_ VOLATILE creates a subkey that would not last beyond the first computer shutdown. The KEY_ALL_ACCESS parameter gives the code permission to read, write, and modify the key. The 0& that follows is the signal to use the default security structure.

The handle of the key you have created appears in hKeyHandle, and lResult can be used to determine whether we have created a new key or opened an existing one. You don't really care, so you can use a variable that will be changed almost immediately. Note that the function's return value is stored in lResult, which overwrites the new/old key value. If successful, lResult holds the constant ERROR_SUCCESS.

The balance of the code in this section is error trapping, which you learned about in Chapter 10, "Problem Solving: Handling Errors and Debugging Your Program."

Running the Program

Press F5 to run the program. Select the HKEY_LOCAL_MACHINE option and enter VB Interactive in the SubKeys textbox. When you click Create Key, the new key is added to the registry. Before you take a look at it, change the SubKeys textbox to read VB6Interactive\1.0 and click Create Key one more time.

Now you can take a look at your results. Start the Regedit program and select HKEY_LOCAL_MACHINE. Expand the SOFTWARE key, and you will find VB Interactive with a plus sign beside it. Expand that subkey, and you find 1.0 as a branch beneath it. Figure 15.10 shows the Registry Editor (RegEdit) with the VB6Interative key and the 1.0 key underneath it.

It won't harm your system if you leave these entries in your Registry. It will cause the size of your Registry to grow, though. To remove Registry entries is identical to removing items from Window Explorer. Select the item you want to remove, and press the Del key.

FIGURE **15.10**

The Registry Editor showing the key VB6Interactive.

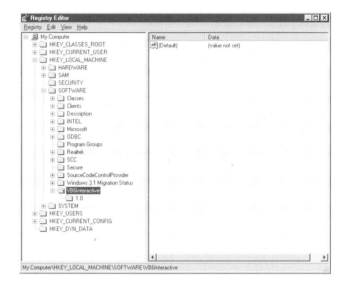

Caution

Be extremely careful when removing keys and subkeys. Deletions are permanent, and there is no Undo feature.

Lesson Summary

This lesson showed you that the Registry is the repository for your system and software configuration. For brevity, this lesson's project was trimmed down. On the CD under Chapter 15, you will find a subdirectory called RegAPI, which is the completed application. Its provided so you can see how to add Subkey values and read values from the Registry.

Unfortuately (or fortunately), this lesson barely scratches the surface of the Windows Registry. There are a number of books that go more in depth on the components of the Registry and how to maintain it, such as *Troubleshooting and Configuring the Windows Nt/95 Registry* (Sams Publishing, 1997) and *Windows 95 and Windows Nt 4.0 Registry & Customization Handbook* (Que Corp., 1997).

In the next lesson, you learn how to use API functions to work with graphic files.

Quiz 4

1. The easiest way to get API constants, declarations and types correctly inserted in your programs is to use

   a. Regedit

   b. Access

   c. Word

   d. The API Text Viewer

2. New keys are placed into the registry using

   a. `RegCreateKeyEx`

   b. `RegInsertKeyEx`

   c. `RegOpenKeyA`

   d. `RegMakeKeyEx`

3. The parameter `REG_OPTION_NON_VOLATILE` tells Windows to

   a. Erase the key when the program is terminated.

   b. Erase the key when the computer is turned off.

   c. Save the key to the registry.

   d. None of the above.

4. The parameter `KEY_ALL_ACCESS` tells Windows

   a. To let everybody access Windows without a password

   b. To add a password to the registry files

   c. To require the keylock to be on before registry access is allowed

   d. To allow read, write, modify, add, and delete privileges of accessing the registry

Exercise 4

Complexity: Easy

1. Write an application that will create a Local Machine key named MyVB6.

Complexity: Easy

2. Write an application that will delete a Current User key.

LESSON 5

Manipulating Bitmaps

As illustrated in Lesson 3 in this chapter, you used the GDI32 API to change the background color of a form. If you didn't already guess, the GDI32 API is used to work with graphics. Within the GDI32, there are three functions that Windows use to transfer bitmap images quickly between locations on the screen and between the screen and memory. Two of the functions can stretch an image, if necessary, to get it to fit into the target location. The other one will fill the target area as a repeating pattern, or like a brush.

All three are block transfer functions using ternary raster operation codes, also known as ROP. *ROP codes* define how the GDI32 combines colors from a source bitmap, a possible brush bitmap, and the destination bitmap to produce the final color in the target bitmap. The block transfer functions are BitBlt, StretchBlt, and PatBlt. BitBlt, pronounced *bit-blit*, stands for bit block transfer. It transfers bitmapped images from one device context (hDC) to an equally sized area of another device context.

StretchBlt stands for Block Transfer and Stretch, and it transfers a bitmapped image from one device context to another device context. Unlike BitBlt, the target device context can be a different or equal sized device context. It can also convert color mapping to monochrome and vice versa.

PatBlt stands for Pattern Block Transfer, and it fills a device context with a pattern. The pattern is determined by a selected brush and by the raster operation (ROP) specified when the function is called.

The three functions are defined in the following code, and Table 15.9 describes the parameters.

```
Declare Function BitBlt Lib "gdi32" Alias "BitBlt" _
    (ByVal hDestDC As Long, ByVal x As Long, ByVal y As Long, _
    ByVal nWidth As Long, ByVal nHeight As Long, _
    ByVal hSrcDC As Long, ByVal xSrc As Long, ByVal ySrc As Long, _
    ByVal dwRop As Long) As Long
Declare Function StretchBlt Lib "gdi32" Alias "StretchBlt" _
    (ByVal hdc As Long, ByVal x As Long, ByVal y As Long, _
    ByVal nWidth As Long, ByVal nHeight As Long, ByVal hSrcDC As Long, _
    ByVal xSrc As Long, ByVal ySrc As Long, ByVal nSrcWidth As Long, _
    ByVal nSrcHeight As Long, ByVal dwRop As Long) As Long
Declare Function PatBlt Lib "gdi32" Alias "PatBlt" _
    (ByVal hdc As Long, ByVal x As Long, ByVal y As Long, _
    ByVal nWidth As Long, ByVal nHeight As Long, _
    ByVal dwRop As Long) As Long
```

TABLE 15.9   Block Transfer Function Parameters

Parameter	Definition
hDC or hDestDC	The destination device context (DC)
x, y	The coordinates of the upper-left corner of a rectangle within the destination device context. The coordinate system will be based on the Picture Box's ScaleMode property
nWidth, nHeight	The width and height of the destination rectangle
nSrc or nSrcDC	The source device context
xSrc, ySrc	The coordinates of the upper-left corner of a rectangle within the source device context. This rectangle will have the same dimension as the one in the destination, but the coordinates of the corner may be different.
dwRop	This is the 32-bit value for the ternary raster operation (ROP) that will combine bitmaps during the transfer

In this lesson, you will use BitBlt to perform a left to right image wiping effect, similar to the transition between slides in Microsoft PowerPoint. First, create a new Standard EXE project and name the project BMPTrans.VBP. In the default form that is created with the project, add two PictureBox controls, a Timer control, and a Command Button. Use Table 15.10 for the property settings of the controls.

TABLE 15.10   BMPTrans' Property for Form Objects

Object	Property	Value
Form	Name	frmWipeBMP
	Caption	"BMP Transition"
Command Button	Name	cmdDoIt
	Caption	"Do It"
PictureBox	Name	picCurrentPicture
	Left	240
	AutoResize	True
	ScaleMode	3-Pixel
	Top	240
PictureBox	Name	picNextPicture
	AutoRedraw	True
	AutoResize	True
	ScaleMode	3-Pixel
Timer	Name	tmrWipe
	Interval	25

The ScaleMode property of the PictureBox controls are set to Pixel because the coordinate scale is more manageable to think in pixels than in *twips*. The AutoRedraw property in the picNextPicture PictureBox is set to True to ensure that Windows forces the picture to refresh itself when data has been transferred to it. If you don't set this to True, you will get a picture full of horizontal lines, because the picture didn't get refreshed as the data was being transferred.

The AutoResize property on both PictureBox controls is set to True. If the size of the bitmap is different than the size of the PictureBox control, the control will resize itself to match the size of the image. Save this form as frmWipeBMP.frm.

In the General Declaration section the form, use the code in Listing 15.14.

LISTING 15.14   frmWipeBMP's General Declarations

```
Option Explicit

Private Declare Function BitBlt Lib "gdi32" _
    (ByVal hDestDC As Long, ByVal x As Long, ByVal y As Long, _
    ByVal nWidth As Long, ByVal nHeight As Long, _
    ByVal hSrcDC As Long, ByVal xSrc As Long, _
    ByVal ySrc As Long, ByVal dwRop As Long) As Long

' This setting will cause the target picture to
' be copied onto the source picture
Const nSRCCOPY = &HCC0020

' The wipe is actually a number of discrete "steps".
' By varying this constant and the Timer interval,
' you can control the wipe speed.
Const nSTEPS = 100

' These variables set up the actual wipe operation.
Dim nCurPicScaleWidth As Long
Dim nWidthChange As Long
Dim nPieceToAdd As Long
Dim nNextPiece As Long
```

You could have assigned the bitmap images to the Picture property of the PictureBox controls, but a lot of times it better to assign them in your code. This way, if you need to change the location of the image or want to change the image, you just have to change the property in your code versus going into each control and changing the Picture property. The drawback by assigning the location in your code is that you need to ensure that the picture file stays where you have specified; otherwise, the image will never be found.

In Listing 15.15, the program references the WINNT256.BMP and LANMA256.BMP files. These images come with Windows NT Workstation and Server. If you're not running Windows NT, you can find these files on the CD in the Chapter 15 directory. Also, rather than defining a definitive path to the picture files, like c:\projects\WINNT256.BMP, the procedure is using the `App.Path` method. By using this method, as long as the files are in the same directory as the application, the images will always be found.

LISTING 15.15   Set the `Picture` Property of Each `PictureBox` as the Form Loads

```
Private Sub Form_Load()

    picCurrentPicture.Picture = LoadPicture(App.Path & "\winnt256.bmp")
    picNextPicture.Picture = LoadPicture(App.Path & "\lanma256.bmp")

End Sub
```

Rather than have to worry if the images will fit in the `PictureBox` controls, add the code in Listing 15.16 to the `Form_Activate` event. The code will resize the form and center the Command button on the form under the `PictureBox` control based on the size the resized `PictureBox` control.

LISTING 15.16   Form Resizing and Command Button Centering

```
Private Sub Form_Activate()

    ' Dynamically resize the form and
    ' center the command button based
    ' on the size of the Current Picture.
    Me.Width = picCurrentPicture.Width + 480
    Me.Height = picCurrentPicture.Height + cmdDoIt.Height + _
        cmdDoIt.Height + 480
    cmdDoIt.Top = picCurrentPicture.Height + picCurrentPicture.Top + 240
    cmdDoIt.Left = (Me.Width / 2) - (cmdDoIt.Width / 2)

End Sub
```

Add the code in Listing 15.17 to the cmdDoIt Command Button's click event. This procedure will compute the amount of vertical or horizontal wipes will need to be processed in the Timer's `Timer` event.

LISTING 15.17   cmdDoIt's `Click` Event in `frmTransBMP`

```
Private Sub cmdDoIt_Click()

    ' Determine how many panels will be needed
    ' to clear the image
    nCurPicScaleWidth = picCurrentPicture.ScaleWidth
    nWidthChange = nCurPicScaleWidth \ nSTEPS
    nPieceToAdd = nWidthChange

    ' Transfer control of the effect to the Timer
    tmrWipe.Enabled = True

End Sub
```

Add the code in List 15.18 to the `tmrWipe_Timer` event. This procedure will cause the illusion that the images are in transition from left to right.

LISTING 15.18   Using the `Timer` Function in the `BltBlt` Function

```
Private Sub tmrWipe_Timer()

    Dim x As Integer 'Counter to keep track of pieces

    ' Each time the timer event executes,
    ' display another piece of the next picture
    nNextPiece = BitBlt(picCurrentPicture.hDC, 0, 0, _
        nPieceToAdd, picCurrentPicture.ScaleHeight, _
        picNextPicture.hDC, 0, 0, nSRCCOPY)
    nPieceToAdd = nPieceToAdd + nWidthChange
    x = x + 1
    ' When all the pieces are displayed, turn off the timer.
    If (x - nSTEPS) > 0 Then tmrWipe.Enabled = False

End Sub
```

Save the project and press F5 to run it. The first image you see is the Windows NT Workstation bitmap. When you click the command button, the first image will appear to be wiped away from the left to the right and will display the Windows NT Server bitmap. Figure 15.11 illustrates the wipe from left to right in transition. By changing the `nSTEP` constant in the General Declarations section and the `Timer`'s Interval property you can adjust the rate of transition. Also by changing the `BitBlt` property in the `Timer` control's `Timer` event, you can change the way the images are wiped, such as right to left and top to bottom.

FIGURE 15.11

The wipe transition from left to right using BitBlt.

Lesson Summary

The three functions that affect graphics—BitBlt, StretchBlt, and PatBlt—all use similar arguments. The difference is in how they work. BitBlt is good for copying images that are the same size from one source to another. StretchBlt enables you to copy an image to a target source that is not necessarily the same size as the original image. PatBlt enables you to fill a target image with the pattern of the original image. Now that you've been introduced to manipulating graphic images, the next lesson will cover how to manipulate text.

Quiz 5

1. What does ROP stand for?

    a. Raster Operator

    b. Raster Operation

    c. Rapper Outreach

    d. Recruiting Opportunity

2. What block transfer function requires both the target and source to be the same size?

    a. PatBlt

    b. StretchBlt

    c. BitBlt

    d. ROP

3. What block transfer function will transfer graphic information from one device context to another, regardless of the source and target size?

   a. `PatBlt`

   b. `BitBlt` and `StretchBlt`

   c. `PatBlt` and `StretchBlt`

   d. None of the above

4. What block transfer function maps color images as well as monochrome?

   a. `BitBlt`

   b. `StretchBlt`

   c. `PatBlt`

   d. None of the above

Exercise 5

Complexity: Moderate

1. Take the application created in this lesson and cause the images to wipe from top to bottom.

Complexity: Moderate

2. Write an application that uses the `StretchBlt` to copy a bitmap image.

LESSON 6

Manipulating Text

You've seen how APIs work with forms and part of the operating system. Now you are going to explore how APIs can help you with text manipulation. Now that you know how to change the background color of a form, wouldn't it be nice to do something with text as well? There are three API functions—`CreateFontIndirect`, `SelectObject`, and `DeleteObject`—along with a user-type, `LOGFONT`, it is possible to rotate text on an object like a picture box, a form, or a Printer object.

The `CreateFontIndirect` function creates a logical font based on the characteristics you specified in the structure LOGFONT, which will be described shortly. The declaration for this API is as follows:

```
Private Declare Function CreateFontIndirect Lib "gdi32" _
    Alias "CreateFontIndirectA" (lpLogFont As LOGFONT) As Long
```

It requires one parameter, `lpLogFont`, which is a data type found in LogFont. The function returns the handle to the logical font if it can successfully create the font; otherwise, it returns a `Null` value.

After you create your logical font, you place it into your target object by calling the `SelectObject` function. The declaration for this function is

```
Private Declare Function SelectObject Lib "gdi32" _
    (ByVal hdc As Long, ByVal hObject As Long) As Long
```

The first parameter, `hDC`, specifies the object the logical font will be placed in. The second parameter, `hObject`, is the handle to the logical font you're going to display. If the function is successful, it will return the handle of the logical font you replace; otherwise, the function returns a zero.

After you're finished displaying your font, you must clean up after yourself. The `DeleteObject` function will return the logical font's resources back to the operating system. The declaration for this function is

```
Private Declare Function DeleteObject Lib "gdi32" _
    (ByVal hObject As Long) As Long
```

The function has one parameter, `hObject`. It contains the handle to the logical font. The function returns True if it was successful in releasing the object; otherwise it returns a zero if it fails.

When you are working with logical fonts, you will need to use the following LogFont, short for *logical font*, data-type structure:

```
Type LOGFONT
        lfHeight As Long
        lfWidth As Long
        lfEscapement As Long
        lfOrientation As Long
        lfWeight As Long
        lfItalic As Byte
        lfUnderline As Byte
        lfStrikeOut As Byte
        lfCharSet As Byte
        lfOutPrecision As Byte
        lfClipPrecision As Byte
        lfQuality As Byte
        lfPitchAndFamily As Byte
        lfFaceName As String * LF_FACESIZE
End Type
```

Note In the API Text Viewer, it defines the lfFaceName as *lfFacename(LF_FACESIZE) As Byte*. This is the wrong definition. The data type definition described previously is the correct way to define this data type.

This data type structure might look intimidating, but it really isn't when you know which ones are required for your task. Let's take a look at them. The logical fonts are built based on a font mapper that is part of the operating system.

Note A lot of this information might not make a lot of sense because it deals with font design. For more information about font design, you can find it in most desktop publishing and/or graphic design books.

The first two fields, lfHeight and lfWidth, determine the height and weight of the font in logical units. The font mapper interprets heights greater than zero as the height of the font cell. Numbers less than zero specifies the character height of the font, which is the height of the cell minus the amount of internal line spacing. If you specify a height of zero, the font mapper uses the default height for the font.

Windows handles font widths similarly. If you specify a width of zero, the font mapper uses a default width based on the font height. The font mapper interprets nonzero widths as the average width for the font.

The lfEscapement parameter specifies the angle for the line of text. The coordinate system is based on a counter-clockwise horizon. This means that zero degrees is on the horizontal access, 90 degrees would mean the text would be rotated backwards; therefore, the text is rotated counter-clockwise, and so on.

Note It's not clearly documented anywhere, but you will need to design your lfEscapement numbers by a factor of 100. This means that if you want to change the angle to 90 degrees, the lfEscapement parameter should be 900.

The lfOrientation parameter is ignored by the Windows operating system. You can place any value in it and it wouldn't make any difference on your rotation result.

The lfWeight parameter specifies the thickness of the font. The character weight ranges from 100 to 900. Table 15.11 describes the font weights more clearly.

TABLE 15.11   Weight for Your Font

Constant Name	Value
FW_DONTCARE	0
FW_THIN	100
FW_EXTRALIGHT	200
FW_LIGHT	300
FW_NORMAL	400
FW_MEDIUM	500
FW_SEMIBOLD	600
FW_BOLD	700
FW_EXTRABOLD	800
FW_HEAVY	900
FW_ULTRALIGHT	FW_EXTRALIGHT
FW_REGULAR	FW_NORMAL
FW_DEMIBOLD	FW_SEMIBOLD
FW_ULTRABOLD	FW_EXTRABOLD
FW_BLACK	FW_HEAVY

The following parameters, lfItalic, lfUnderline, and lfStrikeOut, are fairly self-explanatory. You assign any non-zero value if you want the logical font to have any or all these attributes.

The lfCharSet parameter consists of one of the values in Table 15.12, which identifies which character set the font will be based on.

TABLE 15.12   Character Set from Which the Font Mapper Will Derive the Font

Constant Name	Value
ANSI_CHARSET	0
DEFAULT_CHARSET	1
SYMBOL_CHARSET	2
SHIFTJIS_CHARSET	128
OEM_CHARSET	255

The lfOutPrecision parameter provides guidelines for the font mapper when it comes to matching fonts. It helps in determining the height, width, orientation, escapement, and pitch of the font. Table 15.13 lists all the values you can choose from.

TABLE 15.13   Output Precision

Constant Name	Value
OUT_DEFAULT_PRECIS	0
OUT_STRING_PRECIS	1
OUT_CHARACTER_PRECIS	2
OUT_STROKE_PRECIS	3
OUT_TT_PRECIS	4
OUT_DEVICE_PRECIS	5
OUT_RASTER_PRECIS	6
OUT_TT_ONLY_PRECIS	7

The lfClipPrecision parameter specifies how Windows should clip characters that partially extend outside the clipping region. Table 15.14 lists all the values you can use. The CLIP_CHARACTER_PRECIS contains specifications that Windows should clip the string at character boundary, while the CLIP_STROKE_PRECIS set the clipping at the stroke level.

TABLE 15.14   Character Clip Specifications

Constant Name	Value
CLIP_DEFAULT_PRECIS	0
CLIP_CHARACTER_PRECIS	1
CLIP_STROKE_PRECIS	2

The lfQuality parameters tells the font mapper how close it needs to create the logical font compared to the physical font. Table 15.15 lists the three potential values.

TABLE 15.15   Font Quality Settings

Constant Name	Value
DEFAULT_QUALITY	0
DRAFT_QUALITY	1
PROOF_QUALITY	2

The lfPitchAndFamily parameter lets you select the pitch and family of font you want to use. You can specify the exact font you want to use, but if the font isn't available for some reason, the font mapper tries to substitute a font from a similar family. You can also have the font mapper match the type of Pitch the font is based on. Table 15.16 lists the possible font families you can choose from. Table 15.17 lists the possible font pitches it can use for substitution.

TABLE 15.16   Base Font Families

Constant Name	Value
FF_DONTCARE	0
FF_ROMAN	16
FF_SWISS	32
FF_MODERN	48
FF_SCRIPT	64
FF_DECORATIVE	80

TABLE 15.17   Font Pitch Substitution

Constant Name	Value
DEFAULT_PITCH	0
FIXED_PITCH	1
VARIABLE_PITCH	2

The lfFaceName parameter specifies the name of the typeface you want to use. Just type any typeface name you have installed on your system, for example Arial or Times New Roman, followed by an ampersand and CHR$(0). If this parameter is left as Null, the font mapper will attempt to select a default typeface.

Now, you just went through a lot of parameters. You're probably thinking this is going to be complicated. Well it isn't. The reason why it isn't complicated is because if you don't plan to change any of the default options, you don't have to reference them in your program. You still have to define the complete LOGFONT data type, but the parameters are optional parameters.

Before you get more confused, let's do an example that will illustrate what you just covered. The following example displays a message in a Picture Box with the text flipped upside-down.

Create a new project directory called Text. Create a new Standard EXE and save the project as Text.VBP. In Form1, place Command Button and Picture Box on it. Use the properties listed in Table 15.18 to define the objects. The form should look like that shown in Figure 15.12.

FIGURE 15.12

A view of frmMain
form.

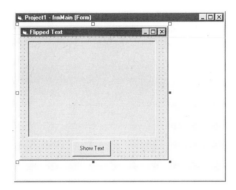

TABLE 15.18   Text.VBP Objects and Properties List

Object	Property	Value
Form	Name	frmMain
	Caption	"Flipped Text"
Command Button	Name	cmdShowText
	Caption	"Show Text"
Picture Box	Name	picDisplay
	Height	3015
	Width	4095

In the General Declaration section of the frmMain form, insert the code in Listing 15.19.

LISTING 15.19   General Declarations for Text.VBP

```
Option Explicit

Private Declare Function CreateFontIndirect Lib "gdi32" _
    Alias "CreateFontIndirectA" (lpLogFont As LOGFONT) As Long
Private Declare Function SelectObject Lib "gdi32" _
    (ByVal hdc As Long, ByVal hObject As Long) As Long
Private Declare Function DeleteObject Lib "gdi32" _
    (ByVal hObject As Long) As Long
Const LF_FACESIZE = 32

Private Type LOGFONT
    lfHeight As Long
    lfWidth As Long
    lfEscapement As Long
    lfOrientation As Long
```

```
        lfWeight As Long
        lfItalic As Byte
        lfUnderline As Byte
        lfStrikeOut As Byte
        lfCharSet As Byte
        lfOutPrecision As Byte
        lfClipPrecision As Byte
        lfQuality As Byte
        lfPitchAndFamily As Byte
        lfFaceName As String * LF_FACESIZE
End Type
```

In the Click event of the cmdShowText command button, insert the code in Listing 15.20.

LISTING 15.20   cmdShowText's Click Event

```
Private Sub cmdShowText_Click()
    Dim cFont As LOGFONT
    Dim prevFont As Long
    Dim hFont As Long
    Dim rc As Long

    Const FONTSIZE = 18
    cFont.lfEscapement = 1800
    cFont.lfFaceName = "Times New Roman" & Chr$(0)
    cFont.lfHeight = (FONTSIZE * -20) / Screen.TwipsPerPixelY
    hFont = CreateFontIndirect(cFont)
    prevFont = SelectObject(picDisplay.hdc, hFont)
    picDisplay.CurrentX = picDisplay.Left + picDisplay.Width / 2
    picDisplay.CurrentY = picDisplay.ScaleHeight / 2
    picDisplay.Print "Rotated Text"
    rc = SelectObject(picDisplay.hdc, prevFont)
    rc = DeleteObject(hFont)
    picDisplay.CurrentY = picDisplay.ScaleHeight / 2
    picDisplay.Print "Normal Text"

End Sub
```

Save the program and execute it by pressing F5. When the form is loaded, press the Show Text command button. The Click event in the cmdShowText command button is triggered. What happens is that two items of text will be printed on the form. One item labeled "Rotated Text" should appear in Times New Roman (or its equivalent if your system doesn't have that font) and it will be inverted. The second item labeled "Normal Text" will appear right-side up in a sans serif font.

Lesson Summary

The amount of form manipulation is virtually endless through the use of API functions. By integrating some of the other lessons with this one, you can develop user interfaces out of the norm without having to invest in a lot of third-party custom controls, because all these functions come with the operating system. Now that you've been exposed to APIs that interact with form, the last lesson will cover how to get information from the Windows operating system itself.

Quiz 6

1. What type of object can use the `CreateFontIndirect`, `SelectObject`, and `DeleteObject` function?

    a. Picture box

    b. Forms

    c. Printer object

    d. All the above

2. The `lfEscapement` parameter is used for what?

    a. Determines whether the ESC button can be used to cancel a process

    b. Specifies the angle text will be displayed

    c. Specifies how a program will terminate

    d. None of the above

3. What is the lfWeight setting for a bold font?

    a. FW_BOLD

    b. FW_HEAVY

    c. 700

    d. Both a and b

4. What parameter can you use to have the font mapper choose a similar font family if the font you specified doesn't exist?

    a. `lfPitchAndFamily`

    b. `lfQuality`

    c. `lfCharSet`

    d. All of the above

Exercise 6

Complexity: Moderate

1. Build an application that will display a line of text rotated every 45 degrees.

Complexity: Moderate

2. Build an application that will print a line of text at a 45-degree angle and move the text from the lower right-hand corner of the form to the upper left-hand corner of the form.

LESSON 7

Refining Time

Note

> "Time is an illusion caused by the passage of history, and history is an illusion caused by the passage of time."
>
> —Douglas Adams, author of the *Hitchhiker's Guide to the Galaxy* series.

We all seem to be fascinated with time. Time is all around us. We never seem to have enough of it and we are always trying to catch up with it. Most of us think of time in hours, minutes, and seconds. When it comes to calculating amounts of times, this isn't the most efficient method, especially when it comes to benchmarking your application. A lot of times you will want to find time down to the millisecond for how long a function takes to process.

There is an easy way to get millisecond timing from the Windows operating system by using the API, GetTickCount. This function returns the number of milliseconds since the system was started. The API looks like the following:

```
Declare Function GetTickCount Lib "kernel32" Alias "GetTickCount" () As Long
```

Note

> This above code came straight from the API Text Viewer. Notice that there is an Alias GetTickCount after the kernel32 reference. This is not required in order to make use of this function. So if you see it in an article or other publication without it, don't panic. It's optional.

This is probably one of the easier API functions to use. To get the time from the function, assign it a variable as follows:

```
lSysTime = GetTickCount()
```

Assuming you defined the lSysTime variable as a Long, the GetTickCount will store the value in the variable in milliseconds.

An example for using this function would be to create a class module that you can reference from any module in your application to calculate the elapsed time of a function or procedure. Create a new Standard EXE project and add a New Class module to your project. In the Properties window of the Class, name the class Timing.

Add the following code in Listing 15.21 in the General Declaration section of the Timing class module. Here you will need to declare the GetTickCount API function in order to have access to the method that returns timing values with milliseconds. The standard Time() function in Visual Basic only provides for seconds.

LISTING 15.21   General Declaration Code for the Timing.Cls Module

```
Option Explicit

' Dimension Read-Only variables for timing events
Dim mStartTime As Long
Dim mFinishTime As Long
Dim mElapsedTime As Long

' Declare API to get system ticks in milliseconds
Declare Function GetTickCount Lib "kernel32" () As Long
```

Add the following methods and properties in Listing 15.22 to the Timing class. These methods and properties will enable you to time the execution of procedures and functions, and have access to the elapsed time value in milliseconds.

LISTING 15.22   Methods and Properties for Calculating Elapsed Time

```
Option Explicit

' Dimension Read-Only variables for timing events
Dim mStartTime As Long
Dim mFinishTime As Long
Dim mElapsedTime As Long

' Declare API to get system ticks in milliseconds
Private Declare Function GetTickCount Lib "kernel32" () As Long
```

```
' Method to store start time
Public Sub Start()
    mStartTime = GetTickCount()
    mFinishTime = 0
    mElapsedTime = 0
End Sub

' Method to store finish time and calculate
' elapsed time in milliseconds
Public Sub Finish()
    mFinishTime = GetTickCount()
    mElapsedTime = mFinishTime - mStartTime
End Sub

' Read-Only property to access elapsed time
' and shows the time up to 100th of a second
Public Property Get ElapsedTime()
    ElapsedTime = mElapsedTime / 1000
End Property
```

Save the Class module as Timing.CLS. You may have noticed that the `GetTickCount` function is declared as a `Private` function. This is because functions in Class modules cannot be public functions. By default, if you don't specify if a function or procedure is private or public, Visual Basic defaults them to public.

Go to the form in this project and place two Command Buttons and a Text Box on it. Set the properties of the Form and Command Button to those in Table 15.19.

TABLE 15.19   The Timing Project's Properties

Object	Property	Value
Form	Name	frmTiming
	Caption	Timing
Command Button	Name	cmdStart
	Caption	Start
Command Button	Name	cmdEnd
	Caption	End
	Enabled	False
Text Box	Name	txtTime
	Locked	True
	Text	íî

Now add the following code in Listing 15.23 to the project.

LISTING 15.23   Code for the Timing Project

```
Option Explicit

Dim otiming As New Timing

Private Sub cmdEnd_Click()

    otiming.Finish
    txtTime.Text = otiming.ElapsedTime
    cmdStart.Enabled = True
    cmdEnd.Enabled = False

End Sub

Private Sub cmdStart_Click()

    otiming.Start
    cmdStart.Enabled = False
    cmdEnd.Enabled = True

End Sub
```

Save the form as Timing.FRM and run the program. Essentially what you have just created is a stopwatch. Click the Start command button to start your timing count. When you want to see how much time has elapsed, click the End command button. The elapsed time will be displayed in the text box. Figure 15.13 illustrates this.

FIGURE 15.13

The Timing program showing how much time has elapsed.

Lesson Summary

The GetTickCount API function is very useful with many sorts of timing issues. The most common usage is for determining how long a procedure or function took to execute. By placing a GetTickCount at the beginning and end of a function, you then calculate the difference for the total processing time.

Quiz 7

1. What API does `GetTickCount` belong to?

    a. GDI32

    b. SYSTEM32

    c. ADVAPI

    d. KERNEL32

2. The `GetTickCount` function does what?

    a. Counts the number of ticks on a clock

    b. Returns how long the operating system has been running in seconds

    c. Returns how long the operating system has been running in milliseconds

    d. Returns how long the operating system has been running in nanoseconds

3. Why would you want to use the `GetTickCount` function versus the `Time` function?

    a. `GetTickCount` is more accurate

    b. Time doesn't count to the millisecond

    c. Both a and b

    d. None of the above

4. How can your reset the Tick count?

    a. FDISK

    b. Log off and log back on

    c. Restart the system

    d. None of the above

Exercise 7

Complexity: Easy

1. Write an application to display the tick count on a status bar. To display the latest tick count, have a command button refresh the screen.

Complexity: Advanced

2. Write an application that will display the tick count in hours, minutes, and seconds.

Chapter Summary

As you can see, Windows APIs can really enhance your application in many ways. A lot of the things you see being done in other applications can be done in yours, assuming you know which API functions they used. A caveat is that if you reference a function incorrectly, there is a good chance you can make your development environment and your operating system unstable if an error occurs. APIs are your friends, but be patient when learning new APIs. Here is a recap of the important points covered in this chapter.

- Passing arguments *By Value* means arguments are passed as strings.

- Passing arguments *By Ref* means arguments are passed based on the memory location of the variable.

- The Windows API Viewer lists all the API functions, constants, and data types. Be advised that some of the API definitions may be the recommended way of declaring them, but some modification might be necessary.

- There are a lot of APIs that will enable you to change the way an application's form looks and acts. The two that were used in this chapter were `FlashWindow` and `RealizePalette`.

- With the Registry APIs, you can add, update and delete any key, subkey and value from your System Registry. These functions may seem simple to use, but can be very disastrous to your system if used recklessly. Use them with caution. It's always a good idea to back up your Registry before doing any manipulation of it.

- When manipulating bitmaps, the three APIs to be familiar with are `BitBlt`, `StretchBlt`, and `PatBlt`.

- When manipulating text, there are three functions to be familiar with. They are `CreateFontIndirect`, `SelectObject`, and `DeleteObject`. Also use the user type, `LogFont`. Any object that has an hDC (handle for a device context) can use these APIs.

- The `GetTickCount` tracks how long a system has been running in milliseconds. This is very useful when you are trying to gauge system performance because the Time function only takes up the second, not millisecond.

This chapter touches the surface of what APIs you have available to you, and how to use them. For more information on the Windows API, you should visit the Microsoft Developers Network on the Internet at `http://www.microsoft.com/msdn`. There you can find more information about all the Windows APIs. As mentioned in the "Lesson Summary" for Lesson 1, for a more comprehensive look at Windows API tailored for the Visual Basic developer, you should refer to Dan Appleman's book, *Dan Appleman's Visual Basic Programmer's Guide to the Win32 API* (Ziff-Davis Press, 1997).

CHAPTER 16

Interfacing with Excel and Other Programs

This chapter introduces a new method of designing and building applications with Visual Basic: using OLE and some ActiveX technology. Using object-oriented techniques and OLE, you can build your own software components. This chapter examines the different features of OLE. It explains how to create applications that use the Visual Basic OLE container control to link and embed documents from Microsoft Word and Microsoft Excel. It explains OLE automation and how to create ActiveX client and server applications. This chapter also provides a review of Visual Basic's system objects and a simple methodology for designing OLE objects.

LESSON 1

What Is OLE?

You have just written a really good application, maybe a slick notepad or text editor. You are showing the application off, and someone asks, "Can you do spell checking?" You think to yourself, spell checking? No way! It would take longer to write a spell checker than it took to develop the entire application! The moral of this story is that people expect more from their applications today.

But all is not lost. A few years ago, Microsoft and several other Integrated System Vendors (ISVs) created an open specification that enables applications to communicate with one another. The specification also defines a programming interface to use another application's objects, including that spell checker. Application developers can use objects from existing applications to enhance their own applications, rather than reinventing the wheel. And now OLE has been extended with ActiveX technology so that it works with intranet and Internet applications. Reusable components mean faster application development and higher quality applications.

The open standard created by Microsoft and the ISVs is Object Linking and Embedding (OLE). Microsoft preached the virtues of OLE to developers with the claim that OLE is a major technology in today's applications. In its infancy, OLE represented the capability to link and embed documents from one application to another. Over time, OLE grew into several standards for interprocess communication, object storage, and object reuse.

So how does ActiveX technology fit into all this? In Microsoft's process to establish an Internet presence, they introduced a new term to the world of developers: *ActiveX*. When it was first defined, it was believed to be variation of OLE. As it turned out, ActiveX technology includes, but is not limited to, OLE. ActiveX and OLE are part of an architecture known as the Component Object Model (COM). It is a general architecture that lays the foundation on which OLE is based on. It establishes common models for interaction among software, such as applications, library modules, system software, and more. Therefore, COM can be implemented with almost any kind of software technology using the guideline layout.

There are a number of books on the subject of OLE, ActiveX, and COM. They go into greater detail on their differences, their similarities, their object models and guidelines, and how they fit in with client/server development. Books such as *Understanding ActiveX and OLE* (Microsoft Press, 1996) and *Visual Basic 6 Client/Server How-To* (Waite Group Press, 1998) just to name a few.

Before you start looking at all of the major technologies that make up OLE, study a few OLE terms to make the discussion more meaningful:

- Compound documents—Documents that contain data from more than one application.
- OLE object—Data that is stored or linked in a compound document, for example, a spreadsheet, a Word document, or a sound file.

- Automation—This makes it possible for one application to manipulate objects implemented in another application, or to *expose* objects so they can be manipulated.
- Visual editing—Objects that activate in place and can be edited without manually switching to another application.

OLE enables you to display and use data from other applications and to edit data from the applications that created them. And OLE enables you to include functionality and objects found in other applications. Consider some of the different ways OLE is used.

Some of the ActiveX terms you should know to make the discussion more meaningful are

- Container/control/client application—An application that can create and manage OLE objects or an ActiveX component.
- Server/object application—An application that creates OLE objects or an ActiveX client.

Compound Documents

Compound documents are an integral part of OLE. They can contain information from a number of different applications—such information as audio tracks, spreadsheet calculations, and word-processed text all within one document. A document can contain data from several applications, and through the technique of linking and embedding, you access the data through a single interface, rather than several different interfaces.

Object Linking and Embedding

Object linking and embedding enables you to create applications that are document centered. You can work with data from several applications without having to exit your application. Object linking and embedding enables you to work with applications with which you are already familiar.

What is the main difference between a linked object and an embedded object? Figure 16.1 shows an example of a linked object.

When an object is linked, the container application contains a pointer or reference to the object and the actual data. If the object is modified, the application that created the object saves the data. Linking a document is useful when you want to share the same data across many users or with different applications. If the linked object is changed by one application, other applications linking to the object will have the changed data. Also, the data can be changed within the host application, which is Excel in this example. Note that to link an Excel chart, Excel must be running and accessible from both computers.

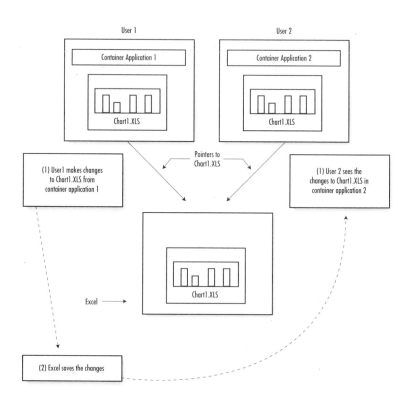

FIGURE 16.1

A linked object.

Figure 16.2 shows an embedded object. With an embedded object, the data exists within the container application. When the object is first created, the object's data is copied into the container application, and no other applications have access to the data. If an application modifies an embedded document, other applications do not see the changes. Embedded objects travel with the container applications. Use embedded objects when you want to display and edit data that was created in another application, while still wanting to maintain the data in its original source file. Unlike a linked object, any changes made to the original source file will not be reflected in the file that contains the embedded information.

Note   Embedded or linked, the objects you access with OLE are accessed by way of a server. The server for an Excel chart, for example, is Excel. Your user must have Excel installed on their system or network in order to use the embedded chart.

FIGURE 16.2

An embedded object.

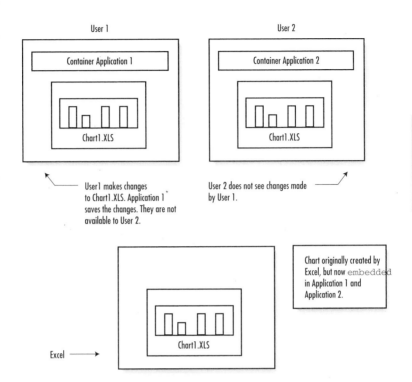

OLE Objects

An OLE object is a component of an application that can be used by another application. A spreadsheet, Word document, and a sound file are examples of OLE objects. Later in this chapter you will find out how to find the OLE objects on your system and how to use them in an application.

Automation

Automation (formerly known as *OLE automation*) is a standard that allows applications to expose their objects and methods so that other applications can use them. Examples include Microsoft Word's spell checker and Excel's calculating capabilities. Sound confusing? Automation is covered in detail in Lesson 3, and Lesson 5 uses automation to integrate Microsoft Word's spell checker into the Notepad application developed in Chapter 12, "Reading and Writing Disk Files."

Visual Editing

Visual editing enables you to edit an OLE object without having to switch to the application that created the object. Embedded objects support visual editing, whereas linked objects do not support it.

Custom Controls

Custom controls have been around since Visual Basic Version 1. They are optional functions that can be added to your toolbar and used on your form's user interface. In VB versions 1 through 3 and version 4 (16-bit), these controls were called VBXs, which stands for Visual Basic eXtensions. Visual Basic version 5 and later use the custom control known as an OCX, which originated from OLE Custom Control, but is now called an ActiveX control.

Even though ActiveX OCX controls look and act like the corresponding VBX controls, they are actually very different. VBXs are tied to the 16-bit architecture of Windows 3.x, and cannot take advantage of the advances in 32-bit Windows. VBXs are fast and use Windows messaging for communication. However, VBXs are not portable to 32-bit and have limited application support. The OCX, however, is based on ActiveX technology. OCXs communicate via OLE interfaces, are 32-bit, and can work with any OLE enabled application.

OCXs are as fast as VBXs because they are implemented as an in-process ActiveX server, meaning that the OCX and the application share the same memory address space so that communication is not across applications, but within the same application.

ActiveX DLLs and Servers

An ActiveX DLL or Server, formerly known as an OLE DLL and OLE Server, contains ActiveX components that can be reused by other applications. An ActiveX DLL, like an ActiveX control, is implemented as an in-process ActiveX component. This means that it and the application that is using it share the same memory address space. ActiveX servers are implemented as an out-of-process ActiveX component, which means that it and the application that is referencing it use their own memory address.

What About DDE?

So what about Dynamic Data Exchange (DDE)? After all, DDE enables you to share data between two applications and is a form of interprocess communication. When do you use DDE over OLE, or vice versa?

Both OLE and DDE provide a method of direct interprocess communication and enable you to display data from other applications and use functions from other applications. However, the capabilities of the two technologies are very different. (OLE is the most able technology.) The following is a comparison:

- DDE exchanges data via a conversation (link) between two applications. While data is being exchanged between the two applications, control is not automatically switched between them. In OLE, control actually transfers to the OLE server application temporarily while the data is being modified.

- DDE does not permit you to display the data from one application as it appears in another application, but OLE allows data from one application to be displayed in another application as it appears in the original application.

- DDE does not provide a method to modify the data from one application in another application. Instead, modifications must be made by sending data and commands between the two applications. OLE provides an interface to another application's objects and methods that can be used programmatically to control the objects. Also, OLE allows the user to edit and modify the data directly from your application using the application menus and methods from the application that created the object.

Lesson Summary

In general, always use OLE instead of DDE; use DDE only in cases where OLE is not yet supported by the application. Nowadays, almost every application supports OLE. OLE is one of Microsoft's standards for an application to be a certified Windows 95 and Windows NT application. You should now have a better understanding of OLE, ActiveX, and their capabilities.

In the next lesson, you will learn how to integrate an OLE Object to your application using the OLE Container Control.

Quiz 1

1. Which of the following is not part of OLE technology?

   a. OCX

   b. OLE automation

   c. Embedding documents

   d. OLE DDE exchange

2. _____ is the equivalent of the VBX it replaced.

    a. ActiveX server

    b. OCX

    c. Automation

    d. OLE container

3. A _____ document can be shared by many applications. Modifications are saved by the application that created the object, and the changes are reflected in the other applications.

    a. Linked

    b. Embedded

    c. OLE automation

    d. Container

4. An embedded document is created from CHART1.XLS. Application 1 modifies the chart significantly. Application 2 then creates an embedded document from CHART1.XLS. The chart displayed in application 1 is

    a. Different than the chart display in application 2.

    b. The same as the chart displayed in application 2.

    c. Invalid because application 2 cannot use CHART1.XLS after application 1 saved the modification.

    d. The same, when application 2 does an OLE refresh.

LESSON 2

Using the OLE Container Control

This lesson demonstrates how to use the OLE container control provided by Visual Basic to integrate object and linking capabilities into your applications. The OLE container control is shown in Figure 16.3.

The OLE container control enables you to link or embed objects from other applications by providing a place to insert objects into your Visual Basic application or display objects you create at runtime. Here are some of the OLE container control properties you will be using.

FIGURE 16.3

The OLE custom control.

The `Class` Property

The `Class` property is used to set or return the class of an embedded object. For example, the class of the embedded Excel chart shown in Figure 16.2 is Excel.Chart.8. The class name identifies the object you are embedding.

> The `Class` property is dependent on the product version you are using. Many software vendors try to keep the `Class` property names independent from the version number to ensure compatibility with multiple product versions.

The `Object` Property

The `Object` property is used to access the methods or properties of an embedded object. It is a read-only property and is not visible in the Properties window.

The `OLEType` Property

The `OLEType` property is available only at runtime and can be used to determine whether the container control is empty or contains a linked or embedded object. Because it is a runtime-only property, it does not appear in the Properties window.

`OLETypeAllowed`

`OLETypeAllowed` can be set at runtime or design time and determines the type of object the container control can contain: linked, embedded, or either.

Using the OLE Container Control to Link and Embed Data

This project helps you learn how to use the OLE container for visual editing, linking, and embedding documents. The following examples use Microsoft Excel 97 and Microsoft Word 97. If you do not have these applications, you will still be able to use the OLE container control using whatever OLE objects are available on your PC.

16

Note

> Don't feel compelled that you have to have the latest version of Microsoft Excel or Word. If you didn't jump on the upgrade bandwagon to Excel 97 or Word 97 and are still using Excel 95 or Word 95, a lot of the steps in this lesson still apply. Also, if you're using a different spreadsheet or word processor other than Microsoft's, as long as its OLE enabled, the concepts still apply, but the object models will vary.

Start a new project and name it LearnOLE. The LearnOLE application will consist of a single form with two OLE container controls, a few command buttons, labels, and text boxes. The objects in the OLE containers of the LearnOLE application are

- An embedded Excel chart to demonstrate embedded documents, visual editing, and in-place activation
- A linked Word document to demonstrate the differences between linking and embedding

To keep things simple and fast, all the OLE container control's objects will be inserted at design time instead of at runtime. Set the properties on the form and objects shown in Table 16.1.

TABLE 16.1   Object and Property Settings for Project LearnOLE

Object	Property	Setting
Form	Caption	VB 6 Interactive Course Learn OLE
	Height	6630
	Name	frmLearnOLE
	Width	6810
Label1	Caption	Class
	Height	315
	Left	2550
	Name	lblClass
	Top	5440
	Width	600

Object	Property	Setting
ComboBox	Height	315
	Left	705
	Name	cboOLE
	Style	2 - Dropdown List
	Top	5400
	Width	1680
TextBox	Height	315
	Left	3195
	Name	txtClass
	Top	5400
	Width	2640

Add the menu items shown in Table 16.2.

TABLE 16.2   Menu for `frmLearnOLE`

Menu Name	Caption
mnuFile	&File
mnuEdit	&Edit

Add an OLE container control to the form. The Insert Object dialog box, shown in Figure 16.4, appears.

FIGURE 16.4

The Insert Object dialog box.

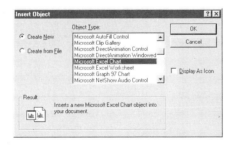

The Insert Object dialog box appears every time you add an OLE control, and is used to insert embedded or linked objects in the container control at design time. Select an object to place in the container control from the list of available objects. If it is available on your PC, select Microsoft Excel Chart. Check the Create New option in the Insert Object dialog box and click the OK button. You have just created an embedded object in the OLE container control. Set the properties for the OLE control as shown in Table 16.3. If Microsoft Excel Chart is not available, you should select an object such as a Wordpad document. At least this way, you can still see automation in action.

TABLE 16.3 Property Settings for OLE Control with an Embedded Excel Chart

Object	Property	Setting
OLE	Height	2550
	Left	645
	Name	oleEmbed
	Top	330
	Width	5340

Add another OLE container control to the application. This time, select the option Create From File on the Insert Object dialog box. If you have Microsoft Word, select the file that comes with this book, `learnole.doc`, or select any document on your PC. After you have selected the file, check the Link box to link the document instead of embedding the document. Click the OK button and the object container will be added to the form. Set the properties for the OLE control as shown in Table 16.4.

TABLE 16.4 Property Settings for OLE Control with a Linked Word Document

Object	Property	Setting
OLE	Height	1980
	Left	645
	Name	oleLink
	Top	3165
	Width	5340

Add the code shown in Listing 16.1 to the form load event.

LISTING 16.1   `frmLearnOLE FormLoad` Event Code

```
Private Sub Form_Load()

        'Add The Following the Combo Box
        cboOLE.AddItem "Link"
        cboOLE.AddItem "Embed"
        cboOLE.ListIndex = 0

End Sub
```

Add the code in Listing 16.2 to the `Click` event of the `ComboBox` to display the `Class` of the selected OLE container control.

LISTING 16.2   `cboOLE ComboBox Click` Event Code

```
Private Sub cboOLE_Click()

        'Display the Object class in the
        'text box - toggle value with the
        'Combo box
        If cboOLE.Text = "Link" Then
            txtClass.Text = oleLink.Class
        Else
            txtClass.Text = oleEmbed.Class
        End If

End Sub
```

Now run the application. First, select Embed in the drop combo box list. Notice the format of the `Class` property, displayed in the text box control for the selected OLE control. Now, activate the embedded object, the Excel chart, by double-clicking the OLE container control. What happened? You have activated the object in the container and invoked visual editing. A border appears around the container control signifying that the control has been activated and that the menu options for the LearnOLE application have been replaced with Excel's menu options, as shown in Figure 16.5.

You can use the menu options in your application as if you were using Excel instead of your application. Try it. Use the menu options to change the chart from 2D to 3D by selecting the Format menu option and then selecting Chart Type. Try some of the other Chart Type options, too.

FIGURE 16.5

The LearnOLE application replaced with Microsoft Excel.

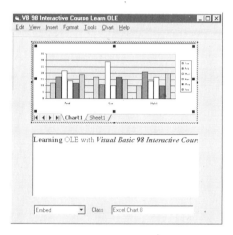

To return the LearnOLE application back to normal, press the Esc key on your keyboard. The menu bar will return back to its original settings of only File and Edit. You might have noticed that they had disappeared when the Excel chart was activated. What is occurring is the embedded object is negotiating menu space with the existing menu bar.

To make your application's menu co-exist with the embedded application's menus, you need to set the NegotiatePosition property in the Menu Editor. This property has four settings:

- None—The host application will not display that menu item when the OLE application is active.
- Left—The host application will place its menu at the left-most position on the menu bar.
- Middle—The host application will place its menu item somewhere in the middle of the OLE application's menu bar.
- Right—The host application will place its menu item at the right-most position on the OLE application's menu bar.

Let's look at the difference between embedded and linked documents. To do so, double-click the OLE container control that holds the Word document. What happens? Microsoft Word is activated and becomes the active window. You can modify the linked document using Microsoft Word. To see this in action, change some text to bold and add something. Then save the changes in Word and exit from Word. What's displayed in the OLE container control after you changed the information? The changed information appears in the OLE container control, of course.

How would you save information in the embedded worksheet? Because the worksheet is embedded, Visual Basic code must be used to save the data to a file and to read the data back at application startup. Do this with the OLE container control methods `SaveToFile` and `ReadFromFile`.

This lesson clearly demonstrates the difference between linked and embedded documents. It also shows the one weakness in OLE linking and embedding: when you activate an OLE document, the OLE container (program) must be loaded before you can edit the document. The very perceptible delay makes your application seem sluggish. You can improve the appearance of speed by using the `Shell` function to load the OLE server for linked documents while your splash screen is showing. The following code loads Word, but leaves it minimized and keeps the focus in your application:

```
Dim dWordID As Double
    dWordID = Shell("C:\MSOFFICE\WINWORD\WINWORD.EXE", vbMinimizedNoFocus)
```

Lesson Summary

This lesson explained how to use the OLE Container Control to link and embed other OLE objects, such as a spreadsheet's worksheet or word processor's document, within your own application. By using this control, you give the OLE objects a placeholder to display their information. Also keep in mind the menu negotiation that takes place within your application with activated OLE objects. If you don't consider how they will be laid out within your menu structure, you can cause confusion to your users.

In the next lesson, you will learn more about OLE objects and how their automation effects the applications they are part of.

Quiz 2

1. The OLE container control enables you to

   a. Easily link and embed OLE documents

   b. Turn your application into an OLE server

   c. Contain OLE applications such as Microsoft Word and Excel

   d. Perform visual editing on a linked document

2. The correct way to represent an Excel Version 5 chart in the `Class` property of an OLE container control is

   a. 5.Chart.Excel

   b. Excel.Chart.5

   c. Microsoft.Excel5.Chart

   d. Excel5.Chart

3. A ____ document supports visual editing.

   a. Linked

   b. Stored

   c. OLE automation

   d. Embedded

4. When an OLE embedded document is activated, the ____ take the appearance of the object creating application.

   a. Form

   b. Menu

   c. Buttons

   d. Text boxes

Exercise 2

Complexity: Moderate

1. Write a program that uses two OLE container controls. Select an OLE object such as a Microsoft Word document or an Excel spreadsheet and link the object to one OLE container control and embed the object in the other control. Run the program and experiment with the differences between a linked and an embedded object.

Complexity: Moderate

2. Add the code to save the changes of the embedded object.

LESSON 3

What Is Automation?

This lesson examines automation. To gain an understanding of what OLE automation is all about, consider the concept of exposed objects.

Exposed Objects

Look to your bank for a good example of exposed objects. As a bank customer, you can go into the lobby of the bank to do your banking, depositing or withdrawing money and checking your account balance. Before computers, that was the only way you could do your banking. Now computers have revolutionized banking; you can use an automatic teller to handle most of your banking chores.

If you think about your bank account as an object and the functions you perform, withdrawing and depositing money, as the methods of the bank account object, then what did the bank do with the ATM? It provided its customers with a programmable interface to execute the methods of the bank account object.

Thinking in OLE programming terms, the bank account is an object with methods, and the ATM is a controlling application that has access to some of the bank account methods. The object (bank account) and methods (deposit) which the bank gives the ATM access to are called exposed objects. Exposed objects are objects that exist in one application and are made available to other applications.

Let's describe another example to make sure that you understand the idea of exposed objects.

Figure 16.6 shows a cartoon figure of a word processor application. The application is holding out two objects, a document object and a drawing object. A third object, the file object, is hidden inside of the word processor with Off Limits and No Trespassing signs. The document and drawing objects are public objects. A public object is an object that can be used by outside applications. The file object, which is hidden in Figure 16.6, is a private object. A private object is not exposed and cannot be used by outside applications.

FIGURE 16.6

A word processor with exposed objects.

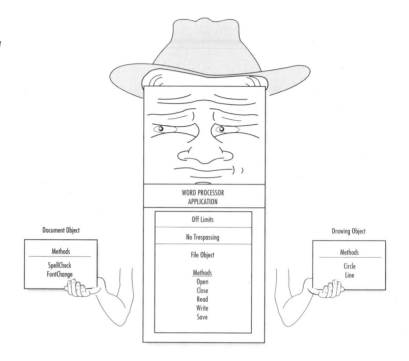

Building with Components

Now you know what an exposed object is, but what use is it? Think about another real world example: a car. A car is a great object that helps you get to and from your favorite places. It also gets you to the dentist, but you can forgive that, can't you?

Once again, think in terms of objects and pieces, or components, this time in terms of a car. A car is built from many different parts and components. A car manufacturer selects many different parts and integrates them to build a car. When you buy the car, you have the capability to modify some of the components that make up your car. You may not like the tires the manufacturer used, so you can swap them for a set of different tires, perhaps a set of racing tires. The point is, in the real world many different objects are built from existing objects to create other objects.

Using OLE, programmers can build software applications in the same way a manufacturer builds a car. The programmer can integrate software components from existing applications into totally new programs. The developer makes component choices, such as selecting a spell-checking component for text editing applications or a graphing component for number-crunching applications. The OLE components that developers so easily integrate into applications are exposed objects from other applications, and the technology that enables an application to create and manipulate these exposed objects is OLE automation.

Automation

Automation enables you to integrate functionality into your application that you may not be capable of writing or may not want to write. Figure 16.7 shows an example of an application using an existing spreadsheet and word processor spell checker via automation. Controlling applications, sometimes referred to as OLE clients, use the exposed objects to perform tasks, such as creating new objects, getting existing objects, setting object properties, or using object methods.

FIGURE 16.7

Automation.

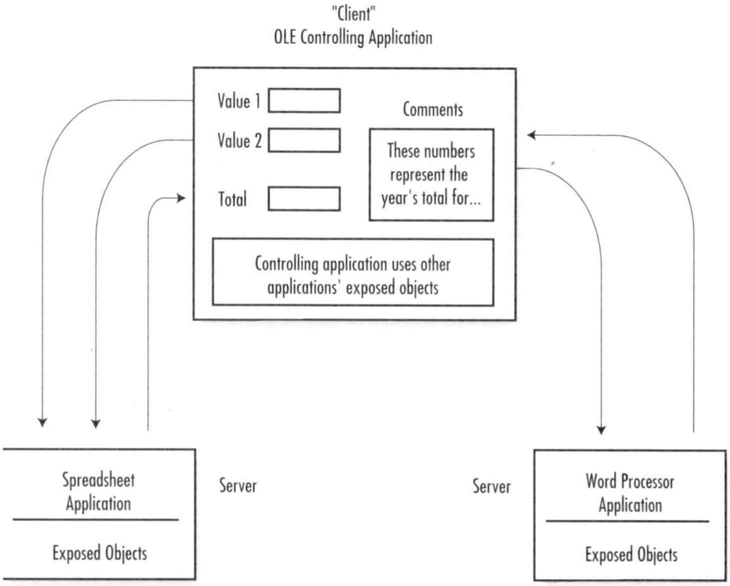

"Client"
OLE Controlling Application

Value 1

Value 2

Total

Comments

These numbers represent the year's total for...

Controlling application uses other applications' exposed objects

Server

Spreadsheet Application

Exposed Objects

Server

Word Processor Application

Exposed Objects

In Figure 16.7, the controlling application uses an existing spreadsheet to compute a total for two numbers and uses the word processor's spell checker to check the spelling of a comment's text box. The object's application shown in Figure 16.7, sometimes referred to as an *OLE server* or *ActiveX Server*, exposes objects and methods to be used by other applications.

OLE servers can be applications in their own right, like Microsoft Word and Microsoft Excel, or they may exist only to support client applications. Automation enables programmers to use existing code from any OLE server without having to rewrite the code.

The use of OLE components follows the object-oriented approach of reusable code, data encapsulation, and easy integration.

In order for an application to be an OLE Server as well as a standalone application like Microsoft Word, the type of Visual Basic project you would create is called an ActiveX EXE. When you create a new project, select the ActiveX EXE icon from the New Project window, as shown in Figure 16.8.

FIGURE 16.8

ActiveX EXE selected in the New Project window.

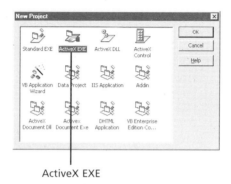

ActiveX EXE

During the course of an application's development cycle, you may discover that the Standard EXE project you've been developing could also be used within other application. To turn your Standard EXE into an OLE server, you don't have to scrap all your hard work and start over. You simply change the Project Type property. To change this property, select the Project's Properties from the Project menu. In the General tab of the Project Properties window, Change the Project Type property from Standard EXE to ActiveX EXE, as shown in Figure 16.9.

FIGURE 16.9

Changing the property type from Standard EXE to ActiveX EXE.

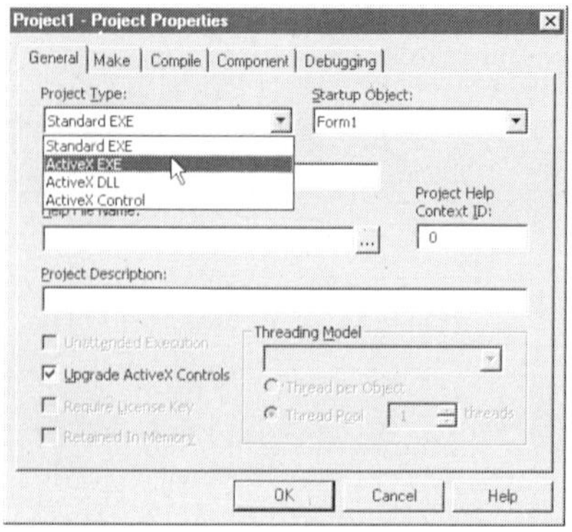

Unfortunately, there is a lot more involved into creating an ActiveX EXE than just changing the Project Type property. Not to tease you, but you will learn how to create an ActiveX EXE later in this chapter in Lesson 6.

Lesson Summary

This lesson reviewed the concept of automation. Visual Basic can be used to create OLE controlling/client applications or OLE object application/servers. Remember that you can only create ActiveX Servers in the Professional and Enterprise editions of Visual Basic. In Lesson 6, you will learn how to create an ActiveX server and use automation to test out the server. But for you get knee deep into something that advanced, there are still some things you need to learn about Objects and their hierarchy, which will be covered in the next lesson.

Quiz 3

1. _____ exist in one application and are made available to other applications.

   a. Private objects

   b. Private properties

   c. OLE properties

   d. Exposed objects

2. An advantage to using objects is that you can create applications:

   a. Using existing software components

   b. Writing existing objects over again

   c. With Visual Basic, writing the application from scratch

   d. Using DLLs instead of objects

3. _____ enable the developer to manipulate objects exposed by other applications.

   a. Linked documents

   b. Embedded documents

   c. OLE automation

   d. Object classes

4. An OLE controlling application is also referred to as a:

    a. OLE server

    b. Linked document

    c. Embedded document

    d. OLE client

LESSON 4

Object Hierarchy and the Object Browser

Before you start using automation in your Visual Basic programs, you must first understand the object hierarchy of the application objects you want to use. The object hierarchy is like a road map. If you wanted to go from your hometown to a city called Visual Basic City several hundred miles away, you would get out a road map to find the correct highways and roads to take. The road map also provides the names of cities and towns along the way where you can stop for meals or lodging.

The object hierarchy of an application provides you with the exposed objects available to your application and with the route to take to get the correct object. In other words, it is a road map of the object. The hierarchy for Excel is shown in Figure 16.10.

FIGURE 16.10

The object hierarchy of Microsoft Excel.

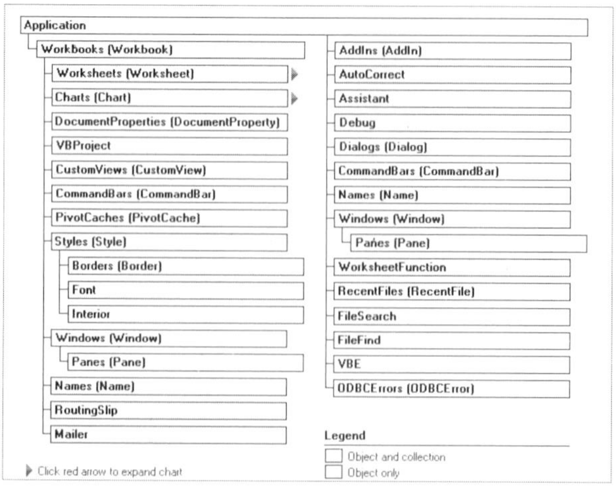

The Legend key shows that the Workbook is part of a collection. The hierarchy also shows the member objects of an Excel Workbook. If you expand the `Worksheet` object, the `Range` object appears. The hierarchy of the `Range` object is shown in Figure 16.11.

FIGURE 16.11

The object hierarchy of the Excel's Range *object.*

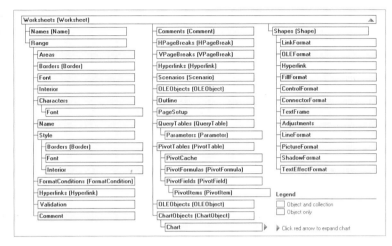

Here's how you figure out the hierarchy diagram in Figure 16.11:

- The `Parent` object, which is Application, is at the top of the hierarchy.
- According to the key, the `Workbook` object is an object and a collection. When that is the case, the name of the collection is the plural of the name of the object. Then, the hierarchy so far is `Application.Worksheets.Worksheet`.
- The `Range` object is an object of `Worksheet`. Thus, the hierarchy of the `Range` object so far is `Application.Worksheets.Worksheet.Range`.

And now you know why people draw hierarchy diagrams instead of trying to describe them in words!

The last concept you need to understand about the object hierarchy is the concept of dependent objects. A *dependent* object is an object in the hierarchy that cannot be created or accessed by itself but is created by using a method of the object on which it is dependent.

In Figure 16.11, the `Range` object is a dependent object of the `Worksheet` object. You cannot access or create an Excel `Range` object; instead, you must create a Worksheet object and then use the Range method to create a Range object. The object hierarchy may seem a bit complex at first, but Visual Basic 5 provides you with a tool to access and navigate that hierarchy, called the Object Browser.

Using the Object Browser

The Object Browser enables you to view exposed objects from other applications as well as classes from object libraries and procedures contained in your Visual Basic project. The following examples use the Object Browser to browse Microsoft Excel's object hierarchy. If you do not have Excel, don't worry. Select any available object and follow through the various exercises. The goal of this section is to teach you how to use the Object Browser to integrate exposed application objects into your applications. First, add Excel or another object to your References profile:

1. Select the Project menu from the Visual Basic menu bar.

2. Select References.

   The References dialog box, shown in Figure 16.12, appears.

FIGURE 16.12

The Visual Basic References dialog box.

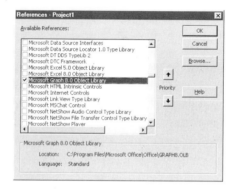

3. If you have Microsoft Excel Version 5 or greater installed on your system, you should see at least a check box that's titled Microsoft Excel 5.0 Object Library. Check the check box of the latest Excel object library if it is not already checked, and click the OK button.

Now you are ready to use the Object Browser to explore Excel's object hierarchy. Click the Object Browser button on the Visual Basic toolbar. The icon is shown in Figure 16.13.

FIGURE **16.13**

The Object Browser button on the Visual Basic menu bar.

Object Browser

Note

If the Object Browser is missing from your toolbar, you can use the Customize option to place it there. You can also open the Object Browser with F2 or from the View menu.

The Object Browser, shown in Figure 16.14, appears.

FIGURE **16.14**

The Object Browser.

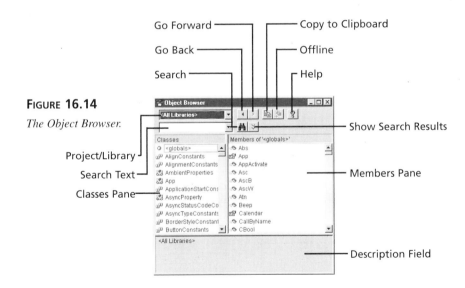

To view Excel's object module, do the following:

1. Select Excel from the Project/Library drop-down list box. This will display all of Excel's the objects and constants.

2. Scroll through the Classes list box and find the Range object.

3. Click the `Range` object. The methods and properties for the object are displayed in the Members of list box. The key to the icons in the list box is shown in Figure 16.15.

FIGURE 16.15

The icon legend for the Members list.

Method
Property
Event
Constant

4. Click the Object Browser's Help button to view the hierarchy of the `Range` object, or

5. Scroll through the Members list and select the member of the property for which you need help. Then click the Object Browser's Help button to bring up detailed help information on the selected method, property, or object.

The help file for objects offers more help than you might think. Figure 16.16 shows the help screen for the `Range` object. The hierarchy is shown at the top. Each item in the hierarchy is a hyperlink that takes you to the help file for that part of the hierarchy. The last item in the hierarchy diagram is labeled Multiple Objects. Clicking that link opens a list of the member objects of the `Range` object.

FIGURE 16.16

The member objects of Excel's `Range` object.

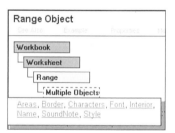

Lesson Summary

All objects have a hierarchy upon which they are built. The hierarchy defines the attributes that make up the entire object. This lesson introduced the concept of an Object Hierarchy and through the use of the Object Browser, you can see pieces of the hierarchy. In the Visual Basic Books Online, you will find a lot of basic object hierarchy. To find other object hierarchies for Microsoft products, refer to the Microsoft Developers Network Library CD and companion Web site (`http://www.microsoft.com/msdn`) to find more information.

If you plan to develop applications using automation with Microsoft Office products, the next lesson will cover using automation with Microsoft Word and Excel in greater depth.

Quiz 4

1. _____ is like a road map that describes objects exposed by applications.

    a. The object map

    b. The object file

    c. The Object Browser

    d. The object hierarchy

2. _____ is a container for other objects. An example is the Microsoft Excel object `Charts`.

    a. An OLE group

    b. An OLE set

    c. A collection object

    d. An object hierarchy

3. _____ cannot be created or accessed by itself, but is created using a method of another object.

    a. A dependent object

    b. A public object

    c. A group object

    d. An independent object

4. _____ enables you to view exposed objects from other applications.

    a. The Object Browser

    b. The Project Viewer

    c. The Object Viewer

    d. The Class Wizard

Exercise 4

Complexity: Easy

1. Create a Standard EXE project and add the Microsoft ActiveX Data Object 2.0 Library and list the members of the `Fields` class.

Complexity: Easy

2. Create a Standard EXE project and add the reference to the Microsoft ActiveMovie Control. Identify the members of the StateContants and their respective constant values.

LESSON 5

Using OLE Automation with Microsoft Word and Excel

This lesson shows how to use OLE automation to integrate Microsoft Word and Microsoft Excel into your applications. Using OLE automation requires five steps:

1. Determine the type of object to use.

   Before you can use an OLE automation object, you must determine the type of object you want to use. Use the Object Browser and the Reference dialog box to determine the OLE objects available to you, and pick the one you need to do the job.

2. Declare an object variable for the object.

   You must declare a variable to store the object. If you have an object library (type library) in the Reference dialog box for the object, you can define the type of object your application will contain at design time. For instance, if you want to use a Microsoft Project Task object, and you have Microsoft Project's object library checked in the References dialog box, you can define an object variable in the following manner:

   ```
   Dim MyTask As Task
   ```

   You are telling the compiler that the variable MyTask will contain a Microsoft Project Task object. If you try to use the variable MyTask to hold an Excel Worksheet object, Visual Basic returns a runtime error message. This method of object declaration is known as early binding because Visual Basic determines the type of object the variable will hold during compilation.

   What do you do if you don't have an object library for the application or if you are not sure of the object type? You can define the variable using the Object data type as follows:

   ```
   Dim MyTask as Object
   ```

Using the `Object` data type is called late binding. When it uses late binding, Visual Basic does not know the object type the variable will contain until the object is created at runtime.

Whenever possible, use early binding when referencing objects. It offers efficiencies in speed because the compiler will know what object library to use and if the method or property you're referencing is available during the program compilation stage rather than at runtime. With late binding, the validation of the object doesn't occur until the program is executed.

3. Get an existing object or create a new object.

   To create a new object, use the command `CreateObject`. The syntax is

   ```
   CreateObject(class)
   ```

   `class` is the class of the object to create.

   The `class` parameter has the following format:

   ```
   appname.objecttype
   ```

   `appname` is the application name, and `objecttype` is the object or class to create.

   For example:

   ```
   Set wd = CreateObject("Word.Basic")
   ```

   To use an existing object, such as a Word document or an Excel spreadsheet, use the command `GetObject`, which has the following syntax:

   ```
   GetObject([pathname][, class])
   ```

   `pathname` is the full path and filename of the object, and `class` is the type of class or object.

   For example:

   ```
   Set wd = GetObject("Word.Basic")
   ```

4. Use the object's properties and methods.

   When you have an instance of the object, use any of the available properties and methods. For example, using an Excel application object:

   ```
   Xl.Visible = True
   ```

5. Close the object, if required, and then release the instance of the object.

When you have completed your task and you no longer need the object, you sometimes must close the object with the close method, and you must always release the object by setting the object variable to `Nothing`. For example:

```
Set Xl = Nothing
```

So let's test what you've just learned. The first project uses OLE automation by integrating Microsoft Word's spell checker into a previous application, the Notepad application developed in Chapter 12, "Reading and Writing Disk Files." Microsoft Word has a very simple object model that has only a single object, the Basic object. All methods and commands for Word are part of the Basic object. This project adds a single routine to the Notepad application. That routine uses Word.Basic to check the spelling of the text in the Notepad, making spelling corrections and then replacing the text in Notepad with the corrected text.

Start by creating a new Standard EXE project. Right-click Form1 in the Project Explorer and remove the form from the project. Right-click in the Project Explorer window again, and use Add File to add frmNotePad from the Notepad project in Chapter 12. Then add File.cls from the same directory. Now open the Project menu and select Project Properties. Change the Startup form to frmNotePad. Finally, use SaveAs to save the project, the form, and the class to a new directory. Name the project SpellPad. (And now you know one way to reuse objects you have already created!)

Add the menu option shown in Table 16.5 to frmNotePad.

TABLE 16.5   Menu Properties for frmNotePad

Caption	Name
&Tools	mnuTools
&Spelling	mnuSpelling

Add the code shown in Listing 16.3 to mnuSpelling_Click.

LISTING 16.3   mnuSpelling_Click Event Code

```
Private Sub mnuSpelling_Click()

    Dim oWord As Object            ' Generic Object Type

    On Error GoTo Word_Error
    If txtBuffer.Text = "" Then
      MsgBox "Notepad is empty - need text to check spelling.", _
          MB_ICONSTOP, "Empty NotePad"
      Exit Sub
    End If

    'Check all of the Text in the NotePad Text box
```

```
    'Create Word object and assign it to object variable

    Set oWord = CreateObject("Word.Basic")

    'Use WordBasic functions as methods of the object
    oWord.FileNewDefault          'Create a New File in Word

    oWord.StartOfDocument         'Move to the start of the document
    oWord.Insert txtBuffer.Text   'Insert the notepad text
    oWord.EditSelectAll           'Select all of the text
    On Error Resume Next          'Ignore Word's message box
    oWord.ToolsSpelling           'Invoke the Spell Checker
    On Error GoTo Word_Error
    oWord.StartOfDocument         'Go to the start of the document
    oWord.EditSelectAll           'Select all of the text
    oWord.EditCut                 'Cut the text to the clip board

    'place the text back in the notepad
    'from the clipboard

    txtBuffer.Text = Clipboard.GetText(vbCFText)

    oWord.FileClose 2       'Close the file without saving
    oWord.FileExit          ' Close the application
    Set oWord = Nothing     'Release the object
EndWordDemo:
    Exit Sub

'Error handler
Word_Error:
    MsgBox Error$(Err)
    If Not (oWord Is Nothing) Then
        'Close Word and release the Object Variable
        oWord.FileClose 2
        Set oWord = Nothing
    End If
    Resume EndWordDemo

End Sub
```

Test the spell-checking feature with the SpellPad application. Enter some text in the SpellPad and select the spelling option under the Tools menu. What happens? Microsoft Word starts up and all of the text in the notepad is selected and placed in a Word document. Word then checks the spelling of the text, prompting you for any changes, as shown in Figure 16.17. When all of the spelling has been checked, the corrected text in the Word document is cut to the clipboard and pasted back into the Notepad. Then

Microsoft Word is closed (without saving the document), and the object variable is released.

FIGURE **16.17**

Microsoft Word's spell checker in action via OLE automation.

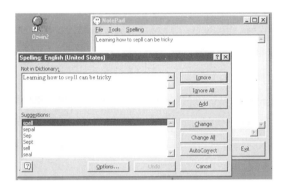

Where Is the Word Basic **Object?**

If you spent any time at all looking for the Basic object or for Microsoft Word with the Object Browser, you discovered that it is not there. How do you learn what objects and methods are in it? Well, if you want to use Word.Basic, open Macros in Word's Tools menu and select Word Commands. There they are: dozens of them—hundreds of them!

The simplest way to get them in the right order to do what you want to do is to record a macro in Word and copy it into your code window. Add your object reference, and it is done. (You probably will need to tweak it a little.)

Using Microsoft Excel

The next project uses OLE automation with Microsoft Excel. It creates a simple application that makes a new Excel worksheet, and then adds four values to the worksheet using the Range object. From those four values, it creates an Excel chart, makes the chart 3D, and rotates it. You can see OLE automation at work; the project makes Excel visible while it manipulates the Excel objects via OLE automation. (Ordinarily Excel would be left invisible.) After the chart is created and rotated, the program calls the Windows API Sleep, and "sleeps" for five seconds so you can view the chart. Finally, the program closes Excel without saving the worksheet or the chart, and sets the object to Nothing.

Begin by creating a new project named ExcelOLE, with a single form and a single command button. Set the properties for the form and command button according to Table 16.6.

TABLE 16.6 Object and Property Settings for ExcelOLE

Object	Property	Setting
Form	Caption	OLE Automation with Excel
	Height	3435
	Name	frmExcelOLE
	Width	5425
CommandButton	Caption	Control Excel
	Height	990
	Left	1320
	Name	cmdControlExcel
	Top	945
	Width	2535

Add the code shown in Listing 16.4 to the click event of the command button.

LISTING 16.4 Command Button Click Event Code to Control Excel via OLE Automation

```
Private Sub cmdControlExcel_Click()

    Dim Xl As Object
    Dim XlChart As Object
    Dim i As Integer

    On Error GoTo OLE_ERROR
    'Create Excel object
    Set Xl = CreateObject("Excel.Application")

    'Normally when using OLE Excel is invisible.
    'For demonstration purposes let's
    'toggle the visible property to True
    'so you can see the different events
    'taking place.
    Xl.Visible = True

    'Add an Excel Workbook
    Xl.Workbooks.Add

    'Put values into some cells using the Range object
```

continues

LISTING 16.4   continued

```
Xl.Range("a1").Value = 3
Xl.Range("a2").Value = 2
Xl.Range("a3").Value = 1
Xl.Range("a4").Value = 5

'Select the data in the cells
Xl.Range("A1:A4").Select

'Create a new chart
Set XlChart = Xl.Charts.Add()

'make the chart 3D Column
XlChart.Type = -4100 'xl constant for 3D Column chart

'rotate the chart
For i = 35 To 175 Step 10
   XlChart.rotation = i
Next

'Sleep for 5 seconds (Using the Sleep API) - so you can see
'the chart created via OLE Automation.
sleep (5000)

'Close the Workbook without saving - could save if we wanted.
'
' Note: Passing the parameter False suppresses the message box
' that asks if the spreadsheet is to be saved.
Xl.Workbooks.Close (False)

'Close Microsoft Excel with the Quit Method
Xl.Application.Quit

'Release the the object Variable
Set Xl = Nothing

EndDemo:
   Exit Sub

'Error handler
OLE_ERROR:
   MsgBox Error$(Err)
   If Not (Xl Is Nothing) Then

      'Close Excel and release the Object Variable
      Set Xl = Nothing
   End If
   Resume EndDemo
End Sub
```

Add a module to the project. Name it `ExcelOLE.bas` and add the following Windows API declaration in the declarations section of the module:

```
Declare Sub Sleep Lib "kernel32" (ByVal dwMilliseconds As Long)
```

Run the application, and click the Control Excel button. What happens? Excel begins to run and becomes visible when your program sets the `Application.Visible` property to `True`. Four values are added to cells in a worksheet. The four cells are selected, and a new chart, shown in Figure 16.18, is created from the values in the four cells. Excel then exits without saving any of the changes.

FIGURE 16.18

The Microsoft Excel chart created with OLE automation.

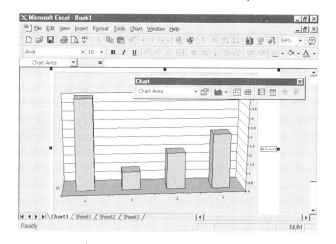

<table>
<tr><td>
Note
</td><td>
In Chapter 15, "Doing the Impossible (and More) with the Windows API," you learned how to get different API functions using the API Text Viewer. Refer to the first lesson to learn more about the API Text Viewer. To learn more about the different API functions, refer to Microsoft Software Developers Kit (SDK) either found online at `http://www.microsoft.com/mdsn` or the Microsoft Developers Network Library CD.

You may be wondering what object methods to use to perform a certain function. Here's a useful tip: If you are using Microsoft Word or Microsoft Excel, use their macro recorders to generate Visual Basic for Applications code. Start the macro recorder, perform the functions you want to do in the application, and then stop the macro recorder. You have now generated Visual Basic for Applications code. You can then copy the code into your Visual Basic applications!
</td></tr>
</table>

Lesson Summary

In this chapter, you learned how automation is done using Microsoft Word and Excel. The example application in this lesson used the concept of late binding to define the application object that was going to be used for automation. To learn more about automation, you should refer to Deborah Kurata's book *Doing Objects in Microsoft Visual Basic 6* (Sams Publishing, 1999). She discusses in great detail the uses of objects within a VB development environment as well as how to work with them.

Quiz 5

1. A _____ defines the type of objects and methods exposed by an application.

    a. Include file

    b. Header file

    c. Type library

    d. Declaration file

2. What does the following code do?

   ```
   Dim wd as Object
   Set wd = CreateObject("Word.Basic")
   ```

    a. Creates a Word Basic object.

    b. Nothing, because `CreateObject` is not a valid Visual Basic function.

    c. Creates a wd object.

    d. The syntax for the `CreateObject` is incorrect.

3. To release an OLE automation object:

    a. Set the object to zero.

    b. Close the object.

    c. Set the object's reference to `Nothing`.

    d. Set the object to `Empty`.

4. If you have an Excel application object variable `Xl`, what does the following code do?

   ```
   Xl.Workbooks.Add
   ```

    a. Executes an Excel macro called `Add`

    b. Adds an Excel workbook

    c. Reads the workbook collection

    d. Adds an `Application` object to the workbook

Exercise 5

Complexity: Moderate

1. Replicate the ExcelOLE project, but this time use early binding. Hint: Use `Excel.Application`

Complexity: Advanced

2. Either using SpellPad or Chapter 12's Notepad as a base, add printing to the application using Microsoft Word as the print engine. This means that all the text entered into your application will be printed using Word.

16

LESSON 6

Exposing Your Own Classes: Creating ActiveX Servers

In the last few lessons, you learned how to use exposed objects from other applications. Up to this point, you have used your Visual Basic programs as a controlling application. Building class modules and using object-oriented programming is valuable, but wouldn't it be great if you could create applications that exposed objects? Think of how easy it would be to reuse code! Maybe you wrote a great database security application, and you want to include the same functionality in a new application. If you can expose the objects in your security application, you can check database security from other applications without rewriting the code.

Visual Basic provides you with the capability to expose your classes and create ActiveX servers! This capability is found in the Visual Basic Professional and Enterprise editions. If you own the Learning Edition, you will not be able to create ActiveX servers, but the ability to create ActiveX servers is so important that you should read through and understand this section anyway.

Note | Important: For this programming exercise to work properly, it is important that you follow the steps in the exact order in which they are written.

The VBCalc Project: An Out-of-Process ActiveX Server

Start a new project, or load VBCalc.VBP from the CD files that come with this book. When the New Project dialog box appears, select ActiveX EXE. The project opens with a Class module and no forms. Open the Properties window, name the class clsCalculator, and set the Instancing property to 5 - Multiuse. This setting makes the class Public, which exposes it for use by other programs and allows several programs to use it at the same time. If you change the setting to 3 - Single Use, then each program that wants to use it must run a separate instance of VBCalc. If you change the setting to 1 - Private, then no programs can use the class except VBCalc.

Note | If you use the files from the CD, they must be copied to your hard disk first, because this project must write to the project's directory.

Open the Project menu and select Properties. Set the project properties according to Table 16.7.

TABLE 16.7   Project Property Settings for VBCalc

Tab	Property	Value
General	Project Type	ActiveX EXE
	Startup Object	(None)
	Project Name	VBCalc
	Project Description	4 Function Calculator
	Upgrade ActiveX Controls	Checked
Make	Title	VBCalc
	Type	Comments
	Value	Four Function
Calculator		OLE Demo
Compile	Compile to Native Code	Checked
	Optimize for Fast Code	Checked

On the Tools menu, select Options. Set the options according to Table 16.8.

TABLE 16.8   Option Settings for `VBCalc`

Tab	Setting	Value
Editor	Autolist Members	Checked
	Default to Full ModuleView	Checked
General	Compile on Demand	Checked
Environment	Prompt to Save Changes	Checked

Add the code in D16.5 to the Declarations section of `clsCalculator`.

LISTING 16.5   Public Property Declarations for `clsCalculator`

```
Option Explicit
Public Result As Double ' Class Property - Result
Public Enum CalcShowMode
    CalcModal = vbModal
    CalcModeless = vbModeless
End Enum
```

Add the Public procedures in Listing 16.6 to `clsCalculator`. These are the methods for the class.

LISTING 16.6   Methods for `clsCalculator`

```
Public Sub Add(x As Double, y As Double)
    If IsNumeric And IsNumeric Then
        Result = x + y
    End If
End Sub

Public Sub Multiply(x As Double, y As Double)
    If IsNumeric And IsNumeric Then
        Result = x * y
    End If
```

continues

LISTING 16.6 continued

```
End Sub

Public Sub Subtract(x As Double, y As Double)
    If IsNumeric And IsNumeric Then
        Result = x - y
    End If
End Sub

Public Sub Divide(x As Double, y As Double)
    On Error GoTo err_Divide
    If IsNumeric And IsNumeric Then
        Result = x / y
    End If
exit_Divide:
    Exit Sub
err_Divide:
    Result = 0
    Resume exit_Divide
End Sub
```

VBCalc is an out-of-process server. In other words, it is an .EXE file that is capable of running on its own, just like Word and Excel. Unlike those applications, however, it does not have a user interface. The following steps show that it is possible for an out-of-process server to display either modal or modeless forms, if needed.

First, select Add Form on the Project menu. Select Form from the dialog box that opens. Add a Command button to the form. Press f4 to open the Properties window, and set the form's properties according to Table 16.9.

TABLE 16.9 Properties for `frmVBCalc`

Object	Property	Value
Form	Name	frmVBCalc
	Caption	VBCalc Modal
	Left	0
	Top	0
	Height	930
	Width	2670
	MaxButton	False
	MinButton	False

Object	Property	Value
CommandButton	Name	cmdExit
	Caption	Exit
	Height	375
	Left	540
	Top	60
	Width	1515

16

Add the following lines of code to cmdExit_Click:

```
Private Sub cmdExit_Click()
    Unload Me
End Sub
```

That's all for the form, but now you must add code to clsCalculator to show the form. Add the code in Listing 16.7 as a new method for clsCalculator.

LISTING 16.7 The ShowForm Method for clsCalculator

```
Public Sub ShowForm(Optional Modality As _
    CalcShowMode = CalcModal)
    Dim frm As New frmVBCalc
    If Modality = CalcModeless Then
        frm.Caption = "VBCalc - Modeless"
    End If
    frm.Show Modality
End Sub
```

A Look at the Code

The methods of clsCalculator are pretty standard stuff. The code in the Divide method contains an error handler that sets Result to zero if a divide error occurs. Division causes more errors than the other simple math functions, so a bit of added safety isn't misplaced.

The ShowForm method uses the Enums to determine whether to show the form as a Modal or Modeless form. If the form is shown Modeless, the caption is changed.

Getting Ready to Run

Before you can use an out-of-process server, the system must have a reference to it, a reference EXE to help your test program maintain its connection to the server. To create your reference EXE, click Make VBCalc.Exe. You need to do this only once.

The program must register its public members with the system registry so your test program can find it. Running the EXE of an out-of-process server automatically registers it. You are not running the EXE, however, because debugging is almost impossible then. Instead, select Start With Full Compile from the Start menu, which does the same thing on a temporary basis.

That's it! You now have an ActiveX Server running. Nothing happened? Sure it did; it just doesn't show the way you're use to see it running. On a Windows 95/98 system, if you press Ctrl+Alt+Delete, you will see that VBCalc is running within the Close Program window. On a Windows NT system, if you bring up the Windows NT Task Manager by pressing Ctrl+Shift+Esc, you will see two entries for VBCalc, as shown in Figure 16.19. One is VBCalc-Microsoft Visual Basic [Run] and the other is just VBCalc. The first one refers to the Visual Basic IDE and the VBCalc project that is loaded within it. The fact that it has "[Run]" after it means that the IDE is currently running the project VBCalc. The VBCalc entry is the ActiveX Server running on the system. To ensure that the VBCalc is working properly, you need to create a program that references the ActiveX Server and uses the properties and methods you programmed.

FIGURE 16.19

Windows NT Task Manager showing VBCalc running.

The `TestCalc` Project

In order to test VBCalc, you must start another instance of Visual Basic. Before you do, minimize the one that is already running to help avoid confusion. (It can get very confusing!) Use the Windows Start menu to open another instance of Visual Basic. The new project will be a standard EXE.

On the Project menu, select References. The project description of VBCalc, 4 Function Calculator, appears in the References list. Select the one that lists its location as the VBP file. (If you select the EXE file, you will not be able to debug the project.) Click OK to add the new component to your project and make its methods and properties available to your code.

Open Options from the Tools menu and place a check on AutoList Members so you can see the new objects as you type.

Before you begin, press F2 and look for clsCalculator in the Object Browser. It is an example of how you can use the Object Browser to learn about programs that expose their objects for use.

Add seven Command buttons, three text boxes, and three labels to the form. Set the properties according to Table 16.10. (The sizes and positions are not listed in the table. Use Figure 16.20 as a guide, and use the Format menu to size and position the controls.)

FIGURE 16.20

Calculating with TestCalc.

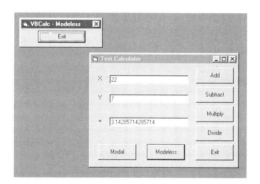

TABLE 16.10 The TestCalc Project

Object	Property	Value
Form	Name	frmTestCalc
	Caption	"Test Calculator"
CommandButton	Name	cmdAdd
	Caption	"Add"
CommandButton	Name	cmdSubtract
	Caption	"Subtract"
CommandButton	Name	cmdMultiply
	Caption	"Multiply"
CommandButton	Name	cmdDivide
	Caption	"Divide"

continues

TABLE 16.10 continued

Object	Property	Value
CommandButton	Name	cmdExit
	Caption	"Exit"
CommandButton	Name	cmdModal
	Caption	"Modal"
CommandButton	Name	cmdModeless
	Caption	"Modeless"
TextBox	Name	txtX
TextBox	Name	txtY
TextBox	Name	txtResult
Label	Name	lblX
	Caption	"X"
Label	Name	lblY
	Caption	"Y"
Label	Name	lblResult
	Caption	"="

Open the Form Layout window and move the form to the right of the screen so it will be out of the way at runtime. (Yes, it really matters.)

None of the part placements are critical. Strive for a layout that pleases you. Add the code in Listing 16.8 to project TestCalc.

LISTING 16.8 The Code for TestCalc

```
Option Explicit
Private x As Double, y As Double
Private Calc As clsCalculator

Private Sub cmdAdd_Click()
    If txtX <> "" And txtY <> "" Then
        x = CDbl(txtX)
        y = CDbl(txtY)
        Calc.Add x, y
        txtResult = Calc.result
    Else
        MsgBox "Must have X and Y Values to do math!", vbOKOnly
    End If
End Sub
```

```
Private Sub cmdDivide_Click()
    If txtX <> "" And txtY <> "" Then
        x = CDbl(txtX)
        y = CDbl(txtY)
        If y <> 0 Then
            Calc.Divide x, y
            txtResult = Calc.result
        Else
            MsgBox "Can't divide by 0!", vbOKOnly
        End If
    Else
        MsgBox "Must have X and Y Values to do math!", vbOKOnly
    End If
End Sub

Private Sub cmdModal_Click()
    Calc.ShowForm VBModal
End Sub

Private Sub cmdModeless_Click()
    Calc.ShowForm vbModeLess
End Sub

Private Sub cmdMultiply_Click()
    If txtX <> "" And txtY <> "" Then
        x = CDbl(txtX)
        y = CDbl(txtY)
        Calc.Multiply x, y
        txtResult = Calc.result
    Else
        MsgBox "Must have X and Y Values to do math!", vbOKOnly
    End If
End Sub

Private Sub cmdQuit_Click()
    Unload Me
End Sub

Private Sub cmdSubtract_Click()
    If txtX <> "" And txtY <> "" Then
        x = CDbl(txtX)
        y = CDbl(txtY)
        Calc.Subtract x, y
        txtResult = Calc.result
    Else
        MsgBox "Must have X and Y Values to do math!", vbOKOnly
    End If
End Sub
```

16

continues

LISTING 16.8 continued

```
Private Sub Form_Load()
    Set Calc = New clsCalculator
    txtResult = 0
End Sub

Private Sub Form_Unload(Cancel As Integer)
    Set Calc = Nothing
End Sub
```

A Look at the Code

The Declarations section early binds Calc as an object of type clsCalculator, and Form_Load creates an instance of the class. Note that Form_Unload releases the object with Set Calc = Nothing.

The math function Command buttons check to be sure that there are numbers typed into the X and Y text boxes before the call on clsCalculator's methods. If either fails the test, a MsgBox informs the user. The Divide button also checks to prevent division by zero.

Finally, the two ShowForm buttons call the ShowForm method of the object, sending appropriate values.

Running TestCalc

Press F5 to run the program. Before you try it out, minimize the VB5 window. The only open window on your screen should be TestCalc. (Windows get lost behind each other a lot in this kind of work. Keep your screen simple to avoid confusion.) Enter some numbers into txtX and txtY and try the different math functions on the numbers. VBCalc performs the calculations and puts the results in the public variable Result. Then TestCalc reads Result from VBCalc and places it into txtResult. You have a running ActiveX server!

Now click Modeless. VBCalc creates an instance of frmVBCalc and shows it. Prove to yourself that you can continue using TestCalc with the Modeless form showing. The running TestCalc and the Modeless form are shown in Figure 16.20.

Close the Modeless form and click the Modal button. Looks a lot like the other one, doesn't it? Try running a new math problem with the Modal form still showing. What's this, an error (see Figure 16.21)? As soon as the running instance of VBCalc displays as a Modal form, it becomes "busy" and is waiting for the form to close before anything else can be done. The Windows error message warns you that the server is not responding and, of course, it can't. Click Switch To, and close the Modal form to resume normal operation.

FIGURE 16.21

Calculating with the Modal form—an error!

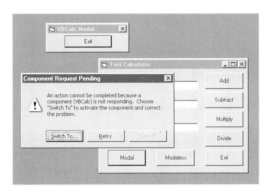

Before you close TestCalc, click Modeless one more time. Now close TestCalc. Hmmm, the Modeless form is still there, which shows that the server is running independently of the test program.

Close the Modeless form, and then maximize the Visual Basic instance that is running VBCalc and click the End button to close the ActiveX server.

The Electric KoolAid Acid Test

Well, you can run two programs and have them communicate via OLE. Do you have to start VBCalc every time you need to use it? That wouldn't be good, would it? And, because it has no internal way of closing itself, how do you stop it? (If there weren't good answers to these questions, would they have been asked?) Follow these steps:

1. If you have made changes to VBCalc since you made your reference EXE, compile the program again. If not, just close that instance of Visual Basic.

2. Now maximize the VB instance with TestCalc, open the Project menu, and click References. There are still two references to the 4 Function Calculator, but the one that is checked says [Missing]. Clear that checkmark, check the one that points to the EXE file instead, and click OK.

3. Now select Make TestCalc.Exe from the File menu. When it is done, close that instance of Visual Basic, too.

4. Use Windows Explorer to find TestCalc.Exe.

5. Double-click the icon to run the program.

6. Try out the same things you did before. They all work!

Because TestCalc is now referencing the EXE file, it creates an instance of clsCalculator by running the VBCalc program. And as soon as there are no references to clsCalculator, VBCalc is closed. The whole thing is transparent to the user, who never needs to know that VBCalc was opened, used, and then closed.

Summary of Building an Out-of-Process ActiveX Server

Out-of-process servers are handy for doing complicated, slow chores for another program while still letting the other program function normally. The following steps outline the normal building process for ActiveX EXE files:

1. Decide what features you want your component to have.

2. List the objects you will need to provide these features. (Each object is a separate class.)

3. If your component will have any forms, design them.

4. Add the properties and methods for your classes. This is the interface for the component.

5. Compile the ActiveX EXE to create a reference EXE.

6. Start the ActiveX EXE with Full Compile.

7. Start a new instance of Visual Basic. Select the VBP version of the new reference so you can debug.

8. Design a test program to exercise all of the features of the ActiveX EXE.

9. When all is working, compile your new ActiveX EXE again. It will now be available for use.

Pros and Cons of ActiveX Servers

When creating just a simple application, you might not really see the advantages of an ActiveX Server. Traditionally, you usually think of an application as a standalone program. That means that you create a program that no other program would use or need to integrate with.

In this lesson's example, you saw an ActiveX server being created to handle the calculations for another application. Imagine that calculation ActiveX server being used by several applications. If you wanted to add more features to the calculation, such as rounding or currency conversion, you only have to make changes to the calculation ActiveX server. If you programmed the calculation functions into every application that used it, the maintenance would be a nightmare, because you would have make sure the changes were applied to a large number of applications.

The flip side of using ActiveX servers is that there will be some performance degradation to your applications. The more you distribute your functions through ActiveX servers, the more your applications will slow down. If you have ActiveX servers loaded throughout your network, your network speed will become part of the performance calculations.

Lesson Summary

This lesson described how to create an ActiveX Server. This concept of ActiveX Servers allows you to develop pieces of applications that can be used by other applications. To learn more about ActiveX Servers and logic partitioning, you can refer to *Visual Basic 6 Client/Server How-To* (Waite Group Press, 1998). This book covers the concept of client/server and the distribution of components such as ActiveX servers in greater detail.

16

Quiz 6

1. For an OLE server, the _____ in the Project Property dialog box identifies the OLE server to the system registry.

    a. Startup form

    b. StartMode check box

    c. Application description

    d. Project name

2. If the class property `Instancing` is set to Private:

    a. Other applications can use the class.

    b. Other applications can use the class, but the class cannot be viewed by the Object Browser.

    c. Other applications can use the class, depending on the setting of the class property `Instancing`.

    d. Other applications cannot use the class.

3. What does the code below do?

    ```
    Dim Calc as Object
    Set Calc = New clsCalculator
    ```

    a. Creates a new instance of the `clsCalculator` object.

    b. Creates a new instance of the application Calculator's class VBCalc.

    c. It is an invalid statement.

    d. Invokes the `Calculator` method of the object VBCalc.

4. Text entered in the Application Description field of the Options dialog box appears in the References dialog and the

    a. Help system when you press f1

    b. Object ToolTips

    c. Object Browser

    d. Debugger

Exercise 6

Complexity: Easy

1. Write an ActiveX server that will calculate the percentage of two numbers, and write a test application that will display the outcome on the form.

Complexity: Moderate

2. Write an ActiveX server that will act as a stopwatch and write an application that will test it. Note: This exercise should use the GetTickCount command introduced in Chapter 15, "Doing the Impossible (and More) with the Windows API."

LESSON 7

Using Visual Basic Built-in Objects

So far you have concentrated on using objects from other applications and creating objects from your own applications. This lesson looks at some often overlooked objects that are a part of Visual Basic. You are already familiar with Visual Basic objects, such as forms and controls, but did you know that there are six system objects in Visual Basic? They are

- App
- Clipboard
- Debug
- Err
- Printer
- Screen

You have already used several system objects. This lesson uses your new perspective on objects to take another look at each Visual Basic object and at how to integrate the object into your Visual Basic applications. For an added bonus to this chapter, use the Object Browser to look at each of the objects in this lesson as you proceed, and try to imagine uses for some of the ones not mentioned here.

Forms and Controls

You have already covered the use of forms and controls. They are mentioned here as a reminder that they are Visual Basic objects. You have already seen that you can create forms and controls dynamically with the Set and New keywords. The Forms collection object is a collection of all the forms in a project. There is always a risk when programs use many forms that a form will be left open when the program closes, using valuable memory resources. Some programmers add the following code in the Form_Unload event of their main form:

```
For j = Forms.Count - 1 to 0, Step -1
    Unload Forms
Next j
```

The App Object

The App object is a system object that was briefly covered in Chapter 12, "Reading and Writing Disk Files." In that chapter, the App.Path property was used to identify the directory the application resided in while running. The App object has other properties that can be useful for creating applications. The PrevInstance property can be used to determine the number of instances of any application running on a PC. To prevent multiple instances of an application running on the same PC, add the following code to the startup form's Load procedure or Sub Main:

```
If App.PrevInstance > 1 Then
    MsgBox "Existing startup - the application " & App.Title _
        & "is already running."
    End
End If
```

In the example above, the App object property Title was used to display the title of the application. The HelpFile property of the App object can be used to find the path and filename of the help file associated with the application, and the CompanyName and LegalCopyright information are often used on splash screens.

The Clipboard Object

The Clipboard object provides the Visual Basic programmer access to the system clipboard. The Clipboard object can be used to cut and paste text or graphics between applications. In Lesson 5, you used the Clipboard object to cut spell-checked text from a Word document and paste it into your Notepad application.

The Clipboard object does not contain any properties that can be set from Visual Basic; however, several methods are available. In the spell-checking Notepad example, you used the GetText method, which returns a text string from the clipboard. To get a graphic from the clipboard, use the GetData method. Graphics or text can be sent to the clipboard by the SetText and SetData methods. The GetFormat method returns the type of data in the clipboard, and the Clear method empties the clipboard.

The Debug Object

The Debug object is used to print messages to the Debug window. You have used the Debug object throughout the book to help debug your applications. The Debug object has no properties and only one method, Print. Debug statements are ignored when an executable is created, but they still increase the size of your executable, so if you want the smallest possible executable, comment out your Debug statements.

The Err Object

The Err object was covered in some detail in Chapter 10, "Problem Solving: Handling Errors and Debugging Your Program." The Err object contains information on Visual Basic runtime errors. The error number and a text description of the error can be found by using the Err object properties Number and Description. The Err object supports two methods, Raise and Clear. Use the Clear method to clear the properties of the Err object. The Raise method is used to generate runtime errors. Set the Err object to a specific error number, which can be very useful when testing your own error handling routines.

The Printer Object

The Printer object was covered in detail in Chapter 9, "Printing." The Printer object enables you to send output to a system printer. Visual Basic also supplies a Collection object called Printers that enables you to scan through the available printers on the system. You can even change the default printer by using the Set statement with the Printers collection.

The Screen Object

The Screen object provides you with useful information that enables you to manipulate the forms in your application based on properties of the Screen object. The Screen object has no methods but several properties. The ActiveControl property specifies the control that has focus. The ActiveForm property specifies the current active window. You can use the ActiveForm property to set properties on the active form.

```
Screen.ActiveForm.MousePointer = DEFAULT
```

The `Height` and `Width` properties are read-only properties that are always measured in twips. Use the `Height` and `Width` properties to resize your forms to fit a screen size or to position the forms on a screen. The following code centers a form on the screen:

```
Public CenterForm (F as Form)
   F.Top = (Screen.Height - Height) / 2 'Set the vertical of the form
   F.Left = (Screen.Width - Width) / 2  'Set the horizontal
End Sub
```

Lesson Summary

This lesson reviewed the six objects that come with Visual Basic. They shouldn't be that new to you. Many of them have been used within other lessons throughout this book. It probably doesn't seem clear when or why you would use them in this lesson. That's because this lesson's purpose was to review them. The `Form` and `Screen` objects are the most commonly used built-in objects. You are constantly referring to the form for objects that are placed on them, and the `Screen` object is used to help provide feedback about the user's system to the user.

The `App` object is used to provide more information about the application itself. The `Printer` object enables you to handle printing within your application. This is covered in greater detail back in Chapter 9. Though a lot of people don't admit they make errors, the `Err` object will help you track down and trap errors when they occur.

The next lesson will wrap up all this talk about objects, their usage, and their importance.

Quiz 7

1. Which one of the following is not a Visual Basic system object?

    a. `App`

    b. `Screen`

    c. `Debug`

    d. `Error`

2. The _____ object can be used to cut and paste text or graphics between applications.

    a. `Clipboard`

    b. `Screen`

    c. `App`

    d. `Printer`

3. The _____ property of the App object can be used to determine the number of instances of any application running on a PC.

    a. NumOfApps

    b. PrevInstance

    c. NumInstance

    d. PrevApp

4. The _____ property of the Screen object specifies the control that has focus.

    a. ActiveControl

    b. GotFocus

    c. ControlFocus

    d. CurrentControl

Exercise 7

Complexity: Easy

   1. Write a program that displays the following properties of the App object: Company Name, hDC, and Application Path.

Complexity: Easy

   2. Write a program that displays the names all the fonts that available to the Screen object and display them using the Debug object.

LESSON 8

Thinking in Objects

The first version of Visual Basic introduced event-driven programming to many programmers. Visual Basic 4 introduced object-oriented programming features similar to those used in C++ and Pascal, and made it possible to build applications from OLE components. Visual Basic 5 brought in ActiveX technology that expanded VB's object orientation even further.

Throughout this book, you have examined the object-oriented features of Visual Basic and learned how to use them. This lesson examines how these features will influence the way you program today and in the future.

Future OLE

ActiveX/OLE is one of the most exciting and important features of Visual Basic. The familiar custom controls, the VBXs, have now been replaced with ActiveX OCXs. To the Visual Basic programmer, the OCX still acts like the previous custom control, but it has many advances. Draw some controls on a form, set a few properties, add some code, and, whamo, you have a working application! The VBX vendors who ported their VBXs to ActiveX OCXs had a whole new marketplace opened up to them. Their OCXs can now be used in other development tools and in applications such as Microsoft Access and even the Internet.

But the most important new OLE feature is the capability to create your own ActiveX servers. Visual Basic's Professional and Enterprise Editions enable you to create ActiveX automation servers (EXE) or in-process ActiveX servers (DLL). Your ActiveX servers can be used and accessed by any application or development tool that can be an OLE controlling application, even over the Internet!

You can now write fully functional applications that can expose objects. You can create applications that have no functionality of their own, but supply objects and methods for other applications. For instance, you can write a single ActiveX server to determine security or business rules for a company. Applications can use that server to check user access, permissions, or business rules. If the business rules were to change, only the ActiveX server code would have to be modified.

Consider the case of building file or database applications where you are performing the same type of task in several different programs. Create a single in-process ActiveX server that handles all of the generic functions required for file I/O or database access. After the code is debugged and tuned, you have a new component to use in future applications. Building applications from ActiveX components results in better, more robust applications that can be created in less time. And the functionality is available to applications outside of Visual Basic!

COM technology, as mentioned early in this chapter, will continue to advance. Microsoft has stated that COM is a major part of its future operating systems, and ActiveX and OLE are an integral part of COM. With the capability to create ActiveX reusable components easily, expect the market for ActiveX servers and new Visual Basic add-in tools to explode. In the marketplace and within your organization, the idea of creating reusable code will become a reality. Remember that COM is an open standard. Look for more and more products and vendors to support COM. To see how easily ActiveX integrates into the Visual Basic environment, add Microsoft Word and Excel to the Visual Basic toolbar:

1. From the Visual Basic menu bar, select Project.

2. Select the option Components.

3. On the Insertable Objects tab, check the boxes marked Microsoft Word Document and Microsoft Excel Chart.

4. Click the OK button.

Figure 16.22 illustrates the Components dialog box as described in the previous steps. Figure 16.23 shows the application objects you have added to the Visual Basic toolbar to create OLE automation objects for your application.

FIGURE 16.22

The Components dialog box with the Insertable Objects tab showing.

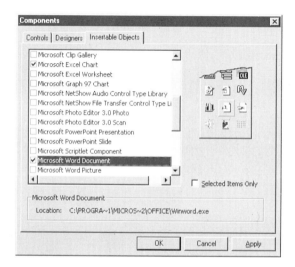

FIGURE 16.23

Word and Excel objects on the Visual Basic toolbar.

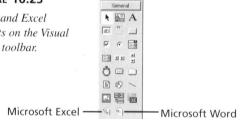

Microsoft Excel ———— Microsoft Word

Designing OLE Objects

Creating Visual Basic ActiveX applications require you to spend more time up front designing the application. Specifically, you must determine which objects will be private and which will be exposed. Here's a quick review of some simple steps you can use when you create an object model for your applications:

1. Determine the objects your application will need.

2. Determine the attributes (properties) and actions (methods) of each object.

3. Determine any possible object dependencies and create an object hierarchy.

4. Determine the objects that should be exposed to other applications.

Follow this everyday example to get an idea of how to design an object model. The project is to draw the door as illustrated in Figure 16.24.

FIGURE 16.24

The door.

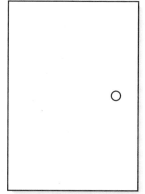

Perform the following steps:

1. First determine the objects required for the Door application. Using Figure 16.24 as a guide, the first object will be the Door object. On the Door object, there is a Doorknob object.

2. Next determine the attributes (properties) that will define the Door and any actions (methods) of the Door object. Figure 16.25 shows the properties and methods for the Door and Doorknob objects. The Door object has two properties, both public: Color and Material. The Door has two methods, Open() and Close(). The Doorknob has two properties, HandleStyle and Material. The Doorknob object has a single method, Turn().

3. Make the Doorknob object dependent on the Door object. This means an application cannot create just a Doorknob object; it first must create a Door object and then use it to create a Doorknob object. Figure 16.26 shows the object hierarchy.

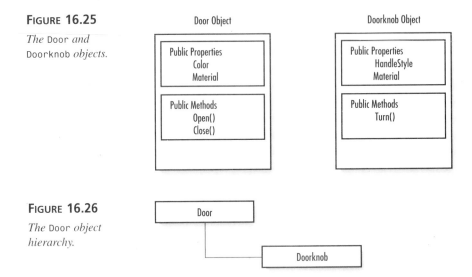

FIGURE 16.25

The Door *and* Doorknob *objects.*

FIGURE 16.26

The Door *object hierarchy.*

4. The last step before you create the class modules is to decide which objects to expose to other applications. In this example, expose both the Door object and the Doorknob object.

Lesson Summary

The important thing to remember, whether you are creating standard Visual Basic applications or ActiveX OLE server applications, is to think objects! Use the Visual Basic object-oriented features to create objects within your applications that can easily be integrated into other applications. The use of classes simplifies and speeds up future application development by creating already working, reusable classes. Building OLE components provides reusable code and functionality to any OLE controlling application on your desktop or in your organization. Soon your development environment and toolbar will be covered with reusable objects, and you will be thinking objects, objects everywhere!

Quiz 8

1. Visual Basic enables you to create OLE servers

   a. That can be used only by other Visual Basic applications

   b. That can be used by any OLE controller applications

    c. That can be used by only Microsoft OLE controller applications

    d. That cannot be used by any OLE controller applications, but only by other OLE server applications

2. A Visual Basic OLE custom control (OCX)

    a. Is not tied to a 16-bit architecture and can easily be used by other development tools besides Visual Basic, such as Microsoft Access

    b. Can only be used by Visual Basic

    c. Is being replaced by the VBX

    d. Is only available in 32-bit architectures and works only with Visual Basic

3. With the capability to easily create OLE reusable components, expect the market for ___ and new Visual Basic add-in tools to explode.

    a. VBXs

    b. OLE controllers

    c. OLE servers

    d. DDE applications

4. The first step in designing an OLE application is to

    a. Determine the objects exposed to other applications.

    b. Determine the attributes (properties) and actions (methods) of each object.

    c. Determine any possible object dependencies and create an object hierarchy.

    d. Determine the objects your application will need.

Exercise 8

Complexity: Easy

1. Write a program with an insertable object such as a Bitmap Image added to the toolbar.

Complexity: Moderate

2. Design an object model for a Login component.

Chapter Summary

This chapter presented the concept of interfacing with other applications using methods such as OLE, automation, and ActiveX. It also introduced the idea that Visual Basic not only can use objects created by other applications, but it can be used to create objects that can be used by other applications. The main points covered in this chapter are the following:

- OLE stands for Object Linking and Embedding and it refers to working with compound documents.

- ActiveX is a technology that grew from the complexity of OLE and is an integral part of Microsoft's COM (Component Object Model) architecture.

- DDE (Dynamic Data Exchange) isn't really used that much anymore because newer applications should be using OLE or ActiveX for exchanging data.

- The OLE Container Control is an easy way to link or embed OLE enabled applications with your VB program.

- Automation, formerly known as OLE automation, enables you to integrate or reference functionality from other applications into your application.

- All objects have a hierarchy in which they are based on. This information is found in the object's object library. The Object Browser enables you to look at the various object library classes and methods available for a given object.

- Late and early binding are the two methods of referencing an object within your application. With late binding, the object isn't linked to until the application references it at runtime. With early binding, you make direct reference to the application during development. This allows VB to know what object and methods are available while you're programming your application.

- ActiveX Servers are special EXE files that run outside the memory space of the application that calls it. This is referred to as an out-of-process server. Certain ActiveX Servers can run as standalone applications as well, such as Microsoft Excel and Word.

- ActiveX DLLs are similar to other dynamic link libraries in that they execute within the same memory space of the application that calls it.

- Visual Basic comes with six built-in objects: `App`, `Clipboard`, `Debug`, `Err`, `Printer`, and `Screen`.

- To create ActiveX servers successfully, you need to understand the use of objects and their model. Becoming familiar with COM will provide you with a good foundation on the use of objects and how to integrate with Visual Basic.

There is a lot reference material on the Internet as well as other books on OLE, automation, and ActiveX/COM. To get a better understanding of objects and how they are used within applications, *Doing Objects in Microsoft Visual Basic 6* (Sams Publishing, 1999) and *Visual Basic 6 Client/Server How-To* (Waite Group Press, 1998) are good resources. On the Internet, you can refer to the Microsoft Developers Network area at `http://www.microsoft.com/msdn`.

16

CHAPTER 17

Advanced ActiveX and Registry API Techniques

In this chapter, we address two topics covered earlier in this book and take them both a step further.

We focus more on ActiveX by introducing you to the ActiveX Interface Wizard and assist you in compiling and distributing your controls.

We show you how to save and retrieve data to the system Registry, review the Registry API, and perform subkey operations.

The ActiveX Interface Wizard is an excellent tool to assist you in control creation, and we'll take you step by step through the entire process. When we finish with that, we'll show you what you can do to distribute it.

With the advance Registry techniques that we'll show you, you will learn how to use the Registry to save specific program information. You'll be able to register your programs with the Windows 95/98 Registry and gain a better understanding of how the Registry works in general.

LESSON 1

The ActiveX Interface Wizard

As you've seen, adding events and properties to a user control is not difficult, but it is detailed. You must remember to put a line or two of code into several different procedures. Make one mistake, and your control doesn't work.

This lesson introduces the ActiveX Control Interface Wizard. Try it—you'll like it.

Running the Wizard

The ActiveX Control Interface Wizard is found on the Add-Ins menu. If it is missing from yours, select the Add-In Manager, and add it to the list of selected add-ins. Open the project NewBtn from the CD.

The second screen of the wizard is shown in Figure 17.1. (The first screen is just an introduction.)

FIGURE 17.1

Starting the ActiveX Control Interface Wizard.

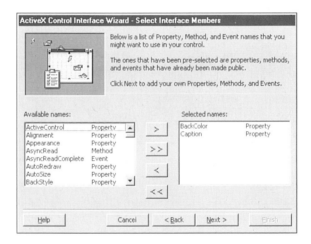

Note

If you do not delete the events you have added, the wizard fails and does not even try to load. You must exit and restart VB 6.

Select the ActiveX Control Interface Wizard from the Add-Ins menu.

The Select Interface Members dialog box provides a list of standard properties, events, and methods for selection. You can select individual items from the Available Names list and click > to move them to the Selected Names list. You can also click >> to move the entire list of Available Names to the Selected Names list. Be careful here, as some of the offerings are not suitable for SButton. Caption and BackColor are already selected because you created those properties manually.

The following items should be selected as in Table 17.1. If they are not, select the properties listed.

TABLE 17.1   Properties and Events for SButton

Name	Type
Click	Event
DblClick	Event
Enabled	Property
Font	Property
FontBold	Property
FontItalic	Property
FontName	Property
FontSize	Property
ForeColor	Property
Picture	Property

Click Next.

The Create Custom Interface Members dialog box opens. The dialog box is shown in Figure 17.2.

If you want to add an interface element that is not part of the standard list, this is where you add it. There are no custom interface elements for this project.

Click Next.

Mapping

The Set Mapping dialog box opens (see Figure 17.3).

The Set Mapping dialog box enables you to map specific properties, events, or methods to the user control or to a specific constituent component of the control. *Mapping* means connecting the property, event, or method to a specific component of the control. For example, you have already mapped the `BackColor` property to the user control, and the `Caption` property to `lblCaption`. Properties and events that are not mapped are added to the user control and all of the constituent components.

FIGURE 17.2

The Create Custom Interface Members dialog box.

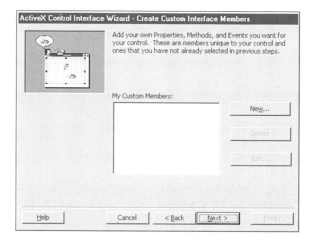

FIGURE 17.3

The Set Mapping dialog box.

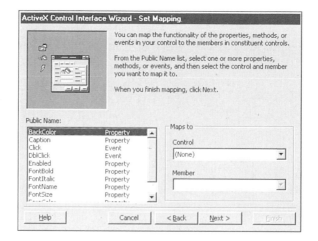

To map the `Enabled` property, perform the following steps:

1. Click Enabled in the Public Name list.

2. Open the Control drop-down list and select UserControl.

3. Map the elements according to Table 17.2.

TABLE 17.2 Map Properties for `SButton`

Element	Map to
BackColor	UserControl
Caption	lblCaption
Font	lblCaption
FontBold	lblCaption
FontItalic	lblCaption
FontName	lblCaption
FontSize	lblCaption
ForeColor	lblCaption
Picture	UserControl

The `Caption` and `BackColor` properties are mapped by the code you have already written. Do not map them again. The `Click` and `DblClick` events must be available to all parts of the control and should not be mapped.

4. Click Next.

The Set Attributes dialog box shown in Figure 17.4 opens. This dialog box enables you to set the attributes of the unmarked elements. You can also add descriptions that will help the developer using your control.

FIGURE 17.4

The Set Attributes dialog box.

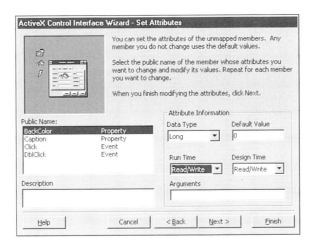

Properties can be made `Read Only`, `Read/Write`, `Write Only`, or `Not Available`. Note that you can set these attributes to be different for runtime and design time.

5. Click Next.

The Finished! dialog box opens. It gives you the option to view a summary report, which gives some advice about what to do next. For the first few times you use the wizard, you will probably want to see the summary.

6. Click Finish.

After a slight delay while the wizard writes some code, you are shown the summary report. If you elect to save the report, it is saved to the current directory as ctlwiz.txt. You can then open the text file with Notepad and print it if you want hard copy.

The ActiveX Control Interface Wizard adds a lot of code to the control. Unfortunately, some of it needs to be changed and some of it is incomplete. If you follow the instructions in the summary report, SButton will not work. The code in Listing 17.1 is the declarations section after the wizard has modified it.

LISTING 17.1 The Modified Declarations Section

```
Option Explicit
Private lBackColor As Long
Const lHighLight = &HE0E0E0
Const lShadow = &H808080
'Event Declarations:
Event Click()
Event DblClick()
```

The wizard has added declarations for the two events. So far, so good. But it has also made the changes in Listing 17.2, some of which are not so good.

LISTING 17.2 Some Other Changes from the Wizard

```
Private Sub UserControl_InitProperties()
'    Caption = Extender.Name
'    BackColor = RGB(192, 192, 192)
End Sub

Private Sub UserControl_ReadProperties(PropBag As PropertyBag)
 Caption = PropBag.ReadProperty("Caption", Extender.Name)
    BackColor = PropBag.ReadProperty("BackColor", RGB(192, 192, 192))
    UserControl.Enabled = PropBag.ReadProperty("Enabled", True)
    lblCaption.FontBold = PropBag.ReadProperty("FontBold", 0)
    lblCaption.FontItalic = PropBag.ReadProperty("FontItalic", 0)
    lblCaption.FontName = PropBag.ReadProperty("FontName", "")
    lblCaption.FontSize = PropBag.ReadProperty("FontSize", 0)
    lblCaption.ForeColor = PropBag.ReadProperty("ForeColor", &HFFFFFF)
```

```
    Set Picture = PropBag.ReadProperty("Picture", Nothing)
    Set lblCaption.Font = PropBag.ReadProperty("Font", Ambient.Font)
End Sub

Private Sub UserControl_WriteProperties(PropBag As PropertyBag)
    PropBag.WriteProperty "Caption", Caption, Extender.Name
    PropBag.WriteProperty "BackColor", BackColor, RGB(192, 192, 192)
    Call PropBag.WriteProperty("Enabled", UserControl.Enabled, True)
    Call PropBag.WriteProperty("FontBold", lblCaption.FontBold, 0)
    Call PropBag.WriteProperty("FontItalic", lblCaption.FontItalic, 0)
    Call PropBag.WriteProperty("FontName", lblCaption.FontName, "")
    Call PropBag.WriteProperty("FontSize", lblCaption.FontSize, 0)
    Call PropBag.WriteProperty("ForeColor", lblCaption.ForeColor, &HFFFFFF)
    Call PropBag.WriteProperty("Picture", Picture, Nothing)
    Call PropBag.WriteProperty("Font", lblCaption.Font, Ambient.Font)
End Sub
```

In `ReadProperties`, for example, we must rem out the lines:

```
Caption = PropBag.ReadProperty("Caption", Extender.Name)
BackColor = PropBag.ReadProperty("BackColor", RGB(192, 192, 192))
```

They have been replaced with

```
UserControl.BackColor = PropBag.ReadProperty("BackColor", &HFF8080)
lblCaption.Caption = PropBag.ReadProperty("Caption", "")
```

The `BackColor` value is not at all what you want, and the default caption is an empty string! Perform the following steps:

1. Change the new lines to read

   ```
   UserControl.BackColor = PropBag.ReadProperty("BackColor", &HC0C0C0)
   lblCaption.Caption = PropBag.ReadProperty("Caption", Extender.Name)
   ```

   You will find a similar change in `WriteProperties`. We must rem out the original lines

   ```
   '    PropBag.WriteProperty "Caption", Caption, Extender.Name
   '    PropBag.WriteProperty "BackColor", BackColor, RGB(192, 192, 192)
   ```

   because they have been replaced with

   ```
   Call PropBag.WriteProperty("BackColor", _
     UserControl.BackColor, &HFF8080)
   Call PropBag.WriteProperty("Caption", _
     lblCaption.Caption, "")
   ```

2. Change the new lines to read

   ```
   Call PropBag.WriteProperty("BackColor", _
       UserControl.BackColor, &HC0C0C0)
     Call PropBag.WriteProperty("Caption", _
       lblCaption.Caption, Extender.Name)
   ```

3. Add the following code to make the events work:

```
Private Sub lblCaption_Click()
    RaiseEvent Click
End Sub

Private Sub lblCaption_DblClick()
    RaiseEvent DblClick
End Sub

Private Sub UserControl_Click()
    RaiseEvent Click
End Sub

Private Sub UserControl_DblClick()
    RaiseEvent DblClick
End Sub
```

One more disaster lurks in the code. The wizard has created code to handle the font for the caption, but it has made one critical error and one critical omission. Look in ReadProperties and you will see

```
lblCaption.FontSize = PropBag.ReadProperty("FontSize", 0)
lblCaption.FontName = PropBag.ReadProperty("FontName", "")
```

And in WriteProperties:

```
Call PropBag.WriteProperty("FontSize", _
    lblCaption.FontSize, 0)
    Call PropBag.WriteProperty("FontName", _
    lblCaption.FontName, "")
```

A FontSize of 0 is too small to see. Worse yet, it generates an error. And an empty string for the FontName property does the same.

4. Change the code to read (changes in bold)

```
lblCaption.FontSize = PropBag.ReadProperty("FontSize", 8)
    lblCaption.FontName = PropBag.ReadProperty("FontName", _"MS Sans
Serif")

    Call PropBag.WriteProperty("FontSize", _
    lblCaption.FontSize, 8)
    Call PropBag.WriteProperty("FontName", _
    lblCaption.FontName, " MS Sans Serif ")
```

The changes provide a default value for the FontSize property and the FontName property. The defaults are consistent, with standard Visual Basic defaults.

5. Delete all of the remmed-out code, just to make it easier to read.

6. Delete any Debug.Print statements that remain.

7. Open the user Control Design window.

8. Select Property Pages and check all four choices.

Congratulations! You just created a new control. Now it's time to test the new control:

1. Click the Close button of the Control Design window to update the control.

2. Open NewBtnDemo.

Take a look at the Properties window now. Your control gives you a totally new access to the properties of a push-button control. Unlike the Command button, SButton has a BackColor property that works. You can even put a picture on it:

1. Select Picture from the Properties window.

2. Select a metafile picture from the VB 6 Graphics directory.

Pretty sharp! Use metafile pictures unless you need something else. Metafiles will stretch to fill SButton. With all of the other available picture types, you must size the button to fit the picture.

What Hath Wiz Wrought?

The ActiveX Interface Wizard takes a lot of the drudgery out of control creation. None of what it does for you is difficult, but there is so much of it! Each new property requires a line or two of code in PropertyGet, PropertyLet and another line in WriteProperties, ReadProperties, and maybe InitProperties. Events and methods must be declared and code written to activate them. Nothing difficult, but nonetheless, a lot of code means plenty of opportunity to make a mistake. The wizard does most of the work for you. What it misses is not hard to detect and is easy to fix, now that you know the mechanics.

This project made you work a little harder than normal. The time to invoke the wizard is when you have decided on the features of your control. Do not add any code or properties to the control until the wizard has done its work. As you saw previously, if you do, it will undo some of your work.

When the wizard is finished, check the default properties it assigned and adjust them to fit your needs.

The hardest part about creating user controls is deciding what functions and features to include before you begin.

Lesson Summary

In this lesson we showed you how to utilize the ActiveX Interface Wizard to assist you in creating controls. We created a project using the wizard to demonstrate how it works. Next, we'll show you how to distribute your control.

Quiz 1

1. Where do you add an interface element that is not part of the standard list?

   a. The Create Custom Interface Members dialog box

   b. The Set Mapping dialog box

   c. The Add an Interface Element dialog box

   d. The Select Interface Members dialog box

2. What provides a list of standard properties, events, and methods for selection?

   a. The Create Custom Interface Members dialog box

   b. The Set Mapping dialog box

   c. The Add an Interface Element dialog box

   d. The Select Interface Members dialog box

3. What enables you to map specific properties, events, or methods to the user control or to a specific component of the control?

   a. The Create Custom Interface Members dialog box

   b. The Set Mapping dialog box

   c. The Add an Interface Element dialog box

   d. The Select Interface Members dialog box

4. Which of the following is not a property that you can map to a user control in the Set Attributes dialog box?

   a. Write Only

   b. Read/Write

   c. Not Available

   d. All Available

LESSON 2

Distributing Your Control and the Setup Wizard

Now that you have a user control all designed and tested, it's time to make it into a real OCX file and consider how to distribute it.

A Last Refinement

If you compile SButton now, developers who want to use it will see the standard user control icon on the ToolBox. It's pretty enough, but ToolBox icons should be unique. In other words, each control you make should have a different icon. Take a look at the Property window with the control builder on the screen. The ToolBox Bitmap property enables you to select a bitmap for the job.

Here's where your artistic talents get their greatest challenge! The ToolBox Bitmap must be 16 x 15 pixels. That's pretty darned small! If you try to draw a 16 x 15 bitmap in Windows Paint, you'll discover how small. There isn't much you can do with it. On the Visual Basic 6 CD is the ImageEdit program. ImageEdit gives you a much better canvas for your design but does not have text. Still, some people come up with some pretty creative designs. (ImageEdit also makes icons.)

There is a bitmap included with the files for this lesson. It is named, with great originality, SBtn.bmp. Perform the following steps:

1. Bring the Control Design window to the front.
2. Click ToolBox Bitmap in the Properties window.
3. Select SBtn.bmp from the CD files, or select one of the bitmaps in the Visual Basic Graphics directory.
4. Close the Control Design window to update the control.

Now SButton has its own icon in the ToolBox.

Making the OCX File

Now it is complete, and it is time to make the OCX file:

1. Click NewBtn in the Project Explorer to select the project.
2. Select Make SButton.ocx from the File menu.
3. Enter SButton.ocx as a filename in the Make Project dialog box.

That does it. Not only does Visual Basic build your OCX file, but it registers it in the system Registry so that other programs can use it. First, though, you need to test it again in the current program.

Test Number One: Testing SButton in the Original NewBtnDemo Program

If you run NewBtnDemo at this point, it will still use the user control that is part of the same project group because that is the connection it has made. To verify the OCX, you must first remove NewBtn.vbp from the project group:

1. Click `NewBtn.vbp` in the Project Explorer to select it.

2. Select Remove Project from the File menu.

   Visual Basic will complain that the project is referenced from another project. That is, of course, because NewBtnDemo contains a reference to it.

3. Click Yes to remove the project.

When NewBtn.vbp is removed, Visual Basic looks for the OCX file in the system Registry. If it exists, it is the reference that was set in the NewBtnDemo project. If it does not exist, the reference was removed and the instances of the control disappear from the form.

1. Select the `SButton` icon and draw another copy of `SButton` on the form.

2. Change the properties of the new `SButton` using the Property Pages. It doesn't matter what you change, just change something (or maybe everything).

3. Press F5 or click the Run button to run the project.

When you are satisfied that the control is working, exit from the NewBtnDemo program. It's time to try the new control with a brand new project:

1. Select New Project from the File menu and start a Standard EXE project.

   The first thing you may notice is that the `SButton` icon is gone from the ToolBox. And after all that work! Never fear.

2. Select Components from the Project menu.

3. If SButton.ocx does not appear on the Controls tab, use the browse button to add it to the list.

4. Check the control and click OK.

   Normal installation of the OCX would put it in the Windows/System directory. Because this is an experimental control (do not market any programs that use it unless you add a lot of error trapping!), it is not in the expected place, which explains having to browse for it.

5. When the control is in the ToolBox, add a few instances of it to Form1.

6. Write some code to show that the control is working. If you can't think of any, try the code in Listing 17.3.

LISTING 17.3 Testing `SButton`

```
Option Explicit

Private Sub SButton1_Click()
    MsgBox "This is SButton1"
```

```
End Sub

Private Sub SButton2_Click()
MsgBox "This is SButton2"
End Sub
```

Run the program and verify the SButton works as advertised.

Distribution Using the Setup Wizard

You can use the Setup Wizard to create distribution copies of your ActiveX controls:

1. Use the Windows Start button to select and run the Setup Wizard.

2. Use the Browse button to select NewBtn.vbp.

3. Remove the checkmark from Rebuild the Project.

4. Click Next.

5. Select your distribution media (Floppy disk, Single Directory, or Disk Directories).

6. If you selected Single Directory or Disk Directories, select a directory for the file on your hard disk drive.

7. Click Next.

8. The project does not use any local ActiveX components. Click Next.

9. The project does use STDOLE2.TLB. Click Next.

10. Click Next to accept the File Summary.

11. Click Finish.

After it analyzes the code for a while, the Setup Wizard creates your distribution files. Note that OCX controls created with Visual Basic require VBRUN600.DLL. If you are distributing only to VB 6 developers, you can omit that file and cut your distribution package by almost a meg.

Another approach to distribution is to distribute the source code instead of the compiled OCX. This can be useful for in-house distribution in particular. For wider distribution, it raises licensing problems, because there is nothing to stop another developer from marketing the program as his or her own.

Licensing

If you develop a control for commercial distribution, then you've spent hundreds of hours building, debugging and testing the control. The world already has enough buggy custom controls, so you spend enough time to make your control really robust. (Robust in computerese means it doesn't break, and it works with anything else a developer may choose to use with it.) The one thing you don't want is for the first developer who purchases your control to "improve" it, making a control project of his or her own that is nothing more than your control with a trivial addition. You market your control as Gadget.OCX, and he or she markets his or hers as IGadget.OCX (for "improved" gadget). Worse yet, he or she undercuts your price by half!

It could happen, but not if you take advantage of the licensing support that is available in Visual Basic. When you add licensing support to a control, VB compiles a license key into the program and adds a .vbl file to the distribution set. When your competitor creates the distribution set for IGadget, your license file is not (and cannot effectively be) included. Developers who buy his or her knockoff product will get a product that refuses to work.

To add licensing to your OCX, perform the following steps:

1. Select Project Properties on the Project menu.
2. Check Require License Key on the General tab.
3. Click OK.

That's all it takes to protect your control from piracy. Because you have added licensing support, the control needs the license file to work. No one can create a distribution set with your control now that it has licensing support.

What About Shareware Distribution?

Shareware distribution is one of the most popular ways small-scale programmers distribute their products. Developers like it too because they can have the "try before you buy" advantage. But how do you keep the developer from distributing programs that use your control and making money without paying you for your work?

There are five basic techniques you can use.

The Honor System

You can just trust people to pay for the software if they use it commercially. As strange as it seems, several topnotch developers use it. A few that come to mind are MacAfee's fine antivirus products, the various incarnations of the WinZip file compression/expansion program, and the Paint Shop Pro graphics manipulation program.

CrippleWare

Some developers leave a few key features out of their shareware distribution product. When someone sends in a check, a fully working copy is sent by regular mail or email. It's an effective technique, but many developers will not consider crippleware programs.

Nags

If a shareware product pops up an opening screen that reminds you to buy it, the screen is called a nag. It's unlikely that a developer would want to market a program that displays your nag, but they do have a fully working copy for evaluation purposes.

Product Support

The idea of product support goes along with trust in the list of possibilities, because it still relies on trust. If your control requires a lot of documentation, an offer of printed docs may elicit a few checks. Add in free product updates and (maybe) telephone support and you have an even better chance. (But be prepared for some really stupid questions at 3:00 a.m.)

Expiration

If you look hard enough, you can find an OCX for sale that includes an expiration date or a usage meter. After a month of use, or a certain number of uses, the program stops working.

Versioning Issues

Now that you have your control in distribution, the suggestions start rolling in: Gee, it would be neat if it could delp a glunder, everyone says. After a few hundred such requests, you study the issue and decide that glunder delping is a really good addition. Better yet, you figure out a really simple way to do it.

You sit down at your computer, and a few dozen hours later, your control delps glunders with the best of them! You recompile the control and announce that Gadget.OCX now has a new feature. Jim D. Veloper buys your upgraded control and adds it to his next project. He is delighted to have a control that does so much and does it so well.

Until he distributes his program, that is. Sue User buys a copy and installs it on the same computer that uses an earlier version of Gadget.OCX. The new program works great, but the earlier program is now broken. Jim D. Veloper now has a most upset customer, and so do you.

How do you prevent this common problem?

- Never remove any functioning parts of the control. You can add all you want.

- Don't remove any properties. If you want to stop using a property, you can mark it as hidden in the Procedure Attributes dialog box. You can remove it from `WriteProperties`, but never remove it from `ReadProperties`, or it will break every program that uses a previous version.

- Don't change procedure attributes for events or methods.
- On the Make tab of the Project Properties dialog box, check Auto Increment. Each new compilation of the OCX will have a higher version number. Setup.exe will not replace an OCX with one that has a lower version number. (It seems to ignore dates.)

Lesson Summary

In this lesson, we take the control we developed in Lesson 1 a step further by making it into an OCX file. We also used the Setup Wizard to create distribution copies of the control, as well as cover licensing and shareware distribution issues. Next, we'll change the topic and revisit the Registry.

Quiz 2

1. Each ToolBox icon should be unique because
    a. Visual Basic requires that all icons be unique
    b. It makes it easier to differentiate from the other ToolBox controls
    c. Both a and b
    d. None of the above

2. When an OCX is newly installed, Windows expects to find it
    a. In the Windows directory
    b. In the Windows/Systems directory
    c. In the system Registry
    d. In the same directory that the OCX was created

3. For other programs to use your OCX file, it must
    a. Be located in the Windows directory
    b. Be registered in the system Registry
    c. Have a license key
    d. Both a and b

4. OCX controls created with Visual Basic require
    a. The Honor System
    b. A license key
    c. Product Support
    d. The file VBRUN600.DLL

LESSON 3

Using the Registry with Built-in VB Commands

Here, we'll manipulate the Registry directly using Visual Basic commands (before you begin this lesson, you may want to refer to Lesson 4 "Using the Registry API" in Chapter 15, "Doing the Impossible (and More) with the Windows API").

Let's say you open a new Windows program and you move and resize the window to a setting that suits your preferences. After using the program for a while, you close the program and go about your business. Later in the day, you open the same program, only to find the window reverted back to full screen again. You realize that no matter what you do to the window, it will never remember your settings and it always reverts back to an undesirable size and position. Soon, you get tired of changing the window settings and would really appreciate a program that remembers its size and position upon opening and closing.

Earlier versions of Windows stored program information in initialization (.INI) files. Some programs used their own .INI files and others used WIN.INI or SYSTEM.INI. Windows 95 and Windows NT can use initialization files, but Microsoft recommends that you store initialization information in a database called the *system Registry*.

You can view the Registry with Regedit. Regedit shows the Registry in tree format, something like Explorer. Start it by selecting Run from the Windows 95 Start menu, entering Regedit on the command line and clicking OK. Figure 17.5 shows what you see.

17

FIGURE 17.5

The Regedit opening screen.

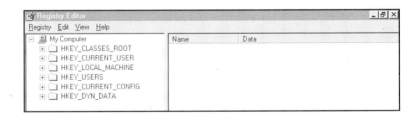

Note

Do not, under any circumstances, actually edit existing items in the system Registry with Regedit unless you have had specific training. You can really mess things up by deleting or changing something you shouldn't.

Click the plus sign next to HKEY_LOCAL_MACHINE to expand that branch, then on the plus sign next to Software, on the plus sign next to Microsoft, the plus sign next to Internet Explorer, and then click Main. You will see something like Figure 17.6. (Mileage will vary: The Registry reflects your computer setup. This illustration is only a typical view of the Registry.)

FIGURE 17.6

Regedit with
HKEY_LOCAL_MACHINE/
Software/Internet
Explorer/Main
expanded.

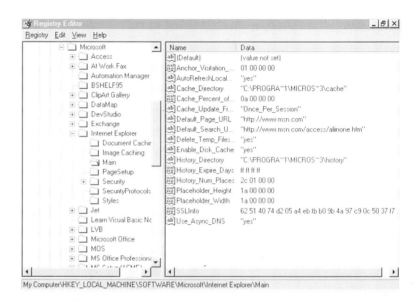

> **Note**
>
> What we have just done is called expanding the Registry. Throughout this chapter, we will use standard directory path notation to refer to a Registry entry. The Internet Explorer entry that we just opened would be referred to as HKEY_LOCAL_MACHINE\Software\Internet Explorer\Main.

The information on the right side of the screen shows the configuration setup for IE on my computer. We won't even try to go into what it all means. The point is that installed software keeps track of things such as window state, window position, paths for other features, and user settings by storing them in the Registry. Your software can do the same thing.

Look again at Figure 17.5. The collapsed Registry tree shows six main roots for the Registry. Table 17.3 lists these roots and explains a little about their purpose.

TABLE 17.3 Registry Roots

Key	Description
HKEY_CLASSES_ROOT	The filename extensions key that tells Windows what application to associate with a file extension. If your application uses a specific extension, it should be added to this key.
HKEY_CURRENT_USER	User-specific data. Used to store configuration information for each user. Each user can have his or her own preferences.
HKEY_LOCAL_MACHINE	Computer-specific data. Data stored here is used by all instances of your application and all users get the same data.
HKEY_USERS	Used by Windows to store data about all of the users.
HKEY_CURRENT_CONFIG	Display and printer configuration information.
HKEY_DYN_DATA	Dynamic data, including performance statistics.

Under the roots are Registry Keys. Your application stores its data in a subkey under the software key. Microsoft recommends the following set of subkeys:

```
HKEY_LOCAL_MACHINE
    Software
        Company Name
            ProductName
                Version
```

The added subkeys are shown in bold print. This type of structure is normally shown the same way we show a path, like this: HKEY_LOCAL_MACHINE\Software\ YourCo\YourApp\1.0.

Each subkey can have a number of values associated with it. The values appear in the right hand pane of the Regedit window, and your program can read those values to determine the paths and the default settings to use when it starts.

Visual Basic and the Registry

Visual Basic makes it easy to store your application information in the Registry. Visual Basic applications automatically create a Registry entry when they are installed. You will find it in HKEY_CURRENT_USER\Software\VB and VBA Program Settings\appname\ section\key. Your first exercise in working with the Registry uses the four commands described next.

The `GetSetting` Function

The `GetSetting` function returns a key setting value from an application's Windows Registry entry. Its syntax is

```
GetSetting(appname, section, key[, default])
```

The components of the syntax are as follows:

- `appname` is a string expression containing the name of the application or project whose key setting is requested.
- `section` is a string expression containing the name of the section where the key setting is found.
- `key` is a string expression containing the name of the key setting to return.
- `default` is an expression containing the value to return if no value is set in the key setting. If omitted, default is assumed to be a zero-length string (`""`).

The `SaveSetting` Statement

The `SaveSetting` statement saves or creates an application entry in the Windows Registry entry. Its syntax is

```
SaveSetting(appname, section, key, setting)
```

The components of the syntax are as follows:

- `appname` is a string expression containing the name of the application or project to which the setting applies.
- `section` is a string expression containing the name of the section where the key setting is being saved.
- `key` is a string expression containing the name of the key setting being saved.
- `setting` is an expression containing the value to which the key is being set.

The `DeleteSetting` Statement

The `DeleteSetting` statement deletes a section or key setting from the Windows Registry entry. The syntax is

```
DeleteSetting(appname, section[, key])
```

The components of the syntax are as follows:

- `appname` is a string expression containing the name of the application or project to which the section or key setting applies.

- `section` is a string expression containing the name of the section where the key setting is being deleted. If only `appname` and `section` are provided, the specified section is deleted, along with all related key settings.

- `key` is a string expression containing the name of the key setting being deleted.

The `GetAllSettings` Function

The `GetAllSettings` function returns a list of key settings and their respective values from an application's Windows Registry entry. The syntax is

```
GetAllSettings(appname, section)
```

The components of the syntax are as follows:

- `appname` is a string expression containing the name of the application or project whose key settings are requested.

- `section` is a string expression containing the name of the section whose key settings are requested. `GetAllSettings` returns a variant whose content is a two-dimensional array of strings containing all the key settings in the specified section and their corresponding values.

Your First Registry Entries

The idea of this project is to have your program save settings when it exits and use them the next time it loads. The Address Book program from Chapter 2, "Object-Oriented Programming," will serve as your experimental platform. You can easily adapt these steps to any of your own applications. Load the Address Book project file. (The version of Address Book that is modified for this project is on the CD in the Chapter 16 folder.) Add a command button, position it near `cmdSave`, and set the properties as shown in Table 17.4.

TABLE 17.4 Properties for the `RegClear` Command Button

Name	Property
Caption	RegClear
Name	cmdRegClear

You will not use this command button in projects that you plan to distribute. The Setup Wizard creates an uninstall file that clears your Registry entries when the program is removed from a computer. Because you are not creating setup disks for this project, you need some way of removing your experimental Registry entries. Add the following code:

In Declarations, enter

```
Option Explicit
Public bDeleted As Boolean
```

The rest of the code is in Listing 17.4.

LISTING 17.4   The Code for Your First Registry Manipulation

```
Private Sub Form_Unload(Cancel As Integer)
' Save the form's size and position if bDeleted is false
If bDeleted = True Then Exit Sub
SaveSetting "AddBook", "Startup", "Left", frmAddressBook.Left
SaveSetting "AddBook", "Startup", "Top", frmAddressBook.Top
SaveSetting "AddBook", "Startup", "Width", frmAddressBook.Width
SaveSetting "AddBook", "Startup", "Height", frmAddressBook.Height
End Sub

Private Sub cmdRegClear_Click()
' Clear the registry and set bDeleted to True
' If there is no registry entry to clear this generates
' an error that we will want to ignore.
On Error Resume Next
DeleteSetting "AddBook"
bDeleted = True
End Sub

Private Sub Form_Load()
'    Reads the registry and sets the form size and position
'    to the settings used in the previous Lesson
Dim iLeft As Integer, iTop As Integer
Dim iWidth As Integer, iHeight As Integer
bDeleted = False
iLeft = Val(GetSetting("AddBook", "Startup", "Left", "0"))
iTop = Val(GetSetting("AddBook", "Startup", "Top", "0"))
iWidth = Val(GetSetting("AddBook", "Startup", "Width", "6500"))
iHeight = Val(GetSetting("AddBook", "Startup", "Height", "4500"))
frmAddressBook.Move iLeft, iTop, iWidth, iHeight
End Sub
```

The variable bDeleted is a global variable used as a flag to indicate whether or not to save the settings. You don't want to save the Registry entries again if you have cleaned out the entries from the Registry by clicking cmdRegClear.

The Form_Load event reads the four values from the Registry and uses the move method to position and size the form according to the previous settings. What happens the first time you run the program? There are no previous keys or key values to read. Look at the following line of code:

```
iWidth = Val(GetSetting("AddBook", "Startup", "Width", "6500"))
```

The last parameter is the default setting, the string that is returned when there is no Registry value to read. The form width is set to 6500 twips when there is no Registry key value read.

The code

```
SaveSetting "AddBook", "Startup", "Width", frmAddressBook.Width
```

saves the "Width" and the form's width from `frmAddressBook.Width` in `HKEY_CURRENT_USER\Software\VB and VBA Program Settings\AddBook\Startup`.

Testing the Program

Press F5 to run the program. Move the form and resize it, and then exit from the program. Then press F5 to run the program again. It should resume running in exactly the same location and at exactly the same size as when you quit the program.

Lesson Summary

In this lesson, you have seen how to save data to the system Registry and how to retrieve that data using statements and functions from Visual Basic. In the next lesson, we will use the API to save settings to `HKEY_LOCAL_MACHINE` and `HKEY_CURRENT_USER`.

Quiz 3

1. What is the purpose of the `GetSetting` statement?

   a. Saves an application entry in the Windows Registry entry

   b. Creates an application entry in the Windows Registry entry

   c. Returns a key setting value from an applications Windows Registry entry

   d. Returns an application entry from the Windows Registry entry

2. What is the purpose of the `SaveSetting` statement?

   a. Saves an application entry in the Windows Registry entry

   b. Returns a key setting value from an application's Window Registry entry

   c. Copies an application entry in the Windows Registry entry

   d. Both a and c

3. What is the purpose of the `DeleteSetting` statement?

    a. Deletes a section from the Windows Registry entry

    b. Deletes a key setting from the Windows Registry entry

    c. Both a and b

    d. None of the above

4. The `GetAllSettings` function

    a. Returns a list of key settings and their respective values from an application's Windows Registry entry

    b. Returns a list of key settings and their respective addresses from an application's Windows Registry entry

    c. Writes a list of key settings to file

    d. None of the above

LESSON 4

Adding Values to Subkeys

In Lesson 4 of Chapter 15, "Doing the Impossible (and More) with the Windows API," and Lesson 3 of this chapter, you learned how to use the Registry API and create a subkey. Now that you have created a subkey, it is time to make it do something useful: store some data. Of course, this means more APIs, but that is the source of your power.

The New Controls

Add another frame to the form, and place two option buttons inside. Add two textboxes and two labels to the form. Again, use Figure 17.3 as a guide to placement. Set the properties for the New controls according to Table 17.5.

TABLE 17.5 Properties for the New Controls

Object	Property	Value
Frame	Name	fraType
	Caption	Value Type
Option Button	Name	optType
	Index	0
	Caption	String
	Value	True

Object	Property	Value
Option Button	Name	optType
	Index	1
	Caption	Number
	Value	False
Label	Name	Label2
	Caption	Value Name
Label	Name	Label3
	Caption	Value
TextBox	Name	txtValueName
	Text	" "
TextBox	Name	txtValue
	Text	" "

17

Adding the Code

Open the API Text Viewer and find RegSetValueEx in the Declares section. Copy the declaration into the declaration section of RegAPI.Bas, as shown in Listing 17.5.

LISTING 17.5   The Declaration of RegSetValueEx

```
Declare Function RegSetValueEx Lib "advapi32.dll" _
  Alias "RegSetValueExA" _
  (ByVal hKey As Long, ByVal lpValueName As String, _
  ByVal Reserved As Long, ByVal dwType As Long, _
  lpData As Any, ByVal cbData As Long) As Long
```

Next, open the Code window for the form and add the code shown in Listing 17.6 to the beginning of Command1_Click:

LISTING 17.6   Additions to Command_Click

```
Dim sType As String    (Existing Code)

If optType Then
 sType = "String"
Else
 sType = "Number"
End If
```

continues

LISTING 17.6   continued

```
' Selects command action (Existing Code)
In the Select-Case section find Case 1 and add the following:
Case 1  ' Create new value or set value
If optKey Then
 SetNewValue HKEY_LOCAL_MACHINE, _
 "\SOFTWARE\" & txtSubKey, _
 sType, _
 txtValueName, _
 txtValue
Else
 SetNewValue HKEY_CURRENT_USER, _
 "\SOFTWARE\" & txtSubKey, _
 sType, _
 txtValueName, _
 txtValue
End If
```

Close the form's Code window, and open the Code window for RegAPI.Bas. Add a
new procedure named SetNewValue, and then enter the code from Listing 17.7 in
SetNewValue:

LISTING 17.7   The SetNewValue Sub

```
Public Sub SetNewValue(lRoot As Long, sSubKey As String, _
 sType As String, sValueName As String, sValue As String)
' Sets or changes values in subkeys
' Parameters:
' lRoot is one of HKEY_CURRENT_USER or HKEY_LOCAL_MACHINE
' (Could be modified for other roots)
' sSubKey is the subkey name (requires leading \)
' sValue is string version of value to save

 Dim lResult As Long, hKeyHandle As Long, sMsg As String
Dim lValue As Long, lType As Long

' make sure that data has been passed to
' create the key

If Len(sValue) = 0 Then
 sMsg = "Bad input to creat value" & vbCrLf
 sMsg = sMsg & "Value = " & sValue
 MsgBox sMsg
 GoTo Exit_SetNewValue
End If

' If the key\subkey does not exist it will be created
```

```vb
' If it does exist it will be opened

lResult = RegCreateKeyEx _
 (lRoot, _
 sSubKey, _
 0&, _
 vbNullString, _
 REG_OPTION_NON_VOLATILE, _
 KEY_ALL_ACCESS, _
 0&, _
 hKeyHandle, _
 lResult)

If lResult <> ERROR_SUCCESS Then
 sMsg = "Could not open key"
 MsgBox sMsg
 GoTo Exit_SetNewValue
End If

Select Case sType
Case "String"
 lType = REG_SZ
 sValue = sValue & Chr$
 lResult = RegSetValueEx _
 (hKeyHandle, _
 sValueName, _
 0&, _
 lType, _
 ByVal sValue, _
 Len(sValue))

Case "Number"
 lType = REG_DWORD
 lValue = Val(sValue)
 lResult = RegSetValueEx _
 (hKeyHandle, _
 sValueName, _
 0&, _
 lType, _
 lValue, _
 4)

Case Else
 sMsg = "Bad input to create value" & vbCrLf
 sMsg = sMsg & "Type = " & sType
 MsgBox sMsg
 lResult = RegCloseKey(hKeyHandle)
 GoTo Exit_SetNewValue
End Select
```

continues

17

LISTING 17.7   continued

```
If lResult <> ERROR_SUCCESS Then
 sMsg = "Could not set value"
 MsgBox sMsg
 GoTo Exit_SetNewValue
Else
 lResult = RegCloseKey(hKeyHandle)
End If

lResult = RegCloseKey(hKeyHandle)

Exit_SetNewValue:
Exit Sub

Error_SetNewValue:
MsgBox Error
Resume Exit_SetNewValue
End Sub
```

A Look at the New Code

The SetNewValue sub uses RegCreateKeyEx to open the key. If the key does not exist, RegCreateKeyEx creates it. The program provides for two different types of values: strings and long integers. Both are inserted under the subkey, but the insertion is done differently, so there are two different calls to RegSetValueEx.

The code that does the work is inside the select-case structure. Strings sent to API functions must be null-terminated. The last line in the following code adds the null as Chr$:

```
Select Case sType
Stype will be one of "String" or "Number"
Case "String"
 lType = REG_SZ
REG_SZ represents a null-terminated string.
        sValue = sValue & Chr$

lResult = RegSetValueEx _
 (hKeyHandle, _
 sValueName, _
 0&, _
 lType, _
 ByVal sValue, _
 Len(sValue))

Case "Number"
 lType = REG_DWORD
```

REG_DWORD is a four-byte number—in other words, a long integer.

```
lValue = Val(sValue)
lResult = RegSetValueEx _
 (hKeyHandle, _
 sValueName, _
 0&, _
 lType, _
 lValue, _
 4)
```

Note the difference between this section and the string section above. The value changes from a string variable (sValue) to a long integer variable (lValue). Note also that sValue is sent ByVal. The other difference is in the final parameter, which is the size of the value.

```
Case Else
 sMsg = "Bad input to create value" & vbCrLf
 sMsg = sMsg & "Type = " & sType
 MsgBox sMsg
 GoTo Exit_SetNewValue
End Select
```

The Case Else handles improper data types. The rest of the program prevents this from happening, but if you reuse the module in another program, you need this protection.

The rest of the code is typical error trapping.

Running the Code

When you ran the previous section, you created two subkeys, VB Interactive and VB Interactive\1.0. Press f5 to run the program again. Select HKEY_LOCAL_MACHINE for the root and String for the value type. Enter VB Interactive\1.0 in the SubKeys textbox, and test in the Value Name text box. Enter your name in the Value text box and click Set Key Value.

Change the value type to Number and the value name to Numeric. Enter a whole number in the Value textbox, and once more click Set Key Value. The SubKeys textbox should still read VB Interactive\1.0. Run Regedit again so you can verify that the data has been written. (If you still had Regedit running from the last lesson, you need to refresh the display: Close the subkey that is open, and click one of the other subkeys. Then reopen the VB Interactive\1.0 subkey.) Both of your values have been saved in the Registry under the subkey.

Lesson Summary

Now you can create new subkeys and store named values in them. The same routine that stores a value can be used to change the value. Now, wouldn't it be nice to be able to recover those values? That is what you do in the next lesson.

Quiz 4

1. The `RegCreateKeyEx` function

    a. Opens a Registry key

    b. Creates a Registry key

    c. Overwrites a previous key

    d. Both a and b

2. `REG_DWORD` is

    a. A four-byte number

    b. A long integer

    c. Both a and b

    d. Neither a or b

3. If the function `RegCreateKeyEx` is called and the key does not exist, it

    a. Creates it

    b. Returns an error

    c. Creates a default key

    d. None of the above

4. The line of code

    `sValue = sValue & Chr$`

    does the following:

    a. Sets `sValue` to `Null`

    b. Appends a `Null` character to the end of the string `sValue`

    c. Appends a `0` character to the end of the string `sValue`

    d. None of the above

LESSON 5

Reading Registry Values

Now it is time to read values back from the Registry. The API that you use for this needs some modification to handle three different chores: learning the type and size of the value that is stored, reading string values, and reading long integer values.

You'll be happy to know that there are no new controls in this lesson. In fact, you have all of the controls you need. All you have to do now is add functionality.

Adding Code to `Command_Click`

Open the form's Code window and add the code from Listing 17.8 to the `Command_Click` event for Command1:

LISTING 17.8 New Code for the `Command_Click` Event

```
Case 2 ' Read a value
If optKey Then
 txtValue = ReadRegValue(HKEY_LOCAL_MACHINE, _
 "SOFTWARE\" & txtSubKey, txtValueName)
Else
 txtValue = ReadRegValue(HKEY_CURRENT_USER, _
 "SOFTWARE\" & txtSubKey, txtValueName)
End If
```

Adding New Code to `RegAPI.Bas`

Close the form Code window and open the Code window for `RegAPI.Bas`. Now open the API Text Viewer again, select `RegQueryValueEx`, and paste three copies of it into the declaration section of `RegAPI.Bas`. To make your new function flexible enough to handle everything you want to do, you will create three new variations of `RegQueryValueEx`: one to determine the details of the value you want to read, one to read strings, and one to read numbers.

Convert the first copy of `RegQueryValueEx` to look like this:

```
Declare Function RegQueryValueExNULL Lib "advapi32.dll" _
 Alias "RegQueryValueExA" _
 (ByVal hKey As Long, ByVal lpValueName As String, _
 ByVal lpReserved As Long, lpType As Long, _
 ByVal lpData As Long, lpcbData As Long) As Long
```

17

This is the version we will use to figure out if the value is a string or a long integer.

Convert the second copy to look like this:

```
Declare Function RegQueryValueExLONG Lib "advapi32.dll" _
 Alias "RegQueryValueExA" _
 (ByVal hKey As Long, ByVal lpValueName As String, _
 ByVal lpReserved As Long, lpType As Long, _
 lpData As Long, lpcbData As Long) As Long
```

This is the version we will use to read long integers.

Convert the third copy to look like this:

```
Declare Function RegQueryValueExSTRING Lib "advapi32.dll" _
 Alias "RegQueryValueExA" _
 (ByVal hKey As Long, ByVal lpValueName As String, _
 ByVal lpReserved As Long, lpType As Long, _
 ByVal lpData As String, lpcbData As Long) As Long
```

This is the version we will use for reading strings.

Now add a new function named ReadRegValue to RegAPI.Bas.

Add the code from Listing 17.9.

LISTING 17.9   The ReadRegValue Function

```
Function ReadRegValue(lRoot As Long, sSubKey As String, _
 sValueName As String) As String
' Reads registry values
' Parameters:
' lRoot is one of HKEY_CURRENT_USER or
' HKEY_LOCAL_MACHINE
' sSubKey is the subkey name (no leading \)
' Returns: String value of registry value

Dim lResult As Long, hKeyHandle As Long
Dim sMsg As String, lType As Long, lValue As Long
Dim lcch As Long, lrc As Long, sValue As String

On Error GoTo Error_ReadRegValue

' Open key

lResult = RegOpenKeyEx(lRoot, sSubKey, 0, KEY_QUERY_VALUE, hKeyHandle)
If lResult <> ERROR_SUCCESS Then
 sMsg = "Could not open key"
 MsgBox sMsg
 GoTo Exit_ReadRegValue
End If
```

```
' Determine the size and type of the data to be read
lrc = RegQueryValueExNULL _
(hKeyHandle, _
sValueName, _
0&, _
lType, _
0&, _
lcch)

Select Case lType
Case REG_SZ
 sValue = String(lcch, 0)
 lrc = RegQueryValueExSTRING(hKeyHandle, sValueName, _
0&, lType, sValue, lcch)
 ReadRegValue = Left(sValue, lcch - 1)

Case REG_DWORD
 lrc = RegQueryValueExLONG(hKeyHandle, sValueName, _
0&, lType, lValue, lcch)
 If lrc = ERROR_SUCCESS Then ReadRegValue = Str(lValue)

Case Else
 lrc = -1

End Select

If lrc <> ERROR_SUCCESS Then
 sMsg = "Could not read Key"
 MsgBox sMsg
 lResult = RegCloseKey(hKeyHandle)
 GoTo Exit_ReadRegValue
End If

lResult = RegCloseKey(hKeyHandle)

Exit_ReadRegValue:
Exit Function

Error_ReadRegValue:
MsgBox Error
Resume Exit_ReadRegValue
End Function
```

By replacing the lpValue parameter with 0&, you ask RegQueryValueExNULL to return the type of the stored value in lType and the size of the data in lcch. The variable lType then determines whether the program calls RegQueryValueExSTRING or RegQueryValueExLONG. A long integer value is converted to a string value before it is returned to Command_Click event. Strings returned from the API are null-terminated strings. The line

```
ReadRegValue = Left(sValue, lcch - 1)
```

removes the null.

Running the Program

You already have values stored in the Registry. Run the program and Select HKEY_LOCAL_MACHINE for the root. Enter VB Interactive\1.0 in the SubKeys textbox and Test in the Value Name textbox, and click the Query Value button. The text value you stored in the Registry appears in the Value text box.

Change the Value Name to Numeric, and click the Query Value button again. The number you saved will now be displayed in the Value text box.

Lesson Summary

Now that you can create keys and subkeys, you can write named data into those keys and subkeys, and you can read that data back. True, this program only displays the data, but you already know other ways to use it.

What remains is to be able to delete values and delete subkeys. In the next lesson, you will learn to do both.

Quiz 5

1. What would the line

   ```
   ReadRegValue = Left(sValue, lcch - 2)
   ```

   do?

      a. Remove lcch from the string

      b. Convert the string to a left-justified string

      c. Remove the terminating Null from the string

      d. Remove the terminating Null, plus a character before the Null

2. The function used to fetch a long integer from the Registry is

      a. RegQueryValueEx

      b. RegQueryValueLong

      c. RegQueryValueExLONG

      d. RegQueryValueEx(Long)

3. The function used to fetch a string from the Registry is

    a. `RegQueryValueEx`

    b. `RegQueryValueString`

    c. `RegQueryValueExSTRING`

    d. `RegQueryValueEx(String)`

4. What does the line of code displayed below do?

    `Lrc = RegQueryValueExNull (hKeyHandle, sValueName, 0&, LType, 0&, Lcch)`

    a. Determine the size of the data to be read

    b. Determine the type of data to be read

    c. Both a and b

    d. Neither a nor b

17

LESSON 6

Deleting Values and Subkeys

You guessed it! More APIs, but simple ones this time. There are times when you'll want to delete values and subkeys from the Registry. We will perform this function with a few Registry functions.

Adding Code to `Command_Click`

Open the form's Code window. You are going to be adding the code for the remaining two command buttons, indexes 3 and 4, as shown in Listing 17.10.

LISTING 17.10 The Remaining Code for `Command_Click`

```
Case 3 ' Delete value
If optKey Then
 DeleteRegValue HKEY_LOCAL_MACHINE, _
 "SOFTWARE\" & txtSubKey, txtValueName
Else
 DeleteRegValue HKEY_CURRENT_USER, _
 "SOFTWARE\" & txtSubKey, txtValueName
End If
txtValueName = ""
txtValue = ""

Case 4 ' Delete Key
```

continues

LISTING 17.10 continued

```
If optKey Then
 DeleteRegKey HKEY_LOCAL_MACHINE, _
 "SOFTWARE\" & txtSubKey
Else
 DeleteRegKey HKEY_CURRENT_USER, _
 "SOFTWARE\" & txtSubKey
End If
txtValueName = ""
txtValue = ""
txtSubKey = ""
```

Both of these routines use optKey to determine the Registry root to use and call the appropriate routine from RegAPI.Bas to accomplish their tasks.

The New Code for RegAPI.Bas

Close the form's Code window and open the Code window for RegAPI.Bas. Open the API Text Viewer and select RegDeleteValue and RegDeleteKey. Copy them, and paste them into the Declarations section of RegAPI.Bas, as shown in Listing 17.11.

LISTING 17.11 Declarations for RegDeleteValue and RegDeleteKey

```
Declare Function RegDeleteValue Lib "advapi32.dll" _
 Alias "RegDeleteValueA" _
 (ByVal hKey As Long, ByVal lpValueName As String) As Long

Declare Function RegDeleteKey Lib "advapi32.dll" _
 Alias "RegDeleteKeyA" _
 (ByVal hKey As Long, ByVal lpSubKey As String) As Long
```

Create a new subkey in RegAPI.Bas named DeleteRegValue. Place the code from Listing 17.12 in it.

LISTING 17.12 The Code for DeleteRegValue

```
Sub DeleteRegValue(lRoot As Long, sSubKey As String, sValueName As String)
 ' Deletes a value from the regisry
 ' Parameters:
 ' lRoot is one of HKEY_CURRENT_USER or HKEY_LOCAL_MACHINE
 ' sSubKey is the subkey name (requires leading \)
 ' sValueName is the name of the value to delete

Dim lResult As Long, hKeyHandle As Long, sMsg As String
```

```
On Error GoTo Error_DeleteRegValue

' Open key

lResult = RegOpenKeyEx(lRoot, sSubKey, 0, KEY_SET_VALUE, hKeyHandle)
If lResult <> ERROR_SUCCESS Then
 sMsg = "Could not open key"
 MsgBox sMsg
 GoTo Exit_DeleteRegValue
End If

lResult = RegDeleteValue(hKeyHandle, sValueName)

If lResult <> ERROR_SUCCESS Then
 sMsg = "Could not delete key value"
 MsgBox sMsg
 lResult = RegCloseKey(hKeyHandle)
 GoTo Exit_DeleteRegValue
End If

lResult = lResult = RegCloseKey(hKeyHandle)

Exit_DeleteRegValue:
Exit Sub

Error_DeleteRegValue:
MsgBox Error
Resume Exit_DeleteRegValue

End Sub
```

Create another new subkey named DeleteRegKey and put the code from Listing 17.13 in it.

LISTING 17.13 The Code for DeleteRegKey

```
Sub DeleteRegKey(lRoot As Long, sSubKey As String)
' Deletes key from registry
' Parameters: lRoot is one of HKEY_CURRENT_USER or
' HKEY_LOCAL_MACHINE
' sSubKey is the subkey name (requires leading \)

Dim lResult As Long, hKeyHandle As Long
Dim sMsg As String

On Error GoTo Error_DeleteRegKey

' Open key
```

continues

LISTING 17.13 continued

```
lResult = RegOpenKeyEx(lRoot, sSubKey, 0, KEY_QUERY_VALUE, hKeyHandle)

If lResult <> ERROR_SUCCESS Then
 sMsg = "Could not open key"
 MsgBox sMsg
 GoTo Exit_DeleteRegKey
End If

lResult = RegDeleteKey(lRoot, sSubKey)
If lResult <> ERROR_SUCCESS Then
 sMsg = "Could not delete key"
 MsgBox sMsg
 GoTo Exit_DeleteRegKey
End If

Exit_DeleteRegKey:
Exit Sub

Error_DeleteRegKey:
MsgBox Error
Resume Error_DeleteRegKey

End Sub
```

A Look at the Code

There is nothing spectacular in either of these routines. Both start by opening the key, and both then call their respective API functions. If there is any difference, it is that after deleting a value, the key must be closed. Note that the access parameter for the functions is KEY_SET_VALUE.

Both RegDeleteValue and RegDeleteKey require the handle of the target Registry key. The handle is provided by the RegOpenKey function.

The function RegDeleteValue deletes a single value from the Registry key, which is then closed by the function RegCloseKey. To remove several values from the key, RegDeleteValue must be called once for each value.

The function RegDeleteKey removes the entire key from the Registry. There is no need to close the key afterward; it no longer exists, and RegCloseKey would return an error.

Running the Program

When you run the program, you can try out both operations. Enter VB Interactive\1.0 in the SubKeys textbox, Test in the Value Name textbox, and click the Delete Value button. Use Regedit to verify that the text value has been removed. Close Regedit before the next step.

Change the SubKeys textbox to read VB Interactive, click the Delete Key button, and run Regedit again to verify that the entire key is gone.

The RegAPI.Bas module can be included in other programs, simplifying your future Registry access.

Lesson Summary

In this lesson, you completed your exploration of the Registry APIs. Although the program itself did nothing with the Registry subkeys and values that it stored, you have already seen some of the things you can do with that data. Other possibilities include registration information, version information, encrypted passwords, serial numbers, and pallets. The RegAPI.Bas module can be included in other programs, simplifying your future Registry access.

Quiz 6

1. Both _____ and _____ require the handle of the target Registry key.
    a. RegDeleteKey and RegDeleteValue
    b. RegDeleteKey and RegRemoveValue
    c. RegRemoveKey and RegRemoveValue
    d. RegCloseKey and RegCloseValue

2. The _____ provides the handle to the target Registry key.
    a. RegGetKey function
    b. RegOpenKey function
    c. RegRetrieveKey function
    d. RegObtainKey function

3. The _____ function deletes a single value from the Registry key.
    a. RegCloseKey
    b. RegFreeKey
    c. RegDeleteValue
    d. RegRemoveKey

4. After an entire key is removed from the Registry, you must then

    a. Call the `RegCloseKey` function.

    b. Call the `RegFreeKey` function.

    c. Do nothing. Calling `RegCloseKey` would return an error.

    d. Call the `RegDeleteValue` function, then `RegCloseKey`.

Chapter Summary

This chapter covered two topics: ActiveX controls and the system Registry.

In Lesson 1, we introduced a powerful tool included with Visual Basic 6 called the ActiveX Interface Wizard. We used the previous project `SButton` and created the control using the wizard. In Lesson 2, we covered all the topics of compiling and distributing your control. Such topics as licensing, shareware distribution and versioning issues were discussed.

The second topic focused on the system Registry. Lesson 3 showed you how to save data to the system Registry and how to retrieve that data using Visual Basic code. Lesson 4 showed you how to add values to the subkeys. In Lesson 5, we wrote code to read Registry values, and in Lesson 6 we covered deleting values and subkeys.

CHAPTER 18

Using Visual Basic for Communications

Communication! It is one of the bywords of modern computing. If you don't have a modem and an Internet account, you are considered impoverished. And it's an ever-expanding field. More and more business software is Internet ready.

This chapter introduces some of the communications capabilities in Visual Basic 6. All the lessons in this chapter require a modem, and some require an Internet account.

LESSON 1

The MSComm Control

In the days of MS-DOS and Windows 3.x, connection to the serial port or a modem was a matter of sending and reading data from hardware addresses called *ports*. Windows 95 strongly discourages direct port access, which is often a source of system problems. Instead, with Windows 95 and Windows NT computers, accessing input/output (I/O) ports is handled through drivers. The result is greater stability for the operating, system, but it has also created problems for people with a need for I/O operations because they could no longer get direct access to the ports.

The MSComm control provides serial communications for Visual Basic programs by providing access to the serial ports. This lesson unravels some of the intricacies of using the MSComm control to talk to your modem.

Start a new project and add the MSComm control to the toolbox. Press Ctrl+T or select Components from the Project menu and select Microsoft MSComm Control 6.0. Click OK. The icon for the MSComm control is shown in Figure 18.1. The completed project is on the CD that comes with this book.

FIGURE 18.1

The MSComm *control in the toolbox.*

Double-click the MSComm icon to place the MSComm control on the form. It has no visible interface, so it doesn't matter where you put it. Add three Command buttons and a text box to the form. Set the properties according to Table 18.1.

TABLE 18.1 Properties for MSComm Project 1

Object	Property	Value
Form	Name	frmComm_1
	Caption	"Comm 1"
	Caption	"Comm 1"
	Height	4725
	Width	7650
CommandButton	Name	cmdQuit
	Caption	"E&xit"
	Height	315
	Left	5940
	TabIndex	2
	Top	540
	Width	1455
CommandButton	Name	cmdStop
	Caption	"Stop"
	Height	315
	Left	180
	TabIndex	1
	Top	540
	Width	1455

Object	Property	Value
CommandButton	Name	cmdStart
	Caption	"Start"
	Height	315
	Left	180
	TabIndex	0
	Top	60
	Width	1455
TextBox	Name	txtInData
	Height	3615
	Left	60
	MultiLine	True
	ScrollBars	2-Vertical
	TabIndex	3
	Top	1020
	Width	7515
MSComm	Name	MSComm1
	DTREnable	True

18

Click Save Project in the File menu and save the project as Comm_1.prj. The design-time form is shown in Figure 18.2.

FIGURE 18.2

frmComm_1 *at design time.*

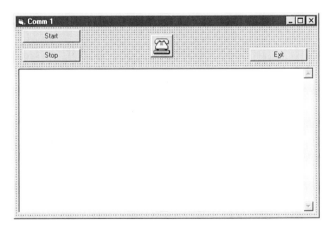

MSComm Properties

The MSComm control has a bewildering array of properties. They are needed to set up the modem, for handshaking between the computer and the modem, and for transferring data to and from the modem.

Modem Setup

If you and Joe User decided to set up two-way radio communications, and you purchased an FM transceiver while Joe purchased an AM transceiver, there would not be a lot of communication. The same is true of computer serial communications. Before a serial port can start communicating, it must be set up so that the port's properties match those of the data source. With the exception of the CommPort property, the parameters listed in Table 18.2 must be the same on both ends for communication to take place.

TABLE 18.2 Setup Property Parameters

Parameter	Settings	Meaning
CommPort	1 through 16	Selects the Com port to use. You must set the CommPort property to match the port you plan to use before you do anything else.
Baud rate	110 through 56000	The number of data bits being transferred per second. If you are connecting to a modem, the number cannot exceed the maximum BPS rate of the modem.
Parity	O, E, N, M, S	An error-checking mechanism based on whether the number of ones in a byte is odd or even. Usually set to N, because modems have better error correcting built into them.
Data bits	4 through 8	An integer representing the number of bits to send as a complete unit.
Stop bits	1, 1.5, 2	An extra bit that is sent with each byte to indicate the end of the byte.

The settings are put together in a comma-delimited string. A typical setting would look like this:

```
MSComm1.Settings = "28800,N,8,1"
```

This setup string means 28,800 baud, no parity, 8-bit data, and one-stop bit. This is typical for modem communications.

If you are communicating via modem, set your baud rate at the highest rate available for your modem. When it connects with another modem, the two modems determine the fastest baud rate they can use together. If you are connecting a serial port directly to another computer or to another device with a serial interface, the two must have the same baud rate settings.

The settings are not sent to the modem, actually, but to an integrated circuit called UART. *UART* stands for *Universal Asynchronous Receiver Transmitter*. The UART handles the conversion of data from parallel (8 bits at a time) format to serial (1 bit at a time) format. It also handles the baud rate, parity, and stop bits.

Other properties are involved in setup, too. Much of the time you can use the default values, but there may be times when a change is needed. These properties are listed in Table 18.3.

TABLE 18.3 Other Setup Properties

Parameter	Settings	Meaning
inBufferSize	0 to 65535	Sets or returns the size of the input buffer. This is the number of consecutive bytes that can be received and stored before the computer reads the input data. If the buffer overflows, an overflow error is generated and some of the data will be lost. Default size is 1,024 (1K) bytes. If this overflows, increase the size.
outBufferSize	0 to 65535	Sets or returns the size of the output buffer. This is the number of bytes stored in the transmit buffer. If the computer attempts to send more data when this buffer is full, an overflow error is generated and some of the data will be lost. Default size is 512 bytes. If this overflows, increase the size.
DTREnable	True or False	If DTREnable is set to True, the computer signals the modem that it is ready to communicate by making the data terminal ready (DTR) line high when the port is opened. Some serial devices require this, but the default setting is False, because most do not.

continues

18

TABLE 18.3   continued

Parameter	Settings	Meaning
RTSEnable	True or False	If RTSEnable is True, the computer will make the request to send (RTS) line high to request permission from the modem before it transmits data. The computer will not send data until the clear to send (CTS) line goes high in response. Some serial devices require this, but the default setting is False, because most do not.
NullDiscard	True or False	Determines whether Nulls are sent to the modem. The default value is True.
EOFEnable	True or False	Determines whether MSComm looks for the end of file (EOF) character. If this is set to True, an EOF character terminates data reception. The default value is False.

Most of these properties can usually be left set to their default values. Do not change them unless you have a specific requirement. There are a couple of other properties that fit in this classification. They are used with event-driven communications, and are covered in a later lesson.

Handshaking

Communication with a modem requires a lot of back-and-forth action between the computer and the modem. Each must be sure that the other is ready before data transfer can take place. The chatter between the modem and the computer—exclusive of actual data transfer—is called *handshaking*. The *handshaking* signals are listed in Table 18.4.

TABLE 18.4   Handshaking Signals

Signal	MSComm1	Purpose/Meaning
None	HandShaking	Establishes the handshaking protocol that will be used for data transfers. The default is None. Other choices are comXOnXOff, which is a form of software handshaking; comRTS, which is hardware handshaking; and comRTSXOnXOff, which uses both.
DTR	None	Data terminal ready signal sent from the computer to the modem to indicate that the computer is ready to establish communication. This is automatic when the DTREnable property is set to True.

Signal	MSComm1	Purpose/Meaning
DSR	DSRHolding	Data set ready is a signal from the modem to the computer indicating that the modem is ready for communications. If DSRHolding is True, communications can be started.
RTS	None	A request to send signal is sent from the computer to the modem before the computer sends output data. This is automatic when the RTSEnable property is set to True.
CTS	CTS	A holding clear to send is a signal sent from the modem to the computer in response to RTS. If CTSHolding is True, data can be transmitted.
CD	CDHolding	When the modem is connected to another modem, there is a steady carrier signal between them, and the modem makes the carrier-detect (CD) signal high. If CDHolding is True, there is a carrier and the CD line is high.
Break	Break	Some communications programs require that a break signal be sent at specific times. Setting Break to True sends the break signal; setting it to False ends the break signal.
InBufferCount		Returns the number of bytes in the input buffer.
OutBufferCount		Returns the number of bytes in the output buffer.

Data Transfer

Once the modem is set up and handshaking has been determined, you are ready for data transfers to take place. (Finally!) And, after all that work, it's a relief to know how simple it is to send and receive data. Use

```
MSComm1.Output = DataString
```

to send data and

```
MSComm1.InputLen = 0
InputString = MSComm1.Input
```

to receive it.

The InputLen property tells the MSComm control how many bytes to read from the input buffer. Setting it to 0 tells it to read all the data that is in the buffer.

Your First Comm Program

It's time to put it all to work now. There's nothing like experience to simplify the complexities. Open the Code window and add a declaration to the General Declarations section:

```
Option Explicit
Private bQuit As Boolean
```

Add the following code to the Click event of cmdStop:

```
Private Sub cmdStop_Click()
    bQuit = True
End Sub
```

Add the following code to the Click event of cmdQuit:

```
Private Sub cmdQuit_Click()
    Unload Me
    End
End Sub
```

Add the code in Listing 18.1 to the Click event of cmdStart.

LISTING 18.1   Making It Work

```
Private Sub cmdStart_Click()
    '   Buffer for input data
    Dim InString As String
    ' Initialize quit command
    bQuit = False
    ' Initialize Com Port
    txtInData = vbCrLf & txtInData & _
      "Opening Com port" & vbCrLf & vbCrLf
    ' Move insertion point to end of text
    txtInData.SelStart = Len(txtInData)
    ' Set Com port to the one in YOUR computer
    MSComm1.CommPort = 2
    ' Send settings: Set Baud rate to the fastest that
    ' YOUR modem can handle. Settings here are
    ' 14400 baud, no parity, 8 data, and 1 stop bit.
    MSComm1.Settings = "14400,N,8,1"
    ' Tell the control to read entire buffer when Input
    ' is used.
    MSComm1.InputLen = 0
    ' Open the port.
    MSComm1.PortOpen = True
    ' Send the attention command to the modem.
    MSComm1.Output = "AT" & vbCrLf
    ' Wait for data to come back to the serial port.
```

```
        Do While Not bQuit
            If MSComm1.InBufferCount Then
                InString = InString & MSComm1.Input
                If InStr(InString, vbCrLf) Then
                    txtInData = txtInData & InString
                    txtInData.SelStart = Len(txtInData)
                    If InStr(InString, "OK") Then Exit Do
                    InString = ""
                    DoEvents
                End If
            End If
            DoEvents
            If bQuit Then Exit Do
        Loop
        txtInData = vbCrLf & vbCrLf & txtInData & _
          "Closing Com port" & vbCrLf & vbCrLf
        txtInData.SelStart = Len(txtInData)
        MSComm1.PortOpen = False
End Sub
```

That's it.

What's Going On?

The code displays messages in txtInData that let you follow the progress of the program. The line

```
txtInData.SelStart = Len(txtInData)
```

keeps the insertion point at the end of the text box, which means you always see the last data that was inserted.

The first working step is to set up the modem. The lines

```
MSComm1.CommPort = 2
MSComm1.Settings = "14400,N,8,1"
MSComm1.InputLen = 0
MSComm1.PortOpen = True
```

do that. Be sure to set the CommPort property to match your computer and the Baud portion of the setup string to the highest baud rate your modem supports.

Next you need to send something to your computer that will make the modem respond. The line

```
MSComm1.Output = "AT" & vbCrLf
```

sends the Attention signal to the modem. The signal is part of the Hayes-compatible command set that is recognized by nearly every modem used in personal computers.

Now comes the hard part: reading the data from the modem and displaying it. The code

```
Do While Not bQuit
        If MSComm1.InBufferCount Then
            InString = InString & MSComm1.Input
            If InStr(InString, vbCrLf) Then
                txtInData = txtInData & InString
                txtInData.SelStart = Len(txtInData)
                If InStr(InString, "OK") Then Exit Do
                InString = ""
                DoEvents
            End If
        End If
        DoEvents
    Loop
```

sets up a Do loop for that. Chances are that your modem, by default, echoes the commands you send back to your computer. If so, it will send back the "AT" & vbCrLf. When InBufferCount is not zero (there is data in the input buffer), the outer If...Then transfers the data from the input buffer to InString. Reading the data from InBuffer also clears the buffer.

The inner If...Then checks for a carriage-return character, which indicates the end of a line of data. When the carriage return is found, the data is copied from InString to the text box, and InString is cleared. The DoEvents gives the computer time to paint the text into the text box.

Hayes-compatible modems respond to every successful command string with OK. Once that OK is received, no further data will be received. The third If...Then looks for OK and exits from the loop when it is found.

What if it is not successful? That's why cmdStop is there. Clicking cmdStop sets the Boolean variable bQuit to True, which also exits from the loop. The code could check for the word ERROR, too, but there may be cases where the modem just _doesn't respond. cmdStop handles that case, too.

Finally, the code in cmdStart closes the Com port.

Running the Program

Press F5 or click the Start button to run the program. Click Start and watch txtData. The running program is shown in Figure 18.3.

Viewing the Handshaking

You can get an idea about some of the handshaking signals by adding a new procedure to this program. Select Add Procedure from the Tools menu. Add a Private procedure named ShowStatus. Add the code in Listing 18.2 to the ShowStatus procedure.

FIGURE **18.3**

prjComm_1 *at runtime*.

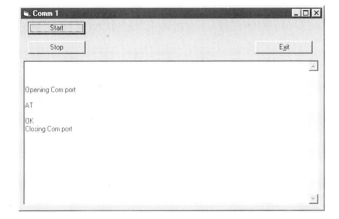

LISTING 18.2   The ShowStatus Procedure

```
Private Sub ShowStatus()
    Debug.Print "CDHolding  " & MSComm1.CDHolding
    Debug.Print "Input Mode " & MSComm1.InputMode
    Debug.Print "CTSHolding " & MSComm1.CTSHolding
    Debug.Print "DSRHolding " & MSComm1.DSRHolding
    Debug.Print "DTREnable  " & MSComm1.DTREnable
    Debug.Print "EOFEnable  " & MSComm1.EOFEnable
    Debug.Print "Handshaking " & MSComm1.Handshaking
    Debug.Print "RTSEnable  " & MSComm1.RTSEnable
End Sub
```

Now change the code in the Click event of cmdStart to that in Listing 18.3 (changes are in bold).

LISTING 18.3   Changes to cmdStart_Click

```
Private Sub cmdStart_Click()
    '   Buffer for input data
    Dim InString As String
    ' Initialize quit command
    bQuit = False
    ' Initialize Com Port
    txtInData = vbCrLf & txtInData & _
      "Opening Com port" & vbCrLf & vbCrLf
    ' Move insertion point to end of text
    txtInData.SelStart = Len(txtInData)
    ' Set Com port to the one in YOUR computer
    MSComm1.CommPort = 2
    ' Send settings: Set Baud rate to the fastest that
```

continues

LISTING 18.3   continued

```
' YOUR modem can handle. Settings here are
' 14400 baud, no parity, 8 data, and 1 stop bit.
MSComm1.Settings = "14400,N,8,1"
' Tell the control to read entire buffer when Input
' is used.
MSComm1.InputLen = 0
' Open the port.
MSComm1.PortOpen = True
' Send the attention command to the modem.
Debug.Print "After Open"
ShowStatus
MSComm1.Output = "AT" & vbCrLf
' Wait for data to come back to the serial port.
Do While Not bQuit
    If MSComm1.InBufferCount Then
        InString = InString & MSComm1.Input
        If InStr(InString, vbCrLf) Then
            txtInData = txtInData & InString
            txtInData.SelStart = Len(txtInData)
            If InStr(InString, "OK") Then Exit Do
            InString = ""
            DoEvents
        End If
    End If
    DoEvents
Loop
txtInData = vbCrLf & vbCrLf & txtInData & _
    "Closing Com port" & vbCrLf & vbCrLf
txtInData.SelStart = Len(txtInData)
MSComm1.PortOpen = False
Debug.Print "After Close"
ShowStatus
End Sub
```

Run the program again. The state of the selected handshaking signals is displayed in the Immediate window.

Lesson Summary

In this lesson introduce the MSComm control and cover its properties. We also learned about modem settings and how they are used. It was all put to work by writing an application that uses the MSComm control. In the next lesson, we cover the modem more thoroughly.

Quiz 1

1. Before a serial port can start communicating, it must be set up so that

    a. All port's properties match those of the data source with exception of the Data bits property

    b. Only the CommPort property matches that of the data source

    c. All the port's properties match those of the data source

    d. All the port's properties are initialized to Null

2. If you are communicating via modem, set your baud rate

    a. At the highest rate available for your modem

    b. At the lowest rate available for your modem

    c. At 14,400 baud

    d. At 28,8000 Rpms

3. The integrated circuit that handles conversion of data parallel format to serial format is called:

    a. A Converter

    b. A TRUART

    c. A Comm Chip

    d. A UART

4. The chatter between the modem and the computer—exclusive of actual data transfer—is called:

    a. Sync-transferring

    b. Backscratching

    c. Handshaking

    d. Protocoling

Exercise 1

Complexity: Easy

1. Change the Comm program by adding three label controls. The first label control will display the comm port that is being used, the second label will display the modem settings, and the third label will display the port status. Place all the code that set the label captions into one routine calledShowModemStatus. Place the calls to this routine in the proper places, so that the port status label reflects the changing of the port status.

Complexity: Moderate

2. Change the Comm program by adding four command buttons and a label field.
   Label each button 9600 Baud, 14400 Baud, 28800 Baud, 56000 Baud. Write the
   program so that when the user clicks one of the buttons, the baud rate is changed
   for the MSComm control. Display the Settings property of the MSComm control in the
   label to show that the changes have been made. In addition, execute the code of the
   9600 Baud button when the form loads, so that the MSComm control and label field
   are initialized.

LESSON 2

More from the Modem

It won't take long before just getting your modem to say OK gets pretty dull. This lesson
uses a different AT command to return the active configuration profile and the configuration profiles that are stored in the modem's nonvolatile RAM. (If that means nothing to
you, don't worry about it.)

Reading the Profiles

This program uses the same form as the last one, but makes substantial changes to the
code, including two new procedures. It's your choice whether to modify the last program, to start a new one, or to read the completed project from the CD that accompanies
this book.

All the code for this project is shown in Listing 18.4.

LISTING 18.4   Code for prjComm_2

```
Option Explicit
Private bQuit As Boolean

Private Sub cmdQuit_Click()
    Unload Me
    End
End Sub

Private Sub cmdStart_Click()
    ' Initialize quit command
    bQuit = False
    ' Initialize Com Port
    If Not MSComm1.PortOpen Then OpenCom
```

```
    ' Request configuration data
    txtInData = txtInData & vbCrLf & "Sending request" & vbCrLf & vbCrLf
    txtInData.SelStart = Len(txtInData)
    ' Send it
    MSComm1.Output = "AT &V" & vbCrLf
    ' Wait for data to come back to the serial port.
    ReadModem
End Sub

Private Sub cmdStop_Click()
    If MSComm1.PortOpen = False Then Exit Sub
    bQuit = True
    txtInData = vbCrLf & txtInData & _
      "Closing Com port" & vbCrLf & vbCrLf
    txtInData.SelStart = Len(txtInData)
    MSComm1.PortOpen = False
    txtInData = vbCrLf & txtInData & _
      "Closed " & vbCrLf & vbCrLf
    txtInData.SelStart = Len(txtInData)
End Sub

Public Sub ReadModem()
    Dim InString As String
    Do
        If MSComm1.InBufferCount Then
            InString = InString & MSComm1.Input
            If InStr(InString, vbCrLf) Then
                txtInData = txtInData & InString
                txtInData.SelStart = Len(txtInData)
                If InStr(InString, "OK") Then Exit Do
                InString = ""
                DoEvents
            End If
        End If
        DoEvents
        If bQuit Then Exit Do
    Loop
End Sub

Public Sub OpenCom()
    txtInData = vbCrLf & txtInData & _
      "Opening Com port" & vbCrLf & vbCrLf
    txtInData.SelStart = Len(txtInData)
    ' Set Com port to the one in YOUR computer
    MSComm1.CommPort = 2
    ' Send settings: Set Baud rate to the fastest that
    ' YOUR modem can handle
    ' 14400 baud, no parity, 8 data, and 1 stop bit.
    MSComm1.Settings = "14400,N,8,1"
```

continues

LISTING 18.4   continued

```
        ' Tell the control to read entire buffer when Input
        ' is used.
        MSComm1.InputLen = 0
        ' Open the port.
        MSComm1.PortOpen = True
End Sub
```

The main difference, aside from the AT command, is that this program divides up the work into more logical units. When you click Start, the code in the cmdStart_Click event tests to see if the Com port is already open. (Trying to open an already open port raises an error.) If the port is not open, the program calls the OpenCom procedure, which contains all the familiar code to open the Com port.

The command AT &V asks the modem to return the current configuration and a listing of all the stored configurations from the modem's nonvolatile RAM (NVRAM). After sending this command to the modem, the program calls the ReadModem procedure, which is also familiar code in a new place. When ReadModem returns to cmdStart_Click, however, there is a change—the Com port is not closed. If you plan to send a series of commands to the modem, you don't want to close the Com port after each one. Closing the Com port after each command resets everything back to its default, undoing the changes you've made.

Running prjComm_2

Run the program by pressing F5 or clicking the Start button. When you click Start, you should get a screen that looks something like Figure 18.4.

FIGURE 18.4

After the AT &V
command.

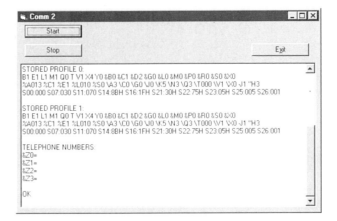

The properties of the MSComm control must match the settings of your modem. For example, if the baud rate or handshaking property is set incorrectly, your modem will not respond correctly.

What is all that stuff? Something like 50 settings are stored in your modem to set it up for communications. Communications programs and Internet dialers set specific values by sending setup strings to the modem. (Values not specifically changed are left with their default values, which are chosen by the modem's manufacturer.) Toward the top of txtData, the current configuration is listed. The stored profiles are sets of configurations that have been stored in NVRAM. If you send "AT &Y1" as a command string, stored profile number 1 will become the active profile.

Getting the correct setup string for an application is tricky. It is the source of more problems in communications than probably any other single issue. Being able to view the current profile can sometimes help you figure out why a modem communication link is not working. Listing and explaining each of the entries in the profile is well beyond the scope of this book. Consult your modem's manual for help.

A Phone Dialer

It doesn't take much to convert this program into a useful phone dialer. Once you can safely send one AT command to your modem, you can send any AT command to your modem. To create the dialer, start by adding a list box to your form and changing the captions on a few of the buttons. Name the list box lstNumbers. Change the caption on the cmdStart to Dial and the caption on cmdStop to Disconnect. The completed project is on the CD that accompanies this book. Use Figure 18.5 as a guide for laying out the form.

FIGURE 18.5

The dialer project.

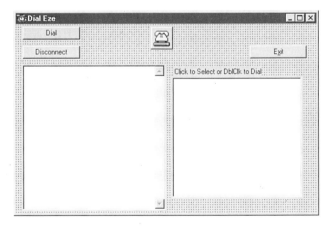

Add the following code to the Form_Load event:

```
Private Sub Form_Load()
    Dim j As Integer
    ' Put names and numbers into array
    PhoneList.Name = "David"
    PhoneList.Number = "555-1234"
    PhoneList.Name = "Mark"
    PhoneList.Number = "(555) 555-1212"
    PhoneList.Name = "Pierre"
    PhoneList.Number = "555-2345"
    j = 1
    ' Put names into listbox
    Do While PhoneList.Name <> ""
        lstNumbers.AddItem PhoneList.Name
        j = j + 1
    Loop
End Sub
```

Substitute the names and numbers of your friends for the dummy names and numbers included here. Of course, if you want to make this into a practical dialer, you need a way to add and delete names and numbers. That exercise is left to your imagination.

Now add the following to the lstNumbers_Click and lstNumbers_DblClick events:

```
Private Sub lstNumbers_Click()
    ' Set index into array
    iIndex = lstNumbers.ListIndex + 1
End Sub

Private Sub lstNumbers_DblClick()
    ' Set index into array
    iIndex = lstNumbers.ListIndex + 1
    ' Dial
    cmdStart_Click
End Subx
```

The Click event returns an index into the array of names and numbers. The second does the same, then clicks the Dial button.

Change the code in cmdStart to the following:

```
Private Sub cmdStart_Click()
    ' Initialize quit command
    bQuit = False
    ' Check for selection
    If iIndex < 1 Then
        MsgBox "No number selected", vbOKOnly, "Sorry"
        Exit Sub
    End If
    ' Get number
```

```
      PhoneNumber = PhoneList(iIndex).Number
      txtInData = txtInData & "Dialing " & _
        PhoneList(iIndex).Name & vbCrLf
      ' Initialize Com Port
      If Not MSComm1.PortOpen Then OpenCom
      ' Dial the number
      ' Use DP for pulse dial
      MSComm1.Output = "AT DT " & PhoneNumber & vbCrLf
      ' Wait for data to come back to the serial port.
      ReadModem
End Sub
```

The first new part of the code makes sure that a number has been selected, and displays a message if it hasn't. The next two lines change the display in txtInDate to reflect the new functionality of the program. The line that does the work is MSComm1.Output = "AT DT " & PhoneNumber & vbCrLf. The AT gets the modem's attention. The D tells it that it is going to dial a number, and the T instructs it to use tone dialing. (If you have a pulse-dial phone, change the T to P.) The phone number can be entered in almost any form: 5551212 555-1212, and (555) 555-1212 all work. When the modem is dialing, it ignores almost everything except the numbers.

Change Sub ReadModem to the following:

```
Public Sub ReadModem()
    Dim InString As String
    Do While Not bQuit
        If MSComm1.InBufferCount Then
            InString = InString & MSComm1.Input
            If InStr(InString, vbCrLf) Then
                txtInData = txtInData & InString
                DoEvents
                txtInData.SelStart = Len(txtInData)
                If InStr(InString, "BUSY") Then bQuit = True
                If InStr(InString, "NO") Then bQuit = True
                InString = ""
            End If
        End If
        DoEvents
    Loop
    cmdStop_Click
End Sub
```

There are two possible responses from the modem, BUSY and NO DIALTONE. If either shows up, ReadModem exits the Do loop and clicks cmdStop to disconnect. Sadly, most modems will not tell you when they get a voice response. (If you have the speaker on the modem turned on, you can usually hear when somebody answers.)

Running the Program

Run the program by pressing F5 or clicking the Start button. Select a number from the list and click the Dial button. After a few seconds, pick up your handset and click the Disconnect button. The modem acts like a second phone on the telephone line and reduces the phone's volume.

Have the program dial your own number so you can see the BUSY response. If you want to see the NO DIALTONE response, unplug the modem from the phone jack before you try to dial a number.

Lesson Summary

In this lesson we took our modem knowledge one step further by writing a dialer program. We communicated with the modem by sending command directly to it and reading the messages it sent back. In the next lesson, we'll communicate with the rest of the world by with the MSComm control.

Quiz 2

1. The command AT &V asks the modem

    a. To return the current configuration and a listing of all the stored configurations from the modem's nonvolatile ROM

    b. To return the current configuration and a listing of all the stored configurations from the modem's nonvolatile RAM

    c. To return the current configuration and a listing of all the stored configurations from the modem's volatile RAM

    d. To return the current configuration and a listing of all the stored configurations from the modem's volatile ROM

2. If you plan to send a series of commands to the modem,

    a. You don't want to close the Com port after each command

    b. You want to close the Com port after each command

    c. It doesn't matter if you close the Com port after each command or not

    d. You have to close the Com port after each command

3. Communications programs set specific values by sending _____ to the modem.

    a. Setup values

    b. Default strings

  c. Initialization strings

  d. Setup strings

4. If Communications programs do not set specific values to the modem, the modem values

  a. Are set to 0

  b. Do not change

  c. Are set to their default values

  d. Are set to their maximum values

Exercise 2

Complexity: Easy

1. Change the Dialer program so that when a busy number or no dial tone is detected, a message box pops up signaling the error.

Complexity: Moderate

2. Add a second form to the Dialer program with two command buttons. Label the first button Retry, the second, Cancel. Only have this form appear when there is a busy tone. When the user clicks Retry, hide the form and have the number dialed again. Add labels to the form explaining that the line is busy, and ask if they would like to retry the number.

18

LESSON 3

Communications with MSComm

It's all well and good to be able to chat with your modem, but the idea of having a modem is to be able to chat with the rest of the world. This lesson explains how to accomplish that daunting task.

You should realize that there are dozens of useful communications programs already written and distributed. They are used by hobbyists and businesses for calling computer bulletin board systems (BBS) and text-only Internet services. The best of them can handle ANSI graphics, a RIP graphics, and provide terminal emulation of a half dozen or so common dumb terminals. They also handle file transfers using any of a dozen different transfer protocols. (A *transfer protocol* is a set of agreed-upon rules for transferring data.)

The program developed in this lesson does none of that. It is not meant to be a replacement for commercial terminal programs. Translating raw ANSI codes into colors and symbols is a complex and time-consuming task that can only interfere with the main point of the lesson. And handling file transfer protocols such as ZModem and HSLink requires purchasing commercial ActiveX controls.

With that out of the way, welcome to Chat! Chat allows you use a modem to chat with someone across the miles.

The OnComm Event

The MSComm programs in Lesson 1 and Lesson 2 use polled communications. Once the Com port is open, the program sits in a Do loop and waits for InBufferCount to indicate that there is data to be read. It works, but it also ties up a lot of processor time just waiting for something to happen.

The MSComm control has one event, the OnComm event. The OnComm event is fired when almost any change occurs at the Com port. When a character arrives or is sent, the OnComm event is fired. When one of the handshaking lines changes, the OnComm event is fired. When an error is raised, the OnComm event is fired. And, when the OnComm event is fired, the CommEvent property returns a numeric code for the event.

The neat thing about OnComm is that it doesn't use any processor time until something happens. It is event driven, just like Command buttons and check boxes. The not-so-neat thing is that all UARTs do not support all the events. The program in this lesson shows you how to use event-driven communications. Perform the following steps:

1. Start a new project in Visual Basic. Set the properties of the form according to Table 18.5. The completed project is on the CD that accompanies this book.

TABLE 18.5   Properties for frmChat

Object	Property	Value
Form	Name	frmChat
	Caption	"Chat"
	Height	4320
	Width	7140
	ControlBox	False
	Icon	Graphics\Icons\Comm\Phone01.Ico
	MaxButton	False
	StartUpPosition	Windows Default

This is the main form for the program, but you need one more.

2. Add a second form to the project by selecting Add Form from the Project menu or clicking the Add Form icon on the toolbar. Set its properties according to Table 18.6.

TABLE 18.6   Properties for frmSetup

Object	Property	Value
Form	Name	frmSetup
	BorderStyle	Fixed Single
	Caption	"Set-Up Modem"
	Height	2415
	Width	2970
	ControlBox	False
	MaxButton	False
	MinButton	False

3. Press Ctrl+T or select Components from the Project menu. Find and select Microsoft MSComm 6.0 and Microsoft Windows Common Controls 6.0; then click OK. Chances are your toolbox must be resized to see all the controls it now holds.

4. Select Properties from the Project menu and set the program's properties according to Table 18.7.

TABLE 18.7   Project Settings

Tab	Property	Value
General	Project Type	Standard EXE
	Startup Object	frmSetup
	Project Name	Chat
Make	Title	Chat
	Icon	frmChat
Compile	Compile to Native Code	Selected
	Optimize for Small Code	Selected

5. Click OK when you are finished, then save the project to disk.

Don't run the project yet; there is no way except Ctrl+Break to exit from frmSetup, which is the startup form.

18

6. Make frmSetup the active window and add two Command buttons. Set their properties according to Table 18.8.

TABLE 18.8   frmSetup Properties

Object	Property	Value
CommandButton	Name	cmdCancel
	Caption	"Cancel"
	Default	False
	Height	375
	Left	480
	TabIndex	1
	Top	1920
	Width	855
CommandButton	Name	cmdOK
	Caption	"OK"
	Default	True
	Height	375
	Left	1440
	TabIndex	0
	Top	1920
	Width	855

When you use a form with no Control box, make sure you provide a way out! This form is used to set up the modem. Figure 18.6 shows frmSetup at design time so you can use it as a guide for the next several steps.

FIGURE 18.6

frmSetup *at design time.*

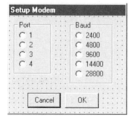

7. Add two frames to the form.

8. Add four Option buttons to Frame 1.

9. Add five Option buttons to Frame 2.

10. Set the properties according to Table 18.9.

TABLE 18.9   The Frames and Option Buttons for frmSetup

Object	Property	Value
Frame	Name	Frame1
	Caption	"Port"
	Height	1335
	Left	120
	Top	120
Frame	ToolTipText	"Select a Baud Rate"
	Width	975
OptionButton	Name	optPort
	Caption	"1"
	Index	0
OptionButton	Name	optPort
	Caption	"2"
	Index	1
OptionButton	Name	optPort
	Caption	"3"
	Index	2
OptionButton	Name	optPort
	Caption	"4"
	Index	3
Frame	Name	Frame2
	Caption	"Baud"
	Height	1575
	Left	1560
	Top	120
	ToolTipText	"Select a Baud Rate"
	Width	1095
OptionButton	Name	optBaud
	Caption	"2400"
	Index	0

18

continues

TABLE 18.9   continued

Object	Property	Value
OptionButton	Name	optBaud
	Caption	"4800"
	Index	1
OptionButton	Name	optBaud
	Caption	"9600"
	Index	2
OptionButton	Name	optBaud
	Caption	"14400"
	Index	3
OptionButton	Name	optBaud
	Caption	"28800"
	Index	4

Use the Format menu to size and position the Option buttons within their respective frames.

Obviously, `frmSetup` is used to select the port number and baud rate. Just as obviously, the user will not want to make the selection every time he or she runs the program, so Chat must save the selected port number and baud rate somewhere. You learned earlier in this book how to use the Windows Registry to store program configuration data. This lesson uses a different idea—a simple text data file—for the same purpose.

11. Open your favorite text editor and enter three lines of text, pressing Enter after each line.

```
0
0
0
```

(Those are zeros, not letter Os.)

12. Save the file in the directory with `Chat.vbp`. Name it `Chat.Dat`.

The first two numbers are indexes into the Option button control arrays and the third indicates whether the settings have been saved to disk by the program (0 = No.)

13. Add the code from Listing 18.5.

LISTING 18.5   Code for `frmSetup`

```
Option Explicit
Private iBaud As Integer, iSet As Integer
Public iPort As Integer, sBaud As String
Private bChanged As Boolean, sDatFile As String

Private Sub Form_Load()
ReadDat
If iSet = 1 Then
    optBaud(iBaud) = True
    optPort(iPort) = True
    sBaud = optBaud(iBaud).Caption
    bChanged = False
    cmdOK_Click
End If
End Sub

Private Sub cmdOK_Click()
If bChanged Then
' Save port and baud data
Open sDatFile For Output As #1
Print #1, iBaud
Print #1, iPort
Print #1, 1
Close #1
bChanged = False
End If
Load frmChat
DoEvents
frmChat.Show
Me.Hide
End Sub

Private Sub Form_Unload(Cancel As Integer)
If bChanged Then
' Save port and baud data
Open sDatFile For Output As #1
Print #1, iBaud
Print #1, iPort
Print #1, 1
Close #1
End If
End
End Sub

Private Sub optBaud_Click(Index As Integer)
bChanged = True
iBaud = Index
```

continues

LISTING 18.5   continued

```
sBaud = optBaud(Index).Caption
End Sub

Private Sub optPort_Click(Index As Integer)
bChanged = True
iPort = Index
End Sub
```

What the Code Is Doing

The Form_Load event opens Chat.Dat and reads three values from the data file. The following lines check the data file to see if it is the dummy file or if it has been saved by the program.

```
If iSet = 1 Then
    optBaud(iBaud) = True
    optPort(iPort) = True
    sBaud = optBaud(iBaud).Caption
    bChanged = False
    cmdOK_Click
End If
```

If it has been saved by the program, the code selects the Option button to match the stored baud rate and port number, then calls cmdOK_Click. The code in cmdOK_Click saves any changed data back to the disk file, loads and shows frmChat, and hides frmSetup.

If the user has changed one or both settings and then decides to cancel the changes, cmdCancel reads the original data back from disk and calls cmdOK_Click. Note that cmdCancel sets bChanged to False to avoid having to save the data back to the same file it just finished reading.

Figure 18.7 shows frmChat at runtime.

FIGURE 18.7

frmChat *at runtime.*

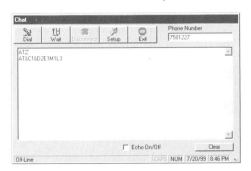

Note that there is still no way to exit from the program while frmSetup is active. That privilege is reserved for the main form, frmChat.

Building frmChat

Save and close frmSetup and bring the Form view of frmChat to the top; then, perform the following steps:

1. Add a toolbar, an image list, and an MSComm control to frmChat.
2. Right-click the image list and select Properties from the Context menu.
3. Select the images shown in Table 18.10.

TABLE 18.10 Icons for the Image List

Image	Index	Key
Graphic\Icons\Comm\Phone13.Ico	1	Call
Graphic\Icons\Comm\Phone14.Ico	2	Wait
Graphic\Icons\Comm\Phone16.Ico	3	Disconnect
Graphic\Icons\Industry\Wrench.Ico	4	Setup
Graphic\Icons\Traffic\Trffc14.Ico	5	Exit

Click OK when you are finished.

4. Click the toolbar and press F4 to open the Properties window.
5. Name the toolbar Tools.
6. Open the Property pages by clicking Custom in the Properties window.
7. On the General tab, set the image list to ImageList1.
8. Switch to the Buttons tab and add five buttons to the toolbar. Set their properties according to Table 18.11.

TABLE 18.11 Toolbar Buttons

Index	Caption	Key	Image
1	Dial	Dial	1
2	Wait	Wait	2
3	Disconnect	Disconnect	3
4	Setup	Setup	4
5	Exit	Exit	5

18

Add ToolTip text if you like.

9. Set the properties for the MSComm control according to Table 18.12.

TABLE 18.12   Properties for MSComm1

Object	Property	Value
MSComm Control	Name	MSComm1
	DTREnable	True
	Handshaking	2
	Rthreshold	1
	RTSEnable	True
	Sthreshold	1

10. Click OK when you are done.

The design-time form up to this point is shown in Figure 18.8.

FIGURE 18.8

frmChat *with ToolBar.*

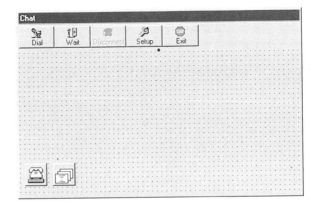

11. Open the Code window and add the code from Listing 18.6.

LISTING 18.6   Code for ToolBar Private Sub DialNumber ()

```
End Sub

Private Sub HangUp ()

End Sub

Private Sub WaitForRing ()
```

```
End Sub

Private Sub SetUp ()

End Sub

Private Sub QuitMe ()
If MSComm1.PortOpen Then MSComm1.PortOpen = False
Unload frmSetup
Unload Me
End
End Sub

Private Sub Tools_ButtonClick(ByVal Button As ComctlLib.Button)
Select Case Button
    Case "Dial"
        DialNumber
    Case "Disconnect"
        HangUp
    Case "Wait"
        WaitForRing
    Case "Setup"
        frmSetup.Show
    Case "Exit"
        QuitMe
End Select
End Sub
```

18

Finally, there is a way to exit from the program! The stubs get filled in later with code to make it all work.

12. Draw two text boxes right on top of the toolbar, one above the other. Set their properties according to Table 18.13.

TABLE 18.13 Text Box Properties and Values

Object	Property	Value
TextBox	Name	txtLabel
	Appearance	Flat
	BackColor	&H80000004&
	BorderStyle	None
	Height	195
	Left	4920
	Locked	True
	TabStop	False

continues

TABLE 18.13   continued

Object	Property	Value
	Text	"Phone Number"
	Top	0
	Width	1935
TextBox	Name	txtNum
	Height	285
	Left	4920
	ToolTipText	"Enter Phone Number"
	Top	240
	Width	2055

13. Add a status bar, a text box, a check box, and a Command button to the form.

14. In the Properties window, name the status bar Status.

15. Set the properties for the text box, the check box, and the Command button according to Table 18.14.

TABLE 18.14   Properties for txtChat, chkEcho, and cmdClear

Object	Property	Value
TextBox	Name	txtChat
	Height	2895
	Left	120
	MultiLine	True
	ScrollBars	Vertical
	Top	720
	Width	6855
CheckBox	Name	chkEcho
	Caption	"Echo On/Off"
	Height	255
	Left	= 3480
	Top	3720
	Width	1575

Object	Property	Value
CommandButton	Name	cmdClear
	Caption	"Clear"
	Height	255
	Left	5760
	Top	3720
	Width	1215

16. Right-click the status bar and select Properties from the Context menu.

17. On the Panels tab, add five panels. Set their properties according to Table 18.15.

TABLE 18.15 Properties for the Status Bar

Index	Key	AutoSize
1Stat	sbrText	sbrSpring
2	sbrCaps	sbrContents
3	sbrNum	sbrContents
4	sbrDate	sbrContents
5	sbrTime	sbrContents

The completed form at design time is shown in Figure 18.9.

FIGURE 18.9

frmChat *at design time.*

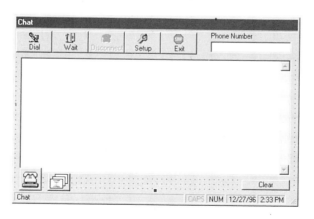

Now it's code time. Switch to the Code window and add the code in Listing 18.7.

LISTING 18.7   Startup Code for `frmChat`

```
Option Explicit
Private sSettings As String, iMyPort As Integer
Private Activity As Integer
Private bEcho As Boolean
Private Const Dialing As Integer = 1, Waiting As Integer = 2

Private Sub Form_Activate()
txtNum.SetFocus
OffLine
Status.Panels("Stat").Text = "Off-Line"
End Sub

Private Sub Form_Load()
iMyPort = frmSetup.iPort + 1
sSettings = frmSetup.sBaud & ",N,8,1"
End Sub

Private Sub cmdClear_Click()
txtChat = ""
End Sub

Private Sub chkEcho_Click()
bEcho = chkEcho.Value
End Sub
```

Nothing spectacular here. The Form_Load event reads two values from frmSetup and uses them to create the settings string for MSComm1. Now to fill in the stubs from that initial code. Start with Listing 18.8.

LISTING 18.8   Dialing Out

```
Private Sub DialNumber()
If txtNum = "" Then
    MsgBox "No number to dial", vbOKOnly, "Sorry."
    Exit Sub
End If
' Clear the chat box
txtChat = ""
If Not MSComm1.PortOpen Then
    OpenCom
    ' Wait for OK
    Do
        DoEvents
```

```
        Loop Until InStr(txtChat, "OK")
    End If
    Status.Panels("Stat").Text = "Dialing"
    ' dial
    MSComm1.Output = "ATDT " & txtNum & vbCrLf
    OnLine
    Activity = Dialing
    txtChat.SetFocus
    txtChat.SelStart = Len(txtChat)
End Sub
```

Before the program can dial a number, it must have a number. DialNumber checks to be sure that something has been entered in txtNum and exits if the text box is empty. If the test is passed, txtChat is cleared and the status of PortOpen is tested. If PortOpen is False, the OpenCom procedure is called, and the code loops until the modem responds with OK.

If the PortOpen is True, or after OpenCom has done its job, MSComm1.Output = "ATDT " & txtNum & vbCrLf dials the number and calls the OnLine procedure.

If you want to receive calls instead of make them, you must take a different tack. Listing 18.9 shows the code from the WaitForRing procedure.

LISTING 18.9   Waiting for a Call

```
Private Sub WaitForRing()
txtChat = ""
If Not MSComm1.PortOpen Then
    OpenCom
' Wait for OK
    Do
        DoEvents
    Loop Until InStr(txtChat, "OK")
End If
' Set autoanswer to one ring
MSComm1.Output = "ATS0=1" & vbCrLf
' Wait for OK
Do
    DoEvents
Loop Until InStr(txtChat, "OK")
OnLine
Activity = Waiting
txtChat.SetFocus
txtChat.SelStart = Len(txtChat)
End Sub
```

This procedure, too, must check the PortOpen property before it can do anything else. Again, if PortOpen is False, the OpenCom procedure is called and the code waits for OK from the modem before it proceeds.

Modems output a Ring Detect signal when they receive ring voltage from the phone line. Unfortunately, all UARTs do not support this signal, so the code in this procedure uses the modem's auto answer feature instead. The line MSComm1.Output = "ATS0=1" & vbCrLf does the job. Setting the modem's S0 register to 1 tells the modem to answer the phone on the first ring. (Be sure not to leave it that way. Callers who get modem negotiation tones when they call you tend to get annoyed!)

Opening the Com Port

The DialNumber procedure and the WaitForRing procedure call on OpenCom if the Com port is not already open. The code is shown in Listing 18.10.

LISTING 18.10 Opening the Com Port

```
Private Sub OpenCom()
Dim i As Integer
If Not MSComm1.PortOpen Then _
  MSComm1.PortOpen = True
' Reset modem
MSComm1.Output = "ATZ" & vbCrLf
' Setup string sets DCD ON (&C1)
' DTR ON (&D2), Echo ON (E1),
' Speaker ON (M1) and Speaker volume MAX (L3)
MSComm1.Output = "AT&C1&D2E1M1L3" & vbCrLf
End Sub
```

Once the Com port is open, this procedure resets it with MSComm1.Output = "ATZ" & vbCrLf. It's always a good idea to reset the modem to factory defaults before you do anything else. Otherwise, you may get some unpleasant surprises. The setup string, AT&C1&D2E1M1L3, does a number of chores:

1. &C1 sets the modem's data carrier detect (DCD) signal so it will follow the state of the received signal. If the modem on the other end hangs up, the DCD signal will switch to low (False).

2. &D2 tells the modem how to handle the data terminal ready (DTR) signal.

3. M1 turns the modem's speaker on while a connection is being made and off after the connection has been made. M0 turns the speaker off.

4. L3 sets the modem speaker's volume. Most modems have three acceptable values: L1, which is the softest; L2, which is medium; and L3, which is the loudest. Feel free to change this to suit your ears.

Hanging Up

No matter how much you like the person on the other end, eventually you will want to hang up and go eat lunch! The code in Listing 18.11 shows you how.

LISTING 18.11 Hanging Up

```
Private Sub HangUp()
If MSComm1.PortOpen Then
    ' Hang up the modem
    MSComm1.Output = "ATH0" & vbCrLf
    ' Turn off autoanswer
    MSComm1.Output = "ATS0=0" & vbCrLf
    ' turn off local echo
    bEcho = False
    chkEcho.Value = False
End If
Activity = 0
Tools.Buttons("Disconnect").Enabled = False
txtNum = ""
Status.Panels("Stat").Text = "Off-Line"
OffLine
End Sub
```

There's nothing special here. ATH0 is the command that tells the modem to hang up. Note that the procedure also turns off autoanswer with ATS0=0 and does a few other house-keeping chores.

All three procedures call on either OnLine or OffLine. They are shown in Listing 18.12.

LISTING 18.12 Online and Offline

```
Private Sub OnLine()
Tools.Buttons("Disconnect").Enabled = True
Tools.Buttons("Dial").Enabled = False
Tools.Buttons("Wait").Enabled = False
Tools.Buttons("Setup").Enabled = False
txtNum.Enabled = False
End Sub
```

continues

LISTING 18.12 continued

```
Private Sub OffLine()
Status.Panels("Stat").Text = "Off-Line"
Tools.Buttons("Disconnect").Enabled = False
Tools.Buttons("Dial").Enabled = True
Tools.Buttons("Wait").Enabled = True
Tools.Buttons("Setup").Enabled = True
txtNum.Enabled = True
End Sub
```

As you can see, these procedures handle the enabling and disabling of buttons on the toolbar so the user can't crash the program by clicking the wrong thing. While you are offline, you really don't need to hang up, and while you are online, there is no good reason to dial a number.

Using the OnComm Event

This program happily sits idle while it waits for signals from the UART to tell it something happened. When something does happen, an OnComm event is triggered. The OnComm event for frmChat is shown in Listing 18.13.

LISTING 18.13 The OnComm Event

```
Private Sub MSComm1_OnComm()
Dim sInBuffer As String
Select Case MSComm1.CommEvent
' Errors
    Case comBreak    ' A Break was received.
        Status.Panels("Stat").Text = "Received Break"
    Case comCDTO     ' CD Timeout.
        Status.Panels("Stat").Text = "CD Timed Out"
    Case comCTSTO    ' CTS Timeout.
        Status.Panels("Stat").Text = "CTS Timed Out"
    Case comDSRTO    ' DSR Timeout.
        Status.Panels("Stat").Text = "BDSR Timed Out"
    Case comFrame    ' Framing Error
        txtChat.SelStart = Len(txtChat.Text)
        txtChat.SelText = vbCrLf & "Framing Error" & vbCrLf
    Case comOverrun ' Data Lost.
        txtChat.SelStart = Len(txtChat)
        txtChat.SelText = vbCrLf & "TX OverRun Error" & vbCrLf
    Case comRxOver   ' Receive buffer overflow.
        txtChat.SelStart = Len(txtChat)
        txtChat.SelText = vbCrLf & "RX OverRun Error" & vbCrLf
    Case comRxParity    ' Parity Error.
        txtChat.SelStart = Len(txtChat)
        txtChat.SelText = vbCrLf & "RX Parity Error" & vbCrLf
```

```
      Case comTxFull   ' Transmit buffer full.
         txtChat.SelStart = Len(txtChat)
         txtChat.SelText = vbCrLf & "Trasmit Buffer Full" & vbCrLf
      Case comDCB ' Unexpected error retrieving DCB]
         txtChat.SelStart = Len(txtChat)
         txtChat.SelText = vbCrLf & "DCB Error" & vbCrLf
      ' Events
      Case comEvCD     ' Change in the CD line.
         If MSComm1.CDHolding Then
            Status.Panels("Stat").Text = "Connected"
            If Activity = Waiting Then
              MSComm1.Output = _
                "You have connected to Chat." & vbCrLf
                Status.Panels("Stat").Text = "Received call"
            End If
         Else
            HangUp
      End If           '
      Case comEvDSR    ' Change in the DSR line.
         If MSComm1.DSRHolding Then
         '   DSRChange
         Else
            Status.Panels("Stat").Text = _
              "Modem Not Ready"
         End If
      Case comEvReceive   ' Received Some Characters
         sInBuffer = MSComm1.Input
         ParseString (sInBuffer)
End Select
End Sub
```

The variable CommEvent reports exactly what caused the event to occur. The program uses a Select Case structure to respond. Take a look at the code.

Chances are you will never see the error messages in action. Modem technology is good enough these days that overflows and framing errors are rare.

The ComEvCD Event

The real work begins with ComEvCD, which is triggered when the carrier detect (CD) signal changes. Recall that the CD signal reports whether or not you are online. The actual status of the CD line is reported by CDHolding.

When CDHolding is True, the modem is connected. Because there are two ways the modem can get connected—placing a call or receiving a call—the Activity variable (you've been wondering about that one, haven't you?) determines what to do next. The If...Then sends out a welcome message when a call is received, but does nothing when the call is outgoing.

18

When CDHolding is False, you have been disconnected, so the code calls the HangUp procedure.

The ComEvDSR Event

The ComEvDSR event changes when the modem switches between ready and not ready. (The modem is the data set and the computer is the data terminal.) The only change of concern is when DSRHolding is False, meaning the modem is not available. It's unlikely you will ever see this event, but it must be handled.

The ComEvReceive Event

The event that gets fired the most is ComEvReceive, which is fired when the receive buffer has RThreshold or more characters. Recall that RThreshold is set to 1; the event is fired for every single character received! Each time it is fired, the characters in the receive buffer are read into the string sInBuffer.

Unfortunately, you can't just dump the characters into txtChat. Some characters are considered *unprintable* characters and leave ugly black lines on the screen. This is true of a linefeed character (vbLf), a carriage-return character (vbCr), and a backspace character (vbBack). To handle this, sInBuffer is sent to the ParseString procedure.

Handling the Unprintable Characters

The ParseString procedure is shown in Listing 18.14.

LISTING 18.14   The ParseString Procedure

```
Private Sub ParseString(sString As String)
' Deals with "Unprintable Characters"
Dim iPos As Integer, iLen
iLen = Len(txtChat)
txtChat.SelStart = iLen
' Start with Backspace
Do
    iPos = InStr(sString, vbBack)
    If iPos Then
        If iPos = 1 Then ' BS is first character
            txtChat.SelStart = iLen - 1
            ' Back up in the existing text
            txtChat.SelLength = 1
            sString = Mid$(sString, iPos + 1)
        Else
            sString = Left$(sString, iPos - 2) & _
              Mid$(sString, iPos + 1)
        End If
    End If
End If
```

```
Loop While iPos
' Strip out all linefeed characters
Do
    iPos = InStr(sString, vbLf)
    If iPos Then
        sString = Left$(sString, iPos - 1) & _
          Mid$(sString, iPos + 1)
    End If
Loop While iPos
' Now add linefeed to all carriage returns
iPos = 1
Do
    iPos = InStr(iPos, sString, vbCr)
    If iPos Then
        sString = Left$(sString, iPos) & _
          vbLf & Mid$(sString, iPos + 1)
        iPos = iPos + 1
    End If
Loop While iPos
' Display the string
txtChat.SelText = sString
txtChat.SelStart = Len(txtChat)
End Sub
```

The ParseString procedure runs through the string three times. The first Do loop deals with vbBack, the backspace character. The only special case is when vbBack is the first character in the string, in which case a character must be deleted from those already in txtChat. That nifty little trick is done by moving txtChat.SelStart back a space. If vbBack is not in the first character position, Left$() and Mid$() concatenate a new string minus one character. Note the code fragment Left$(sString, iPos - 2). The - 2 deletes the preceding character and the backspace character from the string.

The second Do loop removes every linefeed character from the string using concatenation.

The third Do loop puts all the linefeed characters back. Well, sort of. It adds vbLf to the string immediately following every vbCr character. The result, of course, is vbCrLf, which multiline text boxes such as txtChat can handle with ease.

Running Chat

Testing Chat is a little different from testing other programs in this book. As a first test, enter your own phone number in txtNum and click Dial. You should see the following messages appear in txtChat:

```
ATZ
AT&C1&D2E1M1L3
```

OK
ATDT 5551211

BUSY

Between the ATDT and the BUSY, you should hear the modem dialing out.

You can do a more thorough calling-out test if you have an account on a bulletin board system. Before you place the call, log on to the BBS and change your defaults so your account is a text-only connection. Figure 18.10 shows a BBS connection that has sent ANSI graphics to Chat.

FIGURE 18.10

Chat connected to an ANSI BBS.

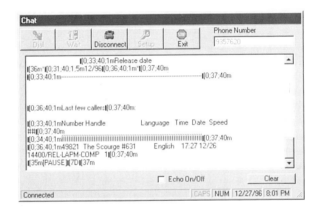

Hard to read, isn't it? All that strange-looking gibberish is code for colors and ANSI symbols. Figure 18.11 shows the same part of the BBS with graphics turned off.

FIGURE 18.11

Chat connected to a text-only BBS.

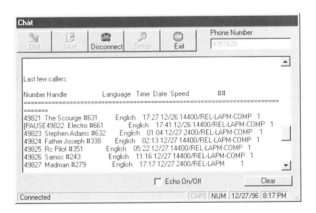

If you want to do a full test of Chat, you will have to install it on a friend's computer. Compile the program by selecting Make Chat.exe from the File menu. Run the Setup Wizard (see Chapter 14, "Advanced Features") and install the program on your friend's computer. At a prearranged time, start Chat and click Wait. Then have your friend use Chat to call your computer. You should be able to chat back and forth.

About Echo

If you type something in Chat and don't see it on your screen, the other computer is not echoing your keystrokes back to your computer. Turn Echo on. If you see double characters, turn Echo off.

Lesson Summary

In this lesson we worked more with the MSComm control by writing a program that allows the user chat with other computers, such as BBS's and text-only Internet services. This program also allows a user to change their modem settings through an interface we created. In the next lesson, we'll connect to the World Wide Web.

Quiz 3

1. The _____ event is fired when almost any change occurs at the Com port.

    a. The ComEvCD event

    b. The ComEvDSR event

    c. The ComEvReceive event

    d. The OnComm event

2. The _____ event changes when the modem switches between ready and not ready.

    a. The ComEvCD event

    b. The ComEvDSR event

    c. The ComEvReceive event

    d. The ComEvReady event

3. The _____ event is triggered when the carrier detect signal changes.

    a. The ComEvCD event

    b. The ComEvDSR event

    c. The ComEvReceive event

    d. The OnComm event

4. The _____ event gets fired when the receive buffer has RThreshold or more characters.

    a. The ComEvCD event

    b. The ComEvDSR event

    c. The ComEvReceive event

    d. The ComEvReady event

Exercise 3

Complexity: Easy

1. Add the baud option of 56000 to the frmSetup of the Chat program so that it will
work with 56k modems.

Complexity: Moderate

2. Create a new button in the Chat program with the caption Select Phone #. When
this button is pushed, display a form with text box where the user can select a
name (like the phone dialer program in lesson 2). That person's phone number
should appear in the phone number box of the Chat form.

LESSON 4

Connecting to the World Wide Web

Welcome to the Internet! By now you have at least some familiarity with the Internet. Be
it at work, home, school, or a friend's house, you most likely have done some surfing. It
is becoming more popular than ever, and it must be part of every programmer's arsenal.

Although there is much more to the Internet than the World Wide Web, it is the Web that
has popularized Internet access. Visual Basic 6 includes the Microsoft WebBrowser control, which makes accessing the World Wide Web as easy as accessing a text file on your
disk.

The Microsoft WebBrowser Control

The WebBrowser control is an ActiveX control that lets you add browsing capabilities to
your applications. It can be used to browse "live" on the Web or to browse files on your
hard drive or on network servers.

It's not that you want to try to create a new Web browser to rival Microsoft's Internet Explorer or Netscape's Navigator. But more and more business software has a need to connect to a specific Web page, perhaps to download the latest sales figures or information about the new products in the company's line. More and more companies are using the Internet (or private intranets) to disseminate information to their employees and customers.

frmMain

The opening form in this project doesn't do much. If you were programming for business, the Web browser would not be the main form in the project. Instead, it would most likely be accessed from a menu. The opening form of this project simulates that:

1. Start a new project named WWW.vbp or load the completed project from the CD that accompanies this book. Set the form's properties according to Table 18.16.

TABLE 18.16   Properties for frmMain

Object	Property	Value
Form	Name	frmMain
	Caption	"Web Viewer"
	Height	3915
	Left	240
	Top	1830
	Width	6630

Recall from Chapter 1, "What's All That Stuff on My Screen?," that you can also have the Application Wizard add browsing capabilities to the programs that it creates.

2. Add a second form to the project. Name it frmBrowser and set its WindowState property to Maximized.

3. Bring frmMain to the top and select Menu Editor from the Tools menu or press Ctrl+E to open the Menu Editor.

4. Create a top-level menu named &File. Add a submenu under File named E&xit.

5. Create a top-level menu named &View. Add a submenu under View named &Web Browser.

The Menu Editor is shown in Figure 18.12.

18

FIGURE 18.12

Building the menus for
WWW.vpb.

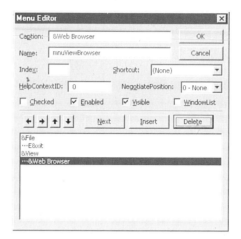

Add the code in Listing 18.15 to frmMain.

LISTING 18.15   Code for frmMain

```
Option Explicit

Private Sub Form_Unload(Cancel As Integer)
Dim i As Integer
'close all sub forms
For i = Forms.Count - 1 To 1 Step -1
    Unload Forms
Next
End Sub

Private Sub mnuViewBrowser_Click()
Dim frmB As New frmBrowser
frmB.StartingAddress = "http://www.mcp.com/waite/ezone/"
frmB.Show
End Sub

Private Sub mnuFileExit_Click()
'unload the form
Unload Me
End Sub
```

That's all the code you need for frmMain. The work is all done in the code for frmBrowser. If you were writing a business application, frmMain would be more involved, but this is only a demonstration project.

Building `frmBrowser`

The Web browser form is where most of the work in this project is done. It is the container for the `WebBrowser` control and the controls that support it:

1. Close `frmMain`. You won't be making any further changes to it.
2. Press Ctrl+T or select Components from the Project menu.
3. Click Microsoft Internet Controls and Microsoft Windows Common Controls 6.0.
4. Click OK.

   Microsoft Internet Controls adds two icons to the toolbox. One is the `WebBrowser` control, which we'll use to build our Web browser (see Figure 18.13). The other is the `ShellFolderViewOC`. We will not be discussing this control, because that would go beyond the scope of this book. We'll focus only on the `WebBrowser` control.

FIGURE 18.13

The `WebBrowser` *control.*

5. Add a toolbar to the form. Name it tbToolBar.
6. Add an `ImageList` control to the form. Name it `tlbrImages`.
7. Open the Property page for the image list, and add the six images in Table 18.17.

TABLE 18.17   Images for `tlbrImages`

Index	Name
1	Back
2	Forward
3	Stop
4	Refresh
5	Home
6	Search

You can find the bitmap files for the images on the CD that comes with this book, in the same directory as the `vbp` files for this project.

8. Close the ImageList Property page.
9. Open the Property page for the toolbar.
10. On the General tab, select tlbrImages as the image list for the toolbar.
11. Switch to the Buttons tab and add six buttons. Use Table 18.18 as a guide.

TABLE 18.18   Toolbar Buttons for frmBrowser

Index	Caption	Key	Image
1	Back	Back	1
2	Forward	Forward	2
3	Stop	Stop	3
4	Refresh	Refresh	4
5	Home	Home	5
6	Search	Search	6

12. Add a picture box to the form. Draw the box immediately beneath the toolbar. Make it the width of the form and 675 twips in height.

13. Add a Timer control to the form.

14. Draw a label into the picture box.

15. Draw a combo box into the picture box.

Use Figure 18.14 as a guide to placing the Label and PictureBox controls.

FIGURE 18.14

frmBrowser *at design time.*

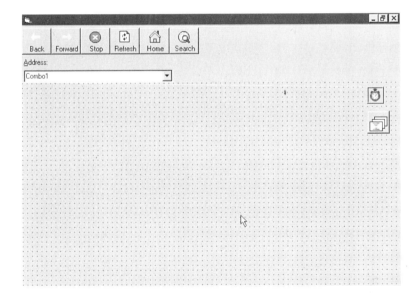

16. Set the properties according to Table 18.19.

TABLE 18.19 Properties for the Address Picture Box

Object	Property	Value
Timer	Name	timTimer
	Enabled	False
	Interval	5
PictureBox	Name	picAddress
	Align	Align Top
	BorderStyle	None
	Height	675
ComboBox	Name	cboAddress
	Height	315
	Left	45
	Top	300
	Width	3795
Label	Name	lblAddress
	Caption	"&Address:"
	Height	255
	Left	45
	Top	60
	Width	3075

17. Finally, add a WebBrowser control to the form and set its properties according to Table 18.20.

TABLE 18.20 Properties for the WebBrowser Control

Object	Property	Value
WebBrowser	Name	brwWebBrowser
	Height	3495
	Left	120
	TabIndex	0
	Top	1440
	Width	5400

Figure 18.15 shows frmBrowser with the WebBrowser control added.

FIGURE 18.15

The WebBrowser *control.*

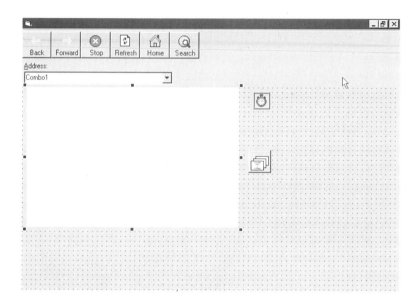

The WebBrowser control offers an array of useful methods, properties, and events. To open an Internet site, for example, use the Navigate method, which has the following syntax:

```
object.Navigate url, flags, TargetFrameName, PostData, Headers
```

The components of the syntax are as follows:

- object is the name you've given to the WebBrowser control.

- url is a required string that evaluates to the URL of the resource to display or the full path of the file to display.

- flags is an optional constant or value that specifies whether to add the resource to the history list, whether to read from or write to the cache, and whether to display the resource in a new window. It can be a combination of the values listed in Table 18.21.

- TargetFrameName is an optional string that evaluates to the name of a frame in which to display the resource.

- PostData is optional data to send to the server during the HTTP POST transaction. This parameter is ignored if the URL is not an HTTP URL.

- Headers is an optional value that specifies additional HTTP headers to send to the server. This parameter is ignored if the URL is not an HTTP URL.

TABLE 18.21 Flags for the Web Browser `Navigate` Method

Constant	Value	Description
navOpenInNewWindow	1	Opens the resource or file in a new window.
navNoHistory	2	Does not add to the history list. The new page replaces the current page in the list.
navNoReadFromCache	4	Does not read from the disk cache for this navigation.
navNoWriteToCache	8	Does not write the results of this navigation to the disk cache. To navigate to the eZone, for example, the `Navigate` method can be called with the following code: `brwWebBrowser.Navigate "http:// www.mcp.com/waite/ezone/", navNoReadFromCache`

The `Flags` parameter is optional. Using `navNoReadFromCache` opens the site and reads the URL from the Internet instead of opening a copy of the page stored in the cache. (The *cache* is a collection of files on your hard disk drive that Web browsers use to speed access to Web sites you have visited recently.)

A number of the Web browser methods correspond to the toolbar buttons. They require no parameters, because the actions they perform are based on the history list and the settings for Internet Explorer. These are listed in Table 18.22.

TABLE 18.22 Toolbar Navigation Methods

Method	Syntax	Action
GoBack	object.GoBack	Jumps back in the history list.
GoForward	object.GoForward	Jumps forward in the history list.
GoHome	object.GoHome	Jumps to Internet Explorer's home page.
GoSearch	object.GoSearch	Navigates to the current search page specified in Internet Explorer and the Internet control panel.
Quit	object.Quit	Closes the Web browser.
Refresh	object.Refresh	Reloads the current page.
Stop	object.Stop	Cancels the current navigation.

The code in Listing 18.16 demonstrates the use of the methods and properties. Enter this code in your program.

18

LISTING 18.16   Code for `frmBrowser`

```
Option Explicit
Public StartingAddress As String
Dim mbDontNavigateNow As Boolean

Private Sub Form_Load()
On Error Resume Next
Me.Show
tbToolBar.Refresh
Form_Resize
cboAddress.Move 50, lblAddress.Top + lblAddress.Height + 15
If Len(StartingAddress) > 0 Then
    cboAddress.Text = StartingAddress
    cboAddress.AddItem cboAddress.Text
    'try to navigate to the starting address
    timTimer.Enabled = True
    brwWebBrowser.Navigate StartingAddress
End If
End Sub

Private Sub Form_Resize()
cboAddress.Width = Me.ScaleWidth - 100
brwWebBrowser.Width = Me.ScaleWidth - 100
brwWebBrowser.Height = Me.ScaleHeight - _
  (picAddress.Top + picAddress.Height) - 100
End Sub

Private Sub brwWebBrowser_DownloadComplete()
On Error Resume Next
Me.Caption = brwWebBrowser.LocationName
End Sub

Private Sub brwWebBrowser_NavigateComplete(ByVal URL As String)
Dim i As Integer
Dim bFound As Boolean
Me.Caption = brwWebBrowser.LocationName
For i = 0 To cboAddress.ListCount - 1
    If cboAddress.List = brwWebBrowser.LocationURL Then
        bFound = True
        Exit For
    End If
Next i
mbDontNavigateNow = True
If bFound Then
    cboAddress.RemoveItem i
End If
cboAddress.AddItem brwWebBrowser.LocationURL, 0
cboAddress.ListIndex = 0
mbDontNavigateNow = False
End Sub
```

```vb
Private Sub cboAddress_Click()
If mbDontNavigateNow Then Exit Sub
timTimer.Enabled = True
brwWebBrowser.Navigate cboAddress.Text
End Sub

Private Sub cboAddress_KeyPress(KeyAscii As Integer)
On Error Resume Next
If KeyAscii = vbKeyReturn Then
    cboAddress_Click
End If
End Sub

Private Sub Form_Resize()
cboAddress.Width = Me.ScaleWidth - 100
brwWebBrowser.Width = Me.ScaleWidth - 100
brwWebBrowser.Height = Me.ScaleHeight - (picAddress.Top + picAddress.Height) -
100
End Sub

Private Sub timTimer_Timer()
If brwWebBrowser.Busy = False Then
    timTimer.Enabled = False
    Me.Caption = brwWebBrowser.LocationName
Else
    Me.Caption = "Working..."
End If
End Sub

Private Sub tbToolBar_ButtonClick(ByVal Button As Button)
On Error Resume Next
timTimer.Enabled = True
Select Case Button.Key
    Case "Back"
        brwWebBrowser.GoBack
    Case "Forward"
        brwWebBrowser.GoForward
    Case "Refresh"
        brwWebBrowser.Refresh
    Case "Home"
        brwWebBrowser.GoHome
    Case "Search"
        brwWebBrowser.GoSearch
    Case "Stop"
        timTimer.Enabled = False
        brwWebBrowser.Stop
        Me.Caption = brwWebBrowser.LocationName
End Select
End Sub
```

18

What's Going On?

When the form is loaded, Form_Load starts with a call to the Form_Resize event. The Form_Resize event sets the width of picAddress and the width and height of the Browser window. When control returns to the Form_Load event, the combo box is moved to a position relative to its label.

Recall that mnuViewBrowser sent the URL to the new frmBrowser instance with the code

```
frmB.StartingAddress = "http://samsteachyourself.com/"
```

The variable is copied into the combo box and also used as the URL parameter for the Navigate method. If the user is already connected to the Internet, the WebBrowser control opens the URL. If the user is not connected to the Internet, the browser opens the Connect To dialog box, as shown in Figure 18.16.

FIGURE 18.16

Connecting to the Internet.

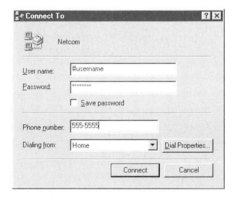

After the connection is made, the timer is enabled and the WebBrowser control navigates to the URL, downloads the page, and displays it. This is shown in Figure 18.17.

The timer checks the Busy property every 5 milliseconds while the Navigate method is attempting to download the page. When Busy is True, the timer displays Working... as the form's caption. When Busy is False, the form's caption is changed to brwBrowser.LocationName, which is the title of the Web page.

Meanwhile, when the URL is located and loaded, the NavigateComplete event is fired. The code here scans through the combo box to see if the URL address is already there. If it is, the code deletes the address and then adds it back in with the AddItem method. Sound silly? The idea is to have the current URL as the first one in the list, but not to have it in the list twice.

FIGURE 18.17

Connected to the eZone!

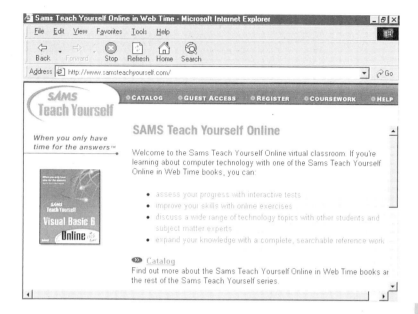

Finally, the toolbar's `ButtonClick` event handles the rest of the work. The only thing notable here is the `Stop` method. Because the timer is enabled when the Navigate method is called, its `Enabled` property must be set to `False`. The `Stop` subroutine must also set the new caption for the form.

Running the Program

When the program runs, `frmMain` opens. Selecting Web Browser from the View menu loads a new instance of `frmBrowser`. That implies, correctly, that you can have several instances running at the same time.

Once the connection is made and the site is connected, you can type other URLs into the text box portion of `cboAddress`. Pressing Enter or clicking the combo box navigates to the new URL.

What's Next?

Programs such as this do not replace Microsoft's Internet Explorer or Netscape's Navigator. They do provide a way for business programs to access specific Internet or intranet Web pages, an important consideration. The control's `BeforeNavigate` event can be used to prevent leaving the startup site or to limit site changes to a specific list. There is even a `ProgressChange` event that you can use to fill a progress bar! Like much of Visual Basic 6, the main limitation is your own imagination.

Lesson Summary

In this lesson we built our own custom Web browser and uses the navigation methods of the `WebBrowser` control. Next, we'll introduce FTP.

Quiz 4

1. To stop a page from loading, use the

    a. `End` method

    b. `Stop` method

    c. `GoStop` method

    d. `StopLoad` method

2. To reload a page, use the

    a. `GoBack` method

    b. `ReDraw` method

    c. `ReFresh` method

    d. `ReLoad` method

3. The _____ event can be used to prevent leaving the startup site.

    a. `RestrictNavigate`

    b. `BeforeNavigate`

    c. `EndNavigate`

    d. `PreventNavigate`

4. The _____ event can be used to fill a progress bar.

    a. `ProgressChange`

    b. `VariableChange`

    c. `Completion`

    d. `NavigateChange`

Exercise 4

Complexity: Easy

1. Using the `mbDontNavigateNow` variable, change the www program by preventing the user from accessing the site `http:/www.waite.com`.

Complexity: Moderate

2. Experiment with the `ProgressChange` event, add a progress bar to the www form, and place it between the form and the toolbar. Make sure it resizes with the form.

LESSON 5

Files, Files, Files: Using FTP

The World Wide Web generates excitement, but it is far from all there is to the Internet. For one thing, a wealth of files is available for download from FTP sites. FTP stands for *file transfer protocol*, the protocol (agreed-upon set of rules) for transferring text and binary files over the Internet.

True, you can find files on the Web, but not all FTP sites are available from the Web. And FTP connections generally run faster because there is less demand for them. Some say they are more reliable, too. FTP also has business uses: Business applications use FTP connections to update distributed database files, sales catalogs, and other business documents.

This lesson explains how to use the Internet Transfer Control to establish an FTP connection and download files.

The Internet Transfer Control

The Internet Transfer Control (ITC) implements either FTP or Hypertext Transfer Protocol (HTTP). When the ITC is set up for FTP, it can be used to create an FTP browser or to download files from a public or private FTP site. It can operate with the default Internet settings from the system registry, with a direct (T1) connection to the Internet, or through a proxy server.

Adding the ITC to the Toolbox

Before you can use the ITC, you must add it to your toolbox:

1. Press Ctrl+T or select Components from the Project Menu.
2. Select Microsoft Internet Transfer Control 6.0.
3. Click OK.

The ITC icon is shown in Figure 18.18.

18

FIGURE **18.18**

The ITC.

The FTP Project

Accessing an FTP site requires navigating to the site, listing directories, changing directories, reading text files, and downloading files. The project in this lesson demonstrates how to add an FTP browser to your programs:

1. Start a new project and add the ITC to your toolbox as described above. The completed project is on the CD that accompanies this book.

2. Press F4 to open the Properties window, and set the form's properties according to Table 18.23.

TABLE 18.23   Properties for `frmFTP`

Object	Property	Value
Form	Name	frmFTP
	Caption	"FTP Client"
	Height	6015
	Width	6360
	Icon	Graphics\Icons\Comm\Net10a.ico
	MaxButton	False

For convenience, the form needs to display the FTP host site, the current FTP directory name, and the commands that are sent to the FTP host.

3. Add three text boxes and three labels to the form. Set their properties according to Table 18.24.

TABLE 18.24   Properties for Labels and Text Boxes on `frmFTP`

Object	Property	Value
TextBox	Name	xtServer
	Height	285
	Left	1440
	Top	240
	Width	4575

Object	Property	Value
TextBox	Name	txtDirectory
	Height	285
	Left	1440
	Locked	True
	TabStop	False
	Top	600
	Width	4575
TextBox	Name	txtCommand
	Height	855
	Left	120
	MultiLine	True
	ScrollBars	Vertical
	Top	5040
	Width	6075
Label	Name	Label1
	AutoSize	True
	Caption	"Working Directory:"
	Left	0
	Top	600
Label	Name	Label2
	AutoSize	True
	Caption	"Host:"
	Left	
	Top	40
Label	Name	lblWhat
	AutoSize	True
	Caption	"lblWhat.Caption"
	Left	0
	Top	0

18

The form also needs a place to display the files and subdirectories in an active directory.

4. Add a list box to the form. Set its properties according to Table 18.25.

TABLE 18.25   Properties of `lstDir`

Object	Property	Value
ListBox	Name	lstDir
	Height	3990
	Left	1440
	Top	960
	Width	4695

The project also requires six Command buttons to send commands to the FTP site.

5. Add six Command buttons to `frmFTP`. Set their properties according to Table 18.26.

TABLE 18.26   Properties for the Command Buttons

Object	Property	Value
CommandButton	Name	cmdConnect
	Caption	"&Connect"
	Height	495
	Left	120
	Top	1020
	Width	1095
CommandButton	Name	cmdDirectory
	Caption	"Get &Directory"
	Enabled	False
	Height	495
	Left	120
	Top	1668
	Width	1095
CommandButton	Name	cmdReadText
	Caption	"Read Text File"
	Enabled	False
	Height	495
	Left	120
	Top	2316
	Width	1095

Object	Property	Value
Command Button	Name	cmdDownLoad
	Caption	"Download File"
	Enabled	False
	Height	495
	Left	120
	Top	2964
	Width	1095
Command Button	Name	cmdClose
	Caption	"C&lose Connection"
	Enabled	False
	Height	495
	Left	120
	Top	3612
	Width	1095
CommandButton	Name	cmdQuit
	Caption	"E&xit"
	Height	495
	Left	120
	Top	4260
	Width	1095

6. Add the ITC to the form. The control is not visible at runtime, so it does not matter where you place it. Set the control's properties according to Table 18.27.

TABLE 18.27   Properties for the ITC

Object	Property	Value
Inet	Name	Inet1
	Protocol	2
	URL	(Leave blank)
	UserName	"anonymous"
	Password	(See text)

Anonymous FTP

Public sites that let you download files are anonymous FTP sites. That means that you do not have to be registered with the site in order to log on and download files. Instead, logon is with the user name anonymous.

The Password property for anonymous FTP is your email address. If you are writing a program to call a single, proprietary FTP site, the URL, user name, and password can be saved in the system registry and set programmatically. You can review these registry operations in Chapter 15, "Doing the Impossible (and More) with the Windows API."

The completed form is shown in Figure 18.19.

FIGURE 18.19

The completed form.

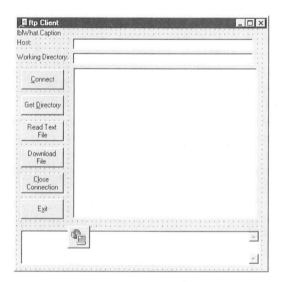

The Internet Transfer Control's Methods

The ITC has only a few methods.

The Execute Method

Most commands to the FTP site are made using the Execute method. The syntax for the Execute method is

```
object.Execute url, operation, data, requestHeaders
```

The components of the syntax are as follows:

- object is the name you gave the ITC.

- url is an optional string that specifies the URL to which the control should connect. If no URL is specified here, the URL specified in the URL property will be used.

- operation is an optional string that specifies the type of operation to be executed. See Table 18.28 for a list of the supported operations.

- data is an optional string that specifies the data for operations. This parameter is not used for FTP.

- requestHeaders is an optional string that specifies additional headers to be sent from the remote server. This parameter is not used for FTP.

TABLE 18.28 FTP Commands

Operation	Description
CD file1	Change directory. Changes to the directory specified in file1.
CDUP	Change to parent directory. Equivalent to CD.
CLOSE	Closes the current FTP connection.
DIR file1	Directory. Searches the directory specified in file1. (Wildcards are permitted but they must be recognized by the remote host.) If no file1 is specified, a full directory of the current working directory is returned. Use the GetChunk method to return the directory data.
GET file1 file2	Retrieves the remote file specified in file1 and creates a new local file specified in file2.
RECV file1 file2	Retrieves the remote file specified in file1 and creates a new local file specified in file2. Equivalent to GET.
LS file1	List. Searches the directory specified in file1. (Wildcards are permitted but the remote host dictates the syntax.) Use the GetChunk method to return the file directory data.
PWD	Print working directory. Returns the current directory name. Use the GetChunk method to return the data.
SIZE file1	Returns the size of the directory specified in file1.
QUIT	Terminates the current user.
* DELETE file1	Deletes the file specified in file1.
* MKDIR file1	Make directory. Creates a directory as specified in file1. Success is dependent on user privileges on the remote host.

18

continues

TABLE 18.28 continued

Operation	Description
* PUT file1 file2	Copies a local file specified in file1 to the remote host specified in file2.
* RENAME file1 file2	Renames the remote file named in file1 to the new name specified in file2. Success is dependent on user privileges on the remote host.
* RMDIR file1	Remove directory. Removes the remote directory specified in file1. Success is dependent on user privileges on the remote host.
* SEND file1 file2	Copies a local file, specified in file1, to the remote host, specified in file2. Equivalent to PUT.

Note The commands marked with an asterisk can be executed only if the user has privileges on the FTP host. Anonymous FTP sites will not allow anyone to create directories or to delete files or directories. Anonymous FTP sites also allow uploads only to certain directories.

The ITC uses the Execute method to start almost every operation. Uploads and downloads are automatic; all you need to do once they begin is wait until they are done. Listing directories and reading text files are more complicated. Both of these operations require the GetChunk method.

The GetChunk Method

The syntax for GetChunk is

```
object.GetChunk( size [,datatype] )
```

The components of the syntax are as follows:

- object is the name you gave to the ITC.
- size is a long numeric expression that determines the size of the chunk to be retrieved.
- datatype is an optional integer parameter that specifies the data type of the retrieved chunk. The datatype may be either icString, which returns string data for reading text files, or icByte, which returns the data as a byte array.

The OpenURL Method

The OpenURL method is used to open and return documents from a site. Its syntax is

```
object.OpenUrl url [,datatype]
```

The components of the syntax are as follows:

- object is the name you gave the ITC object.
- url is the URL of the document to be retrieved.
- datatype is an optional integer that specifies the type. This is identical to the datatype parameter in GetChunk.

The Cancel Method

The only other ITC method that is used by the FTP protocol is the Cancel method. The Cancel method cancels the current operation and closes the connection. The syntax is

```
object.Cancel
```

where object is the name you gave to the ITC.

The StateChanged Event

The ITC has only one event, the StateChanged event. The control receives reports from the FTP site and reports them as State through the StateChanged event. The different states are listed in Table 18.29.

TABLE 18.29   State-Changed Constants

Constant	Value	Description
icNone	0	No state to report.
icHostResolvingHost	1	The control is looking up the IP address of the specified host computer.
icHostResolved	2	The control successfully found the IP address of the specified host computer.
icConnecting	3	The control is connecting to the host computer.
icConnected	4	The control successfully connected to the host computer.
icRequesting	5	The control is sending a request to the host computer.
icRequestSent	6	The control successfully sent the request.

continues

18

TABLE 18.29   continued

Constant	Value	Description
icReceivingResponse	7	The control is receiving a response from the host computer.
icResponseReceived	8	The control successfully received a response from the host computer.
icDisconnecting	9	The control is disconnecting from the host computer.
icDisconnected	10	The control successfully disconnected from the host computer.
icError	11	An error occurred in communicating with the host computer.
icResponseCompleted	12	The request has been completed and all data has been received.

Programs use the StateChanged event to determine what to do and when. Now it's time to look at some code.

Code for **StateChanged**

The control has a single event, but it is a busy event indeed. Add the code in Listing 18.17 to the StateChanged event.

LISTING 18.17   The StateChanged Event

```
Private Sub Inet1_StateChanged(ByVal State As Integer)
'   Fired each time inet control detects a change in state
Dim sMsg As String
On Error GoTo Error_Handler
'   Figure out what to do
Select Case State
    Case icResponseCompleted
    '   All of the preliminaries are done, now get the information
    lblWhat.Caption = "Response Completed "
    '   Display response
    If Inet1.ResponseCode <> 0 Then _
        txtCommand = txtCommand & vbCrLf & Inet1.ResponseCode & _
          ": " & Inet1.ResponseInfo
    txtCommand.SelStart = Len(txtCommand.Text)
    DoEvents
    Select Case iAction
        Case 0, 1, 4: subGetDir  '  Make connection, CDUP, or change directory
        Case 2: '   Read text file — handled in cmdReadText_Click
        Case 3: '   Download a file — handled in cmdDownLoad_Click
    End Select
```

```
    Case icConnecting
        lblWhat.Caption = "Connecting"
        DoEvents
    Case icConnected
        lblWhat.Caption = "Connected"
        DoEvents
    Case icDisconnected
        lblWhat.Caption = "Disconnected"
        DoEvents
    Case icDisconnecting
        lblWhat.Caption = "Disconnecting"
        DoEvents
    Case icHostResolved
        lblWhat.Caption = "Host Resolved"
        DoEvents
    Case icReceivingResponse
        lblWhat.Caption = "Receiving Response "
        DoEvents
    Case icRequesting
        lblWhat.Caption = "Sending Request"
        DoEvents
    Case icRequestSent
        lblWhat.Caption = "Request Sent"
        DoEvents
    Case icResolvingHost
        lblWhat.Caption = "Resolving Host"
        DoEvents
    Case icError
        sMsg = "Error Code " & Inet1.ResponseCode
        sMsg = sMsg & vbCrLf & Inet1.ResponseInfo
        MsgBox sMsg, vbOKOnly, "Error Response Received"
        DoEvents
        Exit Sub
    Case icResponseReceived
        lblWhat.Caption = "Response Received!"
        '   Display response
        If Inet1.ResponseCode <> 0 Then _
            txtCommand = txtCommand & vbCrLf & Inet1.ResponseCode & _
            ": " & Inet1.ResponseInfo
        txtCommand.SelStart = Len(txtCommand.Text)
        DoEvents
    Case Else   '   Should never get here
        lblWhat.Caption = "Unknown State Received"
        DoEvents
End Select
Ok_Exit:
Exit Sub
Error_Handler:
MsgBox "Error # " & Err & " " & Error, vbOKOnly, "State Changed"
GoTo Ok_Exit
End Sub
```

18

Quite a bit there, isn't there? Fortunately, most of it is pretty simple. Skip over icResponseCompleted for the moment. The next eight values of State are informative responses. Each causes a message to be displayed as lblWhat.Caption, providing the user with visual feedback about what is happening.

If State equals icError, an error message is displayed in a message box. When the user clicks OK in the message box, the procedure is exited.

If State equals icResponseReceived, the exact response is added to txtCommand. The user can scroll back in txtCommand to review the commands that were sent to the host and the host's responses to them.

Now take a look at icResponseCompleted. When this state is received, decisions must be made to handle the response. Exactly what to do depends on what the program did to generate the response. When it is making a connection or changing directories, the code must explicitly use the GetChunk method to process the data. When the program is uploading or downloading a file or reading a text file, the action is handled automatically.

Using GetChunk

Recall that the GetChunk method has two parameters, size and datatype. Because directories are always text, the datatype for reading directory contents is icString:

1. Create a new Public procedure by selecting Add Procedure from the Tools menu.

2. Name the procedure GetDir.

3. Enter the code from Listing 18.18 into the procedure.

LISTING 18.18   The GetDir Procedure

```
Public Sub subGetDir()
'    Reads directory or directory name from host
'    called from inet control state changed event
Dim vtData As Variant ' Data variable.
Dim strData As String: strData = ""
Dim bDone As Boolean: bDone = False
' Get first chunk.
vtData = Inet1.GetChunk(1024, icString)
'    continue until no data is in the buffer
Do While Not bDone
    lblWhat.Caption = "Reading DIR "
    DoEvents
    strData = strData & vtData
    ' Get next chunk.
    vtData = Inet1.GetChunk(1024, icString)
```

```
        lblWhat.Caption = "Reading DIR "
        DoEvents
        If Len(vtData) = 0 Then
            bDone = True
        End If
Loop
If iAction = intntGetDirName Then
    txtDirectory = strData
ElseIf iAction = intntConnect Then
    lstDir.Clear
    FillDir (strData)
ElseIf iAction = intntChangeDir Then
    lstDir.Clear
    lstDir.AddItem ".."
    FillDir (strData)
End If
lblWhat.Caption = "Directory Done"
End Sub
```

To allow any type of data to be read, vtData is declared as a variant. The line vtData = Inet1.GetChunk(1024, icString) gets one chunk of data from the host and stores it in vtData. The string in vtData is immediately copied into strData. The Do loop repeats the same action until there is no data left to be read.

The If...ElseIf...End If structure then decides what to do with the data in sData. If iAction is intntGetDirName, which is the case when the command is PWD, sData is copied into txtDirectory.

If iAction is intntConnect, the command was LS. The list box is cleared and sData is passed to the FillDir procedure that breaks it into its separate parts and adds them to the list.

If iAction is intntChangeDir, the command was also LS, but because the connection is already established, the directory being read is not the root directory. The code adds ".." as the first item in the list, then calls the FillDir procedure.

The FillDir Procedure

The FTP site sends its directory as a string that ends with a carriage return/line feed. The string must be parsed so the directory entries can be displayed in the list box:

1. Create a new Public procedure by selecting Add Procedure from the Tools menu.

2. Name the procedure FillDir.

3. Enter the code from Listing 18.19 into the procedure.

LISTING 18.19   The FillDir Procedure

```
Sub FillDir(strData As String)
' Parses strData and fills lstDir with
' directory and file names
Dim iCR As Integer
Dim iStart As Integer: iStart = 1
Do
    ' Find vbCrLf
    iCR = InStr(iStart, strData, vbCrLf)
    ' If not found, exit loop
    If iCR = 0 Then Exit Do
    ' Found, add next item to listbox
    lstDir.AddItem Mid(strData, iStart, iCR - iStart)
    ' Skip start position over vbCrLf (2 characters)
    iStart = iCR + 2
Loop
End Sub
```

The string is downloaded with each directory item delimited by a carriage-return linefeed pair, vbCrLf. The code in FillDir Do loops through the string looking for the next vbCrLf and uses AddItem to add each item to the lstDir.

The Rest of the General Section

There are three more procedures in the General Declarations section of the code.

Create each of the procedures shown in Listing 18.20 and add the code.

LISTING 18.20   Controlling the Command Buttons

```
Sub subConnected()
cmdDirectory.Enabled = True
cmdDownLoad.Enabled = True
cmdReadText.Enabled = True
cmdClose.Enabled = True
cmdConnect.Enabled = False
End Sub

Sub subDisConnected()
cmdDirectory.Enabled = False
cmdDownLoad.Enabled = False
cmdReadText.Enabled = False
cmdClose.Enabled = False
cmdConnect.Enabled = True
End Sub

Public Sub subBusy(bz As Boolean)
```

```
If bz Then
    cmdDirectory.Enabled = False
    cmdDownLoad.Enabled = False
    cmdReadText.Enabled = False
    cmdClose.Enabled = True
    cmdConnect.Enabled = False
Else
    cmdDirectory.Enabled = True
    cmdDownLoad.Enabled = True
    cmdReadText.Enabled = True
    cmdClose.Enabled = True
    cmdConnect.Enabled = False
End If
End Sub
```

These subroutines enable or disable Command buttons depending on what the program is doing. If you are already connected, for example, you should not be able to press Connect again. While data is being retrieved, only the Close button should be enabled (to disconnect if something goes wrong).

Open the Code window of frmFTP, and add the code from Listing 18.21.

LISTING 18.21 Declarations and Form Events for frmFTP

```
Option Explicit
Public sCommand As String
Public sServer As String
Public Action As Integer
' Download Directory Path
Const DownLoadDir As String = "C:\Temp\"
' Activity Constants
Const intntConnect As Integer = 0
Const intntChangeDir As Integer = 1
Const intntGetText As Integer = 2
Const intntGetFile As Integer = 3
Const intntGetDirName As Integer = 4_
Private Sub Form_Load()
lblWhat.Caption = "Enter Server Name"
End Sub

Private Sub Form_Unload(Cancel As Integer)
Dim i As Integer
For i = Forms.Count - 1 To 0 Step -1
    Unload Forms
Next
End
End Sub
```

Note the constant `DownLoadDir`. If your computer does not have a C:\Temp directory, either create one or change the path in the constant to match a directory of your choice.

The activity constants are used elsewhere in the program to control the program's response to codes from the `StateChanged` event.

Note the code in the `Unload` event. The `For` loop assures that all the forms are unloaded, avoiding memory leaks.

Making the Connection

The code in Listing 18.22 opens the connection to the FTP site.

LISTING 18.22   Code for `txtServer` and `cmdConnect`

```
Private Sub txtServer_KeyPress(KeyAscii As Integer)
If KeyAscii = 13 Then
    sServer = txtServer.Text
    cmdConnect_Click
End If
End Sub

Private Sub txtServer_LostFocus()
sServer = txtServer.Text
End Sub

Private Sub txtServer_Change()
    cmdConnect.Enabled = True
End Sub

Private Sub cmdConnect_Click()
On Error GoTo Error_Handler
'   Can't open a non-existent server
If sServer = "" Then
    MsgBox "Must enter server name", vbOKOnly, "Note:"
    Exit Sub
End If
'   OK, open the server and get the directory
With Inet1
    .URL = sServer
    iAction = intntGetDirName
    .Execute , "PWD"
    '   Wait until done before doing anything else
    Do While Inet1.StillExecuting
        DoEvents
    Loop
    iAction = intntConnect
    '   Display command being sent
    txtCommand = txtCommand & vbCrLf & "LS"
```

```
    txtCommand.SelStart = Len(txtCommand.Text)
    .Execute , "LS"
    '   Wait until done before doing anything else
    Do While Inet1.StillExecuting
        DoEvents
    Loop
    Call subConnected
End With
Exit_Normal:
    Exit Sub
Error_Handler:
    MsgBox Err & " " & Error, vbOKOnly, "Connect Error"
    Select Case Err
        Case 35761: Inet1.Cancel     ' Timeout
        Case 35764: Inet1.Cancel     ' Still Executing
    End Select
    Resume Exit_Normal
End Sub
```

When a user types a URL into txtServer and presses ENTER or clicks the Connect button, the text in txtServer is copied into the string sServer. If cmdConnect is disabled, typing into txtServer enables it. (cmdConnect is disabled while the program is online.)

The code in cmdConnect_Click begins by checking to be sure that the user has entered a URL. If so, the With...End With structure copies sServer to the URL property and invokes the Execute method with the command PWD. The Execute method opens the connection to the host site and sends it the PWD command. From here, the StateChanged event takes over for a while.

Note the block of code

```
Do While Inet1.StillExecuting
    DoEvents
Loop
```

This code waits for the StillExecuting property to become False. Because StateChanged depends on the speed of the Internet, the program must wait for the host to catch up after sending it a command.

Once the PWD command is completed, the code issues an LS command to get the directory listing.

Changing Directories

When you log on to an FTP site, the first directory is called the *root directory*. (Sound familiar?) Chances are there is not much there for downloading. You must change directories to get to the good stuff. (Hint: Look for the Pub directory.) The program needs a way to select and switch to a new directory.

Add the following code to `lstDir_DblClick`:

```
Private Sub lstDir_DblClick()
    If Right$(lstDir.List(lstDir.ListIndex), 1) = "/" Then cmdDirectory_Click
End Sub
```

Add the code in Listing 18.23 to the `Click` event of `cmdDirectory`.

LISTING 18.23 Code for `cmdDirectory`

```
Sub cmdDirectory_Click()
On Error GoTo Error_Handler
'   Change directory on remote computer
Dim sDirectory As String
sDirectory = lstDir.List(lstDir.ListIndex)
'   Test for no directory selected
If sDirectory = "" Then
    MsgBox "No directory selected.", vbOKOnly, "Note:"
    Exit Sub
End If
'   Test for file name selected
If sDirectory <> ".." And Right$(sDirectory, 1) <> "/" Then
    MsgBox "File selected.", vbOKOnly, "Note:"
    Exit Sub
End If
'   OK, there is something selected
iAction = intntChangeDir
If sDirectory = ".." Then
    '   Move up
    '   Display activity
    lblWhat = "Moving to parent directory"
    Call subBusy(True)
    DoEvents
    With Inet1
        .URL = sServer
        '   Display command being sent
        txtCommand = txtCommand & vbCrLf & "CD .."
        txtCommand.SelStart = Len(txtCommand.Text)
        sCommand = "CD .."
        .Execute , sCommand
        '   Wait until done before doing anything else
        Do While Inet1.StillExecuting
            DoEvents
        Loop
        '   Display command being sent
        txtCommand = txtCommand & vbCrLf & "PWD"
        txtCommand.SelStart = Len(txtCommand.Text)
        sCommand = "PWD"
        iAction = intntGetDirName
        .Execute , sCommand
```

```
            '   Wait until done before doing anything else
            Do While Inet1.StillExecuting
                DoEvents
            Loop
            '   Display command being sent
            txtCommand = txtCommand & vbCrLf & "LS"
            txtCommand.SelStart = Len(txtCommand.Text)
            sCommand = "LS"
            iAction = intntChangeDir
            .Execute , sCommand
            '   Wait until done before doing anything else
            Do While Inet1.StillExecuting
                DoEvents
            Loop
        End With
'   End of CDUP routine
Else
        '   Move to new directory
        '   Display activity
        lblWhat = "Moving to " & sDirectory
        Call subBusy(True)
        DoEvents
        With Inet1
            .URL = sServer
            sCommand = "CD " & txtDirectory
            If Right$(sCommand, 1) <> "/" Then
                sCommand = sCommand & "/" & sDirectory
            Else
                sCommand = sCommand & sDirectory
            End If
            '   Display command being sent
            txtCommand = txtCommand & vbCrLf & sCommand
            txtCommand.SelStart = Len(txtCommand.Text)
            iAction = intntChangeDir
            .Execute , sCommand
            '   Wait until done before doing anything else
            Do While Inet1.StillExecuting
                DoEvents
            Loop
            iAction = intntGetDirName
            '   Display command being sent
            txtCommand = txtCommand & vbCrLf & "PWD"
            txtCommand.SelStart = Len(txtCommand.Text)
            txtCommand = txtCommand & vbCrLf & "PWD"
            txtCommand.SelStart = Len(txtCommand.Text)
            .Execute , "PWD"
            '   Wait until done before doing anything else
            Do While Inet1.StillExecuting
                DoEvents
```

18

continues

LISTING 18.23   continued

```
            Loop
            iAction = intntChangeDir
            '   Display command being sent
            txtCommand = txtCommand & vbCrLf & "LS"
            txtCommand.SelStart = Len(txtCommand.Text)
            .Execute , "LS"
            '   Wait until done before doing anything else
            Do While Inet1.StillExecuting
                DoEvents
            Loop
        End With
    '   Directory read
    End If
Exit_Normal:
    Call subBusy(False)
    Exit Sub
Error_Handler:
    MsgBox Err & " " & Error, vbOKOnly, "Directory Error"
    Select Case Err
        Case 35761: Inet1.Cancel    ' Timeout
        Case 35764: Inet1.Cancel    ' Still Executing
    End Select
    Resume Exit_Normal
End Sub
```

To change directories, the user first selects a directory and then clicks the Get Directory button. Double-clicking the selection in lstDir calls cmdDirectory_Click automatically. The procedure checks to be sure something has been selected from cmdDir, and then checks for a trailing / to be sure it is a directory.

Changing directories takes three steps:

1. Change the directory.

2. Get the new directory name.

3. List the directory.

There are two possibilities: selecting a new directory or moving up to a higher-level directory. The code issues either "CD..." or "CD " & txtDirectory.

Closing the Connection

You can't break the Internet, so you can close the connection to a site simply by exiting from the program. If you want to explore another site, though, that means you must start the program all over again, which is not very convenient. It is far better to close the connection the "polite" way.

Add the following code to the Click event of cmdClose:

```
Private Sub cmdClose_Click()
    On Error Resume Next
    Inet1.Execute , "CLOSE"
    Call subDisConnected
End Sub
```

The Close command is, perhaps, the only one that operates instantaneously, so you don't need the Do loop here. The subDisconnected procedure enables and disables the appropriate Command buttons.

Reading a Text File

If you are trolling FTP sites instead of looking for specific files, look for files named index.txt and readme.txt. The readme file generally contains information about the site, including the site's rules, whereas the index file provides a list of directories and files on the site.

Clearly, you need a way to read the text files while you are online. The project needs one more form to display text files:

1. Add a new form to the project.
2. Add a Command button and a text box to the form.
3. Set the properties according to Table 18.30.

TABLE 18.30   Properties for frmText

Object	Property	Value
Form	Name	frmText
	Caption	"Text File"
	Height	4410
	Width	7110
	ControlBox	False
TextBox	Name	txtData
	Height	3735
	Left	120
	Locked	True
	MultiLine	True
	ScrollBars	'Both
TextBox	Top	120
	Width	6975

continues

TABLE 18.30   continued

Object	Property	Value
CommandButton	Name	cmdDone
	Caption	"Done"
	Height	375
	Left	240
	Top	3960
	Width	975

The completed form is shown in Figure 18.20.

FIGURE 18.20

frmText *at design time.*

Open the Code window, and add the code in Listing 18.24.

LISTING 18.24   Code for frmText

```
Option Explicit

Private Sub cmdDone_Click()
Me.Hide
frmFTP.Show
End Sub

Private Sub Form_Load()
Form_Resize
End Sub

Private Sub Form_Resize()
txtData.Width = Me.ScaleWidth - 120
txtData.Height = cmdDone.Top - 240
End Sub
```

The only real work in this code is in the Form_Resize event, which sizes txtData to fill the form. Note, also, that the form is hidden by cmdDone, rather than unloaded. This is a supplementary form that is loaded and unloaded only by frmFTP.

You are finished with frmText:

1. Close the Object and Code windows of frmText.

2. Open the Code window of frmFTP.

3. Change the Form_Load procedure as shown below (changes are in bold).

```
Private Sub Form_Load()
Load frmText
lblWhat.Caption = "Enter Server Name"
End Sub
```

Add the code in Listing 18.25 to the Click event of cmdReadText.

LISTING 18.25   Code for cmdReadText_Click

```
Private Sub cmdReadText_Click()
On Error GoTo Error_Handler
'    Read a text file — display it on frmText
Dim sFileName As String
If lstDir.List(lstDir.ListIndex) = "" Then
    MsgBox "No file selected.", vbOKOnly, "Note:"
    Exit Sub
End If
If Right$(lstDir.List(lstDir.ListIndex), 3) <> "txt" Then
    MsgBox "File is not a text file!", vbOKOnly, "Note:"
    Exit Sub
End If
'   ok, got here so set up to read directory
'   Creat filename of directory
If txtDirectory = "/" Then  '    This is the root
    sFileName = txtServer & txtDirectory & lstDir.List(lstDir.ListIndex)
ElseIf Right$(txtDirectory, 1) = "/" Then   '   / is there
    sFileName = txtServer & "/" & _
        txtDirectory & lstDir.List(lstDir.ListIndex)
Else    '    slash is not there, add one
    sFileName = txtServer & "/" & _
        txtDirectory & "/" & lstDir.List(lstDir.ListIndex)
End If
iAction = intntGetText
'   Get file
'   Display activity
lblWhat = "Reading " & lstDir.List(lstDir.ListIndex)
DoEvents
```

continues

LISTING 18.25   continued

```
sCommand = sFileName
'   Display command being sent
txtCommand = txtCommand & vbCrLf & sCommand
txtCommand.SelStart = Len(txtCommand.Text)
Call subBusy(True)
frmText.txtData.Text = Inet1.OpenURL(sCommand)
'   Wait until done before doing anything else
Do While Inet1.StillExecuting
    DoEvents
Loop
'   done reading, display the form
Call subBusy(False)
frmText.Show
lblWhat.Caption = ""
Exit_Normal:
    Exit Sub
Error_Handler:
    MsgBox Err & " " & Error, vbOKOnly, "Read Text"
    Select Case Err
        Case 35761: Inet1.Cancel    ' Timeout
        Case 35764: Inet1.Cancel    ' Still Executing
    End Select
    Resume Exit_Normal
End Sub
```

As always, the procedure starts by validating the request. It verifies that something is selected and that the selection is a really a text file. If the request passes the test, the procedure uses the OpenURL method to retrieve and display the text file. The OpenURL method copies the text file directly into the text box on frmText.

Downloading

Finally! The whole point of FTP is downloading files. Now that you can connect and read the supporting text files, it's time to download. Add the code in Listing 18.26 to cmdDownlod_Click.

LISTING 18.26   Downloading Files

```
Private Sub cmdDownLoad_Click()
'   Download the selected file
Dim sFileName As String, sTemp As String
Dim sDLName As String, iResponse As Integer
On Error GoTo Error_Handler
If lstDir.List(lstDir.ListIndex) = "" Then
    MsgBox "No file selected.", vbOKOnly, "Note:"
    Exit Sub
```

```
'   No file selected, exit this procedure
End If
If Right$(lstDir.List(lstDir.ListIndex), 1) = "/" Then
    MsgBox "Directory selected.", vbOKOnly, "Note:"
    Exit Sub
    '   Not a file — cannot download
End If
'   build the path and filename string
If txtDirectory = "/" Then
    '   Root directory
    sFileName = txtDirectory & lstDir.List(lstDir.ListIndex)
ElseIf Right$(txtDirectory, 1) = "/" Then
    '   has slash. Build path/filename
    sFileName = txtDirectory & lstDir.List(lstDir.ListIndex)
Else
    '   no slash, add it to build path/filename
    sFileName = txtDirectory & "/" & lstDir.List(lstDir.ListIndex)
End If
sDLName = lstDir.List(lstDir.ListIndex)
If Len(Dir(DownLoadDir & sDLName)) Then
    '   File exists in download directory
    iResponse = MsgBox(sDLName & "already in " & DownLoadDir & _
      vbCrLf & "OverWrite?", vbOKCancel, "Warning!")
    ' No? Then exit sub
    If iResponse = vbCancel Then Exit Sub
    ' Yes, then delete old
    sTemp = DownLoadDir & sDLName
    Kill sTemp
End If
Call subBusy(True)
'   Start the download
With Inet1
    sCommand = "GET " & sFileName & " " & DownLoadDir & _
      sDLName
    '   Display command being sent
    txtCommand = txtCommand & vbCrLf & sCommand
    txtCommand.SelStart = Len(txtCommand.Text)
    .Execute , sCommand
    '   Wait until done before doing anything else
    Do While Inet1.StillExecuting
        lblWhat.Font.Bold = Not lblWhat.Font.Bold
        lblWhat.Caption = "Downloading " & lstDir.List(lstDir.ListIndex)
        DoEvents
    Loop
    lblWhat.Caption = "Done Downloading"
    Call subBusy(False)
    Beep
End With
Exit_Normal:
```

18

continues

LISTING 18.26   continued

```
      Exit Sub
Error_Handler:
      MsgBox Err & " " & Error, vbOKOnly, "Download Error"
      Select Case Err
          Case 35761: Inet1.Cancel    ' Timeout
          Case 35764: Inet1.Cancel    ' Still Executing
      End Select
      Resume Exit_Normal
End Sub
```

Downloading is all but automatic. The code checks to be sure that something has been selected and that the selection is not a directory name. It also checks the download directory for a file of the same name. If it finds a match, it offers the option of overwriting the original or exiting from the download operation.

Finally, the code builds the GET command string, sCommand, and issues .Execute sCommand to the ITC. That done, all that remains is to wait in a Do loop until the download is complete. The loop alternates lblWhat's Font.Bold property as an activity indicator.

Exiting

You can now log on to an FTP site, change directories, read text files, download files of any kind, and disconnect from the site. All that remains is a way to exit from the program itself, which is, of course, the reason for cmdQuit.

Add the following code to the Click event of cmdQuit:

```
Private Sub cmdQuit_Click()
'    Exit from the program
Unload Me
End
End Sub
```

Running the Program

Unlike the WebBrowser control, the Internet Transfer Control does not start the logon process for you. Before you can connect to an FTP site with this program, you must connect to your Internet service provider (ISP).

Once that connection is made, enter FTP.microsoft.com into txtServer and press Enter or click Connect. Figure 18.21 shows the program connected to the Microsoft FTP site.

FIGURE 18.21

Connected!

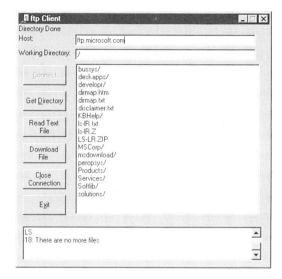

Note the response from the site in txtCommand.

Click disclaimer.txt in the directory listing and then click Read Text File. Figure 18.22 shows the program displaying the text file on frmText.

FIGURE 18.22

Reading a text file.

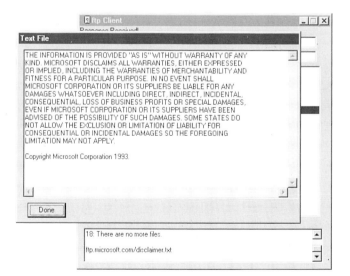

18

Now navigate through the directories. Double-click DEVELOPR. When that directory is completely listed, click BASIC and then click Get Directory to switch to that directory. Finally, double-click KB to change to the Visual Basic Knowledge Base directory.

Click index.txt and then click Download File to download the Knowledge Base index to your computer. When the download is completed, explore the site to your heart's content.

Click Close Connection, followed by Exit when you are finished.

Lesson Summary

The program in this lesson is a rudimentary FTP browser. Its main purpose is to demonstrate how to use the ITC to access FTP sites. If your project involves automatic download, many of the choices that this project leaves to the user—logging on, changing to the correct directory, and even downloading the file—can be done programmatically. In the next lesson, we'll work with the `Winsock` control.

Quiz 5

1. The ITC has only one event, which is the _____ event.

    a. `Execute`

    b. `EvReceive`

    c. `Receive`

    d. `StateChanged`

2. An Anonymous FTP allows a user to

    a. Create directories and uploads only

    b. Create directories and downloads only

    c. Create directories, delete directories, and uploads only

    d. None of the above

3. Which FTP operation is a privileged one?

    a. `SEND`

    b. `CD`

    c. `GET`

    d. `PWD`

4. Which FTP operation is not a privileged one?

    a. MKDIR

    b. RECV

    c. PUT

    d. SEND

Exercise 5

Complexity: Easy

1. Add a Clear button to clear the contents of the txtCommand text box in the FTP program.

Complexity: Moderate

2. Change the FTP program by replacing the txtServer textbox control with a combo box so that it keeps track of the last sites you visited.

LESSON 6

The Microsoft Winsock Control

18

There is one more communication control that this chapter will cover and that is the Microsoft Winsock Control. It is yet one more way to communicate to the Internet. In this lesson, we will write two applications that will explore the capabilities of the Winsock Control.

What Is Winsock?

Winsock is short for *Windows Sockets*. It was created to allow you to connect to a remote computer and exchange data. There are two different types of protocols the Winsock can use to exchange data. They are the *Transmission Control Protocol* (TCP) and the *User Datagram Protocol* (UDP).

Which Protocol Should You Use?

Either protocol can be used to create client and server applications, but there are differences between the two. You have to decide which one is best to use for your application. Let's take a look at the pro's and con's of the two protocols:

The difference between the two protocols is in their connection state.

The TCP protocol is a *connection-based protocol*, which is to say the user must establish a connection before exchanging data. Think of it like a phone: you must wait for a connection on the other end before communicating. The TCP protocol is better suited for transferring large amounts of data in one session, because the connection remains open.

The UDP protocol is a *connectionless protocol*. A connection does not have to be made with the other computer before communicating. It's like mailing a letter. The letter is sent and delivered, but they are not directly connected. The UDP protocol is better suited for tasks that require the transfer of small amounts of data, as well as data that is sent in pieces at a time. If the application doesn't require acknowledgment from the other computer, UDP should be selected.

Chat with the TCP Protocol

Let's try out an example that is similar to the DDE example in Chapter 14, "Advanced Features," Lesson 5. That example demonstrated a one-way communication between a source DDE and destination application. This example will be similar, but instead of the one way data transfer, we'll write a two-way chat program. Start a new project and press Ctrl+T to add the Winsock control to the toolbox. Select Microsoft Winsock Control 6.0 and click OK. The Winsock control is shown in Figure 18.23.

FIGURE 18.23

The Winsock control.

Double-click the Winsock Icon to place it on the form. It doesn't have a visible interface, so it doesn't matter where you put it. Add two text boxes and two labels to the form. Set the properties according to Table 18.31.

TABLE 18.31 Application `TCPServer` Objects and Property Settings

Object	Property	Value
Form	Name	frmServer
	Caption	"TCP Server"
	Height	3600
	Width	5000
TextBox	Name	txtSendData
	Height	255
	Width	3700
	Top	480
	Text	None

Object	Property	Value
TextBox	Name	txtReceiveData
	Height	255
	Width	3700
	Top	2280
	Text	None
Label	Name	lblSend
	Caption	"Outgoing Data"
	Height	255
	Width	3700
	Top	120
Label	Name	lblReceive
	Caption	"Incoming Data"
	Height	255
	Width	3700
	Top	2040
Winsock	Name	tcpServer
	Protocol	0-sckTCPProtocol

Click Save Project in the File menu and save the project as Server.prj. The design-time form is shown in Figure 18.24.

FIGURE 18.24

The TCP Server form at design time.

Open a second Visual Basic session and start a new project. Add a Winsock Control, two Textbox Controls, two labels, and a Command Button. Set the properties according to Table 18.32. The design-time form is shown in Figure 18.25.

FIGURE **18.25**

The TCP Client form
at design time.

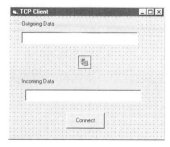

TABLE 18.32   Application `TCPClient` Objects and Property Settings

Object	Property	Value
Form	Name	frmClient
	Caption	"TCP Client"
	Height	4200
	Width	5000
TextBox	Name	txtSendData
	Height	375
	Width	3700
	Top	480
	Left	480
	Text	None
TextBox	Name	txtReceiveData
	Height	375
	Width	3700
	Top	2280
	Left	480
	Text	None
Label	Name	lblSend
	Caption	"Outgoing Data"
	Height	255
	Width	3700
	Top	120
	Left	480

Object	Property	Value
Label	Name	lblReceive
	Caption	"Incoming Data"
	Height	255
	Width	3700
	Top	2040
	Left	480
Winsock	Name	tcpServer
	Protocol	0-sckTCPProtocol
CommandButton	Name	cmdConnect
	Caption	"Connect"
	Height	495
	Width	1215
	Top	3000
	Left	1800

Winsock Properties

Unlike the MSComm Control, the Winsock control doesn't have many properties. For our example, we don't really have to set any other properties but the Protocol. The parameters are listed in Table 18.33. For this example, most properties can remain at the default, because we will be setting most of them within the program code.

TABLE 18.33   Winsock Property Parameters

Parameter	Meaning
Name	The name of the Winsock Control
Local Port	The port number used on the local computer
Protocol	Can be set to sckTCPProtocol or sck UDPProtocol
RemoteHost	The name used to identify the remote computer
RemotePort	The port to be connected to on the remote computer

The TCP Chat Program

Let's get this chat program running. Open up the server project and add the following code to Load event of frmServer:

```
Private Sub Form_Load()
tcpServer.LocalPort = 1003
tcpServer.Listen
End Sub
```

Add the following code to the ConnectionRequest event of tcpServer:

```
Private Sub tcpServer_ConnectionRequest(ByVal requestID As Long)
If tcpServer.State <> sckClosed Then
tcpServer.Close
End If
tcpServer.Accept requestID
End Sub
```

Add the following code to the Change event of txtSendData:

```
Private Sub txtSendData_Change()
tcpServer.SendData txtSendData.Text
End Sub
```

Add the following code to the DataArrival event of tcpServer:

```
Private Sub tcpServer_DataArrival(ByVal bytesTotal As Long)
Dim strData As String
tcpServer.GetData strData
txtReceiveData.Text = strData
End Sub
```

Before we take a look at the code, lets finish the tcpClient program as well. Add the following code to Load event of frmClient:

```
Private Sub Form_Load()
tcpClient.RemoteHost = "127.0.0.1"
tcpClient.RemotePort = 1003
End Sub
```

Add the following code to the Change event of txtSendData:

```
Private Sub txtSendData_Change()
tcpClient.SendData txtSendData.Text
End Sub
```

Add the following code to the DataArrival event of tcpClient:

```
Private Sub tcpClient_DataArrival(ByVal bytesTotal As Long)
Dim strData As String
tcpClient.GetData strData
txtReceiveData.Text = strData
End Sub
```

Add the following code to the Click event of cmdConnect:

```
Private Sub cmdConnect_Click()
tcpClient.Connect
End Sub
```

It's ready to run! But before you do, let's examine some of the code first.

A Look at the Code

It doesn't look like much, but this small example demonstrates the use of the TCP protocol quite well. Let's take a look at some of the lines in code before we run it. We'll look at the server application first.

The line

```
tcpServer.LocalPort = 1003
```

sets the local port to be used by the Winsock Control. It can be any integer number. If the port is unavailable, you must use another one.

The next following that one is

```
tcpServer.Listen
```

This invokes the Listen method of our Winsock Control. This is the major difference between the server application and the client application. The server application will now be "listening" for a connection, much like someone waiting for the phone to ring.

The lines

```
If tcpServer.State <> sckClosed Then
tcpServer.Close
End If
tcpServer.Accept requestID
```

check to see if the server is already connected to a host. If it is, it closes any previous connection and accepts the new one.

```
tcpServer.SendData txtSendData.Text
```

sends any data typed in the txtSendData textbox control for the client application to receive.

```
tcpServer.GetData strData
txtReceiveData.Text = strData
```

When data arrives, the server receives it using the GetData method. The data is then displayed in the txtReceiveData textbox control.

Let's take a look at the code in the client application. The client application must initiate the connection, and does so with the line

```
tcpClient.Connect
```

18

It's as simple as that to initiate the connection. It's up to the server to complete the connection.

There is really only one other line of code to discuss. The code

```
tcpClient.RemoteHost = "127.0.0.1"
```

sets the RemoteHost of the Winsock control to the IP address of the host that it is calling. Think of it like a telephone number; it needs this number to call the host computer to connect. You will have to change this number when calling other hosts with this application. Use the previous IP address to test out the application when you connect to the Internet. It's the same as using your assigned IP address.

Running the Program

Connect to the Internet. Open a Visual Basic session and run the server project. Open a second Visual Basic session and run the client project. Click the button labeled Connect and type characters into the textbox controls labeled Outgoing Data. Both applications should be able to transmit data. Figure 18.26 shows the program at runtime. Next, we'll write the same program using UDP.

FIGURE 18.26

TCP Chat in action.

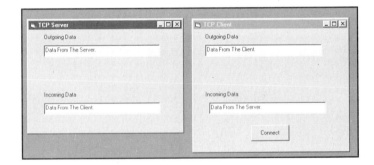

Chat with the UDP Protocol

Now we'll try the same example, but this time we'll use the UDP protocol instead. Because of their different connection requirements, we won't need to run two separate instances of Visual Basic to test the program.

Start a new project and name it UDPChat.prj. Create a form and add a Winsock control, two textboxes, and two labels (see Table 18.34). Use Figure 18.27 as a guide for laying out the form.

FIGURE 18.27

The completed form.

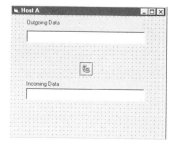

TABLE 18.34   Form A of Application HDPChat Objects and Property Settings

Object	Property	Value
Form	Name	frmHostA
	Caption	"Host A"
	Height	4200
	Width	5000
TextBox	Name	txtSendData
	Height	375
	Width	3700
	Top	480
	Left	480
	Text	None
TextBox	Name	txtReceiveData
	Height	375
	Width	3700
	Top	2280
	Left	480
	Text	None
Label	Name	lblSend
	Caption	"Outgoing Data"
	Height	255
Label	Width	3700
	Top	120
	Left	480

continues

18

TABLE 18.34   continued

Object	Property	Value
Label	Name	lblReceive
	Caption	"Incoming Data"
	Height	255
	Width	3700
	Top	2040
	Left	480
Winsock	Name	tcpServer
	Protocol	0-sckHDProtocol

Add the following code to the Load event of frmHostA:

```
Private Sub Form_Load()
udpHostA.RemoteHost = "127.0.0.1"
udpHostA.RemotePort = 1001
udpHostA.Bind 1002
End Sub
```

Add the following code to the Change event of txtSendData:

```
Private Sub txtSend_Change()
udpHostA.SendData txtSend.Text
End Sub
```

Add the following code to the DataArrival event of udpHostA:

```
Private Sub udphostA_DataArrival(ByVal bytesTotal As Long)
Dim strData As String
udpHostA.GetData strData
txtOutput.Text = strData
End Sub
```

Create a second form in the same application with the same controls. Set the properties according to Table 18.35. Use Figure 18.28 as a guide for laying out the form.

FIGURE 18.28

The completed form.

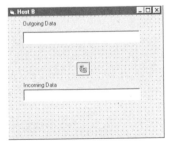

TABLE 18.35 Form B of Application HDPChat Objects and Property Settings

Object	Property	Value
Form	Name	frmHostB
	Caption	"Host B"
	Height	4200
	Width	5000
TextBox	Name	txtSendData
	Height	375
	Width	3700
	Top	480
	Left	480
	Text	None
TextBox	Name	txtReceiveData
	Height	375
	Width	3700
	Top	2280
	Left	480
	Text	None
Label	Name	lblSend
	Caption	"Outgoing Data"
	Height	255
	Width	3700
	Top	120
	Left	480
Label	Name	lblReceive
	Caption	"Incoming Data"
	Height	255
	Width	3700
	Top	2040
	Left	480
Winsock	Name	tcpServer
	Protocol	0-sckHDProtocol

Add the following code to the Load event of frmHostB:

```
Private Sub Form_Load()
udpHostB.RemoteHost = "127.0.0.1"
udpHostB.RemotePort = 1002
udpHostB.Bind 1001
End Sub
```

Add the following code to the Change event of txtSendData:

```
Private Sub txtSend_Change()
udpHostB.SendData txtSend.Text
End Sub
```

Add the following code to the DataArrival event of udpHostB:

```
Private Sub udphostA_DataArrival(ByVal bytesTotal As Long)
Dim strData As String
udpHostB.GetData strData
txtOutput.Text = strData
End Sub
```

That's it! It's a little smaller than the TCP example, but basically does the same thing. We'll examine the code next to see how different.

A Look at the Code

The code is a little bit different than the TCP example. As you would expect, the main difference is in the connection method. In fact, it's the only difference. Let's see how they connect.

The lines

```
udpHostA.RemoteHost = "127.0.0.1"
udpHostA.RemotePort = 1001
```

do the same thing as the TCP example, except this time both sides of the application need to declare the remote host's IP address and port number. Notice that both udpHostA and udpHostB set their RemoteHost property to an IP address. This IP address is like a telephone number to the remote host. They are both set to the same number in this example, as we are testing it on the same computer, thus the source computer and destination computer are the same.

Also notice that both applications need to set the RemotePort property. This must match the port of the destination host.

We set the port of the Winsock Control by binding it to a local port number using the bind method. The line

```
udpHostA.Bind 1002
```

binds the updHostA Winsock to the local port 1002. This port must be used to communicate with the updHostA Windsock. Note that udpHostB has its local port bound to 1001. The bind method reserves that port to the Winsock, and no other application can use that port to listen on. This comes in handy when you want to prevent an application from using a certain port.

Running the Program

Connect to the Internet and run the program. Because you are using the UDP protocol, you no longer need one side to initiate a connection with the other. Just type away and watch the data fly!

Lesson Summary

The programs in this lesson create a simple chat application using both the TCP protocol and the UDP protocol. While the examples mainly focused upon the differences in their methods of connecting, don't forget that there are other differences as well. Remember that the TCP protocol is better suited for transmitting large amounts of data in a single session, while the UDP can transfer smaller pieces of data much more efficiently. Also, the TCP protocol must close its connection before changing the `RemotePort` and `RemoteHost` properties, while the UDP protocol can change them on-the-fly. It's up to you to decide which protocol is best for your application.

18

Quiz 6

1. Which of the following statements is true?

   a. The TCP protocol requires an explicit connection before sending or receiving data.

   b. The UDP protocol requires an explicit connection before sending or receiving data.

   c. The UDP protocol is best suited for transferring large amounts of data.

   d. The TCP protocol is best suited for transferring small amounts of data.

2. Which statement about the TCP protocol is true?

   a. The TCP protocol is a connection-based protocol

   b. The TCP protocol is a connectionless protocol

   c. The TCP protocol be either a connection-based protocol or a connectionless one

   d. None of the above

3. UDP should be selected for an application when

    a. Large amounts of data need to be transferred

    b. The application doesn't require acknowledgment from the other computer when sending data

    c. Both a and b

    d. None of the above

4. UDP stands for

    a. User Data Protocol

    b. Unified Datagram Protocol

    c. Unique Data Protocol

    d. User Datagram Protocol

Exercise 6

Complexity: Easy

1. Add a command button to each form in the UDP example and call them Send. Change the program so that the contents of the outgoing boxes are sent only when the Send button is pressed.

Complexity: Moderate

2. Write a program that uses the UDP control. Create two forms like you did in the UDP example. Name the forms HostA and HostB. Place a set of three option buttons on each form. When HostA clicks an option button, reflect the change in HostB and vice-versa. (Hint: You may want to use a control array for the option buttons.)

Chapter Summary

This chapter covered a wide-range of communication methods and tools. In Lesson 1, you learned how to communicate with the modem using the MSComm control. All the various modem settings were discussed, and we wrote an example that allowed us to talk to the modem.

In Lesson 2, we took what you learned about the MSComm control a step farther and created an application that could dial out into the real world. In Lesson 3, we created a professional interface where we could actually see the data we were receiving from the modem once we connected somewhere, such as a BBS.

In Lesson 4, we explored the WebBrowser Control. Using this control, we built a fully functional custom Web browser, complete with Back, Forward, Stop, Refresh, Home, and Search buttons. Lesson 5 introduced the ITC Control, and with this we built an FTP browser. The Winsock control was covered in Lesson 6, and both protocols of the control were covered: the TCP protocol and the UDP protocol. The advantages and disadvantages of the two were examined, and chat programs using both protocols were created.

18

CHAPTER 19

Using Visual Basic with Internet/Intranet Applications

This chapter explores some of the advanced features and functions that Visual Basic can use with the Internet or an intranet. Some Microsoft applications will be required for some of the lessons, such as Internet Explorer 4.0 and Microsoft Exchange, which are available at the Microsoft Web site.

We will not, however, be showing you how to manipulate an ActiveX control using VBScript, because it would go beyond the scope of this book. VBScript is a subset of the Visual Basic language. It is an interpreter for use in Web browsers and other applications that use ActiveX controls, Java applets, and OLE Automation servers. More and more books are being written on the subject, so you should be able to find one in a bookstore, or you can visit Microsoft on the Web at `http://www.microsoft.com/vbscript/`.

LESSON 1

The ActiveX Document

An ActiveX Document is another type of application that we can create using Visual Basic. An ActiveX Document is an application that requires a container, such as Microsoft Binder or Internet Explorer. The functionality of the container is available to the ActiveX document. If we create an ActiveX document that uses Internet Explorer as its container, we will have access to all the functions and capabilities that Internet Explorer possesses.

When you create an ActiveX Document, you are creating a complete, separate application. Like an ActiveX control, the ActiveX document needs a host application to perform, and all the events, methods, and properties of the host application are available to the ActiveX Document.

When you start a new ActiveX document project, a UserDocument will be available to you for building your application. Like a form, you can add controls to the UserDocument to use with your application. Every control is available to you except the OLE control container. It should also be noted that embedded objects, such as Microsoft Word documents or Excel Worksheets, cannot be used with ActiveX documents.

Start a new project and select ActiveX document EXE from the New Project dialog box. The New Project dialog box is shown in Figure 19.1. Visual Basic will automatically add a UserDocument designer to the project. The default name of the UserDocument will be UserDocument1. Double-click UserDocument1 to display the document and its properties. Add a CommandButton and a TextBox control to the document. Set the properties according to Table 19.1.

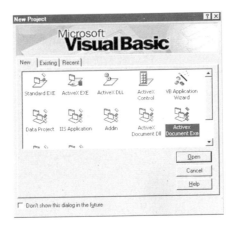

FIGURE 19.1

Starting an ActiveX document project.

TABLE 19.1   Properties for ActiveX Document Project

Object	Property	Value
UserDocument	Name	NavigateDocument
CommandButton	Name	cmdNavigate
	Caption	"Navigate"
	Height	300
	Top	840
	Left	200
TextBox	Name	txtUrl
	Text	(none)
	Top 840	
	Height	300
	Left	1800

Add the following code to the Click event of cmdNavigate:

```
Private Sub cmdNavigate_Click()
Hyperlink.NavigateTo txtUrl.Text
End Sub
```

Click Save Project in the File menu and save the project. The design-time form is shown in Figure 19.2.

FIGURE 19.2

The Navigate Document at design time.

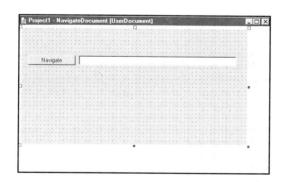

Run the program. It should look just like Figure 19.3. You'll notice that the program runs inside of Internet Explorer, and we are able to take advantage of all the functionality of Internet Explorer in our program. Connect to the Internet if you are not already, and type in the text http://www.microsoft.com.

FIGURE 19.3

*The Navigate
Document at runtime.*

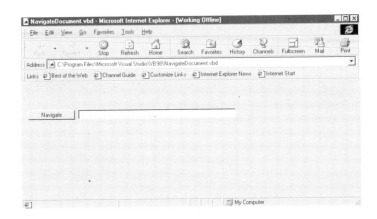

Click the navigate button and you'll see we go right to the Microsoft Web site. The one
line of code we inserted to perform this action

```
Hyperlink.NavigateTo txtUrl.Text
```

uses the Hyperlink object method `NavigateTo` to go to the URL that is typed in `txtUrl`.
Note that we have to include `http://` before the `URL`. This is the protocol portion of
the URL and is required by the `NavigateTo` method.

Because we are using Internet Explorer as our host application, a Visual Basic document
file is created (.vbd) when we compile our project. This file holds the class ID of our
executable file. If we open this .vbd file by our host application (Internet Explorer), we
can view our ActiveX document. Users can view your ActiveX document by opening the
.vbd file in a host application. The file does not have to have the extension .vbd, though.
You may rename it to whatever you want.

Using More than One ActiveX Document

Of course, you may want your application to have more than one ActiveX Document.
Viewing a second ActiveX document is simple, because all you need to know is the path
of the desired ActiveX Document. The following code shows how to load an ActiveX
document entitled Document2.vbd.

```
Hyperlink.NavigateTo "file://C:\Visual Basic Files\Document2.vbd"
```

As you can see, it's pretty simple.

Lesson Summary

The application we wrote in this chapter is just a small example of what can be done
with ActiveX Documents, but what we have covered in this lesson is very powerful. With

what you have learned in Chapter 18, "Using Visual Basic for Communications," you should be able to make a very good Internet/Intranet application, and because it is an ActiveX document, it is easily distributed. ActiveX Documents are very powerful and can perform many more useful functions that are beyond the scope of a beginner's book, but what we have covered here you should find extremely useful.

Quiz 1

1. An ActiveX document requires

    a. A host application to operate

    b. ActiveX controls

    c. Internet Explorer 4.0

    d. An Internet connection

2. Which of the following controls cannot be placed on an ActiveX Document?

    a. The `Image` control

    b. The `OLE` container control

    c. Any ActiveX control

    d. An ActiveX cocument can contain any controls available

3. The extension .vbd stands for

    a. Visual Basic Data

    b. Visual Basic Document

    c. Visual Basic Definition

    d. None of the above

4. Which filename below is a valid name for an ActiveX Document?

    a. MyActive.vbd

    b. MyActive.doc

    c. MyActive

    d. All of the above

Exercise 1

Complexity: Easy

1. Add a command button to the project and label it Next. Add a line of code to the click event that uses the `HyperLink.GoForward` object method.

Complexity: Moderate

2. Add a second UserDocument to the project entitled NavigateDocument2. Add a Label control to the document with the caption Document 2. Add a Command button to both UserDocuments. Set the caption to the button on the first document to To Document 2. Set the caption to the button on the second document to To Document 1. Write code so that when the buttons are clicked, they go to the proper document. Note: You'll have to know the path to where the documents are located.

LESSON 2

Reading Your Email with MAPI

In this lesson, we take our Internet programming a step further by developing a program that deals with email. We will create an application that will enable you to download your email messages, compose a message, attach a file, and send it to whomever you want. The Messaging Application Program Interface (MAPI) controls enable us to perform these powerful operations.

The MAPI controls are a set of components that are used to interact with an underlying message subsystem. In order for us to use the MAPI controls, a MAPI-compliant email system must be installed. Because Microsoft Exchange is a MAPI-compliant email system (and most likely installed on your computer), we will be using this program with our MAPI program examples.

Using the MAPI Controls

There are two steps involved in using the MAPI controls. The first step is establishing a MAPI session. The second step is using the properties and methods to manage an individual Inbox. Such properties and methods include composing and sending a message, retrieving messages, and adding attachments to messages.

Let's jump right in and begin developing an electronic mail application. Start a new project and the MAPI controls to the toolbox. Press Ctrl+T or select Components from the Project menu and select Microsoft MAPI Controls 6.0. The icons for the MAPI controls are shown in Figure 19.4.

Double-click both the MAPIMessages and MAPISession icons to place them on the form. Add six Command buttons, two TextBox controls, one RichTextBox control, and three Label controls. Set the properties according to Table 19.2.

FIGURE 19.4

The MAPIMessages *icon and the* MAPISession *icon.*

TABLE 19.2   Properties for MAPI Project

Object	Property	Value
Form	Name	frmMail
	Caption	"E-Mail"
	Height	8000
	Width	11000
MAPISession	Name	MAPISession1
MAPIMessages	Name	MAPIMessages1
CommandButton	Name	cmdConnect
	Caption	"Connect"
	Height	500
	Width	1200
	Top	120
	Left	100
CommandButton	Name	cmdGetMail
	Caption	"Get Mail"
	Height	500
	Width	1200
	Top	120
	Left	100
CommandButton	Name	cmdDisconnect
	Caption	"Disconnect"
	Height	500
	Width	1200
	Top	6500
	Left	100
CommandButton	Name	cmdPrevious
	Caption	"Previous Message"
	Height	500

19

continues

TABLE 19.2 continued

Object	Property	Value
	Width	1500
	Top	7000
	Left	3000
CommandButton	Name	cmdNext
	Caption	"Next Message"
	Height	500
	Width	1500
	Top	7000
	Left	8500
TextBox	Name	txtAddress
	Text	(none)
	Height	285
	Width	7000
	Top	120
	Left	2760
TextBox	Name	txtSubject
	Text	(none)
	Height	285
	Width	7000
	Top	960
	Left	2760
RichTextBox	Name	txtBody
	Text	(none)
	Height	5000
	Width	7000
	Top	1500
	Left	2760
Label	Name	lblMessage
	Caption	" "
	Height	255
	Width	4455
	Top	120
	Left	4000

Object	Property	Value
Label	Name	lblFrom
	Caption	"From:"
	Height	255
	Width	375
	Top	600
	Left	2280
Label	Name	lblSubject
	Caption	"Subject:"
	Height	255
	Width	615
	Top	960
	Left	2040

The design-time form is shown in Figure 19.5.

FIGURE 19.5

frmMail *at design time.*

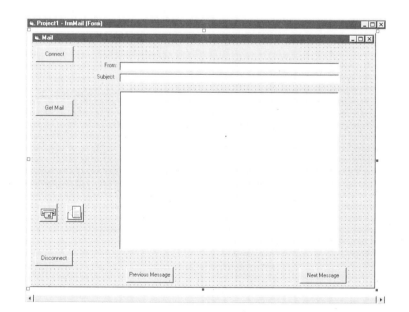

The MAPI Control's Methods

Let's take a closer look at the methods of the MAPISession control and the MAPIMessages control. Both controls work together to build a functional email application as we'll soon see.

The MAPISession Control

The MAPISession control has only two methods. These are listed in Table 19.3.

TABLE 19.3   MAPISession Methods

Method	Description
SignOn	Establish a MAPI connection
SignOff	Close a MAPI connection

The MAPIMessages Control

The MAPIMessages control has methods that correspond to most of the operations you would expect from an email application. These are listed in Table 19.4.

TABLE 19.4   MAPIMessages Methods

Method	Description
Compose	Compose a new message
Copy	Copy a message
Delete	Delete a message, recipient, or attachment
Fetch	Creates a message set from selected messages in the Inbox
Forward	Forward a message
Reply	Reply to a message
ReplyAll	Reply to all message recipients
Save	Save a message
Send	Send a message

The code in Listing 19.1 demonstrates the use of the methods and properties. Enter the code in your program.

LISTING 19.1   An Example of Using the MAPI Controls

```
Option Explicit

Private Sub cmdConnect_Click()
   MAPISession1.SignOn
   MAPIMessages1.SessionID = MAPISession1.SessionID
   MAPIMessages1.Fetch
   Call SetMailFields
End Sub
```

```
Private Sub cmdDisconnect_Click()
    MAPISession1.SignOff
End Sub

Private Sub cmdGetMail_Click()
    MAPIMessages1.Fetch
    MAPIMessages1.MsgIndex = MAPIMessages1.MsgCount - 1
    Call SetMailFields
End Sub

Private Sub cmdNext_Click()
  If (MAPIMessages1.MsgIndex < MAPIMessages1.MsgCount - 1) Then
        MAPIMessages1.MsgIndex = MAPIMessages1.MsgIndex + 1
        Call SetMailFields
    End If
End Sub

Private Sub cmdPrevious_Click()
If (MAPIMessages1.MsgIndex > 0) Then
        MAPIMessages1.MsgIndex = MAPIMessages1.MsgIndex - 1
        Call SetMailFields
  End If
End Sub

Private Sub SetMailFields()
    txtAddress.Text = MAPIMessages1.MsgOrigAddress
    txtSubject.Text = MAPIMessages1.MsgSubject
    txtBody.Text = MAPIMessages1.MsgNoteText
    lblMessage.Caption = "Message " & MAPIMessages1.MsgIndex + 1 & " of " &
 MAPIMessages1.MsgCount
End Sub
```

19

What's Going On?

The program generates a message set from an individual Inbox and displays the messages in the set. Before the program can run properly, the Connect button must be pressed. The line

```
MAPISession1.SignOn
```

establishes a MAPI session. When the session is successfully established, the SessionID property of the MAPIMessages control must be set to the SessionID property of the MAPISession control. By doing this we create an association between the MAPIMessages control and the MAPISession control. We can forget about the MAPISession control from now on until we want to sign off. The following line creates the association between the controls.

```
MAPIMessages1.SessionID = MAPISession1.SessionID
```

Next, we need to create a message set from our selected Inbox. This is performed with the `Fetch` method. When the message set has been created, we can now utilize the property `MsgIndex` to refer to particular message. After the `Fetch` method is completed, the `MsgIndex` property is set to 0, which is the first letter in the Inbox. The following code creates our message set.

```
MAPIMessages1.Fetch
```

When the messages set has been created, we want to view the contents of the first message in our text fields. The code below calls a procedure to set our text fields. Because the `MsgIndex` is set to 0, the first message can be viewed.

```
Call SetMailFields
```

The lines

```
txtAddress.Text = MAPIMessages1.MsgOrigAddress
txtSubject.Text = MAPIMessages1.MsgSubject
txtBody.Text = MAPIMessages1.MsgNoteText
```

set the text boxes to the original address, the subject, and body of the message.

The code

```
lblMessage.Caption = "Message " & MAPIMessages1.MsgIndex + 1 & " of " &
MAPIMessages1.MsgCount
```

displays the current message being viewed out of the total number of messages. The property `MsgCount` holds the value of the total number of messages in the message set.

Next, we want to be able to traverse through the messages in the Inbox. We will do this by incrementing or decrementing the `MsgIndex` by one and then setting the text boxes to the new message contents. We also want to make sure we don't increment the `MsgIndex` beyond the total number of messages or decrement it below zero. The code we have to view the next message is

```
If (MAPIMessages1.MsgIndex < MAPIMessages1.MsgCount - 1) Then
        MAPIMessages1.MsgIndex = MAPIMessages1.MsgIndex + 1
        Call SetMailFields
    End If
```

To view the previous message,

```
If (MAPIMessages1.MsgIndex > 0) Then
        MAPIMessages1.MsgIndex = MAPIMessages1.MsgIndex - 1
        Call SetMailFields
    End If
```

Notice how we call the `SetMailFields` routine after we change the `MsgIndex`.

Finally we use the line of code

```
MAPISession1.SignOff
```

to end MAPI session.

Running the Program

Run the program and click the Connect button. A window will pop up asking you to select a profile. Select Microsoft Outlook and click OK. If you are not already connected to the Internet, another window will appear asking you to connect. Once connected, you can start reading your email through this application.

Composing a Message

Now that we have written a program that can read email, we will take it one step further so that we can compose and send a message!

Add a command button to the form `frmMail` entitled Compose Message with the properties listed in Table 19.5.

TABLE 19.5   Properties for `cmdCompose`

Object	Property	Value
CommandButton	Name	cmdCompose
	Caption	Compose Message
	Height	500
	Width	1200
	Top	3000
	Left	100

Next, add a new form to the project. On the new form, add a Command button, two `TextBox` controls, one `RichTextBox` control, and two `Label` controls. Set the properties according to Table 19.6.

TABLE 19.6   Properties for MAPI Project

Object	Property	Value
Form	Name	frmSend
	Caption	Compose Message
	Height	8000
	Width	11000

continues

TABLE 19.6 continued

Object	Property	Value
CommandButton	Name	cmdSend
	Caption	Send Message
	Height	500
	Width	1200
	Top	1200
	Left	120
TextBox	Name	txtAddress
	Text	(none)
	Height	285
	Width	7000
	Top	120
	Left	3200
TextBox	Name	txtSubject
	Text	(none)
	Height	285
	Width	7000
	Top	480
	Left	3200
RichTextBox	Name	txtBody
	Text	(none)
	Height	5000
	Width	7000
	Top	960
	Left	3200
Label	Name	lblTo
	Caption	To:
	Height	255
	Width	375
	Top	120
	Left	2760

Object	Property	Value
Label	Name	lblSubject
	Caption	Subject:
	Height	255
	Width	615
	Top	480
	Left	2400

The design-time form is shown in Figure 19.6.

FIGURE 19.6

frmSend *at design time.*

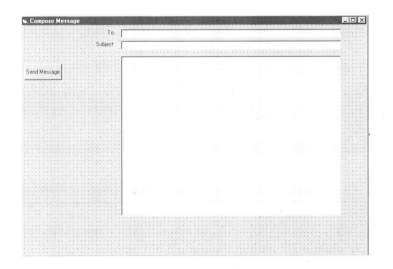

Enter the following code in the cmdSend Click event:

```
Private Sub cmdSend_Click()

    frmMail.MAPIMessages1.Compose

    'E-mail Address
    frmMail.MAPIMessages1.RecipAddress = txtAddress

    ' Resolve recipient name
    frmMail.MAPIMessages1.AddressResolveUI = True
    frmMail.MAPIMessages1.ResolveName
    'Message Subject
    frmMail.MAPIMessages1.MsgSubject = txtSubject
    'Message Body
    frmMail.MAPIMessages1.MsgNoteText = txtBody
```

```
        frmMail.MAPIMessages1.Send False
        frmSend.Hide
        txtAddress.Text = ""
        txtSubject.Text = ""
        txtBody.Text = ""
End Sub
```

What's Going On?

This routine sends an email message. The code

```
frmMail.MAPIMessages1.Compose
```

clears the compose buffer and sets the `MsgIndex` to `-1`. After which, we must set the recipient's email address. The line

```
frmMail.MAPIMessages1.RecipAddress = txtAddress
```

sets the `RecipAddress` property to the text box `txtAddress`.

Next we must verify the recipient's name. This is done by the `ResolveName` method. The name is verified by checking the name against a list of verified users in the email system. The following code determines that the recipient's email name is valid by invoking the `ResolveName` method and setting the `AddressResolveUI` property to True.

```
        frmMail.MAPIMessages1.AddressResolveUI = True
        frmMail.MAPIMessages1.ResolveName
```

Now we are ready to send the subject and body of our message. The code

```
frmMail.MAPIMessages1.MsgSubject = txtSubject
frmMail.MAPIMessages1.MsgNoteText = txtBody
```

sets the subject and body of the message to properties `MsgSubject` and `MsgNoteText`. To send it, we invoke the `Send` method. We can send the message with or without user interaction. If we set the value to TRUE, we would be requiring user interaction, but we want to keep our email application as simple as possible so we will set it to FALSE. The line

```
frmMail.MAPIMessages1.Send False
```

performs this operation.

Attachments

Let's give our email program the capability to send file attachments with our messages. Add a TextBox control and a `Label` control to `frmSend`. Set the properties according to Table 19.7.

TABLE 19.7   Properties for the Attachment Controls

Object	Property	Value
TextBox	Name	txtAttachment
	Text	(none)
	Height	285
	Width	7000
	Top	6000
	Left	3200
Label	Name	lblAttachment
	Caption	Attachment:
	Height	255
	Width	375
	Top	6000
	Left	2160

Will need to use the `AttachmentPathName` property to specify the name and path of the file. If the path name is incorrect or empty, an error will be generated. Add the following lines of code to the `cmdSend` click event right before the `send` method is invoked:

```
If (txtAttachment.Text <> "") Then
    frmMail.MAPIMessages1.AttachmentPathName = txtAttachment.Text
End If
```

The previous code checks to see if `txtAttachment` contains text. If it does, we set the `AttachmentPathName` property to the contents of the `txtAttachment` control. That's all there is to it!

Lesson Summary

We haven't covered all of the features of the MAPI control in this lesson, but we have covered enough to get you started on developing your very own customizable email program. You should have little trouble tackling the more advanced features of the MAPI controls after completing this lesson.

Quiz 2

1. MAPI stands for

    a. Messaging Application Program Interface

    b. Mail Application Programmable Interface

19

    c. Message Application Programmable Information

    d. Mail Application Programmable Information

2. The two MAPI controls required to create mail applications are

    a. The `MAPIMessages` control and `MAPIService` control

    b. The `MAPIMail` control and `MAPIMessages` control

    c. The `MAPIMail` control and `MAPISession` control

    d. The `MAPIMessages` control and `MAPISession` control

3. What must be installed in order to use the MAPI controls?

    a. Microsoft Exchange

    b. Microsoft Internet Explorer

    c. a MAPI-compliant email system

    d. None of the above

4. To create a message set from our selected Inbox, use the

    a. `Retrieve` method

    b. `Set` method

    c. `Fetch` method

    d. `Inbox` method

Exercise 2

Complexity: Easy

1. Change the application so that the first message displayed is the most current mail message in the Inbox.

Complexity: Moderate

2. Remove the `txtAttachment` control from the form `frmSend`. Add a Command button with the caption Attachment. Write the program so that when the user clicks the button, a new form is shown to select the file. Add a `DriveListBox` control, a `DirListBox` control, and a `FileListBox` control to the form. Add two `TextBox` controls, so that one displays the name of the file attachment selected, and the other the path. Include an OK button and a Cancel button as well.

LESSON 3

Introduction to Dynamic HTML Applications

In this lesson we'll take a quick look at creating Dynamic HTML applications for use with intranets. What is Dynamic HTML? *Dynamic HTML* (DHTML) is an extension of HTML. With DHTML, you can access and manipulate every element on a Web page. A Web page can now be treated just like a form. We can now use standard Visual Basic code to process events in HTML pages instead of relying on scripts or server-side processing.

Before we begin, make sure you have Internet Explorer 4.0 or later.

Creating a Dynamic HTML Application

Start a new project in Visual Basic. Select DHTML Application from the New Project dialog box. The New Project dialog box is shown in Figure 19.7.

FIGURE 19.7

Starting a Dynamic HTML document.

Take a look at the toolbox. You'll notice that you now have a different set of controls. These are the only controls you can use when developing a DHTML application. The new toolbox is shown in Figure 19.8.

FIGURE 19.8

The HTML toolbox.

19

Double-click the Designers folder in the Project Explorers window. Double-click the one page in it entitled HTMLPage1. You should now see a window similar to Figure 19.9. This is where we will create our HTML page. Open up the document tree on the left-hand side. This tree will display all the elements of the HTML page.

FIGURE **19.9**

The HTML document design interface.

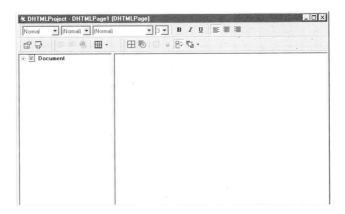

We have nothing in here yet, so let's begin by inserting a heading on top the page. Click in the window on the right side. The cursor will be at the beginning. Let's set the font to a large size such as 5, and click the bold key. Type in the words My Heading. Click the center align button so that it resides in the center of our page. Click the document tree until it is fully expanded. Notice that every element in the page is represented in this tree. Your screen should look similar to Figure 19.10.

FIGURE **19.10**

Viewing our HTML document.

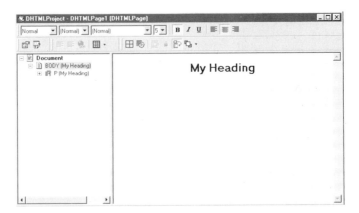

Add one of the controls in the toolbox to our page. Double-click the Button control to place it on the document. You can drag it around just like you would on a form. Add a second button and place it next to the first button. The page layout can be seen in Figure 19.11.

FIGURE 19.11

Displaying the document tree against our HTML document.

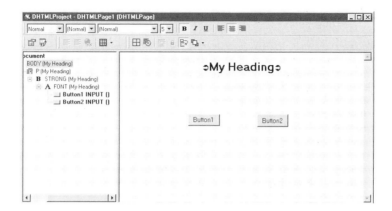

Let's see how we add code to our controls. Double-click the first button to display the code window. Type in the beep command. Do the same to the second button. Run the program. You'll notice that you can click the buttons properly, but no sound emits from your computer. In order for us to test our application properly, we must generate the project's DLL. Click File in the main menu bar and select Make DHTMLProject.DLL. When the process is completed, you can test your program. You'll now hear the buttons beep as they should.

Now we'll dynamically change the contents and appearance of the document. First, we'll change the background color. Enter the code window of the first button and add the line of code

```
Document.bgColor = RGB(255, 0, 0)
```

This will change the background color of the document to blue by setting the property bgColor to an RGB value. We'll make the second button set the background to white with the line

```
Document.bgColor = RGB(255, 255, 255)
```

We can also change the label on the button by clicking inside the button itself once. This will place the cursor inside the button. Change the caption of the first button to Blue, and the second button to White. Run the program to see the results.

Next we'll change the text on the screen. Below the buttons, add a new line and insert the text The Color of the Page is:. On a new line below that, type in the word White. What we want to do is change the word *"White"* to Blue when the document is

19

blue, and vice versa. We can do this easily by setting the ID attribute of the area of text that says "*White.*"

Every object that you want to manipulate on an HTML document must be referred to by a unique ID attribute. The ID attributes of the buttons are Button1 and Button2. To set the ID attribute of our desired text field, select the line where text resides. You'll see the ID property in the Properties window. It should be blank. Type in the word Color. We can now reference this line of the document with this ID attribute. We cannot, however, distinguish a single word of text with this method. We'll utilize the `innertext` property to change the document's contents dynam-_ically. Type the following line of code for Button1

```
Color.Innertext = "Blue"
```

and this code for Button2

```
Color.Innertext = "White"
```

And you thought HTML pages could only just sit there! Figure 19.12 shows our DHTML document in action.

FIGURE 19.12

The HTML document was dynamically changed.

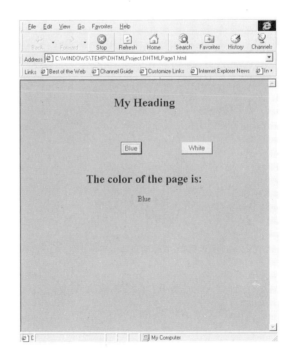

Lesson Summary

We have just scratched the surface on developing Dynamic HTML applications. There is much more you can learn to take advantage of such applications, but this book concentrates on only Visual Basic, and not DHTML. More and more books are popping up covering this relatively new application. You should feel you have learned enough to experiment with the rest of the HTML controls available.

Quiz 3

1. Which of the following statements is true about developing DHTML applications?

   a. DHTML enables you to dynamically change the contents of an HTML document.

   b. DHTML applications are compatible with any version of Internet Explorer.

   c. Any Visual Basic control can be used with a DHTML application.

   d. Controls can be placed anywhere on the document, just like a form.

2. What attribute must be set in order to reference objects on a DHTML document?

   a. The `Name` attribute

   b. The `ID` attribute

   c. The `Reference` attribute

   d. No attribute needs to be set

3. What property is utilized to dynamically change the text in an HTML document?

   a. The `Labeltext` property

   b. The `Textfield` property

   c. The `Innertext` property

   d. The `Idtext` property

4. The object to reference to change the background color of the HTML page is the _____ object.

   a. `HTMLPage`

   b. `HTMLForm`

   c. `Page`

   d. `Document`

19

Exercise 3

Complexity: Easy

1. Add a Hyperlink control that goes to `http://www.microsoft.com` to the exercise. Make sure the link reads To Microsoft!. Hint: An easy way to set the link is to right-click the Hyperlink object after you place it on the form.

Complexity: Moderate

2. Near the bottom of the page, add a line of text that reads **"New Text Here"** and add a button and a `TextField` below it. Change the application so that it enables the user to change the line of text by entering new text in a `TextField` and submitting the contents by pressing the button. Label the button Submit. Note: Don't worry about matching the font size.

Chapter Summary

In this chapter you learned that an ActiveX document is a Visual Basic application that uses a host application. You created an ActiveX document application that used Internet Explorer as its container, and took advantage of some of Internet Explorer's methods and properties.

Next you learned about Message Application Program Interface controls (MAPI). By using these controls, you created your own custom email program that could download mail messages, as well as compose messages that could send attachments. A MAPI-compliant email system, such as Microsoft Exchange, needed to reside on the system in order to use the MAPI controls properly.

In the final lesson, we introduced Dynamic HTML pages, one of latest technologies involving Web pages. Here, we explained how Visual Basic can use DHTML to create powerful Intranet applications, and we created an HTML document that could change dynamically.

APPENDIX A

Quiz Answers

Chapter 1: What's All That Stuff on My Screen?

Lesson 1
1. a
2. b
3. c
4. a

Lesson 2

1. c
2. b
3. d
4. c

Lesson 3

1. d
2. b
3. a
4. b

Lesson 4

1. b
2. a
3. a
4. d

Lesson 5

1. a
2. b
3. b
4. b

Chapter 2: Object-Oriented Programming

Lesson 1

1. d
2. b
3. d
4. a

Lesson 2

1. d
2. a
3. b
4. c

Lesson 3

1. d
2. a
3. b
4. d

Lesson 4

1. c
2. d
3. c
4. a

A

Lesson 5

1. a
2. c
3. d
4. a

Lesson 6

1. b
2. c
3. a
4. d

Lesson 7

1. d
2. d
3. a
4. d

Lesson 8

1. b
2. b
3. c
4. d

Chapter 3: Variable, Constants, and Associated Functions

Lesson 1

1. b
2. a
3. c
4. a

Lesson 2

1. a
2. b
3. b
4. b

Lesson 3

1. c
2. c
3. d
4. c

Lesson 4

1. a
2. a
3. c
4. a

A

Lesson 5

1. b
2. d
3. b
4. d

Lesson 6

1. c
2. a
3. b
4. d

Lesson 7

1. c
2. a
3. c
4. b

Lesson 8

1. b
2. b
3. d
4. b

Chapter 4: Subroutines, Functions, and the Visual Basic 6 Language

Lesson 1

1. d
2. d
3. a
4. b

Lesson 2

1. c
2. d
3. b
4. c

Lesson 3

1. b
2. d
3. a
4. c

Lesson 4

1. d
2. b
3. c
4. d

A

Lesson 5

1. a
2. c
3. c
4. d

Lesson 6

1. a
2. a
3. d
4. c

Lesson 7

1. b
2. d
3. d
4. d

Lesson 8

1. d
2. b
3. c
4. d

Chapter 5: Controls

Lesson 1

1. d
2. b
3. d
4. a

Lesson 2

1. b
2. c
3. d
4. a

Lesson 3

1. b
2. b
3. c
4. c

Lesson 4

1. d
2. a
3. c
4. b

A

Lesson 5

1. a
2. c
3. c
4. d

Lesson 6

1. b
2. a
3. d
4. c

Lesson 7

1. d
2. b
3. b
4. c

Chapter 6: Building the GUI with Forms, Menus, and MDI Forms

Lesson 1

1. a
2. b
3. a
4. c

Lesson 2

1. c
2. a
3. d
4. c

Lesson 3

1. b
2. d
3. b
4. a

Lesson 4

1. d
2. d
3. b
4. b

Lesson 5

1. b
2. c
3. d
4. c

A

Lesson 6

1. a
2. d
3. d
4. a

Lesson 7

1. d
2. c
3. d
4. b

Lesson 8

1. a
2. b
3. c
4. d

Lesson 9

1. a
2. b
3. c
4. d

Chapter 7: Building Classes: The Foundation of Visual Basic OOP

Lesson 1

1. b
2. b
3. c
4. d

Lesson 2

1. a
2. d
3. c
4. b

Lesson 3

1. d
2. d
3. a
4. a

Lesson 4

1. a
2. b
3. c
4. d

Lesson 5

1. b
2. d
3. b
4. d

Lesson 6

1. c
2. b
3. c
4. a

A

Lesson 7

1. b
2. c
3. a
4. b

Lesson 8

1. a
2. d
3. b
4. c

Chapter 8: Using ActiveX Controls

Lesson 1

1. a
2. c
3. d
4. d

Lesson 2

1. d
2. b
3. c
4. d

Lesson 3

1. d
2. d
3. d
4. c

Lesson 4

1. c
2. b
3. a
4. c

Lesson 5

1. b
2. c
3. c
4. d

Lesson 6

1. b
2. c
3. c
4. b

Lesson 7

1. d
2. c
3. b
4. a

A

Lesson 8

1. d
2. b
3. b
4. a

Chapter 9: Printing

Lesson 1

1. d
2. d
3. b
4. c

Lesson 2

1. a
2. b
3. c
4. d

Lesson 3

1. b
2. b
3. a
4. c

Lesson 4

1. c
2. a
3. c
4. d

Lesson 5

1. c
2. b
3. c
4. b

Lesson 6

1. b
2. d
3. d
4. a

Lesson 7

1. d
2. d
3. c
4. a

Lesson 8

1. a
2. a
3. b
4. b

A

Chapter 10: Problem Solving: Handling Errors and Debugging Your Program

Lesson 1

1. a
2. c
3. c
4. d

Lesson 2

1. d
2. c
3. d
4. a

Lesson 3

1. b
2. c
3. a
4. a

Lesson 4

1. a
2. b
3. c
4. d

Lesson 5

1. c
2. d
3. c
4. b

Lesson 6

1. a
2. c
3. b
4. a

Chapter 11: Adding Pizazz with Graphics

Lesson 1

1. b
2. a
3. c
4. a

Lesson 2

1. b
2. a
3. a
4. d

A

Lesson 3

1. b
2. b
3. a
4. c

Lesson 4

1. c
2. a
3. d
4. d

Lesson 5

1. a
2. a
3. b
4. c

Lesson 6

1. a
2. c
3. c
4. d

Lesson 7

1. b
2. c
3. d
4. a

Lesson 8

1. d
2. b
3. d
4. b

Chapter 12: Reading and Writing Disk Files

Lesson 1

1. d
2. b
3. b
4. a

Lesson 2

1. c
2. c
3. b
4. d

Lesson 3

1. c
2. b
3. c
4. a

A

Lesson 4

1. c
2. c
3. a
4. b

Lesson 5

1. b
2. d
3. a
4. b

Lesson 6

1. a
2. c
3. b
4. b

Chapter 13: Database Programming

Lesson 1

1. a
2. c
3. b
4. b

Lesson 2

1. c
2. a
3. d
4. b

Lesson 3

1. b
2. d
3. b
4. d

Lesson 4

1. a
2. c
3. b
4. a

Lesson 5

1. c
2. a
3. a
4. d

A

Lesson 6

1. d
2. c
3. b
4. a

Lesson 7

1. d
2. b
3. a
4. c

Chapter 14: Advanced Features

Lesson 1

1. c
2. b
3. b
4. a

Lesson 2

1. c
2. b
3. a
4. b

Lesson 3

1. b
2. a
3. a
4. d

Lesson 4

1. a
2. a
3. d
4. b

Lesson 5

1. c
2. a
3. d
4. a

Lesson 6

1. d
2. c
3. c
4. d

Lesson 7

1. b
2. a
3. a
4. d

A

Chapter 15: Doing the Impossible (and More) with Windows API

Lesson 1

1. b
2. c
3. d
4. b

Lesson 2

1. c
2. c
3. c
4. b

Lesson 3

1. c
2. c
3. c
4. b

Lesson 4

1. d
2. a
3. c
4. d

Lesson 5

1. a
2. c
3. d
4. b

Lesson 6

1. d
2. b
3. c
4. a

Lesson 7

1. d
2. c
3. c
4. c

Chapter 16: Interfacing with Excel and Other Programs

Lesson 1

1. d
2. b
3. a
4. a

A

Lesson 2

  1. a
  2. b
  3. d
  4. b

Lesson 3

  1. d
  2. a
  3. c
  4. d

Lesson 4

  1. d
  2. c
  3. a
  4. a

Lesson 5

  1. c
  2. a
  3. c
  4. b

Lesson 6

  1. d
  2. d
  3. a
  4. c

Lesson 7

1. d
2. a
3. b
4. a

Lesson 8

1. b
2. a
3. c
4. d

Chapter 17: Advanced ActiveX and Registry API Techniques

Lesson 1

1. a
2. d
3. b
4. d

Lesson 2

1. b
2. b
3. b
4. b

A

Lesson 3

1. c
2. a
3. c
4. a

Lesson 4

1. d
2. c
3. a
4. b

Lesson 5

1. d
2. c
3. c
4. c

Lesson 6

1. a
2. b
3.
4. c

Chapter 18: Using Visual Basic for Communications

Lesson 1

1. c
2. a
3. d
4. c

Lesson 2

1. b
2. a
3. d
4. c

Lesson 3

1. d
2. b
3. a
4. c

Lesson 4

1. b
2. c
3. b
4. a

A

Lesson 5

1. d
2. d
3. a
4. b

Lesson 6

1. a
2. a
3. b
4. d

Chapter 19: Using Visual Basic with Internet/Intranet Applications

Lesson 1

1. a
2. b
3. b
4. d

Lesson 2

1. a
2. d
3. c
4. c

Lesson 3

1. a
2. b
3. c
4. d

A

INDEX